# Time Out

# Hong Kong

**timeout.com/hongkong**

**Penguin Books**

PENGUIN BOOKS

Published by the Penguin Group
Penguin Books Ltd, 80 Strand, London WC2R ORL, England
Penguin Books USA Inc., 375 Hudson Street, New York, New York 10014, USA
Penguin Books Australia Ltd, 250 Camberwell Road, Camberwell, Victoria 3124, Australia
Penguin Books Canada Ltd, 10 Alcorn Avenue, Toronto, Ontario, Canada M4V 3B2
Penguin Books (NZ) Ltd, cnr Rosedale and Airborne Roads, Albany, Auckland, New Zealand

Penguin Books Ltd, Registered Offices: Harmondsworth, Middlesex, England

First published 2001

**Second edition 2004**
10 9 8 7 6 5 4 3 2 1

Copyright © Time Out Group Ltd 2001, 2004
All rights reserved

Colour reprographics by Icon, Crowne House, 56-58 Southwark Street, London SE1 1UN
Printed and bound by Cayfosa-Quebecor, Ctra. de Caldes, Km 3 08 130 Sta, Perpètua de Mogoda, Barcelona, Spain

**Edited and designed by**
**Time Out Guides Limited**
**Universal House**
**251 Tottenham Court Road**
**London W1T 7AB**
**Tel + 44 (0)20 7813 3000**
**Fax + 44 (0)20 7813 6001**
**Email guides@timeout.com**
**www.timeout.com**

### Editorial
**Editor** Lesley McCave
**Deputy Editors** Jonathan Cox, Christi Daugherty
**Listings Checkers** Rehana Sheikh, Vikki Weston
**Proofreaders** Angela Jameson, Rachel Kenney
**Indexer** Jonathan Cox

**Editorial/Managing Director** Peter Fiennes
**Series Editor** Ruth Jarvis
**Deputy Series Editor** Lesley McCave
**Guides Co-ordinator** Anna Norman
**Accountant** Sarah Bostock

### Design
**Art Director** Mandy Martin
**Acting Art Director** Scott Moore
**Acting Art Editor** Tracey Ridgewell
**Acting Senior Designer** Astrid Kogler
**Designer** Sam Lands
**Digital Imaging** Dan Conway
**Ad Make-up** Charlotte Blythe

### Picture Desk
**Picture Editor** Jael Marschner
**Deputy Picture Editor** Kit Burnet
**Picture Researcher** Alex Ortiz

### Advertising
**Sales Director** Mark Phillips
**International Sales Manager** Ross Canadé
**International Sales Executive** James Tuson
**Advertising Sales (Hong Kong)** Herb Moskowitz
**Advertising Assistant** Lucy Butler

### Marketing
**Marketing Manager** Mandy Martinez
**US Publicity & Marketing Associate** Rosella Albanese

### Production
**Guides Production Director** Mark Lamond
**Production Controller** Samantha Furniss

### Time Out Group
**Chairman** Tony Elliott
**Managing Director** Mike Hardwick
**Group Financial Director** Richard Waterlow
**Group Commercial Director** Lesley Gill
**Group Marketing Director** Christine Cort
**Group General Manager** Nichola Coulthard
**Group Art Director** John Oakey
**Online Managing Director** David Pepper

### Contributors
**Introduction** Jason Wordie. **History** Jason Wordie (*Relics of World War II* Andrew Dembina). **Hong Kong Today** Jason Wordie.
**Modern Architecture** Jason Wordie. **Culture & Customs** Andrew Dembina (*Crazy 4 U* Vikki Weston). **Wild Hong Kong** Jason
Wordie. **Where to Stay** Neil Western. **Sightseeing** Jason Wordie (*Introduction* Jonathan Cox; *Lamma, Village vehicle vagabonds*
Andrew Dembina; *Masterstrokes* Chris Baker). **Restaurants** Neil Western, KK Chu. **Pubs & Bars** Neil Western. **Shops &
Services** Reggie Ho (*Shopping in Shenzhen* Ellen McNally; *Super spas* Catharine Nichol). **Festivals & Events** Chris Baker.
**Children** Caroline Courtauld, Fanny Wong. **Film** Vikki Weston, Chris Baker. **Galleries** Clare Tyrrell, Vikki Weston. **Gay & Lesbian**
Chris Baker. **Nightlife** Neil Western. **Performing Arts** Chris Baker. **Sport & Fitness** Catharine Nichol. **Macau** Neil Western.
**Guangzhou** Chris Winnan. **Directory** Rehana Sheikh.

**Maps** JS Graphics (john@jsgrahics.co.uk). Digital data for maps supplied by Apa Publications GmbH & Co. Verlag KG
(Singapore branch).

**Photography** Jon Perugia, except: page 7 AKG; pages 10, 201 Topham Picturepoint; pages 15, 16 Hulton Archive; page 19
Associated Press; page 21 PA News; page 22 AFP; page 39 naturepl.com; page 40 courtesy of Dolphinwatch; page 42
NHPA/B Jones & M Shimlock; page 60 Gareth Brown; page 88 Reuters; pages 103, 109, 187 courtesy of the Hong Kong
Tourism Board; page 202 Kobal; page 233 courtesy of the Hong Kong Dance Company; page 258 courtesy of the Macau
Government Tourist Office.

**The Editor would like to thank** Florence Chan and Keven Chan at the Royal Garden; Lamey Chang and Joanne Brenchley at
the Peninsula; Caroline Courtauld; Carole Klein at the Intercontinental; Portia Lau at the Grand Hyatt; Katharine Liu and Gloria
Si Tou at the Hyatt Regency, Macau; James Mitchell; Daisy Poon; Renee Shaukat Ali; Wen Shi De; Kelly Sum and Ilona Yim at
the Island Shangri-La; Neil Weissman; Jason Williams.

# Contents

# Introduction

Most first-time visitors arrive and depart with the impression that Hong Kong is a cosmopolitan, international city. And so it is, at least in part. But there is much more to it than most people immediately recognise, and even many long-term residents never really get to grips with the place. Some of the impressions are obvious to the point of cliché, and, like all good clichés, they obscure as much as they explain.

Hong Kong is widely portrayed as some sort of near-mystical melding of East and West; an English-speaking ex-British colony that somehow contrives to be more modern than tomorrow and yet still retain significant elements of 'ancient Chinese wisdom'; a concrete jungle, densely clotted with more people per square kilometre than anywhere else on earth. Stir in a liberal measure of shopping and dining and there you have it – the stereotypical Hong Kong experience.

But let's look at the truth. A massive 96 per cent of the population is ethnic Chinese – a surprise to many visitors who presume that a 'cosmopolitan' city must be far more diverse than that. This explains why, unlike in other parts of the former British empire, English is not as widely spoken in Hong Kong as is commonly assumed – another myth exposed.

And what about the city's reputation as a shopper's paradise? Even this was under threat a few years back, when other regional destinations like Bangkok started to catch up. With airfares from Western Europe, Australia and the US costing about the same to the rest of South-east Asia as to Hong Kong – and with far lower accommodation costs while there – it made more sense to shop there instead. And the stampede of globalisation has meant that many formerly expensive items – electronics in particular – now cost the same or less at home than in Hong Kong. Thankfully, local deflation and the lack of sales tax have started to bring a resurgence in the value-for-money shopping scene here, and the trend seems set to continue.

Yet while Hong Kong's image as a shopping mecca is enjoying a renaissance, its reputation for fine dining remains overhyped. International restaurants are pretty much indistinguishable from their counterparts in London, Sydney or New York, at generally the same or higher prices. Hygiene standards remain a perennial problem everywhere in Hong Kong, and cholera outbreaks in seafood restaurants occur almost every summer. Don't get us wrong: the food in Hong Kong can be great, and there are excellent bargains to be had, especially during this time of deflation. It's just that, like everything else here, getting a really good meal takes homework and persistence.

Central's pavements at lunchtime epitomise the grotesquely overcrowded image of Hong Kong. But stand along the waterfront promenade in Tsim Sha Tsui and look across to Hong Kong Island and a very different scene merges above and behind the high-rises – one of massive buildings backed by green mountainsides. Indeed, the wildly lovely side of Hong Kong is one of its most unexplored – and therefore most surprising – aspects.

Of course, any impressions of Hong Kong – whether based on truth or not – have recently been overshadowed by matters beyond the former colony's control. 2003 was an extended rollercoaster ride for Hong Kong, and most of the time it seemed to be heading downhill. It started with SARS but came to a head with a huge demonstration against the Hong Kong Government, seen by the locals as arrogant and indecisive. To some degree, it did the trick: within weeks of the protest the public mood had started to change and improve. The subsequent easing of restrictions on individual travellers visiting Hong Kong from certain parts of the mainland greatly helped the local economy, with visitor numbers surging. By the end of 2003 flights to Hong Kong were mostly full, getting a hotel room was becoming a problem and – a telling marker – the city's renowned hotel buffet spreads were booked out days in advance. To all outward observations, the city's capacity for resilience was demonstrating itself yet again and things were beginning to look up.

In practical terms, Hong Kong's ongoing economic woes and the political shortcomings of its leadership will not have any impact on the casual visitor. In fact, the current period of deflation, and the resulting decreased costs, have convinced more and more overseas travellers that the city is again worth a visit, and having come once, many find that they like it and want to return. They're discovering that the real Hong Kong has a great deal to offer – beyond the age-old clichés.

## ABOUT THE TIME OUT CITY GUIDES

The *Time Out Hong Kong Guide* is one of an expanding series of Time Out City Guides, now numbering 45, produced by the people behind London and New York's successful listings magazines. Our guides are all written and updated by resident experts, who have striven to provide you with all the most up-to-date information you'll need to explore the city, whether you're a local or first-time visitor.

## THE LOWDOWN ON THE LISTINGS

Above all, we've tried to make this book as useful as possible. Addresses, phone numbers, transport information, opening times, admission prices, websites and credit card details are all included in our listings. And, as far as possible, we've given details of facilities, services and events, all checked and correct at the time we went to press. However, since owners and managers can change their arrangements at any time, we always advise readers to telephone and check opening times and other particulars. While every effort has been made to ensure the accuracy of the information contained in this guide, the publishers cannot accept responsibility for any errors it may contain.

## PRICES AND PAYMENT

We have noted whether venues such as shops, hotels and restaurants accept credit cards or not but have only listed the major cards – American Express (**AmEx**), Diners Club (**DC**), MasterCard (**MC**) and Visa (**V**). Many businesses will also accept other cards and travellers' cheques.

The prices we've supplied should be treated as guidelines, not gospel. Fluctuating exchange rates and inflation can cause charges, in shops and restaurants particularly, to change rapidly. If prices vary wildly from those we've quoted, please write and let us know. We aim to give the best and most up-to-date advice, so we always want to know if you've been badly treated or overcharged.

## THE LIE OF THE LAND

Hong Kong falls fairly neatly into four basic areas: Hong Kong Island, the Kowloon peninsula (across Victoria Harbour), the New Territories (the vast swathe of land ballooning out from the north of

Kowloon up to the border with Guangdong province and the rest of China) and the Outlying Islands. Each of these areas has its own chapter within the Sightseeing section, and each is further subdivided into districts. In this guide, in chapters not already divided by area, these districts are included within the addresses. Wherever possible, a map reference is provided for places listed.

## TELEPHONE NUMBERS

The international code for Hong Kong is 852; there is no area code. All phone numbers are eight digits. For more on telephones, see p290.

## ESSENTIAL INFORMATION

For all the practical information you might need for visiting the city – including visa and customs information, disabled access, emergency phone numbers, useful websites and the local transport network – turn to the **Directory** chapter at the back of this guide. It starts on p276.

## MAPS

The maps section at the back of this book, which starts on p305, includes overview maps of Hong Kong, the region and the public transport system, as well as street maps of the city.

## LET US KNOW WHAT YOU THINK

We hope you enjoy the *Time Out Hong Kong Guide*, and we'd like to know what you think of it. We welcome tips for places that you consider we should include in future editions and take notice of your criticism of our choices. There's a reader's reply card at the back of this book – or you can email us on guides@timeout.com.

There is an online version of this book, along with guides to 45 other international cities, at **www.timeout.com**.

# A taste of Time Out City Guides

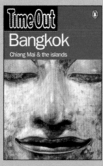

# In Context

## Features

# What Londoners take when they go out.

EVERY WEEK

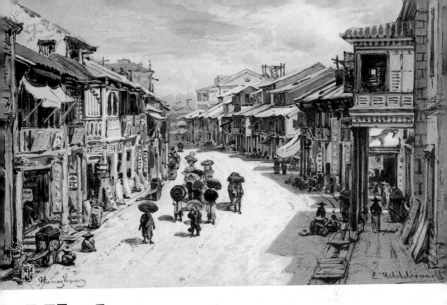

# History

Forever occupied, Hong Kong proves that it's not always easy being popular.

The Portuguese mariner Jorge Alvares was the first European to visit the area surrounding Hong Kong. In 1513 he landed on the island of Lintin, which lies west of the New Territories in the middle of the Pearl River Delta.

### WEST AND EAST COLLIDE

Alvares' mission had started in Malacca, now in Malaysia, which the Portuguese had captured in 1511. He was intent on establishing a sea route to China, so that greater profit could be made on goods purchased direct from their source, rather than through Chinese traders. Chinese porcelain, for example, fetched extremely high prices in Europe, with good-quality ceramics commanding twice their own weight in silver when resold in Goa.

When Alvares arrived on Lintin, the local mandarinate received him in a friendly manner and trade commenced. As a result, Alvares spent most of the next ten months on the island (which is known as 'Solitary Nail' in Chinese, due to its sharply pointed shape), before returning to Malacca when the south-west monsoon winds permitted his little flotilla to sail. Although they were not given much freedom of movement, the traders visiting Lintin were not as closely confined by the Chinese authorities as in later centuries, and, while it is not recorded, it is highly likely that Alvares and his men visited the nearby mainland.

While on Lintin, they erected a *padrão* (or stone) carved with the Portuguese cross and crest, though nothing of it survives today. These stones functioned more as markers of passage for later seafarers than as territorial claims, and were erected wherever the Portuguese mariners sailed, from Mombasa and Ormuz to western India and the Moluccas. Alvares' young son accompanied him on the voyage from Malacca, but he died at Lintin and was buried at the base of the *padrão* erected by his father. Alvares himself made two more voyages to China, in 1519 and in 1521. During the latter, he died and was buried beneath the *padrão* in the same spot as his son.

Other navigators followed in his wake, of course. Periodic trade developed between the Portuguese and Chinese at various locations up and down the coast. These changed from season to season, but one of the most regularly used was the island of Lampacao. It was here

# Foreign devils and big heads

One of the more unappealing and obvious aspects of life in Hong Kong for many local residents – but effectively invisible to the average visitor – is racial discrimination. Being openly looked down upon by the Hong Kong Chinese is an insidious and all-too-frequent part of daily life for thousands of ethnic Hong Kong residents. The problem is made worse by its obvious nature and the official denial that it ever occurs at all.

One doesn't have to live in Hong Kong very long to realise that the place is obsessed with fairness of skin; the darker you are, the lower on the social hierarchy you are perceived to be. Japanese manners, fashions and concepts of beauty are admired, at least partly because of their fair complexions. (There is a tremendous market in Hong Kong for skin-whitening products from Japan.)

Probably Hong Kong's hottest topic in recent years has been the perceived rights and privileges enjoyed by recent mainland migrants to Hong Kong. Almost anything concerning *sun yee mun* (new immigrants) stimulates impassioned debate. More than 150 new entrants come legally into Hong Kong from the mainland every day; a total of 50,000 per year. But one salient fact that most members of the public conveniently forget is that, until relatively recently, almost everyone living in Hong Kong was either a *sun yee mun* or the child of one.

Mainland women are routinely referred to in the Chinese-language tabloid press – especially if they are young, single and pretty – as '*paak kwu*' – a slang term meaning 'northern aunties'. These women are openly dismissed as being on the make and out to snare a husband. The grasping, scheming *paak kwu*, speaking broken, Mandarin-accented Cantonese, is a stock character of Hong Kong soap operas and films.

Pakistani guards are a common sight outside pawn shops, banks and jewellery stores all over the island. Among the Chinese population, the Sikh and Punjabi policemen are known as '*dai tau luk yee*', or 'big heads and green jackets', a reference to the turbans and the colour of their uniforms. Sikhs, Punjabis and other minority groups from the Indian subcontinent face considerable discrimination from the Chinese majority, with Cantonese epithets such as '*chau cha*' ('stinking Indians') and '*dai tau gwai*' ('big head devils') commonly used. Ironically, most

local Indians were born and raised in Hong Kong and are fluent Cantonese speakers who understand fully what is being said about them. There are numerous families of Indian and Pakistani heritage who have lived in Hong Kong for well over a century, and who have as legitimate a claim to being truly 'Hong Kong people' as most Hong Kong Chinese, many of whose parents arrived in the 1950s.

Filipinos, Indonesians and Thais form the majority of Hong Kong's community of domestic workers, which accounts for almost two per cent of the population. These groups are discriminated against, routinely underpaid and overworked. They have few legal rights, and taking a case to the Labour Tribunal is usually more trouble than it is worth. Discouraged from using many shops and facilities – and contemptuously referred to as '*ah bun*' (for Filipinas) or '*nai mui*' (for Indonesians) – they receive little sympathy from the wider community.

Black people fare no better than the rest. They are referred to by the Cantonese as '*haak gwai*', meaning 'black devils', and it is by no means unusual for those in this group to be refused job interviews or to be given poor service in shops or restaurants solely because of their race. Many people of African heritage living in Hong Kong report that on buses and the MTR, Chinese will pointedly get up and walk away if black people sit down near them. Some Hong Kong Chinese openly refer to blacks as dirty and primitive; such slurs even appear now and again in the popular press.

Europeans and those of anglo heritage are generally referred to as '*gweilo*', literally 'devil men', or as '*faan gwai*' (foreign devils). Despite being openly derogatory, the use of *gweilo* is ubiquitous in Hong Kong, and many Europeans openly refer to themselves as *gweilo*. The term '*sai yan*' ('Western person'), is much more polite, though, unfortunately, few Chinese use it.

So far the Hong Kong Government has refused to enact any anti-discrimination legislation at all. One senior government official went so far as to claim, quite astonishingly, that 'as Hong Kong has so few black people, there is almost no racism'. Thus, the daily, officially denied racism routinely endured by many Hong Kong residents remains one of the most shameful open secrets in 'Asia's World City'.

that the Catholic missionary St Francis Xavier died and was buried, later being exhumed and reburied in Malacca, before being removed at a later date to Goa.

At this time, the prevalence of pirates on the islands around the mouth of the Pearl River Delta led to them being dubbed the *Ilhas Ladrones* or 'Islands of Robbers'. In fact, piracy remained a major problem in these waters up to the mid 20th century. But that did not stop trading ships from all over Asia anchoring in the triangle between Lintin, the northern side of Deep Bay and present-day Tuen Mun, in the hope of trading with south China. The Siamese, in particular, had a large seasonal presence, mooring further out by Lantau's northern coast.

## THE EXPANSION OF MACAU

However, when the Portuguese established Macau as a permanent trading settlement with the permission of the local Chinese mandarinate in about 1557, the face of South China trade changed. The tiny port rapidly developed as a centre of *entrepôt* trade between China and Japan, using Portuguese vessels and mariners as carriers. Repeated pirate raids by the Japanese had led to their prohibition from Chinese ports. This, together with Ming Dynasty restrictions on the movement of Chinese abroad, meant that the Portuguese were in the perfect position to act as middlemen, bringing raw Chinese silk to Japan, and returning with silver and copper. Thus, the Portuguese all but monopolised the carrying trade, ushering in a period of wealth and prosperity that Macau has not seen since; 1560 to 1640 is often referred to as the Golden Age of Macau.

In addition to trade, the Portuguese played a major role in exporting Catholic missionaries to Japan, an unwelcome activity that eventually led to the complete closure of Japan to Portuguese trade in 1639.

The first British navigator to reach the China coast, Captain Weddell, had by now landed at Macau (he arrived in 1637), and, in spite of orders by the Chinese not to approach, tried to enter the city of Canton (now Guangzhou) in Guangdong province. He was driven away, and no further British vessels visited these waters for several decades.

The closure of Japan to Portuguese trade was an important factor both in Macau's period of slow decline (which continued until the late 18th century) and the subsequent rise of British and Dutch colonial power in Asia. Throughout this period, Hong Kong remained unnoticed on the other side of the Pearl River Delta, just one more island among hundreds up and down the Guangdong coast, inhabited by only a few fishermen, farmers and pirates.

## CANTON TRADE

For centuries after the establishment of Macau, European traders were not permitted any permanent trading station in China other than Macau itself. Seasonal trade at the port of Canton was permitted, but merchants had to leave the city at the end of the trading season and return to Macau. While in Canton, they were prohibited from bringing their wives and families with them, forbidden to learn Chinese and had their movements around town restricted. Few were allowed to venture beyond their trading compounds, or 'factories', as they were known. These restrictions became increasingly irksome, accompanied as they were by bribery, corruption and constantly changing standards and expectations.

## 'Lord William John Napier's name, unpromisingly, transliterated into Chinese as "laboriously vile".'

The mid 18th century witnessed a growing passion in Europe for tea, silk and other luxury goods, thanks to a long period of steadily rising prosperity. Tea, especially, was in enormous demand and, at this time, China enjoyed a world monopoly on supply. The Chinese insisted that everything be paid for in silver specie (China remained on the silver standard until the early 1930s), which, in due course, led to serious balance of trade deficits in favour of China, as it had little use for European trade goods at the time, other than a few clocks, trinkets and curios. The key to unlocking the Chinese treasure chest was opium.

## INTERNATIONAL TRADE

The British East India Company grew opium under government monopoly in India and sold it at public auction in Calcutta every year. Merchants associated with the company bought opium at the Calcutta auctions and smuggled it to China aboard specially built vessels. Numerous trading houses that later became big names on the China Coast – such as Jardine Matheson, Dent's and Russell's – were heavily involved in the opium trade. Still, while it is the British who are usually vilified for introducing opium to China, it is worth remembering that numerous Scandinavian and American firms were heavily involved as well. The major opium-smuggling depot was located on Lintin, where Alvares had made his China landfall back in 1513. Although numerous opium bans were introduced by the Chinese government, they were largely ineffectual due to local corruption and the active involvement of

The French and British eye up the martial options against China in the 1850s. *See p11.*

Chinese officials in the illicit trade. What's more, a couple of attempts by British East India Company officials to formalise diplomatic relations between Britain and China were rebuffed by the Chinese.

The ever-increasing volume of foreign merchant shipping in the region alarmed the Chinese authorities, and they constructed coastal defences, including forts at Fan Lau and Tung Chung on Lantau island, at the Bocca Tigris (Bogue), some of which still stand today.

### THE FIRST OPIUM WAR

From 1830, there was a gradual increase in tension between the British merchants and the Chinese authorities in Canton over opium. As a result, in 1834, Lord William John Napier was appointed Commissioner of Trade, with the directive to regularise trade and establish diplomatic relations between the two empires. Napier's name, unpromisingly, transliterated into Chinese as 'laboriously vile'.

When Napier died while on official duty, he was succeeded by Captain Charles Elliot. Elliot was in the unenviable position of having to support a trade of which (subsequent correspondence has shown) he did not

personally approve, and negotiate with the Chinese, who – at this time – had no experience of dealing with other nations.

In 1839 Commissioner Lin Tse-hsü was appointed to suppress the opium trade. Lin did his work well, and his campaign resulted in the surrender and destruction of over 20,000 chests of (mostly British-owned) opium at Canton. This action provided the *causus belli* for military action for which many of the merchants had long been agitating in the British Parliament, and a British fleet dispatched from India attacked the Bogue forts on the Pearl River approaches to Canton.

Various attempts at conciliation failed, but eventually the Convention of Chuen Pi (signed in 1841) ended hostilities. The subsequent Treaty of Nanking, signed in 1842, arranged for the opening of five Chinese ports to foreign trade, and for the cession of Hong Kong Island 'in perpetuity' to the British Crown, as a place of permanent, stable, safe British trade.

### WHY HONG KONG ISLAND?

Hong Kong Island was chosen over other larger and more prosperous locations (such as the island of Chusan at the entrance to the Yangtze in eastern China) because it was well known to mariners and possessed an excellent natural harbour. Ships travelling to Canton or further up and down the coast would usually call at Waterfall Bay (near where you'll now find Wah Fu Estate on the western side of Hong Kong Island) for fresh drinking water; they also took shelter from stormy weather and typhoons at Shek Pai Wan (modern Aberdeen). The name Hong Kong is a corruption of Heung Gong, meaning 'fragrant harbour', a reference to the sandalwood incense mills then found at Aberdeen that could be smelled from the sea.

Hong Kong Island was formally occupied on 26 January 1841, and developed rapidly as merchants and traders previously based in Canton and Macau moved to the island.

## EARLY DEVELOPMENTS

Central district was the first area of planned urban development in Hong Kong. At land sales held in June 1841 (five months after the British flag was raised at Possession Point), 51 lots of land were sold to 23 merchant houses for the purpose of building offices and godowns (as warehouses are known in Asia). These firms included Jardine Matheson, which is still prominent today, and its then-rival Dent's (which would later be wiped out in the slump of 1867). Office buildings were constructed between the waterfront and Queen's Road.

## 'Without additional expansion, Hong Kong and Kowloon might still be British today.'

In November 1841 the ridge of land between Albany Nullah (now Garden Road) and Glenealy Nullah (now Glenealy) was set aside for Crown use, and subsequently became known as Government Hill. The Colonial Secretariat, Government House, Albany Government Quarters and St John's Cathedral were all built on this slope. The area extending between Government Hill and Wan Chai was designated for military use. Victoria and Wellington Barracks were built, and the area remained on the defence estate until the late 1970s. This officially created division between the districts of Central and Wan Chai meant that additional residential and commercial areas could only be developed to the east of the military cantonment.

In 1843, after Hong Kong officially became a Crown Colony and, thus, a permanent settlement, the rapidly developing city was named Victoria; it extended over what is now Sheung Wan, Central and Wan Chai. Central became the principal business district and

centre of administration. In addition to the military cantonments to the east of Government Hill, a military camp was built at Stanley soon after the British arrival.

From the 1840s the area around Lyndhurst Terrace, Hollywood Road and Aberdeen Street was a European residential area. From the 1870s onwards, however, increasing numbers of Chinese merchants bought properties in this area, converting the buildings into tenements. So the Europeans moved up the hill to the area around Caine Road and Robinson Road.

The Crown Colony's first two decades were buccaneering in spirit, characterised by corruption, lawlessness, brutality and an attitude of 'make-it-quick, get-out-fast' that some would say has persisted ever since.

A key problem in the beginning was the lack of an efficient civil service, as almost no Government officers for the first 20 or so years of the colony's existence were able to speak or read Chinese. The legal system was hopelessly inadequate, with many government posts filled by almost anyone who happened to be in Hong Kong when a job was going.

There was little interaction between the Chinese and European communities, leading to fear, bigotry and misunderstanding on both sides. An attempted poisoning of the main European bread supply in 1857 caused widespread panic and alienation between the two communities.

The first specially recruited Hong Kong Government administrative cadets to be taught Cantonese were appointed in 1862, and this led to the gradual improvement in government standards and relations between the Europeans and the Chinese in the city.

## THE SECOND OPIUM WAR AND THE DEVELOPMENT OF KOWLOON

A Chinese-led raid on a British registered vessel – the *Arrow* – led to what became known as the Second Opium (or Arrow) War (1857-60). During this conflict, the Summer Palace in Beijing was burned, and afterwards an Anglo-French force governed Canton from 1858 to 1860.

Locally, the conflict led to the cession of the Kowloon peninsula and Stonecutter's Island to Britain in 1860. The new extent of the territory stretched northwards to Boundary Street, and included Tsim Sha Tsui.

The first European settlers in Kowloon were the local Portuguese community, who moved across the harbour from the late 19th century. By the 1920s, Tsim Sha Tsui was almost a Portuguese district, and, until the 1950s, the Portuguese represented the largest non-British, non-Chinese section of the population.

From the 1860s onwards commercial and residential opportunities in Kowloon became apparent, leading to the gradual expansion of the new area. At around the same time, Hong Kong experienced a prolonged economic boom.

The original (pre-1860) land area of Tsim Sha Tsui and the Kowloon peninsula has been greatly enlarged by numerous phases of reclamation over the years; much of which involved removing the tops of the hills that once dominated the area. The result is that the topography has changed completely. The names of some Kowloon streets today, such as Reclamation Street in Yau Ma Tei, provide some clues to the peninsula's former coastlines and hills. *See also p93* **Taking it back**.

The early settlement comprised a British military encampment at Tsim Sha Tsui and a few scattered Chinese hamlets, the most significant being Tai Hang, located near the present-day Granville Road. The military presence continued for many years, with permanent barracks at Gun Club Hill on Austin Road and Whitfield Barracks (now Kowloon Park) on Nathan Road.

## 'The funicular Peak Tram commenced operations in 1888, and has been popular with both visitors and residents ever since.'

Hung Hom further to the east and Sham Shui Po to the north were both early industrial areas, and were established long before the post-war boom in industry that led to Hong Kong's phenomenal growth and resounding international success. The industry that developed here was light manufacturing and included the production of plimsolls, torches and low technology goods.

On Hong Kong Island, the Peak district gradually became more popular as a retreat from hot weather, and the first houses were built there in the 1860s. The hillside funicular Peak Tram commenced operations in 1888, and has been popular with both visitors and residents ever since.

Reclamation work aimed at extending the business district started in 1890 and finished in 1904, adding a large new area. Industry started its initially tentative development at this time with the construction of commercial dockyards at Aberdeen, Hung Hom and Taikoo. These catered to the annually increasing volume of shipping that frequented the colony's harbour. All major and many minor shipping lines called at Hong Kong.

Communications with the world's markets were swift and efficient, as the island became a telecommunications hub; telegraph cables linking Britain and Hong Kong's southern coast (the cable house can still be seen today at Deep Water Bay) were laid in 1870.

## HEALTHCARE AND THE FOUNDING OF TUNG WAH HOSPITAL

For its first 30 years as a British colony, Hong Kong lacked a general hospital. The Government Civil Hospital was established in 1850, and at first catered mainly to the police force and the destitutes they picked up; around 1864 it became accessible to private paying patients as well. The then-expensive fees of HK$1 were a discouragement for most, and very few Chinese wished to use it anyway. Part of this reluctance was due to a general distrust of foreigners, and a deeply held belief that their intentions – however noble they might seem on the surface – were ultimately evil. Western medicine, in particular, emphasised surgery and post-mortem examinations at a time when most Chinese devoutly believed that after death one should return to one's ancestors with an unmutilated body. To an extent they had a point, since 19th-century Western medical science, with its dirty, badly administered hospitals, poorly trained nurses and few specific cures for diseases did little to inspire public confidence – even among those familiar with its practices.

The closest thing that the Chinese had to a hospital was the I Ts'z, where the terminally ill were sent to die because death at home was reckoned to render the house unclean. In 1869, however, the then Governor Sir Richard MacDonnell closed the I Ts'z on account of the appalling conditions, and the idea of a hospital funded and administered by Chinese was proposed. Consequently, the Tung Wah Hospital was established as 'a Chinese hospital for the care and treatment of the indigent sick, to be supported by voluntary contributions', which is how it has largely remained to this day. Sir Richard MacDonnell laid the foundation stone in 1870 on Po Yan Street in Western district, and it is still there today.

The hospital was run by a committee, the members of which were drawn from the comprador (mercantile middle-man) class. Compradors at this time were at the height of their wealth and influence in Hong Kong and the Treaty Ports, but in time their influence declined as Chinese independently engaged in business, medicine or the law took their place. Later still, the compradors were further pushed aside by bankers, department store owners, rich overseas Chinese and émigrés from the 1911 Revolution. This latter group formed a more diversified Chinese elite than existed in the 19th century, and eventually replaced the compradors as arbiters of power and influence within the Tung Wah.

Another important component of the Tung Wah Hospital Committee were the representatives of the various merchant guilds, such as the Nam Pak Hong (dealing mainly with the import of rice and South-East Asian products), the California Merchants Guild (which dealt with the lucrative West Coast trade) and the Chinese Medicine Guild. The guilds elected representative members to the Tung Wah Hospital Committee from among their own number – a forerunner of today's functional constituencies.

*Kaifongs* (street committees), which were found all over Hong Kong, also elected members to the Tung Wah Hospital Committee. *Kaifong* members were simply groups of civic-minded, status-seeking citizens who voted themselves in as a public body. They were accepted – or at least tolerated – by the general public because they were either affluent or 'fixers'; none of their 'constituents' ever actually voted for them. They chose themselves. Elections to the Tung Wah Hospital Committee were conducted from among these closed ranks.

The committee wielded so much influence among the Chinese community that in time it became a sort of 'shadow' Legislative Council, and was often resented and criticised by the Hong Kong government for its wide-ranging power over the Chinese community. However, much later, the more senior members of the committee would be appointed as unofficial Chinese members of the Legislative Council, with the result that their influence was regularised and channelled into political development for the Chinese community.

### THE INCLUSION OF THE LOCAL POPULATION

The first tentative steps at involving representatives of the Chinese community more actively in government affairs in Hong Kong started in the late 1870s. The experiment, which did not prove to be a great success, involved the forward-thinking governor Sir John Pope Hennessy and Ng Choy, also known as Wu Ting Fang.

When Pope Hennessy arrived in Hong Kong in 1877, one of his first thoughts was that the time had come to accord more representation to the Chinese community. The Chinese community had already begun to demand representation, and, in January 1879, sent a memorandum to London arguing that as there

were ten times more Chinese than foreigners in Hong Kong, 'it would be but fair to allow the Chinese community a share in the management of the affairs of the colony'. Regional precedents for such a move existed – Singapore had appointed a Chinese member to the Legislative Council in 1869, and Pope Hennessy had made a similar appointment when he was Governor on Labuan, an island off the Borneo coast.

Pope Hennessy's sympathetic attitude to Asians was partially coloured by his marriage to Kitty, the vivacious and attractive Eurasian daughter of the early Malayan administrator Sir Hugh Low. He certainly had no problem with appointing Ng Choy (a British subject born in Singapore into the famous Canton merchant family of Howqua) to the Legislative Council. Educated from an early age in England, Ng Choy trained as a barrister, becoming the first Chinese person called to the English bar, although he subsequently practised in Hong Kong.

The appointment was criticised by European merchants who felt the move was too conciliatory to the Chinese, and would encourage further demands for participation in public life. They also questioned how it was possible for a Chinese to be loyal to Britain, as questions of race and nationality were so closely intertwined. Ng Choy finally resigned from the Legislative Council in 1883, but, using the name Wu Ting Fang, he later became a national figure on the mainland, serving over the years as Chinese Ambassador to the United States, Peru, Mexico and Cuba, and as China's Foreign Minister.

As a British subject, Ng Choy (who became more nationalistic as he grew older) represented the dilemma of the 'overseas' Chinese. Where did their ultimate loyalties lie? With China or with the countries in which they were born and raised? This question is still faced by overseas Chinese communities in places such as Indonesia today.

### LEASING OF THE NEW TERRITORIES

Towards the end of the 19th century, tensions increased between the various European powers with interests in China. The Germans were heavily involved in Shandong province in northern China, where the city of Tsingtao – still world famous for its brewery today – remained a Teutonic enclave until the Germans were expelled by the Japanese in 1915. The French leased the port of Kwangchowwan between Hong Kong and Haiphong on the Guangdong coast, in 1898 (at the same time as the British leased the New Territories), and remained there until 1943.

It was also in 1898 that the British leased the tiny port of Wei Hai Wei in Shandong, where they remained until 1930. Used as a cool-weather station for the Royal Navy, Wei Hai Wei later played a role in recruiting Shandong men into the Hong Kong Police force.

The principal reason behind the lease of the New Territories was the British belief that it would be impossible to defend Hong Kong Island and Kowloon against attack without having possession of the hills north of the Kowloon peninsula. Unlike the two previous cessions of land from China to Britain (which were essentially the spoils of war and 'unequal treaty'), the New Territories (and around 230 islands) were obtained on a 99-year lease through the 1898 Convention of Peking, sparking off the entire 1997 issue. Without this additional expansion, Hong Kong and Kowloon might still be British today.

Another key element of Hong Kong's relationship with the New Territories has always been fresh water. From the earliest days of British settlement, demand has continually outstripped supply, due to the steady increase in population that the colony's politically stable environment encouraged. Tank streams were quickly over-utilised, and wells in urban areas became contaminated and unsafe.

In the 19th century a number of reservoirs were built on Hong Kong Island. For a while, they were adequate for the needs of the growing city. By the late 1920s, however, the growth of urban Hong Kong made the need for a new reservoir extremely urgent. The only viable location was in the Kowloon hills, at the head of the Shing Mun valley. The project was opposed by the Colonial Office on the grounds that the reservoir would be built in the New Territories, which were leased and would, therefore, revert to China in around 70 years. Building a capital-intensive scheme on someone else's land, as it were, was, they felt, a great waste of money.

This was a view strongly countered by Sir Cecil Clementi, one of Hong Kong's most able and visionary colonial administrators. A possible solution to the problem of the Shing Mun reservoirs, in Clementi's view, lay over a thousand miles to the north of Hong Kong.

Clementi's proposal involved offering to return Wei Hai Wei to Chinese control – as it was a disposable backwater that had never really prospered – in return for outright cession by China of the New Territories, which were vital to Hong Kong's continued growth. His proposal was rejected by the Foreign Office as unnecessary and unworkable, and likely to stir up demands from the Nanking Government for further abandonment of British concessions and privileges elsewhere in China. Yet, in 1930, as a gesture of goodwill, Wei Hai Wei was returned to Chinese rule.

The Shing Mun reservoirs were eventually built anyway, as the growing demand for reliable water supplies overrode all else. Extensive reforestation was undertaken to safeguard the water catchments. Photographs of the Shing Mun area taken in the late 1930s show large areas of thriving new forestry, in stark contrast to the treeless grassy hills in much of the rest of the New Territories. The villages in the valley were removed and their inhabitants were resettled in the north-west New Territories. The village built for them at Kam Tin was named Shing Mun San Tsuen, or Shing Mun New Village. Located between Tai Hong Wai and Wing Lung Wai, the resettlement village still maintains a distinct and separate identity from the rest of the village. There are numerous old people who remember the move from the old village (which has been under water for decades now). Even after more than 60 years, the Shing Mun people are still outsiders at Kam Tin.

## GROWTH OF CHINESE NATIONALISM

In 1900, two years after the New Territories lease was ratified, the Boxer Rebellion broke out in China. Overspill into the Hong Kong region was limited, with the areas most affected being in north China. Support for radical change in China during this period was generated in southern China by Dr Sun Yat-sen and the earlier reformer Kang Yu-hwei (both of whom were Cantonese). Sun Yat-sen attended school in Hong Kong and was a graduate of the Hong Kong College of Medicine. Giving a lecture at Hong Kong University in 1923, he said that it was the peace, prosperity and good government that he had experienced in the British colony, which – contrasted with the chaos and corruption in China itself – had turned him into a revolutionary.

Escalating periods of Chinese nationalist agitation during the years following the fall of the Qing (or Manchu) Dynasty and beginning of the Republican period spilled over into Hong Kong with a tramways strike and boycott in 1912-13, a seamen's strike in 1922 and a General Strike in 1925. The Nationalist (or Kuomintang) Government was based at Canton, and China was divided into numerous feuding warlord fiefdoms. The country was unified under the Nationalists after Chiang Kai-Shek led the Northern Expedition in 1927-8, and subsequently removed the capital to Nanking.

## CHINA VERSUS JAPAN

Around 1853-4 Japan emerged from a period of self-imposed isolation, during which time it was known as *sakoku*, or 'the locked-in country'. Rapidly opening itself up to the West, it modernised every aspect of government, industrialised rapidly and started encroaching on foreign borders.

Japan went to war with – and defeated – the Chinese in 1894-5. Then, while fighting on the Allied side during World War I, it occupied German ports, mines, railway concessions and other enterprises in China, most of which were granted to Japan in the 1919 Versailles Peace Conference.

Throughout the 1920s there was continued Japanese expansion throughout the north-east of China. The rise of Chang Hsueh-liang (known as the Young Marshal) – who only came to power after the Japanese assassinated his father, Manchurian warlord Chang Tso-lin (known as the Old Marshal), at Mukden in 1928 – stemmed the Japanese advance for a time.

However, in 1934, Pu Yi, the last Manchu Emperor of China, was made the puppet Emperor of Manchukuo by the Japanese, formalising their annexation of China's north-eastern provinces. All-out war between Japan and China began in July 1937. The Japanese quickly captured Chinese coastal cities (surrounding Shanghai's International Settlement in the process) and advanced up the Yangtze Valley, where they perpetrated the notorious Rape of Nanking. In October 1938, the city of Canton fell to the Japanese, who advanced to the Shum Chun River (forming the border between the Chinese mainland and Hong Kong) a week or so later.

The Japanese push led to a massive influx of refugees into Hong Kong, which would eventually lead to a post-war housing crisis. Gradually forested from the 1860s to the 1930s, Hong Kong's hills were now deforested by refugees searching for fuel and somewhere to build huts.

> **'After three days of fighting, the line fell and Kowloon was evacuated, crowding Hong Kong Island with refugees.'**

The late 1930s marked the start of Hong Kong's small-scale industrialisation in northern Kowloon and elsewhere in the colony, a process that continued into the 1950s.

In spite of – or perhaps because of – the unsettled conditions on the Chinese mainland, Hong Kong experienced a prolonged period of economic boom. Japanese territorial incursions, which on one occasion included flying over Hong Kong territory and strafing

In the mid 20th century, the most efficient way of getting around Central was by rickshaw.

Europeans flee Hong Kong before the advance of the Japanese during World War II.

a packed refugee train near Fanling, led to a steady strengthening of defensive measures and an increase in the size of the garrison.

## JAPANESE OCCUPATION

In December 1941, at the same time as they launched attacks on Pearl Harbor, the Philippines and north Malaya, the Japanese crossed the border into the New Territories and bombed the airport at Kai Tak. Hong Kong's garrison, while prepared for war, was small and hopelessly outnumbered by the Japanese.

In the late 1930s a string of defensive tunnels, bunkers and machine-gun emplacements had been built in the Kowloon hills as Hong Kong's answer to the Maginot Line. Known then as the Inner Line, post-war it was referred to as the 'gin drinker's line', due to its location between Gin Drinker's Bay (now part of modern Kwai Chung) and Port Shelter. Unfortunately, it did not stand for long. After three days of fighting the line fell and Kowloon was evacuated, crowding Hong Kong Island with refugees. This further added to existing accommodation shortages and caused a water supply crisis that eventually played a large part in forcing the British to surrender.

After waiting almost a week, during which time they sent across two peace missions, the Japanese landed on Hong Kong Island on 18 December 1941. There followed a period of heavy fighting on the eastern side of Hong Kong Island, in the centre of the island at and around Wong Nai Chung Gap, and at Stanley. After 18 days of hostilities, the British finally surrendered on Christmas afternoon 1941, becoming in the process the first British colony to surrender to Japan during the Pacific War.

Partly as a measure of controlling Hong Kong's housing, food and fuel problems, the Japanese immediately initiated a policy of depopulation by forcing the local Chinese to evacuate to their mainland homes. Given the difficult conditions in Hong Kong, many Chinese residents in the urban areas voluntarily returned to their ancestral villages in the hinterland, where, although conditions may have been difficult, there was at least enough to eat.

Following the British surrender, there was widespread co-operation between the erstwhile local elite and the Japanese occupation authorities; these events later prompted a post-war enquiry into collaboration, the findings of which were, perhaps not surprisingly, never released.

Almost the entire Allied civilian population – men, women and children – were interned in a concentration camp at Stanley. Male military prisoners of war were imprisoned in their former barracks in Kowloon; many were later transported to Japan to work as slaves in the mines and on the docks.

One of the most aesthetically pleasing legacies of Japanese rule in Hong Kong is Government House. The original, built in the mid 19th century in tropical Georgian style, was in desperate need of repair when it was renovated by the Japanese. It still stands on Upper Albert Road in Central. The gardens can be visited by the general public once a year when the azaleas are in stunning full bloom.

Throughout their occupation, Chinese guerrillas operating from Kwangtung's East River district harried the Japanese and mounted a number of operations within Hong Kong, including a daring raid on the railway bridge in central Kowloon, but otherwise there was little resistance and the city was remarkably peaceful.

Following the Hiroshima and Nagasaki atomic bombs, the Japanese surrendered on 15 August 1945, much earlier than the Allies had anticipated. This left a brief power vacuum, which was filled by British officials coming out from internment and assuming control from the Japanese. A British fleet was dispatched from Sydney (where it had been undergoing a refit) when the surrender came through; it arrived in Hong Kong on 30 August 1945.

A period of British Military Administration followed, but civilian government was restored in May 1946 under Sir Mark Young, the pre-war governor, who returned to the role after his release as a prisoner of war.

### POST-WAR RECOVERY

As business – and more especially the *entrepôt* trade – had always been Hong Kong's lifeblood, the port was back in full operation very soon after the British returned. The fact that Hong Kong used the dollar rather than sterling, and was able to buy supplies direct from the USA, without having to wait for quotas to be approved from London, meant that the local economy was back on an even footing very swiftly.

# Relics of World War II

Memorials and tombstones abound in Hong Kong commemorating those who died defending the former British colony against the Japanese during World War II. Harder to find are a number of long-discarded concrete pill box gun placements, which were scattered across the territory in a vain attempt to spot and repel Japanese troops. One of the most accessible examples is found on a small ridge off the picnic and playground area on the circular walking track on **Victoria Peak** (*see p78*).

Small networks of bomb-shelter tunnels were cut into hillsides around this time and used in both Japanese air raids and then the ensuing American bombing campaigns when Hong Kong was officially under Japanese occupation. Again, all are now sealed up and many are inaccessible, but one of the easiest to find is in the car park of **St Andrew's Church** in Tsim Sha Tsui, where two bricked up entrances are clearly visible in an adjacent hillock.

Few visitors or residents, though, know that the grand colonial **Peninsula** hotel (*see p53*) played host to a major historic event that occurred during this period. Room 336 was the place where Hong Kong officially

surrendered to invading Japanese troops. When the territory's six defending battalions became overwhelmed on Christmas Day 1941 and retreated to Hong Kong Island, British territorial Commander-in-Chief General CM Maltby informed Governor Mark Young that resistance was no longer possible. The pair was escorted across Victoria Harbour, littered with burned-out vessels, into the Peninsula. There, on behalf of the British Government, they formally surrendered the British colony to Lieutenant-General Sakai. Governor Young remained under guard in this room for two months of interrogation, before he was transferred to a prisoner-of-war camp on the outskirts of Shanghai.

In **Stanley** (*see p83*), on Hong Kong Island's south side, a Commonwealth War Graves Commission cemetery holds the remains of the scores who died fighting the invaders, while part of today's maximum-security prison at Stanley was used by the temporary occupiers as a prisoner of war camp. And **Stanley Main Beach** (*see p84*) was the site of a particularly gruesome episode – the beheading of 33 Hong Kong residents of various ethnic origin by the Japanese – all charged with treason.

Sir Mark Young left Hong Kong in 1947, and was succeeded as governor by Sir Alexander Grantham, a former cadet who had started his administrative career in Hong Kong. For the next ten years, Grantham oversaw a prolonged period of uncertainty. In 1949 civil war and the communist takeover tore apart the mainland. A year later the Korean War broke out and the subsequent American embargo on trade with China – which as far as they were concerned included Hong Kong – stifled the colony's traditional reliance on the *entrepôt* trade.

However, much was also achieved during the decade, including the extension of Kai Tak airport. Rapid and highly efficient industrialisation, mainly fuelled by Shanghainese entrepreneurs who had fled the communists, was in full swing by the mid 1950s. It took advantage of the large pool of refugee labour willing to work for almost any wage.

## 'By the 1980s Hong Kong, formerly known as one of the most corrupt places in Asia, was one of the straightest.'

It was around this time that formerly marginal areas, such as Kwun Tong and Tsuen Wan on the outskirts of Kowloon, rapidly developed into industrial towns, full of spinning, dyeing and weaving mills, toy and plastics factories, and other labour-intensive light industries. Industry of this kind remained a mainstay of the Hong Kong economy until the late 1980s, when the re-opening of China to foreign and overseas investment made manufacturing on the mainland, with its low wages and lax controls, much more economical than in Hong Kong.

In the immediate post-war period, it was thought that many of the refugees who had fled to Hong Kong following the end of the civil war and the communist takeover would return to the mainland as the dust settled, much as waves of refugees had done in the past. Gradually, however, it became apparent that this latest influx had no intention of returning, and provision had to be made for their integration into Hong Kong.

Housing policy (which hitherto had been to tolerate the theoretically temporary squatter settlements that had grown up in various parts of the city) changed dramatically following a massive fire in one of the largest squatter settlements in Kowloon, which made 53,000 people homeless on Christmas Day 1953. The government's response was to develop a public housing programme that is probably post-war Hong Kong's most notable success. The largest single commercial landlord in the world, Hong Kong's Housing Authority, provides subsidised housing to over half the population.

There were other problems around this time. The aftermath of civil war on the mainland often spilled over into Hong Kong, and low-level nationalist/communist confrontations continued throughout the 1950s. Kowloon had serious nationalist-inspired riots in 1956, while the Star Ferry Riots in 1966 were communist-fomented (ironically, considering they were over the increase in price of first-class ferry tickets). Finally, in the summer of 1967, the Cultural Revolution spilled over into Hong Kong and Macau – bombs were thrown and a number of people were killed, but, in the end, the people of Hong Kong came out firmly in favour of the local government.

In addition, rapid industrialisation, massive population movements and a get-rich-quick refugee mentality all led to a spectacular growth of official corruption, especially within the Hong Kong Police. Eventually, the situation became so bad that a special Independent Commission Against Corruption with wide-ranging powers was introduced in 1974. The commission was remarkably effective – by the 1980s Hong Kong, formerly known as one of the most corrupt places in Asia, was one of the straightest and most transparent.

## FINANCIAL GROWTH AND THE JOINT DECLARATION
Under Governor Sir Murray MacLehose, who was in Hong Kong from 1971 to 1981, Hong Kong expanded into a regional financial centre. This resulted in a gradual move away from its traditional *entrepôt* role and the industrial reliance it had developed since the early 1950s.

After the domestic turmoil of the Cultural Revolution (1966-76), China re-emerged as a major consideration, especially as the time for the expiry of the New Territories lease drew closer. By the late 1970s, big businesses were beginning to press for a closer examination of the future of Hong Kong, as the issue of major developmental loans that would still be operational after 1997 needed to be addressed.

In 1979 MacLehose visited Beijing, where he was told by Deng Xiaoping to tell Hong Kong investors to 'put their hearts at ease'. Confidence in the future of Hong Kong soared, as many took this statement to be tacit approval for Hong Kong remaining under British rule beyond 1997. Behind the scenes, however, diplomatic moves were made to determine exactly what the situation was,

The **Star Ferry Riots** of 1966.

and, following Margaret Thatcher's visit to Beijing in 1982, both governments moved towards what eventually became the Joint Declaration, signed in 1984.

The Joint Declaration guaranteed that in 1997 Hong Kong would revert to full Chinese administration (China had, after all, never admitted any British sovereignty), with legal guarantees and safeguards for the future 'stability and prosperity' of Hong Kong.

Confidence, badly eroded in the early 1980s, was restored and Hong Kong continued to prosper. The professional classes, many of whom – or whose families – had fled China in the aftermath of the communist takeover, had no desire to become Chinese subjects, and the 1980s and 1990s saw over 50,000 a year emigrate to Australia, Canada, New Zealand and the United States. Many have since returned, having acquired a foreign passport or permanent residence, creating a returnee backwash with mixed – and at times confused – loyalties, with interesting implications for the future of Hong Kong.

## RUN-UP TO THE HANDOVER

June 1989 saw the violent suppression of student-led protests in Beijing's Tiananmen Square and, for a while, a deteriorated confidence in Hong Kong. Government policy at the time was not to further antagonise the Chinese Government in any way, but this attitude radically changed with the appointment of Chris Patten as the last British governor in 1992.

> **'Finally, on 30 June, the last governor boarded the *Britannia* and sailed away in a flood of his own tears.'**

Patten launched a series of wide-reaching electoral reforms without the backing of the Chinese Government, and a long period ensued when very little constructive was achieved. The small flurry of popular interest in democracy kicked up at the time subsided back into general political apathy within a few years. Urgently needed environmental and education reforms were sidelined due to politics, and are only now being introduced.

June 1997 saw the long-awaited Handover, a media feeding frenzy for the world press, which nevertheless turned into something of a non-event. The riots and unrest that the film crews were not-so-secretly hoping for didn't happen, the People's Liberation Army didn't have any opportunity for an immediate crackdown on the streets of Central, it rained

continually for weeks and, finally, on the night of 30 June, the last governor boarded the *Britannia* and sailed away in a flood of his own tears.

## LIFE AFTER THE HANDOVER

Much of the gloom and disaster somewhat gleefully forecast for Hong Kong by the world's media in the lead-up to the Handover has failed to materialise, although the new Special Administrative Region (SAR) has had more than its fair share of problems over the last six years. The Asian economic crisis in 1997-8, which decimated the so-called 'tiger economies', hit Hong Kong quite badly, and its effects still linger. But the political fallout that rocked other regional economies, such as Indonesia, was cushioned here by massive government intervention in the stock market. Similarly, the Hong Kong dollar remained stable due to considerable intervention on the part of the administration. One lasting casualty was Hong Kong's international reputation as a laissez-faire economy – no bad thing as far as many people were concerned.

Hong Kong's hyper-inflated property sector, which had been in overdrive throughout the 1990s, finally started to lose steam in late 1997, trapping many local property owners in negative equity. The collapse here had nothing to do with the Handover, and everything to do with prices rising to absolutely ridiculous levels. The luxury end of the market was particularly badly hit, with some developments losing between 50 and 70 per cent of their boomtime value. But the decline in property asset value affected the entire housing market, and the incidence of associated problems, including bankruptcies, have soared in recent years and, although there are signs of improvement and general economic recovery, there will be no major improvements any time soon.

A massive avian flu outbreak in 1997, when a deadly virus crossed the species barrier from poultry to people, was partially averted by the slaughter of millions of chickens. Scientists repeatedly warned that the only way to prevent further outbreaks in Hong Kong was to ban live poultry shops from wet markets and centralise slaughtering facilities. Reluctant to antagonise the grass-roots population, which insists that poultry be bought while still alive (it apparently tastes much better that way), the government backed down from this measure and as a result periodic avian flu outbreaks have continued to occur, with resultant mass culls.

An avian flu-like analogy can be made – at least in part – to the 2003 SARS outbreak. This has been conclusively linked in many cases to generally low levels of civic cleanliness

# Shake the disease

After bubbling away virtually undetected in China for a few months, SARS erupted with a vengeance on to the global stage in early 2003, and for a while Hong Kong had the dubious, and at least partially deserved, worldwide reputation as a plague port to be avoided at all costs. Severe Acute Respiratory Syndrome (SARS) must have been one of the world's most unfortunate acronyms – since 1997 the former colony has been a Special Administrative Region (SAR) of China, and the tag seemed to equate Hong Kong with the disease, when in reality this latest pathogen was China's gift to the world.

From the beginning, the Hong Kong Government's response to SARS was quick and relatively efficient, but was – as ever – hampered by a bureaucracy both unable and unwilling to share information beyond its own departments. Neither of the SAR's medical schools, at Chinese University and Hong Kong University, communicated properly on the disease until it was almost too late.

It was no surprise that the other main international areas of infection were those with close business or emigrant links to Hong Kong, such as Singapore and Canada. Both countries imposed stringent health checks on arrival, but nonetheless reported more cases than anywhere outside mainland China.

But there were positive outcomes of the outbreak. SARS seemed to make the Chinese Government realise that a higher level of openness did not necessarily pose a threat to its authority; greater freedom of information was vital in order for facts about how the disease was spread to be communicated.

But from an economic standpoint, the SARS outbreak was an absolute disaster for Hong Kong. Tourist numbers dropped away to almost nothing; flights in all directions were practically empty and shops and restaurants were in dire straits – some closed down altogether. Throughout the outbreak there were more patients in local hospitals with ordinary pneumonia than the atypical kind. But these basic facts, publicised locally but seldom internationally, did much to avert panic.

Despite the scary televised images of near-deserted streets (to heighten the effect, most were taken at around 5am when the streets were quiet anyway), daily life went on. People still went to work, used public transport, had an evening out, and there was, as always in times of real (as opposed to media-manufactured) threat in Hong Kong, a strange sense of calm. Perhaps it was the age-old Chinese stoicism that came through. That said, many expats and wealthy Chinese cleared off to 'healthier' climes, but the majority carried on magnificently, heroically and mostly without recognition.

The worst of the disease passed within six months and though sporadic cases were reported in Asia in late 2003, things are pretty much back to normal, with hotels reporting excellent occupancy levels, airlines doing well again and visitor numbers continuing to rise.

Depressingly, even after the devastation of SARS, general public attitudes towards fairly basic civic hygiene issues such as spitting and littering remain as apathetic as ever. During the very height of the epidemic, it was not uncommon to see local people lower their face masks, gob loudly on the pavement or the floor of a bus, and then continue on their way oblivious. The entrenched Chinese attitude of 'If it's not in my back yard, it's not my problem' continued regardless.

These issues are now being addressed, but even so only sketchily. In the wake of the 1 July demonstrations, the Hong Kong Government has become even more reluctant to antagonise the public further, even when it's transparently in its own best interest.

Out with the old... revellers mark the 1997 **Handover**. *See p20.*

and a lack of awareness of the importance of environmental hygiene. While this is a societal problem that has been obvious to many for years now, without effective leadership little can be achieved in changing public attitudes.

### WIDESPREAD PUBLIC UNREST

Dissatisfaction with the way Hong Kong is run is currently at an all-time high. Barely a week passes without rowdy demonstrations in one form or another taking place through the streets of the city. While some would say that this practice signals continued governmental tolerance towards vocal dissent – undoubtedly a good sign – there are two major downsides to it all. The first is that an awful lot of ordinary people are fed up – the most vocal demonstrations are about everyday livelihood issues such as negative equity and rising unemployment, not the big issues of greater representative government or other political freedoms. Secondly, and perhaps most telling, street protests are not a regular weekly feature of life in London, New York or Sydney – but they are in Hong Kong. Many ordinary residents feel deeply frustrated that their voices are not heard, and that the issues and concerns of the average person are not given enough attention by those in positions of authority. Some critics, though,

also point to the regular protests and plethora of small political parties as evidence of Hong Kong's general level of political immaturity. It seems that there are elements of truth in both assertions.

To its credit, the mainland government has taken an admirable hands-off approach to Hong Kong affairs since the Handover, and without doubt many of the territory's ongoing problems have been exacerbated by a vacillating, indecisive leadership that constantly kowtows to powerful vested interests, especially in the property sectors, at the expense of the rest of the population.

In July 2002 Chief Executive Tung Chee-hwa was appointed to a second term in office, to the surprise of no one and the chagrin of many. This means that he will remain in power until 2007. According to the Basic Law – Hong Kong's mini-constitution published in 1988 – full direct elections to the legislative council are permitted, but it remains anyone's guess whether these will take place as hoped.

Another noticeable and steadily growing trend is a broad sense of wounded national pride and festering disappointment on the part of many local people that – so far, anyway – the much-vaunted pre-Handover concept of Hong Kong people ruling Hong Kong has been a conspicuous flop. The people of Hong Kong don't feel like they are ruling anything.

# Key events

**1513** Portuguese explorer Alvares lands on Lintin in the Pearl River Delta.

**c1557** Macau settled by the Portuguese as a base from which to control the trade between China and Japan.

**1637** First British ship to reach China is driven back from Canton (Guangzhou).

**1639** Japan closed to the Portuguese.

**1685** Limited trade to Canton permitted; the British East India Company starts trading.

**1799** The spread of opium addiction causes Beijing to ban it, driving the trade underground.

**1834** British East India Company loses its opium trade monopoly; Lord Napier aims to regularise Sino-British trade and diplomatic relations.

**1839** Lin Tse-hsü tries to stamp out the opium trade; he confiscates 20,000 chests of opium in Canton, sparking the First Opium (or Anglo-Chinese) War.

**1841** The British attack Canton and occupy its forts. The dispute is settled by the Convention of Chuen Pi, which cedes the island of Hong Kong to Britain, although neither side ratifies the treaty.

**1842** The Treaty of Nanking finally ends the war, confirming British sovereignty over Hong Kong 'in perpetuity' and opening up five Chinese cities to British trade.

**1860** Kowloon and Stonecutter's Island are ceded by China to Britain during the Second Opium (or Arrow) War.

**1862** China signs over Macau to Portugal.

**1870** Founding of the Tung Wah Hospital.

**1898** The British lease the New Territories from China for 99 years.

**1911** Sun Yat-sen overthrows the Qing Dynasty and establishes the Republic of China.

**1922** Seamen's strike in Hong Kong.

**1925** General strike in Hong Kong.

**1945** China's civil war between the communists and the nationalists continues as World War II ends.

**1949** The communists triumph, founding the People's Republic of China; the nationalists flee to Taiwan.

**1956** Riots between nationalists and communists leave dozens dead, with the active involvement of the triads on the nationalist side.

**1966** Rioting in Hong Kong over the increase of the price of first-class tickets on the Star Ferry; the start of the Cultural Revolution.

**1971** Taiwan is replaced in the UN General Assembly by the People's Republic of China; Sir Murray MacLehose appointed as governor.

**1974** Independent Commission Against Corruption (ICAC) formed to combat crime and corruption.

**1979** Opening of Hong Kong's Mass Transit Railway (MTR).

**1982** British Prime Minister Margaret Thatcher visits Hong Kong and Beijing, beginning talks on the future of Hong Kong. China starts to develop Shenzhen as a Special Economic Zone.

**1983** China announces that Hong Kong will become a Special Administrative Region (SAR) after the 1997 Handover, retaining capitalism, its police and judiciary.

**1984** A Sino-British 'Draft Agreement on the Future of Hong Kong' (aka the 'Joint Declaration') is announced.

**1988** Publication of the Basic Law, Hong Kong's post-Handover constitution.

**1989** The Tiananmen Square massacre provokes a huge demonstration in Hong Kong.

**1992** Arrival of Chris Patten, Hong Kong's 28th and last governor. His proposed reforms of the political system are criticised by Beijing.

**1994** Legislative Council passes Patten's proposed electoral reforms; arguments with Beijing continue for three more years.

**1997** Handover of sovereignty from Britain to China at midnight on 30 June. Swearing in of new government; the Beijing-appointed provisional legislature supplants the Legislative Council; Tung Chee-hwa is appointed Chief Executive.

**1997-8** Asian economic crisis seriously damages regional economies; Hong Kong emerges relatively unscathed but with troubling deflation problems.

**1999** Handover of Macau after 442 years of Portuguese rule.

**2001** China joins World Trade Organisation.

**2002** Official celebrations mark the fifth anniversary of the Handover, but meet with lukewarm public response as the economic downturn continues.

**2003** SARS causes worldwide panic; the WHO warns against travel to Hong Kong, and the local economy experiences a severe setback. Over 500,000 people take to the streets on 1 July, protesting unpopular 'national security' legislation. The proposed amendments are scrapped a few days later.

# Hong Kong Today

Pollution and government complacency are ongoing worries, but better value for money makes now a great time to visit.

As dynamic and adjective-defying as it ever was, Hong Kong has undergone considerable changes since the last edition of this guide was published in 2001. Despite – and in some cases because of – the devastating SARS outbreak in the first half of 2003, numerous new social and political developments have begun, which can only be seen as moves in the right direction. Hong Kong is experiencing interesting times, and will continue to do so for the foreseeable future.

Probably the first question asked of long-time residents by newcomers to the city is 'What has changed since the Handover in 1997?' The short answer is – not a lot. Of course, there have been changes, but they will probably not be noticeable to the casual visitor. There are however a few positive developments that are immediately apparent to those who've been here in the past: everything costs less now, and for the first time in decades Hong Kong provides reasonable value for money.

SARS and the general, prolonged economic downturn had the effect of brutally forcing the local tourist industry out of the prosperity-driven complacency it had slipped into during the easy-money years of the 1980s and '90s. The level of interest that the Handover helped fuel has passed, and Hong Kong has had to come up with reasons to visit other than a change of government and a brace of new faces and flags.

On the plus side, six continuous years of deflation and the collapse of the previously superheated property market mean that for the first time since the early 1980s, Hong Kong has become an affordable place to visit. Formerly on a par with London and New York and once almost as expensive as Tokyo, shop rents have come down greatly; as a result, retail outlets needn't charge as much just to cover their overheads, and bars and restaurants are no longer forced to gouge crazy prices out of their customers to stay in business. Harder economic times and more competition have also ensured that general standards of courtesy and customer service – never a Hong Kong strongpoint – have consistently improved. The habit has caught on widely, and more and more people have come to expect decent levels of service for their money. Long may this trend continue.

Yet, despite positive developments in many areas, Hong Kong has numerous besetting problems. The one most visitors will immediately notice, especially during the cooler months, is the truly dire air pollution. Annually worsening levels of air pollution remain a pressing problem, and despite loudly trumpeted statistical improvements, the situation remains chronic. In autumn and winter, when the skies over Hong Kong should be at their clearest, the northern monsoon wind brings down enough airborne crud from China to cloud the air for days. Sometimes the smog is so thick you cannot see across the harbour.

The past two decades' economic liberalisation on the mainland have seen the former rural districts of the Pearl River Delta region surrounding Hong Kong transformed into the 'workshop of the world' – with levels of air and water pollution to match. Despite increasingly strict emission controls in Hong Kong and the move towards cleaner fuels such as liquefied petroleum gas (LPG) and more public transport, the problem simply gets worse the faster China develops. A greater level of cross-border co-operation seems the key to long-term improvements, and while steady progress has been made in this direction, much more still needs to be done.

## 'One prominent legislator even gave the finger to waiting crowds when driven away from a meeting.'

Political consciousness has also increased dramatically in the post-SARS period. Rising public dissatisfaction with the Hong Kong Government's generally dismal performance in the years after the Handover, especially among the middle classes, who saw the value of their property and savings plummet, finally led to a massive yet peaceful public demonstration against the administration on 1 July 2003.

The ostensible reason for the protest march was the Hong Kong Government's proposal to introduce 'national security' legislation, in spite of considerable public disquiet about both its scope and necessity. The government's consultation process was generally seen as sloppy, and the insensitive way in which the debate was managed by the then Secretary

for Security Regina Ip deeply alienated many people. In the wake of the protest marches, Ip resigned and moved to the United States.

The date for the march was well chosen – it was the sixth anniversary of the Handover, and the televised images of flag-raising ceremonies and self-congratulatory speeches by local leaders earlier in the day were completely cancelled out by the sight of half a million marchers converging on the Central Government Offices to voice their discontent. The majority were people who had never taken part in a protest march in their life – they were just ordinary citizens sick of a bumbling administration whose leading members seemed completely indifferent to (and were often openly contemptuous of) their needs and aspirations. One prominent legislator even gave the finger to waiting crowds when being driven away from a meeting; despite an uproar he refused to offer any meaningful apology (he claimed to be a bit drunk at the time) and didn't resign.

Sustained calls were made for unpopular Chief Executive Tung Chee-Hwa and several of his closest appointees to quit, and while no one seriously expected him to do so, this was the clearest indication yet that the way his team managed things had to change, and soon.

Since this timely wake-up call from Mr and Mrs 'Average Hong Kong Person', there have been indications that the government is, at last, becoming more responsive to public wishes and expectations. Perhaps the most interesting development has been the Chinese leadership's public remarks on the issue; the Hong Kong Government has been unequivocally told to be more responsive to the needs of the people it is meant to serve. This has been widely interpreted as an amber light (if not a full green sign) from Beijing for swifter moves towards more genuinely representative government in Hong Kong in coming years.

The basic reality, though, is that, apart from local political developments and SARS (which, even as this guide went to press, continued to raise its ugly head in the form of isolated cases), not a lot has changed in post-Handover Hong Kong. SARS aside, sustained interest in the territory's affairs has largely waned in the world's collective consciousness. As a telling metaphor for this, an escaped pet crocodile in the New Territories in autumn 2003 generated more column inches in the international press than all the other recent political developments in Hong Kong combined. But perhaps that's just the true spirit of the city coming through: there is never any shortage of bizarre and unusual happenings here, and the elusive Yuen Long crocodile is just another one of them.

The **Bank of China Tower**.

In Context

# Modern Architecture

The sky's the limit.

What Hong Kong lacks in reminders of its architectural heritage it more than makes up for in terms of striking, modern buildings. While most of what's been built over the past 40 years is strictly utilitarian – and some of it even rather ugly – there are quite a few very interesting examples. And, best of all, most of them are easily accessible.

Historically, the demand for high-end buildings has been in and around the business district, so most of the really impressive new structures are to be found in Central and the surrounding areas. But that may be about to change. Until Kai Tak Airport closed down in 1998 (superseded by the new international airport at Chek Lap Kok), strict height restrictions in Kowloon were in force. These have since been lifted, with the result that various new buildings are being planned, including a massive tower for the West Kowloon reclamation – a twin for the IFC in Central (*see p29*) – and an enormous

Norman Foster-designed civic centre. All of these promise something to look forward to in a few years' time.

## HONG KONG ISLAND

Hong Kong's best-known modern architectural symbol is probably IM Pei's stunning **Bank of China Tower** (*see p65*), built on the original site of Murray House, a 19th-century British Officers' mess (which has been re-erected out at Stanley; *see p83*). The Bank of China Tower attracted heated controversy from the moment its design was first made public, and this continued for years after its completion in 1990. In feng shui-obsessed, rumour-crazy Hong Kong, the 70-storey building's sharp angles were immediately said – and therefore popularly believed – to be a symbolic mainland dagger aimed at the heart of Hong Kong, its negative vibes radiating towards Government House to foil and distort any administrative decisions made there. Then there were the two white

Jardine House.
*See p29.*

antennae atop the building – they were deemed inauspicious as, according to Chinese custom, two sticks of incense are burned only for the dead. Artificial ponds and waterfalls inside the building help soften the stark exterior effect and – apparently – help mitigate some of the worst feng shui effects. But whatever your cosmic feelings about the tower, it remains one of the city's most striking modern buildings.

Predating the Bank of China Tower by four years, the **Hongkong & Shanghai Banking Corporation Headquarters** (HSBC; *see p65*) was completed in 1985. The third HSBC incarnation to occupy the site, Lord Foster's Meccano-like, steel-and-glass masterpiece has immediately became a recognisable symbol of the Central business district, and it features prominently on most of the territory's banknotes. This building replaced Hong Kong's first true skyscraper – a graceful granite building that opened in 1935, which had centralised air-conditioning, lifts and – best of all in the memories of many – magnificent mosaic ceilings. All that remains of that earlier incarnation are the two large bronze lions at the base of the present one; the lion on the Chater Garden side still bears the scars of Pacific War shrapnel on its flanks. The ground floor of 'The Bank' – as it is popularly, even somewhat reverentially, known in Hong Kong – is completely open, and is actually a thronging pedestrian thoroughfare during the week. It's also a popular gathering spot for legions of off-duty Filipina maids on weekends and public holidays.

> **'Jardine House has attracted an enduring sobriquet – "The House of a Thousand Arseholes".'**

A short distance away from HSBC, across Statue Square, is the **Hong Kong Club**, which first opened in 1985. This tower block replaced a beautiful Italianate structure dating from 1897, which was demolished in 1980. This building was the subject of a bitterly fought heritage conservation battle in the late 1970s, but like most such campaigns in those years, it failed, mainly due to the confluence of powerful vested interests and general public apathy. The new structure is graceful and stylish (the club section is closed to the public), and you can't help but wonder how much of a landmark the older building would have been now, marooned among the packed expressways and soaring office towers.

# Pole position

One of the few sights in Hong Kong that has barely changed in recent decades is bamboo scaffolding, seen all over building sites. Towering skyscrapers clad in bamboo frameworks are one of those emblematic sights that immediately grab visitors' attention, but are so commonplace that local residents often fail to notice.

Flimsy though it looks, once the bamboo framework reaches above a few storeys it becomes immensely strong. Indeed, each 'square' of bamboo – typically a little over a metre in diameter – can support up to a thousand pounds without buckling or breaking. What's even more amazing is that no nails, staples or screws are used in the construction; the bamboo is held together by thousands of thin plastic strips. Workers shinny upwards along the poles lashing it all together.

High-quality bamboo is expensive and, unlike rainforest timber used elsewhere in the local building industry (and invariably thrown away), bamboo is continuously recycled. Its use in construction in China dates back hundreds of years, and it is still preferred to steel because of its excellent tensile qualities and resistance to wind – an important consideration on high-rise buildings.

Erecting bamboo scaffolding is a highly skilled occupation, but these days it's a trade that few young men wish to enter. The work is arduous, and hours and wages are erratic. It's also dangerous. Very few workers use protective equipment, partly because the macho image of the trade discourages it, and partly because of perennially slack Hong Kong legislation. As a result, many bamboo scaffolding workers are injured – and several killed – every year.

Situated almost next to the Star Ferry terminal is **Jardine House** (*see p64*), Hong Kong's oldest modern office tower, built in 1973. The sleek aluminium-clad structure rises more than 50 storeys above the Hong Kong Island waterfront. Now surrounded – dwarfed, in fact – by numerous other buildings like it, Jardine House was the first of its kind in Hong Kong and remains a popular local landmark. Nevertheless, with hundreds of porthole-shaped windows, the building has attracted one of the rudest and most enduring of Hong Kong sobriquets – 'The House of a Thousand Arseholes', directed at both the building and the type of person believed to work within it.

Out on the waterfront reclamation, rising above the Hong Kong terminus of the airport railway, is the **Two International Finance Centre** (officially called Two ifc but commonly referred to as IFC2 or 2IFC; *see p64*). While architecturally stunning, this 88-storey tower (completed in 2003) was, like many buildings in Hong Kong, built without any reference to the surrounding landscape. Seen from the Tsim Sha Tsui waterfront promenade, the Two ifc building completely obscures the view of soaring Victoria Peak behind it. Taking shape next door is the luxury Four Seasons' first foray into Hong Kong, which is slated to open in 2005.

Somewhat irreverently known as the 'disco building' because of its luridly coloured, constantly changing evening illumination, the **Center** (99 Queen's Road, Central; built 1998) is one of Hong Kong's most emblematic recent buildings, immediately visible from all directions; if the weather conditions are right you can even see it flashing at you when you fly into the city. Glassy, gleaming, 73 storeys high, but nevertheless unattractively hemmed in by many other grubby old office buildings, the Center is one of the five tallest structures in Hong Kong – at least for now. A series of horizontal light bars are built into the structure, undetectable during daylight hours and unobtrusive to those in the building. These produce 175 different colour sequences and patterns in shades ranging from electric blue and lime green to flame red and bright purple. While many people love it, and it's certainly eye-catching, the Center is, in some respects, an unintended architectural metaphor for urban Hong Kong: stunning and hypnotic at a distance, but gradually less than amazing (and frankly a bit tacky and OTT) the closer you get to it.

One of Hong Kong's best known and most striking buildings is the **Peak Tower** (*see p79*; built by British architect Terry Farrell in 1996), at the upper terminus of the Peak Tramway, and visible for miles around. To some people it's a

bird with outstretched wings, to others it's a pair of open hands, and to others still it's a gigantic wok straddled across Victoria Gap. However you choose to look at it, it's unmistakable. The cable-operated funicular Peak Tram has connected Hong Kong Island's relatively uncrowded hilltop district with the teeming city since 1888. While for many years nothing more remarkable than a station platform and sedan-chair depot stood here, progressively larger and more expansive terminal buildings – incorporating cafés, souvenir shops and look-out points – were built, culminating in this latest one, which opened in 1995. The tower complex neatly illustrates the split personality of the Peak itself: part exclusive residential area, part tacky tourist trap. But with stunning views in every direction on a clear day, it has to be seen – indeed, experienced – at least once.

Amid the city's air-conditioned steel-and-glass boxes, the notion of sustainable development is reflected in the **Kadoorie Biological Sciences Building** (Pok Fu Lam Road; built 2000) at the University of Hong Kong in the New Territories, which has won numerous awards for its energy-efficient design. Parabolic aluminium shades shield the building from the sun and enhance its 'green' design and energy efficiency. It's well worth making a trip to this somewhat out-of-the-way location to see it.

> **'The massive, government-planned Hong Kong Central Library is hideous beyond all imagination.'**

Built on a small man-made island of reclaimed land off the Wan Chai foreshore, and to some people vaguely reminiscent of Sydney's Opera House, the **Hong Kong Convention & Exhibition Centre** (*see p73*) was begun in 1994 and completed just in time for the 1997 Handover ceremonies to be held inside. Depending on your point of view, the building looks like automotive airfoils, the wings of a bird, lotus petals or a series of semi-open clam shells. A massive, gold-leafed, stylised bauhinia flower on a pedestal is situated in front of the building, which is mainly visited by package-tour groups from the mainland. Few locals bother.

Designed with a sculptural approach, the **Lippo Centre** (*see p69*) opened in 1988 and has been an immediately recognisable feature of the local skyline ever since. Backed by a consortium headed by Australian entrepreneur Alan Bond, the building was first known as the Bond Centre. After Bond's spectacular fall

In Context

from corporate grace in the early 1990s, it was acquired by the Indonesian-controlled Lippo Group and tactfully renamed the Lippo Centre.

Nothing written about modern architecture in Hong Kong can possibly exclude or ignore the massive, government-planned, hideous-beyond-all-imagination **Hong Kong Central Library** (Moreton Terrace, Causeway Bay). With an exterior caked in pale, honey-coloured stone cladding and almost-hilarious Greco-Roman pretensions – including a Parthenon-style pediment – the building was designed by a committee of the now-defunct Urban Council, and the bureaucratic approach certainly shows. Step inside and the lashings of blond wood fittings and escalators to everywhere bring to mind a four-star(ish) hotel anywhere on the mainland, rather than emulating the sober dignity of a world-class library. That said, research facilities within the Central Library are excellent and stand up to comparisons with the best in the world, but no one – except its designers – has found a good word to say for the structure itself. It must be seen to be believed.

Potentially one of Hong Kong's architectural success stories, but in reality probably its most resounding failure, is the Hong Kong Jockey Club-funded **Hong Kong Stadium** (55 Eastern Hospital Road, Causeway Bay). Unveiled in 1994, the enormous scalloped structure quickly became enmeshed in controversy. Situated in a bowl-like valley surrounded by housing, the stadium works like an enormous loudspeaker, amplifying the volume of whatever is taking place there to excruciating levels. In consequence it can only really be used for sporting activities, and is best appreciated during the annual Hong Kong Sevens, the internationally revered rugby event.

Whether you love it or hate it, one thing that's immediately visible from the bend in Repulse Bay Road as you travel along Hong Kong Island's southern coast is the sinuously curving pastel-blue tower between the mountains and the beach. The **Repulse Bay** apartment building (109 Repulse Bay Road) was built to replace the venerable Repulse Bay Hotel, dating from 1920, which was demolished despite strenuous public opposition in 1982. A new version of its famed sea-view veranda restaurant (see p134), using many of the original fittings, was incorporated in the structure. This has proved very successful with a new generation who are charmed by its 'historic' ambience, but many of them are completely unaware that the building they are admiring is a very well-made fake. A large space was left vacant in the new apartment building, which frames the rocky green mountainside behind, rather like a picture window. But, this being Hong Kong, a popular urban legend quickly grew up concerning the alleged feng shui of the building, which had it that the hole was left there so the dragon who lived on the hillside could get down to the sea to bathe. A delightful tale to be sure, and the tourists love it, but the reality behind the decision was much more prosaic: the owner once saw something similar in Florida, and wanted to incorporate the feature back home in Hong Kong.

## KOWLOON AND BEYOND

Over on the Kowloon side, one of the rare examples of a magnificent old building with a sympathetic new addition, the tower extension of the **Peninsula Hotel** (see p53), has been consistently praised since it was unveiled in 1994. The Peninsula proves that a modern addition can actually enhance and improve the original, which retains all the gracious features that have made it such a favourite for both overseas visitors and local residents for the last 75 years. Die-hard avant-garde design fiends go into raptures over the Philippe Starck-designed restaurant Felix, with the harbour and city spread out below it.

Often just passed through on the way to somewhere else, Hong Kong's sprawling new airport complex is worth a longer visit than most visitors give it. The massive **Hong Kong International Airport** (see p276) at Chek Lap Kok on Lantau, with associated highway, railway and bridging works, was the most extensive single civil engineering project ever undertaken in history; now *that* really is a rare superlative. Designed by Norman Foster, who was also responsible for the HSBC building in Central (see p65), immense curves of glass and canvas-like material give you the impression that you're in the clouds when you're still on the ground.

Even on the journey to and from the airport there's more to see – three soaring bridges link Lantau and the international airport with the rest of the urban area: the massive **Tsing Ma Suspension Bridge** (built 1997), which connects the islands of Tsing Yi and Ma Wan, is vaguely reminiscent of San Francisco's Golden Gate Bridge; the smaller **Kap Shui Mun Bridge** (1997), which joins up Ma Wan and Lantau; and the **Ting Kau Bridge** (1998), linking Tsing Yi and the mainland New Territories. All are spectacularly illuminated at night.

For those who want to further explore other iconic modern buildings in Hong Kong – as well as a few incongruous survivors from earlier times – *Skylines Hong Kong* by Peter Moss (Hong Kong, FormAsia, 2000) is a great read.

# Culture & Customs

With its rich cultural heritage, Hong Kong adheres to
a vibrant mix of codes and conduct.

The image that Hong Kong tends to project to
the world is one of a place where East meets
West, in both appearance and mindset – after
all, it was governed by Britain for around 150
years. This perception, however, is way off
the mark: despite an abundance of Western
architecture and a love of European and US
fashion labels, the territory's psyche is firmly
rooted in Chinese tradition.

### WHO'S WHO

Hong Kong is usually regarded as a multicultural, cosmopolitan city, yet 96 per cent of
its population is Chinese. Most of this comprises
**Punti**, or **Cantonese**, who built their power
base through land ownership. In the 19th
century, for example, the five great Cantonese
clans (Tang, Hau, Pang, Liu and Man) had their
own areas over which they ruled. However,
there are still pockets of three other Chinese
races – **Hakkas**, **Hoklos** and **Tankas**.
The Hakkas are the largest of these minority
groups, living together in villages throughout
the New Territories.

The very first inhabitants of the region,
however, were **Yao** and **Maio** peoples (racially
similar to Taiwan's aboriginals and Filipinos);
although clusters still survive in Guangdong
(Canton) and Guangxi provinces, no trace of
them remains in Hong Kong.

These days there is an even greater mix,
with immigrants, both legal and illegal, having
flooded into the territory from other parts
of China – many as political and economic
refugees after 1949, when the country became
communist, and intellectuals and the wealthy
felt threatened. More recently Hong Kong has
seen waves of economic chancers, who believe
that its streets are paved with golden job
opportunities (which was all but true until 1997).
Most of them come from neighbouring provinces
like Guangdong, Fujian and Shanghai.

The remaining four per cent of the population
is composed of non-Chinese, who – despite their
small numbers – form highly visible groups as
they tend to work and hang out in central areas.
Despite Hong Kong's former British colonial
status, not many **British** citizens remain –

**Filipinas** during Chinese New Year festivities.

of some 30,000 Brits registered living here, many are Chinese with UK passports. Pre-1997, British citizens did not need a work visa to get a job in the territory, so many young Brit backpackers would stop off in Hong Kong for a few months and earn some quick cash working in a bar, before continuing the trail around Asia or on to Australia. **Americans** have had a strong presence for several decades, mainly thanks to the large number of businesses with regional head offices in Hong Kong. In fact, American residents outnumber Brits by more than three to one. There's also a smaller mix of other Europeans, including French and Italians. White foreigners are dubbed '*gweilo*' (meaning 'ghost man') or '*gweipor*' ('ghost women') by the Cantonese, a term that some Caucasians find offensive – but most *gweilo* old hands happily accept the tag and even use it themselves.

Over the last couple of decades, the largest immigrant group in Hong Kong has been from the Philippines. There are currently over 120,000 **Filipinas** (they're nearly all female) based here working as maids (or *amahs*) for Chinese or Western employers. Indonesia and Thailand also provide thousands more domestic helpers. They are poorly paid as it is (earning an average of HK$3,670 per month), and often work 14 hours a day, but the situation recently became worse when a ten per cent income tax was introduced (the maids were previously exempt from this). Some people claim this is an attempt by the government to deter them

from coming to work here and a ploy to make such work more appealing to locals during the current period of high unemployment. Maids' pay has always been more than they could earn in their native countries (and this will no doubt continue to be the case, despite the new levy), but in Hong Kong they must also deal with the fact that they are generally relegated to second-class status. Still, every Sunday and on public holidays, thousands of *amahs* gather in the squares and streets of Central to sit on the pavement, eat, chat, sing, worship and relax.

There is a small, but important, **Indian** population – which includes some of Hong Kong's wealthiest families – as well as a number of **Nepalese**, most of whom are the children of Gurkhas who served in the British army. More than 15,000 **Vietnamese** refugees also call Hong Kong home. They are part of the 225,000-plus 'boat people' who escaped their war-torn country from the late 1970s. While 67,000 were repatriated and 143,000 resettled overseas, the remainder have been allowed to stay in Hong Kong. The majority survive on casual manual jobs.

## RELIGIOUS BELIEFS

While it may appear that the Hong Kong dollar is the object of worship for most residents, religion plays an important role in many people's lives. Most of Hong Kong's population is either Buddhist or Taoist, but there are also about half a million Christians, up to 100,000

Muslims and a smattering of Hindus, Sikhs and Jews. Religion is evident throughout the city, from ornate monasteries, temples and cathedrals to tiny shrines outside residents' homes and even inside staff quarters of nightclubs. Indeed, unlike the mainland, the territory enjoys total freedom of religious practice. There are some fears, though, that intimidation from Beijing may interfere with this in future, particularly in light of the crackdown on the Falun Gong, a quasi-religious group.

The earliest religious beliefs are tied to the region's first needs – those of the fishing community. The protector of seafarers, Tin Hau (see p80 **Making waves**), was honoured with temples that used to overlook the South China Sea but, due to land reclamation, they now lie mostly inland. The 40 or more Tin Hau temples here overflow when the **Birthday of Tin Hau** (see p187) is celebrated in spring. Like many local deities, Tin Hau is of Taoist origin. But as the faiths of Taoism and Buddhism frequently blur into one integrated belief system, both tend to be honoured in the same temple.

## 'Somewhat creepily, even *papier-mâché* models of favoured domestic helpers are known to be burned.'

**Taoism**, based on the writings of Lao Tse, aims to put mankind in context with nature. Its esoteric philosophies are in perpetual debate and defy simple explanations: Tao itself is usually translated as 'the way'. The most widely recognised Taoist symbol in the world is the yin-yang pictogram, in which all existence struggles infinitely to find harmony.

**Buddhism**, originally from India, is based on principles of dharma; these spiritual and moral codes are strictly adhered to within Hong Kong's monk and nun fraternities, which are found in monasteries in the New Territories and on Lantau (the Po Lin Monastery being the best known; see p115). Buddha's birthday is celebrated on the eighth day of the fourth moon (he is currently believed to be more than 2,500 years old, though figures vary) – and is a public holiday in Hong Kong.

Taoist deities **Wong Tai Sin** (see p94) and **Che Kung** (see p98), found in temples named after them, are approached for general matters of health, while **Kam Fa** – a saint from Guangdong – is said to protect pregnant women. Two of Hong Kong's most popular deities are polar opposites: Buddhist **Kwun Yum**, goddess of mercy, and Taoist **Kwan Kung**, god of war. The former is regarded as

a compassionate protector of all, while the fearsome-looking latter is the god of choice for both police officers and triads. Porcelain representations of the two deities adorn many homes, often on altars.

The average Hong Konger goes to Taoist or Buddhist temples to appease the deities and, usually, to ask for compassion or good fortune. Gifts of food (in particular fruit) are presented, and incense and paper offerings are burned in respect. Donations are given for the upkeep of the temple. Unlike many other religions, individuals visit temples independently, rather than attend services held by priests; the exception to this rule is when special ceremonies, such as weddings and funerals, take place. Temples often have one or more fortune-tellers in residence who, for a fee, will interpret a visitor's palm, face, foot or the symbol written on a *chim* (bamboo stick), which is selected by gently shaking a bamboo beaker full of *chim* in front of a temple altar until one rises up above the rest of the pack.

Besides idols, domestic altars often carry a memorial plaque to departed relatives, which is regarded as one way of maintaining a spiritual link between ancestors and the living; some families who own space in rural parts of the territory also have ancestral temples in memory of several generations. During the **Ching Ming** and **Chung Yuen** festivals, families flock to these temples (or, alternatively, to cemeteries and crematoria) to clean the memorials of their loved ones and present offerings to be enjoyed symbolically in the afterlife. Popular paper offerings to be burned these days include meticulously crafted mobile phones, home entertainment systems and cars, which join the old staples of money, silver and gold ingots, and smart clothes. Somewhat creepily, even *papier-mâché* models of favoured domestic helpers are known to be burned.

Western missionaries did an efficient job of promoting **Christianity** from the 19th century onwards. There is a pretty even split between Catholic and Anglican/Protestant congregations, with the highest proliferation of churches being in Kowloon Tong, Tsim Sha Tsui (look out for the Rosary Church on Chatham Road South) and the Anglican St John's Cathedral in Central (see p66).

The **Muslim** community is 50 per cent Chinese, while faiths with smaller numbers have predominantly non-Chinese congregations. The mosque on Shelley Street, Mid-Levels, is older and more charming than the main one next to Kowloon Park; not far away from it is the Ohel Leah Synagogue, in the shadow of the Jewish Community Centre, which also has old-world appeal. An impressive **Hindu** temple

# Numbers of the beasts

Before the Brits arrived, Hong Kong, like the rest of China, relied on the Chinese lunar calendar, the longest chronological record in history, dating from 2637 BC. An entire cycle takes 60 years to complete and is made up of five mini cycles of 12 years. We are currently in the 78th cycle, which began in February 1984 and ends in February 2044. From this calendar came the Chinese zodiac, represented by an animal for each lunar year, with 12 in total.

According to legend, it all started when the Buddha summoned all the animals in the world to him to say goodbye before he departed from earth. As only 12 animals appeared to bid him farewell, he named a year after each one in the order that they came to see him. The first one to arrive was the rat (or mouse), then the ox, tiger, rabbit, dragon, snake, horse, sheep (or ram), monkey, rooster (or chicken), dog and boar (or pig). Thus the 12 signs that are still recognised today came into being.

Today, the belief in the Chinese zodiac remains strong in Hong Kong. In general, Hong Kongers pay much more attention to their Chinese zodiac sign and associated astrological readings than their Western ones. The animal ruling the year in which you were born is said to have a profound influence on your life and your character; in the lunar year straddling 2000-2001, pregnancies increased because parents wanted their children to be born in the Year of the Dragon, believed to be the most powerful of all animals.

During the complete 60-year cycle, each of the animal signs (sometimes also referred to as the 12 earth branches) is combined with the five elements of wood, fire, earth, metal and water. The element of your lunar sign will also exercise its influence on your life. No element is called the strongest or weakest – they are dependent on one another.

The lunar year is divided into 12 months of 29 days. Every two and a half years, an intercalary month is added to adjust the calendar. The addition of this month every third year produces the lunar leap year. For easy reference, the beginning of each lunar month is the date of the new moon marked on the Western calendar.

The importance of the lunar calendar remains significant in Hong Kong to this day, and particular care is taken to ensure certain events such as marriages, business openings and ancestral worship take place on the most auspicious days.

The following are some of the characteristics associated with each animal and year. Funnily enough, many seem to echo the nature of the beast in question, so whether or not you believe them is another matter. Note that if you were born before the Chinese New Year (late January/early February) you take the animal from the previous year.

---

in Happy Valley caters to a mostly Indian congregation. Smaller places of worship for Methodists, Mormons, Quakers, Scientologists and Sikhs are scattered around the territory.

## FACE OFF

You've just enjoyed a feast in a restaurant with your local host and the time has come to pay. Your host reaches for his credit card. 'No,' you say, 'I'll pay.' A 'No, I'll get it' to-and-froing then ensues. To end the discussion, you grab the bill and take it to the cashier's desk, where you pay, believing your generosity will be appreciated. Wrong. You've just committed a serious faux pas. Your host has lost 'face' and that's just about the cardinal sin in Hong Kong. If you were hoping to close a business deal, forget it.

Face is a peculiar Chinese value and its importance in Hong Kong can never be underestimated. It can lead to arguments, broken friendships and even fights, so a little care is needed to avoid stepping on people's toes. The concept is like pride in other countries (and everyone has that to a degree), but in Hong Kong face is accorded the utmost seriousness and people are judged by it. Some folk go to great lengths to acquire it by displays of wealth or generosity. It confirms social status. The big shot in the restaurant wearing the chunky Rolex and handing around expensive brandy may look and talk like a billionaire, but he could be a small-time entrepreneur blowing more money than he can really afford just to gain face in front of potential clients.

But issues of face are not always so obvious. Subtlety and sensitivity are needed, since the concept of giving face is easier to explain than the potential for losing it. Complimenting someone on their clothes, hairstyle and business acumen – especially in front of their pals or

## Rat (or mouse)
**Characteristics**: Dynamic, protective, open-minded, thrifty and compassionate.
**Years**: 1924, 1936, 1948, 1960, 1972, 1984, 1996.

## Ox
**Characteristics**: Patient, self-reliant, industrious and sure of foot.
**Years**: 1925, 1937, 1949, 1961, 1973, 1985, 1997.

## Tiger
**Characteristics**: Honourable, hard-working and warm-hearted.
**Years**: 1926, 1938, 1950, 1962, 1974, 1986, 1998.

## Rabbit
**Characteristics**: Popular, artistic, stylish, romantic and calm.
**Years**: 1927, 1939, 1951, 1963, 1975, 1987, 1999.

## Dragon
**Characteristics**: Charismatic, principled, discriminating and self-sufficient.
**Years**: 1928, 1940, 1952, 1964, 1976, 1988, 2000.

## Snake
**Characteristics**: Amusing, discreet, intuitive and philosophical.
**Years**: 1929, 1941, 1953, 1965, 1977, 1989, 2001.

## Horse
**Characteristics**: Warm-hearted, strong-minded and sociable yet independent.
**Years**: 1930, 1942, 1954, 1966, 1978, 1990, 2002.

## Sheep (or ram)
**Characteristics**: Intuitive, creative, generous, modest and sensitive.
**Years**: 1931, 1943, 1955, 1967, 1979, 1991, 2003.

## Monkey
**Characteristics**: Faithful, loving, intelligent, entertaining and candid.
**Years**: 1932, 1944, 1956, 1968, 1980, 1992, 2004.

## Rooster (or chicken)
**Characteristics**: Brave, loyal, hard-working, communicative and witty.
**Years**: 1933, 1945, 1957, 1969, 1981, 1993, 2005.

## Dog
**Characteristics**: Sincere, loyal, affectionate, fair-minded and helpful.
**Years**: 1934, 1946, 1958, 1970, 1982, 1994, 2006.

## Boar (or pig)
**Characteristics**: Sensible, sensual, frank, charitable and amusing.
**Years**: 1935, 1947, 1959, 1971, 1983, 1995, 2007.

colleagues – is a sure-fire winner. Confrontation and criticism are guaranteed face-destroyers. In general, in both China and Hong Kong, Western-style bluntness is not appreciated or expected: a polite and gentle approach is more likely to endear guests to their hosts. That might seem at odds with Hong Kong's very visible boldness and brashness, but behind closed doors, or with friends and acquaintances, manners matter. Common sense, as ever, goes a long way in dealing with the issue. When in doubt, lavish those compliments.

### FENG SHUI
This ancient Chinese belief may be seen in the West as little more than a trendy, almost past-it, fad, but here it's serious business. Although Hong Kong is a commercial, modern city, it still pays great heed to this time-honoured art. Feng shui is more than another quirk of a superstitious culture – many of its principal tenets are the basics of good and effective design. The main aim – of aligning oneself and one's home or workplace within an environment – has been followed by successive generations of Chinese in Hong Kong. There is a general belief that businesses and personal health will flourish if this age-old practice is employed under the direction of an experienced master. Even the biggest multinationals follow it when laying out an office or constructing a building, partly out of deference to their staff and partly out of honouring Chinese custom.

The term feng shui is Mandarin (it is known as *fung shui* in Cantonese) for 'wind water', but this philosophy of how to live in harmony with nature taps into more than just these two elements. Experts in the field claim that the interplay of wood, fire, earth and even gold also have to be taken into account and balanced to obtain the optimum result, which is harmony in all areas of one's life. Believers are convinced good fortune is not determined by chance, but by correct feng shui.

The basic tools of the feng shui practitioner's trade are a multi-ringed compass, astronomical charts and ancient texts on the processes of divination. The master will note the natural and man-made features in the building's environs, and will then decide the direction certain rooms and furniture should face, and the items that should be introduced to enhance positivity. These will usually be mirrors, engraved coins and bamboo flutes, hung on walls, from beams or in the corner of rooms. Water features such as small babbling electric mini fountains or fish aquariums are also often used. Even the number and colour of fish has to be right – if they die over time, this is said to be a sign that they have absorbed bad luck that would otherwise have wreaked havoc on human occupants. Dead fish therefore need to be replaced, to maintain the fortuitous number in the tank.

> ## 'Scoff if you like, but who wouldn't want to live in a home next to a waterfall, a lake and green fields?'

Typically, feng shui has been more strongly adhered to in Hong Kong's rural areas. When tunnelling for the Kowloon–Canton Railway began early last century, for example, no Chinese labourers could be persuaded to work on the project for fear of disturbing the earth spirits. Even in 2001, the Kowloon–Canton Railway Corporation (KCRC) called in a feng shui expert for input in a feasibility study for a proposed new rail link in the New Territories. (Strangely enough, villagers' feng shui problems often seem to disappear when compensation terms are raised.)

Some buildings, although built in accordance with a geomancer's instructions, are believed to give off bad feng shui. The angular **Bank of China Tower** (*see p26 and p65*), for instance, with its prominent criss-cross cladding, is said to shoot out poison arrows from the apex of these exterior panels, some say targeting the former Government House (which was one of the reasons why Chief Executive Tung Chee-hwa declined to live there). A weeping willow is said to have been planted in the grounds of Government House to deflect the negative influence. Other buildings include a large hole in their structure or are built on stilts, in order to prevent energy flows being blocked.

Like partially blocked Chinese temple doorways, which are believed to bar the entry of bad spirits, it is quite common for building entrances to be constructed at an angle – the Mandarin Oriental hotel on Hong Kong Island has one of many angled entrances around town. Some home-owners opt for a staggered entrance into their flat for the same reason.

With space at such a premium in Hong Kong, these days murals are sometimes used as a substitute for natural environments. They will often feature components such as rivers and waterfalls emptying into a lake, surrounded by ripe rice fields and fruit-bearing trees, against a backdrop of hills populated by birds and butterflies. These elements read logically: water stands for money and the full lake ensures it stays plentiful; the rice and fruit symbolise full dinner tables; the hills offer protection; and the fauna represents harmony.

Whether or not feng shui actually works is a matter for debate. But enough people opt for it to make it a real business, as well as a preoccupation for many. And scoff if you like, but who wouldn't want to live in a home next to a waterfall, a lake and green fields?

## TRADITIONAL FESTIVALS

There are five major Chinese festivals celebrated in the calendar – the **Lunar New Year**, the **Dragon Boat Festival**, the **Hungry Ghost Festival**, the **Mid Autumn Festival** and **Ching Ming**. For these and more, *see p186-p190*. Most are used as time off work, rather than for lengthy religious ceremony; as with Christmas in the West, these festivals provide families with an opportunity to come together to eat well and exchange gifts. Christian festivals such as Easter and Christmas are still acknowledged public holidays, even in these post-colonial times.

## CHINESE ARTS

Although Hong Kong is one of the most modern cities in the world, it is still possible to see traditional Chinese arts here. You'll find ancient tea paraphernalia at the **Flagstaff House Museum of Tea Ware** (*see p68*), calligraphy at the **Hong Kong Museum of Art** (*see p86*) and (basic) Chinese opera at **Temple Street Night Market** (*see p90*). But the local arts scene is also in touch with contemporary global trends, so don't be surprised if a West End theatre production is enjoying a run while you're here. For more on traditional music, opera and dance, *see p230* **Chinese performing arts**.

## GAME ON

Besides eating, Hong Kongers traditionally spend their leisure time playing games (from the computer to the finger-guessing variety),

# Crazy 4 U

Hong Kong is a place where fads come and go at a dizzying rate. Many of the trends originate in Japan, with Korea hot on its heels for position of top style arbiter. But whether the craze is for hi-tech gadgets, miniature cuddly toys, manga comics or cute cartoon stickers, three words sum up local preferences: cool, cute and collectable.

Being up to date with what's hot is an expensive business involving a strict regime of magazine browsing and shopping (number one 'hobby' of all Hong Kong kids). Self-respecting youngsters take great pride in flaunting their hi-tech street cred, recording everyday trivia on high-end mini digital cameras, typing in the ring code for the latest Canto-pop hit on their mobiles, or thumbing the latest GameBoy. It's a must to own exactly the right brand-name accessories, be it limited-edition Nike sneakers, the cutest Bapy tote bag or the coolest Bathing Ape T-shirt.

In Hong Kong, as in most of Asia, girls are seemingly never too old to be considered cute, and neither are most guys, for that matter. It's quite common in less-salubrious neighbourhoods to find tattooed and bare-chested young men in their twenties with tea-coloured bleached hair held back with a plastic Alice band. Or to see smart-looking, suited young men in Central toting bags adorned with dangling miniature cuties. Many of the motifs for these key chains and toys are inspired by Japanese or Korean

animations, such as Pokémon, Pucca Love and AstroBoy, or local favourites like McMug, Porkchop, Ah Fu, and the comic turd Excreman. Take a stroll through any street market and you'll see the wide range of cute accessories on offer, from Pom Pom Purin hairclips to plastic briefcases with a Nissan noodle or Calbee crisp print. Despite this, the number-one seller remains Sanrio's Hello Kitty, whose face can be found on everything from fish sticks to credit cards. A few years ago, a Hello Kitty Mastercard ad campaign aimed at career women in their thirties and forties resulted in over 100,000 cards being issued in nine months – more proof that age is no barrier to cuteness.

Whereas what's cool or cute may be debatable, collecting is the one passion that arguably unites Hong Kongers of all ages, sexes and incomes, and regardless of apartment size. Almost anything of limited edition (and potentially appreciable value) is deemed collectable – from stamps to sneakers, plastic figurines to phone cards. When such items are due to go on sale, queues will snake around the block before opening time, and strange patterns of behaviour will be unleashed. A couple of years back, when McDonald's gave away free Hello Kitty fluffy toys with meals, buyers queued for hours just to cram the takeaway boxes straight into overflowing bins, and whisk the prized stuffed toys away home.

singing karaoke, gambling on horses, games or at the casinos in Macau, and keeping fit through martial arts and breathing exercises.

Wherever you are in Hong Kong, chances are you'll hear a furious clatter accompanied by lots of shouting and raucous behaviour emanating from flats and village homes, especially during holidays. The cause of this racket? **Mah-jong** – Hong Kong's favourite game. Tracing its origins as far back as 2350 BC, it is played with 144 tiles made up of three suits (bamboo, Chinese characters and circles), numbered from one to nine, of which there are four of each kind, meaning that there are 36 tiles per suit – and 108 suit tiles in total. The remaining 36 tiles are composed of three groups (flowers, winds and dragons), which have different functions depending on the house rules. It's as complex as bridge in terms of explaining the rules, but there are two certainties – the game will last a long time (with many rounds over several hours) and as much noise as possible will be made clattering the tiles on the table.

**Chinese chess**, or *xiangqi*, is more sedate. The game is one of the four Chinese arts along with *qin* (music), *hua* (brush painting) and *shu* (calligraphy). It involves two players, each of whom is assigned 16 pieces: one king, two chariots, two horses, two elephants, two guards, two cannons and five soldiers. The object, as in Western chess, is to capture the king. Games can be seen being played by elderly men in public areas across Hong Kong – usually surrounded by crowds placing bets.

More sedate is the martial art of **t'ai chi**. As dawn breaks, people (mostly elderly) head for the city's hills, parks and beaches to bend, stretch and meditate in silence. It's an amazing sight. Because t'ai chi emphasises correct form and feeling in each movement, the aim being to improve the flow of internal energy within the body, it is undertaken in a very slow and gentle manner. People who practise it regularly claim it promotes strength, stamina and flexibility, cultivating the link between mind and body, and enhancing balance and co-ordination. If you would like to give it a go, the Hong Kong Tourism Board conducts free t'ai chi classes for tourists (*see p237*).

### THE BEST MEDICINE?

Every district you visit in Hong Kong has old-fashioned shops dispensing Chinese remedies and herbal treatments from shelves stacked with oversized jars and medicine chests with tiny drawers. The largest concentration of these shops is in **Sheung Wan**, where you can see all manner of powders, pills, plants and animal parts, each of which is purported to play a distinctive role in the health of human beings.

Eight out of ten cats prefer Chinese medicine.

Non-Chinese may scoff at their healing powers, and animal rights activists regularly protest at the use of bear gall-bladders, tiger penises and sea horses to boost such functions as sexual virility and hair growth, but there's more to Chinese medicine than age-old myths. An extremely high percentage of Hong Kong people turn to Chinese medics before, or along with, Western doctors when illness strikes.

The origin of Chinese medicine dates back 5,000 years to the genesis of Chinese civilisation, but the first recorded case of diagnosing and treating disease can be traced back to about 1500 BC. The concept is holistic – both in treating and preventing illness – and is as relevant today as it ever was. As well as being credited with remedying ailments and altering states of mind, Chinese medicine is also said to enhance recuperative power, immunity and the capacity for pleasure, work and creativity.

The herbal medicine practice is linked to Chinese cosmology, in the belief that creation is born from the marriage of two polar principles, yin and yang: earth and heaven, winter and summer, night and day, cold and hot, wet and dry, inner and outer, body and mind. Harmony of this union means good health, good weather and good fortune, while disharmony leads to disease, disaster and bad luck.

The strategy of Chinese medicine is to restore harmony. Each human is seen as a world in miniature, with a unique ecology to be maintained. Practitioners assess a person's health by feeling the pulse and observing the colour and form of the face, tongue and body. This information is interpreted in the context of a patient's present and past complaints, working and living habits, environment, family health history and emotional life. Treatments include acupuncture, acupressure, exercise, massage and diet (tonic soups are drunk by everyone, as you'll notice as you explore the city).

The elusive **barking deer**.

# Wild Hong Kong

Dodge the snakes, marvel at the butterflies, but please don't feed the monkeys.

If hiking along mountain ridges with spectacular views, swimming on remote beaches or simply getting away from everything (and everyone) appeals to you, then take a walk on the wild side of Hong Kong. While the territory's monolithic skyscrapers and glittering, densely crowded cityscape is known all over the world, remarkably few visitors – or local residents for that matter – ever really discover its extraordinary natural beauty. But it's well worth taking the time to do so, as it helps put the place in context.

There are few major cities in the world that have such dramatic proximity of mountains, sea and teeming humanity. Some 40 per cent of Hong Kong's land area falls within 22 country parks, and the wide open spaces of the New Territories and 235 outlying islands offer considerable opportunities for getting away from it all, generally very easily.

### HIKING AND WILDERNESS

Wherever you stand in Hong Kong you're at most only 30 minutes away from open countryside and wooded trails. These range from gentle family walks near barbecue sites suitable for children and the elderly to adventurous, full-on hiking routes, such as the MacLehose, Wilson, Hong Kong and Lantau trails, which pass remote sandy beaches, hidden valleys, deserted villages, waterfalls and streams. Most trails are well mapped, and while you can do sections of the 'Big Four', the longest extends for 100 kilometres (62 miles). But what they all offer, regardless of their length, is generous amounts of that rarest of Hong Kong commodities – solitude.

### THE 'BIG FOUR' TRAILS

The 100-kilometre (62-mile) **MacLehose Trail** in the New Territories, named after the hill-loving former governor Sir Murray MacLehose, is divided into ten stages, taking in around 20 mountains and stretching east to west across almost the breadth of the New Territories, starting from Sai Kung Country Park and ending at Perowne Barracks in Tuen Mun. This is one of Hong Kong's most diverse and beautiful trails, and each November several thousand hikers compete in a charity event to

# Dolphin friendly

In recent years one local species has captured the public imagination more than any other – the Chinese white dolphin (*sousa chinensis*). Also known as the Indo-Pacific humpback dolphin, it is found around South Africa, India and Australia, but only along the Chinese coast does it have its unique and highly distinctive coloration. The dolphins are born almost black, but their skin quickly fades to paleish grey, before eventually maturing to a pinky white.

The Pearl River Delta region supports an estimated population of 1,000 white dolphins, but marine pollution and habitat destruction is posing an increasing threat to their survival. Around 190,000 cubic metres of raw sewage is dumped into the western harbour of Hong Kong Island every day (set to sky-rocket to 700,000 per day by 2010), and as a result high doses of organochlorines (such as DDT) have been found in dolphin tissue samples. As if this weren't bad enough, massive overfishing around local waters continues to deplete the dolphins' food supply, and heavy boat traffic –

especially around their main feeding ground near Chek Lap Kok airport – causes injury and further habitat degradation.

**Hong Kong Dolphinwatch** organises trips by extremely knowledgeable local guides. They're well worth the money, but don't expect to see the dolphins jumping over the bow of the boat and snatching fish out of your hands: the dolphins are usually pretty shy and sightings tend to be at a relative distance. The company claims a 96 per cent 'hit' rate; if you're unlucky enough not to spot a dolphin on your trip you can go on another one for free.

## Hong Kong Dolphinwatch

*Head office: 1528A Star House, Tsim Sha Tsui, Kowloon (2984 1414/ www.hkdolphinwatch.com).* **Trips** Wed, Fri, Sat, Sun. **Depart** 8.30am from Mandarin Hotel lobby, Central, HK Island; 9am from Kowloon Hotel lobby, Tsim Sha Tsui, Kowloon. **Return** from Tung Chung pier at 12.30pm, back to Tsim Sha Tsui (1pm) & Central (1.30pm). **Tickets** HK$280; HK$140 under-12s; free under-5s. **Credit** MC, V.

finish the trail in less than 48 hours (*see p188*). The fastest times are around 13 hours; new records are set each year.

The 70-kilometre (44-mile) **Wilson Trail** (named after another ex-governor, Sir David Wilson) is also split into several different sections. It starts near Stanley on Hong Kong Island and heads across Tai Tam Country Park, before hopping over the harbour (on the MTR, no less) to the New Territories. The Wilson Trail crosses the MacLehose Trail at several points and finally ends at the rugged Pat Sin Leng mountain range, not far from Tai Po.

## 'There are 50 species of snake in Hong Kong, the majority of them harmless.'

The 50-kilometre (31-mile) **Hong Kong Trail** is the most 'gentle' of the four, with fewer mountains and inclines, considerably more shade, and easier and more accessible starting and finishing points right across the length of Hong Kong Island. An annual hiking competition, the Green Power Hike, takes place along the trail (usually in February or March).

The 70-kilometre (44-mile) **Lantau Trail** curls around the whole of Lantau island. Considerably larger than Hong Kong Island, Lantau offers some of the city's highest and most scenic mountains, along with magnificent remote bathing beaches. The two most popular mountain hikes within the trail are Lantau Peak and Sunset Peak, both very challenging. Despite its obviously mountainous nature, Lantau is much more than just hills. There are numerous beach hikes at Cheung Sha, and to the hidden waterfalls just outside Tai O. There are also beautiful reservoirs, and island views at Shek Pik and around the coast to Fan Lau. The Lantau Trail is another annual hiking challenge that attracts many competitors.

### FLORA AND FAUNA

Hong Kong's diverse natural landscapes and various micro-ecologies contain an impressive range of plant and animal species – some of them unique to the area. The territory divides roughly into three types of vegetation – woodland, open grassland and rocky, barren slopes – boasting over 2,000 different species of plants, including more than 200 types of fern and 120 types of indigenous orchid. Early summer is the best time to enjoy blossoming trees and scented flowers, while autumn brings forth magnificent colours in mountain grasses and sedges.

The two most common trees in Hong Kong are the casuarina (she-oak) and camphor laurel. The largest remaining expanses of native forest can be found in the New Territories, in the country parks of **Tai Lam**, **Tai Mo Shan** and **Shing Mun** and the **Tai Po Kau Nature Reserve**. Most forested areas are near reservoirs, and were planted to help protect water catchments from siltation.

A severe shortage of firewood during the Japanese occupation in World War II ensured that few very old trees survive in Hong Kong (except in former barrack areas such as Hong Kong Park), but reforested areas abound, with Chinese red pines and American slash pine, as well as Australian species such as acacia, melaleuca and eucalyptus, which were planted for their adaptability and fire-resistant qualities. Many have become interspersed with indigenous species, creating diverse woodland vegetation.

Hong Kong's wildlife is similarly varied, and includes at least 45 species of mammals, 25 kinds of reptiles and 445 varieties of birds. The best spot for wildlife sightings are the rich woodlands of the New Territories, in particular **Tai Mo Shan**, **Shing Mun**, **Tai Po Kau** and around **Plover Cove**, where you can see

# Resources

The following are all useful contacts and information sources for those wanting to explore Hong Kong's wild places.

### Agriculture, Fisheries & Conservation Department

www.afcd.gov.hk

### Friends of the Earth

www.foe.org.hk

### Green Power

www.greenpower.org.hk

### RECOMMENDED BOOKS

*Exploring Hong Kong's Countryside: A Visitor's Companion*, Edward Stokes (HKTB)
*Hong Kong Pathfinder*, Martin Williams (Asia 2000)
*Hong Kong's Wild Places*, Edward Stokes (OUP)
*Lantau Island Explorer's Guide* (HKTB)
*The MacLehose Trail* (CUP)
*Magic Walks*, Kaarlo Schepel (The Alternative Press)
*Trailwalker* (Oxfam Hong Kong)

The poisonous **banded krait**.

In Context

(especially in the early morning or at dusk) larger native mammals, such as small wild boar, pangolin, Chinese porcupine, civet, ferret badger and – even more rarely – the small barking deer. The best places to see monkeys are around **Kam Shan** and **Lion Rock Country Parks**, both in the eastern New Territories. Rhesus and long-tailed macaques are numerous, cheeky and used to visitors. While some can seem tame, this can be deceptive and they can turn nasty if provoked. And under no circumstances feed them: steadily rising monkey populations are a considerable problem and their numbers have reached unsustainable levels in some places.

Hong Kong's reservoirs are well protected and support healthy populations of freshwater turtles, terrapins, snapping turtles and carp.

There are around 50 species of snake found all over Hong Kong (even in quite built-up locations). The vast majority are harmless, but there are several poisonous ones, including the Chinese cobra, the red-necked keelback, the coral snake and the banded krait. Take the usual precautions – walk with a heavy footfall, don't put your hand down any cracks in the rocks, and in the unlikely event of being bitten, stay calm and call 999.

Hong Kong supports an incredible 2,000 species of moths and 225 kinds of butterfly. Of the latter, some pretty varieties to watch out for in March and April are the great orange tip, the grey pansy, the mottled migrant, the bamboo tree brown and the banana skipper. The high-pitched whine of the spotted black cicada is inescapable in many park areas.

Two of the best places to go to appreciate the diversity of Hong Kong's flora and fauna

are the **Kadoorie Farm & Botanic Garden** (*see p104*) and **Mai Po Marshes** (*see p106*), both in the northern New Territories.

### BEING PREPARED

Probably the most important piece of advice you'll ever receive about hiking in Hong Kong is to take a decent map and as much water as you can carry. Excellent maps can be found in book shops around town, as well as the Government Publications Centre (*see p160*), but water is another matter. Each year, several people die from dehydration when hiking in Hong Kong; most of them are local residents who go out unprepared. By the time you feel flushed and thirsty, it's already serious – you're in the early stages of dehydration.

Along with lots of water, it's a sensible idea to pick up some iodine or chlorine tablets from a local pharmacy so you can purify stream/ reservoir water if your own supply runs out. It's also a good idea to carry a small first aid kit.

Many people underestimate just how remote the out-of-the-way parts of Hong Kong are – you can easily be six to eight hours' walk from the nearest main road in some locations. It is also advisable to take a mobile phone with you, just in case. The general accident and emergency number in Hong Kong is 999.

▶ For more walks, *see p82* **Across the Dragon's Back**, *p78* **Peak of fitness** and *p110* **Lamma**.
▶ For more on the city's natural attractions, *see p80-p84* **Hong Kong Island: South & east coasts**, *p97-p109* **The New Territories** and *p110-p119* **The Outlying Islands**.

# Where to Stay

## Features

# Where to Stay

Business travellers may be the local hotel industry's bread and butter, but there are plenty of cheaper alternatives for those not coming on expense accounts.

You may as well know now that hotels in Hong Kong are notoriously expensive. By Asian standards the city remains very costly, and five-star luxury still comes at a price tag that will make anyone but the all-expenses-paid business traveller tremble. But the good news is that things are changing for the better. The continuing Asian economic downturn – not to mention the SARS scare of spring 2003, which spread internationally after several guests staying at the Metropole Hotel in Tsim Sha Tsui contracted it – has led many hotels to reduce official rates and offer big discounts in an effort to boost occupancy. Six months after SARS, however, hotel occupancy was already back to normal, mainly due to an increased number of mainland tourists visiting; the rebound was so strong, in fact, that the government went so far as to suggest, controversially, that flats earmarked for a home-ownership scheme be turned into tourist accommodation. Several more hotels are scheduled to be built over the next five years, including Hong Kong's first boutique hotel, planned for Central by 2005.

Most of the existing major hotels are located in Central, Wan Chai, Causeway Bay and Tsim Sha Tsui. Any of these districts will place you right at the heart of the action. Clusters of luxury hotels can be found facing Admiralty's Supreme Court Road (including the **Island Shangri-La**; *see p46*) or Central's Chater Road (the **Ritz-Carlton**; *see p45*), and the Tsim Sha Tsui and Wan Chai harboursides (among them opulent and impressive five-star landmarks such as the **Peninsula** (*see p53*) and the **Grand Hyatt** (*see p49*), which are among the best hotels in the world).

After being virtually non-existent for years, the mid-range sector is growing. Hotels outside the main districts, such as Western, North Point and further north of Kowloon, offer similar standards to the more central hotels for less money. Hong Kong is a small city with excellent and cheap public transport (or free or bargain-rate shuttle buses), so the minor inconvenience of being further out can be balanced by the savings. The **Ibis North Point** on the east of Hong Kong Island (*see p51*), the **Novotel Century Harbourview Hotel** on the west of the island (*see p46*) and **BP International House** in Jordan, Kowloon (*see p55*), are all good examples.

Next down the scale are the guesthouses. These are mainly concentrated in Causeway Bay and Tsim Sha Tsui. The latter is famous for its guesthouses, which nestle cheek-by-jowl with some of the city's flashiest hotels. Many backpackers end up in **Chungking Mansions** on Nathan Road (*see p54* **Golden oldies**). The rabbit-warren buildings house scores of guesthouses; some are good, some are gritty,

The **Island Shangri-La**.
See p46.

but all offer prime location for a fraction of the price charged by the more upmarket hotels. The worst of the guesthouses offer poor facilities or, worse, poor security, so check out a place before you stay and try to haggle over the price (normally, the longer you commit to staying, the cheaper the daily rate). More guesthouses can be found further along Nathan Road towards Jordan and Yau Ma Tei. If you're walking around with a backpack, touts will come and hand you business cards urging you to stay in one of them.

A good alternative to guesthouses are youth hostels. These do not enjoy such prime locations but often have beautiful settings amidst the extensive country parks near the city. You'll need to be a YHA member to stay at a hostel; membership cards can be bought from YHA offices in your home country, or from the Hong Kong head office (Room 225-226, Block 19, Shek Kip Mei Estate, Sham Shui Po, Kowloon, 2788 1638/fax 2788 3105). An email booking form is available on the Hong Kong Youth Hostels Association (HKYHA) website (www.yha.org.hk).

### THE LOWDOWN ON PRICES

The late autumn months through to Christmas and Chinese New Year usually denote the high season. The best deals are to be found in the spring and during the humid summer months, and can be around 50 per cent of the official rates. In this chapter, we use the following categories, based on lowest double room price: **Deluxe** (HK$3,000 or above), **Expensive** (HK$2,000-$2,999); **Moderate** (HK$1,000-$1,999) and **Cheap** (under HK$1,000); hotels have their own category. Check whether hotel prices are inclusive or exclusive of taxes – the current government surcharge is 13 per cent, and an additional service charge may also be levied. Unless otherwise indicated, rates listed here are official rates, exclusive of taxes and of breakfast.

# Hong Kong Island

## Central

As Central is the business heart of the city, it's no surprise that its few hotels are geared towards business travellers. A six-star Four Seasons (Hong Kong's first) is scheduled to open in the IFC, Central by 2005, as is a boutique hotel in the rebuilt Landmark complex. Admiralty has a cluster of fantastically luxurious hotels – among them the **Island Shangri-La** (*see p46*) – which jut skywards from the vast Pacific Place shopping mall.

## The best Hotels

### For afternoon tea
The **Peninsula**, of course. *See p53.*

### For the best deal in town
The **Salisbury YMCA** – prime location, excellent facilities, affordable prices. *See p55.*

### For business travellers on a budget
Many Hong Kong hotels have free in-room broadband internet access, but the **Best Western Rosedale on the Park** offers that plus other business perks, and at decent rates. *See p49.*

### For foodies
The restaurants at the **Island Shangri-La** (*see p46*), **Peninsula** (*see p53*) and **Intercontinental** (*see p51*) are so good you'll never want to set foot outside.

### For getting away from it all
The award-winning **Pak Sha O Hostel**, is worth the hike into beautiful Sai Kung Country Park. *See p58.*

### For shopping on your doorstep
The **Excelsior** is just a short walk from Causeway Bay's malls. *See p49.*

### For spa treatments
I-Spa at the **Intercontinental**. *See p51.*

### For technophobes
The **Ritz-Carlton** has a dedicated butler on call round the clock to deal with any technological hiccups. *See below.*

### For tickling the underbelly of Hong Kong
**Chungking House.** *See p54* **Golden oldies**.

## Deluxe

### The Ritz-Carlton
*3 Connaught Road (2877 6666/fax 2877 6778/ www.ritzcarlton.com). Central MTR (exit J3)/buses through Central/Central Star Ferry Pier.* **Rates** HK$3,200-$4,200 single/double; HK$7,800-$28,750 suite. **Credit** AmEx, DC, MC, V. **Map** p309 E4.
Located in the Central business district between Chater and Connaught Roads, the Ritz-Carlton attracts a mix of business and leisure travellers. Although it has 216 rooms (many with harbour views), it has an intimate feel, which extends to its six restaurants and the wonderfully discreet Chater

Lounge. The rooms are elegantly furnished, with marble bathrooms and luxuries like the 24-hour 'technology butler' on hand to fix any computer, fax or internet problems you might face. The food is equally impressive: Toscana, the hotel's signature restaurant, is a fine Italian place, and Shanghai Shanghai in the basement is an art-deco gem.

**Hotel services** *Air-conditioning. Babysitting. Bar. Beauty salon. Business services. Concierge. Disabled: adapted rooms. Gym. Laundry. Limousine service. No-smoking floors. Restaurants. Swimming pool (outdoor).* **Room services** *Broadband internet access. Iron. Mini-bar. Room service (24hrs). Telephone. TV: cable/pay movies/satellite.*

## Expensive

### Island Shangri-La

*Pacific Place, 88 Queensway, Admiralty (2877 3838/fax 2521 8742/www.shangri-la.com). Admiralty MTR (exit C1)/buses along Queensway.* **Rates** HK$2,400-$3,450 single; HK$2,600-$3,650 double; HK$5,800-$26,000 suite. **Credit** AmEx, DC, MC, V. **Map** p309 F5.

The tallest hotel in Hong Kong is also one of the most luxurious. No expense has been spared, from the artworks and chandeliers in the lavish lobby, to the 565 rooms (including 34 suites), which are the largest on HK Island and have views of either the Peak or the harbour. In the atrium hangs the 16-storey-high Great Motherland of China, thought to be the largest Chinese silk painting in the world. Business travellers are well catered for, with wireless connectivity in all public areas, and three IDD phone lines in all rooms. But shopaholics will also enjoy it here – the hotel is within the upmarket Pacific Place mall. Dining options, which are among the best in the city, include the casual Café TOO and the award-winning Petrus (for both, *see p124*), with its jaw-dropping views over the harbour. Perks for guests paying rack rates include free laundry and dry-cleaning, late (6pm) checkout and free local phone calls.

**Hotel services** *Air-conditioning. Babysitting. Bars. Beauty salon. Business services. Concierge. Disabled: adapted rooms. Gym. Laundry. Limousine service. No-smoking rooms. Restaurants. Swimming pool (outdoor).* **Room services** *Broadband internet access. Hairdryer. Mini-bar. Room service (24hrs). Telephone. TV: cable/pay movies/satellite.*

### Mandarin Oriental

*5 Connaught Road (2522 0111/fax 2810 6190/ www.mandarinoriental.com). Central MTR (exit F, H)/buses to Central Star Ferry/Central Star Ferry Pier.* **Rates** HK$2,000-$2,950 single/double; HK$5,500 suite. **Credit** AmEx, DC, MC, V. **Map** p309 E3.

The multi-award-winning Mandarin Oriental chain now has hotels around the world, but the original one stands here, in the heart of Central's financial district, with stunning views of Victoria Harbour. Probably the best-located hotel in Hong Kong, the Mandarin is a local institution. Its Mandarin Grill has been the setting for many a deal between *tai pans* (the tycoons who ran the *hongs* in colonial times), while the Chinnery Bar – a men-only club until 1990 – is an old favourite of the social elite.

A towering landmark when it was built in 1963, the hotel is now dwarfed by modern towers, and the balconies now overhang a noisy, busy highway. Thankfully, double glazing cuts all that out and allows you to savour the interior, with flowers, Oriental flourishes and dark wood. The 542 guest rooms and suites are more modest than some newer luxury hotels, but the business and leisure facilities are first class. But above all it's the impeccable service that keeps guests coming back.

**Hotel services** *Air-conditioning. Babysitting. Bars. Beauty salon. Business services. Concierge. Gym. Laundry. Limousine service. No-smoking rooms. Restaurants. Swimming pool (indoor).* **Room services** *Broadband internet access. Hairdryer. Mini-bar. Room services (24hrs). Telephone. TV: cable/pay movies/satellite.*

## Sheung Wan & Mid-Levels

## Moderate

### Novotel Century Harbourview Hotel

*508 Queen's Road West, Kennedy Town, Sheung Wan (2974 1234/fax 2974 0333). Buses to Kennedy Town.* **Rates** HK$1,100 single/double; HK$2,700 suite. **Credit** AmEx, DC, MC, V.

As you might expect, the Novotel offers great sea views from many of its rooms. Rooms are tastefully furnished, and facilities are modern, if only because the hotel is quite young. The area is a bit of a tourist backwater, but the price is good, and if it's real Hong Kong street life you want then this is your place (and if you really must go to Central it's only a short bus or taxi ride away).

**Other locations:** Novotel Century 238 Jaffe Road, Wan Chai, HK Island (2598 8888).

**Hotel services** *Air-conditioning. Babysitting. Bar. Business services. Concierge. Disabled: adapted rooms. Gym. No-smoking rooms. Parking (HK$300/ day). Restaurants. Swimming pool (indoor).* **Room services** *Broadband internet access. Hairdryer. Mini-bar. Room service (11am-midnight). Telephone. TV: cable/pay movies/satellite.*

## Cheap

### Garden View International House

*1 MacDonnell Road, Mid-Levels (2877 3737/fax 2845 6263/www.ywca.org.hk). Taxi from Hong Kong Airport Express Station.* **Rates** HK$880-$990 single/double; $1,800-$2,000 suite. **Credit** AmEx, DC, MC, V.

For such a prime location – in the upmarket Mid-Levels residential area, close to SoHo, Hong Kong Park and the Botanical Gardens – this place is a bargain. Another bonus is the outdoor swimming pool,

Luxury, **Grand Hyatt** style. *See p49.*

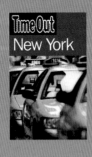
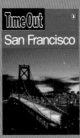

a godsend during the summer heat. The rooms are fairly small and basic (though they do at least have a mini fridge), but if you're using it as a base for exploring then this probably won't bother you. If your budget will allow, pay the extra for a harbour-view room or a suite. The food options aren't great, but there are plenty of excellent restaurants just a short walk away. Hotel minibuses run down to Central every few minutes.
**Hotel services** *Air-conditioning. Bar. Disabled: adapted rooms. Gym. Laundry. No-smoking rooms. Restaurant. Swimming pool (outdoor).* **Room services** *Kitchenette (suites only). Telephone. TV: cable/satellite.*

## Hostel

### Jockey Club Mount Davis Youth Hostel
*Mount Davis Path, Mount Davis, Kennedy Town, Sheung Wan (2817 5715/fax 2788 1638/ www.yha.org.hk). Sheung Wan MTR then taxi or shuttle bus from Shun Tak Centre next door.*
**Rates** HK$40-$65 dorm bed; HK$150-$300 private room. **No credit cards.**
Formerly known as Ma Wui Hall, this hostel enjoys a magnificent setting atop Mount Davis at the west end of Hong Kong Island. The views of Tsing Ma Bridge and Victoria Harbour are breathtaking, and have made the place so popular that it recently expanded from 111 beds to 169. The hostel is just a short bus hop into the main areas of Hong Kong, but be warned: if you miss the hostel shuttle bus, which runs only four times a day, there's a 35-minute walk uphill from the nearest bus stop.
**Hotel services** *Air-conditioning. Kitchen. Laundry.*

## Wan Chai & Causeway Bay

If you want to experience the hustle and bustle of Hong Kong, Wan Chai and Causeway Bay, just east of Central, give you just that. With a 24/7 culture and strip after strip of bars, clubs and shops, these districts never sleep.

## Deluxe

### Grand Hyatt
*1 Harbour Road, Wan Chai (2588 1234/fax 2802 0677/http://hongkong.hyatt.com). Wan Chai MTR (exit A1/C)/A12, 18, 88 bus/Wan Chai Star Ferry Pier.* **Rates** from HK$3,600 single/double; HK$4,400-$25,900 suite. **Credit** AmEx, DC, MC, V. **Map** p310 B2.
Hyatt International's flagship hotel is about the best on Hong Kong Island. The lavish art deco lobby gives way to 572 surprisingly minimalist yet ultra-luxe rooms, most with harbour views. Business travellers are well catered to – each room has a self-contained work station, broadband internet access and fax machine with personal number; an extra $900 buys access to the Grand Club, with private

lounge and complimentary breakfast; and the adjoining convention centre makes it an ideal hotel for delegates. Leisure facilities are equally impressive, and include Hong Kong's largest freeform swimming pool, and two of the city's best restaurants, One Harbour Road (*see p131*), which showcases excellent Cantonese cooking, and Grissini (*see p131*), serving outstanding Italian cuisine; afternoon tea and the evening dessert buffet in the Tiffin Lounge are also memorable experiences. Celebs also get a look-in – there are 13 speciality suites, including two Presidential Suites, plus a Grand Ballroom and a luxury junk for hire should the need arise.
**Hotel services** *Air-conditioning. Babysitting. Bar. Beauty salon. Business services. Concierge. Disabled: adapted rooms. Gym. Laundry. Limousine service. No-smoking floors. Parking (HK$90/2hrs). Restaurants. Swimming pool (outdoor).* **Room services** *Broadband internet access. DVD player (executive floor). Fax. Hairdryer. Iron. Mini-bar. Room service (24hrs). Telephone. TV: cable/pay movies/satellite.*

## Moderate

### Best Western Rosedale on the Park
*8 Shelter Street, Causeway Bay, HK Island (2127 8888/fax 2127 3333). Causeway Bay MTR (exit D3, E)/buses along Gloucester Road.* **Rates** HK$1,280 single/double; HK$1,980-$6,980 suite. **Credit** DC, MC, V. **Map** p311 E/F3.
This good-value hotel across the road from Victoria Park in bustling Causeway Bay opened in 2001, making it a relative newcomer to the Hong Kong hotel scene. Facilities are impressive for the price – rooms are on the small side but have above-average bathrooms and are equipped with an impressive array of facilities. OK, it's not the height of luxury, but if you're a business traveller and/or staying a while you could do a lot worse. The friendly young staff are a further bonus.
**Hotel services** *Bar. Business services. Concierge. Disabled: rooms. Fax. Fitness centre. Laundry. No-smoking rooms. Restaurant.* **Room services** *Broadband internet access. Hairdryer. Mini-bar. Room service (7am-1am). TV: cable.*

### The Excelsior
*281 Gloucester Road, Causeway Bay (2894 8888/fax 2895 6459/www.mandarin-oriental.com/excelsior). Causeway Bay MTR (exit D1)/buses along Gloucester Road.* **Rates** from HK$1,900 single/ double; HK$3,800-$8,000 suite. **Credit** AmEx, DC, MC, V. **Map** p311 E2.
With 863 rooms and 21 suites, the Excelsior is the largest hotel on HK Island. It's run by the Mandarin Oriental group, so the service here is better than you might expect for such a big operation. It's located on the harbour – with great views of the Royal Hong Kong Yacht Club – and near the Noon Day Gun, which is fired every day should you ever oversleep. The hotel is always busy with business travellers,

The spectral towers of Hong Kong Island, as seen from the **Intercontinental**. *See p51.*

tourists and airline personnel drawn by its location in the heart of vibrant Causeway Bay. The rooms are a bit '70s in style, but comfy and spacious nonetheless. Dickens Bar is a lively sports pub, and ToTT's Asian Grill & Bar (*see p224*) is great for a snack. **Hotel services** *Air-conditioning. Babysitting. Bar. Beauty salon. Business services. Concierge. Disabled: adapted rooms. Gym. Laundry. Limousine service. No-smoking floors. Restaurants.* **Room services** *Broadband internet access. Hairdryer. Iron. Mini-bar. Room service (24hrs). Safe. Telephone. TV: cable/pay movies/satellite.*

### Harbour View International House

*4 Harbour Road, Wan Chai (2802 011/fax 2802 9063/www.harbour.ymca.org.hk). Wan Chai MTR (exit A1, C)/taxi from Hong Kong Airport Express Station.* **Rates** HK$1,200-$1,750 single/double. **Credit** AmEx, MC, V. **Map** p310 B3.

Location and cost are the paramount reasons for staying here, as it's close to the throbbing heart of Wan Chai but just enough removed from the madness. It's also close to the Arts Centre and the Academy for Performing Arts, which means it's often packed with touring dancers and musicians. Many rooms in the towerblock hotel – officially a hostel – offer great views. Most of the rooms are quite small and simply decorated, but have reasonable facilities.

**Hotel services** *Air-conditioning. Babysitting. Concierge. Disabled: adapted rooms. Laundry. No-smoking rooms. Restaurant.* **Room services** *Broadband internet access. Mini-bar. Safe. Telephone. TV: cable/satellite.*

### Luk Kwok

*72 Gloucester Road, Wan Chai (2866 2166). Wan Chai MTR (exit A1, C).* **Rates** HK$1,450-$1,600 single/double; HK$2,100-$2,300 executive; HK$3,600-$5,700 suite. **Credit** AmEx, DC, MC, V. **Map** p310 B3.

Built on the site of the hotel where Suzie Wong used to hang out, the Luk Kwok is now a respectable hotel catering to a largely business customer base. The facilities are impressive given the decent prices. **Hotel services** *Babysitting. Bar. Business services. Concierge. Disabled: adapted rooms. Gym. Laundry. Limousine service. No-smoking floor. Restaurants.* **Room services** *Broadband internet access. Hairdryer. Mini-bar. Room service (24hrs). Safe. Telephone. TV: cable/satellite.*

## Cheap

### Hwa Seng Guesthouse

*Block B1, 5/F, Great George Building, 27 Paterson Street, Causeway Bay (2895 6859/ fax 2838 7052/www.guesthouse.com.hk). Causeway*

*MTR (exit E)/buses along Yee Wo Street.* **Rates** from HK$400 single/double. **No credit cards.** **Map** p311 E2.

This family-run guesthouse offers small but decent rooms for a reasonable price. It's close to Causeway Bay MTR station, and right in the heart of a shopping and entertainment hub. Some rooms have private baths.

**Room services** *Air-conditioning. Telephone. TV.*

### Wesley

*22 Hennessy Road, Wan Chai (2866 6688/fax 2866 6633/www.grandhotel.com.hk/wesley/index.htm). Wan Chai MTR (exit B1)/shuttle bus from Hong Kong Airport Express station/buses along Hennessy Road.* **Rates** HK$700-$1,050 single/double. **Credit** AmEx, DC, MC, V. **Map** p310 B3.

If you're planning on spending two weeks or longer in Hong Kong and money is an object, you might think seriously about the Wesley. It offers bargain long-term accommodation (from HK$8,000 per month) and is popular with temporary residents – so popular, in fact, that some have stayed here years. Situated on the border of Admiralty and Wan Chai, it's very convenient for entertainment, shops and public transport. The hotel's restaurants are average, but many better places to eat can be found nearby.

**Hotel services** *Air-conditioning. Business services. Concierge. Disabled: adapted rooms. Laundry. Limousine service. No-smoking rooms. Restaurant.* **Room services** *Dataport. Hairdryer. Mini-bar. TV: cable/satellite.*

## Hostels

### Noble Hostel

*Flat A3, 17/F, Great George Building, 27 Paterson Street, Causeway Bay (2576 6148). Causeway MTR (exit E)/buses along Yee Wo Street.* **Rates** HK$180-$300 single; HK$250-$450 double; HK$350-$550 triple. **No credit cards. Map** p311 E2.

In the same building as Hwa Seng (*see p50*), Noble Hostel is another excellent guesthouse, especially for those who want assurance that slumming it doesn't mean dirty rooms. Rooms are air-conditioned and spotlessly clean.

**Hotel services** *Air-conditioning. Laundry.* **Room services** *TV.*

### Wang Fat Hostel

*Flat A2, 3/F, Paterson Building, 47 Paterson Street, Causeway Bay (2895 1015/fax 2576 7509/ www.wangfathostel.com.hk). Causeway MTR (exit E)/buses along Yee Wo Street.* **Rates** HK$150 single; HK$280 double; HK$140 dorm. **No credit cards. Map** p311 E2.

The recently renovated Wang Fat Hostel offers everything from single rooms to dorms. The rooms are immaculate, the decor modern, and the staff friendly. Best of all, though, are the plum location and the free net access in the reception area.

**Hotel services** *Air-conditioning. Internet access. Laundry.* **Room services** *Telephone. TV.*

## East

## Cheap

### Ibis North Point

*136-42 Java Road, North Point (2588 1111/fax 2588 1123). North Point MTR (exit A1, A2)/10 bus.* **Rates** HK$500-$600 single/double; HK$2,859 suite. **Credit** AmEx, DC, MC, V.

Staying out of the main commercial areas means you get more for your dollar. But in this case, because North Point is accessible by MTR, tram and bus, inconvenience isn't really an issue. Also on the plus side, the hotel is well equipped, many rooms have harbour views and all have satellite television. As if that weren't enough, the business centre offers net facilities, computer hire and mobile phone rental.

**Hotel services** *Business services. Disabled: adapted rooms. Laundry. No-smoking rooms. Restaurant.* **Room services** *Broadband internet access. Hairdryer. Safe. Telephone. TV.*

# Kowloon

## Tsim Sha Tsui

The southern tip of the Kowloon peninsula is where most people stay when they come to Hong Kong, either in a cheap guesthouse or at one of the flash five-star hotels. It's a great area to wander around, with the promenade offering the jaw-dropping night-time view of the Hong Kong Island skyline. There are also plenty of museums and shops and good transport links to anywhere in the city.

## Deluxe

### The Intercontinental

*18 Salisbury Road (2721 1211/fax 2739 4546/ www.intercontinental.com). Tsim Sha Tsui MTR (exit E)/buses along Salisbury Road/Tsim Sha Tsui Star Ferry Pier.* **Rates** HK$3,100-$3,500 single/ double; HK$5,500-$28,000 suite. **Credit** AmEx, DC, MC, V. **Map** p313 C6.

Formerly the Regent (and still known as such by many cab drivers), the Intercontinental underwent a revamp a few years back, bringing it in line with the Peninsula, its nearest competitor (both in terms of luxury and location). Situated right on the waterfront at Tsim Sha Tsui, the hotel has some of the best views of Hong Kong harbour. The open-plan lounge, and most of the restaurants and 514 rooms also enjoy these views (the rest overlook the lovely pool and sun deck). The Intercontinental has among the best business services in Hong Kong, and for an extra HK$500 a day (plus tax and service), guests get access to the business lounge, with business services, free local calls, and complimentary breakfast,

afternoon tea and evening drinks and nibbles. But leisure travellers will also feel thoroughly spoiled with the facilities, which include the excellent I-Spa (*see p180*), a swimming pool and three spa pools overlooking the harbour. And the rooms? Spacious, luxurious, with huge bathrooms featuring spa tubs and luxury showers; and 24-hour butler service. Dining options are also among Hong Kong's best, and include Yü (*see p141*) and a branch of Alain Ducasse's upmarket international chain, Spoon (*see p138*). A real gem.

**Hotel services** *Babysitting. Bar. Beauty salon. Business services. Concierge. Disabled: adapted rooms. Gym. Laundry. Limousine service. No-smoking floors. Parking (HK$130/2hrs). Restaurants. Swimming pool (outdoor).* **Room services** *Air-conditioning. Broadband internet access. CD player (suites only). Hairdryer. Iron. Mini-bar. Room service (24hrs). Telephone. TV: pay movies/satellite.*

### The Peninsula

*Salisbury Road (2920 2888/fax 2722 4170/ www.peninsula.com). Tsim Sha Tsui MTR (exit E)/ shuttle bus from Kowloon Airport Express Station/ buses to Tsim Sha Tsui Ferry Pier & along Salisbury Road/Tsim Sha Tsui Star Ferry Pier.* **Rates** HK$3,000-$4,900 double/twin; HK$5,600-$39,000 suite. **Credit** AmEx, DC, MC, V. **Map** p313 B/C6.

The Grand Old Lady of Kowloon turned 75 in 2003 but remains as distinguished as ever. The jewel in the crown of the city's five-star hotel industry, the Pen is a destination in its own right, and it's no surprise that royalty (and *hoi polloi*) from around the world choose to stay here whenever they're in town. All are attracted by the hotel's elegance, restrained luxury and impeccable service. Even a 30-storey extension in 1994, which almost doubled the number of rooms to 300 (including 54 suites), managed to be in keeping with the rest of the building.

Rooms are spacious, featuring opulent Western decor with classical oriental furniture and motifs, but are kept up to date with high-speed internet access, fax and laser-disc/CD players. The marble bathrooms have huge tubs, and the suites have jacuzzis, many of which have a 180-degree panoramic view. The list of facilities is endless, with a faux Roman swimming pool, a large sun terrace overlooking the harbour, and a spa (*see p181*) in a well-equipped gym. Helicopter tours of the city are offered from the rooftop's twin helipads, while a fleet of 13 Rolls-Royce Silver Spur IIIs is at the disposal of guests. You can even take a class in anything from brush-writing to traditional Chinese medicine.

All this comes at a high price, of course, but even if you can't afford to stay here, try at least to experience one of the hotel's eight restaurants and bars. These include the opulent French restaurant Gaddi's (*see p137*), the Cantonese Spring Moon (*see p136*) and the Philippe Starck-designed restaurant and bar, Felix (*see p154*). Afternoon tea in the lobby (HK$180 per person, exclusive of service) is also a splendid way to relive the colonial days.

**Hotel services** *Air-conditioning. Bars. Beauty salon. Business services. Concierge. Disabled: adapted rooms, facilities. Gym. Laundry. Limousine service. No-smoking floors. Restaurants. Swimming pool (indoor).* **Room services** *Broadband internet access. CD/DVD player. Fax. Hairdryer. Iron. Mini-bar. Room service (24hrs). Safe. Telephone. TV: cable/pay movies/satellite.*

## Expensive

### Holiday Inn Golden Mile

*50 Nathan Road (2369 3111/fax 2369 8016/ http://goldenmile-hk.holiday-inn.com). Tsim Sha Tsui MTR (exit C1, C2)/buses along Nathan Road.* **Rates** from HK$1,900 single; from HK$2,500 double; from HK$5,800 suite. **Credit** AmEx, DC, MC, V. **Map** p313 C6.

This isn't the pick of the hotels on the 'Golden Mile', but it still has plenty to offer. A web of escalators and elevators take you between its thriving bars and restaurants, of which Loong Yuen is the best, offering decent dim sum and award-winning fried rice (yes, really). The hotel's 600 rooms are on the small side but are comfy and feature marble bathrooms.

**Hotel services** *Air-conditioning. Babysitting. Bar. Beauty salon. Business services. Concierge. Disabled: adapted rooms. Gym. Laundry. Limousine service. No-smoking floors. Parking (HK$130/2hrs). Restaurants. Swimming pool (outdoor).* **Room services** *Broadband internet access. Hairdryer. Iron. Mini-bar. Room service (24hrs). Safe. Telephone. TV: cable/pay movies/satellite.*

### Royal Garden Hong Kong

*69 Mody Road (2721 5215/fax 2369 9976/ www.theroyalgardenhotel.com.hk). Tsim Sha Tsui MTR (exit C1)/203, 973 bus/buses along Chatham Road South & Salisbury Road.* **Rates** HK$2,100-$2,950 single; HK$2,250-$3,150 double; HK$3,700-$13,700 suite. **Credit** AmEx, DC, MC, V. **Map** p313 C6.

Step inside the Royal Garden and for a moment you forget you're in the heart of Tsim Sha Tsui. The central atrium, with its lush greenery, is a haven from the bustling streets outside. It's unbeatable for the price; rooms aren't as lavish as in higher-end hotels, but are on the right side of luxurious, with bathrooms with powerful showers and deep tubs. And all the necessary facilities are present and correct: business centre (with private boardroom), gym, sauna and massage treatments, and a gorgeous rooftop pool (covered in winter) with stunning views over the harbour. Like many other Hong Kong hotels, the Royal Garden has excellent dining and drinking facilities – in this case the Japanese restaurant Inagiku (*see p141*), Sabatini, with its upmarket Italian food, and the sleek Martini Bar.

**Hotel services** *Air-conditioning. Babysitting. Bar. Business services. Concierge. Gym. No-smoking floors. Parking. Restaurant. Swimming pool (outdoor).* **Room services** *Broadband internet access. Hairdryer. Mini-bar. Room service (24hrs). Telephone. Safe. TV: pay movies/satellite.*

# Golden oldies

Backpackers usually find Hong Kong's hotels well beyond their meagre budgets. But rather than head for the youth hostels in the hills, they usually go to a tangled warren of old mansions slap bang on Nathan Road's 'Golden Mile'. Here, run-down and ramshackle buildings are home to scores of guesthouses, ranging from the shabby to the the not-too-shabby, as well as curry houses and tiny shops. The itinerant population can be a bit intimidating, especially for single women, but avoid dark corners at night and you should be safe enough. Most guesthouses have staff on duty 24 hours a day, but never leave valuables in your room.

The most famous – or rather infamous – of these crumbling buildings is **Chungking Mansions**, which inspired Wong Kar-wai's classic film *Chungking Express*, which holds myriad guesthouses within its rambling walls (including **Chungking House**; *pictured*). The **Delhi Guest House** is a decent, less-famous, alternative. For more upmarket choices in the area, *see p51-p56*.

## Chungking House

*Block A, 4F & 5F, Chungking Mansions, 40 Nathan Road, Tsim Sha Tsui, Kowloon (2366 5362/fax 2721 3570). Tsim Sha Tsui MTR (exit E)/buses along Nathan Road/Tsim Sha Tsui Star Ferry Pier.* **Rates** HK$200-$380 single; HK$260-$400 double. **No credit cards**. **Map** p313 C6.
This is without doubt the best guesthouse in Chungking. It has more than 100 rooms, but they're often all full as they're clean, have the luxury of air-con, televisions and phones (some even have private baths). You pay up to 50 per cent more than at smaller guesthouses, but it's money well spent.
**Hotel services** *Air-conditioning.*
**Room services** *Telephone. TV.*

## Delhi Guest House

*Block B, Flat B2, 5/F, Chungking Mansions, 40 Nathan Road, Tsim Sha Tsui, Kowloon (2368 1682. Tsim Sha Tsui MTR (exit E)/buses along Nathan Road & Salisbury Road/Tsim Sha Tsui Star Ferry Pier.* **Rates** from HK$200 single/double. **Credit** MC. **Map** p313 C6.
The Delhi is your typical no-frills Chungking guesthouse, with sparsely furnished, basic rooms and shared facilities. But it's cheap, which is why it (and others like it) have been in business for decades. The phone number here is for a restaurant owned by the proprietors – it's the best way of reaching them.
**Hotel services** *Air-conditioning.*
**Room services** *Telephone. TV.*

## Moderate

### BP International House
*8 Austin Road (2376 1111/fax 2376 1333/ www.megahotels.com.hk). Jordan MTR (exit C1, D)/shuttle bus from Kowloon Airport Express Station/A21 bus from the airport/buses along Nathan Road.* **Rates** from HK$1,050 single/double; HK$2,950-$3,350 suite. **Credit** AmEx, DC, MC, V. **Map** p313 C5.
Despite its name, this hotel has nothing to do with the oil multinational. It is handily located between the consumer mecca of Tsim Sha Tsui and the busy nightlife of Jordan, and offers value for money for those on a budget who don't want to go quite as downmarket as a guesthouse. Rooms are satisfactory and clean, and if you're lucky you might get one with a view over Victoria Harbour.
**Hotel services** *Air-conditioning. Babysitting. Bar. Business services. Disabled: adapted rooms. Laundry (self-service). Limousine service. No-smoking rooms. Parking (HK$100/24hrs).* **Room services** *Broadband internet access. Safe. Telephone. TV: cable/pay movies/satellite.*

### Kowloon Hotel
*19 Nathan Road (2929 2888/fax 2739 9811/ http://fasttrack.kowloon.peninsula.com). Tsim Sha Tsui MTR (exit E)/shuttle bus from Kowloon Airport Express Station/buses along Nathan Road & Salisbury Road/Tsim Sha Tsui Star Ferry Pier.* **Rates** HK$1,300-$2,200 single/double; HK$3,600-$5,100 suite. **Credit** AmEx, DC, MC, V. **Map** p313 B6.
If convenience and communication are your watchwords, this hi-tech hotel should be top of your list. The Kowloon has a combined TV/computer monitor in each room, offering high-speed internet access. You'll even get an email address and fax number under the hotel's network. The 736 rooms (including 17 suites) are fairly small but comfortable enough, and some have a harbour view. Sitting in the heart of Tsim Sha Tsui's entertainment and shopping district behind the famed Peninsula hotel (*see p53*), the Kowloon is part of the same group, meaning service here is exemplary. Guests also enjoy signing privileges at the Pen, although the Kowloon's Wan Loong Court (Cantonese) and Pizzeria (Italian) are also excellent dining options.
**Hotel services** *Air-conditioning. Babysitting. Bar. Beauty salon. Business services. Concierge. Laundry. No-smoking rooms. Restaurants.* **Room services** *Broadband internet access. Hairdryer. Mini-bar. Telephone. TV: cable/pay movies/satellite.*

### Ramada
*73-5 Chatham Road South (2311 1100/fax 2311 6000). Tsim Sha Tsui MTR (exit B1)/973 bus.* **Rates** HK$1,500-$2,050 single/double; HK$2,800-$4,200 suite. **Credit** AmEx, DC, MC, V. **Map** p313 C5.
Chinese businessmen tend to fill up the Ramada, if only because it is near the KCR train terminus, with a direct service to China. This might explain why the hotel has all the necessary business amenities –

from internet connections to conference facilities. Leisure travellers headed to China might also find this a convenient place to stay, especially if they're only in Hong Kong for one or two nights.
**Hotel services** *Air-conditioning. Babysitting. Bar. Business services. Concierge. Disabled: adapted rooms. Laundry. No-smoking rooms. Restaurant.* **Room services** *Dataport. Hairdryer. Mini-bar. Room service (7am-6pm). Telephone. TV: cable/pay movies/satellite.*

## Cheap

### Holy Carpenter Guesthouse
*1 Dyer Avenue, Hung Hom (2362 0301/fax 2362 2193). Kowloon KCR/buses along Hung Hom South Road/Hung Hom Ferry Pier.* **Rates** HK$424 single/double. **Credit** MC, V. **Map** p313 E4.
Bigger and brighter than the guesthouses down the road at Chungking, the Holy Carpenter is a pleasant budget option, and even has conference facilities (admittedly not the plushest).
**Hotel services** *Air-conditioning. Business services.* **Room services** *TV. Telephone.*

### Nathan Hotel
*378 Nathan Road, Tsim Sha Tsui, Kowloon (2388 5141/2770 4262). Jordan MTR (exit B1)/A21 bus from the airport/buses along Nathan Road.* **Rates** HK$400-$750 single; HK$450-$1,250 double; HK$1,250-$2,000 suite. **Credit** AmEx, DC, MC, V. **Map** p313 B4.
Another cheap-ish alternative on the 'Golden Mile', the Nathan makes a useful exploration base. The rooms are a bit poky and well worn, but the facilities are pretty good and you'll find plenty of 24-hour entertainment right outside.
**Hotel services** *Air-conditioning. Bar. Business services. Laundry. Restaurant.* **Room services** *Hairdryer. Mini-bar. Room service (24hrs). Telephone. TV.*

### Salisbury YMCA
*41 Salisbury Road (2369 2211/fax 2739 9315/ www.ymcahk.org.hk). Tsim Sha Tsui MTR (exit E)/buses to Tsim Sha Tsui Ferry Pier & along Salisbury Road/Tsim Sha Tsui Ferry Pier.* **Rates** HK$210 dorm bed; HK$580-$650 single/double; HK$1,200-$1,400 suite. **Credit** MC, V. **Map** p313 B6.
You might find the price a bit steep for a YMCA, but this Y is no hostel. Instead it's a hotel in every sense – and an excellent one at that. From the well-equipped, well-designed rooms to the quality service and facilities, the Salisbury offers outstanding value for money. But what make this place a real steal is its location next to the city's premier hotel, the Peninsula. Here you can enjoy the same panorama of the harbour for a fraction of the price (it's certainly worth paying a little extra for a high-floor harbour-view room). There's also a well-equipped gym (extra cost) and an indoor swimming pool.
**Hotel services** *Air-conditioning. Babysitting. Business services. Beauty salon. Concierge. Disabled: facilities. Gym. Laundry. No-smoking rooms.*

Restaurants. Swimming pool (indoor). **Room services** Broadband internet access. Hairdryer. Mini-bar. Room service (7am-midnight). Telephone. TV: cable/satellite.

### Stanford Hillview

*13-17 Observatory Road (2722 7822/fax 2723 3718/www.stanfordhillview.com). Tsim Sha Tsui MTR (exit B2)/shuttle bus from Kowloon Airport Express Station/buses along Nathan Road.* **Rates** HK$880-$1,580 single/double; HK$2,380 suite. **Credit** AmEx, DC, MC, V. **Map** p313 C5.

This place isn't much to look at from the outside, but inside it has a certain charm, albeit with a retro feel. The 170 rooms are standard but have all the necessary facilities, and there's a café, bar and lounge to relax in, plus a fitness facility and two driving nets for golfers. The view of the observatory isn't bad from here, and it's close to Knutsford Terrace, Tsim Sha Tsui's leading bar and restaurant district. If going out sounds too strenuous, unwind in the hotel's cocktail lounge.

**Hotel services** Air-conditioning. Bar. Business services. Concierge. Disabled: facilities. Gym. Laundry. Limousine service. No-smoking rooms. Restaurant. **Room services** Broadband internet access. Hairdryer. Mini-bar. Room service (24hrs). Telephone. TV: cable/pay movies.

## Yau Ma Tei, Mong Kok & around

## Moderate

### Eaton Hotel

*380 Nathan Road, Yau Ma Tei (2782 1818/fax 2782 5563/www.eaton-hotel.com). Jordan MTR (exit A, B1)/A21 bus from the airport/buses along Nathan Road.* **Rates** from HK$1,050 single/double; from HK$2,050 suite. **Credit** AmEx, DC, MC, V. **Map** p313 B4.

What makes this place stand out from the crowd is its friendly and helpful service. That should be a given, of course, but sadly not in this part of town. Rooms aren't very big, but they do have all the necessities (as well as some luxuries, like broadband internet access). The MTR is pretty close and there's plenty of life in the neighbourhood.

**Hotel services** Air-conditioning. Babysitting. Bar. Business services. Disabled: adapted rooms. Gym. Laundry. Limousine service. No-smoking rooms. Restaurants. Swimming pool (outdoor). **Room services** Broadband internet access. Fax. Hairdryer. Mini-bar. Room service (7am-2am). Telephone. TV: satellite.

## Cheap

### Anne Black Guest House (YWCA)

*5 Man Fuk Road, Ho Man Tin (2713 9211/ fax 2761 1269/www.ywca.org.hk). Yau Ma Tei/ Mong Kok MTR then taxi or 20min walk/shuttle*

bus from the airport/3, 7, 103, 111, 170 bus. **Rates** HK$480 single/double. **Credit** AmEx, DC, MC, V.

If you don't mind being a little out of the action, the Anne Black is a great, affordable choice. The 169 rooms (with en suite facilities) are clean and safe, and service is friendly. And if you're on your own but would like to meet fellow travellers, there's a restaurant, reading room and common room for guests' use. Shopping and dining are also available in Ho Man Tin and nearby Mong Kok.

**Hotel services** Air-conditioning. Laundry. No-smoking rooms. Restaurant. **Room services** Telephone. TV.

### Booth Lodge

*11 Wing Sing Lane, Yau Ma Tei (2771 9266/fax 2385 1140). Yau Ma Tei MTR (exit C, D) then 10min walk/A21 bus from the airport.* **Rates** HK$620-$1,500 single/double. **Credit** AmEx, MC, V. **Map** p312 C3.

This award-winning hotel is run by the Salvation Army and is a reasonable deal. With rooms more suited to a hotel chain, plus a decent restaurant and al fresco dining in its coffee shop, Booth Lodge is more than just a place to crash out. Its distinctive (read: ugly), sloping front makes it a landmark in Yau Ma Tei. It's pretty far removed from the action, but if you like your night-time decibels low, that's a bonus.

**Hotel services** Air-conditioning. Concierge. No-smoking rooms. Restaurant. **Room services** Hairdryer. Iron. Mini-bar. Telephone. TV: satellite.

### Caritas Bianchi Lodge

*4 Cliff Road, Yau Ma Tei (2388 1111/fax 2770 6669). Yau Ma Tei MTR (exit C, D)/A21 bus from the airport/buses along Nathan Road.* **Rates** HK$420-$920 single/double/triple. **Credit** AmEx, MC, V.

A true bargain. Run by Caritas, the official social welfare bureau of the Roman Catholic Church in Hong Kong, Bianchi Lodge has a welcoming atmosphere. The rooms are clean with good-sized beds and en suite bathrooms, and triple rooms are available for families or groups. Perched on top of the Caritas Bianchi adult school facing Nathan Road, the location is convenient for shopping.

**Hotel services** Air-conditioning. Laundry. **Room services** Hairdryer. Mini-bar. Telephone. TV: cable.

### Dorsett Seaview

*268 Shanghai Street, Yau Ma Tei (2782 0882/fax 2781 8800/www.dorsettseaview.com.hk). Yau Ma Tei MTR (exit C)/buses along Nathan Road.* **Rates** HK$880-$1,280 single/double; HK$2,400-$3,000 suite. **Credit** AmEx, DC, MC, V. **Map** p312 B3.

This tower block may have a partial sea view from the top-floor lounge, but don't expect a panorama of the harbour from your room. The best thing about Dorsett Seaview's location is that it's next to the thriving Temple Street night market, which is spilling over with curios and kitsch. The 257 rooms are reasonably decorated and have decent facilities.

Feel on top of the world at the **Jockey Club Mount Davis Youth Hostel**. *See p49.*

**Hotel services** *Air-conditioning. Bar. Babysitting. Concierge. Business services. Disabled: adapted rooms. Laundry. Limousine service. No-smoking floor.* **Room services** *Broadband internet access. Hairdryer. Mini-bar. Room service (24hrs). Telephone. TV: pay-movies.*

## Rent A Room

*Flat A, 2/F, Knight Garden, 7-8 Tak Hing Street, Jordan (2366 301/fax 2366 3588/ http://rentaroomhk.com). Jordan MTR (exit E)/buses along Nathan Road.* **Rates** HK$150 dorm bed; HK$300 single; HK$360 double. **No credit cards.**
At the Jordan end of the 'Golden Mile', this pragmatically named place is experienced in catering to the needs of budget travellers. The rooms are a snip too, considering each has an en suite shower, TV, phone and air-con. Service is efficient, and there's even a patio for sunbathing. What's more, Tsim Sha Tsui's many attractions are just a short stroll away.
**Hotel services** *Kitchen. Laundry (self-service).* **Room services** *Air-conditioning. Dataport. Telephone. TV.*

## Stanford Hotel

*118 Soy Street, Mong Kok (2781 1881/fax 2388 3733/www.stanfordhongkong.com). Mong Kok MTR (exit E2)/buses along Nathan Road.* **Rates** HK$780-$830 single/double. **Credit** AmEx, DC, MC, V.

The poor relation to Stanford Hillview (*see p56*), the Stanford offers the same facilities but in a less attractive environment. This area isn't for everybody – Mong Kok is dirty and crowded, with drug dealers, illegal hawkers and brothels dotted in among the bars and shops – but it's action-packed, and with the Ladies Market nearby is actually a pretty safe place to stroll around.
**Hotel services** *Air-conditioning. Babysitting. Bar. Business services. Concierge. Laundry. Limousine service. No-smoking rooms. Restaurant.* **Room services** *Dataport. Hairdryer. Mini-bar. Room service (7am-11pm). Telephone. TV: cable/ pay movies.*

## YMCA International House

*23 Waterloo Road, Mong Kok (2771 9111). Yau Ma Tei MTR (exit D)/A21 bus from the airport/buses along Nathan Road.* **Rates** HK$780 single/double; HK$1,800 suite. **Credit** AmEx, DC, MC, V.
This 391-room tower has all the amenities of a top hotel, for a third of the price. Along with a bar, coffee shop and banqueting facilities, it boasts tennis and squash courts, a health centre and sauna. The best feature is the swimming pool – a great attraction on a muggy summer's day. There's also a Western-style restaurant, a relaxing lounge and even a chapel. Rooms have simple and comfortable furnishings.

*Hotel services Air-conditioning. Gym. No-smoking rooms. Restaurant. Swimming pool (indoor).* **Room services** *Broadband internet access. Mini-bar. Telephone. TV: cable.*

# The New Territories

## Hostel

### Sze Lok Yuen Hostel

*Tai Mo Shan, Tsuen Wan (2488 8188/fax 2788 1638/www.yha.org.hk). Tsuen Wan MTR then 51 bus (call for onward directions).* **Rates** HK$35 dorm bed; HK$16 tent pitch. **No credit cards.** **Map** p307.

Hikers love this place. It's perched on top of Tai Mo Shan (Hong Kong's tallest mountain), so the only way to get here is on foot. By the time you arrive you'll settle for a bed anywhere, which is just as well as there is no air-conditioning – not even an electric fan – so summer nights can be practically unbearable. The hostel has a kitchen and barbecue pits, but you'll have to bring your own food.

## East New Territories

## Hostels

### Bradbury Hall Hostel

*Chek Keng, Sai Kung (2328 2458/fax 2788 1638/www.yha.org.hk). Choi Hung MTR then minibus (call for onward directions).* **Rates** HK$45 dorm bed; HK$16 tent pitch. **No credit cards.** **Map** p307.

This 100-bed hostel mainly takes in hikers mid hike; thus, the facilities and decoration are rather basic. It does, however, have barbecue pits, use of a kitchen, and a nice view of the neighbouring hillside.

### Bradbury Lodge

*66 Tai Mei Tuk Road, Tai Mei Tuk, Tai Po (2662 5123/fax 2788 1638/www.yha.org.hk). Tai Po Market KCR then 75K bus.* **Rates** HK$55 dorm bed; HK$150-$240 single/double; HK$60 tent pitch. **No credit cards.** **Map** p307.

The facilities in this of 94-bed lodge are better than in most hostels. It offers more than a brief stop on your hiking route as it is located near the waterfront and has a watersports centre nearby. Air-conditioning is included in the cost of the two- and four-bed rooms, but costs extra per night in the dorms. The campsite has a wonderful bay view.

### Pak Sha O Hostel

*Pak Sha O, Hoi Ha Road, Sai Kung (2328 2327/fax 2788 1638/www.yha.org.hk). Choi Hung MTR to Sai Kung then 92 bus (call for onward directions).* **Rates** HK$45 dorm bed; HK$16 tent pitch. **No credit cards.** **Map** p307.

Built inside an abandoned village school, this beautiful development has won awards for design. It holds up to 112 people and has a campsite too. Located in Sai Kung Country Park, it's hard to reach, but is worth it for the spectacular views. There is also a huge barbecue area and a basketball court.

# The Outlying Islands

## Lantau

## Hostels

### Hongkong Bank Foundation SG Davis Hostel

*Ngong Ping (2985 5610/fax 2788 1638/www.yha.org.hk). Bus 23 from Tung Chung/bus 2 from Mui Wo Ferry Pier.* **Rates** HK$45 dorm bed; HK$150 double room; HK$16 tent pitch. **No credit cards.** **Map** p306.

Formerly known more simply as the SG Davis Hostel, this place is located near the Big Buddha, high in Lantau's beautiful mountains, and the quaint Tai O fishing village is just about within walking distance. The hostel has only 52 beds and offers plenty of facilities, including a kitchen, barbecue pits and badminton court, so get in quick.

### Jockey Club Mong Tung Wan Hostel

*Mong Tung Wan (2984 1389/fax 2788 1638/www.yha.org.hk). Taxi from Mui Wo Ferry Pier/sampan to Mong Tung Wan Pier.* **Rates** HK$45 dorm bed; HK$16 tent pitch. **No credit cards.** **Map** p306.

This is the newest of Hong Kong's seven hostels and consequently offers clean rooms and modern facilities. It can hold up to 88 people, mostly hikers exploring Lantau's verdant trails or nearby beaches. Pluses included the lovely view of the sea from the hostel and the communal kitchen. Camping is permitted.

## Cheung Chau

## Cheap

### Cheung Chau Warwick

*East Bay (2981 0081/fax 2981 9174). Cheung Chau Ferry Pier then 15min walk.* **Rates** HK$495-$695 single/double. **Credit** AmEx, MC, V. **Map** p306.

This hotel is dated and fairly run-down, but it is close to a nice beach and is pretty cheap. The design certainly won't win any awards – it's a dark concrete blot on Cheung Chau's traditional Chinese landscape – but the views from the balcony of the seafront rooms make it worth staying a night, especially for watersports fans, who can go windsurfing or sea kayaking from the beach below.

**Hotel services** *Air-conditioning. Restaurant.* **Room services** *Laundry. Mini-bar. Telephone. TV.*

# Sightseeing

# Introduction

Explore one of the world's most dynamic cities, and its peaceful hinterland.

Though at first glance Hong Kong may look like a homogeneous mass of skyscrapers, that's just one part of the picture. Even if you're only here for a day, that's still plenty of time to explore the different areas that comprise the Special Administrative Region (as the former colony is now known), each of which has its own character and points of interest for visitors.

Depending on where you are staying, the first areas you are likely to explore are those that line Hong Kong harbour. **Central**, on the northern coast of **Hong Kong Island**, is a natural starting point, being home to the seat of government and the all-important financial district. Its highlights include glamorous shopping, some striking modern architecture, a lovely park and a thriving nightlife.

**Sheung Wan** may only be minutes to the west of Central, but it is worlds apart in terms of atmosphere. This is where you'll get a feel for an older, and distinctly more Chinese, Hong Kong, packed with antiques, Chinese medicine, dried food and funeral shops.

To the east of Central, **Wan Chai** and **Causeway Bay** are primarily dedicated to nightlife and shopping, respectively. Heavily built up, the urban crush is relieved by the large open space of Victoria Park and Happy Valley Racecourse, just to the south.

Towering above Central is the **Peak**, best reached via the old Peak Tram; the fantastic panoramas from up here should not be missed. There are fine walks up here too.

Most visitors also enjoy a trip to the comparatively rural parts in the centre of the island and along the **south and east coasts**. Here you can hike, relax on a beach, potter around a market or have fun in a theme park.

Across the harbour from Central, **Kowloon** – particularly the district of **Tsim Sha Tsui** on the peninsula's tip – contains the greatest concentration of museums. It's also a great place from which to admire Hong Kong Island's stunning skyline. Shop-lined Nathan Road, forming the spine of Kowloon, starts here and extends north through the districts of **Yau Ma Tei** and **Mong Kok**, which are home to a number of specialist markets.

Once you've spent a couple of days exploring the more built-up areas of the city, travel out into the **New Territories** to discover a side of Hong Kong that few visitors experience. There's a fair amount of unsightly industrial and urban sprawl in places, but also interesting museums and walled villages, plus – and this is the most surprising attraction – great swathes of unspoiled countryside criss-crossed by hiking trails, and some remote, pristine beaches.

An alternative is to head the **Outlying Islands**. Depending on your interests, you can explore the peaceful monasteries of huge, hilly Lantau, the laid-back charm and seafood restaurants of Lamma or villagey Cheung Chau.

And if you have the time, a visit to the former Portuguese colony of **Macau** or the dynamic city of **Guangzhou** is well worthwhile.

**Hong Kong Island**, as seen from Kowloon.

# Essential Hong Kong

## ... in a day

● Take a tram to **Western Market**, mooch around **Sheung Wan**, then browse the antiques shops on **Hollywood Road** (for all, *see p70*).
● Head to **Hong Kong Park** (*see p68*) for an al fresco lunch.
● Take the Peak Tram up to **Victoria Peak** (*see p78*).
● Stroll around Lugard and Harlech roads (*see p78* **Peak of fitness**), and up to the Peak itself, taking in the stunning panoramas.
● Return to Central by the Peak Tram and walk down to the Star Ferry pier, crossing over to Tsim Sha Tsui to admire the Hong Kong Island skyline.
● Enjoy afternoon tea in the **Peninsula** hotel (*see p53*) or early evening drinks in the hotel's sky-high **Felix** bar (*see p154*).
● Either ride the MTR to **Temple Street Night Market** (*see p90*) and chance your luck at a street-side *dai pai dong* food stall, or return via the Star Ferry for dinner and drinking in **Lan Kwai Fong** (*see p66*) or **SoHo** (*see p72*).

## ... in 48 hours

Day two:
● Spend the morning walking the **Dragon's Back** (*see p82* **Across the Dragon's Back**) or, if you have kids, at **Ocean Park** (*see p193*).
● If you do the walk, lunch in **Shek O** (*see p84*), then relax on the beach for a couple of hours; if you take the Ocean Park option, then, afterwards, catch the bus into **Stanley** to eat and peruse the market (*see p83*).
● Take the bus and MTR to **Causeway Bay** (*see p74*) for a bit of late-afternoon shopping.
● End the day by exploring **Wan Chai**'s nightlife (*see p215-p224*) or, if the day and season are right, go to **Happy Valley** for a night at the races (*see p76*).

## ... in 72 hours

Day three:
● Rise early to practise **t'ai chi** on the Tsim Sha Tsui waterfront (*see p237*).
● Spend the morning visiting whichever museum in Tsim Sha Tsui is of interest, be it **Art** or **Space** (for both, *see p86*), **Science** or **History** (for both, *see p89*).
● Take the Star Ferry across the harbour for dim sum at **City Hall Maxim's Palace** (*see p143*).
● Walk to the nearby Outlying Islands Ferry Piers and catch a ferry to **Yung Shue Wan** on Lamma (*see p110*).

● Walk across the island to **Sok Kwu Wan** (*see p111*), stopping off at a beach along the way; eat an early seafood dinner and catch the ferry back to Central.

## ... in 96 hours

Day four:
● Early in the morning, take the KCR north into the New Territories to Sha Tin and visit the **Hong Kong Heritage Museum** (*see p99*) and the **Ten Thousand Buddhas Monastery** (*see p99*).
● Grab a bite to eat in **Sha Tin** (*see p99*), before taking a taxi to the **Sai Kung Peninsula** (*see p108*).
● Hire a sampan from Sai Kung's main ferry pier if you wish to spend the afternoon on a secluded beach (*see p109*) or, if you're feeling more energetic, hike through the countryside around **Pak Tam Chung** (*see p108*).
● Dine in one of several good restaurants in Sai Kung (*see p145*) before heading back to the city.

## ... in 120 hours or more

Day five:
● Venture further afield, with a day or two in the intriguing ex-Portuguese colony of **Macau** (*see p244*) or the chaotic, buzzy city of **Guangzhou** (*see p260*).

**Sightseeing**

# Hong Kong Island

Urban buzz and rural tranquillity, side by side.

One of the most enduring curiosities about Hong Kong is that, despite being less than a kilometre across the water from each other, those who live on Hong Kong Island rarely visit Kowloon, and vice versa. Residents of the island, however, definitely consider themselves superior to their counterparts on the north side of the harbour – and have done since the 19th century.

Much of this perceived superiority has to do with the fact that Victoria, the administrative centre and official capital, is on Hong Kong Island. It is also partly because the smartest shopping centres, social clubs and residential areas are all found on the island, but this geographical and psychological division very accurately reflects just how truly insular and small town this big city can be at times.

Hong Kong Island certainly has it all: a plethora of business opportunities, shops galore, its fair share of sights, the SAR's only theme park (at least until Disney opens on Lantau in 2005), some good beaches, several very beautiful country parks and a thriving nightlife that rivals the best in the world.

## Central

Vertiginous skyscrapers, impatient crowds, streaming traffic, disorientating tangles of raised pedestrian walkways: Hong Kong's political, financial and commercial centre is an undeniably exciting, occasionally overwhelming and often rather ugly place. Squeezed into a narrow coastal strip between harbour and hillside, along the western end of Hong Kong Island's northern side, **Central** is where it all happens – or starts happening.

In many respects Central is a glittering temple to high-end conspicuous consumption, and fashion victims will have no problem finding every possible designer boutique in which to part company with their money. In broader cultural terms, however, offerings are far more meagre compared with almost any other city of its size – and certainly in the West. Constantly re-inventing itself, and without the slightest vestige of sentimentality (or sense of history, its critics would argue), Central epitomises here-and-now Hong Kong – the few remnants of its built heritage that survive are little more than scraps and fragments, which half a century's inexorable development and

land reclamation (*see p93* **Taking it back**) have left marooned like waifs from another time among the towers of steel and glass.

Despite these caveats, there is still plenty to see and do in Central. Some of its most impressive modern buildings can be examined up close; Lan Kwai Fong is, along with nearby SoHo, the main drinking, eating and partying enclave and a lively lunch- and night-time destination; and there are even a couple of green open spaces, such as Hong Kong Park and the Botanical Gardens, in which to take a breather.

### Star Ferry & the waterfront

By far the most breathtaking way to approach Central is to take the eight-minute **Star Ferry** ride across Victoria Harbour from Kowloon (costing a mere HK$2.20 for a seat on the first-class, upper deck). These double-ended, green-and-cream ferries have been ploughing across the waters here since 1874, and it's no exaggeration to say (and it has been said many, many times before) that this short crossing remains one of the world's great ferry journeys.

Comparisons with the Manhattan skyline aren't entirely fanciful, the north side of Hong Kong Island having the added element of a backdrop of deep green, thickly wooded mountains, rearing majestic and indifferent above the bustle and the clamour. Although undeniably the most romantic approach to Central, the Star Ferry is just one spoke in the district's transport hub and unless you're travelling directly from somewhere close to the pier in Tsim Sha Tsui to a similar destination in Central, it is probably not the fastest or most convenient transport option.

Plans are in place to move the Star Ferry Pier out another 200 metres (650 feet) or so to the completed reclamation, where it will be adjacent to the Outlying Districts Piers. This is slated to happen in the next couple of years, when the reclamation is completed, though the gloomy local economic outlook means that the plans may well be delayed.

The Airport Express line from Chek Lap Kok terminates at Hong Kong Station, just west of the Central Star Ferry Pier. North of the station are the Outlying Districts piers, where you can catch ferries to Lantau, Lamma, Cheung Chau and other islands. Hong Kong Station is

Hong Kong Island, as seen from Kowloon; and the city's efficent MTR underground system.

The **Mid-Levels Escalator**. *See p70.*

connected by underground walkway to the busy Central MTR (metro) station, and most bus routes along the north side of the island pass along one of three parallel roads: Connaught Road/Harcourt Road, Des Voeux Road/Chater Road and Queen's Road Central/Queensway.

### RECENT DEVELOPMENTS

For most visitors, Central's most interesting 'sights' are architectural. The district has changed beyond all recognition since the 1970s, and the profusion of modern towers that have sprung up in the last 20 or so years – some markedly more aesthetically appealing than others – all define modern Hong Kong.

Just west of the Star Ferry Pier is the **General Post Office** and beyond that, accessible by elevated walkway, stands the **Exchange Square** complex (1985), where Hong Kong's Stock Exchange has operated since the merger of its four exchanges in 1986. Swiss architect Remo Riva's strategy of 'architecture as sculpture' is best appreciated from mid harbour on the Star Ferry. Close up, the scale and layout of its three interlinked buildings doesn't really work and can be quite confusing to get around. More pleasing is its open piazza, with its fountains and Henry Moore's *Single Oval* sculpture, Dame Elizabeth Frink's bronzes and Taiwanese artist Chu Ming's stylised human figure in t'ai chi pose. It's an agreeable spot to sit out with a snack or a drink – there are plenty of bars, cafés and restaurants nearby – and watch the stockbroker types scurrying by.

Out on the waterfront reclamation, rising above the Hong Kong terminus of the airport railway, are the two modern towers of the **International Finance Centre**, better known locally as IFC . While architecturally stunning, the 88-storey **IFC2** tower (*see also p29*) was nevertheless – like many buildings in Hong Kong – built without any reference to the surrounding landscape and has been likened by some critics to a gigantic nose-hair clipper. Less happily, the IFC development was also built in complete contravention of existing town-planning guidelines, which clearly stated that new buildings should not block the view of Victoria Peak from the Tsim Sha Tsui waterfront promenade, one of urban Hong Kong's most magnificent viewing points. Despite this 'safeguard', the Two ifc building almost completely obscures the Peak – yet another example of Hong Kong's vested interests getting their own way regardless. Next door a Four Seasons hotel is under construction (due to open in 2005).

Just east of Exchange Square, opposite the General Post Office, stands **Jardine House** (1973; *see also p29*), known locally as the 'House of a Thousand Arseholes' (partly due to its 1,700-plus porthole-style windows, partly as a comment on those who work behind them). This 52-storey structure, once the tallest building in Asia, is the Hong Kong headquarters of Jardine Matheson, one of the major trading houses that virtually founded commerce in Hong Kong (the company moved its official domicile to Bermuda in 1984). Another Henry Moore piece, *Double Oval*, can be seen in a small outdoor area to the east of the building.

On a prime waterfront site east of the Star Ferry Pier stands Hong Kong's **City Hall** (*see p226*). Its two blocks, with their 1960s civic architecture, reflect the general disregard for aesthetics, especially when you compare them with (a picture of) the original – a rather grand mid 19th-century French classical incarnation. The Low Block contains a theatre and a concert hall, as well as a pleasant enclosed garden, which was built by public subscription in memory of the Hong Kong Volunteer Defence Corps who died during World War Two. The High Block, to the rear, houses a succession of libraries, a recital hall and various committee rooms. The Chinese restaurant on the second floor, with views out over Kowloon, is rightly famed for its dim sum (see p143).

Further to the east is the **Chinese People's Liberation Army Forces Hong Kong Building**, formerly known as the Prince of Wales Building (and sometimes compared to an upturned gin bottle – look at it closely and you'll immediately understand why). Also previously known as HMS Tamar (named after the naval vessel that was moored here and used as a floating naval base until it was scuttled in World War II), this former British naval headquarters is now occupied, in a very low-key way, by the PLA.

## Heading south

The old colonial area of Hong Kong centres around **Statue Square**, which was once flanked by granite colonial buildings with columned verandas. The square was originally named for a bronze statue of Queen Victoria; in Chinese the area is still referred to as the 'Empress' Statue Square'. Along with other statues in the area she was removed by the Japanese during World War II, but was recovered and later replaced in Causeway Bay, where she can still be seen today. Today, Statue Square has just one statue; the former HSBC Chief Manager Sir Thomas Jackson. The square is best known – at least on weekends – for the hundreds of Filipina maids who gather here on Sundays (and in many other open spaces on the Island) to enjoy their day off.

On the eastern edge of the square stands one of the few remaining colonial buildings, the neoclassical, granite **Legislative Council Building**. Originally built as the Supreme Court – the scales of justice can still be seen outside – it now houses the Hong Kong Legislative Council, the closest thing the SAR has to a parliament. The eastern side of the Legislative Council Building faces **Chater Garden**, which was the site of the Hong Kong Cricket Club until the mid 1970s. A pleasant enough public park, it has been a popular gathering place for political activists and pressure groups to loudly vent their disapproval of various official policies.

Along Des Voeux Road, on Statue Square's southern side, Hong Kong's clattering old trams have trundled between Kennedy Town and Shau Kei Wan since 1904. With a HK$2 flat fare, these wood-panelled relics are a cheap and enjoyable way to travel along the northern side of the island. But they are definitely not recommended for anyone in a hurry.

Dominating the south side of Statue Square is Norman Foster's phenomenally expensive (HK$5.2 billion) **HSBC Building** (see also p27). The world's costliest building when it was completed in 1985, this colossal structure made of steel and glass rests on four tall pillars, creating an airy, open-air forum that remains a public space. It is worth taking the escalator up to the quiet business-like first floor for a sense of the scale of the place, and to feel for a moment like nothing more than one of the stick people in an architectural concept drawing.

According to those 'in the know', the building has some of the best feng shui in Hong Kong. Its unencumbered views of the harbour and the hills behind it are favourable, but, more significantly, it sits at the only local junction of five dragon lines (magnetic fields thought to follow the direction of underground water flows, which carry powerful channels of positive chi, or life-force energy). This energy is said to be sucked inside the huge atrium of the bank by the angled escalators and the undulating floor. The two huge lions guarding the entrance – war-damaged remnants of the earlier building – help block negative energy and are also supposed to confer good luck on passers-by who rub their paws.

Corporate competition between the HSBC and the Bank of China extended to a feng shui war when the **Bank of China Tower** (see also p26) was built. Its knife-like structure, inauspicious chopstick-shaped antennae and dominant position undid much of the HSBC's allegedly good feng shui, until local tycoon Lee Ka-shing built the **Cheung Kong Center** between them, restoring much of the harmony and energy flow – or so the urban legend relates.

The Bank of China Tower is also one of the buildings that encroached on the feng shui of the old Government House and was one of the reasons that Chief Executive Tung Chee-hwa gave for preferring not to move into the traditional seat of power.

When the Bank of China outgrew its former home alongside the HSBC, Chinese-American architect IM Pei was commissioned to build the new headquarters. The result is probably the city's most striking modern building. Completed in 1990, its elegant, dynamic, asymmetrical geometry, resembling black, triangular building blocks, presents an unmistakable aspect from every angle. It's well worth going up to the 47th-floor viewing gallery for a panoramic view on a clear day.

## COLONIAL FRAGMENTS

South of the HSBC Building, up the hill, lie a few lingering reminders of Hong Kong's colonial heritage. Climb the steps up to Battery Path and the cathedral precinct and you'll find whitewashed, cool and quiet **St John's Cathedral** (*see below*), which was completed in 1849. Its entrance doors are made from the wood salvaged from HMS *Tamar*, the Royal Navy's floating HQ that was scuttled during World War II, and numerous moving memorials and other historical relics are hidden away inside.

Across from the cathedral is Hong Kong's **Court of Final Appeal**, housed in the charming red-brick, green-shuttered, neoclassical **French Mission Building**, which dates in part from the 1860s. French Catholic missionaries added a chapel to the original building when they took it over in 1917.

On the other side of Lower Albert Road and further up the hill stands **Government House**, residence of Hong Kong's British governors since 1855. Originally constructed in a tropical Georgian style, the structure was completely rebuilt by the occupying Japanese, who added its distinctive central tower. The building, which is closed to the public, is still used for official functions. The pretty gardens are opened to the public once a year when the azaleas are in bloom (call the HKTB for details). While it used to enjoy a prime location, with uninterrupted views of the harbour, the building is now hemmed in from all sides by corporate towers – neatly illustrating how quickly Hong Kong turns its back on its past.

Not far away, at the junction of Ice House Street and Lower Albert Road, stands the early 20th-century, brown-and-cream brick old **Dairy Farm Building**, which now houses the **Fringe Club** (*see p222*), the excellent **M at the Fringe** restaurant (*see p125*) and the Foreign Correspondents' Club. Ice House Street gained its name from an ice storage facility that stood at the bottom of the road in the days when ice was imported from North America. Opposite is the gracious old **Bishop's House**, with its tower/study, dating from 1848 and one of Hong Kong's oldest surviving European buildings.

### St John's Cathedral

*4-8 Garden Road (2523 4157/www.stjohns cathedral.org.hk). Central MTR (exit K)/buses along Garden Road.* **Open** 9am-5pm Mon-Fri; 9am-noon Sat, Sun. **Admission** free. **Map** p309 E4.

Now marooned by ultra-modern towers, St John's is one of the oldest Anglican churches in Asia (its foundation stone was laid in 1847 and it was completed in 1849 – and later extended in 1873). Within, the cathedral is pleasingly airy and light, but there is little evidence of its former parishioners – the memorial brasses that marked the deaths of prominent local residents were removed during World War II by occupying Japanese forces (who used the church as a social club). In a side chapel are some old flags and standards belonging to the Hong Kong Volunteers, who were buried to avoid their capture by the Japanese in 1941 and only unearthed in the late 1950s.

# Lan Kwai Fong & around

The backstreets to the west of the old Dairy Farm Building are largely devoted to restaurants, bars and shops. The best concentration of drinking and eating joints is on and around **Lan Kwai Fong**, off D'Aguilar Street. During the day the place is not much to look at – and is actually rather grubby – but after work hours, particularly on Fridays, the neon shines brightly above a raucous procession of diners, drinkers, demob-happy suits and pre-clubbers. For a quintessential Hong Kong experience, be sure to grab a plastic stool, a bottle of Singha and a fine curry outside **Good Luck Thai Café** (*see p127*) on Wing Wah Lane and enjoy the street life. These days, however, more discerning expats tend to favour the burgeoning drinking and dining scene of the area (west of here) informally known as SoHo (*see p72*).

Close by, north of Queen's Road Central, stands one of Central's biggest upmarket shopping complexes: the **Landmark**, containing most of the area's swankiest boutiques (with prices to match). If it's relative bargains you're after, head for Pedder Street and explore the **Pedder Building** – one of the last old office buildings in the area – which houses a series of small shops selling a mixture of genuine, cut-price and fake labels, beautiful embroidered shawls and a fair helping of tat. Also on the first floor of the Pedder Building, looking down on the throng of Pedder Street, is the China Tee Club, a cool, quiet restaurant and café with a faux colonial air, thanks to the old ceiling fans, dark wood furniture and trilling song birds in antique cages. On the ground floor is **Shanghai Tang** (*see p172*), a stylishly retro and tongue-in-cheek kitsch boutique, selling some beautiful fabrics, Chinese-style clothes, ornaments and chic, fun gifts. It's not cheap, though, and numerous imitations have sprung up in recent years, selling virtually the same items for much less.

The crowded sky over **Central.**

Running between Des Voeux Road Central and Queen's Road Central, a few minutes' walk north-west, are Li Yuen Street East and Li Yuen Street West (known as 'The Lanes'; see p156), which are crowded with cheap clothing, beads, handbag stalls and shoppers. It's a place to come as much for the spectacle as for the bargain hunting. Similar fare is also on offer in nearby Pottinger Street. A little further beyond, at the foot of the Mid-Levels Escalator (see p70), stands **Central Market**. For many years, this wet market has provided a lively contrast to Central's homogeneous shopping streets and malls, but it is presently under threat of redevelopment.

## Nearby green spaces

When the swirling maelstrom of Central becomes too much, it's worth remembering that there are a few green havens in among the concrete and the crowds. The extensive **Hong Kong Zoological & Botanical Gardens** (see p69) overlook Government House across Upper Albert Road. Featuring dozens of animal (mainly primates) and bird species, and more than 1,000 types of flora, the gardens are small but full of interest, as well as being peaceful and well shaded – very important on a sweltering Hong Kong summer's day.

To the east of the gardens, beyond the Peak Tram Lower Terminal, is **Hong Kong Park** (see p69), located on the old Victoria Cantonment. Spread across one square kilometre (0.38 square miles) of prime real estate, the park is proof positive that Hong Kong doesn't always put money over quality of life. Spectacularly bordered by some of

Central's most striking tower blocks, the park contains landscaped gardens, an artificial lake (complete with multicoloured fish and sunbathing terrapins), a children's playground, a t'ai chi garden, an amphitheatre, a restaurant and bar, and the architecturally stunning **Edward Youde Aviary** (see p69). This elegant expanse of undulating mesh, stretched over a series of arches, manages to be both spectacular and discreet, and provides a perfect setting in which to wander along the raised wooden walkway, trying to spot the 150 species of South-east Asian birdlife therein.

Also in the park is the **Flagstaff House Museum of Tea Ware** (see p69), occupying an elegant colonial building constructed between 1844 and 1846, which, until 1978, served as official residence of the Commander of British Forces in Hong Kong. Now devoted to Chinese tea and tea ware, the building itself is a well-preserved gem, and worth a visit in its own right.

As well as being a marvellous expanse of open space within the city, Hong Kong Park is one of the best places to see Hong Kong's identikit wedding couples, dressed in flouncy white wedding dresses and completely unfeasible tuxedos. Photo shoots in the park after a quick trip to the Registry Office within the park's boundaries are a near-obligatory part of getting married in Hong Kong. The Cultural Centre environs in Tsim Sha Tsui offer a Kowloon version of the same somewhat cheesy experience.

If all this open space and massed greenery proves overwhelming, shopping junkies can cross Supreme Court Road and immerse themselves in **Pacific Place**, an immense multi-storey mall (see p165). A food court and

Hong Kong Park. See p69.

restaurants provide plenty of decent eating and drinking choices, although most are on the pricey side. This area, linking Central and Wan Chai, is known as **Admiralty**, due to the long-vanished Royal Naval Dockyard that stood across the road here until the late 1950s. Its most interesting buildings are the two glittering silver towers of the **Lippo Centre** (made all the more startling by their proximity to the golden **Far East Finance Centre**), overlooking Hong Kong Park. Designed by American architect Paul Rudolph in 1988, the Centre has something of an aura of bad luck, having seen three large corporate occupants go bankrupt, including the Australian entrepreneur Alan Bond, after whom the building was originally named.

## Edward Youde Aviary

*Hong Kong Park, Cotton Tree Drive (2521 5041/2521 5092/www.lcsd.gov.hk). Admiralty MTR (exit B)/buses & trams along Queensway/buses along Cotton Tree Drive.* **Open** 9am-5pm daily. **Admission** free. **Map** p309 E5.

For many the highlight of a visit to Hong Kong Park, this imaginative aviary contains a whole other world below its spectacular expanse of steel netting. An aerial walkway passes through the aviary, offering excellent branch-high vantage points. All the birds here are from South-east Asia, and more than a few are increasingly endangered in their natural habitats, especially in Indonesia. Almost every variety of parrot found in the region can be seen here, including vivid purple and green eclectus parrots from Papua, lively white-and-yellow lesser sulphur-crested cockatoos from the eastern Moluccas, fire-red Ambon parrots, and massive hornbills from Borneo. You don't have to be an amateur naturalist to enjoy this well-designed complex, which really is stunning.

## Flagstaff House Museum of Tea Ware

*Hong Kong Park, 10 Cotton Tree Drive (2869 0690/2869 6690/www.lcsd.gov.hk). Admiralty MTR (exit B)/buses & trams along Queensway/buses along Cotton Tree Drive.* **Open** 10am-5pm Mon, Wed-Sun. **Admission** free. **Map** p309 F5.

This small museum offers a comprehensive, if somewhat unexciting, display of tea ware and the different types of tea and tea preparation, but there are some beautiful and extraordinarily well-crafted antique and modern pieces. A couple of dozen different teas are for sale in the museum shop – some are rare and rather expensive, while others are much more reasonably priced. The China Products Department Stores probably offer as good a selection as the Museum of Tea Ware, for somewhat lower prices. There are also plenty of teapots for sale; among the most popular are the Yixing teapots made from a special variety of clay. While quality here is high, prices are too, and similar items can

often be obtained from Shenzhen for substantially less. The best reason to visit the museum, though, is for the marvellous old colonial building itself.

## Hong Kong Park

*19 Cotton Tree Drive (2521 5041/5092/www.lcsd.gov.hk). Admiralty MTR (exit B, C1)/buses & trams along Queensway/buses along Cotton Tree Drive.* **Open** 6.30am-11pm daily. **Admission** free. **Map** p309 E5.

Opened in 1991 on the site of the sprawling old Victoria Barracks complex, this delightful, unusual park, dwarfed by surrounding corporate towers and endlessly busy flyovers, centres around a large artificial lake, replete with multi-hued fish, mostly koi and goerami. Among its numerous attractions are a bar/café, an observatory (open 9am-5pm daily), a pleasant t'ai chi garden, a children's playground and the very impressive walk-through Edward Youde Aviary (*see above*).

## Hong Kong Zoological & Botanical Gardens

*Albany Road (2530 0154/www.lcsd.gov.hk). Buses along Upper Albert Road.* **Open** 6am-7pm daily. **Admission** free. **Map** p308 C5/p309 D5.

The western side of the gardens, which were founded in 1864, is where you'll find most of the animal enclosures. There's an impressive collection of primates, including macaques, tamarins and a family of bored-looking orang-utans, including Datu, an immense, pot-bellied and impressively grumpy male. Other exotic residents are a tree kangaroo and a family of improbably cute ring-tailed lemurs. It's not a place for those who object to seeing caged animals as the enclosures are not huge, although most of the creatures look fairly content. In the eastern half of the gardens, on the other side of Albany Road, there are several bird enclosures, housing dozens of pink, stick-legged African flamingos and a flock of vivid scarlet ibis. You'll also find a large fountain, lawns, well-tended flowerbeds and a bronze statue of King George VI presiding over it all.

## Sheung Wan & Mid-Levels

Blending into Central on its western side, Sheung Wan (also known as Western) is the Chinese heart of old Hong Kong. It's a vibrant, colourful area that's best explored on foot. Although development has obliterated most of the formerly distinct streetscapes, there's still a real old-fashioned Chinese character to the area, and few of the bland mega-malls that dominate so much of the north of the island. As you climb the hill – or ride the world's longest escalator – you'll cross over Hollywood Road (the main centre for Hong Kong's important antiques and curio trade, and the location of the atmospheric Man Mo Temple) and reach the trendy bar and restaurant enclave of SoHo, prior to the upmarket residential district of Mid-Levels.

## Sheung Wan

In **Sheung Wan**, the area around the MTR makes for some of the most colourful and interesting sightseeing in Hong Kong.

Many of the streets around here specialise in specific trades. For instance, head to Man Wa Lane for name chop stalls. Chops are usually made from pieces of wood, bamboo or bone, on to which Chinese names are carved. You can watch them being carved and have one made with a Chinese translation of your name for about HK$100.

Wing Lok Street, Queen's Road West and many of the neighbouring streets are filled with shops piled high with sacks of dried seafood and other ingredients used both for Chinese medicine in soups and other dishes. If you know what to look for, you can uncover entire desiccated deer foetuses, dog's penises, dried seahorses and horse bezoars (hard balls of hair or vegetable fibre that collect in their stomachs; said to make an excellent antidote to poison).

This is also the centre of the completely out-of-control shark's fin trade, which is sharply reducing shark populations around the world. Most of the fins collected here are resold to emerging markets on the mainland. Good-quality shark's fin soup sells for about HK$300 a bowl, and the import trade was estimated to have been worth HK$3.5 billion in 2002. Several shops in the area also seem to base their businesses entirely on the sale of ginseng roots or swifts' nests, the latter gathered at great risk from the frighteningly high sides of caves in Borneo, Vietnam and southern Thailand. Constructed of swifts' spittle, they are used in a number of Chinese dishes, but most commonly for bird's nest soup, which is often served as a starter at formal dinners. (If you want to sample some, check out the snappily named Golden Ship Swallow Nests & Sea Products Restaurant at G/F, 78A Bonham Strand East; 2541 5837.) Despite its alleged health-giving properties, bird's nest tastes much like ordinary egg albumen.

Another popular ingredient in both Chinese medicine and cuisine can be found sleeping in a rather dingy shop at 13 Hillier Street: snakes. Their blood, flesh and, particularly, their bile are favoured as a warming food, and are very popular during the winter months. Snake is not available during the summer – the Chinese consider their flesh too 'heaty' to consume at that time.

A good place to browse for knick-knacks is the red-brick and granite, Edwardian-style **Western Market**, just west of Sheung Wan MTR. It's a light, airy three-storey building, built in 1906 and renovated in the 1990s (after

80 or so years as a food market). On the ground floor are stalls selling jade trinkets, Hong Kong memorabilia of varying grades of authenticity, faux opium pipes, antique cameras and clocks. The second floor is dedicated to the sale of fabrics and the third floor is home to the Treasure Inn Restaurant, a popular lunch venue.

Continuing westwards from Sheung Wan, the tram line terminates at **Kennedy Town** (named after 19th-century governor Sir Arthur Kennedy). Few visitors make it this far, as there is little to see other than an authentic working district of Hong Kong. **Mount Davis** rises 269 metres (883 feet) behind Kennedy Town and is well worth a climb. Along the summit are several disused gun batteries and a popular youth hostel (*see p49*).

## The Mid-Levels Escalator

In 1993, in a (not very successful) attempt to ease traffic congestion, a 792-metre-long (2,600-foot) escalator opened between Central Market and the residential area of Mid-Levels. It is actually a series of 20 escalators and three travelators, with exits to all of the streets across which it cuts. It's a good way to reach the hip bars and restaurants of SoHo, and to get to the concrete canyons of the Mid-Levels, but otherwise not of much use. The Escalator heads downwards from 6am to 10.20am (taking commuters to work in Central), but then changes direction and remains running uphill until midnight. Worth trying at least once.

## Hollywood Road & Tai Ping Shan

**Hollywood Road**, along with many of its neighbouring side streets, is almost entirely taken up by shops selling real and replica antique furniture, ornaments, statues, trinkets and curios. The more upmarket stores tend to congregate at its eastern end, where you'll also find a couple of surviving colonial structures: **Central Police Station** and the adjacent **Victoria Prison**.

Running parallel to Hollywood Road, but further west, is **Upper Lascar Row**, also known as Cat Street, which is well known as a hunting ground for cheap antiques, bric-a-brac and plain junk. Although its days as the place to find bargain antiques have, like most shopping experiences in Hong Kong, long since passed, there is still plenty to look at. Found here are various items such as jade, jewellery, old photos of Hong Kong and plenty of kitsch memorabilia, like Chairman Mao ashtrays, ornaments and badges. Something may well take your fancy along here but be prepared to bargain hard.

The busy harbour at **Sheung Wan** on Hong Kong Island's north-western tip. *See p69.*

Close by, at the corner of Hollywood Road and Ladder Street, stands **Man Mo Temple** (*see p72*), one of the most atmospheric places on Hong Kong Island. Dating from the late 1840s, and still a popular place of worship, its incense-blackened interior is dimly lit by red lanterns. Sandalwood smoke hangs thick in the air from the coils of incense suspended from the ceiling, the largest of which take a couple of weeks to burn through. To propitiate the spirits of the dead, Chinese burn paper offerings in two huge iron urns. There's quite a choice of spirit world combustibles available in nearby specialist shops. The most popular are 'Bank of Hell' banknotes, but you can also send up in flames complete mini-sets of kitchenware, cars, and gold and silver ingots, as well as computers and portable compact disc players. The temple became a cultural and political focal point for the Chinese community soon after it opened. Meetings were held, grievances aired and a customary tribunal established by and for Chinese residents. If you've seen the film of Richard Mason's Hong Kong novel *The World of Suzie Wong*, then this part of town may look at least superficially familiar, as several scenes were filmed around here. Although visiting the temple is free, any donations made go towards local charities.

More temples can be found a little further west at the junction of Tai Ping Shan Street with Pound Lane (which lies just south of Hollywood Road). The district of **Tai Ping Shan** (meaning 'peaceful mountain') was one of the first areas to be settled by the Chinese after the colony was founded. It was anything but peaceful, being notorious for its overcrowded housing and periodic outbreaks of plague, and as an early haunt of the Hong Kong triad

societies. Above street level, the temples are easily missed, resembling parts of homes rather than places of worship, an impression that persists until you see the incense sticks.

The **Kuan Yin Temple** is dedicated to the Buddhist goddess of Mercy (very popular with prostitutes), while the **Sui Tsing Pak Temple** next door holds a statue of the god Sui Tsing Pak, known as the 'pacifying general' and revered for his ability to cure illnesses (the statue was brought here in 1894 during a particularly virulent outbreak of plague). One of the rooms is used by fortune tellers, and there are rows of *tai sui* – statues of 60 different gods, each relating to a specific year in the 60-year cycle of the Chinese calendar (*see also p34* **Numbers of the beasts**). In times of strife, or to avert trouble, people make offerings to the god of their year of birth.

There are a number of shrines nearby, the most interesting of which is the **Pak Sing** ('hundred surnames') **Ancestral Hall**. Originally created in the mid 19th century, it was rebuilt in 1895, when all the buildings in the area were razed because of the plague. Used to store the bodies of those awaiting burial back in China, it still houses ancestral tablets (little wooden boards bearing the name and date of birth of dead people, and sometimes a photograph too). Some of these tablets are hardly recognisable, they have been so completely blackened by years of incense and smoke. The incinerator in the courtyard behind the altar is for burning paper offerings to the dead.

Nearby, the **Hong Kong Museum of Medical Sciences** (*see p72*) gives an interesting overview of the history of public health and medical services in Hong Kong,

**Time Out** Hong Kong **71**

and the building itself (built in 1906) is an attractive reminder of how the Mid-Levels looked before the tower blocks.

Across Hollywood Road from Pound Lane is **Possession Street**. It was here, above the one-time shoreline, that the British planted the Union Jack and officially took possession of Hong Kong Island in 1841. No memorial marks the occasion or the location, though one stood here till the mid 1970s. The considerable distance from here to today's harbourfront illustrates the extent of land reclamation in Hong Kong (*see p93* **Taking it back**).

At the far western end of Hollywood Road is **Hollywood Road Park**, a small but charming place with pagoda-style tiled walls and roofs, running water, goldfish ponds and plenty of shade under venerable old trees. Opposite are several coffin makers, with some massive Chinese-style caskets on display, the cheapest of which are very expensive.

## Hong Kong Museum of Medical Sciences

*2 Caine Lane, off Caine Road (2549 5123/ www.hkmms.org.hk). Bus 23, 40, 26/8, 22 minibus.* **Open** 10am-5pm Tue-Sat; 1-5pm Sun. **Admission** HK$10; HK$5 concessions. **No credit cards.** **Map** p308 A3.

Located in the Old Bacteriological Institute (established in 1906; later known as the Pathological Institute), the three floors of this small museum have displays of old medical equipment and some basic information on public health and the treatment of disease in Hong Kong. A handful of exhibits make it worth a quick visit, though; most notably, the story of the 1894 outbreak and treatment of the bubonic plague in Hong Kong. A potentially interesting section on Chinese medicine is, alas, only labelled in Chinese.

## Man Mo Temple

*126 Hollywood Road (2540 0350). Sheung Wan MTR (exit A2)/26 bus.* **Open** 8am-6pm daily. **Admission** free; donations appreciated. **Map** p308 B3.

This popular, atmospheric temple is dedicated to Man, the god of literature and civil servants, and Mo, the god of war. They are reputed to have been real men, who were deified by later emperors. Zhang Yazi (Man) was a celebrated administrator from the third century, while Guan Yu (Mo) was a successful military leader from the second century. The statues of Man and Mo sit at the far end of the temple. Against the eastern wall rest the elaborately carved, gold-plated sedan chairs on which the statues are taken out during processions.

## SoHo

The Mid-Levels Escalator may have done little to decrease traffic congestion, but it has opened up a previously overlooked tangle of streets between Hollywood Road and the swanky Mid-Levels residential blocks. This area, informally known as **SoHo** (**So**uth of **Ho**llywood Road), has become the hippest – and according to some critics one of the priciest and most pretentious – places to hang out in Hong Kong over the past few years.

On Staunton, Elgin, Shelley and surrounding streets, a cool new bar or restaurant seems to be opening up (or closing down) almost every week. Whereas once Hong Kong's main nightlife options were a cheap bowl of noodles, a pretentious Italian or French meal or a pie and a pint in a beery expat boozer, you can now eat and drink in fashionable bars and cosmopolitan eateries that wouldn't look out of place in London, Sydney or New York – and with prices in excess of those places. And – for the moment at least – SoHo remains one of Hong Kong's most mixed and characterful areas, with traditional Chinese businesses that have been there for decades operating beside the latest DJ bars and cutting-edge restaurants. Take it for what it offers.

A red sign on Staunton Street marks the former headquarters of Xing Zhong Hui (Revive China Society), the revolutionary organisation established by Dr Sun Yat-sen in 1895 and dedicated to overthrowing the Qing Dynasty in China. It marks the start of the **Sun Yat-sen Historical Trail,** an easy-to-follow walk around 13 sites bearing marker plaques (no extant buildings survive, however) related to the revolutionary's life, all in and around Hollywood Road, where he lived briefly during the 1890s.

Much further west is the entrance to the main campus of the **University of Hong Kong** (founded in 1912) on Bonham Road (Sun Yat-sen was a student of the Hong Kong College of Medicine that preceded it). If you have any interest in Chinese art and archaeology, it's worth visiting the **University Museum & Art Gallery** (*see below*) – its collection of antique bronzes, ceramics and paintings is exquisite, and the attractive old buildings are a lovely reminder of times past.

## University Museum & Art Gallery

*University of Hong Kong, 94 Bonham Road, Pok Fu Lam (2241 5500/www.hku.hk/hkumag). Bus 3B, 23, 40, 40M, 103.* **Open** 9.30am-6pm Mon-Sat; 1.30-5.30pm Sun. **Admission** free.

This collection of Chinese pottery, paintings and artefacts spanning 5,000 years is small, but contains some beautiful exhibits from the Han Dynasty, including terracotta horses and blue and white Ming porcelain. It also features the world's largest collection of bronze crosses belonging to the Christian Nestorian church. In addition, the museum hosts art exhibitions, which change every couple of months.

## Wan Chai & Causeway Bay

Wan Chai and Causeway Bay hug the northern edge of the island to the east of Central. Wan Chai's colourful 1950s and 1960s past, evoked in Richard Mason's novel *The World of Suzie Wong*, has faded as it has become more of an extension of Central. The seedy streets of a once-considerable red light district have given way to ongoing new development – but the sleaze continues in a couple of areas. Two of Wan Chai's least attractive aspects are its heavy pollution and an almost total lack of open space. There have been various proposals mooted to make more of the area's features and create some green spaces and al fresco dining and drinking areas, but so far these have come to nothing.

For relief, though, a stiff climb up towards Wan Chai Gap to traffic-free Bowen Road affords pleasant walking and some fine views out through the crowded towers and over the harbour.

At first sight, Causeway Bay's huge – and numerous – department stores make it just another sprawling shopping district. The area has various points of interest, which many people manage to overlook. Victoria Park, Hong Kong's largest (and one of its best) public parks, lies at the far end of Causeway Bay. And there are a few relics from its colonial past, most notably the Noon Day Gun, fired daily from the edge of the Typhoon Shelter, and a bronze statue of Queen Victoria herself, which once stood in Central's Statue Square (that's where the name comes from).

South of these two districts you'll find the island's celebrated racecourse at Happy Valley, a terrifically atmospheric place during mid-week race nights.

## Wan Chai

Just to the east of Central, **Wan Chai** is easily accessible by foot, tram, bus, MTR or taxi. Wan Chai MTR is a good starting point for a walking tour. Wan Chai can be divided into the area of land reclamation north of Hennessy Road, crowned by the massive and grandiose Hong Kong Convention & Exhibition Centre, and the warren of narrow streets of 'old' Wan Chai between Johnston Road and Queen's Road East, where you'll still find a few interesting corners.

### NORTH OF HENNESSY ROAD

A walk along **Lockhart Road**, which runs east to west parallel to the waterfront, reveals the area's few remaining ties with *The World of Suzie Wong*. Along a 100-metre (328-foot) strip,

you'll find a handful of sorry-looking topless bars rejoicing in classy names, such as Club Lady and Club Romance; this is where the successors of Mason's 1950s' muses plied their trade. These seedy places are notorious for their extortionate, sometimes invisible, extra charges just for entering and ordering a drink; but then having a drink is not the point of going. Most of these venues today are staffed by Filipinas, not Chinese. A better place to sample some of the area's character without being ripped off is the Old China Hand, a rakish but friendly pub in the midst of all the seedier joints (though a refurbishment has left it far less dingy than previously). Local denizens, sometimes with working girls in tow, frequent the pub. Happy hour here lasts all afternoon.

A five-minute walk north of the MTR exit on Lockhart Road is **Central Plaza**, the tallest skyscraper in Hong Kong at the time of its construction in 1992 (374 metres/1,227 feet). Apart from its height, Central Plaza is fairly undistinguished, but it does at least allow visitors to enjoy its views. Walk through the lofty, marble-clad foyer and take the escalator up to the lift lobby. The vantage point on the 46th floor has tall plate glass windows, offering spectacular views of the city's streets and harbour.

Facing Central Plaza across Harbour Road is the **Hong Kong Convention & Exhibition Centre** (*see p29 and p226*). Its extension, which juts out into the harbour and marks the most northerly section of the extensive land reclamation in Wan Chai, is one of the city's most striking buildings. Costing HK$4.8 billion, the sweeping lines of the extension are intended to create the impression of a bird taking flight. This was the appropriately impressive venue for the 1997 Handover ceremony. Although most of the building is given up to exhibition space, it's definitely worth a wander round. Gaze at the harbour through high glass windows, sip coffee or eat at one of several cafés and restaurants, or surf the internet for free at a couple of access points. Outside, there's a large promenade around the edge of the building and a sitting-out area that's perfect for making the most of the breeze. There's also a black obelisk marking the Handover, which is inscribed with a rhetorical celebration of the SAR's return to Chinese rule. Flag-raising ceremonies are held here with police bands – these parades are very popular photo-opportunities for mainland Chinese tour groups, and largely ignored by the rest of the population.

The **Hong Kong Arts Centre** (*see p226*) and the **Hong Kong Academy for Performing Arts** (*see p225*) are both a couple of minutes' walk west of here. The Arts Centre,

Sightseeing

on Harbour Road, hosts regular exhibitions of art and photography, while *Artslink*, its monthly magazine, contains full listings for, and reviews of, the local arts scene. It also has a café serving reasonable food.

### SOUTH OF HENNESSY ROAD

The narrow streets and older tenement buildings between Johnston Road and Queen's Road East offer a flavour of older Wan Chai. Wander along any one of these streets and you're sure to stumble across something a little out of the ordinary – be it a market stall, shop or small factory turning out anything from metalwork and printed matter to furniture. Queen's Road East has been the high-end furniture centre of Hong Kong for over a century; a selection of shops along here specialise in rattan, mahogany and rosewood; most will readily take orders or commissions.

Dating from the 1860s, the small, smoke-caked **Hung Shing Temple** stands at 129 Queen's Road East. It is dedicated to a government official from the Tang dynasty who became a patron saint of seafarers due to his excellent weather-forecasting skills. It used to be right next to the sea, before land reclamation marooned it far inland.

The revolving restaurant on the top (and 62nd) floor of the tall, tubular **Hopewell Centre** on Queen's Road East makes a scenic lunch stop, with particularly good views over the harbour and east towards Happy Valley. Even if you don't want to eat, the ride up the glass escalators on the outside of the building is a good way to get a glimpse of the surrounding area; definitely not for those afflicted with vertigo.

Further east along Queen's Road East, under a venerable old mango tree, is the **Old Wan Chai Post Office**, built in 1912-13. This small, one-storey building ceased service in 1992, and now houses an Environmental Resources Centre. It also marks the start of the steep one-and-a-half-kilometre (one-mile) Green Trail. The early stage consists of a rather pitiful selection of plaques pointing out unremarkable (but in Wan Chai, rare) trees. The second section is rather better as it winds up Wan Chai Gap Road into the woods. It ends close to Wan Chai Gap, near one of the entrances to Aberdeen Country Park and the small **Police Museum** (*see below*) at Coombe Road.

Further along Queen's Road East, close to Happy Valley and just past the entrance to the Ruttonjee Hospital, is **Wan Chai Park**, a small, unremarkable but precious speck of green space in among the tower blocks, which is very popular with students from nearby schools.

### Police Museum

*27 Coombe Road, Wan Chai Gap (2849 7019/ www.info.gov.hk/police). Bus 15, 15B.* **Open** 2-5pm Tue; 9am-5pm Wed-Sun. **Admission** free.

This small museum at the top of Wan Chai Gap Road is worth dropping by on the way to or from the Peak. The mostly static displays include a motor bike and field gun, and the exhibits themselves tell an interesting and coherent story of the Hong Kong Police. There is a small but interesting section containing ritual items from the triads.

## Causeway Bay

At the beginning of **Causeway Bay**, by the busy Canal Road flyover, **Bowrington Road Market** has separate floors for fruit and vegetables, fish and meat. Walk along the side streets nearby and you'll find similar items, at slightly lower prices. The colourful produce on offer here, including fresh steaming white bean curd being scooped from massive wooden tubs, makes for great photos.

All manner of seafood, including writhing eels and fidgeting crustaceans, is picked live from its tub and dismembered before your eyes, while frogs and turtles blink nonchalantly in baskets nearby. Hanging from hooks overhead, meanwhile, is every imaginable cut of cow and pig, including whole heads, tails, lungs and brains. For sensitive souls, it's probably not a good idea to linger too long around the poultry stalls, where live birds are dispatched with a casual flick of a blade and stuffed still twitching into a vat of hot water, after which they are tossed into a plucking machine. Perhaps the most absorbing and grisly sight, though, is the spectacle of live fish being deftly sliced lengthways and expertly gutted, while the exposed heart keeps beating.

Across Canal Road in Causeway Bay, the huge **Times Square** shopping mall (*see p165*) marks the start of Hong Kong's busiest shopping district. It's packed with stores of every description, from less-expensive chains to upmarket boutiques. There are also a number of department stores, including the Japanese giant **Sogo** (*see p163*) and the local **Wing On** (*see p163*), selling everyday household goods. This is one of the most popular places for young Hong Kongers to hang out to see and be seen.

East of Times Square, close to Causeway Bay MTR station, are two small streets, **Jardine's Bazaar** and **Jardine's Crescent**, which are crammed with market stalls selling food and bargain-priced clothes.

From here it's a couple of minutes' walk east to sprawling **Victoria Park** (*see p76*), Hong Kong's largest public park. Beyond the park, on **Tin Hau Temple Road**, is a small

**Causeway Bay.**
*See p73.*

and fairly typical temple to Tin Hau, the goddess of the sea. As one of Hong Kong's most popular Taoist gods, there are at least 40 temples in the SAR dedicated to her (*see p80* **Making waves**).

A major road separates the northern side of Victoria Park from the **Causeway Bay Typhoon Shelter**. By the side of the shelter, roughly in front of the Excelsior Hotel, stands the **Noon Day Gun**, fired daily since the 19th century and celebrated in the song *Mad Dogs and Englishmen* by Noël Coward. A small plaque details the (completely apocryphal) story of the gun. According to its own legend, Jardine Matheson, one of the largest and oldest trading houses in Hong Kong, often fired the gun to salute the arrival of its senior managers in port, which so incensed a particular naval officer's sense of protocol that he ordered Jardine's to fire the gun daily as a punishment for its presumption. The firing of the gun is now something of a charity fund-raising event, with Jardine's distributing the money that people pay to fire it to local charities. The small enclosure housing the gun is open for half an hour after noon. From Victoria Park, the gun is best reached via the walkway crossing Victoria Park Road, or from Causeway Bay via a badly signposted underpass, the entrance to which is in the multi-storey car park below the World Trade Centre Mall.

In the Typhoon Shelter there are about a dozen tiny houseboats, which are essentially sampans converted into floating residences, neatly kept with flower boxes on their 'porches'. On a promontory at the western end of the typhoon shelter stands the **Royal Hong Kong Yacht Club** (*see p239*). Keen or aspiring sailors should leave their details on a noticeboard outside the club's bar if they wish to join the crew of any yacht sailing out of Hong Kong. There's more chance of those with experience being signed on, but it's not unheard of for an inexperienced but willing deckhand to hitch a ride.

### Victoria Park

*Between Gloucester Road, Victoria Park Road, Causeway Road and Hing Fat Street.* **Open** 24hrs daily. **Map** p311 E/F2.

Aside from plenty of open space, the park contains a running track, a 50-metre (164-foot) swimming pool, basketball and tennis courts, and a model boating lake. This deservedly popular park is the venue for large gatherings, such as at Chinese New Year, when a popular flower fair is held here.

## Happy Valley

From Causeway Bay, one of Hong Kong's most powerful institutions, the **Happy Valley Racecourse** (closed July and August; *see p242*), is just to the south. The easiest way to get to the racecourse is to hop on a tram to Happy Valley. Although smaller than its sister site at Sha Tin in the New Territories, the Happy Valley Racecourse, in use since 1846, is the traditional home of horse racing in the city. An evening's racing here, with the stands packed out with more than 55,000 enthusiastic spectators, is still one of the quintessential Hong Kong experiences.

Unparalleled views from **The Peak**. *See p78.*

Ironically named Happy Valley when still a mosquito and malaria-ridden marsh, the site was chosen because it was the only piece of flat ground on the island large enough for a race track. Wednesday evenings are the best time to visit the brightly floodlit track. With the lights of apartments twinkling in the high-rises beyond, the excitement is palpable. It seems that every second person is a chain smoker and, if you stand at the bottom of the huge racing stand you will see, caught in the glare, a thick smoke plume rising from the cigarettes of thousands of nervous punters.

**The Peak**

LUGARD ROAD

▲ Victoria Peak
552m

See p308

To Central

Victoria Peak Garden

MOUNT AUSTIN ROAD

LUGARD ROAD

OLD PEAK ROAD

THE GOVERNOR'S WALK

HARLECH ROAD

MOUNT AUSTIN ROAD

Peak Tower

Peak Tram Upper Terminal

Tramway

FINDLAY ROAD

0    300 m

0    300 yds

© Copyright Time Out Group 2004

VICTORIA GAP

Pok Fu Lam Country Park

PEAK ROAD

Peak Galleria

*Sightseeing*

The small, well laid-out **Hong Kong Racing Museum** (*see below*), on the second floor of the stand, records the history of racing in Hong Kong. You can stop off for a bite to eat at the Moon Koon (2966 7111) next door, a reasonably priced Chinese restaurant with good food and terrific views on to the racetrack through the large plate-glass windows.

The old cemeteries at Happy Valley – an interesting glimpse into Hong Kong's cosmopolitan past – are well worth a wander if you're in the area. In particular, the well-kept **Hong Kong Cemetery**, more popularly known as the Old Colonial Cemetery, merits a wander, with magnificent trees and views out across the racecourse from the upper levels.

### Hong Kong Racing Museum

*2/F, Happy Valley Stand, Happy Valley (2966 8065/ www.hongkongjockeyclub.com). Trams to Happy Valley.* **Open** 10am-5pm Tue-Sun. **Admission** free. **Map** p311 D5.

Hong Kong's racing history and Chinese depictions of the horse in art are the focus of this museum. Through eight galleries, it tells the story of horse racing in Hong Kong from the early days of Happy Valley in the 1840s, and of horse breeding and trading in China and Mongolia, where the most prized ponies were raised. The skeleton of Hong Kong's legendary champion racehorse Silver Lining is mounted in pride of place.

### Further east

Beyond Causeway Bay, the monotonous residential and commercial towers continue to stretch east through North Point and Quarry Bay to Shau Kei Wan, where one of Hong Kong's newest museums, the **Hong Kong Museum of Coastal Defence** (*see below*), is situated.

### Hong Kong Museum of Coastal Defence

*175 Tung Hei Road, Shau Kei Wan (2569 1500/ www.lcsd.gov.hk). Shau Kei Wan MTR (exit B2)/ 84, 85 bus.* **Open** 10am-5pm Mon-Wed, Fri-Sun. **Admission** HK$10; HK$5 concessions; HK$7 per person in a group of 20 or more. Free to all Wed. **No credit cards. Map** p307.

This HK$300 million branch of the Hong Kong Museum of History (*see p89*) opened in 2000 within the 120-year-old Lei Yue Mun Fort. The core of the museum is the Redoubt, featuring an exhibition on '600 Years of Hong Kong's Coastal Defence', which is supplemented by a range of artefacts and multimedia displays. Other historic military structures on the site, such as the gun batteries and the Brennan Torpedo, have been restored; follow the Historical Trail that links the various parts of the fort together. The museum is a 15-minute walk from Shau Kei Wan MTR; there is also a free shuttle bus to the museum from Heng Fa Chuen MTR on Saturdays and Sundays.

# Peak of fitness

One of the best ways to enjoy the Peak area is to meander along the paved, pushchair-friendly three-kilometre (two-mile) circular path that follows the base of the Peak, along Lugard Road and back along Harlech Road. It's a pretty, tree-shaded route affording spectacular panoramic views of land and sea, and some tantalising glimpses of some of the Peak's most expensive properties. At night it is fully lit and the views are particularly impressive.

Another easy five-kilometre (three-mile) walk starts from outside the Peak Galleria and heads down Pok Fu Lam Reservoir Road, through the wooded **Pok Fu Lam Country Park**, to the reservoir and back. If you can't face the trudge back up the hill, you can always walk down to Pok Fu Lam Road,

from where there are plenty of buses back into Central. More adventurous ramblers can also walk to **Aberdeen** (*see p81*), turning left halfway down Reservoir Road, and along the side of Mount Kellett.

Victoria Gap is also the starting point for the 50-kilometre (31-mile) **Hong Kong Trail** (*see p41*), which passes through the island's four country parks, ending at Shek O (*see p84*).

A short circular tour of **Mount Gough**, along Findlay Road, east from the Peak Tower, will take you past some more of the area's swankiest properties and more superb views. Be aware, though, you'll have to walk along the road itself for much of its length, and some of the corners are very tight. Traffic is busiest at the weekends.

## The Peak

Towering above the commercial heart of Hong Kong Island, **Victoria Peak** – otherwise simply known as 'the Peak' – offers the most spectacular views in Hong Kong. On a rare clear day, the 552-metre (1,810-foot) summit overlooks not just the improbable towers of the north side of Hong Kong Island, but also Victoria Harbour, Kowloon and the hills of the New Territories beyond. To the south, the lush vegetation of the south side of Hong Kong Island leads down towards Lamma island (the chimneys of its power station are very prominent); while to the west lie the islands of Cheung Chau, Peng Chau and massive Lantau. The vistas are just as spectacular by night. Don't bother coming up if the weather is foggy – you won't see a thing.

The Peak is also the starting point for a number of fine walks, ranging from the gentle to the arduous (*see above* **Peak of fitness**).

Its milder temperatures (an average 5ºC lower than at sea level) and extraordinary vantage points have long made the Peak the most sought-after address in Hong Kong. Governor Sir Richard MacDonnell built a summer house here around 1868, when the trip from Central, by horse, sedan chair or on foot, took around an hour. The commencement of the **Peak Tram** services in 1888 cut the arduous journey down to just under ten minutes, making it an increasingly popular residential area. Remarkably, the tram (actually a funicular railway) has never suffered any fatal accidents – its most

serious setback occurred during a severe typhoon in the 1960s, when much of the track was washed away. The arrival of the tram also opened the Peak up to substantial development (it was intended as a commuter service, not a tourist ride). Today the Peak is among the most expensive places in the world to buy property, and many of Hong Kong's movers and shakers live here.

Taking a stroll in **Stanley**. *See p83.*

At their height in 1997, Hong Kong's property prices were briefly the highest (square foot for square foot) in the world – up to HK$20,000 per square foot at one point. Houses on the Peak regularly went for more than HK$100 million, and at the time their purchase was thought to have been a popular way for triads to launder large amounts of money. A subsequent property slump led to prices dropping by up to half. Property has long been the base on which tycoons, triads and middle-class folk in Hong Kong have built their wealth and long-term prosperity. The severe drop in the market has, therefore, plunged many citizens into negative equity, a legacy that is likely to linger; it remains a major source of discontent in the territory.

### Peak Tram

**Lower Terminal** *Garden Road, Central* **Upper Terminal** *Lugard Road, The Peak (2849 7654/www.thepeak.com.hk).* **Open** 7am-midnight daily (every 15mins). **Tickets** (single) HK$20; HK$6 concessions; (return) HK$30; HK$9 concessions. **Credit** (over HK$350) MC, V. **Map** p77.

### Victoria Gap

Bus 15 and minibus 1 run from the Central Star Ferry Pier up to the Peak, but the classic ascent is to take the Peak Tram from its Lower Terminal on Garden Road (reached by taking

the 15C shuttle bus from the Ferry Pier). Victoria Gap – not the Peak itself – is the final stop on the 373-metre (1,224-foot) steep (up to 27°) tram ride up from Mid-Levels – make sure you sit on the right-hand side going up for the best views.

The tram empties into Terry Farrell's **Peak Tower** (*see also p29*), an ugly development of extremely tacky shops and tourist-trap 'attractions' that opened in 1996. On its seven floors you'll find restaurants, cafés, a motion-simulator ride called the Peak Explorer (HK$55; HK$35 concessions), the Rise of the Dragon dark ride ('experience the sights, smells and sounds of old Hong Kong'), the local **Madame Tussaud's** and **Ripley's Believe It or Not! Odditorium** (for both, *see p80*). The viewing terrace on the fifth level affords some excellent views (Hong Kong's fickle weather and increasingly bad air pollution permitting), as does the outdoor seating at the noodle shop on the second level, which is also a good place to enjoy an inexpensive drink and some decent, cheap noodles.

Next to the Peak Tower is the **Peak Galleria**, which shares with its neighbour a plethora of tacky tourist shops, more cafés, restaurants and a supermarket. For westward views towards the outlying islands, head across the road to the **Peak Lookout** (*see p133*), a comfortable, well-appointed but pricier place for lunch, dinner or refreshments.

Dip your toes in the South China Sea at **Stanley Main Beach**. *See p84.*

# Making waves

**Tin Hau**, the goddess of the sea, is one of the most popular deities in Hong Kong, which is not surprising, given the historical importance of fishing to local people. The SAR has at least 40 Tin Hau temples, all of them originally built on the waterfront, but most now far inland thanks to ongoing land reclamation.

The compassionate Taoist goddess Tin Hau was the saintly daughter of a tenth-century fisherman from Fujian province who was said to be able to forecast the weather, calm the waves and generally help fishermen to land a decent catch. However, she died at an early age trying to save the lives of her two brothers. Several years later, fishermen started claiming that her apparition had appeared to save them from death at sea. As a result, ships began carrying her image, and numerous shrines to Tin Hau were built along the South China coast. In the 12th century, she was canonised as a 'Saintly and Diligent Saviour', and,

in 1683, promoted to the exulted rank of 'Queen of Heaven' ('Tin Hau' in Cantonese).

The festival held to celebrate the birthday of Tin Hau is usually held in late April or early May (the 23rd day of the third lunar month). It's one of Hong Kong's most colourful festivals, with events taking place at all the Tin Hau temples scattered throughout Hong Kong (though the festival focuses on those in Joss House Bay and Yuen Long). The goddess herself is supposed to visit the temple at Joss House Bay during the festival, so around 20,000 people usually turn up to experience her presence.

In tribute to Tin Hau, fishing boats are decorated with colourful flags, there are parades, opera performances and lion dances, and family shrines are carried to the shore to be blessed by Taoist priests. In addition, offerings in the form of different kinds of food, including pink dumplings, are made – particularly by fishermen – as a mark of respect.

## Madame Tussaud's

*Level 2, Peak Tower, 128 Peak Road (2849 6966/Ticketek advance booking 3128 8288/ www.madame-tussauds.com). Peak Tram/15 bus/ 1 minibus.* **Open** noon-8pm daily. **Admission** HK$90; HK$50 concessions. **Credit** AmEx, MC, V. **Map** p77.

Madame Tussaud's first venture into Asia opened in summer 2000, with more than 100 waxy celebs to bump into. As in London, the credulous can hang out with Sly, Arnie, Jacko and friends, see likenesses of David Beckham and his pop-star missus, or be snapped posing next to local heroes actor Jackie Chan, Olympic gold-winning windsurfer Lee Lai-shan and (only in Hong Kong) top business supremo Li Ka-shing.

## Ripley's Believe It or Not! Odditorium

*Levels 2 & 3, Peak Tower, 128 Peak Road (2849 0818/www.ripleys.com). Peak Tram/15 bus/ 1 minibus.* **Open** 9am-10pm daily. **Admission** HK$75; HK$50 concessions. **Credit** (over HK$350) MC, V. **Map** p77.

This inexplicable freak show chain offers a haphazard collection of strange facts and anthropological bric-a-brac, some of it truly gruesome, such as a plastic model of the world's fattest man. Perhaps the most interesting thing to witness here is observing the mainland Chinese tour groups taking photos of each other and shaking their heads in disbelief at the items on display.

## Victoria Peak

Surprisingly, the buildings at Victoria Gap offer no information about, or signposts to, the summit of Victoria Peak, although the tourist board recently rectified this. The Peak itself, immediately to the west of Victoria Gap, is a steep 20-minute walk up Mount Austin Road. For a gentler and longer stroll, head along Harlech Road (until its junction with Lugard Road on the south-west side of the Peak) and head up the Governor's Walk, which threads a gently rising path up to the small, but well-tended **Victoria Peak Garden**. Located on the site of the old Governor's lodge, which was demolished after World War II, it offers viewing areas looking west, south and east. The very summit of the Peak is occupied by telephone masts and surrounded by a large fenced-off area.

## South & east coasts

When the hustle and hassle of the northern coast of Hong Kong Island becomes too much, jump on a bus and head over to the more relaxed south and east coasts, where the pace of life is slower and a variety of man-made and natural attractions awaits. Aberdeen is a vibrant – if rather smelly – mixed commercial/

industrial fishing town with a busy harbour.
Close to it is Ocean Park, a sprawling, varied
and spectacularly situated amusement park.
Further south are the beaches of Repulse and
Deep Water Bays and the pretty seaside town
of Stanley. To really get away from it all, the
sleepy village of Shek O at the far south-eastern
end of the island offers a striking coastline
and great beaches. And don't neglect the hilly
interior of the island, which features great
hiking and superb views.

## Aberdeen

Drab high-rise blocks edge **Aberdeen** harbour.
Ignore the ugly town centre and head to the
typhoon shelter, which is always jammed with
dozens of fishing boats – most of them the old-
fashioned, high-prowed wooden type. Tyre-
festooned sampans dodge deftly among them
and at the harbour edge small-scale shipyards
refit ageing vessels. Towards the western end
of the harbour is the large, and often frantically
busy, wholesale fish and seafood market.
During the day it's crowded with merchants
and restaurateurs buying all kinds of seafood
and loading up their trucks.

Sampan tours of the harbour are available
from pushy elderly women lying in wait for
meandering tourists, or from the Aberdeen
Sampan Company, prominently signposted east
of the wholesale market. HK$60 (less if there's
more than one passenger – be prepared to
haggle a bit) will buy a 15-minute tour of the
harbour. You won't get much out of your 'guide'
– unless you speak Cantonese – but she will
point out the few remaining family junks,
which used to be a common sight here. Most
of the folk who once lived on their fishing
boats have moved into the new developments

around Aberdeen over the last 30 years,
completely transforming an age-old way of life.

The ferry that constantly shuttles diners from
the quayside to the three giant floating seafood
restaurants moored out towards the southern
end of the typhoon shelter will provide you with
a slightly less extensive, but free, tour of the
harbour. These floating restaurants are what
put Aberdeen on the map for many tourists.

The most famous, and by far the most
elaborate and garish, is the red and gold hulk of
the **Jumbo Floating Restaurant**, resembling
something between a technicolour pagoda and
a Mississippi paddle steamer-turned-casino.
There's a production line approach to business
at the Jumbo, with the result that an estimated
30 million people have dined here since it
opened in the 1970s. The impersonal approach
extends to the assigning of tables (for which
you are issued with a ticket at busy times),
the service and the food itself, which does not
have a particularly great reputation and is by
no means cheap. None of this seems to deter
diners – tourists and locals alike pack it out at
weekends. The Jumbo also organises a number
of tours that usually involve a cruise and meal –
details are available at any HKTB centre.

If the Jumbo experience does not appeal,
and time permits, you can always catch a ferry
from Aberdeen to the much better seafood
restaurants on Lamma island. Go either to Yung
Shue Wan, the main settlement (*see p110*), or the
quieter (and closer) Sok Kwu Wan (*see p111*) on
the east side of the island for a seafood dinner
which – while not that cheap either – will not
have you taking out a second mortgage.

Incidentally, Aberdeen has no connection
with the Scottish city of the same name.
It's named after Lord Aberdeen – Secretary of
State for the Colonies in the mid 19th century.

**Big Wave Bay.**
*See p84.*

## Deep Water Bay & Repulse Bays

Travelling east along the south coast from Aberdeen towards Stanley takes you past **Ocean Park** (*see p193*) and a number of decent beaches. **Deep Water Bay** is a pretty spot long-favoured by the wealthy – as the number of plush houses in the area testifies. The long stretch of beach, lined by trees, has an almost Riviera-like air. As with most major beaches in Hong Kong, there are barbecue areas, but be warned that on Sundays legions of Filipina and Indonesian domestic workers on their day off are likely to have staked their claim to every barbecue pit very early in the morning.

Just around a headland to the south, huge, upmarket and expensive apartment blocks, populated by well-paid executives, surround the long, well-tended beach at **Repulse Bay**. The beach is a popular destination in the summer and gets very crowded. Above it, the Verandah restaurant (*see p134*) is a lovely, if expensive, place for a drink or afternoon tea. Behind the

# Across the Dragon's Back

The **Dragon's Back** is one of Hong Kong Island's easiest and most popular hiking routes. Although the very beginning of the walk is at Big Wave Bay (*see p84*), this shorter version is a perfect beginner's hike and one that you can take kids on too.

Starting near Mount Collinson (named after the maker of the first detailed topographical map of Hong Kong Island), this walk ends in the former fishing village of Shek O on the island's east coast. The eight-kilometre (five-mile) trek rarely takes more than two hours, even at a leisurely pace, and is easy to reach via public transport.

Walking along the gentle ridge reveals unrivalled views of the South China Sea, the outlying islands, Tai Tam Country Park's reservoirs, Mounts Parker and Butler, and Violet Hill, as well as clear views of Stanley, the Red Hill Peninsula and parts of Kowloon. On most weekend afternoons, you can spot paragliders leaping off the Dragon's Back, enjoying some of Asia's finest thermals and then floating down to land on one of Shek O's smaller beaches. The reward at the end of the hike is the laid-back village of Shek O, which has a great beach, several restaurants and a small headland to explore (*see p84*).

## GETTING THERE

Catch the MTR to Shau Kei Wan station (exit A3) and take the number 9 bus to Shek O from the bus station outside. Stay on the bus for about five kilometres (three miles) and ring the bell as soon as you see a mini roundabout (the only one along this road), so that you can get off at the next stop.

## THE HIKE

Remain on the same side of the road as the bus stop. Walk straight ahead and you will see a set of steps. Climb the steps and

turn right at the top by the women's prison. Walk past the prison and up a concrete water-catchment road. At the top, the road forks. A sign indicates a path to the left that leads to the surfer hangout of Big Wave Bay, but for Shek O continue ahead along a muddy, worn path lined by trees and bushes. (Don't worry about getting lost; there are no turn-offs along this route.)

After about 30-40 minutes, look for a knee-high wooden post (No.90). Shortly after this you'll see another post next to a right-hand turning. Take this right turn, and walk uphill for about five minutes (off path). When you reach the top you are officially at the start of the Dragon's Back. Turn right at the top (the sea is on your left) and walk along the whole of the Dragon's Back. Looking down the hill, you will see the village of Shek O on your left side and Tai Tam Harbour on your right. The path runs out after about 30-40 minutes of ridge walking (a seat marks the end of the trail) and you'll see a path and steps leading downhill. Follow them for about 15 minutes and you'll reach the main road (Shek O Road) next to a bus stop. Rather than walk on the main road (there is no path and traffic is fast), hop back on to the number 9 bus – it is a five-minute journey into Shek O, where the bus terminates.

## THE AFTER-HIKE REWARDS

There are a couple of inexpensive, casual restaurants in Shek O. A good hiker hangout is the Shek O Chinese-Thai Seafood Restaurant (*see p84 and p135*), which was a popular haunt of Chris Patten. There are plenty of others with similar food, prices and standards nearby, although reservations are recommended, especially at weekends, when things can get pretty busy.

Verandah, there's a supermarket and a couple of cafés.

At the southern end of the beach is the Hong Kong Life Guards' Club, which resembles a Chinese temple. Among the canoes and lifesaving equipment you'll find scores of statues of gods, animals and fabulous beasts dotted around its grounds. For example, there are huge statues of Kwun Yam, the goddess of mercy, and Tin Hau, plus several bronze Buddhas, their bald heads and ample bellies polished bright by hundreds of human hands.

**Middle Bay**, just around the coast between Repulse Bay and South Bay, is Hong Kong's popular gay beach (for Middle Bay and South Bay, *see p213* **Splashing out**) and is always thronged with cruising males, whatever the weather.

## Stanley

The pretty town and sandy beaches of **Stanley** are a 25-minute bus ride from Central (take bus 6, 6A, 6X or 260) or ten minutes by minibus from Aberdeen. Stanley – known as Chek Chue – was a Chinese settlement long before the British arrival. Until the 1960s it was a thriving fishing village, but that industry has declined over the last 30 years and today it feels more like an English seaside town, complete with pubs and red-faced Europeans roasting in the sun. But despite extensive and at times unsympathetic development, Stanley still retains considerable charm and it's possible to spend a leisurely half-day wandering around the town.

The extensive sprawl of **Stanley Market**'s 'stalls' (many of them now actual shops; *see also p170* **Market places**) is one of the main reasons for Stanley's continued popularity with visitors. There are perhaps a couple of hundred outlets selling export-order clothes, beachwear, silk, accessories, jewellery, jade, trinkets, paintings, DVDs and furniture, usually cheaper than in central Hong Kong or Kowloon (though

the days of real bargains – as in Hong Kong generally – has long-since gone). The market is open from around 11am to 6pm daily.

A pleasant promenade links the market area with the quiet seafront, populated by several restaurants serving Italian, Thai, Spanish, Vietnamese and Chinese food, as well as the friendly Smugglers Inn on Stanley Main Road. This is also where you'll find the old Police Station, a historical landmark and the oldest surviving police station building in Hong Kong (built 1859), which has been converted into – believe it or not – a supermarket. A new shopping development at the western end of the promenade has been introduced with, by Hong Kong standards at least, some sensitivity. Five storeys high, it is tucked unobtrusively away and includes a supermarket, car park and attractive square facing the sea, which is covered by a large canopy with seating for public events.

The large neoclassical building beside the square is **Murray House**. It contains some smart but reasonably priced restaurants with views over the bay. The original building stood for a century and a half in Central (at the spot now occupied by the Bank of China Tower) until 1982, when it was dismantled, the granite details numbered and put into storage. It was only recently that it was reassembled here over a concrete shell; look closely and you'll see that some of the numbers labelling each block for the move are still visible. One of the earliest colonial structures in Hong Kong, it dates to 1843, when it was used as a mess for British army officers.

Nearby is Stanley's **Tin Hau Temple**, which can trace its origins back to 1767, making it one of the oldest – and, inside at least, most evocative – temples on the island. Incense coils fill it with scented smoke, while the altar is populated by elaborate statuary depicting Tin Hau (*see p80* **Making waves**) and a bodyguard of grimacing warriors.

On the other side of town is **Stanley War Cemetery**, a beautifully kept place in which you can trace the earliest colonial days through the gravestones of military personnel and their families. The toll taken by disease is shocking, particularly on young children and babies, but perhaps most moving is the profusion of stones marking the deaths of some 4,500 British and Commonwealth servicemen, who perished during the fall of Hong Kong in 1941 and, subsequently, as Japan's prisoners of war. A memorial at the entrance details the desperate defence of the New Territories and the island by British and Commonwealth forces, who finally surrendered on Christmas Day 1941.

Below the cemetery is the relatively clean **St Stephen's Beach**, with views towards Stanley and across to Lamma island. South of the beach lies **Stanley Peninsula**, home to **Stanley Fort**, which was previously occupied by the British Army and is now used by the People's Liberation Army. It is not accessible without a permit.

On the other side of the peninsula, a short distance from the bus terminus in the centre of town, is **Stanley Main Beach**, a good long stretch of sand and the venue for the local dragon boat race in June.

## Shek O

The tiny, sleepy village of **Shek O**, which clusters on a small headland at the far south-eastern corner of Hong Kong Island, has so far escaped any unsightly development. This is the place to go for a day of sea breezes, great beaches and peace (especially on weekdays). It's a thoroughly relaxing spot with some dramatic shoreline and great South China Sea views.

Shek O is also one of the finishing points for the **Dragon's Back Trail** (*see p82* **Across the Dragon's Back**) and the **Hong Kong Trail** (*see p41*). It is most easily reached by taking the number 9 bus, which runs every 15 minutes from the bus terminus just outside

Shau Kei Wan MTR. At the end of the long, winding and scenic route, the bus drops you in the centre of the village. From the bus stop, turn right at the mini roundabout for the main beach, an immaculately kept stretch of golden sand with changing facilities and lifeguards. It's also worth taking a walk to the small rocky islet at the tip of the headland (straight ahead across the roundabout from the bus stop). The five-minute walk will take you past Shek O's mix of small, pretty, weather-beaten dwellings and the larger mansions on the edges of the headland. On the shoreline there's usually a strong, fresh breeze blowing and large waves crashing against the strikingly pitted and fissured rocks.

From the headland there's a footbridge to a small island called **Tai Tau Chau**, from where there are great views across to the New Territories. Eating and drinking choices are limited in Shek O to the restaurants that circle the mini-roundabout. The largest is the **Shek O Chinese-Thai Seafood Restaurant** (*see p82 and p135*), which offers average prices and quality but an extensive menu, including the theatrical 'Chicken on Fire', which is flambéed in brandy at your table.

Close to the roundabout, tucked down a narrow alley off Headland Road is a small but immaculately kept and very pretty **Tin Hau Temple** (*see p80* **Making waves**). The flowers decked outside and the smiles on the faces of the statues make it one of the most cheerful on the island.

**Big Wave Bay**, a couple of kilometres to the north, has a good sandy beach set between ruggedly beautiful cliffs and rocks. It's virtually the only place – with the exception of a few remote spots in the New Territories – where Hong Kong's small surfing community can go to catch a wave. It's an easy, but not particularly pleasant, walk from Shek O along the road to Big Wave Bay; there's no pavement so watch out for passing traffic. The road cuts through the Shek O golf course and passes several large mansions set in extensive grounds, homes to some of Hong Kong's wealthiest residents.

If surfing is the idea, there are two hire shops by the beach, although they are closed at quiet times of year. Long and short boards can be hired for about HK$50 a day, plus a HK$100 deposit.

At the far north-eastern end of the bay, close to the furthest lifeguard's station, is one of Hong Kong's ancient rock carvings, thought to date back to the Bronze Age between 2,500 and 3,000 BC. Faint geometric designs and stylised animal figures can just be made out on a small area of rock inside the small protective shelter.

# Kowloon

Gritty rather than glitzy, Kowloon feels a million miles away from its flashier cross-harbour neighbour.

There are no more memorable experiences in Hong Kong than standing at the southern tip of the Kowloon peninsula and gazing out over Victoria Harbour at the jostling ranks of gleaming towers crowding the northern shore of Hong Kong Island, with richly wooded hills and the Peak beyond (admittedly now half obscured by the IFC2 tower). But Kowloon offers much more than just a vantage point. Though it certainly lacks the polish of its island neighbour, it has a far more tangible Chinese feel to it, superb shopping opportunities and the territory's major concentration of museums and galleries.

The peninsula's 12-square kilometres (four-and-a-half-square miles) are densely packed with shops, bars, hotels and housing in a vibrant, untidy jumble of new skyscrapers and old low-rise tenements. Within this relatively small area lie a half dozen temples and museums, the Cultural Centre and, hidden away on its side-streets, atmospheric old Chinese neighbourhoods and extensive street markets waiting to be explored.

Kowloon's name derives from the Cantonese phrase *gau lung*, or 'nine dragons'. According to local legend, the peninsula was named eight centuries ago when the boy emperor Zhao Bing, the last emperor of the Southern Song Dynasty, arrived in the area while fleeing invading Mongols. It is said that he pointed to the eight hills above the peninsula and announced that eight dragons must dwell there – one for each hill. He was then reminded that, as emperors were also considered dragons, his own presence meant that there were nine dragons in the area. No giant lizards saved the little emperor, though, as he met his end to the west of present-day Macau, throwing himself into the sea to escape the approaching Mongols. Today, the dragons of the Kowloon hills look down upon serried ranks of public housing blocks, one of Hong Kong's most unsung post-war success stories.

When the British claimed Hong Kong Island in 1841, Kowloon was not included in the settlement. It was soon realised that the close proximity of potentially hostile territory represented an emergent threat to the fledgling colony. Following the Second Opium War in 1860, the peninsula was ceded 'in perpetuity' to Great Britain. Around three kilometres (two

miles) inland, Boundary Street, which runs west to east in a ruler-straight line, once defined the frontier between British Hong Kong and China.

The roads criss-crossing Kowloon may be as jammed as those in Central, but they encroach less on pedestrian space than over the water, so getting about on foot is a realistic option. And when you tire, just hop on the MTR or one of the numerous buses patrolling Nathan Road, which forms the spine of Kowloon from Tsim Sha Tsui in the south through the districts of Yau Ma Tei and Mong Kok.

## Tsim Sha Tsui

**Tsim Sha Tsui** (pronounced 'Chim Sa Choy'), at the very southern tip of Kowloon, is the grubbier cousin of Central, which it faces across the harbour. Its major thoroughfare, shop-lined **Nathan Road**, is a wide, straight highway that has attempted to adopt the nickname 'the Golden Mile'. In truth, the epithet is overly flattering – as a rule, shops here are far less glitzy than those of Central – and inaccurate, as it's considerably longer than a mile. Hundreds of electronics stores, clothing shops, a handful of topless bars and, every few yards it seems, Indian tailors or their touts, line Nathan Road and its side-streets.

Tsim Sha Tsui isn't entirely devoted to commercial activities, however: it also contains most of Hong Kong's museums and the excellent, though very ugly, Cultural Centre. This area of the city is also a major tourist accommodation area, with hotels available from the cheapest backpacker doss-house (nevertheless very expensive by Indian or South-east Asian standards) to some of the world's finest five-star hotels.

When setting out to explore Kowloon, a natural starting point is the **Tsim Sha Tsui Star Ferry Pier** – where cross-harbour ferries arrive from Central and Wan Chai. Within the Star Ferry Pier, there is a branch of the **Hong Kong Tourism Board**; it's worth stopping by to pick up free maps, brochures, and information on local tours and upcoming events.

Next to the Star Ferry Pier is the old **Kowloon–Canton Railway Station clock tower**. Overlooking the tip of the peninsula, the 44-metre (144-foot) tower is all that remains of the southern terminus of the Kowloon–Canton Railway, which stood here from 1915 until it was demolished in 1978. A new underground KCR extension is currently under construction, at enormous cost, to re-link Tsim Sha Tsui with the main station at Hung Hom (a new station, East Tsim Sha Tsui, will emerge in Middle Road). So much for long-term civic planning.

Near the Star Ferry Pier are two sprawling shopping arcades. The nearer (and smaller) one, **Star House**, is known for its extensive offerings of Asian arts and crafts, and holds the massive **Chinese Arts & Crafts** store (*see p179*), selling an impressive array of jewellery, ornaments, furniture, embroidered tablecloths, clothing and jade. Larger – and somewhat more upmarket – **Harbour City** (incorporating Ocean Terminal and Ocean Centre; *see p165*) features an enormous number of high-end shops, alongside a handy first-floor café with free internet access.

From the pier, sweeping past the clock and beyond, there is a long waterfront promenade, which gives fabulous views by day and night over the water towards Hong Kong Island. Such a prime site would seem made in heaven for outdoor cafés and waterfront bars – but there are none, mainly because of arcane licensing laws and other seemingly insurmountable bureaucratic difficulties.

Just to the east of the Star Ferry Pier (along the waterfront promenade) is the **Hong Kong Cultural Centre**, one of the territory's greatest wasted architectural opportunities. When the Kowloon–Canton Railway station was demolished in 1978 it freed up one of Hong Kong's – and indeed the world's – most spectacular sites. Facing the incomparable city-and-mountains vista on the northern side of Hong Kong Island, what was built to replace it? A soulless structure without any windows, clad in insipid pink-beige lavatory-style tiles, the whole thing resembling an outsize public toilet cross-bred with a ski-jump. Its only saving grace is that it at least provides a wide-ranging cultural programme within its excellent concert hall and two theatres (*see p226*).

On the waterfront next door to the Cultural Centre, the **Hong Kong Museum of Art** (*see p89*) hosts excellent permanent exhibitions of Asian ceramics and a pictorial history of Chinese art, with an emphasis on classic and contemporary Hong Kong art.

Sandwiched between the art museum and the Peninsula hotel, the **Hong Kong Space Museum** has a few interesting interactive displays (*see p89*). Inside a tiled hemisphere within the museum's lobby is the Space Theatre. At regular intervals, so-called 'sky shows' are projected onto its domed ceiling;

not surprisingly, these 30-minute shows are very popular with rowdy local school groups.

At the opposite end of the architectural universe, and directly across Salisbury Road, is the handsome, neo-classical exterior of the **Peninsula** hotel (*see p53*), with its sympathetic tower extension. Arguably the grandest hotel in Hong Kong, this effortlessly classy place is a must-see. Even if you can't stretch to staying the night, don't miss the chance to take afternoon tea in the elegant, high-ceilinged and pillar-bedecked lobby (served between 2pm and 7pm every day, but most popular on Sundays). If you mistakenly think that the Pen is stuck in the past, go to the top floor and visit the Philippe Starck-designed Felix restaurant and bar. Floor-to-ceiling windows deliver astonishing views over the harbour to Hong Kong Island on one side and back over Kowloon towards the New Territories on the other. Gents shouldn't miss going to the loos – the urinals are placed in front of vast windows, giving the user the somewhat god-like feeling that he is relieving himself over all of Kowloon.

A couple of minutes' walk east of the Peninsula along Salisbury Road is the tiny, somewhat secluded **Signal Hill Garden**. This little-appreciated green corner contains a steep hill topped by a tower (open 9-11am, 4-6pm daily) offering a good vantage point. The tower was originally built in 1904 to send signals to ships in the harbour, thus enabling seafarers to verify the accuracy of their chronographs. Over time, though, more advanced technology rendered it redundant.

An inescapable feature of this southern tip of Tsim Sha Tsui – at least for the next couple of years – is construction work for the new KCR extension. Roads are partially blocked off and the noise level from pile-drivers and other equipment can be excruciating. In short, it all makes the area not very pleasant to wander around. While it won't last for ever (very little does in Hong Kong), the situation is something we're stuck with for a bit longer.

If all the uproar is making you crave more expansive greenery, walk up Nathan Road to **Kowloon Park** (*see p89*), one of Hong Kong's larger and most precious open spaces.

Just past the south-eastern edge of the park, the minarets of the **Jamia Masjid Islamic Centre** rise near the intersection of Nathan and Cameron roads. Hong Kong's largest mosque, it was built in the early 1980s to replace a 19th-century mosque that had been constructed for the use of British Indian troops. Tourists are not allowed inside.

For a choice of places to eat and drink, head down Kimberley Road opposite the park. Tucked away off the street is a short strip of

The **Hong Kong Cultural Centre**. *See p86.*

# Masterstrokes

The subject of essays, documentaries and local folklore, octogenarian Tsang Tsou-choi is renowned throughout the territory for his graffiti. Wielding a Chinese calligraphy brush in preference to a can of spray paint, Tsang, otherwise known as the 'King of Kowloon', has been writing on Hong Kong's walls, electric transformer boxes and freeway overpasses for more than 40 years.

Tsang's 'calligraffiti' consists of incomprehensible texts that include the names of family members, ancestors, Chinese and British historical figures and various places in Hong Kong. His big strokes have a childlike boldness to them and, despite being on crutches since an accident a decade ago, and almost daily run-ins with the police, Tsang continues to cover the Kowloon peninsula with his cipher of names of people and places.

Variously dubbed a working-class hero, a public nuisance and a madman, Tsang is known to just about everyone in Hong Kong. Parents have scolded their young children for following his example, bohemians have praised his spirit and audacity, and for the most part, city officials have turned a blind eye to his acts of artistic anarchy. His spats with authorities are the stuff of legend and during a long and infamous career, he has publicly accused the British government of stealing his land and been threatened with wilful damage charges by the SAR administration.

In the lead up to the Handover, several of Hong Kong's intelligentsia held up the work of Tsang as a metaphor for the fragility of free speech and championed his right to deface the city. With this new high profile, his texts and style were elaborately critiqued by several members of the Hong Kong arts community. In 1997, one art critic staged an exhibition of Tsang's calligraphy at the Hong Kong Goethe Institut, claiming that his work descended from the masters of Classical Chinese calligraphy. While the literati and *cognoscenti* reviewed the exhibition, Tsang muttered to himself in a corner and continued to paint.

Tsang's calligraphy has also been admired overseas. Following the success of his debut exhibition, his work inspired a fashion show by the internationally acclaimed Hong Kong designer William Tang. Wearing fabrics patterned with variations of Tsang's graffiti, a leggy catwalk model paraded the old man's words to great applause at Germany's über-cool Insel Hombroich Museum.

If you'd like to see some of Tsang's work, you can purchase a documentary about the man (*King of Kowloon*) and his writing by Joanne Shen and Martin Egan at www.films.bigstep.com/generic.jhtml?pid=2. Or, better still, take a walk under the freeways of Kowloon and perhaps see the master himself, propped up on crutches, in action.

restaurants and bars, on **Knutsford Terrace**. It may not rival Lan Kwai Fong in Central, but it is one of the few areas in Kowloon to offer some version of al fresco dining. A massive new area is being created off Mody Road, to be imitatively known as KLKF – Kowloon Lan Kwai Fong (*see also p149*) – but it remains to be seen whether it develops into more than just a wannabe version of the one across the harbour.

To the east, across Chatham Road South, are two major museums: the **Hong Kong Museum of History** (*see below*) and the popular, hands-on **Hong Kong Science Museum** (*see below*). There is also the delightful old **Rosary Church**, one of Kowloon's oldest surviving places of worship, which was paid for at the end of the 19th century by a prominent local Portuguese medical doctor.

### Hong Kong Museum of Art

*10 Salisbury Road (2721 0116/www.lcsd.gov.hk/hkma). Tsim Sha Tsui MTR (exit E)/buses to Tsim Sha Tsui Star Ferry Pier & along Salisbury Road/Tsim Sha Tsui Star Ferry Pier.* **Open** 10am-6pm Mon-Wed, Fri-Sun. **Admission** HK$10; HK$5 concessions. Free to all Wed. **No credit cards. Map** p313 C6.

Despite its relatively small size, this waterfront museum has enough to keep visitors occupied for at least a couple of hours. Works are arranged in six galleries, five of which house permanent displays. The sixth accommodates visiting exhibits from China and further afield, of frankly variable quality. Among the permanent displays are an extensive collection of crafts from southern China and elsewhere in Asia dating from neolithic times to the present day.

While the exhibitions are wide-ranging, porcelain and other ceramic items form the museum's core display, with an extensive collection of extraordinarily fine pieces, and a useful explanation of the manufacturing process and the development of porcelain-making techniques. There is also a permanent exhibition of historical paintings and lithographs of Hong Kong, Macau and Canton (now Guangzhou) in colonial and pre-colonial days, and a small collection of contemporary art from the region.

Audio guides (available for HK$10) help explain some of the exhibits, but for the most part the information is heavy on facts and thin on context, which can be frustrating for those without much prior knowledge. On the ground floor, there's a well-stocked shop selling art books, prints and postcards, many at very reasonable prices. *See also p207.*

### Hong Kong Museum of History

*100 Chatham Road South (2724 9042/www.lcsd.gov.hk/CE/Museum/History). Buses along Chatham Road South.* **Open** 10am-6pm Mon, Wed-Sat; 10am-7pm Sun. **Admission** HK$10; HK$5 concessions. Free to all Wed. **No credit cards. Map** p313 C5.

Opened in 2001, this long-awaited museum gives a magisterial overview of Hong Kong's history from palaeolithic times to the present. Well-curated displays and sensitive captions mean there's something for nearly everyone. Political correctness has not been allowed to rear its sanctimonious head here, and even a few unlikely candidates have been included among the displays – there are pictures of the Tiananmen Square incident in 1989, for instance. Not to be missed for those who want to know more about how and why Hong Kong came about.

### Hong Kong Science Museum

*2 Science Museum Road, Tsim Sha Tsui East (2732 3232/www.lcsd.gov.hk/CE/Museum/Science/index.htm). Buses along Chatham Road South.* **Open** 1-9pm Mon-Wed, Fri; 10am-9pm Sat, Sun. **Admission** HK$25; HK$12.50 concessions. Free to all Wed. **No credit cards. Map** p313 C5.

The four floors of this museum are almost entirely filled with excellent interactive displays neatly demonstrating the basic principles of physics, electricity, chemistry and everyday technology. A popular destination for parents and children of all ages, it's a fun, boisterous place, often filled with excitable local school parties. Most adults – especially visitors with limited time – can live without a visit here, though.

### Hong Kong Space Museum

*10 Salisbury Road (2721 0226/www.lcsd.gov.hk/CE/Museum/Space/e_index.htm). Tsim Sha Tsui MTR (exit E)/buses to Kowloon Star Ferry Pier & along Salisbury Road/Kowloon Star Ferry Pier.* **Open** 1-9pm Mon, Wed-Fri; 10am-9pm Sat, Sun. **Admission** *Museum* free. *Omnimax Theatre* HK$24-$32; HK$12-$16 concessions. **No credit cards. Map** p313 C6.

This is not the most thrilling museum in Hong Kong, but children will like the four or five good interactive exhibits, including rides simulating the gravity on the moon and the landing of the lunar module, a centrifuge and a gyroscope. Displays explaining the workings of rockets, the solar system and the stars are reasonably well put together but, like the Science Museum, are more for kids than adults. In addition, some of the displays are starting to show their age, and many are poorly explained. The same goes for the Sculpture Garden outside; some of its dozen or so pieces are labelled, but otherwise there's little information available about either the works or their creators. Documentaries in Cantonese, Mandarin and Japanese (in English via headphones) are shown every day in the Omnimax Theatre.

### Kowloon Park

*Between Kowloon Park Drive & Nathan Road. Tsim Sha Tsui MTR (exit A1).* **Open** 6am-midnight daily. **Map** p313 B5.

One of the city's best-loved green spaces, Kowloon Park was previously the site of Whitfield Barracks, which was used for British (in practice, though, mostly Indian) soldiers. It is well designed, so there's lots to see, plus plenty of space in which to stroll or just sit and relax. An attractive open-plan swimming area (open daily, April-October) takes up the northern section of the park – be warned: it gets very busy. (There's also an Olympic-sized indoor heated pool). Just south of the pools is an aviary alive with birdlife and a pond crowded with flamingos and waterfowl alongside a secluded Chinese garden. On the park's eastern edge is a small, waist-high maze, a lovely sculpture garden and a number of fountains and other water features.

## Hung Hom

East of the museums lies the area called **Hung Hom**. At its southern end stands the 12,500-seater **Hong Kong Coliseum** (see p221), an inverted pyramid that plays host to major sporting events and music concerts. Next door is Hung Hom Station, the terminus of the Kowloon–Canton Railway (KCR). Trains depart from here to the New Territories, Guangzhou, Shanghai, Beijing and other places in China. The reclaimed land on the eastern edge of Hung Hom – formerly the site of the Hong Kong and Whampoa Dock Company, better known as the Kowloon Docks – has been developed into a largely utilitarian area of housing, shops and office blocks known as **Whampoa Gardens**. A mirage rises up from the thicket of retail outlets on Hung Hom Road – you can't miss the massive hull of the **Whampoa** (visible from the path to Tsim Sha Tsui; on Shung King Street at Tak Fung Street), a ship-shaped hunk of concrete that will never set sail, as it is, in fact, a shopping mall. With four levels (or 'decks'), the 100-metre-long (328-foot) ship houses upmarket shops, restaurants, a playground and a cinema.

Aside from the Whampoa, there are only a few other parts of Hung Hom worth visiting. Close by, on the waterfront near the bus terminus, is the impressive five-star **Harbour Plaza**. The bar/restaurant outside is a relaxed, if somewhat expensive, place for snacks in an al fresco setting with easterly views of the harbour.

A hidden gem worth seeking out in the area is **Sung Kit Street**, a pedestrian alley off Bailey Street that is crowded with – unusually for Hong Kong – cheap and unpretentious Japanese restaurants; elsewhere in the city such places are often both pricey and posey.

Conveniently, the Star Ferry sails frequently from the Hung Hom Ferry Pier (just in front of the bus terminus) to Wan Chai and Central.

## Yau Ma Tei & Mong Kok

North of Kowloon Park, Tsim Sha Tsui melds imperceptibly into the district of **Yau Ma Tei**. This, along with **Mong Kok** further north, is a gritty but very interesting district. Yau Ma Tei

means 'hemp oil ground' in Cantonese, although the only examples to be found in this completely urbanised area today are in shops. But what the area does have to offer are street markets, temples and masses of authentic backstreet atmosphere. Both Yau Ma Tei and Mong Kok are crammed with markets, including the perennially popular Jade Market in Yau Ma Tei and the bustling, fragrant Mong Kok Flower Market on – you guessed it – Flower Market Road.

## Yau Ma Tei

Jordan MTR is a good starting point from which to explore Yau Ma Tei. To find the heart of the district, take exit A out of the MTR station and head west along Jordan Road to Temple Street and walk north. This is where you'll find the heart of the **Temple Street Night Market** (see p170), which, as its name implies, is at its best after dark. There is a good deal of junk on sale here, but you can usually find a few decent buys – particularly cheap designer fakes – if you look hard enough. On the corner of Temple and Pak Hoi Streets, half a dozen or so inexpensive canteen-style restaurants operate out of a small covered area, serving food until late. The squeamish may want to avoid it, however, as the table etiquette here, as in most basic Chinese establishments, regards spitting gristle and bone fragments on to the plastic table tops as entirely acceptable.

If you haven't already seen a Chinese food and produce market, Reclamation Street, which runs parallel with Temple Street (two blocks to the west), hosts a large **food market** during the day. Virtually the entire area around the street, stretching between Argyle Street to the north, Ferry Street to the west and Nathan Road to the east, is full of interesting Chinese shops and businesses, including funeral parlours, herbalists and health tea shops. **Ning Po Street** is particularly impressive: check out the shop at No.21, which specialises in snake products; its walls are lined with jars of pickled reptiles. You'll also find a number of paper shops here selling items destined to be burnt at funerals, such as paper clothes, cars, paper money, mah-jong sets and fragile paper houses.

At the end of Temple Street (on Kansu Street under the flyover just west of the top end of Temple Street) is the famous **Jade Market** (see p170). Inside the small covered market, around 50 stalls sell jade ornaments and jewellery, as well as carved bone trinkets. Be prepared for some heavy-duty bargaining, and know how much the items cost elsewhere before you buy. Unless you're a jade expert (or have one handily in tow), don't part with any

**Kowloon Park**
(*see p89*) and around.

**Tin Hau Temple** in Yau Ma Tei.

significant sums – it's all too easy for novices to be ripped off. The market officially stays open till 6pm but it's best to go early in the day as some vendors close up shop around lunchtime.

A minute's walk north-east of the Jade Market is Yau Ma Tei's sizeable **Tin Hau Temple** (open 8am-6pm daily), divided into three separate areas for the worship of Hong Kong's favourite deities: Tin Hau (the sea goddess), Shing Wong, the city god, and To Tei, the earth god. It costs nothing to enter and look around, but it is considered polite to make a small contribution. Photography is frowned upon, though not expressly forbidden. In the evenings, numerous fortune-tellers gather outside the temple to offer their services. There is a choice of face and palm readers, as well as 'birds of fortune' (small birds that supposedly tell your fortune by picking out tarot-style cards when they're released from their cages). A couple more fortune-tellers, one of them advertising fortunes told in English, also operate from the annexe at the far end of the temple building during the day.

## Mong Kok

Most of the sights and shopping in Mong Kok are located to the east of Mong Kok MTR. One of its busiest markets is known as the **Ladies' Market** (running the length of Tung Choi Street), even though it sells a huge range of goods not necessarily restricted to female tastes. Clothes, CDs, luggage, sandals, feather boas and wigs are all here in abundance, along with other essentials like clothes-fluff removers and eyelash curlers.

Running parallel to the market is **Fa Yuen Street**, where dozens of shops sell trainers and other sports goods, while at the northern end of the market, along Tung Choi Street, is the **Goldfish Market**, which is more a cluster of well-stocked goldfish shops than an actual market. Goldfish are extremely popular among the Chinese (they are believed to bring good luck and to help absorb bad vibes – and are good quiet pets for small noisy flats), and there is a fascinating variety of breeds on offer. While most are reasonably priced, some are mind-bogglingly expensive.

A short walk north of here along Prince Edward Road West brings you to the **Flower Market**. This delightful place consists of a long line of shops and stalls selling a huge array of exotic flowers and budding branches, often at very reasonable prices. This vivid street teems with customers year round, but is particularly crowded around Chinese New Year.

A stretch of garden running alongside Yuen Po Street at the far end of Flower Market Road is a gathering place for local bird lovers. The **Bird Market** (*see also p170*) is alive with the twitter and chirp of many species of songbird and parrot (many illegally smuggled). Many enthusiasts take their own birds along, usually in delicately wrought (and often wretchedly tiny) cages. A dozen or so stalls sell birds, bird food and accessories, including bags of grasshoppers, which are fed to the birds using chopsticks. The ornate cages make fine souvenirs themselves and are reasonably priced.

At the top end of the garden runs **Boundary Street**, the old Kowloon–China border. After Britain forced China to cede the Kowloon Peninsula to them in 1860, they then became worried that it wasn't enough. As fears about the growing influence of other Western powers over China grew (particularly considering new gunnery technology that increased the range of artillery) and concerns about the lack of a fresh water supply for the colony were raised, the British persuaded the Chinese government into leasing the New Territories to them for 99 years in 1898. The decision to ask for only a temporary lease on the land made for tremendous administrative and diplomatic problems in subsequent decades. Hong Kong Island and Kowloon had been permanently ceded, but the necessity of returning the New Territories to China in 1997, and the overspill of development from the 1910s onwards, made the retention of the rest of the colony untenable.

## Eastern Kowloon

Although the area just to the north of Boundary Street is officially part of the New Territories, it became locally known as 'New Kowloon' in the early 20th century; that designation has long-since lapsed, and today the sprawling conurbation goes by the name of **Eastern Kowloon**.

While much of it is of little interest to tourists, there are a handful of places worth visiting. To the east along the Quarry Bay MTR line are the large, busy Wong Tai Sin Temple and the beautiful and strange Kowloon Walled City Park, while to the west along the Tsuen Wan MTR line is the cheap clothes and goods market of Sham Shui Po.

## East along the Quarry Bay line

When you arrive in Eastern Kowloon, you are likely to feel that you've wandered into a massive building site – much of it is continually being torn down and replaced by newer, taller tower blocks, shopping centres and office blocks. (The height restrictions in Kowloon, necessary while the old Kai Tak airport was in use, have now been lifted.) The construction noise is easily avoided, however, and a good starting point for exploring the area on foot is the Lok Fu MTR station. When you come out of the station, walk down Wang Tau Hom East Road and turn left at the T-junction along Junction Road. On the left-hand side of the road you'll see the **Chinese Christian Cemetery**,

**Sightseeing**

# Taking it back

If you take one of the earliest maps of the city from the 1840s and lay it over a present-day version, the difference is astonishing. Today's Hong Kong is, unsurprisingly, vastly bigger, but it's the pattern of growth that's unusual. Rather than creep outwards across the land, Hong Kong takes earth from the quarries and uses it to fill in the sea. Jagged coastlines have been steadily transformed into straight lines, and entire bays have disappeared. Even Victoria Harbour is smaller than it used to be – originally 7,000 hectares in area (27 square miles), it's now a mere 3,839 hectares (about 12 square miles).

One of the main reasons why land reclamation has such a long history here is to do with Hong Kong's system of land tenure and the various means that have been employed to generate revenue. Land holdings are all ultimately vested in the government, and supply has always been kept restricted to maintain an artificially high price. To this day, land sales provide the government with a sizeable chunk of its annual income.

In the 19th century the government raised revenue from the sale of monopolies on retail alcohol and opium sales and – bizarrely – nightsoil collection for fertiliser, as well as land sales. There were no customs duties, limited excise, no VAT and no income taxes until after World War II; even now, more than 70 per cent of the population pays little or no tax.

So the money for roads, sewers, waterworks and hospitals has had to come from elsewhere, and land sales have traditionally filled the gap. In areas such as Central, where land for building has already

been exhausted, filling in the adjacent sea bed becomes an attractive option, made even more tempting by the fact that land created by reclamation is relatively cheap to make and can be sold for a massive premium.

To get some perspective on the full extent of land reclamation, consider two examples. The electric tramlines running along the northern side of Hong Kong Island, from Kennedy Town to Shau Kei Wan, roughly follow the original 1841 shoreline; anything to the north – including most of the business district – is built on landfill. On the Kowloon side, Yau Ma Tei's Tin Hau Temple was once on the shoreline, as befits a shrine to the goddess of the sea. It is now marooned almost three kilometres (two miles) inland. The road in front of the temple, Reclamation Street, is named after the first phase of harbour fill undertaken here in the late 19th century.

So what does the future hold for Victoria Harbour? Of course, this is one of Hong Kong's major scenic assets, and has huge recreational potential if pollution is brought under control. Progressive narrowing of the harbour has already significantly increased wave size and choppiness around the piers, even in calm conditions; as a result ferries now take longer to berth. On the plus side, public attitudes towards marine reclamation are changing, and people are realising that, as far as near-indiscriminate harbour fill is concerned, enough is enough. Grass-roots action groups have emerged, and, following sustained, well-articulated public protests, the government recently scrapped large reclamation plans for the western harbour area around Green Island.

with its graves stacked up and squeezed into every available piece of ground. Nearby is the tiny and very lovely **Hau Wong Temple** (open 8am-5pm daily), built in 1737 and shaded by tall feathery bamboo. The temple is dedicated to one of the exiled boy-emperor Zhao Bing's most loyal generals.

Close to the temple is an oasis of fountains, elaborate topiary, sculptures and meandering walkways in the **Kowloon Walled City Park** (open 6.30am-11pm daily). Inside the old almshouse, facing the main entrance on Tung Tsing Road, is a display about the intriguing history of the Walled City, which once stood where the garden is today. Built by the Chinese in the mid 19th century as part of the empire's southern coastal defences, the fortress was inexplicably left out of the lease of the New Territories by the British in 1898. After World War II, much of the fort was levelled by Japanese forces, and high-rise apartments sprang up. Squatters and, later, triads moved in, creating a lawless underworld that thrived until 1992, when the buildings were pulled down.

Also worth a visit is **Wong Tai Sin Temple** (*see below*). Located close to the Wong Tai Sin MTR station, one stop from Lok Fu, the temple is one of Hong Kong's largest, busiest and most interesting places of worship. The complex contains altars and shrines to several Buddhist, Confucian and Taoist deities, and is regularly filled with thronging worshippers, an almost unbelievable level of noise and – inevitably – swirling incense. Near the main temple is a large covered area containing more than 100 fortune-teller stalls. Several of these soothsayers can reveal your fortune in English, mostly through palm and face reading. You're likely to be quoted about HK$300 for a five-minute consultation, but it should be possible to haggle them down to HK$100 or even less. Kneeling in front of the main temple's altar, many Chinese can be seen and heard solemnly shaking small canisters of bamboo sticks – known as *chim* – until one finally emerges from the can. Each stick is marked with a numeral and a corresponding meaning. Many users immediately head to the fortune-tellers to have their stick interpreted.

An alternative method of divination known as *sing pei,* or 'Buddha's lips', uses *bui,* two pieces of wood shaped like orange segments. A question is asked, the *bui* are thrown and the 'lips' answer 'yes' or 'no', depending on which way they land.

The next stop on the MTR line is Diamond Hill, from where it is a short and well-signposted walk to the austerely beautiful **Chi Lin Buddhist Nunnery** (*see below*),

larger but more serene than Wong Tai Sin Temple. Its yellow cedar timbers and elegantly tiled roof are new (although built in the ancient Tang style of architecture), while the carefully contrived layout of the large courtyard, temple and gardens all contribute to a sense of order and calm. The temples hold large and finely sculpted golden statues of various incarnations of the Buddha.

The small, charming village of **Lei Yue Mun**, which has long been a favourite destination for seafood lovers, lies at the very southern tip of Kowloon in the eastern part of Victoria harbour. (To get there, take the MTR to Kwun Tong station, and then the number 14C bus to its terminus at Sam Ka Tsuen typhoon shelter.) Once you arrive in the village, walk east from the edge of the small harbour (past the large modern library) and turn right around the edge of the harbour to find the heart of the village. Here, there are dark narrow alleyways, hemmed in by hundreds of tanks filled with marine life, and, further into the village, several seafood restaurants. Prices aren't cheap – most people are attracted more by the experience of eating in the village's bucolic environs than the food itself. But there's the advantage of being able to choose and buy your dinner from one of the seafood vendors; the restaurants will then cook it for a fee. Make sure you agree on a price first, as tourist rip-offs occur here with tiresome regularity.

Aside from the seafood restaurants, Lei Yue Mun is still a thriving coastal village and there's plenty going on throughout the week. If you make it out here on a weekday, wander further into the village, past the boisterously playing children in the primary school playground, which is filled with concrete animals, and along the shore towards the small Tin Hau Temple on the shoreline, where you can see dozens of rod fishermen crouching on the rocks.

### Chi Lin Buddhist Nunnery
*5 Chi Lin Drive, Diamond Hill (2354 1730/ www.chilin.org). Diamond Hill MTR (exit C2).* **Open** 9am-4.30pm daily. **Admission** free. **Map** p307.
This elegant and peaceful complex was first constructed in the 1930s and substantially rebuilt in the 1990s in the style of the Tang Dynasty (AD 618-907). The attached nunnery contains some fine statues of the Sakyamuni Buddha, and the water lily ponds in the courtyards are extremely beautiful.

### Wong Tai Sin Temple
*2 Chuk Yuen, Wong Tai Sin (2328 0270/2327 8141/www.siksikyuen.org.hk). Wong Tai Sin MTR (exit B2).* **Open** 7am-5.30pm daily. **Admission** free. **Map** p307.

The **Jamia Masjid Islamic Centre**. *See p86.*

Facing the past at the **Hong Kong Museum of History**. *See p89*.

This sprawling temple complex is primarily dedicated to the god Wong Tai Sin. Before he was deified, Wong Tai Sin was a shepherd from Zhejiang Province who was taught how to make a healing potion by a *xian* ('fairy immortal'). He then went on to perform many miracles among the sick, and was deified. Religious devotion in the temple is not strictly limited to Wong Tai Sin, however, as it also takes in a broad sweep of Taoist, Confucian and Buddhist deities. One of the best-known temples in Hong Kong, it is thronged with visitors, many of them tourists from the mainland, Taiwan and South-east Asia. The excellent website has useful background information.

## West along the Tsuen Wan line

Travelling west through New Kowloon, one of the first worthwhile stops is **Sham Shui Po Market**, close to Sham Shui Po MTR station. Although this open-air market and its surrounding shops are not unique, they do sell a diverse range of goods and the prices are very low. Outside the Apliu Street exit of the MTR, the extensive street market stretches away in all directions. Here, luggage and clothes are probably as cheap as they get this side of the Chinese border, although the choice is not as great as in Shenzhen.

To the north-west of the MTR station, on Yen Chow Street, there's a large computer market in the upstairs section of the Golden Shopping Centre; prices are marginally

better than in Kowloon. A few metres away at 100 Yen Chow Street, a good VCD and DVD shop has an extremely comprehensive selection of US and UK TV series, as well as hundreds of (mostly Cantonese-language) films. For more on Apliu Street Market, *see p170* **Market places**.

After perusing the wares on offer at the centre, get back on to the MTR and head one stop north-west to Cheung Sha Wan, home of the **Lei Cheng Uk Han Tomb Museum** (*see below*), located an easy and well-signposted walk from the station. Turn left up Tonkin Street and the museum is just over Po On Road, past the public garden.

## Lei Cheng Uk Han Tomb Museum

*41 Tonkin Street, Sham Shui Po (2386 2863/ www.lcsd.gov.hk/CE/Museum/History/leicheng/ english/index.html). Cheung Sha Wan MTR (exit A2, A3)/bus 2 from Kowloon Star Ferry.* **Open** 10am-1pm, 2-6pm Mon-Wed, Fri, Sat; 1-6pm Sun. **Admission** free. **Map** p307.
This Han-era tomb chamber dates to the Eastern Han Dynasty (AD 24-220). Uncovered by workmen in 1955 while building a public housing estate, this ancient burial tomb is worth a quick look if you're in the area. There's a small display of the finds (mostly pottery) excavated from the tomb. The tomb itself, visible through a Perspex sheet and resembling a small brick kiln, is outside in the courtyard. Alas, there's very little information about who built the complex and for whom it was constructed. Don't come expecting anything like Tutankhamen's Tomb, or you'll be very disappointed.

# The New Territories

Largely ignored by tourists, the other face of Hong Kong is home to stunning natural parks and wide open spaces.

The New Territories – extending from Boundary Street in the middle of downtown Kowloon northwards to the Shum Chun River – were leased from China in 1898 for 99 years under the Convention of Peking – hence the beginning of the entire '1997' issue. This dramatically beautiful region of lowland valleys, jagged mountain ranges, deeply incised coastline and hundreds of islands is the lesser-known side of Hong Kong that most casual visitors to the territory never see.

Today, more than three million people (over 40 per cent of Hong Kong's total population) live in this extensive region. Despite some unsightly, badly planned urban, commercial and industrial developments (particularly in the west), large tracts of unspoiled countryside still remain, and hundreds of square kilometres are given over to country parks. More than 40 per cent of Hong Kong's total land mass comprises country parks, and wonderful hiking and wildlife-watching are to be had along the New Territories' many mountainous trails. In addition, many of Hong Kong's finest beaches are in the remote and difficult to access north-east New Territories.

Significant rural settlements have existed here for hundreds of years, and as a result there is a considerable amount of authentic Chinese village heritage in the area. Dozens of temples, ancestral halls and walled villages – some dating back several centuries – are dotted around the countryside. Just don't expect to find the Forbidden City, the Great Wall or other

The **Hong Kong Heritage Museum**. *See p99.*

Tai Po's **Wishing Tree**. See p100.

impressive Imperial Chinese treasures here; the New Territories' heritage is overwhelmingly small-scale and rural. As a result, the real attractions are the mountains and countryside.

Happily, despite the region's lingering rural feel and considerable size, travel is very easy here. The Kowloon–Canton Railway (KCR), the Light Rail Transit (LRT) and West Rail in the west, the Mass Transit Railway (MTR) along Lantau's northern coast, excellent bus and minibus services and ferries all make even quite remote areas fairly accessible for the day-tripper. Note that the West Rail extension opened as this guide went to press, and visitors are advised to check local transportation before planning a trip.

Before exploring the mainland New Territories or the outlying islands, pay a visit to the Government Publications Centre (see p160) for one of the Countryside series of maps. These are an inexpensive way to help you get your bearings, plan your journey and make the most of what the region has to offer. Various small local outfits can help you organise guided walks and visits to the New Territories. While most trips can be done fairly easily on your own, for those with limited time who still want to experience something of this 'other Hong Kong', www.walkhongkong.com and resources listed on p41 may be of use. For further inspiration, see p39-p42 and p234-p242.

## Central New Territories

A day trip along the Kowloon-Canton Railway line from Sha Tin to Sheung Shui is a convenient way to experience something of life beyond the Kowloon hills, especially if you're only in Hong Kong for a short time. Along here you'll find hillside temples, two sprawling New Towns (Sha Tin and Tai Po) that are the 'real Hong Kong' for millions of local residents these days, Sha Tin's excellent Hong Kong Heritage Museum (see p99), and, glimpsed through the smog on a clear day, Shenzhen, Hong Kong's neighbouring Special Economic Zone.

### Tai Wai

The first stop on the KCR after passing through the Kowloon hills is **Tai Wai** (which today virtually merges into Sha Tin; see p99). **Amah Rock**, said to resemble a woman who was turned to stone by the gods after her husband failed to return from a fishing expedition (though it's actually a pre-Chinese phallic symbol), is the most prominent sight in the area. The stone can be reached from the station via Hung Miu Kuk Road and a subsequent path.

Closer to the station on Che Kung Miu Road is the popular **Che Kung Temple** (see p99), while another ten minutes' walk up the road is the impressive walled village known as **Tsang Tai Uk**. Translated as 'Tsang's big house', this mid 19th-century structure was built for members of the Tsang clan and is very well preserved, unlike other New Territories walled villages, most of which are squalid and badly decayed.

## Che Kung Temple

*7 Che Kung Miu Road (no phone). Tai Wai KCR. Follow exit sign to the temple; take the pedestrian subway.* **Open** 7am-6pm daily. **Admission** free. **Map** p307.

Dedicated to Che Kung, a legendary general who reputedly rid part of Guangdong province of plague, this is one of Hong Kong's most popular local temples and is especially thronged around the Lunar New Year period.

## Sha Tin

Hong Kong's first 'New Town', **Sha Tin** is large, well planned and extensive – and for many people a surprisingly attractive and interesting place, with generous expanses of parkland running along its riverfront.

The Sha Tin KCR station empties into the sprawling **New Town Plaza**, a popular shopping destination that, like many in other New Towns, represents the new face of the 'real Hong Kong'.

A 15-minute walk from the northern exit of the KCR is the **Ten Thousand Buddhas Monastery** (*see below*). Cross the road in front of the station and follow the signposts to the temple at the top of a wooded hill. You'll know you're on the right path when, after about five minutes or so, you begin to see the large, golden, scarlet-lipped Buddhas lining the steep route. Over 400 steps must be climbed to reach the temple, but it's worth the effort – there are more than 10,000 Buddha statues inside (as well as the mummified, gilded corpse of a former abbot inside a glass case).

Within walking distance of Sha Tin KCR station (and situated next to the Shing Mun riverside park), is the **Hong Kong Heritage Museum** (*see below*). This superb facility offers a fascinating and comprehensive social and anthropological history of Hong Kong – dating back to the region's geological formation. Its extensive static displays, audio-visual exhibits and interactive terminals cover more than 6,000 years of human existence in the region; it's well worth a visit.

Sha Tin's other main attraction – especially for legions of locals – is the **racecourse** (*see below*). Opened in 1980, this huge, high-tech stadium is strikingly juxtaposed against the backdrop of nearby hills. Tens of millions of dollars are wagered here every race-night.

## Hong Kong Heritage Museum

*1 Man Lam Road (2180 8188/www.heritage museum.gov.hk). Sha Tin KCR or Tai Wai KCR then 15min walk/A41, E42, 72A, 80M, 86, 89, N271, 282 bus.* **Open** 10am-6pm Mon, Wed-Sat; 10am-7pm Sun, public hols. **Admission** HK$10; concessions HK$5; free to all Wed. **No credit cards. Map** p307.

Opened in December 2000, the Hong Kong Heritage Museum, along with the Hong Kong Museum of History in Kowloon (*see p89*), is one of Hong Kong's best museums. There are six excellent permanent collections, plus plenty of space for temporary displays. The best, and largest, of the permanent exhibitions is the New Territories Heritage Hall. It explains how the landscape was formed, and illustrates the arrival of animal and prehistoric human life, the rise of the traditional village society, eventual colonial rule and the large-scale development of the New Territories towns. While you could spend all day in this one gallery, there's much more to see. Beautiful calligraphy and renderings of plants and animals by the acclaimed Lingnan artist Zhao Shao'ang hang from scrolls on the first floor, while the TT Tsui Gallery holds a wide range of ceramics dating back to neolithic times. There's also a colourful, educational exhibition on Cantonese Opera that explains some of the elaborate ritual involved.

## Sha Tin Racecourse

*Sha Tin (2966 8111/www.shatinracetrack.com). Racecourse KCR; phone for more detailed information.* **Admission** varies. **No credit cards. Map** p307.

While it does not quite have the atmosphere of the night races at Happy Valley (*see p242*), the vast scale of Sha Tin Racecourse is nonetheless impressive. Its backdrop of wide-open spaces and rugged hills is perhaps its greatest appeal. During the racing season (September-June), visitors can either pay the regular admission fee or stump up HK$50 to enter the Members' Enclosure, which guarantees entry to busy race meetings (you must be over 18, have been in Hong Kong for less than 21 days and bring your passport with you for inspection). Alternatively, join one of the excursions organised by the Hong Kong Tourism Board, which includes a decent buffet meal. *See also p242.*

## Ten Thousand Buddhas Monastery

*Sha Tin (2691 1067/www.10kbuddhas.org). Sha Tin KCR (exit B) then 20min walk via pedestrian bridge towards Grand Central Plaza.* **Open** 9am-5pm daily. **Admission** free. **Map** p307.

After a rather arduous climb up to the monastery's main building (especially taxing in the summer heat), you are rewarded at the top by the delightful sight of thousands of tiny golden Buddhas in hundreds of poses lining shelves that reach to the ceiling. More Buddha images can be found outside – there's a Buddha astride a giant white elephant and another atop a huge dog. Nearby, Buddha statues peer down from a bright red nine-storey pagoda. In a small annexe above the main temple lies the body of the

*Sightseeing*

temple's founding monk, who died in 1965. This annexe was recently closed to the public for repairs, but should it be open when you're here you can see him lying inside a glass case, covered in gold leaf. If the climb has made you peckish, the vegetarian canteen next to the main temple is cheap and tasty (a meal will set you back about HK$50).

## University

Two stops north of Sha Tin on the KCR is University station, serving the **Chinese University of Hong Kong**. Constantly changing exhibitions at the **Chinese University Art Museum** (*see below*) make the otherwise fairly ugly, 1960s-style campus worth a visit. The museum has a good – and extensive – collection that includes gold jewellery and jade ornaments, as well as numerous paintings and other items. (To reach the museum, exit the KCR on the campus (west) side, turn right and board the free campus shuttle bus. Get off at the second stop – the museum is close to the library and the administration building. The buildings are on the south side of the road, but are not immediately obvious and are badly signposted, so you may have to ask one of the students to point it out if you're in doubt.)

The area around the University KCR station is an ideal location to launch a boat trip to the islands of **Tap Mun Chau** ('Grassy Island'; *see p119*) and **Ping Chau** near the mainland coast, as well as to the remoter parts of the Sai Kung Peninsula at the mouth of Tolo Harbour. Ferries to the islands can be caught at Ma Liu Shui, a 15-minute walk from the station. Tap Mun is notable for its rugged peacefulness, beautiful beaches, the caves along its shores, its fishing village and a small **Tin Hau Temple** that dates back to the Qing dynasty. Also worth seeing is much smaller Ping Chau for its white sand beaches, soft coral formations and excellent beaches – beware of sharks here, though.

### Chinese University Art Museum

*Chinese University of Hong Kong, Tai Po Road (2609 7416/www.cuhk.edu.hk/ics/amm). University KCR then bus/coach.* **Open** 10am-4.45pm Mon-Sat; 12.30-5.30pm Sun. **Admission** free. **Map** p307.
The Hong Kong Museum of Art in Kowloon (*see p89*) and the Hong Kong Heritage Museum in Sha Tin (*see p99*) both have more interesting tradition-al Chinese paintings than the permanent collection on display here, but the museum is worth a visit for its large, impressive collection of decorative arts including fine ceramics, sculptures and jade. Some of the more than 7,000 items displayed date back to neolithic times. These, and other special collections, are shown on rotation, so, if you particularly want to see something specific, it's advisable to check what's on display before setting out.

## Tai Po

While at first glance **Tai Po** is just another of the newly created towns that dot the New Territories countryside, it is in fact centred around one of the area's oldest market towns and there are plenty of sites of interest here, including numerous buildings from the early British period.

One feature that has become very popular in recent years – but was unknown before – is the **Wishing Tree**. This large Chinese banyan lies a 20-minute bus ride from Tai Po Market station (take the number 64K bus to the Fong Ma Po stop). For a few dollars, the stallholders around the tree – you can't miss it, it's covered in oranges and paper streamers – will sell you an orange with a vividly coloured streamer attached to it. Write your wish on the streamer and hurl the orange at the tree. If the fruit lodges among the branches, your wish will come true.

You can wander around **Tai Po Market** for an hour or so, and the old district office and police station on the hillside can also be visited. Both are popular nesting places for egrets: hundreds of the bony creatures can be seen perched on the trees surrounding the buildings.

The **Hong Kong Railway Museum** (*see below*) near the market also warrants a peek if you are a train lover. The Chinese-style station is a reminder of what all the original KCR stations looked like. Nearby on Fu Shin Street is the 19th-century **Man Mo Temple**.

From Tai Po you can board a bus for the wild country and walking trails around the man-made **Plover Cove reservoir**. This inlet on the Tolo harbour was dammed in the 1960s; it's a popular spot for weekend strollers.

Nature lovers should also make the effort to visit the lovely **Kadoorie Farm & Botanic Garden** (*see p104*), a pioneering education and conservation project outside Tai Po

### Hong Kong Railway Museum

*13 Shung Tak Street, Tai Po Market (2653 3455/ www.heritagemuseum.gov.hk/english/branch.htm). Tai Po Market KCR then minibus 25K.* **Open** 9am-5pm Mon, Wed-Sun, public hols. **Admission** free. **Map** p307.
It's hardly a must-see sight, but rail enthusiasts and those with time to kill can peruse exhibits that include an old narrow-gauge engine, a few railway carriages and some models. Photos of the old water-front Tsim Sha Tsui KCR railway station provide interesting glimpses of Kowloon in earlier times.

## Fanling & Lo Wai

Continuing north along the KCR, the biggest attraction for most visitors to the small town of **Fanling** is the Lung Yuek Tau Heritage Trail.

**Chuk Lam Shim Yuen Monastery.**
*See p105.*

Before setting off on the hike, pop into the **Fung Ying Sin Koon Temple** (open 9am-5pm daily), located a three-minute walk from the west exit of the station. A large, modern Taoist temple, it includes a section dedicated to the deities of particular years (past, current and future) and their corresponding Chinese birth signs. Worshippers pray, bow and make offerings to the idol corresponding to their own birth sign.

A ten-minute ride on the number 54K bus from the eastern side of the KCR will bring you to the **Tang Chung Ling Ancestral Hall** (*see below*), one of the largest of its kind in the New Territories. The hall lies along the **Lung Yuek Tau Heritage Trail**, which passes five *wai tsuen* (walled villages) and six *uk tsuen* (unwalled villages), within a couple of kilometres of each other. The Ancestral Hall is the best starting point for hitting the trail – it is on a bus route and there's a detailed map posted outside. Walking the trail is easily accomplished in a morning or afternoon, but be aware that the signposting is patchy along the way.

Probably the best-preserved walled village on the trail is **Lo Wai**. The village gate and watchtower, along with the old walls, are all still intact. Tourists are welcome to visit, but don't prowl around too close to private houses. Nearby **Ma Wat Wai** still has its well-preserved main entrance, first built in the 1700s, along with its iron chain-link gate.

### Tang Chung Ling Ancestral Hall

*Ping Che Road, Lo Wai (Antiquities & Monuments Office 2721 2326/www.lcsd.gov.hk/CE/Museum/Monument). Fanling KCR then minibus 54K.* **Open** 9am-1pm, 2-5pm Mon, Wed-Sun. **Admission** free. **Map** p307.

Dating back more than 500 years, this large ancestral hall was founded by the Tang clan, one of the five great New Territories clans. You'll find some ancient and ornate ancestral tablets at the end of the temple, including those of the *Wong Kwu* (Emperor's Aunt), a 12th-century princess of the southern Song Dynasty who married into the Tang clan after escaping the invading Mongol hordes. Despite its popularity with tourists and visitors, Tang Chung Ling is still an active meeting hall where clan members pay respects to their ancestors, and hold meetings and celebrations, much as their families have done for centuries.

### Sheung Shui & beyond

**Sheung Shui** is the last stop on the KCR before it reaches the border at Lo Wu. Sheung Shui is the most convenient stop for bird-watching trips to the world-famous **Mai Po Marshes** (*see p106*), seasonal home to numerous species of migratory birds. Not far

from Sheung Shui, near the village of Wing Ping Tsuen, is **Tai Fu Tai** (*see below*), a mansion known locally – and somewhat erroneously – as the 'Mandarin's House'. This attractive Chinese home incorporates various European decorative elements. It was first built in 1865 by a senior member of the Man clan from nearby San Tin. (To get here, take the number 76K bus from outside Sheung Shui KCR station, or the No.17 minibus – alight when you see San Tin post office. Signposts mark the way to Tai Fu Tai, which is located a few minutes' walk north of the post office.)

Two kilometres (one and a quarter miles) to the north-east of Tai Fu Tai is the old border lookout of **Lok Ma Chau** (while it's possible to walk the route from Tai Fu Tai, it's certainly simpler and much faster to take a taxi). The lookout is just a few hundred metres from the Shum Chun River, the border between the Hong Kong Special Administrative Region and the neighbouring city of **Shenzhen** (*see p163* **Shopping in Shenzhen**). Shenzhen has grown rapidly over the past two decades, changing from a quiet country village into the bustling modern city it is today.

### Tai Fu Tai

*Antiquities & Monuments Office 2721 2326/www.lcsd.gov.hk/CE/Museum/Monument. Sheung Shui KCR then 76K bus/17 minibus towards Yuen Long; alight at Wing Ping Tsuen.* **Open** 9am-1pm, 2-5pm Mon, Wed-Sun, public hols. **Admission** free.

This large, ornate house, built in about 1865, is one of the New Territories' better restored heritage sites. It was once the home of Man Chung-luen, a senior Qing Dynasty civil servant, or *dai fu*.

## West New Territories

Large, modern satellite towns dominate much of the southern coast and low-lying valleys of the western New Territories. Beyond them are vast expanses of wilderness, much of it contained within the borders of country parks at Lam Tsuen, Tai Lam and Tai Mo Shan. Mai Po Marshes, one of Hong Kong's most pristine wilderness areas, is also nearby along the southern shores of Deep Bay.

### Tsuen Wan & Tai Mo Shan

An industrial/residential/commercial agglomeration at the end of the MTR line, **Tsuen Wan** gradually developed in the immediate post-war era from a small market settlement into a major industrial area. While at first glance it is rather ugly, crowded and traffic-congested, Tsuen Wan and places like

View from **Tai Mo Shan**, looking south towards Hong Kong Island.

it are nevertheless the 'real Hong Kong' and merit a visit for a flavour of that authenticity, if for nothing else.

A five-minute walk east of the MTR (take exit B3 to Sai Lau Kok Road) is the **Sam Tung Uk Museum** (*see p106*). Actually an 18th-century walled village, it was only recently made into a museum, because until then it was an active residential site – home to members of the Chan clan who migrated from the Fujian province. In 1980, when the last residents finally moved out, it was turned into a museum. Many people feel that its authenticity was damaged when it was subjected to a restoration programme, and while worth a look, like many village museums, it has a curiously dead air about it.

If the intricacies of large-scale engineering projects are your thing (and only then), you'll be interested in the **Airport Core Programme Exhibition Centre** (*see p104*), just west of the Ting Kau bridge. This small exhibition details the huge project of building Hong Kong's new international airport on the levelled island of Chek Lap Kok. Along with the associated bridges, highways and tunnels, Chek Lap Kok was the single most extensive civil engineering project ever undertaken at one time in history, anywhere. Like it or not, the sheer scale of the achievement is impressive.

Other things to be enjoyed near Tsuen Wan are a walk in the hills nearby. Up above the city is one of the area's best temple complexes –

**Chuk Lam Shim Yuen Monastery** ('Bamboo Forest Monastery'; *see p105*), a working Buddhist retreat, founded in 1927. Unfortunately, it's not a particularly pleasant stroll to reach the monastery from the town – as much of it is along and under busy highways – so it is more sensible to treat yourself to a taxi (about HK$30).

A short distance away is another temple facility, the **Yuen Yuen Institute** (*see p106*), which is the one sight that most visitors to Tsuen Wan want to see. It's a large active facility housing Buddhist, Taoist and Confucianist temples.

On the hillside just above the institute are footpaths leading up to **Tai Mo Shan**, Hong Kong's highest peak (its name means 'Big Hat Mountain', a reference to its shape as seen from a distance). It's a serious climb to the top, and you'll need to be well prepared: equip yourself with a decent map, plenty of water and suitable attire. You'll need to allow about six hours for a round trip from Tsuen Wan. There are no facilities or shops on the way or at the summit (except a small kiosk at the visitors' centre on Route Twisk open only on weekends and public holidays), and there's no fast ride down on a funicular if you get tired or bored. The route is pretty, although more spectacular trails to the top lie along the **MacLehose Trail** (*see also p39*), which runs roughly east to west on either side of Tai Mo

# Kadoorie Farm & Botanic Garden

For several decades after British rule was extended in 1898 the New Territories remained, for the most part, an underprivileged, under-serviced, under-policed rural backwater. Contrary to popular belief, the massive post-war population influx that greatly transformed Hong Kong did not only settle in the urban areas. Many New Territories villagers, especially in the northern areas, had relatives on the other side of what until 1950 was a porous, largely theoretical land border. Communist campaigns against rich peasants and rural landlords in the early 1950s saw many villagers moving across to the British side of the Shum Chun River, thus putting further population pressure on existing villages and farmland.

In response to this situation, in 1951 prominent Sephardic Jewish businessmen (Lord) Lawrence and (Sir) Horace Kadoorie set up a rural improvement project, the Kadoorie Agricultural Aid Association (KAAA), to help alleviate the situation. Priority was given to providing much-needed facilities that would have long-term benefits, thus producing self-reliance rather than ongoing welfare dependency. Many rural pathways and bridges over small streams in more remote parts of the New Territories, now mostly used by weekend ramblers, were originally paid for by the KAAA to help improve village access. Far-flung outlying islands were given piers to enable farmers to take produce to market and bring back fertilizers and supplies; the Association also made gifts of sampans and outboard motors where necessary. Small dams, wells and irrigation sumps were built; sumps – small concrete tanks set below ground level with steps leading in and out – were especially welcome as they

are a great time- and labour-saver for farmers who would otherwise have to water their vegetable fields with watering cans.

With the decline in commercial farming in Hong Kong over the past two decades the organisation now focuses more on education and conservation, based at the magnificent **Kadoorie Farm & Botanic Garden** (KFBG), which nestles below Kwun Yum Shan (Goddess of Mercy Mountain) in the Central New Territories. More than a half of all the diverse plants found within Hong Kong are now growing at the KFBG, but its activities don't stop with the study and preservation of flora. Many of Hong Kong's larger mammals, as well as amphibians, reptiles and insects, can also be seen here, and there is also an organic farm where you can purchase fresh produce.

One of the KFBG's particular concerns is the protection of native orchids and other rare flora and the rehabilitation of raptors (birds of prey) originally destined for restaurant tables. Other features include a waterfowl enclosure, a butterfly house and a deer haven and an animal rescue centre.

Except for Sunday, when no cars are allowed, people can hike up or drive up to all the exhibits. Guided tours for groups of 20 are offered but advance booking is required. Indeed, phoning before a visit is the normal procedure (parking space can also be reserved). It's worth asking about special activities, which include tree planting, Earth Day celebrations and an organic festival.

## Kadoorie Farm & Botanic Garden

*Lam Kam Road, Tai Po (2488 1317/ www.kfbg.org.hk). Tai Po Market or Tai Wo KCR then 64K bus.* **Open** by prior appointment only 9.30am-5pm daily. **Admission** free. **Map** p307.

Shan's summit. The peak is dominated by a telecommunications complex, which is off-limits to the public, but there are still good views of the countryside, and you should be able to take photos that aren't filled with aluminium scaffolding and cables.

Nevertheless, despite the direct line of sight across to Hong Kong Island, it is likely to be almost totally obscured, even on a cloudless day, by smog. But if you're lucky and hit the trail on a really clear day, the views are absolutely stunning. The best way back to

the city is to walk down the road to the edge of **Tai Mo Shan Country Park** and then catch the number 51 bus back to Tsuen Wan MTR station.

## Airport Core Programme Exhibition Centre

*401 Castle Peak Road, Ting Kau (2491 9202/ www.info.gov.hk/.napco/exhibition.html). Tsuen Wan MTR (exit E) then 96M bus; alight at Ting Kau.* **Open** 10am-5pm Tue-Fri; 10am-6.30pm Sat, Sun, public hols. **Admission** free. **Map** p306.

This expensively mounted exhibition offers plenty of impressive statistics about the ten large infrastructure projects connected with the new Chek Lap Kok airport – like how many times the huge steel cables used to construct the bridges could stretch round the world. While there are a few decent visuals, the exhibition doesn't really do justice to the enormity of the civil engineering that went into the creation of the airport. The Centre's best feature is the viewing platform on the roof, which offers good views over the harbour and across to the Tsing Ma and Ting Kau bridges – on a rare clear day, that is.

## Chuk Lam Shim Yuen Monastery

*Fu Yung Shan, Tsuen Wan (2490 3392). Tsuen Wan MTR (exit B1) then taxi/minibus 85 from Shiu Wo Street to Fu Yung Shan.* **Open** 9am-5pm daily. **Admission** free. **Map** p306.

This hillside facility houses several large and precious statues of the Buddha. On most days, monks clad in mustard-coloured robes can be seen chanting and offering prayers in the temple at the far end of the complex. With its large grounds and tranquil setting, the monastery is atmospheric and often free of tourists – it's almost worth visiting for that reason alone.

## Sam Tung Uk Museum

*2 Kwu Uk Lane, Tsuen Wan (2411 2001/*
*www.lcsd.gov.hk/stum). Tsuen Wan MTR (exit E)*
*then 10min walk/40, 43X, 905 bus.* **Open** 9am-5pm
Mon, Wed-Sun. **Admission** free. **Map** p306.

Those looking for bustling village authenticity may
be a little disappointed, as this walled village was
largely rebuilt when the last residents were resettled
in nearby high-rise estates more than 20 years ago.
In addition, many of the materials used in the
reconstruction were sourced from southern China.
However, it's an interesting and creditable (if somewhat sanitised) attempt to paint a picture of life in a
New Territories walled village a century or so ago.

## Yuen Yuen Institute

*Sam Dip Tam, Tsuen Wan (2492 2220/*
*www.yuenyuen.org.hk). Tsuen Wan MTR (exit B1)*
*then minibus 81 from Shiu Wo Street.* **Open** 8.30am-
5pm daily. **Admission** free. **Map** p306.

This highly popular Buddhist, Confucianist and
Taoist complex is on the agenda of most New
Territories tourists, as well as worshipping locals
making offerings. It includes a temple dedicated to
the deities in charge of certain years and birth signs

(similar to the Fung Ying Sin Koon temple in
Fanling; *see p102*). The statues within are all finely
carved, while a sign outside updates believers as to
which birth signs might have trouble with the earth
god of the current year and suggests making offerings to the relevant deity at the beginning and end
of the year to help balance out the potential ill effects.
The on-site vegetarian restaurant is also popular
with both local worshippers and tourists – the
former including mostly elderly or retired people.

## Along the LRT line from
## Tuen Mun towards Yuen Long

**Tuen Mun** was the site of the first known
landfall in China by European mariners;
Portuguese sailor Jorge Alvares landed there in
1513 and returned again in 1524. The district is
now a large New Town close to the far western
edge of the New Territories, and dominated by
dramatically beautiful **Castle Peak**.

Although unpromising on first sight,
the Tuen Mun district contains a couple of
interesting and accessible temples, as well as

# Mai Po Marshes

Within sight and sound of neighbouring
Shenzhen, a surprising amount of (mostly
avian) wildlife flourishes in Hong Kong's
richest habitat: Mai Po. Extensive fish ponds,
mangroves and Deep Bay's marshy coastline
attract a huge variety of bird and animal life to
this globally significant wetland. Cormorants,
egrets, kingfishers and herons are just some
of the bird species populating the marshes
(around 60,000 birds winter here each year).
The 38-square kilometre (15-square mile)
reserve is also the New Territories' last
haven for otters, and one of the last habitats
for the critically endangered black-faced
spoonbill and Saunders' gull. Tens of
thousands of migratory birds pass through
here – some fly on from Mai Po to Australia
without feeding, a journey of more than
6,500 kilometres (4,000 miles). Mai Po is
also the only remaining area where *gei wai*,
traditional Chinese prawn ponds, are still
maintained and farmed, though they remain
a common feature elsewhere in the Pearl
River Delta region.

The reserve is very flat, which makes
for easy walking. Several bird hides provide
good cover and the main hide is equipped
with powerful binoculars. Due to the gradual
disappearance of similar regional habitats
as development and pollution have taken

their toll, Mai Po has become more
ecologically significant in recent years. But
like most parts of Hong Kong, the marshes
have not escaped pollution. Sewage and
industrial waste flushed into Deep Bay
from Hong Kong and mainland China have
drastically affected the area's food chain
since the early 1980s, and are thought to be
the main reason behind an alarming decline
in bird numbers in recent years.

Mai Po lies within the Closed Border Area
adjoining the mainland frontier. As it is
a restricted area, entry requires a permit.
The easiest way to visit is as part of a World
Wildlife Fund (WWF) tour, run every weekend
and on public holidays. Tours last about three
hours and cost HK$70 per person (binoculars
can be hired for HK$20). Tour bookings are
taken two weeks in advance and are run in
the mornings and afternoons. Tours in English
require a minimum of ten people. To reach
Mai Po, take the KCR to Sheung Shui, then
the 76K bus towards Yuen Long until you get
to the reserve entrance. On the way back,
either catch the bus back to Sheung Shui
or continue to Yuen Long, taking the 968
bus to Causeway Bay.

For further information on the marshes,
phone WWF on 2526 1011 or visit its
website: www.wwf.org.hk/eng/maipo.

the Ping Shan Heritage Trail close to Yuen Long. Getting to Tuen Mun is easy – take the number 960 or 962 bus from Central and around an hour later you'll be here. Once you're here, it shouldn't take long to get the hang of the excellent Light Rail Transit (LRT), a very simple, efficient and cheap tram network. The LRT links Tuen Mun with Yuen Long further east and the sprawling conurbation between them. (Octopus cards – *see p278* – are accepted on the LRT and must be validated at the correct terminal before boarding and again when alighting.)

As soon as you arrive, your first stop should be the **Ching Chung Koon Temple** (*see below*), a Taoist temple set in lovely, carefully cultivated grounds. Climbing back on to the LRT and travelling two stops further north to Lam Tei LRT station will bring you to the modern and elaborately endowed **Miu Fat Buddhist Monastery** (*see below*).

Perhaps the most rewarding place to spend an hour or so in the western New Territories is a few stops further up the line, where the short **Ping Shan Heritage Trail** starts just south of Yuen Long. Like the Lung Yuek Tau Heritage Trail outside Fanling (*see p102*), the Ping Shan trail features several historic buildings dating back hundreds of years. The first two buildings you'll come across en route are the 18th-century **Hung Shing Temple** and the beautifully painted, high-ceilinged **Kun Ting Study Hall**, which was built in the 19th century as a place where members of the Tang clan could study for their imperial civil service examination. (Unfortunately, the study hall has been closed to the public for over a decade due to a long-running dispute between local villagers and the government.) Also on the trail you'll find the recently restored 700-year-old **Tang Ancestral Hall** – one of the finest in Hong Kong – and the 16th-century **Yu Kiu Ancestral Hall**.

Keep an eye out for the narrow alleyways and tiny houses of **Sheung Cheung Wai**, a walled village that is still inhabited today. Also at Ping Shan is the **Tsui Shing Lau**, a small pagoda built several hundred years ago for geomantic reasons. Though hemmed in by developments and surrounded by general village squalor, it is nevertheless worth a visit and is an integral part of the Ping Shan Heritage Trail. (To reach the trail, take the LRT to Ping Shan station and walk west from the tram/road crossing for about five minutes. Look on the right side of the road for the map detailing the route of the trail, which begins at the Hung Shing Temple. It's best to be armed with a map from the start, as the signposting from the LRT to the trail is not clear.) Villagers at Ping Shan take a mixed view

of visitors – you may be welcomed, and then again you may not be; best to take a chance and see how it feels on the day.)

Another sight worth visiting in the Tuen Mun area is the Buddhist **Ching Shan Monastery** (*see below*), perched halfway up a steep hillside south-west of town.

### Ching Chung Koon Temple

*Tsing Chung Path, Tsing Chung Koon Road, Tuen Mun (2393 7495/www.daoist.org/ccta/ccta.htm). Kwai Fong MTR then 58M bus/Mong Kok MTR then 58X bus/Admiralty MTR then 960 bus/Ching Chung LRT then short walk.* **Open** 9am-6pm daily. **Admission** free. **Map** p306.
This Taoist complex is a peaceful oasis, complete with ponds, sculptures, fountains and hundreds of venerable bonsai trees. In addition, if you happen to be in the area during the third or seventh lunar months, you might stumble upon one of the large religious ceremonies held in its ancestral memorial halls.

### Ching Shan Monastery

*Ching Shan Tsuen, nr Tuen Mun (no phone). Bus to Tuen Mun then taxi.* **Open** 9am-5pm daily. **Admission** free. **Map** p306.
This Buddhist monastery is a rare quiet corner in generally noisy Hong Kong, with cool breezes blowing in from the sea. Inside, chanted prayers seem to come from nowhere (but are actually broadcast by a concealed modern sound system). The nearest LRT stop is Ching Shan Tsuen, but it's a hard, steep trudge of about one and a half kilometres (one mile) to the monastery from the station. An easier means of access is to take a taxi up the hill to the monastery (about HK\$30 from the town centre) and then walk back down to the LRT station.

### Miu Fat Buddhist Monastery

*18 Castle Peak Road, Lam Tei (2461 8567/ miufat@hongkong.com). Tsing Yi MTR then 263M bus to Lam Tei LRT/Kwai Hing MTR then 68A bus to Lam Tei LRT.* **Open** 9am-5pm daily. **Admission** free. **Map** p306.
Two large dragons coil up the pillars by the front door, flanked by two temple lions. This is a lavish, active and modern monastery with plenty of gold and marble, huge chandeliers, and the obligatory surfeit of large and small golden Buddha statues. There's a popular vegetarian canteen on the second floor serving reasonable Chinese vegetarian food. The monastery is located a five-minute walk north of the LRT station, on the eastern side of a busy highway – you can see it from the pedestrian bridge at the station.

## East New Territories

The eastern New Territories is the most sparsely inhabited and least developed part of the SAR. To the north is the jagged peninsula containing the remote and very lovely Pat Sing Leng and Plover Cove Country Parks. To the south is the extensive Sai Kung Peninsula, with its long hiking trails, spectacular scenery and rock formations, and numerous beautiful, isolated beaches.

## Plover Cove & the north-east

Prior to the development of the New Territories, the few incursions by humans into the wilderness of the north-east amounted to little more than small pearl fisheries and tiny Hakka settlements (the Hakka people migrated from north to southern China centuries ago, and first settled in Hong Kong in the late 17th century; most are farmers and you will still see the women working as labourers, wearing distinctive bamboo hats with black cloth fringes).

Even today the area remains a haven for adventurous hikers and wildlife enthusiasts. The **Wilson Trail** (*see p41*) winds north of **Plover Cove**, the huge reservoir that was created when a natural seawater bay was sealed with a massive dam. Larger fauna, such as barking deer and wild boar, still thrive in the area, although sightings from the trails are increasingly rare.

The best way to get here is to catch the number 75K bus from Tai Po Market KCR station – it'll take about 40 minutes to reach Tai Mei Tuk. Here you will find a youth hostel and a watersports centre (which unfortunately does not allow the casual hire of boats or windsurfing equipment).

There are numerous walking opportunities in this district, ranging from ambitious hikes to easy family walks. Probably the easiest is the gentle path around **Bride's Pool** – a naturally formed pool with a waterfall at the end of Bride's Pool Road, just under five kilometres (three miles) from Tai Mei Tuk. You can even make a picnic out of it, as there are barbecue areas close to the pool and at various points along the road.

For stronger walkers, Bride's Pool lies at the end of another walk – the well-marked six-kilometre (four-mile) **Pat Sing Leng Nature Trail**, which begins just above the Plover Cove Park Visitor Centre (a ten-minute walk east along Ting Kok Road from the Tai Mei Tuk bus stop). The route offers wonderful views of Plover Cove Reservoir and Tolo Harbour. A taxi ride from the bus stop back to Tai Po Market KCR station should cost around HK$40.

## Sai Kung & the south-east

This more easily accessible area of the New Territories takes in fine parkland, golden beaches, rolling surf and – in Sai Kung and Clearwater Bay – numerous waterfront cafés,

bars and seafood restaurants. You can hire a sampan to see the islands offshore from Sai Kung, or simply wander to the gorgeous beaches near Wong Shek.

**Sai Kung** town is a quiet place – at least during the week – with a small boat harbour that has become a popular refuge for expats, who enjoy the area's beaches and open spaces. But while it's surrounded by a fairly wild mountainous area, Sai Kung itself offers a pleasant haven of civilisation, with a reasonable selection of restaurants, cafés, pubs and bars.

If heading out on to the water is your goal, your best bet is to start near the main ferry pier, where middle-aged women offer sampan rides around the harbour. Sampan hire costs about HK$50 per half hour, although it's always worthwhile trying to haggle the price down. The sampans are the only way to get to the small, secluded beaches on the islands close to Sai Kung (although the best beaches lie on the south-eastern tip of the peninsula). If you do hire a sampan, the tiny island of **Yim Tin Tsai** is worth a stop. Most of its devout Christian residents have departed, and many of the buildings are dilapidated – including **St Joseph's Chapel** at the top of the hill – but the remaining community is of interest.

Visiting the beaches at the south-eastern edge of Sai Kung is much more difficult, but it is feasible in a day if you set off early. Bus 94 runs from Sai Kung to the coast at **Wong Shek Pier** every half hour (every hour at weekends); this is a strategic spot from which to head for the beaches, and from which to begin walks to the north and east of the peninsula. One particularly dramatic day-long hike hugs the southern edge of the High Island Reservoir, ending at the lovely beach of **Long Ke Wan**. If you want to spend more than a day in the area, you can either camp or stay at the youth hostels in Wong Shek.

If time and/or energy are in short supply, there are walks closer to Sai Kung at Pak Tam Chung. For instance, if you take the 94 bus to the **Pak Tam Chung Visitor Centre** from Sai Kung, a short stroll along the nearby nature trail will take you past the well-preserved, but otherwise underwhelming, **Sheung Yiu Folk Museum** (*see p109*). This partially rebuilt 19th-century Hakka village is a branch of the Hong Kong Heritage Museum (*see p99*). It's also worth popping into the visitor centre, which has some good displays on the wildlife and geology of the area.

Note that getting into, out of and around the wilderness on the Sai Kung Peninsula does take time and it would be best to allow at least a very full day out to explore the area. Careful planning and quite an early start will be necessary for all but the shortest walks. The 92 bus to Sai Kung leaves frequently from Diamond Hill MTR.

The scenery and wilderness of **Clearwater Bay**, ten or so kilometres south of Sai Kung, may be less spectacular than in Sai Kung or Plover Cove, but the area has some good, easily accessible beaches. (Take the 91 bus, which departs regularly from Diamond Hill MTR station.) The best two are those with the not particularly descriptive names of **Beach One** and **Beach Two**, where the water is clear and the golden sand is clean. They also have lifeguards and good facilities. Perhaps not surprisingly, these beaches are popular and tend to be very busy at weekends. Under no circumstances should you be tempted to stop at Silverstrand Beach, which – despite its nicer name – is fairly unappealing; its dingy shores are lapped by dirty water awash with detritus. And there have been numerous shark attacks here in recent years – some of them fatal.

Aside from sunbathing and swimming, there's not much to do at Clearwater Bay, which isn't necessarily a bad thing. However, if you can tear yourself away from the surf there are a few short excursions worth making. Two kilometres (one and a half miles) from Beach Two is the oldest (by descent) Tin Hau Temple in Hong Kong, which dates back to 1274. Although it has been rebuilt and renovated numerous times since then, it's still one of the most impressive and atmospheric of Hong Kong's many Tin Hau temples. The walk to the temple is fairly flat, and follows the road from the Clearwater Bay bus stop south to Clearwater Bay Country Club. The path from the Club to the temple is not clearly marked, but lies immediately to the right of the Club's guardhouse.

When your day in the sun is over, you can either take the number 91 bus all the way back to Diamond Hill MTR station or as far as the Pik Uk prison on Clearwater Bay Road, where you can change to the number 101 bus that continues on to Sai Kung town.

### Sheung Yiu Folk Museum

*Pak Tam Chung Nature Trail, Sai Kung (2792 6365/ www.heritagemuseum.gov.hk/english/branch.htm). Choi Hung MTR (exit C) then 94 bus to Sai Kung Town then minibus 1A.* **Open** 9am-4pm Mon, Wed-Sun. **Admission** free. **Map** p307.

This museum was once a fortified village. Built in the late 19th century, it includes dwellings, animal sheds and a watchtower. The displays feature farm implements, household goods and everyday belongings of Hakka people. In many ways, it's a smaller version of the Sam Tung Uk Museum located in Tsuen Wan (*see p106*).

**Tap Mun Chau**. See p100.

# The Outlying Islands

Peace at last.

Sunset at **Sai Wan**. Cheung Chau. *See p118.*

When you've had your fill of the frenetic urban buzz of Central and Tsim Sha Tsui and crave greenery and solitude, make for the ferry piers in Central and head to one of the many unspoiled islands scattered to the west and south of Hong Kong Island. Secluded bays, isolated swimming beaches, stunning hiking and plenty of seafood restaurants are a short journey away.

For energetic hikes through dramatic mountainous landscapes or relaxing on quiet beaches, head for Lantau. For gentler walking and superb seafood restaurants or just sitting in a bar and watching the world go by, try Lamma. Or spend a day enjoying the varied attractions of the smaller outlying islands such as Cheung Chau and Peng Chau.

## Lamma

At 13 square kilometres (five square miles) the third largest island in Hong Kong, **Lamma** is locally renowned for its excellent open-air seafood restaurants, lack of motorised transport (*see p115* **Village vehicle vagabonds**), pleasant greenery and abundant hillside trails. You could spend the day walking across the island, taking in the sun on one of the beaches or just lounging about in the bars, pubs and cafés.

Most ferry departures from Central and Aberdeen on head to the main settlement of Yung Shue Wan on the island's north-west tip, but it is also worth taking the boat to Sok Kwu Wan on the south-east coast for its stretch of waterside seafood restaurants, and the secluded walks and beaches nearby. The best compromise is to head out to one destination, then walk the four kilometres (two and a half miles) across the island and depart from the other. The most usual route is to start at Yung Shue Wan, take in some of the cafés and complete the relatively gentle hike (though it is quite draining on a hot day) to Sok Kwu Wan's seafood restaurants, in time for supper.

As it's one of the most easily reached pieces of greenery in Hong Kong, many urban residents head to Lamma at weekends, so weekdays offer the best chances to enjoy the fresh sea air without having to share it with thousands of other people. If you just can't tear yourself away from Lamma, there are several modest guesthouses and a youth hostel on the island.

### Yung Shue Wan

At first sight fairly ramshackle, **Yung Shue Wan** straggles around a small inlet, which can be a bit smelly when the tide goes out. This was

Sightseeing

an isolated fishing settlement until after World War II, and thereafter grew only slowly, with much of its income earned from factories that churned out plastic goods in the 1970s. Today it's a busy, charming place with plenty of expats, attracted by lower rents, cleaner air, and a friendlier and more relaxed atmosphere than on Hong Kong Island. In the 1990s, it drew in an alternative foreign crowd of hippies, New Agers and Eurotrash partiers, but since the Handover their numbers – and something of the frenetic, end-of-an-era party spirit – have diminished. However, their influence remains in the form of veggie cafés and the occasional full moon party held on the beach next to the power station.

As you leave the ferry at Yung Shue Wan, look to the left and you'll see a smaller harbour with fishing boats and stilt houses overhanging the rocks and water. To the right is the narrow main street with most of Lamma's shops, restaurants and bars. While the island's seafood restaurants are not particularly cheap, as most of them source their seafood from outside Hong Kong's over-fished, heavily polluted waters, there are a couple of good ones worth trying. But if fish isn't really your thing there are other culinary options. The Sampan serves good, cheap dim sum until about noon, while the Green Cottage next door has some outdoor seating and offers health food. For a drink with a waterside view, head to the superbly named Deli-Lamma (*see p155*). The cheerfully alternative Bookworm Café (*see p146*), towards the far end of the main street, is a peaceful place to have a drink, eat excellent veggie food and read a book (from its library-cum-bookshop).

### Beaches

There are two beaches close to Yung Shue Wan, both within a 15-minute walk of the village. The first, **Tai Wan To**, is overlooked by Lamma's

huge power station, which supplies most of Hong Kong Island's electricity requirements. Despite the industrial-era view, it's not a bad stretch of sand, and is conveniently close to Yung Shue Wan. It's also known by many residents – perhaps unsurprisingly – as 'Power Station Beach'.

A few minutes' walk further south, past the island's small police station, there's an excellent and popular beach at **Hung Shing Ye**. The Concerto Inn overlooking the beach is a cheap, cheerful café with holiday accommodation.

### Sok Kwu Wan & southern Lamma

Hung Shing Ye beach is just off the main concrete path to Sok Kwu Wan, which is about an hour's steady walk from Yung Shue Wan. The more rugged dirt trail running over the hills, with fantastic views over the harbour and Hong Kong Island, offers a dramatically scenic route to the south of the island via Mount Stenhouse, but you'll need a decent map and plenty of time in case you lose your way; the path along here is not always obvious.

In the geographical centre of Lamma, at its narrowest point, is **Lo So Shing**, an excellent, secluded beach that is also has an archaeological site. Whichever route you decide to take, you should see signs to the **Kamikaze Caves** on your right as you hit the eastern shore, very close to Sok Kwu Wan. Created by Japanese occupying forces during World War II, the caves were designed to hide small speedboats packed with explosives intended for suicide attacks on Allied shipping, but the war ended before they were ever employed.

**Sok Kwu Wan** has about a dozen seafood restaurants, none of which are cheap. All have views over the harbour, and while there's not much to differentiate them, the Lamma Hilton is consistently good, the Lamma Mandarin Seafood

---

**Don't miss** Island experiences

#### Lamma
A hippie hangout, with views, beaches, walking trails... and a power station. *See p110.*

#### Lantau
Famous for its Big Buddha, this huge island is also home to expats, and sharks. *See p112.*

#### Cheung Chau
Foodie heaven – there's cheap, decent seafood year-round, and, in May, a bun festival. *See p117.*

#### Peng Chau
Small but perfectly formed, with an alluring laid-back atmosphere. *See p118.*

#### Po Toi
Steep walking trails and glorious views are the reason for visiting this rocky island. *See p119.*

#### Tap Mun Chau
Excellent, clean beaches are tiny Tap Mun Chau's main draw. *See p119.*

Restaurant is well known for its pigeon dishes, and Rainbow Seafood (*see p146*) is always popular. The huge quarry facing the restaurants is gradually being filled and landscaped.

If you're not ready to eat, there's a fairly flat, circular five-kilometre (three-mile) walk to the southern tip of the island that offers good shoreline views. You'll also come across the sleepy hamlet of **Shek Pai Wan**; this isolated place is about as far from Hong Kong's built-up areas as it's possible to imagine. The lovely south-facing beach, like many stretches of coastline elsewhere in Hong Kong, is somewhat marred by broken glass flotsam, so take care if you go paddling. There's also a small temple to the sea god Hung Shing (who was a Tang Dynasty official credited with developing a basic form of meteorology), sacred to fishermen. **Tung O**, the small, all but deserted village nearby, is where Chow Yun-fat, star of *Crouching Tiger, Hidden Dragon*, was born and raised.

Perhaps the best and most secluded beach on Lamma is just on the other side of the headland at **Sham Wan** – it is only accessible via a very narrow, overgrown track. This is the only beach in Hong Kong where green turtles still lay their eggs (it's closed from June to October during nesting season). It's also an archaeological site, where finds dating back 6,000 years have been discovered. The oldest known settlement in Hong Kong, it was inhabited by the Yueh, a little-known pre-Chinese people.

A steep climb away to the west, on the circular path back to Sok Kwu Wan, is **Mount Stenhouse**. The 353-metre-high (1,150-feet) summit is a spectacular vantage point, offering an almost complete view of Lamma, fine vistas of Hong Kong Island to the north and Lantau to the west, and vertiginous views down to the wave-battered rocks below. The route up is a tough scramble along a rocky, overgrown path, but well worth the effort if you're reasonably fit. On a clear day the island and sea views from here are amazing.

## Lantau

Although twice the size of Hong Kong Island, **Lantau** remains largely unspoiled, except for the massive development around Chek Lap Kok – the site of the international airport on the northern coast. Many parts of the island look much as they did when the island was acquired along with the mainland New Territories in 1898. Two huge country parks contain the peaks that form the backbone of the island and numerous hiking trails. On a misty day, the steep wooded hillsides are reminiscent of the Scottish Highlands, a comparison that has been made by travelling writers since the late 19th century.

The development of the new airport on Chek Lap Kok and the Tsing Ma Bridge linking the northern coast of Lantau with the mainland have not had a hugely noticeable impact on the rest of the island – so far. However, the opening of the new Disneyland at Penny's Bay in late 2005 or early 2006, which is expected to attract 18 million (mostly mainland Chinese) visitors annually looks likely to change all that.

Today the main settlements are limited to the mostly expat enclave of Discovery Bay (a California-style toy-town settlement where transport is by golf-cart – honestly), the town of Tung Chung across from the new airport, the area around the ferry terminal at Mui Wo, and the nearby valley. Plenty of open space can be found all over the island, particularly at the south-western end, making the place a terrific retreat from the noise and crowds so prevalent elsewhere in Hong Kong. The seclusion offered on Lantau has made it a popular retreat for (mainly Buddhist) religious orders. Probably the most striking sacred site is the Po Lin Monastery, high in the hills near Lantau Peak, which is home to one of the world's largest outdoor Buddha statues.

There are some good beaches along the southern coast of Lantau, as well as some very wild and inaccessible areas inland. One of the few remaining (and probably the most interesting) traditional fishing settlements in Hong Kong clings to the western coast of Lantau at Tai O. Here, you will still find a large cluster of traditional stilt houses on the muddy banks of the small estuary. Tai O has terrific character and a wander around this sleepy town is highly recommended. It's also a good place to stock up on dried fish and seafood items.

## Discovery Bay

**Discovery Bay** lies just north-east of the ferry port of Mui Wo (*see p114*). The settlement here is like nowhere else in Hong Kong. For some of its residents, that's the whole point of the bay's existence, while for other Hong Kong citizens, nothing would induce them to live there. Love it or hate it, Discovery Bay is a fascinating glimpse into the way at least some Hong Kong people choose to live. Apartment blocks here have names like Brilliance Court, Bijou Hamlet and Neo Horizon. With no cars allowed, golf buggies are the norm; parked all over the place, some have baby seats while others sport football stickers in their windscreens. Other than people-watching, probably the main reasons for coming here are the long sandy beach, the scenic short walk to the Trappist Monastery (*see p114*) and the *kaido* (small ferry) to Peng Chau (*see p118*). (The fast, smart catamaran to Discovery

The **Big Buddha**, Lantau. *See p115.*

Making incense offerings at **Po Lin Monastery**, Lantau. *See p116.*

Bay takes about 25 minutes from Central, costs HK$25 and empties onto the neat piazza next to the pier.) With a numerically significant, mostly well-heeled resident population, there are some good, although not outstanding, restaurants here, and a few coffee shops. The clean, man-made beach just north of the ferry pier is pleasant enough and the water looks relatively clean, but if the wind is blowing from behind the beach it whips up a stinging sandstorm.

*Kaidos* to **Peng Chau** run hourly from the quayside at the southern edge of the headland that divides Discovery Bay from the small harbour and beach of **Nim Shue Wan**. From the plaza by the Discovery Bay ferry terminal, walk to the far end of the bus station, turn left and then walk along the small quayside, looking out for a very small timetable and steps, from where the *kaidos* depart. If you fancy a short hike, there's a well signposted two-kilometre (one-mile) or so shoreline path starting at the top of Nim Shue Wan beach, which leads to the **Trappist Monastery**. From there, you can also jump on a *kaido* to Peng Chau, although only ten run each day and none operates between 12.20pm and 3pm. Both *kaido* rides cost just a few dollars and take about ten minutes.

If you don't feel like walking, there are also a few *kaidos* each day that go to Peng Chau via the ferry pier leading to the Trappist Monastery. From there, it's a short, steep trudge up to the monastery. The way is lined – appropriately enough – with the Stations of the Cross.

## Mui Wo & the southern beaches

**Mui Wo**, also known as **Silvermine Bay**, is the main jumping-off point for Lantau and the place to catch buses to most other destinations

on the island. It's 40 minutes and HK$10.50 away on the ferry from Central, and the bus terminus is right outside the Mui Wo ferry terminal. Catch a bus from here to the beaches on Lantau's southern coast, to Ngong Ping for the Big Buddha and Lantau Peak (*see p115*), and to the fishing village of Tai O on the south-western coast (*see p116*).

On its own, Mui Wo is a pleasant enough place, but there are more interesting destinations nearby. If you want to spend some time here, though, Mui Wo's long stretch of beach, complete with shark net, is a five-minute walk north along the edge of the bay. Another pleasant option is a walk through the valley towards the mountains, past clear streams, village houses and deserted farms and fields.

There are a few bars and some restaurants at Mui Wo, mostly around the ferry and bus terminals. The cooked food market above the bus station has several eateries with cheap, if not hugely appetising, canteen fare. The Sea View offers dim sum from 6am to 1pm. A number of pricier – but better – places just west of the bus station serve up everything from curry to pizza.

One possible excursion from Mui Wo is the three-kilometre (two-mile) walk to the Trappist Monastery (*see above*) north-west of town, although the route is steep in parts. Be sure to take a good map with you.

A number of beaches run along the southern coast, and most are deserted during the week. Two of the best, in terms of cleanliness and facilities, are **Pui O Wan** and **Cheung Sha**. All buses leaving Mui Wo (except for the number 7, which only goes as far as Pui O) pass them.

**Cheung Sha** (which appropriately enough means Long Sand) is just over two kilometres (one mile) further west of Pui O. Look out for the signs marking Cheung Sha and ring the bell for the stop just after the police station, which you should see on the right. The path to the beach is a few metres further west along the road. The beach here is excellent (long, clean and empty, with changing facilities and a gay section; *see p213* **Splashing out**), while the water is as clean as anywhere in Hong Kong, although excitingly, there's no shark net. There are a couple of places to eat, including Stoep (*see also p146*), which offers a mix of good value Mediterranean and South African food. The house speciality is the barbecue menu, which includes home-made *boerewors*, a type of South African sausage.

## Ngong Ping, Po Lin Monastery & the Big Buddha

From Mui Wo, it's a bumpy, winding 16-kilometre (ten-mile) journey on the number 2 bus to **Ngong Ping**. En route, the bus passes along the edge of **Lantau South Country Park** and **Shek Pik Reservoir**. If it's a clear day and you're sitting on the right-hand side of the bus, you will get a good view of the 34-metre-high (110-foot) Buddha statue at Ngong Ping as the bus passes the reservoir. When the bus finally reaches its destination, tourists and devotees (the former usually greatly

outnumbering the latter) disgorge and head for the nearby **Po Lin Monastery** and the **Big Buddha** (*see p116*) – the largest bronze outdoor seated Buddha in the world.

Buddhist monks from China began arriving on Lantau in the early 20th century, but the monastery really developed in the 1920s when the first abbot was appointed and the great hall built. It further expanded in the 1940s and from the '60s has experienced constant growth and development. Its popularity means that it can be very crowded and noisy – not quite what many would expect from a Buddhist retreat.

Ngong Ping is also a good starting point from which to tackle the steep slopes of **Fung Wong Shan** or **Lantau Peak**, the second-highest mountain in Hong Kong. The route up begins to the east of the monastery past the **Tea Farm**, formerly owned by Brook Bernacchi, a local barrister. Many walkers stay overnight at the **Hongkong Bank Foundation SG Davis Youth Hostel** (*see p58*) and get up early to make it up the peak in time for sunrise. Call ahead to book a bed and check opening times, as the hostel is often closed during the day.

Other walking options from the monastery include the relatively gentle trek down from the monastery north to **Tung Chung**, which is about six and a half kilometres (four miles) away. From there, a fast train will take you back

**Sightseeing**

# Village vehicle vagabonds

On Lamma island's quiet streets, where cars and motorcycles are strictly forbidden, pedestrians can be lulled into a false sense of ambulatory security. Until, that is, they discover just how the island's wannabe wide boys have got around the anti-car law. One minute you're walking along the footpath, the next a miniature tractor-truck hybrid is bearing down on you at breakneck speed.

And the driver is laughing.

A loophole in Hong Kong's motorised vehicle legislation allows the use of so-called 'village vehicles'. These are legal forms of transport in rural parts of the New Territories and outlying islands where conventional forms of motorised road vehicle are not permitted. Licences were originally granted for farmers and ranchers to operate small tractors and trucks that are no longer than 3.2 metres (ten feet), and no wider than 1.2 metres (four feet), to till the soil and carry harvested produce.

These days, Hong Kong's version of wide boys are often to be found at the wheel of

regulation-size toytown-like trucks, hired for things like transporting construction supplies to building sites, or for bringing goods to shops. Fun though this looks, passengers are not allowed.

If you're on Lamma long enough, you can be sure that you will encounter these vehicles, whose would-be triad drivers usually wear a vest or no top at all, the better to show off their tattoos. They can often be recognised by their peroxided mop, and the way that they enjoy playing 'chicken' at high speed with pedestrians. They also hurtle themselves at irresponsible speeds around blind corners on Lamma's network of footpaths.

Day-trippers may be surprised to hear the unmistakable sound of an emergency vehicle siren from time to time on the island. What finally comes into view is either a tiny ambulance or one of the new wide-axle, beach-buggy-like fire engines. The resident police force, rather embarrassingly, has to make do with bright yellow push-bikes.

to Central (a single ticket costs HK$23). Take care if you intend to tackle the concrete path, as parts are slick with moss and very slippery after rain. On the way down, you'll pass two Buddhist monasteries. The path takes you through the gardens of the first; these are often tended by nuns, and smell of incense and freshly dug earth. It's a place of quiet religious retreat, so visitors are not usually permitted to enter the buildings. At the bottom of the path, where it meets the road, you'll find the more welcoming **Lo Hon Monastery** (2988 1419). It serves a vegetarian lunch every day, costing HK$60.

## Po Lin Monastery

*Ngong Ping (2985 5248/polin@plm.org.hk). Mui Wo Ferry Pier then bus 2/Tung Chung MTR then bus 23.* **Open** 10am-5pm daily. **Admission** free. **Map** p306. The monastery is grand, although somewhat out-shone by the towering Buddha. Inside the grounds are bauhinia and orchid gardens. Two canteens inside the grand hall serve decent vegetarian food. The filling, if somewhat stodgy, snack menu (noodles and dim sum) costs HK$28, while the full vegetarian lunch costs HK$60 for the basic and HK$100 for the deluxe menu. Meals are served between 11.30am and 5pm. You buy a meal ticket at the foot of the steps to the Buddha statue – this also grants access to the display rooms underneath the Buddha, which tell the story of Buddha's path to enlightenment.

## The Fan Lau Trail

An excellent day-long hike, taking in old ruined villages, stunning sea views and beaches, and a Qing Dynasty fort, the trail snakes around the edges of the south-western coast of Lantau to Tai O. There are two possible routes. The first, flatter option follows the path that starts at the south-western tip of Shek Pik Reservoir (*see p115*) and hugs the coastline all the way. The second, steeper and more dramatic route starts from the top of a hill on the Lantau Trail (*see p41*), just to the north-west of the reservoir. The distances covered are both around 12 to 14 kilometres (seven to nines), depending on the detours taken. Both trails take between five and six hours to complete, and end up at Tai O (*see below*). If you take the first option, there are a couple of places to camp along the way.

**Fan Lau** has an old Tin Hau temple, an abandoned school house and a few elderly residents. There's also a ruined Chinese fort built in the early 1800s, which is a good place to gaze out to sea and watch the Macau-bound jetfoils streak past. The path becomes much easier once you've passed the abandoned village of **Yi O San Tsuen** on the western side of the spur, as it has been concreted pretty much all the way into Tai O. A good map and plenty of water are essential if you want to tackle this trail.

## Tai O

A large but quiet village perched on the far south-western coast of Lantau, **Tai O** is one of the last remaining fishing villages with stilt houses, which were first built here by the Tanka people (nomadic boat people who have fished in Hong Kong's waters for centuries) hundreds of years ago. If you're not walking to Tai O, you should take the number 1 bus from Mui Wo – a journey that takes about 40 minutes and costs HK$8 (a bit more on Sundays). From the bus station, the village clusters around the mouth of a small estuary. A walk over the short pedestrian bridge will take you into the heart of the settlement. Close to Tai O Market Street, you'll find a temple dedicated to Kwan Tai, the god of loyalty and righteousness, which dates back to the 1530s. The main cluster of stilt houses lies a short walk east along the street. Walk behind them and you'll find that there is a small boat moored at almost every house.

The left-hand fork on Tai O Market Street (in front of the Kwan Tai temple) leads to the western edge of town, past the fire station, complete with tiny fire tenders, and a couple of pungent-smelling *haam-ha* (shrimp paste) manufacturers. You will probably pick up the distinctive smell of the paste before you see the blue plastic tubs in which the stuff ferments in the sun. If it still seems like a good idea to you after seeing how it's made, you can buy jars of shrimp paste and shrimp sauce here for between HK$15 and HK$30. These sharp, powerful sauces are similar to Thai fish paste or Indonesian *terasi*, and impart a strong fishy flavour to simple dishes like stir-fried vegetables. It's used to add dimension to squid dishes in many of the seafood restaurants on the outlying islands.

About 200 metres (650 feet) beyond the shrimp paste manufacturers, you'll come across the old Tai O police station. Built in 1902, it dominates the edge of the island. The ferries to Sha Lo Wan (further north along the coast) and Tuen Mun (in the New Territories; *see p106*) stop here. There are two sailings each way, one in the morning and one in the afternoon, from Monday to Friday; three sailings on Saturday and five on Sunday. The fare is about HK$15 to Sha Lo Wan and HK$28 to Tuen Mun.

Food in Tai O is very basic Cantonese fare and, needless to say, seafood dishes dominate. The **Fook Moon Lam Restaurant**, next door to the Kwan Tai temple on Tai O Market Street, does good seafood. The **Wing Fat Restaurant** close to the bus stop (before you head over the bridge) has a varied menu of simple Cantonese dishes and Western snacks. Prices are very reasonable.

A family outing to **Hung Shing Ye** beach, Lamma. *See p111.*

## Cheung Chau

West of Hong Kong Island and off the southern
coast of Lantau, the tiny former pirate haven
of **Cheung Chau** supports a population of
around 20,000. It somehow accommodates them
all without ever seeming too crowded – except,
of course, when visitors from the rest of Hong
Kong flock here at-weekends. Even when it's
packed, though, this is an intriguing place with
secluded areas and good beaches. It's perfectly
feasible to spend some time here, so allow a
couple of days to relax and explore. Orienting
yourself on the island is simple: the narrow
spine where the ferries dock forms the centre of
town, while the blocks of land to the south and
north (once two separate islands) contain
walking trails and smaller beaches to explore.

Ferries from Central or Lantau berth next to
a wide road running the length of the harbour
that is mostly occupied by seafood restaurants.
In terms of going out and eating, Cheung Chau
does not have the diversity of Lamma, but on
the other hand, the seafood here is cheaper (*see
p146*). Standards and prices are pretty uniform,
but one of the most popular places (with
Westerners and Chinese alike) is the **Baccarat**
towards the northern end of the harbour.

The small alleys running off Pak She and San
Hing streets contain dozens of small Chinese
shops and businesses, selling incense, paper
offerings, Chinese medicine and all manner
of daily necessities. A couple of minutes' walk
away from the ferry pier is the recently rebuilt
**Pak Tai Temple** opposite the basketball
court at the top of Pak She Street. The god Pak

Tai is credited with bringing to an end
a virulent outbreak of the plague in 1777,
prompting the grateful islanders to build an
ornate temple in his honour in 1783.

The temple is the centre of the religious
fervour that brings the entire island to a
standstill every May during the famous **Cheung
Chau Bun Festival** (*see also p187*). This
religious festival has evolved into a busy three-
day carnival attracting thousands of visitors. It
all goes back about 100 years, to a time when an
episode of bad luck and illness beset the island.
In response, the islanders started offering lotus-
paste buns to the spirits of the dead. Health and
prosperity returned, so the locals decided to
make the ceremony an annual event – just in
case. As part of the event, three 13-metre-high
(40-feet) bamboo towers covered in thousands
of steamed buns are erected in front of the
Pak Tai Temple and left out for three days.
Taoist priests hold the requisite ceremonies
to encourage the return of all the restless ghosts
to the underworld. Before they come back, the
spirits consume the 'essence' of the buns, while
islanders and visitors eat the remains. The
chaotic scramble to reach the luckiest buns at the
top of the pile was once one of the striking events
in the festival, but this mad rush was banned
years ago after a (seemingly inevitable) serious
accident. Today the focus of the festival is on
the procession of floats, lion dancers and the
colourful 'floating' children, representing
characters from myth and legend, who are
strapped to cleverly hidden poles and seem to
float above the crowd. Despite the height and the
crowds, few ever become visibly distressed.

Dozens of small temples and shrines dot the island, many of them dedicated to *To Tei Kung* earth spirits. One of the most important is the banyan tree on Tung Wan Road, close to the bottom end of San Hing Street. The tree and the spirits said to inhabit it are held in such esteem that when the road needed to be widened, a restaurant opposite was demolished instead of the tree.

One of the best (and most popular) beaches in this area is **Tung Wan**, which you'll find at the eastern end of Tung Wan Road. The beach is fairly large by Hong Kong standards and is well kept. The shark nets are removed and the facilities closed between November and April, but it is still possible to swim with due care.

Although there are some pleasant, secluded paths in the northern section of the island, the southern part of Cheung Chau offers the best walks. From Tung Wan beach, head south around the back of the Warwick Hotel and go past the Kwun Yum temple. Slopes are gentle and it's an easy walk to the south-western tip of the island along Peak Road West. When you reach the cemetery, make a detour down to **Pak Tso Wan**, one of the nicer small beaches in southern Cheung Chau.

Peak Road West heads into the small village of **Sai Wan**, where you can catch the constantly shuttling HK$2.50 sampan back into the centre of Cheung Chau. Not only handy, this is also a good way to see the harbour. Turning sharp left opposite the main Cheung Chau pier will take you along the path to the far western tip of the island, where signs point to a tiny cave with dubious claims that it is the place where the 19th-century pirate Cheung Po-tsai hid the plunder from his raids on shipping in the area. There's not much to see, but the rocky outcrop offers good sea views and it's a pleasant walk. The cave itself is really just a small hole; you'll need a torch to see inside it.

## Other islands

There are hundreds of small islands scattered in Hong Kong's waters, many of them uninhabited and inaccessible without a boat. Unless you hire a boat for the day or evening, you will be tied to infrequent ferry services to Po Toi and Tap Mun Chau. Access to Peng Chau is much easier as it, like Cheung Chau, is a popular commuter island. Hiring a junk with a crew is not out of the question if you are in a group of five or more. Prices start at about HK$2,000 for a day, although you may be able to haggle the price down on weekdays. The *Yellow Pages* has extensive junk hire listings.

### Peng Chau

The tiny island of **Peng Chau** lies just across the water from Discovery Bay on Lantau. Partly owing to its size, there's less to see here than on the other populated islands. Peng Chau's charm lies in its very quiet village character, which is in sharp contrast to the Costa del Something-or-Other feel of Discovery Bay (*see p112*).

The main settlement around the ferry pier is a compact area of small interlinking alleys, local shops and tiny temples, all echoing to the clatter of mah-jong tiles. As Peng Chau covers less than one square kilometre (half a square mile), the island has few extensive beaches and fairly limited eating and drinking options. An hour or two is all that's needed to stroll around the entire island. A good place to head first is south down Wing On Street and Shing Ka Road, then east along Nam Shan Road to **Finger Hill**, Peng Chau's highest point. It's only about ten minutes' walk from the ferry pier, but the final stretch is steep. The reward is to share the view over the island with the black kites that hover lazily around the summit.

**Pak Tai Temple**, Cheung Chau.
*See p117.*

The little township near the pier, thus far largely untouched by development, is the only place to go for food or drink. Although the seafood restaurants here are not especially celebrated, they are relatively cheap, and are popular at weekends. If you crave Western snack food, try the Jungle and the Sea Breeze, next door to each other at 38 and 40 Wing Hing Street. The outside seating at the former looks across to the ferry pier and Lantau. In recent years the construction of a new road and rocky breakwater along the edge of the small harbour at Tung Wan on the other side of Peng Chau has essentially destroyed the beach. It's not a great loss, however, as both water and beach have long since been polluted to the point where few bathers dare to go in.

Peng Chau is easily accessible from the outlying islands ferry pier in Central, with ferries leaving every 45 minutes. A single fare on the slow ferry, which takes about 45 minutes, costs HK$10.50. The single fare on the slightly faster express costs HK$21. There are also less frequent ferry and *kaido* services from Discovery Bay and Mui Wo on Lantau and from Cheung Chau. Some of the *kaidos* plying their trade between Discovery Bay and Peng Chau also stop at the ferry pier near the Trappist Monastery.

## Po Toi

The hills and cliffs of the small rocky island of **Po Toi** shelve steeply into the ocean a few kilometres south of Hong Kong Island. The island has some rugged walking trails, which give terrific views over the South China Sea and across to Hong Kong Island, and a Neolithic rock carving. The tiny, pretty harbour and beach of **Tai Wan** contains one good seafood restaurant, the **Ming Kee**, which is open every day.

Despite its close proximity to Hong Kong, Po Toi is remote and sparsely populated. Travelling to the island without chartering a boat is only really practical on Sunday, as there's no return ferry during the week and the island has no accommodation or flat ground on which to camp. However, you can go to Po Toi during the week – and it's especially good for seafood – if you hire a junk for the day.

There are several walking routes around the island, ranging from concrete paths to rocky, semi-overgrown trails. The most dramatic walking is on the eastern side of the island, on the steep (and often slippery) trail above the Tin Hau temple. One of Hong Kong's ancient rock carvings, thought to date back to the Bronze Age and similar to the one found at Shek O (*see p84*), is on the western side of the island. It's not far, and in two hours you should have circumnavigated the island.

The *kaido* from the ferry pier at St Stephen's beach in Stanley takes about 40 minutes and costs HK$40 return; on the way out, you'll need to tell the operator which afternoon boat you intend to return on. The *kaido* leaves Stanley on Sunday at 10am and 11am, and returns at 3pm and 4.30pm. A ferry also leaves from Aberdeen (right next to the fish market) at 8am on Sunday and returns at 6pm.

## Tap Mun Chau

**Tap Mun Chau** (*see also p100*) is a tiny island just over two kilometres long (one mile) and about one kilometre wide (half a mile), located off the north-east tip of the Sai Kung Peninsula. It's a real out-of-the-way place with considerable charm, clean water and some small but good beaches on its eastern side. There's a large and pretty **Tin Hau Temple** in the village of **Tap Mun**, whose few inhabitants still largely live off the sea. It's one of the few places in Hong Kong where you can still see seafood – mostly fish and squid – drying in the sun.

The short walk past the police post to the eastern shore goes through Tap Mun Chau's open countryside. A refreshing breeze blows off the South China Sea and big waves break against the striking rock formations. Unfortunately – and typically for Hong Kong – many weekend visitors to the island dump their rubbish along here and so it is strewn all over this side of the island. In fact, the only rubbish-free places on the island are its rubbish bins.

Boats for Tap Mun Chau depart from Ma Liu Shui ferry pier on the outskirts of Sha Tin. To reach the ferry pier, exit the Sha Tin KCR station on the east side and walk north past the station. The path goes over and then under the busy carriageway. As you emerge from the short tunnel, the ferry pier will be visible a couple of hundred metres to the north. As there are only two sailings a day to Tap Mun Chau, it's advisable to plan ahead. You can either go early and spend the whole day there, or you can take the afternoon sailing, which will give you an hour to look around the island. The journey takes about an hour on the slow old *kaido*, and costs HK$16 each way during the week and HK$25 each way at the weekend. The *kaido* leaves Ma Liu Shui at 8.30am and 3pm, returning at 11.10am and 5.30pm, Monday to Friday. Weekend departures are at 8.30am, 12.30pm and 3pm, with return journeys at 11.10am, 1.45pm and 5.30pm. However, you should phone the ferry company (2527 2513) to double-check times.

Sightseeing

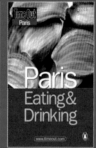

# Eat, Drink, Shop

# Restaurants

From slurping to splurging, all tastes are catered to in the culinary capital of Asia.

Visitors to Hong Kong need never go hungry. In survey after survey on favourite destinations for food lovers, only France and Italy come higher on the list. There are literally thousands of places to eat and drink – so many, in fact, that the options can be bewildering. Besides the native Cantonese fare, other popular Chinese cuisines include those of Sichuan, Chiu Chow, Beijing and Shanghai (*see p134* **Chinese cuisines**). Asian food of all kinds abounds, with scores of Japanese, Vietnamese and Thai eateries, while the international repertoire here is as good as you'll find anywhere in the world, spanning everything from French to Australian.

## The best Restaurants

### For al fresco dining
Stoep. See p146.

### For the best Peking duck
Spring Moon (*see p136*); Yung Kee (*see p124*).

### For brunch
Nicholini's. See p127.

### For a cheap bite
Fat Angelo's (*see p138*); Good Luck Thai Café (*see p127*); Noodle Box (*see p128*).

### For Chinese with style
Water Margin. See p131.

### For insider knowledge
The chef's table at Gaddi's. See p137.

### For seafood (Chinese)
Man Fung Seafood Restaurant (*see p146*); Tung Kee Restaurant (*see p145*).

### For seafood (general)
Yü. See p141.

### For stunning harbour views
Aqua (*see p138*); Petrus (*see p124*).

### For top food at palatable prices
M at the Fringe See p125.

The city is home to many expensive restaurants, but it's often in the cheaper venues – such as the steaming noodle bars or cacophonous dim sum joints – that you really get a taste of true local life. People in Hong Kong eat out regularly, so there are basic Cantonese diners everywhere, and much joy can be found in a bowl of goose noodles for a humble HK$20.

Though many Chinese restaurants have no English menus, most display their signature items in the window – strips of golden barbecued pork, yellow-skinned boiled chickens or a cooked goose hanging by its neck. You can also look at what's in the bowls of other diners and point if you fancy the same, although a busy waiter might not be able – or willing – to tell you in English what the ingredients are. In general, courtesies are dispensed with at most busy restaurants, with rushed staff tending to be abrupt and keen to usher you out before you can say '*mei dan, mgoi*' ('bill, please'). Cultural differences also extend to table manners. In Hong Kong people don't nibble chicken or fish, they pile everything in and spit out the bones on the table.

While you may not have the stomach to try some of the more exotic foods that are popular with locals – frog, snake, duck tongues, offal and chicken feet are all staples – there are more familiar alternatives, such as chicken, goose and pork. And a trip to Hong Kong without sampling dim sum (*see p143* **Dim sum**) is unforgivable. The seafood restaurants found in the Outlying Islands or on the coast of Sai Kung in the New Territories are an essential experience. Pick your catch of the day from one of the many crowded aquariums and pay for the crustacean or fish according to its weight.

Hygiene standards vary, as they do everywhere. Since the SARS outbreak in spring 2003 many lax restaurants have upped standards, but they are likely to slip again. If you end up in a suspicious-looking Chinese restaurant, wash your chopsticks in the hot tea, though if the toilet and crockery are clean you're probably OK. As usual, common sense prevails.

## PRICING GUIDELINES

When it comes to Western food, prices tend to jump considerably. Even in a standard restaurant, dinner for two with wine can easily

A Hong Kong classic: the ever-busy kitchen at **Yung Kee**. *See p124.*

Eat, Drink, Shop

top HK$1,000, while a serious high-end restaurant will dent your wallet by upwards of HK$2,500. Many of the latter places are located in the city's five-star hotels, but scores of independent world-class restaurants have opened in the past few years. Because of high rents, most are small and cosy (some might say cramped). Menus in these places tend to feature classic Western dishes and often creative contemporary fusion cuisine, combining traditional Western ingredients with Asian spices.

Note that a ten per cent service charge is automatically added to most restaurant bills in Hong Kong (but not to those in noodle bars, cafés and coffee shops). Unfortunately, however, this is rarely passed on to the staff, so a further gratuity is normal; the amount is discretionary.

We have given the ranges of main course prices where applicable, but note that many places also offer set lunch and/or dinner menus in addition to (and occasionally instead of) à la carte menus. These can help keep the price of the meal to acceptable levels, especially within the posher hotels.

In addition to the places within this chapter, many of the pubs and bars listed on p147-p155 also offer excellent food.

# Hong Kong Island

## Central

### American

#### Archie B's
*7-9 Staunton Street (2522 1262/ www.hotpastramihk.com). Central MTR (exit D2)/ Mid-Levels Escalator/buses along Des Voeux Road.* **Open** 10am-10pm daily. **Main courses** HK$60-$100. **Credit** MC, V. **Map** p308 B3.
This New York deli-style place serves pastrami and Reuben sandwiches, matzo ball soup, chopped liver, pickles, and, to finish, cheesecake and black and white cookies. The high metal stools aren't particularly comfortable, and the walls are plastered with auto-graphed photos of Madonna and other superstars who have surely never been here, but it's as close to the Big Apple as you're going to get in Hong Kong.

### Chinese

#### Café de Lan Kwai Fong
*G/F, 20-22 D'Aguilar Street (2525 6628). Central MTR (exit D1/D2).* **Open** 7.30am-2.30pm, 6pm-midnight daily. **Main courses** HK$70-$100. **Credit** DC, MC, V. **Map** p308 C4.

This retro diner isn't much food-wise, but is worth a visit for two reasons. The first is to check out the '60s-style interior. The second is to try the Hong Kong Western dishes, one of the city's unheralded native cuisines, which aren't to everyone's tastes but are well executed here. It serves cheap noodle and rice dishes too, and the afternoon set tea starts at just HK$28.

### Shui Hu Ju

*Shop E, G/F, 51A Graham Street (2869 6927). Central MTR (exit C)/Mid-Levels Escalator/buses along Des Voeux Road.* **Open** 6.30pm-midnight daily. **Main courses** HK$58-$200. **Credit** DC, MC, V. **Map** p308 C3.

The first restaurant on Graham Street proved so popular the owners opened a second place just blocks away on Peel Street. They're both done out stylishly in retro Chinese decor, and it's obvious that thought and care has gone into everything from the delicious food to the way the bill is presented (in an antique-looking wooden box). The menus differ slightly, but the food at both places is primarily Northern Chinese, with heavy flavours and lots of spices. The boneless deep-fried lamb ribs are not to be missed, and the dumplings and noodles equally good.
**Other locations**: G/F, 68 Peel Street, Central, HK Island (2869 6927).

### Tsim Chai Kee Noodle Shop

*Shop B, 98-102 Wellington Street (2850 6471). Central MTR (exit D2).* **Open** 10am-9pm daily. **Main courses** HK$10. **No credit cards**. **Map** p308 C3.

Tsim Chai Kee sells its egg and rice noodles topped with only three things: prawn dumplings, fish balls or sliced beef. It's all HK$10 a bowl, while a small plate of fresh veg is HK$5. Diners sit at communal tables on uncomfortable stools, so this is no place to linger, but with prices this low who's complaining?

### Yung Kee

*32-40 Wellington Street (2522 1624/www.yungkee. com.hk). Central MTR (exit D1, D2, G)/12M, 13, 23A, 40M, 43 bus.* **Open** 11am-11.30pm daily. **Main courses** HK$80-$320. **Credit** AmEx, DC, MC, V. **Map** p308 C3.

No trip to Hong Kong would be complete without a visit to Yung Kee. It's famous for its classic Cantonese fare, especially roast goose and barbecued pork. The 1,000-year-old duck eggs (they're not really that old, just preserved) served with fresh ginger are given to every table on arrival, but this can be an acquired taste. Staff are helpful and an English menu is available. You can just drop in, but book if you can – it's a large place but tends to be very busy.

## French

### Chez Moi

*10 Arbuthnot Road (2801 6768). Central MTR (exit G)/40M, 12, 13 bus.* **Open** noon-2.30pm, 7-11pm Mon-Sat. **Set lunch** HK$135-$185. **Set dinner** HK$495-HK$595. **Credit** AmEx, DC, MC, V. **Map** p308 C4.

Dine in a cosy, romantic room filled with whimsical knick-nacks. There's a husband and wife team (chef and pastry chef) in the kitchen, between them dishing up cuisine with all the Gallic flair you could wish for. The menu always lists a couple of rich game dishes as well as lighter fare. The quality of the food and luxurious setting make it worth the price.

### Petrus

*56/F, Island Shangri-La Hotel, Pacific Place, 88 Queensway, Admiralty (2877 3838). Admiralty MTR (exit C1)/buses along Queensway.* **Open** noon-2.30pm, 6.30-10pm daily. **Main courses** HK$250-$400. **Credit** AmEx, DC, MC, V. **Map** p309 F5.

Petrus is the kind of place where if you have to ask how much something is you can't afford it. Mind you, you probably wouldn't want to eat here every day anyway as the food is so rich and luxurious – plenty of foie gras and black truffles – but it's perfect for a special occasion. As to be expected, the wine list is impressive.

### Le Tire Bouchon

*45A Graham Street (2523 5459). Mid-Levels Escalator/26 bus.* **Open** *Bar* 11am-11pm Mon-Sat. *Restaurant* noon-2.30pm, 7-10.30pm Mon-Sat. **Main courses** HK$165-$215. **Credit** AmEx, DC, MC, V. **Map** p308 C3.

Central's oldest independent French restaurant is a hidden treasure. The entrance is almost cave-like, but the interior is extensive, homely and ideal for a romantic meal or group get together. The Gallic staff are knowledgeable about their classic French cuisine – the pièce de résistance being the tournedos rossini (beef fillet in a port and shallot sauce with duck liver). On the lighter side there is a good range of seasonally changing fish dishes. For dessert, the soufflés are wonderful.

## Indian

### Veda

*1/F, 8 Arbuthnot Road (2868 5885). Central MTR (exit K/H)/13, 12M, 23A, 40M bus.* **Open** noon-3pm, 7-11pm daily. **Main courses** HK$148-$260. **Credit** MC, V. **Map** p308 C4.

Radically changing the image of Indian food, this minimalist, stylish space offers light and even healthy contemporary Indian cuisine. The buffet lunches (HK$98) are a bargain, encompassing spiced salads, curries and tandoori meats. Dinners are a lot pricier but the imported jet-fresh ingredients are excellent and vegetarians are well catered for. A popular hangout for *tai tais* (rich housewives who lunch).

## International

### Café TOO

*7/F, Island Shangri-La Hotel, Pacific Place, 88 Queensway, Admiralty (2877 3838). Admiralty MTR (exit C1)/buses along Queensway.* **Open** 6.30am-1am daily. **Set lunch** HK$288. **Set dinner** HK$368. **Credit** AmEX, DC, MC, V. **Map** p309 F5.

Go global at the Island Shangri-La's terrific **Café TOO**. *See p124.*

The Island Shangri-La may be home to one of Hong Kong's swankiest and best French restaurants (Petrus; *see p124*) but it also houses this great buzzing café. It's self service, but the choice is endless, and you can go back as many times as you want (or as many times as your stomach can handle). There are seven 'food stations' covering cuisines such as Thai, Japanese, Indian and seafood, plus a noodle bar and a fantastic range of desserts. There is also an à la carte menu for those with a smaller appetite.

### M at the Fringe

*2 Lower Albert Road (2877 4000/m-onthebund.com/ at_the_fringe). Central MTR (exit D1)/23A bus.* **Open** noon-2.30pm, 7-10.30pm Mon-Sat. **Main courses** HK$200-$280. **Credit** AmEx, DC, MC, V. **Map** p308 C4.

This is one of Hong Kong's oldest 'independent' Western restaurants and there are many reasons it has lasted so long. The food is reliably excellent and reflects the international, eclectic tastes of the 'M' behind the name, Michelle Garnaut, who also owns the M on the Bund in Shanghai. The ever-changing menu always has a Middle Eastern dish or two as well as organ meats that appeal to the adventurous diner. Try the lamb baked in a salt crust, or the roasted suckling pig. Save room for something sweet to end the meal – the pavlova is wonderful, and the dessert platter for two could easily feed four. The dining room is whimsical yet cosy and the staff are always spot-on.

### Peak Café Bar

*9-13 Shelley Street (2140 6877). Mid-Levels Escalator/buses along Caine Road.* **Open** 11am-2am Mon-Fri; 9am-2am Sat, Sun. **Main courses** HK$75-$145. **Credit** AmEx, DC, MC, V. **Map** p308 B4.

The Peak Café was originally located where you might expect it – up on beautiful Victoria Peak with views over Hong Kong Island. When the restaurant lost its lease on the government-owned property, there was a big but unsuccessful hue and cry (the Peak Lookout, opened by a different restaurant group, is now housed in the original property; *see p133*); the Peak Café Bar packed up its successful formula and moved it here. The new menu seems shorter than before but it offers the same eclectic mix of dishes, including pizza, Thai, Indian and Western.

# Coffee break

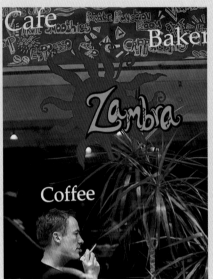

The Chinese may be a nation of tea drinkers, but these days they are in a froth over the coffee bean. Dozens of shops offering cappuccinos and espressos have sprouted up across the city in the past few years, and are especially popular with younger people and business folk.

The two main chains are **Pacific Coffee** and, inevitably, **Starbucks**, which each have more than 30 shops around town. Each group's outlets all boast comfy armchairs, newspapers to read, plus a wide range of coffees and snacks. Pacific Coffee also offers computers for net surfing and wireless access for anyone with a laptop, but Starbucks has the edge in terms of quality of coffee and food.

There are plenty of other options around too. A smaller, upmarket third chain you might come across is **Cova**, which has an excellent range of salads and sandwiches, but costs more. Two other extensive chains dotted around town are **Oliver's Super Sandwiches** and **Délifrance**. Both offer good cheap meals and sandwiches, but the coffee and tea are nothing special. **Pret A Manger** is also establishing a presence in Hong Kong. Most of the big hotels also have coffee shops

that serve exquisite cakes and snacks, but the bill will come in far higher than at a high-street chain.

For coffee connoisseurs, however, there are one or two special places worth seeking out. **Café Zambra** (239 Jaffe Road, Wan Chai, Hong Kong Island, 2535 9198; *pictured*) does more than merely serve perfectly made coffee: owner Blair Donaldson gives talks on how to perfectly roast and grind beans, which are sold in the shop. In the New Territories, **Coffee Culture** (Shop 15-16, L1, 1/F, Old Market, Maritime Square, Tsing Yi, 2880 5622) offers a quaint setting for relaxing over a beverage, while in Tsim Sha Tsui, **My Coffee** (Shop 6E, 6 Ashley Road, 2737 2500) is another good independent shop where care is taken to get the most aroma out of the bean.

Another fad to have taken hold in Hong Kong is for Taiwanese tea. You will find shops selling these unusual but delicious drinks in all the main shopping hubs such as Causeway Bay and Tsim Sha Tsui. The outlets are easy to spot because they are open-fronted and display pictures of brightly coloured drinks that look like milk shakes. A range of exotic-flavoured iced fruit teas – lychee, sesame, taro – are available. Some contain pea-sized pieces of tapioca or *nata de coco*, which are sucked through a giant straw and chewed – but be careful they don't shoot straight down your throat. Another ubiquitous tea chain is the oddly named **rbt**, which has more than 20 outlets around town.

Juice shops too are found on most street corners in Hong Kong, with blenders constantly whirring up watermelon or kiwi juices. These are cheap, healthy and delicious, although sometimes sugar solution is added to sweeten the juice. The best juice shop in town is undoubtedly the **Mix** (Shop 11, Standard & Chartered Bank Building, 3 Queen's Road, Central, 2523 7396), which as well as serving up fantastic juice and smoothie combos has sofas, computers, ambient music and an extensive range of magazines to flick through. The Mix is opening up other outlets around town too and while the drinks are expensive, at around HK$24-$36, they are worth it.

Eat, Drink, Shop

## Italian

### Nicholini's

*8/F, Conrad Hotel, Pacific Place, 88 Queensway, Admiralty (2521 3838). Admiralty MTR (exit C1)/buses along Queensway.* **Open** noon-3pm, 6.30-11pm Mon-Sat; 11am-3pm, 6.30-11pm Sun. **Main courses** HK$220-$350. **Credit** AmEx, DC, MC, V. **Map** p309 F5.

Top-notch Italian food is served in the Conrad's luxurious, somewhat formal surroundings. On the whole it's expensive, but the weekday lunch is a pretty good deal – for less than HK$250 you get an antipasti buffet and a hot main course cooked to order, plus tea or coffee. It's popular for Sunday brunch, which is one of the best in town. The floor-to-ceiling windows mean views of the harbour, so try to bag one of the window seats. Be sure to book.

### Pasta e Pizza

*11 Lyndhurst Terrace (2545 1675). Central MTR (exit D2)/Mid-Levels Escalator/12M, 40M, 23A bus/buses along Lyndhurst Terrace.* **Open** noon-3pm, 6-10.30pm Mon-Sat. **Main courses** HK$60-$90. **Credit** AmEx, MC, V. **Map** p308 C3.

Just down the road from the corporate familiarity of Pizza Express, this place offers a more Italian feel, with red and white checked tablecloths, carafes of wine and friendly waiters. The name tells you all you need to know about the menu, and the simple dishes are pretty good, especially for the cheap prices in this part of town. A jazz band plays late on Saturday nights.

## Mexican

### El Taco Loco

*LG/F, 7 Staunton Street (2522 0215/ www.tacolocohk.com). Central MTR (exit D2)/Mid-Levels Escalator/buses along Lyndhurst Terrace.* **Open** noon-midnight daily. **Main courses** HK$12-$48. **No credit cards.** **Map** p308 B3.

Here's a place where you can have your fill of Mexican food and walk out with change from HK$100. Tacos come either steamed or fried, while burritos are so stuffed they could feed an army. This is a semi self-service restaurant – you place your order at the front and pick up your food at the back, along with whatever salsa or hot sauce (from mildly spicy to incendiary) your mouth can handle.

## Middle Eastern

### Assaf Lebanese Cuisine

*G/F Lyndhurst Building, 37 Lyndhurst Terrace (2851 6550). Central MTR (exit D2)/Mid-Levels Escalator/buses along Lyndhurst Terrace.* **Open** noon-3pm, 6pm-midnight daily. **Main courses** HK$120. **Credit** AmEx, DC, MC, V. **Map** p308 C3.

This is the sister restaurant to Beyrouth Café next door (which is more of a takeaway, although it does have a few tall stools to perch on), but since Assaf is a sit-down place, prices are more expensive here. Balls of falafel are crisp and delicious, while lamb schwarma is well seasoned and not too greasy.

### Habibi/Koshary Café

**Habibi** *G/F, 112-14 Wellington Street (2544 9298). Central MTR (exit D2)/Mid-Levels Escalator/buses along Wellington Street.* **Open** 11.30am-11.30pm Mon-Sat. **Main courses** HK$80-$200. **Map** p308 C3. **Koshary Café** *Shop A, 112-114 Wellington Street (2544 3886).* **Open** 9am-midnight daily. **Main courses** HK$80-$95. **Credit** AmEx, DC, MC, V. **Map** p308 C3.

Habibi was so popular that the restaurant's owners decided to open a place next door to serve cheaper dishes. With low lights, comfy banquettes and chairs and a belly dancer who makes an appearance on weekends, Habibi is the more atmospheric of the two but the food at both is delicious and authentic. Try Koshary's namesake dish – a healthy mix of rice, pasta, grain and vegetables.

## Pan-Asian

### Bo

*1/F & 2/F, TM Leung Building, Bankers Café, 16 Gilman's Bazaar (2850 8371). Sheung Wan MTR (exit E1/E2)/buses along Des Voeux Road.* **Open** noon-2pm, 6.30-11pm daily. **Set lunch** HK$130-$220. **Set dinner** HK$600. **Credit** DC, MC, V. **Map** p308 C2.

At Bo you can eat delicious, beautifully presented Japanese cuisine in a serene, art-filled room. Everything is stylish, from the food to the music system. A *kaiseki* dinner is composed by the chef to reflect the seasons; he uses only the finest ingredients and displays an astonishing array of cooking styles. There will always be pristine fresh sashimi, ethereally light tempura and steamed or braised items, all exquisitely presented as if each dish were a still life.

### Eating Plus

*Shop 1009, 1/F, International Finance Centre (2868 0599). Central MTR Station (exit A)/buses along Connaught Road.* **Open** 7.30am-10pm daily. **Main courses** HK$60-$70. **Credit** AmEx, DC, MC, V. **Map** p309 D2.

Healthy but delicious dining is not always easy to find in Hong Kong, but Eating Plus excels at dishes that are both tasty and nutritious. From the selection of vegetable and fruit juices – the ginger juice is especially rejuvenating – to the salmon sashimi, spicy ramen noodles and tangy salads, the food is modern, innovative and is never known to disappoint. The location is ideal for weary travellers – it's in the mall above the Airport Express Central terminus.

### Good Luck Thai Café

*13 Wing Wah Lane, Lan Kwai Fong (2877 2971). Central MTR (exit D2, G)/12M, 13, 23A, 40M, 43 bus.* **Open** 11am-1pm Mon-Sat. **Main courses** HK$40-$70. **Credit** MC, V. **Map** p308 C4.

Residents may nickname Wing Wah Lane 'rat alley' but expats still come here in droves to perch on a tiny stool in this bustling side street and tuck into top Thai tucker. The tom yam and roast chicken are especially delicious. Several rival alfresco restaurants have opened nearby serving Malaysisan and Vietnamese food, but this one remains our pick. It's not for the unadventurous, but it must be doing something right as on most evenings it's still hard to find a stool.

### Indochine 1929

*2/F, California Tower, Lan Kwai Fong (2869 7399). Central MTR (exit D2/G)/12M, 13, 23A, 40M, 43 bus.* **Open** *noon-2.30pm, 6.30-10.30pm Sun.* **Main courses** HK$116-$200. **Credit** AmEx, DC, MC, V. **Map** p308 C4.

One of the best dining experiences in Hong Kong, this place is as much about atmosphere as food – though that's first class too. The decor harks back to French colonial Indochina, and is ideal for both a romantic dinner or a group gathering. The Vietnamese food here is perhaps the best in Hong Kong, while the budget-conscious can eat reasonably inexpensively if they mix and match starters rather than opt for the pricier mains. Vegetarians will delight in the crunchy sautéed lotus root with water chestnuts, snow peas and walnuts.

### Kyoto Joe

*LG/F & G/F, The Plaza, 21 D'Aguilar Street (2804 6800). Central MTR (exit D2).* **Open** *noon-2.30pm, 6.30-10.45pm Mon-Sat.* **Main courses** HK$150-$300. **Credit** AmEx, DC, MC, V. **Map** p308 C4.

A younger sister to Tokio Joe around the corner at 16 Lan Kwai Fong, Kyoto Joe is brighter and more modern. The food is excellent at both – from the sushi and sashimi platters (the soft-shell crab roll is sensational) to the *robatayaki* grill and innovative mains. It's not cheap, but then good Japanese restaurants rarely are.

## Top five

# Hotel restaurants

### Gaddi's
See p137.

### Grissini
See p131.

### One Harbour Road
See p131.

### Petrus
See p124.

### Spoon
See p138.

### Noodle Box

*30-32 Wyndham Street (2536 0571). Central MTR (exit D1, G)/bus 13, 26, 43.* **Open** *11.30am-10pm Mon-Sat.* **Main courses** HK$30-$55. **No credit cards.** **Map** p308 C4.

With more than a dozen bowls of noodles to choose from, either fried or in broth, the Noodle Box is great for traditional food in a modern setting. The spicy seafood or chicken in coconut curry sauce is irresistible, as is the green papaya salad. But the best thing about this place is its weekday happy hour between 3.30pm and 6pm, when prices for main course noodle dishes are slashed to just HK$30, making them a bargain.

### Pearl

*G/F, 7 Wo On Lane, Lan Kwai Fong (2522 4223). Central MTR (exit D2/G)/buses along Wellington Street.* **Open** *11am-9pm Mon-Fri.* **Main courses** HK$15-$33. **No credit cards.** **Map** p308 C4.

Pearl gets crowded during the weekday lunch rush but the pace is more leisurely at dinner. The food is inexpensive – not authentically Vietnamese, but still good. Fried spring rolls are hot and crisp, while the Vietnamese version of ravioli is smooth and flavourful. If you're dining upstairs, beware of the low ceilings.

## Spanish

### Olé

*1/F, Shun Ho Tower, 24-30 Ice House Street (2523 8624). Central MTR (exit D2, G)/13, 23A, 26, 43 bus.* **Open** *noon-3pm, 6.30-11.30pm daily.* **Main courses** HK$100-$360. **Credit** AmEx, DC, MC, V. **Map** p309 D4.

Authentic Spanish food is served up with true passion at Olé. The excellent paella is the highlight of the menu, but if you feel like splurging try the delicate suckling pig. The atmosphere is informal, with musicians serenading diners and the sangria flowing freely.

## Sheung Wan

### British

### Phoenix

*G/F, 5 U Lam Terrace, nr Bellevue Place (2546 2110). Bus 13, 23, 23A, 23B.* **Open** *6.30-11.30pm Mon-Fri; 11am-11pm Sat, Sun.* **Main courses** HK$100-$150. **Credit** MC, V. **Map** p308 B3.

This gastropub is a short walk up the steps from Man Mo Temple near SoHo. The menu is constantly changing and while the bangers and mash or roast may set you back more than usual, the quality is high. Weekend breakfasts are authentic full English affairs and British newspapers are provided to further soothe homesick expats. It's also BYOB, meaning you can drastically cut down your drinks bill.

Enjoy prime molluscs and priceless views at the Sheraton's **Oyster & Wine Bar**. *See p137.*

## Wan Chai, Causeway Bay & Happy Valley

### Chinese

#### American (Peking) Restaurant

*20 Lockhart Road, Wan Chai (2527 7277). Wan Chai MTR (exit C)/buses along Hennessy Road.* **Open** 11.30am-10.30pm daily. **Main courses** HK$80-$140. **Credit** AmEx, DC, MC, V. **Map** p310 B3.

Expats and tourists love the American, fuelling criticism that it's too Westernised. But it's an institution and the mainly Beijing dishes are rooted in the capital's rich culinary heritage, from the sinfully delicious Peking duck to the moreish minced pigeon in lettuce leaves. Beware the MSG rush at the meal's end. It's a busy place, so book ahead.

#### FF Hotpot

*340-44 Marsh Road ,Wan Chai (2838 9392). Causeway Bay MTR (exit B)/buses along Hennessy Road.* **Open** 11am-4.30am daily. **Credit** V.

'Fay fay', as this place is known to its fans, serves only Sichuanese hotpot, but there's still plenty of choice. You can order your broth in varying degrees

of spiciness, or you can opt for a plainer broth (try a split pot of spicy and non-spicy, preferably the one with preserved egg). Then you have to decide which of the myriad meat, seafood, vegetables and noodles (each costing around HK$20-$50) to cook in the broth. It's a tough decision to make. If you don't like offal, there are many alternatives – sliced beef, chicken or pork, or fish, prawns and other seafood. Even vegetarians can come out of here stuffed on gluten puffs, fried beancurd and a vast array of vegetables.

#### King's Palace Congee & Noodle Bar

*G/F, 22 Sing Woo Road, Happy Valley (2838 4444). Bus 1, 19/Tram to Happy Valley.* **Open** 11.30am-midnight daily. **Main courses** HK$35-$120. **Credit** DC, MC, V.

A top place to come at weekends, especially if you've overdone it on the alcohol the night before. Congee is brilliant for sensitive stomachs as it's light, subtle and comforting. And whereas many other congee places are not conducive to soothing throbbing heads and bleary eyes – they tend to be bright, loud and filled with cigarette fumes – King's Palace has comfortable booths, plays classical music at a low volume and makes outstanding congee (especially the one with fresh crab) and noodles.

**Red Pepper.** *See p131.*

## Lao Ching Hing
*Basement, Century Hotel, 257 Lockhart Road, Wan Chai (2598 6080). Wan Chai MTR (exit A1)/buses along Gloucester Road.* **Open** 11am-11pm daily. **Main courses** HK$50-$250. **Credit** AmEx, MC, V. **Map** p310 C3.
Because of its location, in the basement of an average hotel, this roomy restaurant is often overlooked by those not in the know, but the Shanghainese cuisine here is first rate. From staple dishes such as tofu noodles to more unusual specialities like braised lion-head meatballs and drunken Shanghai crab, the food is a great introduction to Shanghainese fare.

## One Harbour Road
*7/F-8/F, Grand Hyatt Hotel, 1 Harbour Road, Wan Chai (2588 1234, ext 7338). Wan Chai MTR (exit A1/C)/A12, 18, 88 bus/Wan Chai Star Ferry Pier.* **Open** noon-2.30pm, 6.30-10.30pm daily. **Main courses** HK$300-$400. **Credit** AmEx, DC, MC, V. **Map** p308 B2.
The Grand Hyatt's opulent art deco dining room may seem a strange venue for Cantonese cuisine, but somehow it works. And the dishes may sound familiar (chicken with shallots and black bean sauce, hot and sour soup), but here they're given such expert treatment, and have such delicate spicing, that you'd hardly recognise them. Service is exemplary, and the wide-ranging wine list and great harbour views are further draws. Note that the dress code is smart.

## Red Pepper
*G/F, 7 Lan Fong Road, Causeway Bay (2577 3811). Causeway Bay MTR (exit B)/buses along Percival Street & Leighton Road.* **Open** 11.30am-midnight daily. **Main courses** HK$200-$300. **Credit** AmEx, DC, MC, V. **Map** p311 E3.
Red Pepper has been winning awards for many years, but recent diners have given mixed reports. Admittedly, its decor is looking a bit long in the tooth and the dishes can be hit-or-miss, but they're all as spicy and intensely flavoured as Sichuan cuisine demands. Try the sizzling chilli prawns, sour and pepper soup or the dry-fried spring beans with minced pork.

## Water Margin
*Shop 1205, 12/F, Food Forum, Times Square, Causeway Bay (3102 0088). Causeway Bay MTR (exit A)/tram to Happy Valley.* **Open** noon-3pm, 6-11pm daily. **Main courses** HK$50-$200. **Credit** DC, MC, V. **Map** p311 D3.
This Northern Chinese restaurant is a 'wealthy relation' to the Shui Hu Ju restaurants in Central (*see p124*) – it's a much bigger, more stylish space and the menu is far more extensive (and a little more expensive). Fortunately, the owners haven't toned down the rich, spicy flavours. The cooks here are known for using some unusual ingredients in delicious ways – the fried pig's palate with onions and coriander shouldn't be missed by more adventurous diners.

# French

## Olala
*G/F, Hung Dak Building, 1 Electric Street, Wan Chai (2294 0450). Buses along Queen's Road East.* **Open** noon-3pm, 6.30pm-midnight daily. **Set lunch** HK$280. **Set dinner** (8 courses) HK$500-$680. **Credit** MC, V. **Map** p310 A4.
There's no menu at Olala. At lunchtime, the owner comes out, tells the customers what ingredients he has and composes a meal around what they like and how hungry they are. At dinner, you just sit down and eat what the chefs have decided to cook. French haute cuisine this isn't – the food is served 'family style', on plates in the middle of the table so everybody can help themselves, but it's always plentiful, innovative and delicious. The service is just as casual.

# Indian

## Viceroy
*2/F, Sun Hung Kai Centre, 30 Harbour Road, Wan Chai (2827 7777/www.harilela.com.hk). Wan Chai MTR (exit A1)/buses along Gloucester Road.* **Open** noon-2.30pm daily. **Main courses** HK$70-$108. **Credit** AmEx, DC, MC, V. **Map** p310 C3.
The harbour view from the terrace makes Viceroy a popular venue for parties and comedy nights, but mostly it's a fine Indian restaurant. Efficient, friendly staff serve up food that's fit for a rajah, with piquant curries and mouthwateringly tender tandooris. It's swisher than your average curry house, and on the whole worth the extra you have to pay. The buffet lunch costs HK$98.

# International

## Open Kitchen
*6/F, Hong Kong Arts Centre, 2 Harbour Road, Wan Chai (2827 2923). Wan Chai MTR (exit A1, C)/A12, 18, 88 bus/Wan Chai Star Ferry Pier.* **Open** 11am-9pm Mon-Fri; 10am-11pm Sat, Sun. **Main courses** HK$60-$150. **Credit** AmEx, MC, V. **Map** p310 B3.
This has to be one of the best deals in town – decent food (although you have to choose carefully), reasonable prices and a great view overlooking the harbour. The front area has standard, ready-cooked dishes – casseroles, lasagne, baked potatoes and a salad bar – while the back area has a line of cooks ready to make an eclectic selection of dishes to order. Avoid the pastas and opt for the fish and chips or the spicy Singaporean laksa.

# Italian

## Grissini
*2/F, Grand Hyatt Hotel, 1 Harbour Road, Wan Chai (2588 1234, ext 7313). Wan Chai MTR (exit A1/C)/A12, 18, 88 bus/Wan Chai Star*

Seafood specialist **Yü**, where presentation is an art form. *See p141.*

*Ferry Pier.* **Open** noon-2.30pm, 7-11pm daily.
**Main courses** HK$300-$350. **Credit** AmEx, DC,
MC, V. **Map** p310 B2.
This is one of the finest Italian restaurants in Hong
Kong; with the highest-quality lobster, veal and
homemade pastas on the menu, the hardest thing
is choosing what to have. Seasonal specials – in
particular ones incorporating white and black
truffles – are astounding. The crowd tends towards
businessmen on expense accounts at lunchtimes, but
broadens to anyone who appreciates good food at
dinner. Provided they can afford it, that is.

### Milano

*2/F, Sun Hung Kai Centre, 30 Harbour Road,
Wan Chai (2598 1222). Wan Chai MTR (exit A)/
buses along Gloucester Road/Wan Chai Star
Ferry Pier.* **Open** noon-3pm, 6-11pm daily. **Main
courses** HK$58-$188. **Credit** AmEx, MC, DC, V.
**Map** p310 C3.
Walk in the entrance and turn right for Italian food
at Milano (or left for Vietnamese cuisine at sister
restaurant Saigon). If you can't decide between the
two, the staff will let you order from both menus.
Milano's most coveted seats are on the small terrace
with its view of the harbour and Tsim Sha Tsui. The
pasta dishes are dependable, as are the pizzas, with
thin, crisp crusts.

## Middle Eastern

### Zahra's

*409A Jaffe Road, Wan Chai (2838 4597). Causeway
Bay MTR (exit C)/buses along Hennessy Road.* **Open**
6.45-11pm Mon-Sat. **Main courses** HK$70-$150.
**Credit** MC, DC, V. **Map** p310 D3.
Residents in the know head to this tiny eaterie for
their fix of Lebanese food. Booking is advisable as
there are just a few tables packed into the drab-
looking space. The food, however, is a different
story: from the bean dips to the roast meats and
spicy prawn dishes, everything is flavourful.

## Pan-Asian

### Chili Club

*1/F, 88 Lockhart Road, Wan Chai (2527 2872).
Wan Chai MTR (exit C)/buses along Hennessy Road.*
**Open** noon-3pm, 6-10.30pm daily. **Main courses**
HK$45-$130. **Credit** AmEx, MC, V. **Map** p310 B3.
Don't come here for the service, which can be atro-
cious, but for the sizzling hot food at cool prices. The
steamed fish arrives simmering in a sauce bubbling
with fresh chillis and coriander. The tom yam soup,
pad Thai and curries are also good. All dishes are
big enough to share, so try not to over-order.

## Kokage

*Starcrest, 9 Star Street, Wan Chai (2529 6138).*
*Admiralty MTR (exit F)/buses along Queen's Road*
*East.* **Open** noon-2.30pm Mon-Fri; 6-11.30pm Sat.
**Main courses** HK$142-$168. **Credit** AmEx, DC,
MC. **Map** p310 A4.

Chef Bryan Nagao left the Peninsula's famed
Felix restaurant to set up Kokage, a contemporary
Japanese restaurant in the heart of this rejuvenated
part of Wan Chai. Although there is a fantastic sushi
bar, the mains are chiefly Western dishes with a
Japanese twist, such as prime US steak with wasabi
sauce. The wine and drinks list is outstanding, and
the crowd assuredly cool.

## Perfume River

*G/F, 89 Percival Street, Causeway Bay (2576 2240).*
*Causeway Bay MTR (exit A).* **Open** 11am-11pm
daily. **Main courses** HK$28-$65. **Credit** AmEx,
DC, MC, V. **Map** p311 D3.

This joint doesn't look anything special, but the food
is always good and the low bills even better. The
huge menu is all over the place, but take a few
minutes and you'll soon find some tempting dishes.
The frog's leg curry is a good alternative to the usual
chicken, and the prawn crackers topped with spicy
minced pork make an excellent starter. The decor is
nothing to write home about… and be careful not to
bump your head on the low ceiling upstairs.

## WasabiSabi

*13/F, Food Forum, Times Square, 1 Matheson*
*Street, Causeway Bay (2506 0009). Causeway Bay*
*MTR (exit A).* **Open** noon-midnight Mon-Thur,
Sun; noon-2am Fri, Sat. *Food served* noon-3pm,
6-10.45pm Mon-Thur, Sun; noon-3pm, 6-11pm Fri,
Sat. **Main courses** HK$78-$300. **Credit** DC, MC, V.
**Map** p311 D3.

WasabiSabi's sleek compartmentalised interior,
separated by flowing chain curtains and with plush
red furnishings, is big on the 'wow' factor. The food
is contemporary Japanese – think traditional dishes
with a modern twist. The sushi platter comes without wasabi, but is topped with mouthwatering
extras. A DJ spins until late on Saturday nights for
those who wish to linger.

# Vegetarian

## Nice Fragrance Vegetarian Kitchen

*105-107 Thompson Road, Wan Chai (2838 3608).*
*Wan Chai MTR (exit A3)/buses along Johnston*
*Road.* **Open** 11am-11pm daily. **Main courses**
HK$40-$70. **Credit** MC, V. **Map** p310 B/C3.

Chinese vegetarian food tends to be 'mock meat'
simulations of real meat dishes – there's mock goose,
mock chicken, and even mock shark's fin. Actually,
these dishes taste fine on their own merits, but they
bear no similarities to meat. At this restaurant you
can taste a good variety of vegetarian dishes – not
just mock meat, but also more interesting items
such as oyster mushrooms with eggplant and chilli
and beancurd balls with mushrooms.

# The Peak

## International

### Café Deco

*1/F & 2/F, Peak Galleria, 118 Peak Road (2849*
*5111). Peak Tram Upper Terminus/15, 15B bus.*
**Open** 11am-11pm Mon-Thur, Sun; 11am-midnight
Fri, Sat. **Main courses** HK$200-$240. **Credit**
AmEx, DC, MC, V. **Map** p77.

This is a huge, impressive space and the setting is
stunning, especially if you're lucky enough to get
one of the window seats. As to be expected from the
name, authentic art deco touches are everywhere.
The menu is eclectic but features lots of beautifully
fresh seafood. If you can tear your eyes away from
the magnificent view of Hong Kong, you can watch
the chefs at work in the open kitchen.

### EAT Noodles

*Shop 201, 2/F, Peak Tower, 128 Peak Road*
*(2849 5777). Peak Tram/15 bus.* **Open** 11.30am-
8pm daily. **Main courses** HK$16-$45. **Credit** MC,
V. **Map** p77.

Not surprisingly, Eat Noodles specialises in noodle
dishes from all over Asia, including stir-fried and
soup noodles from China, Thailand and Singapore.
The menu also has non-noodle snacks such as several types of satay. There's a balcony with a great
view, while inside is great for people-watching.
**Other locations: EAT at Pacific Place** Shop
008, LG/F, Pacific Place, 88 Queensway, Admiralty,
HK Island (2868 3235); **EAT on Ice** Shop 136, 1/F,
City Plaza, Taikoo Shing (2567 8608).

### Peak Lookout

*121 Peak Road (2849 1000). Peak Tram/15 bus.*
**Open** 10.30am-11.30pm Mon-Fri; 8.30am-1am Sat,
Sun. **Main courses** HK$230-$300. **Credit** AmEx,
MC, V. **Map** p77.

This restaurant replaced the much-loved Peak Café,
which relocated to Central a few years ago (*see*
*p125*). The new owners were smart enough to let the
magnificent space speak for itself, and they also kept
the same mix of East and West dishes that proved
so popular in the past. If it's a balmy day or evening,
try to get a seat outside, where the aromas from the
outdoor barbecue will get your tummy rumbling.

# South & east coasts

## International

### Black Sheep

*G/F, 452 Shek O Village (2809 2021). Shau Kei*
*Wan MTR/9 bus.* **Open** 1-10pm daily. **Main**
**courses** HK$75-$165. **Credit** AmEx, MC, V.

Diners flock to this fussily decorated former shop
for mainly European food in a cosy village atmosphere. The menu is pretty varied but the fish and
seafood dishes are the things to go for. A reasonable
selection of wines and beers completes the picture.

Eat, Drink, Shop

# Chinese cuisines

Chinese people are renowned for eating practically anything. In practice, this means anything that's not poisonous. This extends to some items most of us wouldn't immediately think of as being edible, such as bird's nests, snakes' blood and turtle shells. China is huge, and producing enough food to feed so many people (1.3 billion at the last count) is difficult. And while some ingredients might once have been used out of necessity, skilled Chinese chefs have turned them into delicacies.

In the West, people would never say, 'Let's go out for European food' – instead they would specify French, Italian, German or whatever. In the same way, Chinese people in Hong Kong don't say, 'Let's go out for Chinese food' – they pin it down to Cantonese, Shanghainese, Sichuanese and so on. Cuisines from most provinces of China are available in Hong Kong, although some are more popular than others.

## CANTONESE AND HONG KONG

Hong Kong is made up mostly of Chinese people from the south (Guangdong province), from the city previously known as Canton (now Guangzhou). It's not surprising, then, that the most popular cuisine in Hong Kong is Cantonese. In this type of cooking, the freshness of ingredients is paramount and cooking techniques (especially steaming) are evolved to highlight the freshness. Because subtlety of flavours is so important, Cantonese cooks use a light, delicate hand with seasonings. To those who prefer more robust flavours, Cantonese food might seem bland.

Many restaurants show exactly how fresh their seafood is by displaying it alive in large tanks. The variety is extensive, not just the expected fish, lobsters, crabs, prawns and scallops, but also more unusual items such as squilla (called 'pissing prawns' because they squirt water), horseshoe crabs and foot-long cuttlefish. The fish and seafood is ordered, scooped from the tank and brought in nets to the table so guests can inspect their order for liveliness. The 'victim' is then taken to the kitchen to be dispatched and cooked, often by steaming. Fish is steamed with soy sauce and shredded ginger; after it's removed from the steamer, it is covered with spring onions and fresh coriander and hot oil is poured over to wilt the vegetables. Scallops in their shells (with the roe still attached) and baby long-necked clams are cooked in a similar method, sometimes with fried garlic in place of spring onions, while fresh abalone is steamed with black beans.

Another traditional Cantonese cooking technique (although it's used all over China) is stir-frying, which seals in the flavour of

### The Verandah

*1/F, Repulse Bay Hotel, 109 Repulse Bay Road, Repulse Bay (2812 2722). Bus 6, 6A, 6X, 61, 66, 260, 262.* **Open** *noon-2.30pm, 3-5.30pm, 6.30-10.30pm Mon-Sat; 11am-2.30pm Sun.* **Main courses** HK$200-$300. **Credit** AmEx, DC, MC, V.
A superb romantic setting inside the landmark Repulse Bay Hotel, with lazy overhead fans and stately decor, the Verandah is a blast from the colonial past. The view of the bay is sublime, the food classic (the likes of foie gras) and the list of wines and *digestifs* extensive. The Sunday brunch is legendary, so book weeks in advance.

### Wildfire

*Murray House, Stanley Plaza, Stanley (2813 6060/ www.igors.com). Bus 6, 6A, 6X, 61, 66, 260, 262.* **Open** *11.30am-10.30pm daily.* **Main courses** HK$99-$188. **Credit** DC, MC, V. **Map** p83.
The speciality at Wildfire is thin-crust pizzas baked in a wood-fired oven. There's a huge choice, from a simple margharita to a fancier black forest (with mushrooms, roasted garlic, spinach, parmesan and pine nuts). Pastas are also popular, as are the grilled meats, served on long metal skewers.

**Other locations**: 13 Bonham Road, Central, HK Island (2540 6669); 21 Elgin Street, Central, HK Island (2810 0670).

## Mediterranean

### Lucy's

*G/F, 64 Stanley Main Street, Stanley (2813 9055). Bus 6, 6A, 6X, 61, 66, 260, 262.* **Open** *noon-3pm, 7-10.30pm daily.* **Main courses** HK$150-$190. **Credit** MC, V. **Map** p83.
Hidden in the rabbit warren of Stanley Market, Lucy's offers an oasis of calm amid the shopping madness. Its bamboo furniture reflects its unpretentious atmosphere, which also extends to the good, simple food, including couscous, salads and pastas.

## Pan-Asian

### Chilli N Spice

*Shop 101, Murray House, Stanley Plaza, Stanley (2899 0147). Bus 6, 6A, 6X, 61, 66, 260, 262.* **Open** *noon-midnight daily.* **Main courses** HK$50-$100. **Credit** AmEx, DC, MC, V. **Map** p83.

foods by cooking it quickly over high heat for no more than a minute. Much prized by the discerning diner is *wok hay*, which translates as the 'breath of a wok' – an elusive aroma and flavour that comes when a skilled chef cooks in a well-seasoned wok.

The most popular meat for most Chinese (except those who belong to the Muslim or Jewish faiths) is pork. Cantonese cooks marinate long strips of slightly fatty pork in a sweet and savoury sauce and then barbecue the meat to make *char siu*, or else they roast whole pigs until the skin becomes blistered and crisp. Both of these are commonly available at roast meat shops that also sell soy sauce chicken and roast duck or goose. Even the best home cooks will rarely make any of these meats, preferring to leave it to the experts.

Because Hong Kong is affluent compared to most of mainland China, and is also more influenced by other Asian countries and the West, many agree that it has developed a cuisine of its own. Hong Kong cuisine takes the form of Cantonese dishes that incorporate less-than-traditional ingredients. Some unusual dishes you'll find here include crab or shrimp and mayonnaise in fried dumplings, and lobster with cheese sauce and noodles. Outside influences are also seen in the so-

called Hong Kong-Western restaurants, which combine rather old-fashioned Russian, British, American and 'Continental' cuisine in an unusual way. The menus have borscht and chicken Kiev, steaks covered in brown sauce served on sizzling platters and accompanied by spaghetti in tomato sauce, and for dessert, black forest gateau or crème brûlée.

### SHANGHAINESE

This is probably the second most popular cuisine in Hong Kong. Shanghainese people tend to be wealthy, and many government officials, including the Chief Executive Tung Chee-hwa, are originally from Shanghai. The cuisine, too, is rich, both in flavour and texture. Heavy, unctuous brown sauces are used for braising meats such as pork shanks or knuckle, or to simmer fatty pork balls with vegetables. Dumplings are popular, and very different from the lighter Cantonese variety. The most famous Shanghainese dumplings are *xiao long bao*, which are filled with pork and flavourful broth made solid with gelatine. The gelatine melts in the heat of the steamer and fills the interior of the dumpling with liquid. They're then dipped in a sauce made with Shanghainese brown vinegar and shreds of ginger. This unusual vinegar is an essential flavouring to other dishes – it's an ingredient ▶

The seafront setting of this colonial-style building makes this a great choice. The speciality is spicy South-east Asian food – Singaporean, Thai, Vietnamese and Malaysian – but as flavours are toned down for the more timid Hong Kong palate, if you can take the heat be sure to inform your waiter.

### Shek O Chinese-Thai Seafood

*303 Shek O Village (2809 4426). Shau Kei Wan MTR/9 bus.* **Open** 11.15am-10pm daily. **Main courses** HK$50-$60. **Credit** AmEx, MC, V.

You can't miss this big open restaurant situated next to the main bus stop and right on the only round-about in Shek O. It dishes up everything from fried rice and steamed fish Cantonese-style to spicier curries and hot chilli dishes typical of Thailand. Brightly lit and sparsely decorated, the restaurant is most popular with hikers looking for a filling meal and a few beers after walking the Dragon's Back (*see p82* **Across the Dragon's Back**).

### Sukho Thai

*Stanley Beach Villa, 90 Stanley Street, Stanley (2899 0999). Bus 6, 6A, 6X, 61, 66, 260, 262.* **Open** noon-3pm, 6.30-10.30pm daily.

**Main courses** HK$80-$138. **Credit** DC, MC, V. **Map** p83.

Overlooking Stanley's main street with a view of the beach, this place serves up the spicy, aromatic and refreshing flavours that Thai cuisine is known for. Try the stir-fried roast duck with chilli paste and basil leaves, or the prawns with dried shrimp, egg-plant and tamarind lime sauce. If it's a nice day, be sure to reserve a window seat.

# Kowloon

## Tsim Sha Tsui

## Chinese

### Heaven on Earth

*G/F & 1/F, 6 Knutsford Terrace (2367 8428). Tsim Sha Tsui MTR (exit B1, B2).* **Open** 4.30pm-2am Mon-Thur; 4.30pm-3am Fri, Sat; 4.30pm-1am Sun. **Main courses** HK$80-$150. **Credit** AmEx, DC, MC, V. **Map** p313 C5.

in some braising sauces and stir-fries and is drizzled over seafood, including delicate freshwater shrimp.

While the main starch of Chinese from the South is rice, the Shanghainese prefer bread to accompany their dishes. The poetically named 'silver threads' bread (so called because the interior dough is formed into long, thin strands and then wrapped in a flat sheet of dough) is subtly sweet and comes either steamed or fried; the former is better for sopping up juices.

Shanghainese also specialise in so-called 'cold dishes', which are not actually cold, but room temperature or tepid. They're most often eaten as an appetiser but are so delicious and varied it's easy to make an entire meal of them. They include jellyfish flavoured with sesame oil, mashed soybeans with preserved vegetables, sweet and crispy fried eel, and 'drunken' chicken or pigeon, which has been marinated in rice wine until the flavour permeates the meat.

### SICHUANESE
Most people think of Sichuan food as hot and spicy, although this isn't always the case – it's more that it has strong flavours. When chillies (both dried and fresh) are used, they're usually paired with tiny, reddish-brown Sichuan

peppercorns, which have a unique, numbing/tingling effect on the tongue. Sichuan food is hearty and rich, with sauces that ideally blend sweet, sour and spicy flavours. Hot and sour soup is probably the Sichuanese dish best known in the West – it combines vinegar, pepper and chillies to make a powerful, sinus-clearing broth. Dumplings and breads are also popular in Sichuanese cuisine. Plain steamed buns are usually served with tea-smoked duck; meat dumplings look similar to Cantonese won ton, but instead of being served in a subtle broth, they're smothered in a sauce of soy, garlic and chillies.

### BEIJING
Beijing has been the capital of China since the time of the emperors, and, as such, developed an imperial cuisine. Unfortunately, much of this highly developed, intricate cuisine was lost during Mao's 'Great Leap Forward' in the late 1950s. Some restaurants in Hong Kong serve abbreviated version of imperial Beijing banquets, but they are hard to come by.

Beijing cuisine is rich and oily. Lamb and mutton are popular, and stir-fried slivers of meat and vegetables are frequently served stuffed into pockets of sesame-coated baked breads. The cuisine's most famous dish is

The busy restaurant area of Knutsford Terrace is hidden from the busy streets of Tsim Sha Tsui, but it's worth searching out. Heaven on Earth has a popular bar on the ground floor and a quieter restaurant upstairs. Staff are friendly and will recommend their favourites from the menu, which lists mostly Beijing and Sichuan specialities. The cold dishes, such as the spicy green bean noodles and the unusual 'jade' vegetable, are particularly good,

### Spring Deer
*1/F, 42 Mody Road (2366 4012). Tsim Sha Tsui MTR (exit D2)/buses along Nathan Road.* **Open** noon-3pm, 6-11pm daily. **Main courses** HK$80-$200. **Credit** AmEx, DC, MC, V. **Map** p313 C6.
There's one reason to come here: Peking duck. Every table orders one because it's one of the best versions in town (and reasonably priced too). Waiters scurry around with trolleys and carve the golden brown skin of the basted bird on to a platter ready for you to roll up with cucumber, celery and the sweet, tangy hoisin sauce. There are plenty of other choices, but if you skip the duck you'll never forgive yourself.

### Spring Moon
*1/F, Peninsula Hotel, Salisbury Road (2315 3160). Tsim Sha Tsui MTR (exit E)/buses to Tsim Sha Tsui Ferry Pier & along Salisbury Road/Tsim Sha Tsui Star Ferry Pier.* **Open** 11.30am-3pm, 6-11pm daily. **Main courses** HK$180-$300. **Credit** AmEx, DC, MC, V. **Map** p313B/C6.
Located inside the timeless Peninsula hotel, Spring Moon lives up to expectations. Classic and creative Cantonese cuisine is served to a cultured crowd who don't mind working through their wallet for dining of the highest quality. Whether you plump for the duck, goose, abalone or lobster, everything is magnificently done and served up with a large helping of style.

## Fish/seafood

### Island Seafood & Oyster Bar
*G/F, 10 Knutsford Terrace, Kimberly Road (2312 6663). Tsim Sha Tsui MTR (exit B1, B2)/buses along Nathan Road.* **Open** noon-11pm daily. **Main courses** HK$160-$290. **Credit** AmEx, DC, MC, V. **Map** p313 C5.

Peking duck. It is always served with great ceremony by a white-gloved waiter carving off the deep, mahogany-coloured skin, wrapping the pieces in a thin pancake with a dab of plum sauce and a sliver of spring onion. When it's good, the skin is the best part of the duck – it should be crisp, flavourful and with just a hint of fat. Traditionally, the meat comes as a separate course – usually stir-fried with vegetables – while the bones are simmered into soup and served at the end of the meal.

### CHIU CHOW

The Chiu Chow region of south-east Guangdong province in home to a popular Cantonese splinter cuisine. It's easy to recognise Chiu Chow restaurants – they always have whole cooked goose, crabs and other pre-cooked dishes displayed at the front. These dishes are served at room temperature – never hot. The goose is simmered in a strong broth, chopped to order and served with a sauce of garlicky white vinegar; the same dipping sauce is used for the flower crabs (so called because of the pattern on the shells).

One characteristic of Chiu Chow cuisine is pickled vegetables, which are eaten as a condiment or cooked with other ingredients.

The chefs make extensive use of finely ground white pepper, which flavours soups and other dishes. A small shaker of white pepper is always served with a typical Chiu Chow dish of *ho jai jook* (congee with preserved vegetables and small oysters). These small oysters are also used in oyster omelette, again served with white pepper.

### HAKKA

The Hakka are a nomadic group of people, many of whom ultimately settled in Hong Kong (they can be seen mostly in the New Territories farmlands – they're recognised by their distinctive triangular straw hats). There's nothing subtle about Hakka cuisine – it's oily and flavourful. Because Hakka people were traditionally poor, their cuisine makes great use of inexpensive ingredients, especially offal. A popular dish is *jah dai cheung* – lengths of pig's intestine, sometimes stuffed with whole spring onions, and fried so it has a crackling crisp exterior. Fresh pork belly is braised with preserved vegetables or taro. The most famous Hakka dish is salt-baked chicken – a whole chicken is wrapped in paper, buried in salt and baked, which seals in the flavour. It's served with two dipping sauces – one made with thick sesame paste and the other with spring onions, ginger and oil.

**Eat, Drink, Shop**

This high-ceilinged, multi-level restaurant is great not just for its food, but also for watching the people wandering by on Knutsford Terrace. The seafood and raw oysters are delicious, but there are also enough dishes to satisfy meat eaters. The oyster varieties change according to the season, and there's always an extensive choice.
**Other locations**: Shop C, Towning Mansion, 55-6 Paterson Street, Causeway Bay, Central, HK Island (2915 7110).

### Oyster & Wine Bar

*18/F, Sheraton Hong Kong Hotel & Towers, 20 Nathan Road (2369 1111). Tsim Sha Tsui MTR (exit E)/buses along Nathan Road/Tsim Sha Tsui Star Ferry Pier.* **Open** 6.30pm-1am Mon-Thur; 6.30pm-2am Fri, Sat. **Main courses** HK$90-$600. **Credit** AmEx, DC, MC, V. **Map** p313 C6.
The view alone is worth a visit to this place, but the oysters are the main event. Stroll to the oyster bar and choose from the 20 or more varieties nestled in ice – if necessary, the chef can advise on which order to eat them in. The oysters are then shucked and rushed to your table. Plenty of mains are offered and the wine list is extensive.

## French

### Gaddi's

*1/F, Peninsula Hotel, Salisbury Road (2315 3171). Tsim Sha Tsui MTR (exit E)/buses to Tsim Sha Tsui Ferry Pier & along Salisbury Road/Tsim Sha Tsui Star Ferry Pier.* **Open** noon-3pm, 7-11pm Mon-Sat. **Main courses** HK$300-$450. **Credit** AmEx, DC, MC, V. **Map** p313 B/C6.
Gaddi's celebrated its 50th anniversary in October 2003 – testament to the quality food that has kept gourmets through several culinary eras. With irrepressible Brit Philip Sedgwick adding a creative flair to the traditional luxury ingredients that the place is famous for – foie gras, caviar, lobster and so on – the restaurant's stock is rising again. If you book ahead you can reserve the 'chef's table' in the kitchen and watch the man himself in action. The space has an air of grandeur, but the once-stuffy dress code has been relaxed, meaning smart-casual for lunch and jacket but no tie at dinner. You can even dance to the sultry live jazz singer and band. For real gourmets, the ten-course tasting menu shouldn't be missed.

### Spoon

*Intercontinental Hotel, 18 Salisbury Road (2313 2256). Tsim Sha Tsui MTR (exit E)/buses along Salisbury Road/Tsim Sha Tsui Star Ferry Pier.* **Open** 6-11.30pm daily. **Main courses** HK$200-$400. **Credit** AmEx, DC, MC, V. **Map** p313 C6.

A recent addition to the international haute cuisine chain created by French superchef Alain Ducasse, Spoon enjoys a fantastic harbourfront location. Following a mix'n'match concept, whereby diners choose any main ingredient (steak, fish etc) and combine it with a sauce and side dish, the choices are almost limitless. Of course, eating at a Ducasse restaurant isn't cheap, but it's worth it, especially as there's a sommelier on hand to marry your meal with a wine, and the service is top notch.

## Indian

### Gaylord

*1/F, Ashley Centre, 23-5 Ashley Road (2376 1001). Tsim Sha Tsui MTR (exit C1, C2)/Tsim Sha Tsui Star Ferry Pier.* **Open** noon-3pm, 6-10.45pm daily. **Main courses** HK$70-$150. **Credit** AmEx, DC, MC, V. **Map** p313 B6.

Rated by many as Hong Kong's best traditional curry house, Gaylord is always packed with Indian diners, which must be a good sign. The restaurant is more upmarket than other Kowloon curry houses and has live Indian music every night. As for the food, the tandoor oven cooks fish, chicken and lamb to perfection, and the curries are not too greasy.

### Khyber Pass

*Block E, 7/F, Chungking Mansions, 36-44 Nathan Road (2721 2786). Tsim Sha Tsui MTR (exit C1, D1).* **Open** Mon-Thur, Sat, Sun; 1.45-3.30pm, 6-11.30pm Fri. **Main courses** HK$30-$50. **No credit cards**. **Map** p313 C6.

Chungking Mansions is a labyrinth of shops, restaurants, dirt-cheap hostels and vice. It can be a bit scary, but as with so many other things its reputation is worse than reality. You should, however, take all the usual precautions if venturing inside – don't go alone, leave any jewellery back at the hotel and don't flash around wads of cash. Khyber Pass is much better than most of the other Indian restaurants in Chungking Mansions – it's clean (although very basic), and the food is piping hot.

## International

### Aqua

*29/F & 30/F, One Peking Road (3427 2288). Tsim Sha Tsui MTR (exit C1, E)/Tsim Sha Tsui Star Ferry Pier.* **Open** noon-1am Fri-Sun. **Main courses** HK$100-$200. **Credit** AmEx, DC, MC, V. **Map** p313 B6.

It's all about glass and mirrors at this dazzling restaurant in the penthouse of this shopping and dining complex. The harbour views from almost any angle are second to none and the design inside is just as good. The food, meanwhile, includes Japanese and Italian dishes and is likely to win as many international awards as the original Aqua did when it opened in Central in 2000, before relocating here in 2003.

### Mint

*122-6 Canton Road (2735 5887). Tsim Sha Tsui MTR (exit A1)/buses along Canton Road/Tsim Sha Tsui Star Ferry Pier.* **Open** 11.30am-12.30am daily. **Main courses** HK$100-$208. **Credit** AmEx, DC, MC, V. **Map** p313 B5/6.

A hip young crowd is usually found at this European restaurant with a difference. As in Cantonese restaurants, you can choose individual servings or huge portions to share. Tasteful green-hued decor and friendly staff make this an excellent place to enjoy fancy food at not-too-fancy prices. Several decent wines are available by the glass if you don't want to overdo things.

## Italian

### Fat Angelo's

*G/F, Kowloon Centre, 35 Ashley Road (2730 4788/ www.fatangelo.com). Tsim Sha Tsui MTR (exit C1)/buses along Nathan Road/Tsim Sha Tsui Star Ferry Pier.* **Open** noon-2.30pm, 6-11pm daily. **Main courses** HK$125-$195. **Credit** AmEx, DC, MC, V. **Map** p313 B6.

Giant servings of food and a convivial ambience have made this cheap and cheerful Italian mini chain a huge success. As soon as you sit down there are complimentary salads and hot chunks of bread to tuck in to. Mains include pasta and meat dishes, and while none are spectacular they're decent enough. An ordinary serving is enough for two to four people, while bigger portions can feed up to eight, so be careful not to over-order.

**Other locations:** 49A-C Elgin Street, Central, HK Island (2973 6808); 414 Jaffe Road, Wan Chai, HK Island (2574 6263).

## Pan-Asian

### Daidaya

*2/F, Empire Hotel, 62 Kimberley Road (2367 3666). Tsim Sha Tsui MTR (exit B1, B2)/buses along Nathan Road.* **Open** noon-3pm, 6-11pm daily. **Main courses** HK$70-$300. **Credit** AmEx, DC, MC, V. **Map** p313 C5.

Daidaya serves what's known as 'fusion Japanese' – but don't let that put you off. The creative chefs are influenced by many other cuisines, including French, Korean and Italian. The 'king of kimchee' is an unusual-sounding dish that works – raw fish and vegetables are wrapped in spicy Korean pickled cabbage. Foie gras is present in several dishes, including *chawan mushi* (steamed egg custard). This is a beautifully designed restaurant, so take a little time to explore the space.

Smiling faces are guaranteed at Lamma's famed **Rainbow Seafood**. *See p146.*

# Happy endings

Eat, Drink, Shop

There is a common assumption that the Chinese don't 'do' desserts. This may be true if your idea of a pudding is something more elaborate than a plate of fresh fruit, which is how most traditional Chinese people, when eating at home, usually finish their meals.

But if you're dining at any Chinese restaurant (apart from the very cheapest), the server will almost certainly come around to suggest something sweet to finish. At the simplest places, it might be only bowls of sweet, warm, red bean soup, flavoured star anise or dried tangerine peel. Or the popular cold mango pudding, turned out on to a plate and drizzled with condensed milk. At the cheaper restaurants, this dessert will be glow-in-the-dark orange, so stiff with gelatine it seems impenetrable to the touch of a spoon, artificially flavoured and so sweet it makes your teeth ache. Better restaurants make

it from scratch and serve it studded with chunks of fresh mango.

Unless it's a top place (or, indeed, a luxury hotel such as the Grand Hyatt; *pictured*), where desserts can be as good as the rest of the meal, diners often eschew the restaurant's offerings and go to a speciality shop.

**Hui Lau Shau** is a chain of shops throughout Hong Kong, easily recognised by its bright red frontage and rows of blenders filled with puréed fresh fruit juices. These juices, sweetened with sugar syrup, are available as drinks, but many of Hui Lau Shau's special desserts are also based on the puréed fruits – a large variety that includes mango, papaya, watermelon and strawberry. One of the most popular desserts is juice (often two or more flavours, poured carefully into the bowl so the purées stay separate) with tiny pearls of sago (tapioca) and chunks of fresh fruit. The coconut ice-cream, served with more fresh fruit, including the unusual, jelly-like 'sea coconut', is also rightly popular for its cooling effect, while the fresh mango pudding is tender and delicate. Turtle jelly – made from the shells of turtle and flavoured with medicinal herbs and served hot or cold – has its fans, despite its bitter flavour. Served with sugar syrup to tone down the sharpness, it is regarded as having 'cooling' properties thought to improve the complexion. Hui Lau Shau has become so popular that many places have tried to copy the formula, but this chain is still the best.

While these fruit-based desserts are especially refreshing during Hong Kong's hot and humid weather (which lasts at least six months of the year), a good winter dessert is sweet nut soups. These warm, silken soups are made from everything from peanuts and cashews to black or white sesame seeds.

Other popular desserts found throughout Hong Kong are delicate steamed custards (served hot or cold, and often flavoured with ginger), dense, hot sago pudding (similar to rice pudding) and glutinous rice-flour balls stuffed with sesame paste or nut brittle and served in ginger syrup.

### Inagiku
*1/F, Royal Garden Hotel, 69 Mody Road (2733 2933). Tsim Sha Tsui MTR (exit C1)/ 203, 973 bus/buses along Chatham Road South & Salisbury Road.* **Open** noon-3pm, 6-11pm daily. **Main courses** HK$100-$200. **Credit** AmEx, DC, MC, V. **Map** p313 C6.
At Inagiku you get authentic Japanese food in exquisite, work-of-art presentations. Tempura is the speciality, but virtually everything is excellent. Sushi and sashimi come with fresh wasabi, which is a revelation if you've only ever had the powdered stuff – it's astonishingly delicate.

### Robotayaki
*Harbour Plaza Hotel, 20 Tak Fung Street (2621 3188). Buses to Hung Hom/Wan Chai Ferry to Hung Hom.* **Open** noon-2.30pm, 6-10.30pm daily. **Main courses** HK$100-$800. **Credit** AmEx, DC, MC, V.
At a *robatayaki* restaurant, you sit around a communal grill with other customers and watch the chef cook your meal. It's casual, interactive and fun, though perhaps not the ideal place for a private discussion. While this restaurant also serves other types of Japanese food – including sushi, sashimi and tempura – the *robatayaki* chef's the star.

## Seafood

### Yü
*Intercontinental Hotel, 18 Salisbury Road (2721 1211/www.intercontinental.com). Tsim Sha Tsui MTR (exit E)/buses along Salisbury Road/Tsim Sha Tsui Star Ferry Pier.* **Open** noon-2.30pm, 6.30-11.30pm daily. **Main courses** HK$200-$280. **Credit** AmEx, DC, MC, V. **Map** p313 C6.
Though the menu at Yü changes seasonally, it always includes a wide range of fish and seafood, flown in fresh then put in holding tanks to recover from jetlag. Standout dishes include the signature seafood platter, a mountain of ice topped with shellfish and served with six different sauces. Not cheap, as you might expect from its upmarket hotel surroundings, but definitely worth it.

## Steakhouses

### Morton's of Chicago
*4/F, Sheraton Hong Kong Hotel & Towers, 20 Nathan Road (2732 2343/www.mortons.com). Tsim Sha Tsui MTR (exit E)/buses along Nathan Road/Tsim Sha Tsui Star Ferry Pier.* **Open** 5.30-10.30pm Mon-Sat; 5-11pm Sun. **Main courses** HK$250-$550. **Credit** AmEx, DC, MC, V. **Map** p313 C6.
Don't come here to Morton's in search of a light meal – the portions are American-size. Steaks are excellent, whether it's filet mignon, rib-eye or the enormous porterhouse. Starters, side dishes and desserts are also huge, so those with smaller appetites – or who are on a diet – might want to share one steak and a plate of vegetables.

### Ruth's Chris Steakhouse
*G/F, Empire Centre, 98 Mody Road (2366 6000/ www.ruthchris.com). Tsim Sha Tsui MTR (exit D1, D2)/buses along Chatham Road.* **Open** noon-3pm, 6.30-11pm daily. **Main courses** HK$240-$550. **Credit** AmEx, MC, DC, V. **Map** p313 C6.
As with Morton's, this New Orleans-based chain serves steak, and lots of it. The beef is top quality, which is reflected by the prices – don't come here if you're on a budget or a diet. Fortunately, you get what you pay for: the steaks are perfectly cooked, beefy and tender.
**Other locations:** G/F, Lippo Centre, 89 Queensway, Admiralty, HK Island (2522 9090).

## Yau Ma Tei

## Chinese

### Sun Dau Kee Seafood Restaurant
*G/F, 120 Woo Sung Street, Jordan Road, Yau Ma Tei (2730 6827). Jordan MTR (exit A)/buses along Nathan Road.* **Open** 4.30pm-4.30am daily. **Main courses** HK$80-$230. **Credit** V. **Map** p313 B4.
Sun Dau Kee doesn't look any different from any other Hong Kong seafood restaurant, but here the quality is reliably excellent, even with the non-seafood dishes. The sweet and sour pork is a revelation, especially if all the other versions you've tasted have been cloyingly sweet and brightly coloured – at this restaurant it's subtle and well balanced. Pigeon is another speciality, as is the fried fish with sweetcorn.

## Vegetarian

### Light Vegetarian Restaurant
*G/F, New Lucky House, 13 Jordan Road, Yau Ma Tei (2384 2833). Jordan MTR (exit B2)/buses along Nathan Road.* **Open** 11am-10.30pm daily. **Main courses** HK$30-$50. **Credit** DC, MC, V. **Map** p313 B4.
This restaurant's mock meats are passable, but the best dishes are those that don't pretend to be anything else, like the fried beancurd and mushroom rice and stir-fried vegetables. OK, it's not great, but while vegetarians risk finding unadvertised bits of meat in dishes in many restaurants in this part of town, at least here they can rest easy. The lunch buffet costs HK$44, the dinner buffet HK$78.

## Kowloon City & Kowloon Tong

## Pan-Asian

### Cambo Thai Restaurant
*14-15 Nga Tsin Long Road, Kowloon City (2716 7318). Bus 101, 104, 110.* **Open** 11.30am-1am daily. **Main courses** HK$30-$50. **Credit** MC, V.

The **Chinese Vegetarian Restaurant** at Po Lin Monastery on Lantau. *See p146.*

Since the old Kai Tak airport closed there has been little reason to head out to Kowloon City, but the area remains a treasure trove of South-east Asian food if you're prepared to make the journey. What you'll find are around a dozen no-nonsense Thai restaurants, which serve the large Thai community resident here. There not much to choose between many of them, but Cambo is assuredly one of the best. The chilli in the *tom yum gung* will force you bolt upright, the fish cakes are moreish and the salads will have you reaching for the fire extinguisher.

### Mi

*LG2, Festival Walk, 80 Tat Chee Avenue, Kowloon Tong (2265 8308). Kowloon Tong MTR (exit C1, C2).* **Open** noon-10.30pm Mon-Sat; 11am-10.30pm Sun. **Main courses** HK$30-$60. **Credit** AmEx, DC, MC, V.

This high-tech, funky 1,500sq m (16,000sq ft) space is a revolution in food hall cuisine. It combines a restaurant atmosphere and service with some 20 outlets offering more than 300 dishes from Hong Kong, China, Malaysia, Singapore, Thailand, South Korea and Japan. It may sound overwhelming, but most dishes are on display so you can see what you're getting. Try the Hainan chicken, stingray *sambal* (in a Malaysian spicy sauce) or Malaysian *bakuteh* (pork rib and herb soup). The design is swish and there is a bar so you can linger before paying at the till.

### Wing Chun Vietnamese Restaurant

*16 & 18 Lion Rock Road, Kowloon City (2716 6122). Bus 101, 104, 110.* **Open** 11am-midnight daily. **Main courses** HK$15-$50. **Credit** V.

Wing Chun is certainly not a place to linger – fast food doesn't come much speedier than here. But the cuisine is good enough to justify popping in, with tasty meat and seafood stomach-filling dishes, often fried with lemongrass, chilli and garlic. The cold glass noodle dishes and soft-shell crabs are also worth a try.

# The New Territories

## Central New Territories

### Chinese

#### Royal Park Chinese Restaurant

*2/F Royal Park Hotel, 8 Pak Hok Ting Street, Sha Tin (2601 2111). Kowloon Tong MTR/Sha Tin KCR.* **Open** 24hrs daily. **Main courses** HK$60-$250. **Credit** AmEx, DC, MC, V.

The nearby New Town Plaza is often overflowing with shoppers, so this hotel restaurant feels like an oasis. Cantonese standards are up for grabs here, along with decent dim sum at the weekends (from HK$18; book in advance).

Eat, Drink, Shop

# Dim sum

Dim sum (meaning 'to touch the heart') is one of the most interesting aspects of Chinese cuisine. As with tapas in Spain, many small dishes are ordered and shared, in this case often with a platter of stir-fried vegetables and noodles or fried rice on the side.

Dim sum is traditionally eaten for breakfast and lunch, although at least one restaurant in Hong Kong serves it all day (**Dim Sum** in Happy Valley), and some places are starting to serve it late at night, after the normal dinner hours. On weekends and public holidays, restaurants are packed with families enjoying tucking in.

Hot tea is an integral part of the dim sum meal, and as you sit down at your table, the waiter will ask what kind of tea you want. Favourites are bitter black teas, which are thought to aid digestion, and fragrant flower teas, such as jasmine and chrysanthemum.

Dim sum houses used to be deafening places, as diners tried to converse over the din of waitresses loudly announcing their offerings as they pushed around carts of steaming hot dishes. Nowadays, many restaurants – especially the more expensive places – are much more sedate. Dishes are listed on small menus, diners tick off what they want and everything is cooked to order.

When eating dim sum, it's best to go in a group of at least four so you can try as much as possible. Many dishes will be steamed, a cooking technique much appreciated by the Chinese because it best displays the freshness of the ingredients. Old favourites that you'll find almost everywhere are *har gau* (chopped or whole shrimp wrapped in a thin, translucent skin), *siu mai* (open-faced shrimp and minced pork dumplings with wheat-flour skins) and *cheung fun* (rice-flour rolls wrapped around shrimp, meat or vegetables). However, baked and fried items are also popular – try *wu tau guo* (minced meats and seafood in a delicate, lacy coating of fried taro), *XO cheung fun* (rice-flour rolls stir-fried with XO sauce), *lo baak goh* (a savoury cake made of shredded Chinese radish, and dried shrimp) and *daan taat* (sweet, baked custard tarts). If you love fried spring rolls, a dim sum house is one of the few places in Hong Kong where you're virtually guaranteed to find them.

One of the best things about the dim sum experience is the convivial atmosphere. People are always getting up to greet friends, so you won't be out of place if you take a walk around the restaurant and look at the tables to see what everybody else is ordering. If you see something you might like, just point it out to a waiter, ask him what it is, and if it sounds enticing, order a portion for yourself.

Sadly, there aren't many restaurants left in Hong Kong that specialise in dim sum. Here are our favourites.

## City Hall Maxim's Palace

*2/F, Low Block, City Hall, 7 Edinburgh Place, Central, HK Island (2521 1303). Central MTR (exit A, J3)/buses along Connaught Road/ Central Star Ferry Pier.* **Open** 11am-11.30pm daily. *Dim sum* 5.30-11.30pm daily. **Main courses** HK$80-$100. *Dim sum* HK$17-$45. **Credit** AmEx, MC, V. **Map** p309 E3.
With its fashioned charm, and elderly women pushing around trolleys packed with savoury treats, Maxim's was always being voted the city's best dim sum joint. So what did the owners do? Refurbished it so it looks like any other fancy Chinese restaurant, of course. Prices went up and the ambience was lost, but the food is still good and the views of the harbour still enticing. Reservations required.

## Dim Sum

*63 Sing Woo Road, Happy Valley, HK Island (2834 8893). Bus 1, 19/trams to Happy Valley.* **Open** 11am-4pm, 6-9.30pm daily. **Main courses** HK$60-$120. **Credit** AmEx, DC, MC, V.
Dim sum usually equates with crowded, noisy restaurants, but this place is all about style. The dark wood interior exudes stately elegance, while the dim sum is luxurious, with abalone and lobster as well as the staple pork and shrimp. Not cheap, but worth it.

## Zen

*G/25, Basement, Festival Walk, 80 Tat Chee Avenue, Kowloon Tong (2265 7328). Kowloon Tong KCR or MTR (exit C1, C2)/2C, 203 bus.* **Open** 11am-midnight Mon-Sat; 10am-11pm Sun. **Main courses** HK$70-$125. **Credit** AmEx, DC, MC, V.
A stylish restaurant that's a cut above the rest, with water features and spotless tablecloths. The dim sum, including deep-fried ducks' tongues, is popular at lunchtimes, while the main courses, including suckling pig and roast pigeon, are best at dinner. **Other locations**: LG1, Pacific Place, 88 Queensway, Admiralty, HK Island (2845 4555).

Eat, Drink, Shop

## Pan-Asian

### Chung Shing Thai Curry House

*69 Tai Mei Tuk Village, Ting Kok Road, Tai Po (2664 5218). Tai Po Market KCR then 75K bus.* **Open** 9am-midnight daily. **Main courses** HK$20-$40. **No credit cards**.

If you're in the New Territories and it isn't rainy season, you'll probably want to eat alfresco. The strip along this road has many options, but locals always pack this place out first. The curried crab and chilli prawns are delicious, especially when paired with a cool beer. You can't book, but the wait for a table on busy nights is worth it.

### Cosmopolitan Curry House

*80 Kwong Fuk Road, Tai Po Market (2650 7056). Tai Po Market KCR/72 bus.* **Open** 11am-11.30pm daily. **Main courses** HK$50-$100. **Credit** DC, MC, V.

This gem of a restaurant is located close to Tai Po Market KCR station. Its culinary remit stretches over most of South-east Asia. Here you'll find Indonesian, Thai and Malaysian versions of curries, with many inventive flavour combinations, such as prawn and mango. Comfort may be distinctly lacking and the high decibel level of chattering diners can be an annoyance, but the queues outside the door tell you just how good Cosmopolitan is. Booking is recommended.

# Street snacks

Chinese people are inveterate snackers and those living in Hong Kong are no exception. The range of nibbles sold at noodle stands and street hawkers is extensive. The latter group includes licensed vendors set up in established areas such as the **Ladies' Market** in Mong Kok (*see p92*) or **Temple Street Night Market** in Jordan (*see p170*).

These 'street food' snacks have only one thing in common – they're inexpensive. And for the first-time visitor to Hong Kong, they're essential. Dishes to try include:

● *Chau dou fu* – beancurd that's been allowed to ferment until it is pungent, then deep-fried and served with chilli paste.

● *Gai dan jai* – crisp, sweet hollow balls baked in specially designed moulds over a charcoal brazier.

● *Jah dai cheung* – deep-fried pig's intestines, fried until crisp outside and soft and fatty within.

● *Loong so tong* – 'Dragon's beard' – strands of stretched sugar paste rolled in sugar, nuts and sesame seeds.

● *Yeung cheng jiu* – chillies, peppers or beancurd stuffed with fish paste and fried to order.

● *Yu daan* – minced fish rolled into balls (plain or in a curry broth) and skewered on to a stick.

# West New Territories

## Indian

### Shaffi's Indian Restaurant

*14 Fau Tsoi Street, off Main Road, Yuen Long
(2476 7885). Tuen Mun Ferry Pier then 610,
614, 615 bus.* **Open** 11am-3pm, 5.30-11pm
daily. **Main courses** HK$50-$100. **Credit** DC,
MC, V.

Shaffi's owner Liaqat Ali cooked for British troops
at Shek Kong army barracks (as did his uncle
before him); when the soldiers sailed away in 1997
after the Handover he set up on his own restaurant.
Now civilians can have a taste of what they were
missing: namely creamy, spicy curries that go well
with big, fluffy naan breads.

# East New Territories

## Chinese

### Tung Kee Restaurant

*96-102 Man Nin Street, Sai Kung (2792 7453).
Choi Hung then 1A minibus.* **Open** 11am-11pm
daily. **Main courses** HK$50-$100. **Credit** AmEx,
DC, MC, V.

Sai Kung's waterfront is typical of South China
Sea ports – junks bobbing in the harbour filled
with old fishermen hawking the day's catch, tanks
(over-) filled with a range of exotic sea creatures,
and screeching restaurateurs begging you to dine
at one of the hundreds of alfresco tables. Until
recently, these tables were banned. Luckily the
bureaucrats finally saw sense and allowed Sai
Kung's best feature – the great outdoors – to be
appreciated with a good meal. Further along the
street, Chinese-Thai Seafood Restaurant offers a
spicier seafood option.

## Indian

### Dia Indian Restaurant

*Shop 2, 42-56 Fuk Man Road, Sai Kung (2791
4466). Choi Hung MTR (exit C2) then 1A
minibus.* **Open** 11am-3pm Mon-Fri; 11am-11pm
Sat, Sun. **Main courses** HK$68-$130. **Credit**
MC, V.

The Curry Hut was for a long time the only option
for lovers of Indian cuisine in Sai Kung. Dia's, with
its soothing blue and bamboo decor, is a welcome
newcomer to the local scene, offering good (if
perhaps a little pricey) subcontinental food. Overall,
it's the ambience, which is positively Goan, that
wins diners over.

### Jaspas

*G/F 13 Sha Tsui Path, Sai Kung (2792 6388).
Choi Hung MTR (exit B) then 1A minibus.* **Open**
8am-1.30pm daily. **Main courses** HK$60-$150.
**Credit** MC, V.

Australian-style food in Sai Kung – comfortable,
casual and laid back. Portions are big, the staff
friendly and welcoming and the food flavourful and
plentiful. The menu features plenty of seafood,
cooked here with light, Asian influences.
**Other locations:** 28 Staunton Street, Central,
HK Island (2869 0733).

### Osteria No.1

*183D Po Tung Road, Sai Kung (2792 5296). Choi
Hung MTR then 1A minibus.* **Open** 10am-10.30pm
daily. **Main courses** HK$90-$150. **Credit** MC, V.

This restaurant's friendly Italian owners are always
present to welcome you and have a nice chat. Pastas
(which can be ordered as half-portion starters) are
excellent – especially the homemade ravioli with
ricotta and spinach. *Osso bucco* is also delicious here,
as is the *saltimbocca*.

### Pepperoni's

*1592 Po Tung Road, Sai Kung (2792 2083). Choi
Hung MTR (exit C2) then 1A minibus.* **Open** 9am-
11pm daily. **Main courses** HK$95-$115. **Credit** V.

Now a large chain with outlets across Hong Kong,
the Pepperoni's concept began in Sai Kung more
than a decade ago. The recipe for its success: big
portions of old favourites like nachos, spaghetti
carbonara, deep-fried calamari, pork knuckle and an
exotic array of pizzas. It's all filling and pretty tasty.
**Other locations:** throughout the city.

### Sauce

*9 Sha Tsui Path, Sai Kung (2791 2348/
www.sauce.com.hk). Choi Hung MTR (exit C2)
then 1A minibus.* **Open** noon-11pm daily. **Main
courses** HK$90-$135. **Credit** AmEx, MC, V.

Sai Kung's Sha Tsui Path is always a great place to
watch the world go by, but now this welcome addition has made it even better. The restaurant excels
at the basics – top-notch, delicious European fare
(including fresh pasta dishes and hearty desserts
such as sticky toffee pudding), tasteful decor, outdoor seating, friendly service and a value-for-money
wine list. There's live music every Monday.

## Seafood/fish

### Anthony's Catch

*G/F Lot 1826B, Po Tung Road, Sai Kung (2792
8474/www.anthonyscatch.com). Choi Hung MTR
(exit C2) then 1A minibus.* **Open** 6-10pm Mon-Wed;
6pm-midnight Thur-Sun. **Brunch** 10.30am-3.30pm
Sun. **Main courses** HK$100-$150. **Credit** AmEx,
DC, MC, V.

So many of the Western restaurants in Sai Kung are
characterised by friendly service, big portions and
comfortable surroundings; this place is no exception.
Try to come here on a Sunday, when Anthony's
does a champagne brunch. There are worse ways
to spend a lazy Sunday than with unlimited
bubbly (a California sparkler rather than real French
champagne) and good food, such as waffles with
maple syrup and fresh fruit.

**Eat, Drink, Shop**

# The Outlying Islands

## Lamma

### Chinese

**Han Lok Yuen**
*16-17 Hung Shing Ye (2982 0680). Yung Shue Wan Ferry Pier.* **Open** 11.30am-10pm Tue-Sat; 11.30am-7pm Sun. **Main courses** HK$80-$150. **Credit** AmEx, DC, MC, V.
The short hike from Lamma's main beach to this hilltop eaterie is well worth it, even in the summer heat. It's nicknamed the 'pigeon restaurant' after its speciality dish, and the roast pigeon is the best in Hong Kong. Chris Patten, known by the Chinese as *fei pang* ('fatty Patten'), regularly made the trek. The minced quail eaten in rolled-up lettuce leaves is also delicious, as are the vegetable dishes.

**Man Fung Seafood Restaurant**
*Main Street, Yung Shue Wan (2982 0719). Yung Shue Wan Ferry Pier.* **Open** 11am-10pm daily. **Main courses** HK$100-$200. **Credit** AmEx, MC, V.
Lamma's busiest harbour, Yung Shue Wan, is lined with Cantonese seafood restaurants and its view of the fishing boats and junks is more picturesque than Sok Kwu Wan. Man Fung is the first one you reach from the ferry pier and probably the best. Here you'll find live crabs, prawns and fish swimming in tanks – choose the one you want, and minutes later they turn up sizzling hot on a plate. The delicious house speciality is the crab sticky rice hotpot. One stop along, the Sampan is also worth a visit.

**Rainbow Seafood**
*16-20 First Street, Sok Kwu Wan (2982 8100). Yung Shue Wan Ferry Pier/free private ferry (Rainbow) from Queens Pier, Central.* **Open** 11am-11pm daily. **Main courses** HK$110-$300. **Credit** AmEx, DC, MC, V.
Sok Kwu Wan is the less-populous end of Lamma, with fewer expats and bars. Nonetheless, many daytrippers come here for lunch or dinner at the row of waterfront seafood restaurants immediately next to the ferry pier. There are tanks filled with live lobsters, fish of many colours and all manner of sea creatures clambering over each other in a vain attempt to escape the chef's hands.

### Vegetarian

**Bookworm Café**
*79 Main Street, Yung Shue Wan (2982 4838). Yung Shue Wan Ferry Pier.* **Open** 10am-9pm Mon-Fri, 9am-10pm Sat. **Main courses** HK$65-$80. **Credit** MC, V.
Bookworm is as right-on as you can get. Everything is vegetarian and organic, although the food is pretty basic – beans on toast and poached eggs both feature on the menu. It can feel a bit like New Age overload, but at least it's downright cheap.

## Lantau

### International

**Stoep**
*32 Lower Cheung Sha Village (2980 2699/9465 9226). Tung Chung MTR then 3M, 13, A35 bus/ Mui Wo Ferry Pier then any bus (except 7) towards Lower Cheung Sha Beach.* **Open** 10am-10pm Tue-Sun. **Main courses** HK$45-$150. **Credit** MC, V.
Stoep enjoys the best location in Hong Kong – slap bang on one of the most beautiful stretches of sand. Food is served alfresco, and South African barbecued meats are the speciality, although there are also plenty of European dishes and an impressive wine list. The place to go if you're looking for peace on Lantau.

### Vegetarian

**Chinese Vegetarian Restaurant**
*Po Lin Monastery, Ngong Ping, Po Lin (2985 5248). Mui Wo Ferry Pier then 2 bus/Tung Chung MTR then 23 bus.* **Open** noon-4.30pm daily. **Main courses** HK$50-$88. **Credit** MC, V.
No visit to Po Lin Monastery would be complete without a trip to the large dining hall, where there is a large buffet of vegetarian delights. For less than HK$100 you can gorge on beancurd, mock-meat dishes and a wide range of vegetables. *See also p115.*

## Cheung Chau

### Chinese

**Golden Lake Restaurant**
*Pak She 4th Lane, Cheung Chau (2981 3402). Cheung Chau Ferry Pier then 10min walk.* **Open** noon-midnight daily. **Main courses** HK$40-$120. **No credit cards.**
The row of waterfront restaurants to the left of the ferry pier when you disembark offer a great range of live seafood and fish. Some also serve excellent dim sum, but Golden Lake is the best for fruits de mer – it's especially fresh as the owners have their own seafood store next door. There's a good range of Cantonese treats on the menu too, including the salty fish eggplant bowl, which, trust us, tastes better than it sounds.

### International

**Morocco's/India Curry House**
*71 San Hing Praya Street (2986 9767). Cheung Chau Ferry Pier.* **Open** noon-2am Mon, Tue, Thur-Sun. **Main courses** HK$52-$100. **No credit cards.**
This is an odd but useful eaterie. 'Jack of all trades' springs to mind when looking at the menu, which covers all bases from standard British pub grub to decent Indian curries – but it's the Thai food that the regulars wisely go for.

# Pubs & Bars

Want a swanky bar or an earthy watering hole? Who cares... just get drinking.

Whatever time of day or night, there's always somewhere to drink in Hong Kong. In recent years the city's bar and restaurant scene has undergone a not-so-quiet revolution, with new wine bars, theme pubs and restaurant bars cropping up all over the place. Many are stylish, comfortable spaces with good air-conditioning – and the glass- and open-fronted bars, in particular, make for great people-watching. Although the SARS outbreak hurt many and sounded a death knell to some, dozens of new bars cropped up once the epidemic was over.

All this development has come at a price, however. When people first arrive in Hong Kong and order a round of drinks, the cost often makes them splutter out their first mouthful. A long night of drinking can leave you nursing not only a hangover but an economic depression. Still, with so many bars opening to increase the level of competition, along with the general effects of the prolonged Asian financial slowdown, cocktail prices have not gone up much in recent years. A swanky bar or club might sting you for HK$90 for a fancy martini, but beer and spirits are still around HK$40 to HK$50 in most places.

Thankfully, there are several ways a canny drinker can cut the cost of an evening out by almost half. Happy hours are very popular in Hong Kong and – contrary to the name – usually run for a long part of the day or evening. Each place has a different happy hour schedule, so you can find one at pretty much any time of day or night. Happy hour in Hong Kong usually means cut-price drinks – they're often slashed by about 30 per cent – but can also get you two drinks for the price of one. House policies vary and not all drinks are necessarily included, so check with bar staff before ordering.

## NAME YOUR POISON

In terms of beers, San Miguel and Carlsberg are brewed locally, but, whether on tap or in a bottle, have a tendency to taste chemical and to leave your head pounding in the morning. Tsing Tao (made at a German-modelled brewery in China) is worth a try, while Heineken appears to have won the battle of the imports – it's usually as cheap as local brews and tastes better. Recently Stella Artois has made inroads, while Irish bars serve Kilkenny and Guinness (minus the Liffey water as it's brewed in Malaysia, but the taste is still reasonably authentic). Local micro-breweries do exist, but they are small and rare. If you can find them, Stone Cutter's and Red Dragon, brewed by the South China Brewing Company, are both pretty good.

Agave. See p149.

# Bars

## Agave
Kick into action with the best Margaritas in town and the biggest range of tequila in Asia outside Japan. *See p149.*

## Club Feather Boa
Kick back and hang out in splendid living-room comfort. *See p150.*

## Felix
Men get to piss with panache at the urinals overlooking Kowloon. Women just get top cocktails. *See p154.*

## Groovy Mule
Brilliant choice if you like to dance on the tables – or at least watch the staff do it. *See p153.*

## KBG – Klong Bar & Grill
Has a full-moon party every month – great excuse for a big session. *See p153.*

## 1/5
Where the glitterati sip champagne through a straw on weekends. *See p153.*

## Tango Martini
A hangout for wannabe 007s. *See p153.*

Wine is expensive as excessive import duties have been placed on it by the cash-strapped (and presumably teetotal) local government. Not all bars have a good choice of wines, but there are more places springing up offering a decent range by the glass. Cocktails tend to be well made and often give better value than standard spirits and mixers, since you get two or three shots in a glass for just a few extra dollars.

### DRINKING BY DISTRICT
Although you can find a watering hole in just about any part of town, there are several districts with thriving bar and restaurant subcultures. A bar crawl here can include ten very different places in just one block.

Hong Kong's best-known drinking area is **Lan Kwai Fong** in Central. Over the past 20 years it has grown from a cluster of ragtrade go-downs to a world-class entertainment centre. There's a huge variety of bars and eateries here, most under the ownership of tycoon Allan Zeman, often dubbed 'Mr Lan Kwai Fong'. It can be a good place to start for first-time visitors, since every taxi driver knows it and everything is clustered together. Although

called Lan Kwai Fong, the district also includes neighbouring **D'Aguilar Street**, **Wo On Lane** and **Wing Wah Lane**. It's busy every night, when no traffic is allowed, so drinkers have staggering space. The downside to the area is that it seems to comprise merely suits and expats, as trendier bar-hoppers venture further afield.

A short walk from Lan Kwai Fong takes you to **SoHo** – centred around **Staunton Street** and **Elgin Street**, which cut across the Mid-Levels Escalator. As Lan Kwai Fong became clichéd, this place took over as the most vibrant and happening hotspot. Over the past decade, SoHo has seen a similar exponential growth like the one LKF went through in the 1980s. Most of the old Chinese ceramic and dried-food shops have been replaced by bars and restaurants as rents skyrocketed. The area has grown and most surrounding roads are now part of SoHo; indeed, the bit downhill, to the north of Hollywood Road (NoHo), is also getting in on the act, especially the cobbled **Pottinger Street**. SoHo shuts down earlier than LKF, as restrictive licensing authorities have set midnight – or 2am for some establishments – as the curfew to protect residents from noise. NoHo, Hollywood Road and Wyndham Street above Lan Kwai Fong all open later.

**Wan Chai** is the other main bar area on Hong Kong Island. A gradual facelift has seen an increase in upmarket bars here, but it remains the liveliest and earthiest part of town to drink. If you like to let your hair down or are out on the pull, this is where you come. Also worth checking out nearby are **Causeway Bay**, particularly around Yiu Wa Street (behind Times Square), frequented mainly by trendy locals, and **Happy Valley**, which offers a range of quieter, more intimate watering holes.

Across the harbour, bustling **Tsim Sha Tsui** used to be the heart of Hong Kong's nightlife. But from the 1980s onwards it fell into decline. Currently undergoing much upheaval and blighted by roadworks as new underground train lines are built, it remains an awkward place to get around. Thankfully, things are about to change. The cluster of bars and restaurants on **Knutsford Terrace** has been expanding and a new development, **Knutsford Steps**, is scheduled to open adjacent some time in 2004, offering new places to drink and dine on Mediterranean-style terraces and verandas. **Ashley Road** is also picking up, although the cul-de-sac is grim looking, with its motorcycle parking area and vans often blocking the road. Local traders are constantly campaigning for the street to be pedestrianised.

Eat, Drink, Shop

East of Nathan Road another development is sprouting up, which is being touted as **'Kowloon Lan Kwai Fong'**. The plan is for a giant screen and stage to be built to provide a focal point for al fresco drinkers once the empty premises are turned into bars and restaurants. That said, until these changes happen (if they ever do), the scene remains disjointed and some of the older pubs are downright shoddy. Visitors should certainly explore TST, but be aware there are better options across the harbour.

# Hong Kong Island

## Central

### Agave

*33 D'Aguilar Street (2521 2010). Central MTR (exit D1, D2)/12M, 13, 23A, 40M bus.* **Open** 5pm-2am Mon-Thur, Sun; 5pm-4am Fri, Sat. **Credit** AmEx, DC, MC, V. **Map** p308 C4.
Mexican bars are usually good for kickstarting a night out, and Agave is no exception. Besides the chili-filled quesadillas and tasty tacos on the menu,

there are more than more than 100 imported tequilas (Agave has the biggest choice in Asia outside Japan). The Margaritas are the best in town.

### Alibi

*73 Wyndham Street (2167 1676). Central MTR (exit D1, D2)/12M, 13, 23A, 26, 40M bus.* **Open** noon-late daily. **Credit** AmEx, DC, MC, V. **Map** p308 C4.
Since opening a few years ago, Alibi has continued to attract an upmarket crowd. It's a place where the city's many global citizens like to network, and, although there is a certain snob value, it can also be fun. Downstairs is a New York-style marble-and-glass lounge bar with laid-back music, while upstairs is a swish restaurant, which opens later than most others in the area. Girlie girls might want to try the martini and manicure nights held each week.

### Area

*G/F, 28 Gough Street (2542 3138). Sheung Wan MTR (exit A2, E2)/buses along Queen's Road Central.* **Open** 5.30pm-midnight Mon-Sat. **Credit** AmEx, DC, MC, V. **Map** p308 B3.
This spacious DJ bar is tricky to find as it's a bit off the beaten track, and its sign is unusually discreet for Hong Kong. It's worth the effort, however, as

Making the most of **1/5** during a quieter moment. *See p153.*

Eat, Drink, Shop

it's a friendly place, with a hip crowd. The dance-floor gets going properly around midnight, although sadly Area's residential location means customers are turfed out around midnight, just when they're beginning to have fun.

### Baby Buddha

*18 Wo On Lane (2167 7244). Central MTR (exit D1, D2)/12M, 13, 23A, 40M bus.* **Open** 5pm-2.30am Mon-Thur; 5pm-4.30am Fri; 6pm-4.30am Sat; 7pm-2am Sun. **Credit** AmEx, DC, MC, V. **Map** p309 D4.

After the success of Claude Challe's Buddha Bar in Paris, the god's name has been taken in vain by bars and clubs worldwide. Baby Buddha, born in early 2003, is as small as the name implies. It's an open-fronted bar, occupying what was once a tiny alley, and borders a recently redeveloped small public square that leads up to Pottinger Street. It can be a bit chilly during the winter but the laid-back vibe more than compensates.

### Boca

*65 Peel Street (2548 1717). Central MTR (exit D1, D2)/Mid-Levels Escalator/buses along Caine Road.* **Open** 10pm-2am daily. **Credit** AmEx, DC, MC, V. **Map** p308 C3.

The choice of wines by the glass here is among the best in Hong Kong, and the tapas (both traditional and fusion) are pretty good too. But what makes Boca stand out above everything are its sumptuous couches and seats, on which you can idle away many pleasant hours. Evenings and weekend afternoons are prime chilling-out times.

### Chapter Three

*Basement, 23 Hollywood Road (2526 5566). Central MTR (exit D1, D2)/12M, 13, 23A, 26, 40M bus.* **Open** 5pm-1am Mon-Fri; 7pm-3am Sat; 6pm-1am Sun. **Credit** AmEx, DC, MC, V. **Map** p308 C3.

With its entrance on Cochrane Street, beneath a branch of Pacific Coffee Shop, this DJ bar attracts a young and trendy crowd. It's only a small space but somehow manages to feel cosy rather than cramped. With a glowing red interior and beats pumping until the early hours of the morning, it's an ideal venue to get you in the mood for a full-on night of clubbing.

### Club Feather Boa

*38 Staunton Street (2857 2586). Mid-Levels Escalator/12M, 13, 23A, 26, 40M bus.* **Open** 6pm-late daily. **Credit** AmEx, DC, MC, V. **Map** p308 C3.

The ambience at the Feather Boa is part boudoir, part bordello – giving its customers a feeling of intimacy, as if they had been invited into the home of its genial host, Stella. This former antiques shop stays true to its roots, elegantly furnished with heavy drapes, candelabras and paintings, while drinks come in generous measures served in large, ornate glasses. If you're feeling daring, try the more-ish chocolate martini (trust us: it's impossible to have just a couple). The Boa stays open till the wee hours, but for guaranteed comfort try to get here early and nab one of the two sofas.

### Club 1911

*27 Staunton Street (2810 6681). Mid-Levels Escalator/12M, 13, 23A, 26, 40M bus.* **Open** 5pm-1am Mon-Thur, Sun; 5pm-2am Fri, Sat. **Credit** AmEx, DC, MC, V. **Map** p308 C3.

This small, British-owned place is named in honour of Chinese revolutionary leader Sun Yat-sen, who once lived on this street, before playing a role in China's 1911 revolution. The club underwent a makeover a while back, and is now a relaxed, quiet setting for a pint and a chinwag. Good complimentary nibbles are served too.

### Club 64

*12-14 Wing Wah Lane (2523 2801). Central MTR (exit D1, D2)/12M, 13, 23A, 40M bus.* **Open** noon-2am Mon-Sat; 6pm-1am Sun. **No credit cards.** **Map** p308 C4.

For more than a decade Club 64 has been a meeting point for artists, intellectuals, media types and would-be revolutionaries. After all, it is named in commemoration of the 1989 Tiananmen Square massacre (which occurred on 4 June, a date on which the club always closes). The back room often plays host to live music or community group meetings, while the front bar hosts art exhibitions. The air is often thick with smoke and stimulating conversation, but you can take your drink out front to the bustling alley if you prefer.

### Dublin Jack

*37 Cochrane Street (2543 0081). Central MTR (exit D1, D2)/Mid-Levels Escalator/buses along Queen's Road Central.* **Open** 11.30am-2am daily. **Credit** AmEx, DC, MC, V. **Map** p308 C3.

One of the better Irish theme pubs, the Dublin Jack serves the black stuff and other Irish ales, as well as reasonable food. It's popular with sports fans because it has a big screen on each level – it has even been known to show live football, cricket and rugby at the same time.

### Elements

*55 Elgin Street (8105 0155). Central MTR (exit D1, D2)/Mid-Levels Escalator/12M, 13, 23A, 40M bus.* **Open** 3pm-2am Mon-Sat; noon-midnight Sun. **Credit** AmEx, MC, V. **Map** p308 B3.

This flashy two-storey bar/lounge has white sofas and a windowed front for those who like to see and be seen. Not that there's much to look at at this end of Elgin Street. Still, Elements is a good spot to while away a few hours over a bottle of wine, of which there is a good selection.

### Le Jardin

*10 Wing Wah Lane (2526 2717). Central MTR (exit D1, D2)/12M, 13, 23A, 40M bus.* **Open** noon-2am Mon-Sat. **Credit** MC, V. **Map** p308 C4.

A hidden-away hotspot in Lan Kwai Fong, Le Jardin has a huge outdoor terrace. It's up, up and away from the bustling streets below – you'll find the steps leading to it at the end of Wing Wah Lane past the cluttered al fresco dining area. The jukebox has one of the best choices of sounds in town.

Eat, Drink, Shop

End your evening **On the Rocks**. See p154.

### Jewel

*37-43 Pottinger Street (2541 5988). Central MTR (exit D1, D2)/12M, 13, 23A, 40M bus.* **Open** 6pm-2am Mon-Thur; 6pm-4am Fri, Sat. **Credit** AmEx, DC, MC, V. **Map** p309 D3.

A huge space with plenty of sofas to lounge about on. Incense burns while DJ spins hip-hop and R&B for a sophisticated twentysomething crowd. There's a great range of cocktails, although they're pricey at around $90. If the music isn't blaring (which it usually is at weekends), Jewel is an ideal place to chill out after dinner or before hitting the nearby clubs.

### Metro

*G/F, The Workstation, 43-5 Lyndhurst Terrace (2815 9880). Central MTR (exit D1, D2)/12M, 13, 23A, 40M bus.* **Open** noon-2am Mon-Fri; 11am-2am Sat, Sun. **Credit** AmEx, DC, MC, V. **Map** p308 C3.

Replacing the fancy Blue restaurant, Metro has retained the glass walls but relaxed the atmosphere and switched to a more casual bar-restaurant concept. There are 20 wines by the glass and a decent cocktail list. If you can't choose between them, order a Metrotini, made with fresh strawberries and blueberries and given a kick with honey vodka.

### Post 97

*1/F, 9 Lan Kwai Fong (2810 9333). Central MTR (exit D1, D2)/12M, 13, 23A, 40M bus.* **Open** 9.30am-1am Mon-Thur; 9.30am-2am Sat; 9.30pm-midnight Sun. **Credit** AmEx, DC, MC, V. **Map** p308 C4.

The city's most relaxed supper venue, Post 97 has been the late night hangout of stars and the 'it' crowd for more than a decade. Great food, a good selection of wine by the glass and surroundings you can flop

Eat, Drink, Shop

# Look out Elvis...

Karaoke may conjure up images of drunken saddos grappling for the microphone, but in Hong Kong it's a much more serious affair. Here, wannabe singers closet themselves away for hours in private rooms, belting out Abba and the Spice Girls to their heart's content. It seems that everyone under 30 loves to hold a mic and pretend they're a pop star – even if it's only their loved one in the audience. If you want to sample the real Hong Kong, a trip to a karaoke 'box' is essential.

Like most local crazes, karaoke was imported from Japan during the 1980s. But unlike other fads, karaoke has remained an integral part of the culture ever since. During the '90s karaoke boxes sprang up all over town. These are rabbit warrens packed with dozens of small rooms for singers to strut their stuff. Instead of risking public humiliation, groups of two or more people hide themselves away in sound-proofed cubicles with a TV set, remote control and at least two microphones. (Home karaoke machines once did brisk business around here but those are not so much in use these days – probably because of complaints from angry neighbours.) A typical karaoke box is dimly lit, with upholstered seats and a glass panel in the door, the window being essential to peek through after a trip to the toilet to make sure you enter the right room; bursting in on a bunch of strangers can be pretty embarrassing all round. Drinks and snacks (other than the free crisps and nuts on offer) are ordered by phone and delivered quicker than you can sing 'shoo-be-doo'.

Because of their popularity, karaoke boxes are often full – especially on Friday and Saturday nights, so you may have to wait. Some venues accept bookings, but even then you may still have to wait when you turn up.

Discount rates are available in the afternoon and lunchtime is often the cheapest (yes, workers like to warble during office hours too). Staff don't speak much English, but enough to give you a room and drinks, and to take your money. The charge is usually levied per person per session, which can last between three and six hours. A couple who spend three hours in a karaoke box and drink six beers will probably part with around HK$300 in total.

Once inside the room you have to master the technology. It's generally simple, but made that bit more difficult by the fact that the remote control and TV instructions are in Chinese. Normally there is one button you press to bring up a list of English-language songs on the TV screen, and staff are usually on hand to offer help if need be. There are usually more than 100 English songs, although there are far more in Chinese.

Karaoke boxes can be found all over town, especially in Causeway Bay, Tsim Sha Tsui and Mong Kok. The ones listed below are the main ones to look out for. Where they have more than one branch in Hong Kong, the first address given is for their flagship establishments. Prices listed here are per person per session and are exclusive of service charge.

## Big Echo

*Causeway Bay Plaza Phase II, 463-83 Lockhart Road, Causeway Bay, HK Island (2591 1288). Causeway Bay MTR (exit C)/buses & trams along Hennessy Road.* **Open** 11am-6am daily. **Admission** HK$25-$69. **Credit** AmEx, MC, V. **Map** p311 D3. **Other locations**: 3/F, Silvercord, 30 Canton Road, Tsim Sha Tsui, Kowloon (2199 7779).

## Green Box

*8/F, Windsor House, Great George Street, Causeway Bay, HK Island (2881 5088). Causeway Bay MTR (exit E)/buses along Hennessy Road.* **Open** 11am-6am daily. **Admission** HK$29-$45. **Credit** AmEx, MC, V. **Map** p311 E3.

## Neway

*3/F, Causeway Bay Plaza Phase I, 489 Hennessy Road, Causeway Bay, HK Island (2559 8989). Causeway Bay MTR (exit B)/buses along Hennessy Road.* **Open** 11am-6am daily. **Admission** from HK$45. **Credit** AmEx, MC, V. **Map** p311 D3. **Other locations**: 13/F, Harbour Crystal Center, 100 Granville Road, Tsim Sha Tsui, Kowloon (2721 3303).

## Red Box

*9/F, Windsor House, Great George Street, Causeway Bay, HK Island (2882 6188). Causeway Bay MTR (exit E)/buses along Hennessy Road.* **Open** 4pm-6am Mon-Thur; 11am-6am Fri-Sun. **Admission** HK$26-$79. **Credit** AmEx, MC, V. **Map** p311 E3. **Other locations**: Basement, Miramar Shopping Centre, Nathan Road, Tsim Sha Tsui, Kowloon (2366 3899).

in make it the perfect chill-out zone. It's a popular weekend brunch setting too, and has good buffet lunches on weekdays.

### Staunton's

*10-12 Staunton Street (2973 6611). Mid-Levels Escalator/12M, 13, 23A, 26, 40M bus.* **Open** 8am-2am daily. **Credit** AmEx, DC, MC, V. **Map** p308 C3. Located right next to the Mid-Levels Escalator, Staunton's is busy seven nights a week. Its glass windows make it a perfect spot for people-watching, and it's understandably popular with trendy twenty- and thirtysomethings. Food is pricey here, so many use it solely as a watering hole.

## Wan Chai, Causeway Bay & Happy Valley

### The Bridge

*107 Lockhart Road, Wan Chai (2865 5586). Wan Chai MTR (exit A1, C)/buses along Hennessy Road.* **Open** 24hrs daily. **Credit** DC, MC, V. **Map** p310 C3. Ever since the famed Old China Hand (a bar that has been around since the days of Suzie Wong) opted for a makeover and decided to open a mere 21 hours a day, those who want to keep drinking between 5am and 8am come to the Bridge. It's a decent enough watering hole with a good range of beers and spirits.

### Brown

*18A Sing Woo Road, Happy Valley (2891 8558). Bus 5A/tram to Happy Valley.* **Open** 10am-2am daily. **Credit** AmEx, MC, V. A sophisticated bar in Happy Valley, Brown is owned by an architect – the clean lines and dark wood interior are a bit of a giveaway. Divided into three small areas, including a terrace out the back, it's is an ideal place to sample top-shelf spirits and good wine, and it also offers a good menu of modern but inexpensive fusion cuisine.

### Delaney's

*G/F & 1/F, One Capital Place, 18 Luard Street, Wan Chai (2804 2880). Wan Chai MTR (A1, C)/buses along Gloucester Road & Hennessy Road.* **Open** noon-2am Mon-Thur, Sun; noon-3am Fri, Sat. **Credit** AmEx, DC, MC, V. **Map** p310 B3. The prices would make a Dubliner wince (HK$60 for a pint of Guinness), but Delaney's is Hong Kong's best Irish pub. Much better value is its excellent pub grub – the daily lunch carvery is among the best in town. Downstairs is a great setting to sip your beer, while upstairs is more action packed, with a big-screen TV showing football and rugby. **Other locations**: Basement, Mary Building, 71-7 Peking Road, Tsim Sha Tsui, Kowloon (2301 3980).

### Dimples

*10 Yiu Wa Street, Causeway Bay (2893 1839). Causeway Bay MTR (exit A)/5, 10 bus.* **Open** 5pm-3am daily. **Credit** DC, MC, V. **Map** p311 D3.

There are plenty of cosy little bars along Yiu Wa Street and most offer a good respite from the madness of Causeway Bay. The pop art prints on the wall make Dimples an attractive drinking spot, and the locals certainly love it. In this area you should beware of being charged for the mysterious trays of peanuts on your table that you didn't order. If you don't want them, send them straight back.

### Groovy Mule

*37-9 Lockhart Road, Wan Chai (2527 2077). Wan Chai MTR (exit A1, C)/buses along Hennessy Road.* **Open** noon-1am daily. **Credit** DC, MC, V. **Map** p310 C3. Inspired by the rash of Coyote Ugly-style bars, the Groovy Mule has a cast of waiters and waitresses who intermittently leap on to the bar and tables and get jiggy with it. It's so infectious that by the end of the night everyone's up and dancing to mainstream pop and rock. But if this one gets too hectic, there are a few lively late-night bars nearby.

### KBG – Klong Bar & Grill

*G/F, The Broadway, 54-62 Lockhart Road, Wan Chai (2217 8330). Wan Chai MTR (exit A1, C)/ buses along Hennessy Road.* **Open** 5pm-3am daily. **Credit** AmEx, DC, MC, V. **Map** p310 C3. A little slice of Bangkok, Klong captures the spirit of the Thai capital with cosy sections modelled on opium dens and poles for dancers to slink around. The drinks list offers Mekhong whisky and Sang Thip rum – though why people will pay Hong Kong prices to drink Thai firewater is anyone's guess. The Thai food, however, is well worth the extra. There's a wild full-moon party here every month.

### 1/5

*Starcrest, 9 Star Street, Wan Chai (2520 2515). Bus 5, 5A, 10.* **Open** 6pm-1am Mon-Thur; 6pm-3am Fri, Sat. **Credit** AmEx, DC, MC, V. **Map** p310 A4. The opening of this large loft-type bar in a quiet part of Wan Chai has rejuvenated the area. It has also attracted an exclusive crowd; at weekends it's glamour galore here, along with plenty of off-duty suits. With high ceilings and dark wood, the place has a classy feel, but although it is spacious it can get uncomfortably crowded unless you grab a booth.

### Tango Martini

*3/F, Empire Land Commercial Centre, 81-5 Lockhart Road, Wan Chai (2528 0855). Wan Chai MTR (exit A1, C)/buses along Hennessy Road.* **Open** noon-3pm, 6pm-2am daily. **Credit** AmEx, DC, MC, V. **Map** p310 C3. James Bond and Pussy Galore would be happy canoodling on the zebra-skin couches at this place. Prices are high for Wan Chai, but the vodka and gin measures are generous, and the fruit martinis slip down far too easily. Jazz features on Sunday evenings.

## The Peak

**Café Deco** and **Peak Lookout** are highly recommended (for both, *see p133*).

Eat, Drink, Shop

## South & east coasts

### Beaches
*92B Stanley Main Street, Stanley (2813 7313). Bus 6, 260, 973.* **Open** *9.30am-1am Sat.* **Credit** AmEx, DC, MC, V. **Map** p83.
Stanley Main Street is packed each weekend with an odd assortment of expat families, young Chinese couples and Hell's Angels (OK, so they're off-duty accountants with a fetish for Harleys and leather). Beaches is one of the more relaxed venues along the waterfront, and along with booze it serves simple pastas and pub grub at cheap prices.

### Boathouse
*86-8 Stanley Main Street, Stanley (2813 4467). Bus 6, 260, 973.* **Open** *11am-midnight daily.* **Credit** DC, MC, V. **Map** p83.
One of the fancier bar restaurants along the strip, the Boathouse attracts an expat crowd and is particularly busy in the months leading up to the June Dragon Boat Races (*see p188*) as thirsty crews seek refreshment after a few hours' practice on the sea. After dark it serves good dinners, with plenty of fish and seafood on the menu.

### On the Rocks
*Main Beach, Shek O (2809 2021). Bus 9.* **Open** *9pm-4am Fri, Sat.* **No credit cards. Map** p307.
Tucked away at the far end of the main beach, On the Rocks is Shek O's hippest hangout. It only opens at weekends but has a core of regulars and plenty of customers who head out of the city for a night to party by the beach. There's an African feel to the place, with zebra-skin couches and bump 'n' grind music. Not surprising, it's popular with African immigrants. The bar's owner lays on a free shuttle bus to and from the hostels in Tsim Sha Tsui, where many of them stay.

# Kowloon

## Tsim Sha Tsui

### Bahama Mama's
*4-5 Knutsford Terrace (2368 2121). Tsim Sha Tsui MTR (exit B2)/buses along Nathan Road & Chatham Road South.* **Open** *5pm-3am Mon-Thur, Sun; 5pm-4am Fri, Sat.* **Credit** AmEx, DC, MC, V. **Map** p313 C5.
Nearing a decade in existence (almost a miracle in fickle Hong Kong), this tropical theme bar was one of the first on the now-thriving scene of Knutsford Terrace. It's an odd place – a mix of faux foliage, table football and dance music – but with a terrace out front it keeps pulling in the punters.

### Chemical Suzy
*2 Austin Avenue (2736 0087). Tsim Sha Tsui MTR (exit B2)/buses along Chatham Road South.* **Open** *6pm-4am Mon-Sat; 9pm-4am Sun.* **No credit cards. Map** p313 C5.

Austin Road has a strange mix of karaoke bars and very Chinese bars, but this is the most international, especially for fans of Britpop. Posters of Oasis grace the walls and the jukebox features all the genre's biggest names. It's popular with young people and Japanese residents, partly because of the computer games that keep customers amused.

### Felix
*28/F, Peninsula Hotel, Salisbury Road (2366 6251). Tsim Sha Tsui MTR (exit E)/buses to Tsim Sha Tsui Ferry Pier & along Salisbury Road/Tsim Sha Tsui Star Ferry Pier.* **Open** *6pm-2am daily.* **Credit** AmEx, DC, MC, V. **Map** p313 B/C6.
This place is rated by some as the city's finest bar, and it certainly boasts the best view – a magnificent panorama of the Hong Kong skyline. Perched at the top of the Peninsula hotel (*see p53*), it attracts a chic crowd and has a feel of exclusivity to rival anywhere in the world. The Philippe Starck-designed interior is a visual treat, with a cool island bar and cocooned private rooms. The bar here gets most of the acclaim, but the restaurant's fusion food is a bigger draw (that said, Spring Moon – *see p136* and Gaddi's – *see p137* – offer better fare). Oh, and don't miss the gents' loos, whose urinals look out over Kowloon.

### Hard Rock Café
*G-1/F, Silvercord Centre, 30 Canton Road (2375 1323). Tsim Sha Tsui MTR (exit A1).* **Open** *11am-12.30am Mon-Thur, Sun; 11am-2.30am Fri, Sat.* **Credit** AmEx, DC, MC, V. **Map** p313 B6.
If you want corporate American familiarity – and a raucous atmosphere – this branch of the worldwide chain serves Bud, burgers and fries in a roomy environment. The usual rock'n'roll mementoes adorn the walls and the service is friendly.

### Mes Amis
*15 Ashley Road (2730 3038). Tsim Sha Tsui MTR (exit A1, C1).* **Open** *noon-2am daily.* **Credit** AmEx, DC, MC, V. **Map** p313 B6.
The latest in the Mes Amis chain of bars, this place adds some Central style to Tsim Sha Tsui's rough and ragged drinking scene. This is the pick of the crop on Ashley Road, although there are plenty of other options in the cul-de-sac. Attention has been paid to the decor, and the atmosphere is friendly, lively and sophisticated. Food platters and an extensive choice of wines by the glass are further draws. There are several other branches in Hong Kong – phone this one for details.

### Rick's Café
*53-5 Kimberley Road (2311 2255). Tsim Sha Tsui MTR (exit B1, B2)/buses along Nathan Road.* **Open** *5pm-3am Mon-Thur, Sun; 5pm-5am Fri, Sat.* **Credit** AmEx, DC, MC, V. **Map** p313 C5.
Rick's is less Casablanca than a typical Western-style bar and disco, but it's a great place to meet local people (expats, in particular, come here to meet Chinese women). The atmosphere is fun and unpretentious, with mainstream pop and dance music throughout the night.

**Mes Amis.** *See p154.*

# The New Territories

## East New Territories

### Cheers Sports Bar & Restaurant

*28 Yi Chun Street, Sai Kung (2791 6789). Choi Hung MTR then minibus 12.* **Open** 11.30am-2am daily. **Credit** AmEx, MC, V. **Map** p307.

Sai Kung has a large expat population, so the pubs in the area tend to get quite lively in the evening, especially when football and rugby are shown on the big TV screens. Many bars around here stay open until the wee small hours and Cheers is no exception. In terms of clientele, there's a good mix of local Chinese and expats, who are drawn by the friendly atmosphere. Above-average pub grub is served in the restaurant upstairs.

### Steamers

*18-32 Chan Man Street, Sai Kung (2792 6991). Choi Hung MTR then minibus 12.* **Open** 9am-2am daily. **Credit** AmEx, MC, V. **Map** p307.

This is another bright and cheery Sai Kung bar with an emphasis on sports. There's a decent choice of beer and wine, and the menu offers some good meat and seafood dishes alongside standard pub fare. It's an ideal place after a browse around town or walk through the surrounding country park.

# The Outlying Islands

## Lamma

### Deli-Lamma

*36 Main Street, Yung Shue Wan (2982 1583). Yung Shue Wan Ferry Pier.* **Open** 9am-late daily. **Credit** AmEx, DC, MC, V. **Map** p306.

A young, hip crowd packs the Deli in the evenings, partaking of its on-tap cider and Stella. The food is your basic pub fare – pizzas, curries, Sunday roasts – and the terrace backs right on to the harbour.

### Diesel Sports Bar

*51 Main Street, Yung Shue Wan (2982 4116). Yung Shue Wan Ferry Pier.* **Open** 6pm-late Mon-Fri, Sun; noon-late Sat. **No credit cards. Map** p306.

Like most pubs on Lamma, this one is a hangout for the sizeable expat community. It's rammed on Saturday nights, when live football and rugby are played on the big screen, but since it's tiny inside, punters tend to spill on to the pavement.

### Island Bar

*6 Main Street, Yung Shue Wan (2982 1376). Yung Shue Wan Ferry Pier.* **Open** 5pm-2am Mon-Fri; noon-2am Sat, Sun. **No credit cards. Map** p306.

Lamma is no longer the hippie hangout it was before 1997 – nowadays it's home to young families and Terence Conran-loving couples. This open-fronted bar close to the ferry pier is a favourite watering hole for the new yuppie class; unfortunately, the middle-aged, middle-England clientele make it a fairly middle-of-the-road choice.

## Lantau

### China Bear

*Mui Wo Centre, Mui Wo (2984 9720). Mui Wo Ferry Pier.* **Open** 10am-2am daily. **No credit cards. Map** p306.

This glass-fronted pub with outdoor seating is close to the ferry pier and bus terminal, making it an ideal place to unwind before catching the ferry back to the city. There's a good range of beers, including local microbrews, and the British pub food isn't bad.

## Cheung Chau

### Cheung Chau Windsurfing Centre & Outdoor Café

*1 Hak Pai Road (2981 8316). Cheung Chau Ferry Pier.* **Open** 10am-7pm daily. **Credit** MC, V. **Map** p306.

This is a great spot to sip a beer or cocktail as the sun goes down. It serves sandwiches, omelettes and noodles, but many people drop in because of its celebrity connection – windsurfer Lee Lai-Shan, Hong Kong's only Olympic gold medallist, grew up nearby and trained here before her success in Atlanta in 1996. Her family still runs the café.

**Eat, Drink, Shop**

# Shops & Services

Mall culture may have cost the city its individuality, but visitors who dig around will be rewarded.

Eat, Drink, Shop

Malls, and more malls. In the past couple of decades, Hong Kong probably hasn't seen one year in which a mall wasn't being built. In the SAR you find malls underground, you find malls at the Peak and you find malls in all major MTR stations. The mall culture has become so out of control that one has even been built in Stanley, an area that's better known for being a tranquil waterfront village.

While malls are not all bad – they are great when it rains or when Hong Kong's summer heat takes its toll – malls are still malls and the shopping experience they offer is still rather homogenised. Luckily, Hong Kong does offer some shopping diversity. Those who would rather stay in the 'safe' zone can choose from four main shopping areas in the centre: Tsim Sha Tsui, at the southern tip of Kowloon, and Central, Admiralty and Causeway Bay on the north side of Hong Kong Island. All four are located along the busy Victoria Harbour, where people are pretty English-savvy. For the more adventurous travellers, the inner areas of Kowloon, especially Mong Kok and Sham Shui Po, are mazes of shops offering an indigenous retail experience. But few proprietors speak English so if you come, bring along your phrase book or be prepared to use a lot of body language.

## AREA BREAKDOWN

Trawled by tourists, **Tsim Sha Tsui** is a kaleidoscope of retail outlets ranging from dodgy to sublime. If you're coming by the ferry, your first stop is **Harbour City**, a shopping complex consisting of hundreds of shops alongside hotels, restaurants and cinemas (*see p165*). It's also where the cruise liner terminal is located. Nearby is the Peninsula, arguably Hong Kong's most luxurious hotel. But the glamour fades somewhat when you head inland, where streets such as **Cameron Road** and **Mody Road** are crammed with smaller, cheaper shops. This part of Tsim Sha Tsui is also scattered with tourist traps, especially in the form of electronics shops. So unless it's a big name with uniformed staff, beware of possible scams. Things improve again as you approach **Kimberley Road** and **Chatham Road**, where many trendy boutiques feature the latest fashions by local designers. For

clothing bargains, **Granville Road**, running between Nathan Road and Chatham Road South, is a must. The shops lining this street stock everything from separates for as little as HK$40 to pricey designer labels – if you're lucky, you may even come across a little DKNY number tucked away at the back of a cramped maze of rails. These are not imitations, but mostly excess production from last season's collection that have found their way through the back door from a factory in China.

Go north to **Mong Kok**, and you'll find a chaotic hub of small shops selling local products and latest gadgets from Japan. In many of the dingy malls, pirated CDs are sold from equally dingy shops manned by suspicious-looking characters. North-west of Mong Kok, two stops away on the MTR, is **Sham Shui Po**. Take the exit to **Ap Liu Street** and you'll find a congregation of stalls selling second-hand electronics and electrical appliances. Very traditional shops selling locally made rattan fans and clay pots can also be found here.

Across the harbour, shopping in **Central** is generally more upmarket, with the allure of classy arcades, malls, department stores and shops by international heavyweights. But there is also a scattering of shops selling inexpensive clothing. Then there are '**The Lanes**'. As old as Hong Kong itself, the three narrow alleyways of Douglas Lane, Li Yuen Street East and Li Yuen Street West run parallel to each other between Des Voeux and Queen's roads. Stalls here sell pretty much everything: watches, toys, lighters, shoes, clothes and souvenirs in particular. This is a good place to try out your bargaining skills (*see p160* **Cheap at half the price**), as even if there's a marked price, you can usually get it reduced it by a good few dollars.

**Hollywood Road**, which begins in Central above Lan Kwai Fong and runs west all the way to Sheung Wan, houses most of Hong Kong's reputable antiques shops. Among them you'll be able to find everything from ancient opium beds to Ming dynasty vases, but there are also plenty of cheaper items and lashings of the beautiful, simple, dark wood furniture that is proving increasingly popular in the West.

Zee Stone Gallery.
See p159.

Lying between Central and Wan Chai is **Admiralty**, where all shops are in malls and arcades. Air-conditioned bridges link up all the buildings, so you don't even have to walk on the streets unless you're catching a bus. Here, one of the biggest destinations for shoppers is **Pacific Place** (*see p165*), which houses lots of glossy shops and flashy department stores like **Lane Crawford** and **Seibu** (for both, *see p162*).

Unquestionably, **Causeway Bay** is one of the busiest areas in Hong Kong: it's both a mob scene and shopper's dream. It is extremely popular with the local Chinese, and there are lots of smaller shops on secluded side streets that are definitely worth investigating. A good starting point, however, is the megastore **Sogo** (*see p163*), which holds a prime space above a main MTR exit. Once that's been explored, step outside and follow your nose on a tour of the area's alleys and arcades. If you don't fancy trekking around and would rather stick to a sure thing, **Times Square** (*see p165*), above another Causeway Bay MTR exit, is a worthwhile destination. Causeway Bay is also

a good place to go if you're looking for original computer hardware and software, mobile phones or anything techno.

### SEASONAL SALES, OPENING TIMES
Expect to find some bargains during the sales, which are generally held in June and October. During the Chinese New Year some shops may change their opening times or close altogether.

### IT'S A RIP-OFF
Like many big cities in the world, Hong Kong is both consumer haven and tourist trap. In order to avoid tourists being scammed, the HKTB has introduced the Quality Tourism Services (QTS) scheme as a means of identifying those shops and restaurants that have proven to offer excellent service. Look for the QTS sticker.

## Antiques

### Altfield Gallery
*248-9 Prince's Building, 10 Chater Road, Central, HK Island (2537 6370). Central MTR (exit H)/buses & trams through Central.* **Open** *10am-7pm Mon-Sat; 11am-5pm Sun.* **Credit** *AmEx, MC, V.* **Map** *p309 E4.*

Altfield has two different outlets – Altfield Gallery and Altfield Interiors (*see p181*). While this shop deals in antique Chinese furniture, it also has a penchant for ancient prints (which have their own room) and fantastic Asian maps. These date back as far as the 1500s, and, not surprisingly, come at a steep price.

## Arch Angel Antiques

*53-5 Hollywood Road, Central, HK Island (2851 6828). Central MTR (exit D1, D2, G)/Mid-Levels Escalator/12M, 13, 23A, 26, 40M, 43 bus.* **Open** 9.30am-6.30pm daily. **Credit** AmEx, DC, MC, V. **Map** p308 C3.
This established fixture on Hollywood Road stocks a good range of quality Chinese antiques, and also does repairs and restorations.

## Artemis

*46 Wyndham Street, Central, HK Island (2530 2320). Central MTR (exit D1, D2, G)/13, 26, 43 bus.* **Open** 10am-6pm Mon-Sat. **Credit** AmEx, MC, V. **Map** p308 C4.
This well set-out shop offers room to move, so you can work your way around the wealth of merchandise. And while it's not exactly cheap, it does have stock that you'd be hard pushed to find elsewhere.

## Gallery One

*G/F, 31-3 Hollywood Road, Central, HK Island (2545 6436). Central MTR (exit D1, D2, G)/Mid-Levels Escalator/12M, 13, 23A, 26, 40M, 43 bus.* **Open** 10am-6pm Mon-Sat. **Credit** AmEx, DC, MC, V. **Map** p308 C3.
If you're looking for antique jewellery, Gallery One is the shop for you. It sells a wonderful selection of necklaces, bracelets and rings, as well as Buddhist walnut carvings – you'll just have to shift through the mess to find your perfect purchase.

## Gorgeous Arts & Crafts

*Shop A, UG/F, 30 Hollywood Road, Central, HK Island (2973 0034). Central MTR (exit D1, D2, G)/Mid-Levels Escalator/12M, 13, 23A, 26, 40M, 43 bus.* **Open** 10.30am-7pm Mon-Sat; 1-7pm Sun. **Credit** AmEx, MC, V. **Map** p308 C3.
Located close to the Mid-Levels Escalator, this place can be difficult to find – although you can see its window, stacked high with stock, above Gallery One (*see above*) on Hollywood Road. This shop has a wonderful selection of Chinese antiques at reasonable prices, and staff are friendly.

## Honeychurch Antiques

*29 Hollywood Road, Central, HK Island (2543 2433). Central MTR (exit D1, D2, G)/Mid-Levels Escalator/12M, 13, 23A, 26, 40M, 43 bus.* **Open** 10am-6pm Mon-Sat. **Credit** AmEx, DC, MC, V. **Map** p308 C3.
Conspicuously located opposite Central Police Station, Honeychurch prides itself on reliability, honesty and courteous salesmanship. If you're not sure of what you're buying, you can trust the staff to explain the ins and outs of whatever's caught your eye. For the serious patron, it also handles English and Chinese silverware, a superb range of jewellery and a heady collection of Asian antiques.

## Martin Fung Antiques & Furniture Company

*Shop 321, Pacific Place, 88 Queensway, Admiralty, HK Island (2524 3306). Admiralty MTR (exit C1)/buses & trams through Central.* **Open** 10am-6pm daily. **Credit** AmEx, DC, MC, V. **Map** p309 F5.
Hidden away on the top level of Pacific Place are several arts, antiques and craft stores, including this one. It has no specific bent, meaning there's a good mix of merchandise: paintings, sculptures, furniture and porcelain are all on offer, at very decent prices.

## Wonder Dragon

*30 Hollywood Road, Central, HK Island (2526 8863). Central MTR (exit D1, D2, G)/Mid-Levels Escalator/12M, 13, 23A, 26, 40M, 43 bus.* **Open** 10.30am-6.30pm Mon-Sat; 1.30-6pm Sun. **Credit** AmEx, DC, MC, V. **Map** p308 C3.
Wonder Dragon was established in the 1970s and is still going strong. The interior is awkward and cramped, but not only does it sell a fantastic variety of Chinese antiques, but it also has old upright phones, gramophones and typewriters. Sadly, service can be curt and somewhat haughty.

## Zee Stone Gallery

*G/F, Yu Yet Lai Building, 43-55 Wyndham Street, Central, HK Island (2810 5895/www.zeestone.com). Central MTR (exit D1, G)/13, 26, 43 bus.* **Open** 10am-7pm Mon-Sat; 1-6pm Sun. **Credit** AmEx, DC, MC, V. **Map** p308 C4.
This gallery deals in a sophisticated selection of Chinese works of art, as well as antique furniture and Tibetan rugs. Staff are friendly and helpful.

# Art supplies & stationery

## The Artland Company

*3/F, Lockhart Centre, 301-307 Lockhart Road, Wan Chai, HK Island (2511 4845). Buses along Hennessy Road.* **Open** 9am-7pm Mon-Fri; 9am-5pm Sat. **Credit** MC, V. **Map** p310 C3.
An adequate assortment of art supplies is sold here, including the usual necessities like felt-tip pens, paints, crayons, paper and inks. Prices are fair.

## Fit Copy Equipment Co/ Da Fat Stationery

*52 Lyndhurst Terrace, Central, HK Island (2544 1917). Central MTR (exit D1, D2, G)/Mid-Levels Escalator/12M, 13, 23A, 40M, 43 bus.* **Open** 9am-7pm Mon-Sat. **No credit cards. Map** p308 C3.
This tiny place sells the simplest of stationery products – pens, Filofaxes, paper and envelopes – and deals with all your photocopying needs. Service is efficient and fast, just the way Hong Kongers like it.

## PaperArt

*46 Lyndhurst Terrace, Central, HK Island (2545 8985). Central MTR (exit D1, D2, G)/Mid-Levels Escalator/12M, 13, 23A, 40M, 43 bus.* **Open** 10.30am-7.30pm Mon-Sat. **Credit** AmEx, MC, V. **Map** p308 C3.

# Cheap at half the price

Bargaining is an essential and expected part of shopping in Hong Kong, but it rarely comes easily to Western visitors. Haggling won't, admittedly, cut much ice in department stores or at Gucci, but it's a must at markets, and is certainly worth a try at antiques shops.

Think of it as a game of skill, and always keep a smile on your face – anger and aggression will be met by indifference. The outraged ('how much?!') smile is always a good start, followed, perhaps, by the incredulous ('you must be joking!') smile. After these come the more conciliatory ('that's a bit more like it, but...') smile, and finally the satisfied ('it's a deal') smile. Don't feel under any pressure – chances are that there's another stall selling exactly the same merchandise around the corner, and you're the one holding the trump card – you can always just walk away. Indeed, it's always wise to do a bit of price shopping

first before making a final purchase, since many of the stalls sell exactly the same things for slightly different prices. You can also always use the 'I'll give you HK$100 for two' ploy. Don't fall for the you're-taking-food-out-of-my-children's-mouths' line – if stall owners are not making a decent profit, they simply won't sell.

Vendors in Hong Kong are not as unbridled as their counterparts in China when it comes to ripping off tourists, so you may consider yourself successful if you get 30 to 40 per cent off the asking price. And don't underestimate the satisfaction of some good-natured sparring and the eventual striking of that mutually acceptable bargain – it'll give you a genuine insight into, and interaction with, traditional Chinese life. And, sadly, it's an experience that is getting harder and harder to come by in increasingly cosmopolitan Hong Kong.

More a gift shop than a stationer's, PaperArt stocks rubber stamps from the US, handmade paper and artsy greeting cards, all at fairly high prices.

## Books & magazines

Note that import tax on overseas publications tends to be high.

### Bookazine

*Shop 309-13, Prince's Building, 10 Chater Road, Central, HK Island (2522 1785). Central MTR (exit J1, J2, J3)/buses & trams through Central/Central Star Ferry Pier.* **Open** 9am-7pm Mon-Sat; 10am-6pm Sun. **Credit** AmEx, MC, V. **Map** p309 E4.
These stores stock a good selection of fiction, non-fiction and imported magazines.
**Other locations**: throughout the city.

### Commercial Press (HK) Limited

*9-15 Yee Wo Street, Causeway Bay, HK Island (2890 8028). Causeway Bay MTR (exit E)/buses along Hennessy Road.* **Open** 11am-9pm daily. **Credit** AmEx, MC, V. **Map** p311 E3.
This large bookshop stocks both Chinese and English literature, with a focus on paperbacks.
**Other locations**: 608 Nathan Road, Mong Kok, Kowloon (2384 8228).

### Dymocks

*Shop EPI, Central Star Ferry Concourse, Central, HK Island (2522 1012). Central MTR (exit A)/ Central Star Ferry Pier/buses along Connaught Road.* **Open** 8am-10.30pm Mon-Sat; 9am-10pm Sun. **Credit** AmEx, DC, MC, V. **Map** p309 E3.

There are various Dymocks outlets all over Hong Kong, of which this small, cramped and crowded branch in the Central Star Ferry Concourse is one of the most accessible. Much like its rival Bookazine, Dymocks stocks a good choice of US and UK magazines, along with fiction and non-fiction books. Coffee-table books are a strong point.
**Other locations**: throughout the city.

### Government Publications Centre

*Room 402, 4/F, Murray Building, Garden Road, Central, HK Island (2537 1910). Admiralty MTR (exit B)/40M bus/buses through Garden Road.* **Open** 9am-6pm Mon-Fri; 9am-1pm Sat. **No credit cards**. **Map** p309 E5.
Located beside the main entrance of Pacific Place, this shop has the unappealing feel of a schoolroom-cum-dole office. It stocks everything relating to the inner and outer workings of the region, like the annual budget and exam reference books for schools, as well as, on a more useful level, excellent maps of Hong Kong.

### Hong Kong Book Centre

*LG/F, 25 Des Voeux Road, Central, HK Island (2522 7064). Central MTR (exit B, C)/buses & trams through Central.* **Open** 9am-6.30pm Mon-Fri; 9am-5.30pm Sat. **Credit** AmEx, MC, V. **Map** p309 D3.
Under the same ownership as the Swindon Book Company (*see p161*), the Hong Kong Book Centre is a demure, well-stocked bookworm's haven. The stock is wide-ranging, though fiction is a forte, and there's always a good selection of international magazines to peruse.

## Kelly & Walsh

*Shop 348, Level 3, Pacific Place, 88 Queensway, Admiralty, HK Island (2522 7893). Admiralty MTR (exit C1)/buses & trams through Central.* **Open** 9.30am-8pm Mon-Sat; 11am-8pm Sun. **Credit** AmEx, MC, V. **Map** p309 F5.

The inside of Kelly & Walsh looks more like a stationer's than a bookshop, but it does stock a fantastic mix of local and imported magazines, as well as certain overseas newspapers that can be hard to come by in Hong Kong. It's somewhat cluttered, somewhat pricey, but always busy with a mix of locals and tourists.

## Page One

*B1, Times Square, 1 Matheson Street, Causeway Bay, HK Island (2506 0381). Causeway Bay MTR (exit A)/63, 108, 117, 170, N170 bus.* **Open** 10.30am-10pm Mon-Thur, Sun; 10.30am-11pm Fri, Sat. **Credit** AmEx, DC, MC, V. **Map** p311 D3.

Page One carries an extensive, comprehensive collection of fiction and non-fiction in both Chinese and English.
**Other locations:** Festival Walk, 80 Tat Chee Avenue, Kowloon Tong, Kowloon (2778 2808).

## Swindon Book Company

*13-15 Lock Road, Tsim Sha Tsui, Kowloon (2366 8001). Tsim Sha Tsui MTR (exit C1, E)/ buses along Nathan Road/Tsim Sha Tsui Star Ferry Pier.* **Open** 9am-6.30pm Mon-Thur; 9am-7.30pm Fri, Sat; 12.30-6.30pm Sun. **Credit** AmEx, MC, V. **Map** p313 B6.

This is the bigger Swindon Book Company outlet. It stocks a wide range of English-language titles stretching across two floors. Pricing is reasonable

considering that most of the stock is imported, and the American paperbacks here tend to be the cheapest in town.
**Other locations:** Shop 310-18, Ocean Centre, Harbour City, 5 Canton Road, Tsim Sha Tsui, Kowloon (2735 9881).

# Antiquarian/second-hand

## Flow

*1-2/F, 40 Lyndhurst Terrace, Central, HK Island (2964 9483). Central MTR (exit D1, D2, G)/Mid-Levels Escalator/12M, 13, 23A, 40M, 43 bus.* **Open** 12.30-8pm Tue-Sat; 12.30-7pm Sun.
**No credit cards. Map** p308 C3.

This second-hand bookshop is a dream come true for those who read regularly and end up being bitten by the high prices of imported paperbacks. Flow will exchange your old books, CDs and videos for cash or products sold in the store.

# Department stores & malls

## Department stores

## Jusco

*Kornhill Plaza 2, Kornhill Road, Quarry Bay, HK Island (2884 6888). Quarry Bay MTR.* **Open** 9.30am-10.30pm daily. **Credit** AmEx, DC, MC, V.

Jusco, one of the largest department stores in Japan, set up its first Hong Kong outlet in Quarry Bay back in 1987. Although some branches are showing their age, they are all exceptionally large and well stocked with fashion, food and household items.

**Kelly & Walsh**: the place to go for magazines.

Much-loved department store **Lane Crawford**.

Another bonus is that prices are quite low, making it a better choice than other Japanese megastores. **Other locations**: throughout the city.

## Lane Crawford
*Pacific Place, 88 Queensway, Admiralty, HK Island (2845 1838). Admiralty MTR (exit C1)/buses & trams through Central.* **Open** 10am-9pm daily. **Credit** AmEx, DC, MC, V. **Map** p309 F5.
One of the city's largest and oldest department stores, Lane Crawford is Hong Kong's answer to Harrods. Set over several floors, it's home to quality ranges such as Aveda, plus excellent household, shoe and handbag sections. The Causeway Bay location is pitched towards the younger market, while the other outlets cater to a more mature clientele.
**Other locations**: 70 Queen's Road, Central, HK Island (2118 3388); G-1/F, Times Square, 1 Matheson Street, Causeway Bay, HK Island (2118 3638); Shop 100, Ocean Terminal, Harbour City, 5 Canton Road, Tsim Sha Tsui, Kowloon (2118 3428).

## Marks & Spencer
*Central Tower, B-1/F, 28 Queen's Road, Central, HK Island (2921 8303/www.marksandspencer.com). Central MTR (exit D1, D2, G).* **Open** 10.30am-8.30pm Mon-Fri; 10.30am-8pm Sat, Sun. **Credit** DC, MC, V. **Map** p309 D4.
This is the most accessible of Hong Kong's M&S stores, and it also has the best grocery section.

While the stock mirrors that of the UK outlets, the prices are considerably higher. There's a good choice of clothing, and small but adequate food and cosmetics sections.
**Other locations**: Shop 254, Ocean Centre, Harbour City, 5 Canton Road, Tsim Sha Tsui, Kowloon (2926 3346); Shops 120 & 229, Pacific Place, 88 Queensway, Admiralty, HK Island (2921 8891); 329-39 New Town Plaza 1, Sha Tin, New Territories (2929 4332).

## Seibu
*Pacific Place, 88 Queensway, Admiralty, HK Island (2971 3888). Admiralty MTR (exit C1)/buses & trams through Central.* **Open** 10.30am-8pm Mon-Wed, Sun; 10.30am-9pm Thur-Sat. **Credit** DC, MC, V. **Map** p309 F5.
Although it has a Japanese name, the Hong Kong Seibu shops are actually owned by Dickson 'Harvey Nichols' Poon and are decidedly cosmopolitan. The chic four-floor store in Pacific Place houses the food hall – the city's answer to Dean & Deluca – in the basement, while the other floors brim with a mix of desirable cosmetics, gifts, household items, kitchenware, accessories, shoes and clothes – from brands such as French Connection to Vivienne Westwood and various Japanese labels. Both branches have a different feel – the one in Causeway Bay is geared towards young street fashion.
**Other locations**: Windsor House, 311 Gloucester Road, Causeway Bay, HK Island (2890 0333).

## Sogo

*555 Hennessy Road, Causeway Bay, HK Island
(2833 8338). Causeway Bay MTR (exit B, D2)/buses
along Hennessy Road.* **Open** 10am-10pm daily.
**Credit** AmEx, DC, MC, V. **Map** p311 D3.

This Japanese store has a little bit of everything, and
is very popular among the local well-heeled Chinese.
However, it's not quite as flush – or as well set out
– as its rival, Seibu (*see p162*). But it does have a
good assortment of household accessories such as
glass, plates and vases, not to mention necessities
like irons, kettles, teapots and electrical merchandise. Much of the stock is Japanese and well priced.

## Wing On

*Wing On Centre, 211 Des Voeux Road, Central,
Sheung Wan, HK Island (2852 1888/www.wingon
net.com). Sheung Wan MTR (exit E3)/buses & trams
through Central.* **Open** 10am-7.30pm daily. **Credit**
AmEx, DC, MC, V. **Map** p308 C2.

One of the oldest department stores in the city (founded 1907) but it is constantly upgraded. Its motto is
'value for money', and it stays true to its word. Prices
are very reasonable, and the choice is fantastic and
aimed mainly at the Chinese market. Merchandise
includes cosmetics, clothing and homeware.
**Other locations**: throughout the city.

# Shopping in Shenzhen

Once known as the city of copy bags and
other pirated goods, Shenzhen is now touted
as China's most 'cosmopolitan Chinese' city.
Everywhere you walk, dialects from every
region of the country are overheard.
Skyscrapers cover the landscape.

These days, tourists and Hong Kong locals
alike rush in to take advantage of all the city
has to offer, namely significantly lower prices
for quality goods and services. The big draw
is **Lowu Commercial City**, a huge mall with
1,500 small shops located at the exit of the
Chinese customs office. The mall is just 40
minutes from the centre of Hong Kong (not
counting time waiting in customs) and offers
more variety per square foot than anywhere
else in Shenzhen. Armed with a visa and
HK dollars, shoppers can find a tailor, fabric
and get a suit or any other garment custom-
tailored at short notice by heading to the
Fabric Mall on the fifth floor of the mall.
Expect to pay upwards of (the equivalent of)
US$80 for a man's custom-made suit, and
US$35 for a woman's.

Handbag and shoe shops are to be found on
every floor of the centre. The styles are current
and the prices are low by any standard. Even
so, bargaining is *de rigueur*, and you can often
negotiate the price down at least 50 per cent.

The jewellery section on the second floor
has stalls selling freshwater pearls, semi-
precious stones, jade, all kinds of beads
and even what's claimed to be dinosaur eggs!
The touting and haggling frenzy is enough to
drive you to the massage centre, which in
fact, is a wonderful way to end the day.

Most tourists never get past LCC, but some
venture into the **Dongmen** area and the newer
shopping heart of the city, the **Hua Qiang Bei
Lu** area. Here, the children's market and the
women's market offer up various floors of row

after row of small stores in the style of Lowu
Commercial City. The area is also surrounded
by big new shopping malls full of concessions.
Nearby, world-class golf courses have started
sprouting up, along with skating rinks, kite-
flying parks and various theme parks.

### PRACTICALITIES

Foreign passport holders travelling to
Shenzhen need to get a separate visa. Most
travellers can just get a single-entry, five-day
visa at the checkpoint for HK$150 (holders
of US and some other passports have to pay
HK$450). However, there is no need to get a
special visa for Shenzhen if you already have
one for China. If you do get one here, it takes
about half an hour. But be warned: the
immigration authority of Shenzhen has been
known to give a hard time to British passport
holders and even refuse on-the-spot visas, so
you might want to cut out the hassle and get
one in advance (for details, *see p283*).

Once you've got the necessary paperwork,
it's fairly easy to get to Shenzhen by MTR
and KCR, after changing lines at Kowloon
Tong station. The border is extremely busy,
especially at weekends, so travel on a
weekday if at all possible.

If going to various malls in Shenzhen, or
to other parts of China, you are advised to
change some HK dollars to renminbi (RMB).
Although most stores accept HK dollars, they
will not give you exact change.

Last but not least, although safety in
Shenzhen is improving by the day, it is still a
relatively crime-ridden city compared to Hong
Kong. So do not flaunt your expensive camera
and keep your guard up.

*Ellen McNally is the author of* Shop in
Shenzhen, An Insider's Guide *(HK$95,
sold at book stores around town). For more
information, go to www.shopinshenzhen.com.*

Eat, Drink, Shop

# timeout.com

**The online guide to the world's greatest cities**

## Malls

### Fashion Walk

*Kingston Street, Causeway Bay, Causeway Bay, HK Island. Causeway Bay MTR (exit E)/A11, 103, 170, N170 bus.* **Open** 11am-11pm daily. **Credit** varies. **Map** p311 E2.

This sheltered pedestrianised street is lined with restaurants with outdoor tables as well as trendy boutiques, many of them featuring local designs.

### Festival Walk

*80 Tat Chee Avenue, Kowloon Tong, Kowloon. Kowloon Tong MTR.* **Open** 10.30am-8pm daily. **Credit** varies.

Although Festival Walk resembles Pacific Place (*see below*) in appearance, its target clientele is more mid market. The mall also has an ice rink, an AMC cinemaplex and some decent restaurants.

### Harbour City

*5 Canton Road, Tsim Sha Tsui, Kowloon. Tsim Sha Tsui MTR (exit E)/buses to Tsim Sha Tsui Star Ferry Pier & along Salisbury Road/Tsim Sha Tsui Star Ferry Pier.* **Open** 10.30am-8pm daily. **Credit** varies. **Map** p313 B5/6.

A short walk from the Star Ferry terminal, Harbour City is divided into five interconnected shopping arcades, including the massive Ocean Terminal and Ocean Centre. This gigantic mall is undoubtedly the largest shopping emporium in Tsim Sha Tsui and it's easy to get lost (pick up a guide on your way into the mall). A concept store, LCX, recently opened here, incorporating a mix of clothing and accessories as well as international restaurants with harbour views.

### The Landmark

*16 Des Voeux Road, Central, HK Island. Central MTR (exit G)/buses & trams through Central/Central Star Ferry Pier.* **Open** 10am-7.30pm daily. **Credit** varies. **Map** p309 D4.

The Landmark may be one of the older malls in Hong Kong, but it has managed to maintain its prestigious status and elegant appearance. Inside, there's a huge central atrium and a wide range of shops, which are worth checking out for their flash window displays, even if you're not in a buying mood. All boutiques here are of exclusive brand names, among them Alberta Ferretti, Louis Vuitton and Versace.

### Lee Gardens

*33 Hysan Avenue, Causeway Bay, HK Island. Causeway Bay MTR (exit F).* **Open** 10.30am-8pm daily. **Credit** varies. **Map** p311 E3.

Lee Gardens provides a relaxed environment in which the most prestigious (and expensive) brands congregate. Hermès, Louis Vuitton, Chanel, Cartier, Tiffany and Dior are just a few examples.

### Pacific Place

*88 Queensway, Admiralty, HK Island (2844 8988). Admiralty MTR (exit C1)/buses & trams through Central.* **Open** 10.30am-8pm daily. **Credit** varies. **Map** p309 F5.

Pacific Place's exit from the MTR station is sleek and chic – just like the four-storey mall itself. Well designed and easily accessible, its outlets (particularly the department stores Lane Crawford, Seibu and Marks & Spencer; for all, *see p162*) cater to a wide range of clientele.

### Rise Commercial Building

*5-11 Granville Circuit, Tsim Sha Tsui, Kowloon. Tsim Sha Tsui MTR (exit B1, B2)/buses along Nathan Road/Tsim Sha Tsui Star Ferry Pier.* **Open** daily (times vary). **Credit** varies. **Map** p313 C5.

Despite its rather rundown appearance, this arcade is the current fashion hotspot. Tucked away from view near the factory outlets in Granville Road, the four floors draw a younger crowd, attracted by the lesser-known designers, henna tattoo parlour, homeware shops and other quirky stores.

### Times Square

*Russell Street, Causeway Bay, HK Island. Causeway Bay MTR (exit A)/buses along Hennessy Road.* **Open** 10.30am-9pm daily. **Credit** varies. **Map** p311 D3.

This Causeway Bay landmark building caters to a wide range of shoppers. On the ground floor and at The Lobby on 2/F are Gucci, Ferragamo and the like, whereas floors 3-9 are allocated for themes such as Suit & Dress, Casual Living, Electronics World and Kids. The 10th-14th floors house the Food Forum, a hub of restaurants, while the basement has the Marketplace, for fast food and supermarkets. There's also a Lane Crawford (*see p162*) on the first floor.

### Winning Commercial Centre

*46-8 Hillwood Road, Tsim Sha Tsui, Kowloon. Jordan MTR (exit D).* **Open** daily (times vary). **No credit cards. Map** p313 C5.

As Rise Commercial Building (*see above*) is saturated, young designers are looking for the next hot spot, and they seem to have found it here. It's a bit off the beaten track, but that's exactly why free-spirited, trendy types love it. Besides local fashion labels, there are also many shops selling unique imported fashion and second-hand clothing.

## Dry cleaners

### Goodwins of London

*Shop 27, G/F, Central Building, 1 Pedder Street, Central, HK Island (2525 0605). Central MTR (exit D1, G)/buses & trams through Central/Central Star Ferry Pier.* **Open** 8.15am-7.30pm Mon-Sat; 10.30am-6.30pm Sun. **Credit** MC, V. **Map** p309 D4.

An all-English, extra-refined dry cleaners that provides a reliable, careful service for cleaning clothes. **Other locations**: G/F, Pacific Place, 88 Queensway, Admiralty, HK Island (2918 1400).

### Jeeves

*Shop 2, Lobby Floor, Bank of East Asia Building, 10 Des Voeux Road, Central, HK Island (2973 0101). Central MTR (exit H)/buses & trams through Central/Central Star Ferry Pier.* **Open** 8am-7pm Mon-Sat. **Credit** AmEx, DC, MC, V. **Map** p309 D4.

Eat, Drink, Shop

# Hong Kong in fashion

Long gone are the days when Hong Kong factory workers churned out mass-produced garments from assembly lines. The territory is a fashionable place that is also the birthplace of many fashion design talents; some have even made marks on the international catwalk scene. One such case is **Barney Cheng**, whose reputation for pricey couture creations has placed him in the global spotlight. The high-profile **Flora Cheong-Leen**, whose work heavily employs Chinese symbolism, and **William Tang**, notoriously known as Hong Kong's 'bad boy', have also found lucrative markets overseas. An up-and-coming star is **Johanna Ho**, whose first collection in 1998 was immediately snapped up by Barneys New York.

Ironically, it is those who have chosen to focus on their native Hong Kong who face the most struggle, due to general indifference, overriding commercial concerns and an underlying conservatism. The first generation of Hong Kong fashion designers, such as Eddie Lau Pui Kei and Ragence Lam, have largely redirected their businesses from couture to manufacturing, or simply retired.

Most of those who have the opportunity are shifting their concentration to overseas markets. **Silvio Chan**, who created 37 º 2 In The Morning, has closed all his outlets in Hong Kong. The picture is even greyer for menswear, because the market share is miniscule. 'Men rarely shop any more,' laments **Amus Yeung**, who has his own boutique at Rise Commercial Building. He now devotes much of his time to womenswear – small and slim ladies only need apply – and designs only a handful of items for men each season.

With a fast-emerging market in mainland China, however, the future for Hong Kong design is promising. Already many designers have become beneficiaries of the country's new openness. **Pacino Wan**, who has been named 'the most imaginative designer in Hong Kong' by *Newsweek* and one of the 'Ten Best Asian Designers' by *Four Seasons* magazine in New York, has also set up an office in Shenzhen. His tongue-in-cheek creations (*pictured*) have included pictures of the Queen and instant noodle packets. **Lulu Cheung**, who achieves recognition for taking her retailing business to a mainstream context, now sells her collections of low-key, subtle womenswear in nine stores in Hong Kong and China. Other labels that continue to do well in Hong Kong, China and around the world are **Ruby Li**, whose designs are infused with a young street attitude, characterised by clashing contrasts; **Modele de Prudence**, a creative yet wearable label

One of the city's older dry-cleaning establishments, this is an upmarket place for the upwardly mobile. In other words, prices are steep.

### Robinson Dry Cleaning

*73B Caine Road, Mid-Levels, HK Island (2523 8317). Mid-Levels Escalator/buses along Caine Road.* **Open** 8am-8pm Mon-Sat; 8am-6pm Sun. **No credit cards. Map** p308 B4.

An amiable, dependable dry cleaner situated outside the main hubbub of Central, with fair pricing.

## Electronics

Tsim Sha Tsui is packed with electronics and camera shops, but your chance of being ripped off is high. For peace of mind, stick to **Fortress** or **Citicall** stores, or check out the honest dealers on **Queen Victoria Street** in Central. The **Sham Shui Po** district of Kowloon is the biggest centre for computer goods (both the legitimate and, more famously, the pirated).

Eat, Drink, Shop

### Lulu Cheung
Shop 303, Ocean Terminal, Harbour City, 5 Canton Road, Tsim Sha Tsui, Kowloon (2117 0682). Tsim Sha Tsui MTR (exit C1, E)/buses along Canton Road/Tsim Sha Tsui Star Ferry Pier. **Open** 10.30am-8pm daily. **Credit** AmEx, DC, MC, V. **Map** p313 B6.

### Modele de Prudence
Shop 13, 1/F (menswear), and Shop B317, Basement (ladieswear) Prudential Centre, 216-28A Nathan Road, Tsim Sha Tsui, Kowloon (2736 7006). Jordan MTR (exit D). **Open** 1-10pm daily. **Credit** AmEx, MC, V. **Map** p313 B5.

### 9"
Flat 1A, Hyde Park Mansion, 53 Paterson Street, Causeway Bay, HK Island (2368 1808). Causeway Bay MTR (exit E). **Open** noon-10pm daily. **Credit** AmEx, DC, MC, V. **Map** p311 E2.
**Other locations**: Shops 307 & 310, Rise Commercial Building, 5-11 Granville Circuit, Tsim Sha Tsui, Kowloon (2312 1080).

### Pacino Wan
Shop 2045, Miramar Shopping Centre, 1-23 Kimberley Road, Tsim Sha Tsui, Kowloon (2375 6718). Tsim Sha Tsui MTR (exit B1, B2)/buses along Nathan Road. **Open** 1-10pm daily. **Credit** AmEx, DC, MC, V. **Map** p313 C5.
**Other locations**: throughout the city.

### Ruby Li
Shop 410, 4/F, Rise Commercial Building, 5-11 Granville Circuit, Tsim Sha Tsui, Kowloon (2307 2007). Tsim Sha Tsui MTR (exit B1, B2)/buses along Chatham Road South. **Open** 1-9.30pm daily. **Credit** AmEx, DC, MC, V. **Map** p313 C5.
**Other locations**: Flat B, 1/F, Vienna Mansion, 55 Paterson Street, Causeway Bay, HK Island (2882 9309).

for women and men; and **9"** (Nine Inches), a unisex line that's popular among clubbers.
What's virtually taken as read is that Hong Kong, with a more established background as a cosmopolitan city, will continue to lead as China's fashion capital. Local interest is kept alive by twice-yearly fashion shows in the city, held by the Trade Development Council in January and July. For further details, check out the fashion section at www.tdctrade.com.

### Amus Yeung
Shop 413, Rise Commercial Building, 5-11 Granville Circuit, Tsim Sha Tsui, Kowloon (2366 0413). Tsim Sha Tsui MTR (exit B1, B2)/buses along Chatham Road South. **Open** 4-10pm daily. **Credit** MC, V. **Map** p313 C5.

In Causeway Bay, **Windsor House** (on the corner of Great George Street and Gloucester Road) has several floors of shops dedicated to Mac and PC wares. Prices are competitive, so have a look around before you buy. The pirate CD, DVD, VCD and software market still thrives in Hong Kong. One of its focuses is a crazy warren of stores packed into three floors at 298 Hennessy Road in Wan Chai. If you're lucky, a shifty looking gent will say something along the lines of, 'Looking for products?', then send you off in the direction of a short-lived copy market, stocking all the latest gear. As this is illegal, many of the goods on offer, especially the VCDs, can be shoddy, so don't be too seduced by the low, low costs. After all, you tend to get what you pay for. Just remember, the real thing isn't that much more expensive in Hong Kong.

### Broadway

*Shops 704 & 714, Times Square, Causeway Bay,*
*HK Island (2506 1330/2506 0228). Causeway*
*Bay MTR (exit A).* **Open** 11am-9.30pm Mon-Thur,
Sun; 11am-10pm Fri, Sat. **Credit** DC, MC, V.
**Map** p311 D3.
Like its rival Fortress (*see below*), Broadway also
has branches scattered all over town. Smart
shoppers visit them both to compare prices before
making a purchase.
**Other locations**: throughout the city.

### Citicall

*G/F, Hung Kei Mansion, 5-8 Queen Victoria Street,*
*Central, HK Island (2391 4366). Central MTR (exit*
*B)/buses & trams through Central.* **Open** 10am-8pm
daily. **Credit** MC, V. **Map** p308 C3.
From its humble beginnings as a small camera
shop in Mong Kok, Citicall has blossomed into a
chain of electronics and visual/audio shops that
rivals corporation-backed Fortress and Broadway.
Prices are considerably cheaper as the owner has
the connections that allow him to cut out the
middleman. Don't be put off by the chaos inside
the stores – the staff are usually friendly and willing to give a good price.
**Other locations**: throughout the city.

### Fortress

*Shop 3320, Level 3, Harbour City, 5 Canton Road,*
*Tsim Sha Tsui, Kowloon (2116 1022). Tsim Sha*
*Tsui MTR (exit C1, E)/buses to Tsim Sha Tsui*
*Star Ferry Pier/Tsim Sha Tsui Star Ferry Pier.*
**Open** 11am-9pm daily. **Credit** AmEx, DC, MC, V.
**Map** p313 B5/6.
If you're after a TV, camera, stereo, CD player, plug
or hairdryer, one of the many Fortress outlets
around town will no doubt stock it. They also
have a small collection of CDs, DVDs and VCDs.
These, like the rest of the store's stock, are reliable
and the prices always low. The friendly, helpful staff
are another pull.
**Other locations**: throughout the city.

### Fortress Zoom/Fortress Digital

*59 Russell Street, Causeway Bay, HK Island*
*(2504 4525). Causeway Bay MTR (exit A).*
**Open** noon-10pm daily. **Credit** AmEx, DC, MC, V.
**Map** p311 D3.
Part of the Fortress group, these Zoom/Digital
branches around town specialise in personal
electronic products including audio-visual, photo-
graphic and portable computing products.
**Other locations**: throughout the city.

## Fashion

For high-end shopping, head for Central or
Admiralty; for streetwear, go to Causeway
Bay; and for factory outlets, try Tsim Sha Tsui.
The more adventurous can trek further up the
Kowloon peninsula to Temple Street Night
Market (*see p170* **Market places**) and Mong
Kok for local bargains.

## Accessories

For a wide range of accessories and knick-
knacks, try the street stalls on **Jardine's
Crescent** in Causeway Bay, HK Island.

### Mandarina Duck

*Shop B60, The Landmark, 16 Des Voeux Road,*
*Central, HK Island (2845 4898). Central MTR*
*(exit G)/buses & trams through Central/Central Star*
*Ferry Pier.* **Open** 10am-7pm daily. **Credit** AmEx,
DC, MC, V. **Map** p309 D4.
Every self-respecting dapper local has probably
owned a Mandarina Duck bag at some stage. The
neat, compact designs, often made from hardened
man-made fabric, have an almost sci-fi appearance.
OK, they're pricey, but they wear well.

### Mayfair Leather

*92 Nathan Road, Tsim Sha Tsui, Kowloon*
*(2366 2588). Tsim Sha Tsui MTR (exit B1)/buses*
*along Nathan Road.* **Open** 9.30am-11pm daily.
**Credit** AmEx, DC, MC, V. **Map** p313 C6.
Mayfair Leather is a rather sleek store that stocks
leather accessories including handbags, briefcases
and shoes. Prices aren't too hard on the wallet, and
service comes with a smile.

### Renommé

*Flat B, 13/F, North Point Mansions, 702 King's*
*Road, North Point, HK Island (2522 6435).*
*Quarry Bay MTR (exit B4)/buses along King's Road.*
**Open** 10am-6pm Mon-Fri; by appointment Sat.
**No credit cards.**
This shop is run by a group of Filipinos, who design
superb hats for every occasion. They also allow the
customer to be involved in the creation, so you can
bring your own materials and fabric if you choose.

### Samsonite

*2 Sun Wui Road, Causeway Bay, HK Island*
*(2972 2656). Causeway Bay MTR (exit F)/23B bus.*
**Open** 10am-9pm daily. **Credit** AmEx, MC, V.
**Map** p311 E3.
If you're in need of an extra suitcase (or two) to carry
home your wealth of Hong Kong purchases,
Samsonite is the place to go for its famously robust
cases and travel bags.

### Style

*35 Granville Road, Tsim Sha Tsui, Kowloon (2721*
*0110). Tsim Sha Tsui MTR (exit B2)/buses along*
*Chatham Road South.* **Open** 9.30am-midnight daily.
**Credit** MC, V. **Map** p313 C5.
This trinket store stocks all manner of cheap acces-
sories, from hairclips to wigs and feathered masks.

## Budget

### Bossini

*G/F, On Lok Yuen Building, 27A Des Voeux Road,*
*Central, HK Island (2524 9313). Central MTR (exit*
*A).* **Open** 10am-8pm daily. **Credit** AmEx, DC, MC,
V. **Map** p309 D3.

*Eat, Drink, Shop*

The various branches of the Chinese Crocodile label sell the Western look (trainers, T-shirts, jeans and more) at exceptionally low prices, but this outlet carries one of the biggest kids' departments.
**Other locations**: throughout the city.

### Kingkow

*Shop 023, B/F, Ocean Terminal, Harbour City, 5 Canton Road, Tsim Sha Tsui, Kowloon (2317 4088). Tsim Sha Tsui MTR (exit C1, E)/ buses along Chatham Road South.* **Open** 10am-8pm daily. **Credit** AmEx, DC, MC, V. **Map** p313 B6.

Kingkow stocks inexpensive clothes for kids (under the age of 16 years) to suit any occasion.

## Designer: international

### Birkin

*Shop C, Causeway Bay Mansion, 42-8 Paterson Street, Causeway Bay, HK Island (2577 9323). Causeway Bay MTR (exit E)/A11, 103, 170, N170 bus.* **Open** noon-10pm daily. **Credit** AmEx, DC, MC, V. **Map** p311 E2.

Come to Birkin for the latest from pieces from Prada, Miu Miu and Gucci, all at lower prices than at the official outlets.
**Other locations**: Basement, Sun Arcade, 28 Canton Road, Tsim Sha Tsui, Kowloon (2377 2880).

### Donna Karan/DKNY

*Hang Lung Centre, Paterson Street, Causeway Bay, HK Island (2970 2288). Causeway Bay MTR (exit E)/A11, 103, 170, N170 bus.* **Open** 10.30am-10pm daily. **Credit** AmEx, DC, MC, V. **Map** p311 E2.

Donna Karan infiltrated the capacious wardrobes of many Hong Kong *tai-tais* (ladies who lunch) a long time ago. The diffusion label DKNY represents a funkier option.

### ETE

*Shop B, G/F, 53 Paterson Street, Causeway Bay, HK Island (2881 1865). Causeway Bay MTR (exit E).* **Open** noon-10pm daily. **Credit** AmEx, DC, MC, V. **Map** p311 E2.

Part of the IT group (*see p171*), the ETE shops sell mostly accessories; among the labels you'll find are Marc Jacobs, Costume National, DKNY Jeans and Dirk Bikkembergs.
**Other locations**: throughout the city.

### Extravaganza

*Shop F-16, Fashion Island, 11-19 Great George Street, Causeway Bay, HK Island (2915 0051). Causeway Bay MTR (exit E)/buses along Hennessy Road.* **Open** noon-10pm Mon-Thur, Sun; noon-10.30pm Sat. **Credit** AmEx, DC, MC, V. **Map** p311 E3.

Like Birkin (*see above*), Extravaganza offers the latest designer brands at prices lower than at the official outlets.
**Other locations**: Miramar Shopping Centre, 1-23 Kimberley Road, Tsim Sha Tsui, Kowloon (2730 0500).

Bag heaven: **Mandarina Duck**. *See p168.*

Luckily for budget shoppers, there's a Bossini outlet on almost every street in Hong Kong. Aside from its well-made basics, the store's seasonal collections tend to put many high-street labels to shame.
**Other locations**: throughout the city.

### Giordano

*Shop 4, G/F, China Building, 29 Queen's Road, Central, HK Island (2921 2028). Central MTR (exit D1, D2, G)/buses along Queen's Road Central.* **Open** 10am-8.30pm Mon-Sat; 11am-8pm Sun. **Credit** AmEx, MC, V. **Map** p309 D4.

Like Bossini, Giordano is everywhere in town and offers good basics, from accessories to jeans and T-shirts. As for the pricing, it's so low it's a sin. In recent years, the label has established an upmarket – and pricier – line, Giordano Ladies, which features high-quality fabrics and cuttings (confusingly, for both men and women). Note that not all branches sell this newer range.
**Other locations**: throughout the city.

## Children

### Crocodile for Kids

*Shop 2105-7, Ocean Terminal, Harbour City, 5 Canton Road, Tsim Sha Tsui, Kowloon (2735 5136). Tsim Sha Tsui MTR (exit C1, E)/buses along Chatham Road South.* **Open** 11am-8pm daily. **Credit** AmEx, DC, MC, V. **Map** p313 B6.

**Eat, Drink, Shop**

# Market places

A visit to a market in Hong Kong is a must, whether you're up for a full-on haggling session (*see p160* **Cheap at half the price**) or just want to immerse yourself in the atmosphere. Here's our pick of the best.

## Apliu Street Market

*Sham Shui Po, Kowloon. Sham Shui Po MTR (exit A2/C2)/2, 2C, 6, 6A, 12 bus.* **Open** noon-10pm daily.

Apliu Street is a haven for gadgets and second-hand electronic goods. The former are available from the shops on both sides of the street, while the latter are displayed at the street-side stalls or even just on the roadside on top of a tablecloth. Old coins, 'antique' clocks and watches and even 'vintage' clothes are sold from these vendors, although the antiquity of these goods is questionable. Perhaps the most enjoyable part of a visit here is the chance to sample indigenous foods from the snack stalls.

## Bird Market

*Bird Park, off Flower Market Road, Mong Kok. Prince Edward MTR (exit B1).* **Open** 7am-8pm daily. **Map** p312 C1.

The Bird Market is surprisingly clean and pristine. Much-prized songbirds kept in cages fill the air with cacophonous sounds. Also on sale are wonderfully carved wooden bird cages, which are ornaments in themselves and reasonably priced. If you're an animal lover of any sort, give the place a miss.

## Jade Market

*Kansu & Shanghai Streets, Yau Ma Tei, Kowloon. Yau Ma Tei MTR (exit C) or Jordan MTR (exit A, B1).* **Open** 10am-3.30pm daily. **Map** p313 B4.

The earlier you arrive at the Jade Market the more likely you are to bag a bargain, but recognising such a deal may not be so easy. Jade is priced according to a complicated system that merits the consistency of its colour, the thickness, translucency and purity of the material. Unless you really know what you're doing, stick to cheap trinkets or the freshwater pearls sold alongside the jade.

## Lai Chi Kok Market

*Lai Chi Kok, Kowloon. Lai Chi Kok MTR.* **Open** 1-2pm Mon-Fri.

If you fancy a meander through industrial Hong Kong, trek out to Lai Chi Kok Market. Located in an area of clothing factories and

wholesalers (behind the MTR station close to Wing Hong Street), this remarkably busy market sells stuff (including clothes) that might well have walked out of the back door of nearby factories. This is the kind of place you'll find real bargains.

## Spring Garden Lane Market

*Spring Garden Lane, Wan Chai, HK Island. Wan Chai MTR (exit A3)/trams through Wan Chai/23, 23A, 23b, 25, 25 bus.* **Open** 9am-10pm daily. **Map** p310 B4.

Very few places on Hong Kong Island retain their local heritage as well as this street in Wan Chai. It is where some of the oldest buildings in the city still stand, especially at the intersection with Johnston Road across from Southorn Playground. Here you also find a line-up of factory outlets – places that sell brand-new designer sportswear items from the last season at cut-throat prices. The surrounding wet market is a mix of fresh-produce stalls and Asian grocery stores selling herbs, spices, wicker items and some damn cheap and good tropical-print shirts and trunks. Be sure to don your worn-out sneakers or heavy-duty boots as the path is constantly wet, slippery and covered in fruit peels.

## Stanley Market

*Stanley, HK Island. Buses to Stanley.* **Open** 11am-6pm daily. **Map** p83.

At one time Stanley Market was known for its rock-bottom prices, but, as tourists discovered the market, they've gradually risen. However, you can still uncover some decent souvenirs, factory seconds, fake goods, trinkets and arts and crafts. The bus ride from Central is a pleasure in itself.

## Temple Street Night Market

*Jordan, Temple Street, Kowloon. Jordan MTR (exit A, C2).* **Open** 2-10pm daily. **Map** p313 B4.

After 6pm, Temple Street comes alive with market stalls, entertainers and buzzing crowds. It's a good place to give your bargaining skills a go, especially if you're after copy CDs, watches or bags. At the far end are fortune tellers and rows of small street shows performing Chinese opera, which are aimed more at the locals than tourists. Not far away, north of Yau Ma Tei MTR, on Tung Choi Street, are the cheap clothes and accessories of the Ladies' Market and Goldfish Market (for both, *see p92*).

**Giorgio Armani.**

## Giorgio Armani

*Chater House, 11 Chater Road, Central, HK Island (2532 7700). Central MTR (exit B). Buses through Des Voeux Road Central.* **Open** 10am-7.30pm daily. **Credit** AmEx, DC, MC, V. **Map** p309 D3.

With 2,000sq m (21,500sq ft) of retail space, this Armani superstore has everything you could possibly want from the legendary Italian design house. When all the browsing has worn you out, nourishment can be had at the instore café.

## Gucci

*G1, The Landmark, 16 Des Voeux Road, Central, HK Island (2524 4492). Central MTR (exit G)/ buses & trams through Central/Central Star Ferry Pier.* **Open** 10.30am-7.30pm Mon-Sat; 11am-7pm Sun. **Credit** AmEx, DC, MC, V. **Map** p309 D4.

If you've got cash in your pocket and/or credit on your card, Gucci's temple of extravagance is a favourite place to head.

**Other locations**: Shop 368, Pacific Place, 88 Queensway, Admiralty, HK Island (2524 2721).

## IT

*Sino Plaza, 255-7 Gloucester Road, Causeway Bay, HK Island (2834 4393/www.ithk.com). Causeway Bay MTR (exit C)/buses along Gloucester Road.* **Open** noon-10pm daily. **Credit** AmEx, MC, V. **Map** p311 D2.

The IT chain stocks favourite brands like Paul Smith, Helmut Lang, Vivienne Westwood and Comme des Garçons, as well as desirable furniture and selected homewares. This two-storey outlet is decked out like an early '80s disco, with smoked glass, mirror balls and dark furnishings, which doesn't exactly make for a comfortable shopping experience. If the prices are beyond your budget, there's a sale shop at 72-119 Silvercord (2377 9466) over the road.

**Other locations**: 8 & 10 Queen's Road, Central, HK Island (2167 8287/2868 9448); Shops G107 & 268, 2/F, Ocean Centre, Harbour City, 5 Canton Road, Tsim Sha Tsui, Kowloon (2114 0268).

## Joyce

*106 Canton Road, Tsim Sha Tsui, Kowloon (2367 8128). Tsim Sha Tsui MTR (exit C1/E)/buses along Nathan Road/Tsim Sha Tsui Star Ferry Pier.* **Open** noon-10.30pm Mon-Sat; noon-7pm Sun. **Credit** DC, MC, V. **Map** p313 B6.

Named after its founder, Joyce Ma, this store is a bit of an institution in Hong Kong. Several outlets around the city stock designer names such as Comme des Garçons, Dolce & Gabbana, Anna Sui and Ghost, alongside top-brand shoes, accessories and cosmetics. The Tsim Sha Tsui outlet is the mainstream venue (and has a Prada concession); the Central store is reserved for more upmarket brands; and the Admiralty branch is geared to the young and trendy. The Joyce empire also controls individual boutiques for Dries Van Noten, Dolce & Gabbana, Missoni (all in The Landmark; *see p165*), Jil Sander (Alexandra House, 16-20 Chater Road, Central), Costume National, Y's by Yohji Yamamoto (both Lee Gardens; *see p165*) and Boss (Pacific Place; *see p165*). In fact, Joyce is such an entity that it even publishes its own magazine, entitled – you guessed it – *Joyce*.

**Other locations**: New World Tower, 16 Queen's Road, Central, HK Island (2810 1120); Shop 334, Pacific Place, 88 Queensway, Admiralty, HK Island (2523 5944).

## Joyce Warehouse

*21/F, Horizon Plaza, South Horizon, 2 Lee Wing Street, Ap Lei Chau, HK Island (2814 8313). Bus 90B, 590.* **Open** 10am-7pm Tue-Sat; noon-6pm Sun. **Credit** DC, MC, V.

Joyce Warehouse may be hard to get to, but keen shoppers will be rewarded by the range and prices – womenswear is often vastly reduced.

## Prada

*Shop 213, The Landmark, 16 Des Voeux Road, Central, HK Island (2845 6678). Central MTR (exit G)/buses & trams through Central/Central Star Ferry Pier.* **Open** 10.30am-7.30pm Mon-Sat; 11am-6pm Sun. **Credit** AmEx, DC, MC, V. **Map** p309 D4.

Like many other designer stores in this city, Prada has armed security at the entrance, which is odd, because shoot-outs in classy clothing shops are rare. Still, you never know.
**Other locations**: Shop G28, Sogo, 555 Hennessy Road, Causeway Bay, HK Island (2836 5686).

## The Swank Shop

*Shops 104-5 & 128-9, The Landmark, 16 Des Voeux Road, Central, HK Island (2810 0769/ 2868 6990). Central MTR (exit G)/buses & trams through Central/Central Star Ferry Pier.* **Open** 10.30am-7.30pm daily. **Credit** AmEx, DC, MC, V. **Map** p309 D4.

Don't be put off by the naff name – the Swank Shop is one of the city's oldest fashion stores. It sells an odd but extensive assortment of designer labels, like Gianfranco Ferre and Valentino, for both men and women. Even if these names aren't for you, there's a slick collection of accessories on offer as well.
**Other locations**: Shop 111, 201 Lee Gardens, 33 Hysan Avenue, Causeway Bay, HK Island (2907 3525); Shop 335-6, Pacific Place, 88 Queensway, Admiralty, HK Island (2845 4929); Shop L103, The Place, New World Centre, Tsim Sha Tsui, Kowloon (2736 0280).

## Versace

*G124, Times Square, 2 Matheson Street, Causeway Bay, HK Island (2506 2281). Causeway Bay MTR (exit A)/63, 108, 117, 170, N170 bus.* **Open** 11am-8.30pm daily. **Credit** AmEx, DC, MC, V. **Map** p311 D3.

The Versace label has a large following in Hong Kong and, therefore, plenty of outlets. All are cold and crisp, topped off by service with a (thin) smile.
**Other locations**: throughout the city.

## Vivienne Tam

*Shop 215, Times Square, 2 Matheson Street, Causeway Bay, HK Island (2506 1162). Causeway Bay MTR (exit A)/63, 108, 117, 170, N170 bus.* **Open** 11am-8pm Mon-Thur, Sun; 11am-9pm Fri, Sat. **Credit** AmEx, DC, MC, V. **Map** p311 D3.

Sometimes you'll wander into a store selling the New York-based Chinese designer Vivienne Tam's latest collection and be wowed by her exquisite sexy silk dresses covered in intricate Chinese embroidery. Other times, you'll be appalled by the downmarket nylon fabrics and cheap-looking T-shirts. Still, as one of the territory's greatest design exports, Tam is something of a local treasure.
**Other locations**: Shop 209, Pacific Place, 88 Queensway, Admiralty, HK Island (2523 6620).

# Designer: local

For further ideas, *see p166* **Hong Kong in fashion**.

## Baboon

*Shop 3002, 30/F, Soundwill Plaza, 38 Russell Street, Causeway Bay, HK Island (2368-3099). Causeway Bay MTR (exit A)/.* **Open** 11am-10pm daily. **Credit** AmEx, DC, MC, V. **Map** p311 D3.

Baboon is a fun place for people who like to do their own mixing and matching. In addition to its eponymous label, the shop has also brought in avant-garde designer labels from the US, Europe and Asia. The two other branches are within Extravaganza stores.
**Other locations**: **Extravaganza** Miramar Shopping Centre, 1-23 Kimberley Road, Tsim Sha Tsui, Kowloon (2175 0028); LG 18, **Extravaganza** Silvercord, 30 Canton Road, Tsim Sha Tsui, Kowloon (2574 1265).

## G2000

*Shop 31-4, G/F, Miramar Shopping Centre, 1-23 Kimberley Road, Tsim Sha Tsui, Kowloon (2377 1167). Tsim Sha Tsui MTR (exit B1).* **Open** 11am-11.30pm daily. **Credit** MC, V. **Map** p313 C5.

G2000 is a very popular local brand for suits and classic sportswear. Most of its suits are made from European fabrics, and workmanship is very good. Prices are extremely reasonable for what you get.
**Other locations**: throughout the city.

## Gay Giano

*Shop 2336-7, Level 2, Harbour City, 5 Canton Road, Tsim Sha Tsui, Kowloon (2117 0619). Tsim Sha Tsui MTR (exit A1)/Tsim Sha Tsui Star Ferry Pier.* **Open** 11.30am-8.30pm daily. **Credit** AmEx, DC, MC, V. **Map** p313 B5/6.

Gay Giano could easily be mistaken for an Italian brand – indeed, many Hong Kongers don't know it's actually a local label. All items are well designed and of very high quality, and only a fraction of the price you'd pay for something genuinely Italian.
**Other locations**: throughout the city.

## http://www.izzue.com

*UG/F, 10 Queen's Road, Central, HK Island (2868 4066/www.izzue.com). Central MTR (exit B, C)* 10.30am-7.30pm daily. **Credit** AmEx, DC, MC, V. **Map** p309 D3.

Founded just a few years ago, this local fashion company has already captured the hearts of local youngsters with its hip-hop and street styles. The only downside is that most stock seems to be geared to Asian (ie petite) people. Some branches also have cafés and gadget showcases.
**Other locations**: throughout the city.

## Shanghai Tang

*G/F, Pedder Building, 12 Pedder Street, Central, HK Island (2525 7333/www.shanghaitang.com). Central MTR (exit D1, G)/buses & trams through Central/Central Star Ferry Pier.* **Open** 10am-8pm Mon-Fri; noon-6pm Sat, Sun. **Credit** AmEx, DC, MC, V. **Map** p309 D4.

IT – a two-storey temple of designer style. *See p171.*

The money-making brainchild of local entrepreneur David Tang (*see p183* **David's new toy**), Shanghai Tang is a favourite shopping spot for many. Trad China with a kitsch twist, the shop sells everything from silk-covered diaries to Mao clocks, and leather coats to cheongsams. The store also has its own troupe of tailors, some of whom can still create a real cheongsam – those worn by Maggie Cheung in *In The Mood For Love* were made here.
**Other locations**: Shop ML2-3, Peninsula Hotel, Salisbury Road, Tsim Sha Tsui, Kowloon (2537 2888).

### 'SPY' by Henry Lau

*11 Sharp Street East, Causeway Bay, HK Island (2893 7799). Causeway Bay MTR (exit A).* **Open** 1-11pm daily. **Credit** AmEx, DC, MC, V. **Map** p311 D3.
With shops in Japan, Taiwan, Canada and Macau, Lau is one of the few local designers to enjoy an international profile. His flamboyant designs mix street chic with splashes of the theatrical.
**Other locations**: Shop 406-7, Rise Commercial Building, 5-11 Granville Circuit, Tsim Sha Tsui, Kowloon (2366 5866).

### U2

*Shop 527-8, Times Square, 1 Matheson Street, Causeway Bay, HK Island (2576 3172). Causeway Bay MTR (exit A).* **Open** noon-10pm Mon-Fri; 11.30am-10pm Sat, Sun. **Credit** AmEx, DC, MC, V. **Map** p311 D3.
With a number of locations around town, U2 is the popular sportswear line of G2000 (*see p172*) and sells good-quality casualwear, in both classic

and trendy styles, for men and women. On the whole, prices are incredibly reasonable.
**Other locations**: throughout the city.

## Factory outlets

### Arbutus

*29B Granville Road, Tsim Sha Tsui, Kowloon (2366 5200). Tsim Sha Tsui MTR (exit B1, B2)/ buses along Nathan Road.* **Open** 11am-11pm daily. **Credit** MC, V. **Map** p313 C5.
Arbutus is known for its hip sports clothes and popular active brands. Note that some shops in the same street sell counterfeits.

### Granville Road & Kimberley Road

*Tsim Sha Tsui, Kowloon. Tsim Sha Tsui MTR (exit B1, B2)/buses along Nathan Road.* **Map** p313 C5.
Two parallel streets where lots of factory outlets sell competitively priced clothes.

## Fetish/erotic

### Fetish Fashion

*The 'Cockloft', Merlin Building, 32 Cochrane Street, Central, HK Island (2544 1155). Mid-Levels Escalator/buses along Queen's Road Central.* **Open** noon-10pm Mon-Sat. **Credit** AmEx, MC, V. **Map** p308 C3.
If latex, whips and adult accessories are your thing, Fetish Fashion is the place to go. It sells a heady line of rubber clothes, bondage gear and accessories, as well as sex toys and books.

# Second-hand

## Beatniks

*Shop 1, Rise Commercial Building, 5-11 Granville Circuit, Tsim Sha Tsui, Kowloon (2739 8494). Tsim Sha Tsui MTR (exit B1, B2)/buses along Chatham Road South.* **Open** 2-11pm daily. **Credit** AmEx, DC, MC, V. **Map** p313 C5.

A well-known name among second-hand clothing fans, Beatniks has many vintage fashion items targeted at the grunge type. But don't think that means things are cheap here – it costs big bucks to dress down in Hong Kong.

**Other locations**: 19-21 Shelter Street, Causeway Bay, HK Island (2881 7153).

## Oldish Renascence

*Shop 20-27, G/F, Winning Commercial Building, 46-8 Hillwood Road, Tsim Sha Tsui, Kowloon (no phone). Jordan MTR (exit D).* **Open** 2.30-11pm daily. **No credit cards**. **Map** p313 C5.

Owner Taiji Leung knows his stuff and he collects everything from limited-edition Levi's to rare Adidas. Cool curios like beat-up leather suitcases covered in old airlines stickers and Jackie O shades also feature.

## Salvation Army Thrift Store

*11 Wing Sing Lane, Yau Ma Tei, Kowloon (2332 4433/4531). Yau Ma Tei MTR (exit C).* **Open** 9am-12.30pm, 1.45-5pm Mon-Fri. **No credit cards**. **Map** p312 B3.

The Salvation Army runs the city's most established line of thrift stores and, even better, it's all for charity. But don't think that thrift stores sell only rubbish: many of the items on offer here are well-known labels, and if you dig in you might even come across a Donna Karan or Gaultier.

**Other locations**: throughout the city.

# Shoes

## Millie's

*Shop 13, G/F, Central Building, 1 Pedder Street, Central, HK Island (2523 8001). Central MTR (exit D1, G)/buses & trams through Central/ Central Star Ferry Pier.* **Open** 10am-8pm Mon-Sat; 10am-7pm Sun. **Credit** AmEx, DC, MC, V. **Map** p309 D4.

This long-established shop stocks a decent collection of Italian shoes and handbags. Prices are fair and the designs flatter any modern man or woman.

## Ming Kee

*30 Bowring Street, Jordan, Kowloon (2730 4815) Jordan MTR (exit C1, C2)/buses along Nathan Road.* **Open** 11am-9pm Mon-Sat. **No credit cards**. **Map** p313 B4.

This is where local pop and movie stars have their glitzy shoes made. Orders normally take two weeks, but a rush job can be done in ten days. Bring a sketch or picture of the shoe you want copied. Expect to pay upwards of HK$650.

## Nine West

*Shop 11-12, Central Building, 1 Pedder Street, Central, HK Island (2921 2628). Central MTR (exit D1, G)/buses & trams through Central/ Central Star Ferry Pier.* **Open** 9.30am-7.30pm daily. **Credit** AmEx, DC, MC, V. **Map** p309 D4.

Having conquered the US and UK markets, Nine West has become every gal's favourite shoe store. If you're lucky enough to be around during the sales, prices are slashed by more than half.

**Other locations**: throughout the city.

# Streetwear/clubwear

## D-Mop

*11-15 On Lan Street, Central, HK Island (2840 0822/www.d-mop.com). Central MTR (exit D1, G)/13, 26, 43 bus/buses along Queen's Road Central.* **Open** 11am-8pm Mon-Sat; noon-7pm Sun. **Credit** AmEx, DC, MC, V. **Map** p309 D4.

D-Mop is one of the trendier shops in Hong Kong, selling stuff that no self-respecting, fashion-conscious guru would be without. Patrick Cox and Komodo woollies, clothes by Martine Sitbon, and a great selection of jeans, including good old ever-fashionable Levi's, are all stocked.

**Other locations**: 8 Kingston Street, Causeway Bay, HK Island (2203 4130).

# Tailors

## The Couples

*Shop 38-9, G/F, Beverley Commercial Centre, 87-105 Chatham Road South, Tsim Sha Tsui, Kowloon (2317 6855). Buses along Chatham Road South.* **Open** 1-9.30pm daily. **Credit** AmEx, DC, MC, V. **Map** p313 C5.

Orders here usually take a week, but rush jobs can be done in as little as two days. A basic design costs HK$500.

## Linva Tailor

*38 Cochrane Street, Central, HK Island (2544 2456). Mid-Levels Escalator/buses along Queen's Road Central.* **Open** 9.30am-6pm Mon-Sat. **Credit** AmEx, DC, MC, V. **Map** p308 C3.

This small tailor offers friendly, reliable, well-priced custom-made clothing, and also does alterations.

## Sam's Tailor

*94 Nathan Road, Tsim Sha Tsui, Kowloon (2367 9423/www.samstailor.com). Tsim Sha Tsui MTR (exit B1)/buses along Nathan Road.* **Open** 10am-7.30pm Mon-Sat; 10am-midnight Sun. **Credit** AmEx, DC, MC, V. **Map** p313 C6.

Despite its location, in a rundown arcade on Nathan Road, this tiny shop caters to the stars, as you can tell by the photos and letters that adorn the walls and counter. From Bill Clinton to Princess Diana, there's only one place celebrities go – Sam the tailor. The nice thing about Sam is that you don't have to be rich to see him – he's a very easy-going bloke and is willing to cater to different budgets.

Eat, Drink, Shop

### Sze Sze

*83C Percival Street, Causeway Bay, HK Island (2576 6233). Causeway Bay MTR (exit A)/buses along Gloucester Road.* **Open** 10am-7pm Mon-Sat. **No credit cards. Map** p313 D3.

Located around the corner from Times Square in Causeway Bay, this traditional ladies' tailor has been around since the 1950s. For a tailored cheongsam, expect to part with HK$2,000-$3,000 for labour and around HK$3,000 for the silk. An order normally takes a fortnight, but an emergency job can be completed in a week.

## Underwear

### Jilian

*31C-D Wyndham Street, Central, HK Island (2826 9295). Central MTR (exit D2).* **Open** 11am-8pm Mon-Sat; 11am-6pm Sun. **Credit** V. **Map** p308 C4.

Buying good lingerie can take time, and that is exactly the concept behind this shop. The staff pamper you – even the fitting room is softened by

a fluffy rug. The brand names carried here are mostly European (Argentovivo, Aubade), and cover everything from push-up bras to corsets.

### Lily Co

*17 Li Yuen Street East, Central, HK Island (2810 7178). Central MTR (exit C)/buses & trams through Central.* **Open** 10am-7pm daily. **Credit** MC, V. **Map** p309 D3.

Concealed by the chaotic market stalls of Li Yuen Street East, Lily Co has possibly the best selection of knickers a girl could wish for – at good prices. Jockey and Sloggi sit among other well-known labels, but more obscure brands also feature.

## Watches

### City Chain

*G/F, General Commercial Building, 156 Des Voeux Road, Central, HK Island (2815 3556). Sheung Wan MTR (exit E3)/5, 5B, 5C, M47 bus.* **Open** 10am-8pm daily. **Credit** AmEx, DC, MC, V. **Map** p309 D3.

**Fook Ming Tong Tea Shop.** *See p176.*

Eat, Drink, Shop

It can seem like there is a City Chain watch outlet on virtually every street corner in Hong Kong, selling the best-known brands of watches such as Seiko, Adidas, Cat and Esprit. Don't expect anything too impressive from the service and you won't be disappointed.
**Other locations**: throughout the city.

### Eldorado Watch Co Ltd
*Peter Building, 58-62 Queen's Road, Central, HK Island (2522 7155). Central MTR (exit D1, D2, G)/buses along Queen's Road Central.*
**Open** 10am-6pm daily. **Credit** AmEx, DC, MC, V. **Map** p309 D3.
This gigantic store oozes elegance and sells chic, sleek watches. As well as being the official agent for Omega in Hong Kong, it also has a range of Cartier and Rolex timepieces.

### Masterpiece (by King Fook)
*Shop 216-7, Level 2, Pacific Place, 88 Queensway, Admiralty, HK Island (2845 6766). Admiralty MTR (exit C1)/buses & trams through Central.*
**Open** 10.30am-8pm Mon-Sat; 11.30am-8pm Sun. **Credit** AmEx, DC, MC, V. **Map** p309 F5.
If you're after a major brand of watch, you'll find most brands on display at Masterpiece's two stores in Central.
**Other locations**: Shop 21, Central Building, 1-3 Pedder Street, Central, HK Island (2526 6733).

## Florists

### Anglo-Chinese Florist
*50 Wellington Street, Central, HK Island (2845 4212). Central MTR (exit D1, G)/12M, 13, 23A, 40M, 43 bus.* **Open** 8am-11pm daily. **Credit** AmEx, MC, V. **Map** p308 C4.
This small florist sells a wonderful selection of flowers for any event, and plants for the home. Delivery is available.

### GOD
*Basement, Leighton Centre, 77 Leighton Road (entrance on Sharp East Street), Causeway Bay, HK Island (2881 0908/www.god.com.hk). Causeway Bay MTR (exit A).* **Open** noon-9pm daily. **Credit** AmEx, DC, MC, V. **Map** p311 D3.
The only GOD location that has a separate florist with fresh flowers and plants of all types. But be prepared to splash out for them.
**Other locations**: 3/F, Shop 8D, Ocean Terminal, Harbour City, 5 Canton Road, Tsim Sha Tsui, Kowloon (2736 0098); G-1F, 48 Hollywood Road, Central, HK Island (2805 1876).

### Sim's Flower Workshop
*Shop 9, 1 Lyndhurst Terrace, Central, HK Island (2542 4544). Central MTR (exit D1, D2, G)/Mid-Levels Escalator/12M, 13, 23A, 40M, 43 bus.*
**Open** 9am-6.30pm Mon-Fri; 9am-5.30pm Sat. **Credit** AmEx, MC, V. **Map** p308 C3.
Sim's Flower Workshop is a long, lean shop, filled with sweet-smelling flora that can be made up into bouquets. Service is polite.

# Food & drink

## Bakeries & confectioners

### Cova Pasticceria & Confetteria
*Shop B01, B1 Lee Gardens, 33 Hysan Avenue, Causeway Bay, HK Island (2576 4233). Causeway Bay MTR (exit F).* **Open** 10am-9pm daily. **Credit** AmEx, DC, MC, V. **Map** p311 E3.
This Milan-based company, which was founded nearly two centuries ago, is home to some of the best Italian chocolates and freshly baked cakes in town.
**Other locations**: throughout the city.

### Godiva
*Shop 309-10, Lee Gardens, 33 Hysan Avenue, Causeway Bay, HK Island (2907 4818). Causeway Bay MTR (exit F).* **Open** 10.30am-8pm Mon-Sat; noon-7pm Sun. **Credit** AmEx, MC, V. **Map** p311 E3.
Belgian chocolatier Godiva dishes up the crème de la crème of chocolates in Hong Kong. The assortment of sweet stuff is heady, as are the prices.

## Coffee & tea

For **Starbucks** and **Pacific Coffee Company**, *see p126.*

### Fook Ming Tong Tea Shop
*G3-4, The Landmark, 16 Des Voeux Road, Central, HK Island (2521 0337/www.fookmingtong.com). Central MTR (exit G)/buses & trams through Central/Central Star Ferry Pier.* **Open** 10am-7.30pm Mon-Sat; 11am-6pm Sun. **Credit** AmEx, DC, MC, V. **Map** p309 D4.
The people at Fook Ming Tong are accommodating and ready to help you with your every tea whim. They'll not only grant on-the-spot tastings, but they stock the most remarkable array of tea-leaves.
**Other locations**: Shop 124, Ocean Terminal, Harbour City, 5 Canton Road, Tsim Sha Tsui, Kowloon (2735 1077); B2, Sogo, 555 Hennessy Road, Causeway Bay, HK Island (2834 9978).

### Moon Garden Tea House
*5 Hoi Ping Road, Causeway Bay, HK Island (2882 6878). Causeway Bay MTR (exit F)/8X, 10, 26, 63, 108 bus.* **Open** noon-midnight daily. **Credit** AmEx, DC, MC, V. **Map** p311 E3.
A tea-drinker's dream. As well as selling an excellent selection of leaves – including the ever-popular jasmine, rose and Chinese green tea – Moon Garden also runs courses in tea tasting.

### Tsit Wing
*1/F, 2 Queen Victoria Street, Central, HK Island (2522 9795/www.twcoffee.com). Central MTR (exit A, B, C)/buses to Kennedy Town.* **Open** 10am-7pm Mon-Sat. **Credit** AmEx, DC, MC, V. **Map** p308 C3.
Founded in 1932 as a grocery store, Tsit Wing was the first company to popularise coffee- and tea-drinking among the Chinese in Hong Kong. With

a repackaged image, the shop now runs reasonably stylish cafés and still serves up some of the best coffee that you will find in Hong Kong.
**Other locations**: 2-10 Lyndhurst Terrace, Central, HK Island (2544 2237).

## Delicatessens

Others options include **Castello del Vino** (*see p179*), **CitySuper** (*see below*) and **Great Food Hall** (*see below*).

### Oliver's Delicatessen

*Shop 233, 2/F, Prince's Building, 10 Chater Road, Central, HK Island (2905 1122/2810 7710). Central MTR (exit J1, J2, J3)/buses & trams through Central/Central Star Ferry Pier.* **Open** 9am-8pm daily. **Credit** MC, V. **Map** p309 E4.
If you're after some good old European tucker, Oliver's is the place for you – the shelves here are stocked with items that are difficult to find elsewhere. Further draws come in the form of tempting meat, fish, cheese, salad and pâtisserie counters.

**Oliver's Delicatessen** has fans of all ages.

## Supermarkets

### CitySuper

*Basement One, Times Square, Causeway Bay, HK Island (2506 2888). Causeway Bay MTR (exit A).* **Open** 10.30am-10pm Mon-Thur, Sun; 10.30am-11pm Fri, Sat. **Credit** AmEx, DC, MC, V. **Map** p311 D3.
CitySuper is the biggest upscale supermarket in town, and it stocks an extensive selection of gourmet grocery items from around the world, including fine cheeses and wines.
**Other locations**: Shop 3001, Level 3, Harbour City, 5 Canton Road, Tsim Sha Tsui, Kowloon (2375 8222); Shop 1041-9, IFC Mall, Central, HK Island (2234 7128).

### Great Food Hall

*Shop 9, LG1, Pacific Place, 88 Queensway, Admiralty, HK Island (2918 9986). Admiralty MTR (exit C1)/buses & trams through Central.* **Open** 7.30am-10.30pm daily. **Credit** AmEx, DC, MC, V. **Map** p309 F5.
Like CitySuper, Great Food Hall is also a heaven for gourmands. It carries well-known brands including Harrods, Harvey Nichols and Fortnum & Mason.

### Indian Provisions Store

*18 Spring Garden Lane, Wan Chai, HK Island (2572 7725). Wan Chai MTR (exit A3)/buses along Queen's Road East & Hennessy Road.* **Open** 8am-7pm daily. **No credit cards**. **Map** p310 B4.
This shop has the most extensive assortment of spices in town, with herbs and seasonings from Malaysia, Indonesia, Thailand and, of course, India. There is also a full range of other goodies to make the perfect curry.

### Park 'n' Shop

*Basement 3, Hennessy Centre, 500 Hennessy Road, Causeway Bay, HK Island (2504 5026). Causeway Bay MTR (exit F)/trams through Hennessy Road/ 2, 23, 23A, 23B, 25, 26 bus.* **Open** 8am-11pm daily. **Open** 8am-9pm daily. **Credit** AmEx, MC, V. **Map** p311 D3.
The biggest problem with Hong Kong's supermarkets is the selection of food, which inevitably lies somewhere between Chinese and American. But if you fancy turning out a proper stir-fry or sampling some microwave dim sum, then this is the place. Don't expect much in the way of service, though.
**Other locations**: throughout the city.

### Wellcome

*25-9 Great George Street, G/F, Causeway Bay, HK Island (2577 4958/3215). Causeway Bay MTR (exit B, D2)/buses through Causeway Bay.* **Open** 24hrs daily. **Credit** AmEx, MC, V. **Map** p311 E3.
Much like its rival Park 'n' Shop, Wellcome sells a mix of foods catering for local tastes. But its 'superstores', such as this one, offer more international foods, fresh grocery counters and delicatessens. Many, but not all, outlets are open 24 hours.
**Other locations**: throughout the city.

**Eat, Drink, Shop**

# God's gifts

Though it's a relatively Westernised city, Hong Kong still retains a lot of Chinese-ness in its culture. Such is the case when it comes to the practice of Buddhism, according to which everything from the kitchen to the sea has a deity attached to it.

For believers, Hong Kong's temples are holy houses to visit on important days. The extremely religious, however, go one step further by setting up an altar at home. If you're thinking of taking your Buddhist interest to that level – or just fancy a gander at what there is to offer – the place to pick up altar necessities is **Shanghai Street** in Yau Ma Tei, Kowloon. The 'god shops' here have been around for decades, although none of the proprietors are quite sure why they first sprang up in this particular place.

The first thing that you need is obviously the structure itself. Depending on the type of wood, an altar 41-46 centimetres (16-18 inches) tall goes for anything from HK$680 to HK$1,200. Aim higher, so to speak, and you're talking at least HK$3,000.

Once you've procured the altar, you can choose which god to worship at home. One of the more commonly seen ones is Kuan Yin (or Guanyin, Goon Yam), literally meaning 'observer of the world's voice'. This androgynous deity (popularly portrayed as a woman, but also as a man in certain legends) is said to oversee the world's pain and suffering, and offers assistance to those in need. Other favourite gods include Fook, Luk, Sau, a trio representing fortune, success and longevity; and Guan Gong (or Kwan Kung), the seemingly multi-purpose god of honour, loyalty, integrity, justice, courage and strength. The latter is worshipped by both the police and the triads. Porcelain figurines of these gods can be bought for as little as HK$100, or as much as HK$1,000, depending on the workmanship and the type of clay.

But not all altars are thousand-dollar investments. A more common practice is the placement of a land god altar at the front door. This deity is believed to help you safeguard your household from misfortune. All you need is a wooden plate at the door, inscribed with 'the god of wealth and land' and a burner for incense, and the investment can be as little as HK$20. A stove god altar in the kitchen, for ensuring there is always bread on the table, can be assembled for about the same.

But if you do go the whole hog and get a bigger altar, remember that to set things in motion there has to be a ceremony of *hoi guong*, literally meaning 'turning on the light'. This involves having a child dotting the eyes of the figurines with a new brush pen – this is believed to give life to the clay statues.

---

## Wine, beers & spirits

### Boutique Wines

*Shop 1603, Horizon Plaza, South Horizon, 2 Lee Wing Street, Ap Lei Chau, HK Island (2525 3899). Bus 90B, 590.* **Open** 9am-5pm Mon-Fri; 11am-5pm Sat; 2-5pm Sun. **Credit** MC, V.

This place is a bit off the beaten track (just to the south of Aberdeen, on the south side of Hong Kong Island), but if you happen to be shopping for cut-price designer clothes at Joyce Warehouse (*see p171*) you may want to pop in for a look. Australian and New Zealand wines are specialities, but there's also a good stock of champagne.

### Castello del Vino
*12 Anton Street, Wan Chai, HK Island (2866 0587).*
*Admiralty MTR (exit F).* **Open** 10.30am-6.30pm
daily. **Credit** AmEx, MC, V. **Map** p310 A3.
This small shop with lovely service specialises
in Italian wines and fine foods.
**Other locations**: Shop 23, Basement, Luk Hoi Tong
Building, 31 Queen's Road, Central, HK Island (2866
0577).

### Watson's Wine Cellar
*36 Queen's Road, Central, HK Island (2147 3641).*
*Central MTR (exit D1, D2, G)/buses along Queen's
Road Central.* **Open** 8am-9pm daily. **Credit** AmEx,
MC, V. **Map** p309 D3.
Your best bet for a good international selection of
wines, plus beers, spirits and liqueurs.
**Other locations**: throughout the city.

## Gifts & souvenirs

### Chinese Arts & Crafts
*Star House, 3 Salisbury Road, Tsim Sha Tsui,
Kowloon (2735 4061). Tsim Sha Tsui MTR (exit
E)/buses to Tsim Sha Tsui Star Ferry Pier & along
Salisbury Road/Tsim Sha Tsui Star Ferry Pier.*
**Open** 10am-9.30pm daily. **Credit** AmEx, DC, MC, V.
**Map** p313 B6.
If you're looking for Chinese gifts to take home
(antiques, linens, clothes, bags, embroidered goods)
this is a great one-stop destination. The jewellery
section is one of the best in town, with an extensive
collection of pearls, jade, precious and semi-precious
stones, all at very reasonable prices.

### Just Gold
*27A Nathan Road, Tsim Sha Tsui, Kowloon
(2312 1120). Tsim Sha Tsui MTR (exit E)/buses
along Nathan Road/Tsim Sha Tsui Star Ferry Pier.*
**Open** 11am-8pm Mon-Thur; 11am-8.30pm Fri-Sun.
**Credit** AmEx, DC, MC, V. **Map** p313 C6.
Just Gold produces everything from earrings to
gifts in gold, at reasonable prices.

### King & Country
*Shop 362, Level 3, Pacific Place, 88 Queensway,
Admiralty, HK Island (2525 8603). Admiralty
MTR (exit C1)/buses & trams through Central.*
**Open** 10.30am-8pm Mon-Sat; 11am-7pm Sun.
**Credit** AmEx, DC, MC, V. **Map** p309 F5.
Beautifully wrought Victorian-style model soldiers
and scenes – heaven for boys of all ages.

### Mountain Folkcraft
*12 Wo On Lane, Central, HK Island (2525 3199).
Central MTR (exit D1)/12M, 13, 23A, 40M, 43 bus.*
**Open** 9.30am-6.30pm Mon-Sat. **Credit** AmEx, DC,
MC, V. **Map** p308 C4.
This tiny but popular Aladdin's cave of a store has
knick-knacks from all over Asia.

### My House
*57 Yung Shue Wan Main Street, Lamma (8105
0044). Yung Shue Wan Ferry Pier.* **Open** 12.30-
7.30pm Mon, Wed-Sun. **Credit** (over HK$200) MC, V.

As well as kiddies' toys and accessories, My House
also offers girlie bits and bobs such as mirrors and
ornaments. The staff are friendly, the prices are
decent and the stock is cute.

### Oriental Crafts
*Shop B, G/F, 53-5 Hollywood Road, Central, HK
Island (2541 8840). Central MTR (exit D1, D2,
G)/Mid-Levels Escalator/12M, 13, 23A, 26, 40M,
43 bus.* **Open** 10am-6pm daily. **Credit** AmEx,
MC, V. **Map** p308 C3.
For a gift with a difference, stop by this tiny, jum-
bled shop, which deals (allegedly) in mammoth – as
in the extinct animal – carvings. All kinds of sizes
and shapes are on offer, from minute ornaments to
gigantic carved boats with a crew of skeletons.

### Vincent Sum Collection
*15 Lyndhurst Terrace, Central, HK Island
(2542 2610). Central MTR (exit D1, D2, G)/
Mid-Levels Escalator/12M, 13, 23A, 40M, 43 bus.*
**Open** 10am-6.30pm Mon-Sat. **Credit** AmEx, DC,
MC, V. **Map** p308 C3.
Vincent Sum's shop has been around for 20 years,
selling Thai silks, Indonesian ornaments and Indian
imported goods at very reasonable prices.

### Yue Hwa
*301-309 Nathan Road, Jordan, Kowloon (2384
0084). Jordan MTR (exit A)/buses along Nathan
Road.* **Open** 10am-10pm daily. **Credit** AmEx, DC,
MC, V. **Map** p313 B4.
This main branch in Jordan is an emporium for
everything Chinese, from the sort of rosewood
furniture that is now hugely popular in the West to
cheongsams and other items of traditional clothing.
This shop may be a decade old but it now sells many
fashion items that can rival Shanghai Tang's, but at
a fraction of the cost.
**Other locations**: throughout the city.

## Health & beauty

### The Body Shop
*Shop 121, Pacific Place, 88 Queensway, Admiralty,
HK Island (2537 7072). Admiralty MTR (exit
C1)/buses & trams through Central.* **Open** 10am-
8pm Mon-Sat; 11am-7pm Sun. **Credit** AmEx, DC,
MC, V. **Map** p309 F5.
The Body Shop franchise appeared in Hong Kong
in the late 1980s and now has branches scattered
through the city, selling its familiar ranges of eco-
friendly toiletries.
**Other locations**: throughout the city.

### Crabtree & Evelyn
*Shop 245, Pacific Place, 88 Queensway, Admiralty,
HK Island (2523 8668). Admiralty MTR (exit
C1)/buses & trams through Central.* **Open** 10am-
8pm daily. **Credit** AmEx, DC, MC, V. **Map** p309 F5.
Sweet-smelling products are sold at this international favourite, including a sumptuous range of
bubble baths, home fragrances, body lotions and
other goodies.

# Super spas

## Charlie's Acupressure & Massage Centre of the Blind

*Room 903, 9/F Canton House, 54-6 Queen's Road, Central, HK Island (2810 6666). Central MTR (exit D2)/buses along Queen's Road Central.* **Open** *9am-9pm daily.* **No credit cards. Map** *p309 D3.*

Blind people are said to have a greater sense of touch than sighted. Massages here are a bargain, at around HK$240 per hour. It's usually by appointment but it's worth stopping by on the off chance.

## Elemis Day Spa

*9/F Century Square, 1 D'Aguilar Street, Central, HK Island (2521 6660). Central MTR (exit D1, D2)/23A, 40M bus.* **Open** *10am-10pm Mon-Fri; 9am-8pm Sat; 10am-8pm Sun.* **Credit** *AmEx, DC, MC, V.* **Map** *p308 C4.*

The ambience of relaxation and indulgence is felt as soon as you step out of the lift at this spa, one of the most luxurious in Hong Kong. Specialities include the temple room for two people, and the 'Hawaiian wave' four-hands massage. A standard facial costs from around HK$420.

## Frederique

*4/F Wilson House, 19-27 Wyndham Street, Central, HK Island (2522 3054/ www.frederique.com.hk). Central MTR (exit D1, D2)/13, 26, 43 bus.* **Open** *9am-9pm Mon-Fri; 9am-5pm Sat.* **Credit** *AmEx, DC, MC, V.* **Map** *p308 C4.*

Another top-notch retreat, whose enormous menu of treatments could keep you coming here for years. Frederique's Darphin facial (HK$880) includes two different masks plus a head, neck and shoulder massage. Expect to shell out HK$600 or more for a massage.

## Sunny Paradise Sauna

*341 Lockhart Road, Wan Chai, HK Island (2831 0123). Causeway Bay MTR (exit B)/ buses along Hennessy Road.* **Open** *noon-6am daily.* **Credit** *AmEx, DC, MC, V.* **Map** *p311 D3.*

Yes, the name sounds a bit dodgy, and yes, it's in Wan Chai, but no, there are no extras here... or at least not of that kind. Paper panties and hooks in the shape of little penises are all the rage at this budget spa, and definitely add to the experience. Refreshments run to Chinese tea and fish balls, and entertainment is a Cantonese TV channel. However, all this is worth it when you consider that you can pop in at most times of the day, spend as long as you like chilling out and enjoying the steam room, sauna and free cigarettes (!!) and an hour's massage, all for around HK$250.

## Ziz Clinical Skincare for Men

*5/F Hang Shun Building, 10-12 Wyndham Street, Central, HK Island (2111 2767/ www.ziz.com.hk). Central MTR (exit D1, D2).* **Open** *11am-8pm Mon-Fri; 11am-6pm Sat, Sun.* **Credit** *AmEx, DC, MC, V.* **Map** *p308 C4.*

Exclusively for men, this bijou spa concentrates on facials but also offers other treatments. Most popular as a gift for stressed-out guys is the Complete Rejuvenation Treatment (HK$1,688 for 135 minutes). Facials go from HK$460.

## HOTEL SPAS

Most decent Hong Kong hotels have some kind of beauty treatment facilities, but check first that they're available to non-residents.

## I-Spa at the Inter-Continental Hong Kong

*Intercontinental Hotel, 18 Salisbury Road, Tsim Sha Tsui, Kowloon (2721 1211/ www.intercontinental.com). Tsim Sha Tsui*

## Professional Hair Products

*49A Wellington Street, Central, HK Island (2536 0603). Central MTR (exit D1, D2, G).* **Open** *10am-8pm Mon-Sat.* **Map** *p308 C3.*
On offer here is a fantastic collection of haircare goods for stylists and ordinary punters alike.

## Sasa Cosmetic Company

*62 Queen's Road, Central, HK Island (2521 2928). Central MTR (exit D1, D2, G)/buses along Queen's Road Central.* **Open** *9.30am-8.30pm daily.* **Credit** *AmEx, DC, MC, V.* **Map** *p308 C3.*

Sasa is quickly taking over Hong Kong's cosmetics market – the number of outlets is staggering. Though some of the brands and lines may be limited or out of stock, all is forgiven when you see the low prices. **Other locations**: throughout the city.

## Shu Uemura Beauty Boutique

*Shop 204, Ocean Centre, 5 Canton Road, Tsim Sha Tsui, Kowloon (2735 1767). Tsim Sha Tsui MTR (exit C1, E)/buses along Canton Road/Tsim Sha Tsui Star Ferry Pier.* **Open** *10.30am-7.30pm Mon-Sat; 12.30-6pm Sun.* **Credit** *AmEx, DC, MC, V.* **Map** *p313 B6.*

MTR (exit E)/buses along Salisbury Road/
Tsim Sha Tsui Star Ferry Pier. **Open** 9am-9pm
daily. **Credit** AmEx, DC, MC, V. **Map** p313 C6.
A real treat of a spa, designed in accordance
with the principles of feng shui. There's
an outdoor pool and several spa pools,
and private spa rooms for one or two people.
Treatments include jetlag relief, Oriental
healing and treatment packages. A body
polish is around HK$400, while massages
start at HK$750. See also p51.

### Mandarin Oriental
5 Connaught Road, Central, HK Island (2522
0111/www.mandarinoriental.com). Central
MTR (exit F, H)/buses to Central Star
Ferry/Central Star Ferry Pier.
Beauty salon & barber shop 2/F (2825
4800). **Open** 8am-7pm Mon-Sat.
Health centre 24/F (2825 4093). **Open** 6am-
10pm daily. Massages 9am-9pm daily.
Both **Credit** AmEx, DC, MC, V. **Map** p309 E3.
The Mandarin doesn't yet have a spa to end
all spas, although new facilities are being
planned. What it does have, however, are

a few top-quality centres where you are
looked after like royalty. At the beauty salon,
signature treatments include party packages,
while the barber shop does a luxurious
traditional shave or moustache trim for
the discerning gent, and the health centre on
the 24th floor boasts an indoor Roman-style
marble pool. A one-visit pass allowing use of
all the facilities costs HK$400. See also p46.

### The Peninsula Spa
7/F, Peninsula Hotel, Salisbury Road, Tsim
Sha Tsui, Kowloon (2315 3271). Tsim Sha
Tsui MTR (exit E)/buses to Tsim Sha Tsui
Ferry Pier & along Salisbury Road/Tsim
Sha Tsui Star Ferry Pier. **Open** 10am-9pm
Mon-Sat; 10am-6pm Sun. **Credit** AmEx, DC,
MC, V. **Map** p313 B/C6.
You'd expect the best hotel in Hong Kong to
have a top spa, and it does. The all-weather
swimming pool boasts a panoramic view of
the city and the spa offers individual Clarins
treatments and packages such as a three-hour
jet lag treatment (HK$ 1,650). Facials begin at
a more affordable HK$460. See also p53.

### The Spa at The Excelsior
4/F, 281 Gloucester Road, Causeway Bay,
HK Island (2837 6837/www.excelsior
hongkong.com). Causeway Bay MTR
(exit D1)/buses along Gloucester Road.
**Open** 6am-10pm Mon-Fri; 7am-9pm Sat;
8am-9pm Sun. **Credit** AmEx, DC, MC, V.
**Map** p311 E2.
Part of the exclusive Spa Health Clubs
group, the Spa at The Excelsior offers 370
square metres (4,000 square feet) of modern
health club. With a gym, beauty and massage
facilities, steam rooms and saunas, you'd
need a month to sample everything. Facials
cost HK$450-$880, massages HK$400-
$700. Ask for details of other locations.
See also p49.

Shu Uemura's range of brushes and make-up is
every girl's dream. This place is like a paint box
dedicated to beautifying oneself, but the prices will
strain the average wallet.
**Other locations**: Shop B25, The Landmark, 16 Des
Voeux Road, Central, HK Island (2845 3987).

## Interiors, furniture & fabrics

There are a number of fabric shops in Kowloon
– in particular on Bowring Street and just off
Nathan Road.

### Altfield Interiors
*Shop 223-225, Prince's Building, 10 Chater Road,
Central, HK Island (2524 7526). Central MTR (exit
H)/buses & trams through Central.* **Open** 10am-7pm
Mon-Sat; 11am-5pm Sun. **Credit** AmEx, MC, V.
**Map** p309 E4.
Dedicated to soft furnishings, with a wide range of
lamps and lights, elegant cushions and repro furni-
ture, Altfield promises to make your home into a cosy
comfort zone. The nearby fabric department at Shop
605, 9 Queen's Road, Central (2524 3318), deals with
upholstery orders. For the Altfield Gallery, see p157.

## Aluminium

*4 Lyndhurst Terrace, Central, HK Island (2546 5904). Central MTR (exit D1, D2, G)/Mid-Levels Escalator/12M, 13, 23A, 40M, 43 bus.* **Open** 4-8pm Mon-Fri; 1-6pm Sat. **Credit** AmEx, MC, V. **Map** p308 C3.

Aluminium stocks some of the coolest European furniture and PC accessories that you'll find in Hong Kong. The emphasis is on colourful, space-age, 1970s-style pieces, so if you happen to be looking for a bubble chair or a JVC Videosphere TV, this is where you'll find it.
**Other locations**: Shop D, G/F, 8 Kingston Street, Causeway Bay, HK Island (2577 4766).

## Graham 32

*32 Graham Street, Central, HK Island (2815 5188). Mid-Levels Escalator/26 bus.* **Open** 11am-8pm Mon-Fri; 11am-7.30pm Sat; noon-6pm Sun. **Credit** AmEx, MC, V. **Map** p308 C3.

Promoted as a 'style concept' store, Graham 32 is home to a range of hip homeware as well as a small line of casual clothes.

## Ito Futon

*G/F, 64-6 Wellington Street, Central, HK Island (2845 1138). Central MTR (exit D1, D2, G)/12M, 13, 23A, 40M, 43 bus.* **Open** 10am-7pm Mon-Sat. **Credit** AmEx, MC, V. **Map** p308 C3.

No matter what size, style, status or colour you desire in a futon, Ito Futon will have one to suit you. It also does a funky range of bed covers and Japanese lights.

## Kinari

*Shop 3, 43-55 Wyndham Street, Central, HK Island (2869 6827). Central MTR (exit D1). Mid-Levels Escalator/12M, 13, 23A, 40M bus.* **Open** 10am-7.30pm Mon-Sat. **Credit** AmEx, MC, V. **Map** p308 C4.

Kinari is a treasure trove of products from Thailand and Burma. Ornate carved wooden pieces, big beds, silver Buddhas and lacquered boxes cover the shop's floor, although, not surprisingly, such riches come with high price tags.

## Tequila Kola

*Horizon Plaza, South Horizon, 2 Lee Wing Street Ap Lei Chau, HK Island (2877 3295). Bus 90B, 590.* **Open** 10am-7pm Mon-Fri; 10am-6pm Sat; noon-5pm Sun. **Credit** AmEx, DC, MC, V.

Since Tequila Kola opened in the early 1990s, it has acquired a dedicated cluster of rich clients. It stocks an extensive (and expensive) mix of furniture, including teak tables, wrought-iron beds and big mirrors.

## The Work Shop

*24 Gough Street, Central, HK Island (2813 2572). Sheung Wan MTR (exit A2)/26 bus.* **Open** 11am-8pm Mon-Sat. **Credit** AmEx, MC, V. **Map** p308 B3.

It takes a while to find this place but it's well worth the effort. It features everything from furniture to kitchenware, all of it stylish and unique.

# Music

## HMV

*1/F, Central Building, 1 Pedder Street, Central, HK Island (2739 0268). Central MTR (exit D1, G)/buses & trams through Central/Central Star Ferry Pier.* **Open** 9am-10pm daily. **Credit** AmEx, DC, MC, V. **Map** p309 D4.

This mega music store sells everything and anything for watching and listening to. Prices of CDs are comparable to those in the US, while magazines are almost half the price of those on sale in bookshops and at newsstands. The Tsim Sha Tsui branch is the largest.
**Other locations**: 1/F, Windsor House, 311 Gloucester Road, Causeway Bay, HK Island (2504 3669); G/F-4/F, Sands Building, 12 Peking Road, Tsim Sha Tsui, Kowloon (2302 0122); Shop 408D, New Town Plaza, Phase 1, Sha Tin, New Territories (2602 3931).

## Shun Cheong Record Showroom

*Shop 801, Bank Centre, 636 Nathan Road, Mong Kok, Kowloon (2332 2397). Mong Kok MTR (exit E2).* **Open** 11am-7pm Mon-Sat. **Credit** MC, V. **Map** p312 B2.

A haven for classical music lovers, Sun Cheong has been around for more than 30 years. Its selection includes many albums that you just can't find at mainstream record stores. Along with classical, expect to find jazz and New Age.
**Other locations**: 3/F, Chung Nam House, 59 Des Voeux Road, Central, HK Island (2189 7363).

## Tom Lee Music

*G/F, 1-9 Cameron Lane, Tsim Sha Tsui, Kowloon (2723 9932). Tsim Sha Tsui MTR (exit B2).* **Open** 10am-8pm Mon-Thur, Sun; 10am-9pm Fri, Sat. **Credit** MC, V. **Map** p313 C5.

The Tom Lee Music chain stocks instruments, accessories, written music and instructional videos.The company is also a music promoter, selling tickets for major concerts.
**Other locations**: throughout the city.

# Opticians & eyewear

## Optical 88

*17 Cameron Road, Tsim Sha Tsui, Kowloon (2367 3200). Tsim Sha Tsui MTR (exit A1)/buses along Canton Road/Tsim Sha Tsui Star Ferry Pier.* **Open** 10.30am-9.30pm daily. **Credit** AmEx, DC, MC, V. **Map** p313 C5.

This big, bright shop has opticians to test your eyes, and assistants to see to all your eyewear needs.
**Other locations**: Shop 105, Man Yee Arcade, 50-58 Des Voeux Road, Central, HK Island (2259 5188).

## The Optical Shop

*G/F, China Building, 29 Queen's Road, Central, HK Island (2810 6022). Central MTR (exit D1, D2, G)/buses along Queen's Road Central.* **Open** 9am-7.30pm Mon-Sat; 10am-7pm Sun. **Credit** AmEx, DC, MC, V. **Map** p309 D4.

The Optical Shop will happily test your eyes and equip you with a funky pair of bifocals or comfy contacts. And if Hong Kong is too bright for you, it's also got a choice collection of sunglasses – DKNY, Calvin Klein, Gucci, Ray Ban and so on.
**Other locations**: Shop 108, Pacific Place, 88 Queensway, Admiralty, HK Island (2845 9442).

### Senses Optik

*1/F, 28 Wellington Street, Central, HK Island (2869 5111). Central MTR (exit D1, D2, G)/ 12M, 13, 23A, 40M, 43 bus.* **Open** 10am-8.30pm Mon-Sat; 11am-6pm Sun. **Credit** AmEx, DC, MC, V. **Map** p308 C3.
The Senses Optik assistants will test your eyes and kit you out with a classy pair of specs. A good range of sunglasses is also sold, from standard to designer.

## Pharmacies

### Watson's

*G/F, Melbourne Plaza, 33 Queen's Road, Central, HK Island (2523 0666). Central MTR (exit D1, D2, G)/buses along Queen's Road Central.* **Open** 9am-9pm daily. **Credit** AmEx, DC, MC, V. **Map** p309 D3.
Watson's is a megastore of a chemist, with lots of outlets throughout the region. It sells a wide range of hair products and designer make-up, and has a useful drug counter with helpful staff.
**Other locations**: throughout the city.

## Photography & film processing

### Fotomax

*G/F, Far East Plaza, 5-6 Middle Road, Tsim Sha Tsui, Kowloon (2722 0639). Tsim Sha Tsui MTR (exit E).* **Open** 8.30am-8pm Mon-Sat; 10.30am-8pm Sun. **Credit** AmEx, DC, MC, V. **Map** p313 B6.
One of the most established names in photo processing, Fotomax has stores all over town. Staff can help you with anything from simple developing to complicated jobs involving image enhancement.
**Other locations**: throughout the city.

### Hing Lee Camera Company

*25 Lyndhurst Terrace, Central, HK Island (2544 7593). Central MTR (exit D1, D2, G)/ Mid-Levels Escalator/12M, 13, 23A, 40M, 43 bus.* **Open** 9.30am-7pm Mon-Sat. **No credit cards.** **Map** p308 C3.
Hing Lee sells guaranteed stock, including famous brands like Nikon, Kodak and Olympus, at a good price. Staff are laid-back, honest and helpful, which adds to the attraction.

### Robert Lam Color

*33 Johnston Road, Wan Chai, HK Island (2898 8418). Wan Chai MTR (exit A3)/trams through Wan Chai/buses 25, 26.* **Open** 9am-4pm Mon-Sat. **Credit** AmEx, DC, MC, V. **Map** p310 B4.

# David's new toy

A visit to Shanghai Tang (*see p172*) is as essential as a ride on the Star Ferry when you're in Hong Kong. The chinoiserie store, which also has shops in London and New York, sells clothes, fabrics and all manner of objects bearing the signature 'Made By Chinese'. In the past, traffic havoc has ensued after icons such as Hillary Clinton and Princess Diana dropped by with their entourages to drop some cash and do a little shopping for stylish silk suits and cheongsams in vivid colours; ornate embroidery and hand-woven buttons; or maybe even slightly tacky Mao suits, PLA caps and fortune sticks.

The store will always be a destination, but the man who created it – businessman, bon viveur, culture vulture and cigar-chomping celebrity, David Tang – has left the operation to his partners and moved on to other things. Under his Pacific Cigar Company, which he founded in 1992 as the exclusive importer of Cuban cigars to many parts of Asia including Hong Kong, Tang has opened up

**Red Chamber Cigar Divan.** The imperial-red cigar shop is named after a Chinese folk tale and its decor is designed to resemble an opium house. 'There was a sense of romance to those opium houses in the old days, they were places for smoking...', Tang enthuses, 'and smoking cigars can be that way too.'

From a business point of view, Red Chamber is Tang's way of raising the benchmark in his cigar retail operation. It replaces the Nurse, the hospital-white cigar shop at the Ritz-Carlton that Tang has relocated to Bangkok and, besides having a more glamorous theme and a bigger space, it features 120 private lockers for customers, with half of them within in a dedicated walk-in humidor. A selection of fine wines and spirits completes the stock.

### Red Chamber Cigar Divan

*Shop M1, Pedder Building, 12 Pedder Street, Central, HK Island (2537 0977). Central MTR (exit D1, G)/buses & trams through Central/ Central Star Ferry Pier.* **Open** 11am-9pm Mon-Sat. **Credit** AmEx, DC, MC, V. **Map** p309 D3.

Professional photographers have been coming to Robert Lam Color for years to get their photos processed. And if you're looking for a specific kind of slide film or photo paper, the able staff will be happy to assist you.

### Union Photo Supplies

*13 Queen Victoria Street, Central, HK Island (2526 6281). Central MTR (exit B)/buses & trams through Central.* **Open** 9.30am-6pm Mon-Sat. **Credit** MC, V. **Map** p308 C3.

Union Photo Supplies is a pristine store that oozes professionalism. It boasts an extensive and well-priced stock of cameras, lenses, filters, films, photo paper and other accessories and friendly, knowledgeable staff.

## Sport

### Giga Sports

*Shop 220, Pacific Place, 88 Queensway, Admiralty, HK Island (2918 9088). Admiralty MTR (exit C1)/buses & trams through Central.* **Open** 10.30am-9.30pm daily. **Credit** AmEx, DC, MC, V. **Map** p309 F5.

Make just one stop to Giga Sports and you can find everything you need for your next sporting adventure or gym workout.
**Other locations**: throughout the city.

### The Golf House

*Shop 621, Times Square, 1 Matheson Street, Causeway Bay, HK Island (2506 0111). Causeway Bay MTR (exit A).* **Open** noon-9pm Mon-Fri; 11.30am-9.30pm Sat, Sun. **Credit** AmEx, DC, MC, V. **Map** p311 D3.

The Golf House is stuffed with a comprehensive selection of golfing gear, from clubs and bags to balls and tees.

### Marathon Sports

*543 Lockhart Road, Causeway Bay, HK Island (2831 9872).Causeway Bay MTR (exit D1).* **Open** 11.30am-11pm Mon-Sat; 11am-11pm Sun. **Credit** AmEx, DC, MC, V. **Map** p311 D3.

There are almost 30 Marathon Sports outlets across Hong Kong and the New Territories. The Pacific Place shop is one of the longest established and specialises in trainers. Brands such as Puma, Adidas, Converse and Diesel all feature, alongside a small line of sports clothing and accessories.
**Other locations**: throughout the city.

### Running Bare

*Shop 1, G/F, Wyndham Mansion, 32 Wyndham Street, Central, HK Island (2526 0620). Central MTR (exit D1, G)/13, 26, 43 bus.* **Open** 11am-7pm Mon-Sat. **Credit** AmEx, DC, MC, V. **Map** p308 C4.

Having already built up a string of clients selling sportswear from her flat, Lynn Fong Boseley has now opened this tiny store in Central. Running Bare sells her own label, plus Wahini bikinis and the Rival range.

### X Game

*Shop A1, L/G, Wilson House, 19-27 Wyndham Street, Central, HK Island (2366 9293). Central MTR (exit D2).* **Open** 10am-8pm Mon-Fri; 10am-7pm Sat. **Credit** AmEx, DC, MC, V. **Map** p308 C4.

X Game is almost a little club for the surfer dudes and dudettes in town. Experienced players can find the flashy and high-performance gear that suits their status, while novices come to get tips from the helpful staff and to sign up for the courses. Stock covers all the latest surfer fashions.
**Other locations**: 1/F, 11 Pak Sha Road, Causeway Bay, HK Island (2881 8960); China Minmetals Tower, 79 Chatham Road South, Tsim Sha Tsui, Kowloon (2375 0225).

## Tobacconists

For David Tang's Red Chamber, *see p183* David's new toy.

### Cohiba Cigar Divan

*Lobby, Mandarin Oriental Hotel, 5 Connaught Road, Central, HK Island (2825 4074). Central MTR (exit F, H)/buses to Central Star Ferry Pier/Central Star Ferry Pier.* **Open** 10am-9pm Mon-Sat; noon-6pm Sun. **Credit** AmEx, DC, MC, V. **Map** p309 E3.

This sleek, sweet-smelling cigar shop is the place to pick up a choice Cohiba or two. Service is appropriately charming.

### Davidoff

*Lobby, Peninsula Hotel, Salisbury Road, Tsim Sha Tsui, Kowloon (2368 5774). Tsim Sha Tsui MTR (exit E)/buses to Tsim Sha Tsui Star Ferry Pier & along Salisbury Road/Tsim Sha Tsui StarPier.* **Open** 10am-8pm daily. **Credit** AmEx, DC, MC, V. **Map** p313 B6.

Davidoff sells all sorts of cigars, and staff are happy to help you make an informed choice. But be warned, none of them are cheap.

## Toys & games

### Mothercare

*303-304 Prince's Building, Central, HK Island (2523 5704). Central MTR (exit H)/buses & trams through Central.* **Open** 10am-7pm Mon-Sat; 10am-5pm Sun. **Credit** AmEx, DC, MC, V. **Map** p309 E4.

Like its sister stores worldwide, Mothercare in Hong Kong stocks everything a parent – or child – needs, from nappies, bibs and dummies to toys.
**Other locations**: throughout the city.

### Toys 'R' Us

*Shop 32, B/F, Ocean Terminal, Harbour City, 5 Canton Road, Tsim Sha Tsui, Kowloon (2730 9462). Tsim Sha Tsui MTR (exit C1, E)/buses along Chatham Road South.* **Open** 10am-9pm daily. **Credit** AmEx, MC, V. **Map** p313 B6.

This huge international toy emporium is every kid's dream (and some parents' nightmare). Along its aisles are clothes, toys, games and sporting goods.

# Arts & Entertainment

## Features

# Festivals & Events

From serious arts festivals to laugh-riot bun fights, the territory has it covered.

Like Hong Kong itself, the territory's calendar of festivals and events is densely crowded, cross-cultural and brimming with contrasts and surprises. At the core of this Chinese city's celebrations are half a dozen important traditional festivals linked to the lunar calendar and mirroring the rhythms of the seasons. Often expressing renewal and ancestral worship, these rich and poetic festivals draw upon ancient rural folklore and the rituals of Taoist, Buddhist and Confucian traditions. Among these are the colourful **Birthday of Tin Hau**, the **Hungry Ghost Festival** and the vivid and popular **Dragon Boat Festival**.

Acknowledging its colonial history and its multicultural institutions, Hong Kong also celebrates major Western holidays. While most of the Chinese community do not attach religious importance to Christmas or Easter, these are still public holidays. Hong Kong's romantics celebrate Valentine's Day with great seriousness, and, on Hallowe'en, a local fascination with ghost stories and the supernatural mixes with US-style trick-or-treating.

The local calendar is also dotted with annual artistic, cultural and sporting events, like the reliably good **Hong Kong Arts Festival**, the **CityJan Festival** and arguably the best film festival in the whole of Asia, the **Hong Kong International Film Festival**. These combine to form an impressive cultural season at the beginning of the year, while annual running, motor racing, golf, and horse racing events bring the year to an exciting close.

## TICKETS AND INFORMATION

The Discover Hong Kong website (www.discoverhongkong.com) is the first place to look for details about annual and seasonal events, though the local press is a useful source of information about individual events. It's always wise to check the dates/times of a particular event nearer the time. Tickets to events are available directly from venues and many can also be purchased from **URBTIX** (2734 9009, www.urbtix.gov.hk; *see also p225*) and **HK Ticketing** (3128 8288, www.hkticketing.com; *see also p225*).

For a list of public holidays, *see p293*. For the New Vision Arts Festival, *see p233*. For gay-oriented festivals, *see p214*. For more film festivals, *see p205*. For other sports events, *see p234-p242*.

## Spring

### Hong Kong International Literary Festival

*9300 2592/2511 4211/www.festival.org.hk.* **Date** Mar. This week-long festival focuses on world-class literature written in English but with Asian roots. The programme includes readings, writing workshops and on-stage debates. Local poets, screenwriters and publishers are featured alongside international literary stars: past festivals have included readings by Yann Martel, Hanif Kureishi, Pramoedya Toer, Bei Ling and PK Leung. Events are held at venues across town, and tickets (around HK$100) are available from HK Ticketing and the Fringe Club, among others.

### Art Walk

**Date** 1st Fri of Mar.
This annual fund-raising evening is essentially an unguided tour of a dozen art galleries in the Central and Soho neighbourhoods. After buying a programme that gives gallery names, addresses and maps, you can stroll from one to another, enjoying the art and free food and drink provided by sponsor restaurants. Some galleries feature music and other entertainment, and the evening ends with a party.

## Top five Festivals

### Cheung Chau Bun Festival
A festival based on buns? It'd be rude not to take part. *See p187.*

### Chinese New Year
The biggest event of the year is mainly one for locals, but the fireworks and lantern displays can be enjoyed by all. *See p190.*

### Christmas
Witness as Hong Kong's skyscrapers are turned into towers of tacky tinsel. *See p190.*

### Dragon Boat (Tuen Ng) Festival
Watch the beautiful boats compete in this fast and furious race, which dates back two centuries. *See p188.*

### Hong Kong International Film Festival
This major player among the world's biggest cinematic events is a must-see. *See p187.*

Here be dragons: the thrill of the 2,000-year-old **Dragon Boat Festival**. *See p188*.

All proceeds go to AIDS Concern. Tickets are available directly from the galleries and from the offices of *HK Magazine*, which organises the event.

### Cathay Pacific/Credit Suisse First Boston Hong Kong Rugby Sevens

*Hong Kong Stadium, 55 Eastern Hospital Road, So Kon Po, Causeway Bay, HK Island (2504 8311/ www.hksevens.com.hk). Bus 5B.* **Map** p311 E/F4. **Date** late Mar.

First played in 1976, the three-day Hong Kong Sevens rugby tournament is the most prestigious leg of the International Rugby Board's World Sevens Series. See some of the world's finest players in action, and some wild partying from the fans. *See also p242*.

### Hong Kong International Film Festival

*2734 9009/www.hkiff.org.hk.* **Date** Apr.

The best of eastern and western film-making is showcased in this huge, highly respected two-week festival. Films are shown in venues around the city in four main categories: Hong Kong panorama, Hong Kong cinema retrospective, Asian cinema and world cinema. Many screenings feature Q&A sessions with directors, and each year the programme includes a major retrospective of works by an international name. Postal bookings can be made about a month before the festival begins; all remaining seats are sold on a first-come, first-served basis through URBTIX. Though tickets sometimes sell out in advance, it is often possible to pick up single tickets for about HK$50 a few nights before a screening.

### Le French May Festival of Arts

*3196 6200/Credit card bookings 3128 8288/ www.frenchmay.com.* **Date** late Apr-early June.

This annual month-long celebration of all things Gallic is the biggest French festival in Asia. Expect an eclectic, high-quality range of performers, shows, exhibitions, films and concerts at venues across the territory. Tickets are sold through URBTIX.

### Birthday of Tin Hau

**Date** Apr/May (23rd day of the 3rd lunar mth).

Tin Hau, the goddess of the sea, occupies a special place in the heart of the Harbour City. To celebrate her birthday, fishermen decorate their boats and head to temples dedicated to the goddess to pray for good catches during the coming year. It makes for a colourful and very local holiday. Traditional birthday rites can be seen at the Tin Hau Temple in Joss House Bay (in the eastern New Territories) and in the 40 or so other temples to Tin Hau around the territory. A birthday parade with colourful floats and lion dances also takes place in Yuen Long in the western New Territories. *See also p33 and p80* **Making waves**.

### Cheung Chau Bun Festival

*Pak Tai Temple, Cheung Chau Island. Outlying Islands Ferry Pier 5 from Central.* **Map** p306. **Date** 1 wk in Apr/May/June.

What is surely the world's one and only bun festival takes place on the island of Cheung Chau. This week-long village fiesta is dedicated to peace, renewal, harmony and, well, buns. The dates of the festival are divined by Taoist priests (although cynics note that the most colourful celebrations often coincide with a weekend, thus enabling more visitors to attend). During the festival, three 20-metre (66-foot) bamboo towers (representing heaven,' earth and man), studded with sweet buns, are raised in front of the Pak Tai Temple. The buns are stamped with auspicious pink symbols and are intended, some say, as offerings to the ghosts of pirates. In the past, young men scrambled up the towers in a mad race to collect the highest buns on each tower. This dash ended in 1978 when several people were injured. Nowadays buns are safely handed out to patiently queuing crowds. A highlight of the festival is a large procession that features 'floating' children who are (almost invisibly) carried on supporting poles hidden beneath their elaborate costumes. It's advisable to get a return ticket for the ferry.

# Summer

## Dragon Boat (Tuen Ng) Festival
**Date** June (5th day of the 5th lunar mth).
The 2,000-year-old Dragon Boat ('Tuen Ng') Festival is one of Hong Kong's most exciting annual events. It features elaborately decorated 10-metre (33-foot) dragon boats with crews of 20 paddlers racing to the sounds of pounding drums and the screams of spectators. The festival commemorates the death of the popular Chinese national hero Qu Yuan, who, in the 3rd century BC, drowned himself as a protest against the corrupt government. Legend has it that as the hero threw himself into the river, the townspeople raced to rescue him, beating their drums to scare away fish and throwing dumplings into the sea to keep them from eating the martyr's body. Today, the eating of rice and meat dumplings commemorates this part of the story, while the races symbolise the attempt to rescue Qu Yuan. Dragon boats can be seen at Aberdeen, Chai Wan, Sha Tin, Tai Po and Stanley (which has the rowdiest crowds), with the action starting at around 8.30am and lasting throughout the day.

## Hungry Ghost Festival (Yue Laan)
**Date** mid-late Aug (for 1 lunar mth).
According to cheery local lore, this is the time of the year when the mouth of hell opens and renegade spirits come looking for a place to stay. To keep spirits out of their houses, people leave offerings of food on the street and burn paper money and gold. The festival is celebrated all over the territory, but older and more traditional neighbourhoods like Sheung Wan (especially the King George V Memorial Park), Wan Chai and Cheung Chau village are the most fascinating places to experience the event. *See also p36.*

# Autumn

## Mid Autumn Festival
**Date** late Sept/early Oct.
As the northwest monsoon begins to cool Hong Kong, families and friends gather in the evening to watch the full moon rise and to eat traditional lotus paste 'moon cakes'. This lovely ritual commemorates a 14th-century uprising against the Mongols, when Chinese rebels are said to have slipped pieces of paper into the cakes, which were smuggled to their compatriots. The festival is a peaceful affair and Hong Kong's streets glow with lanterns in all shapes, sizes and colours. Local children stay up late, public transport runs all night and the celebration is followed by a public holiday. The most popular spots to light lanterns and feast on cakes are Victoria Park, Repulse Bay, Cheung Chau's beaches and the Peak.

## China National Day
**Date** 1 Oct.
Every year, to celebrate the founding of the People's Republic, Hong Kong puts on a dazzling night-time fireworks display in the harbour. The best viewing spot is the Tsim Sha Tsui esplanade, although the square in front of City Hall on Hong Kong Island is much less crowded. During the National Day holiday week in mainland China there is very heavy traffic at the border crossings between Hong Kong and Shenzhen and between Macau and Zhuhai.

## Hong Kong Chinese Arts Festival
*information 2370 1044.* **Date** Oct/Nov.
This three-week event held every two years showcases world-renowned artists and performing ensembles from mainland China, Taiwan and Hong Kong. The festival revolves around a different theme each year ('The great times of China' in 2003) and includes performances, workshops and seminars, free outdoor shows and exhibitions. Previous festivals have included exhibitions of traditional musical instruments, Chinese music parades and tributes to street opera. Venues include the Hong Kong Cultural Centre and town halls in the New Territories. As well as the ticketed events (HK$8-$200), free performances take place in the Hong Kong Cultural Centre's foyer and piazza. *See also p232.*

## Hong Kong Youth Arts Festival
*Visual Arts 2802 9455/Performing Arts 2877 2656/www.hkyaf.com.* **Date** Nov.
This month-long celebration of the arts, aimed at everyone from five-year-olds to 25-year-olds, offers a multifaceted range of events taking in the visual and performing arts and literature. Various venues host performances, and some events are free.

## Trailwalker
*www.trailwalker.org.hk.* **Date** Nov.
This popular and tough charity walk takes place along the 100-kilometre (62-mile) MacLehose Trail (*see p39 and p103*). Pre-registered, sponsored walkers have to finish the course (which takes in 20 hills and mountains, including Tai Mo Shan, Hong Kong's tallest) within 48 hours, which means continuing through the night. Trailwalker unofficially marks the start of the Hong Kong hiking season.

# Winter

For the **Macau Grand Prix**, held in November, *see p258* **Making tracks**.

## Winter Solstice Festival (Dong Zhi)
**Date** 22 Dec.
If you're walking the streets of Hong Kong on this day, you'll probably notice the late-afternoon stampede of office workers dashing off to gather round a table with their families. It's been said that to understand Chinese culture, one needs to appreciate rituals associated with family and food. This holiday, marked by a shared meal, rather than organised public festivities, affords an opportunity to observe both. If you can, try to go to a Chinese restaurant to experience the warmth and rites that bond familial relationships across generations.

**Chinese New Year**. *See p190.*

## Christmas

**Date** run-up to 25 Dec.

Taking a boat trip across the harbour or a stroll along the Tsim Sha Tsui East esplanade is an exhilarating experience the week before Christmas. Hong Kong welcomes the season with an amazing display of lights and decorations. Shopping centres are draped in baubles and tinsel and entire skyscrapers are turned into giant neon Yuletide scenes. A recent favourite was a gigantic neon Santa pedalling a bicycle above the Bank of China's soaring geometric entrance. Trying to outdo each other, Hong Kong's most impressive buildings radiate with light and colour. Many of the Christmas lights are cleverly reconfigured a few weeks later for Chinese New Year, when Santa might miraculously morph into the Chinese god of prosperity.

Hong Kong's churches are well attended over Christmas and the New Year (and also at Easter). Catholic and Protestant services are delivered in English, Cantonese, Mandarin and Tagalog (the language spoken in the Philippines). Many of the territory's large community of Filipino domestic helpers worship every Sunday and when joined by sporadic expatriate churchgoers at Christmas and Easter, churches are filled to capacity.

## CityJam Festival

*Fringe Club, 2 Lower Albert Road, Central, HK Island (2521 7251/www.hkfringe.com.hk). Central MTR (exit D1)/23A bus.* **Map** p309 D4. **Date** 3wks in Jan/Feb.

The former Fringe Festival is now a scaled-down but diverse celebration of performance, live music, art and photography exhibitions. The line-up incorporates an eclectic range of international and local performers and artists, and includes workshops and an all-night open-air music, film and food event on the Fringe Club's rooftop.

## Chinese New Year

**Date** late Jan/early Feb.

Chinese (or Lunar) New Year is the biggest festival of the calendar, and the three-day public holiday involves great preparation and ritual. Businesses (including many restaurants) close, families travel across the border to be reunited, and this is the only time of the year when street vendors shut up shop and take a well-earned rest. On the eve of the holiday, throngs of smiling people promenade the streets. Victoria Park becomes a giant outdoor market and the flower markets in Mong Kok are packed with families buying kumquat trees, narcissus and pussy willow, which signify new beginnings, prosperity and good luck. Children and unmarried young adults receive *lai see* (gifts of freshly minted notes in red envelopes) and the greeting of '*kung hei fat choi*' (prosperous wishes) can be heard as people visit relatives and friends.

Although the holiday is primarily a family celebration (and tourists who don't have friends here can feel a bit left out of the proceedings), there are still things for visitors to enjoy, including fantastic lighting displays, beautiful lantern decorations outside the Cultural Centre in Tsim Sha Tsui, and a parade of floats through the streets of Central on the first day of the New Year. A visit to Wong Tai Sing Temple in Kowloon makes for a most auspicious beginning to the year, and the fireworks above Victoria Harbour (on the evening of the second day of the New Year) are consistently spectacular.

## Carlsberg Cup/Chinese New Year Football Tournament

*Hong Kong Stadium, 55 Eastern Hospital Road, So Kon Po, Causeway Bay, HK Island (2504 8311/www.carlsberg.com.hk). Bus 5B.* **Map** p311 E/F4. **Date** late Jan/early Feb.

Soccer is hugely popular in Hong Kong, even if the SAR's team remains no more than a minnow within the football world. To coincide with the Chinese New Year holidays, three international football teams compete for the Carlsberg Cup, Hong Kong's most popular annual soccer tournament. In recent years, the Czech Republic, Norway, South Korea, Denmark, Japan and Mexico have battled on the pitch. Expect to pay around HK$140-$380 for tickets.

## Hong Kong Arts Festival

*2824 3555/programme enquiry hotline 2824 2430/ www.hk.artsfestival.org.* **Date** early Feb-early Mar.

One of the world's premier arts festivals, this month-long feast of classical music, ballet, opera, theatre and popular performances attracts first-rank names such as Yo-Yo Ma, the Royal Shakespeare Company, Mikhail Baryshnikov and the Hamburg Ballet. Since its beginnings in 1973, the festival has followed a tried-and-tested formula that guarantees at least one major visiting orchestra, several classical recitals and chamber concerts, a splashy imported opera event, a range of dance and theatre productions and a performance by a jazz legend. In recent years the Tallis Scholars, José Carreras, members of the Buena Vista Social Club, the London Symphony Orchestra, Cesaria Evora and Herbie Hancock have all taken the stage. Venues include the Hong Kong Arts Centre and the Hong Kong Academy for Performing Arts.

Festival programmes are available in early November from the Cultural Centre, City Hall and Hong Kong Tourism Board centres. Preferential tickets can be ordered on the internet or by fax on 2802 8160 until 1 December, then remaining seats go on sale through URBTIX box offices.

## Standard Chartered Hong Kong Marathon

*2577 0800/www.hkmarathon.com.* **Date** early Feb.

Attracting world-class competitors, this day of races also features a half marathon and a 10K race. All three races start at the Cultural Centre on the Tsim Sha Tsui waterfront and finish at the Convention & Exhibition Centre in Wan Chai. Runners can enter as individuals or as a team (write to the Marathon Secretariat, PO Box 98843, Tsim Sha Tsui, Kowloon; fees are from HK$270).

# Children

Hot, sweaty, noisy and exhilarating, Hong Kong is the perfect playground for young visitors.

Kids love Hong Kong, and it's easy to see why. The glitzy nightlife may be off limits to them, but even in the daytime the streets are full of adventure – weird food, creaking trams, old men taking birds for walks – and the burst of energy that greets all visitors here will enliven even the moodiest teenager.

The excitement begins even before you land: as your plane circles over Hong Kong's archipelago of 235 islands, the view is an exhilarating one of ships and sparkling water. Once through the airport, the visual journey continues. First there are the majestic bridges that connect the islands to Kowloon, then comes the view of Victoria Harbour, with the Peak towering behind rows of high-rise buildings guarding the shoreline; when the sun is shining their glass and steel glitters, while on a grey day clouds cling to the tallest towers, making them loom out of the mist. For a child it's sheer magic.

It may not boast as many world-class museums as, say, London or New York, but the SAR nonetheless offers a wealth of things to see and do. And thanks to its efficient and good-value public transport system, a lot can be packed into one day. If you plan carefully you can easily spend at least a day in a different area of the territory. Thankfully, with all manner of restaurants and fast-food chains, you'll never be far from refreshments.

## Hong Kong Island

### Central

Chances are that jet lag will have got you and you'll be awake in the early hours. If so, grab the opportunity to watch people practising the graceful martial art of t'ai chi. Groups gather in both **Chater Garden** (*see p65*) and the **Botanical Gardens** (*see p68*) around 7am. (There are also free classes at 8am at the piazza of the **Hong Kong Cultural Centre** in Kowloon; *see p86*). In the Botanical Gardens, t'ai chi is performed around the fountain (opposite the Government House entrance). Nearby, the caged orang-utans will be enjoying their breakfast. If you have food in mind yourself, you can take the Government House exit, walk down Garden

Road and into Queen's Road Central and there beside the HSBC building is **Mix** (*see p126*), a restaurant serving delicious breakfast wraps and smoothies.

Reinvigorated, take a trip around the **HSBC** HQ itself (*see p65*). Enter under the portcullis, ride the escalator up into the mouth of the banking hall, circle around the atrium and then go back down in one of the inside-out lifts. A visit to the 47th-floor viewing gallery of the **Bank of China Tower** next door (*see p65*) is an obvious next step, if heights don't scare you or the little ones.

Continuing eastwards, kids can explore the huge linked malls of **Queensway Plaza** and **Pacific Place** (*see p68 and p165*) in air-conditioned comfort. Two shops in Pacific Place might specifically interest young shoppers. **King & Country** (*see p179*), on Level 3, sells military and other models, including ones of Hong Kong street life at the turn of the 19th century: look out for the rickshaw man and the street dentist. On the same level is **Kelly & Walsh** (*see p161*), a good bookshop with

**The best** Kids' stuff

**The harbour**
Join **Dolphinwatch** to visit the 'pink' dolphins. See p194.

**Hong Kong Island**
Marvel at the traditional shops with dried sea horses and snakes in jars in **Sheung Wan**. See p192.

**Kowloon**
Explore the old streets and sounds in the **Hong Kong Museum of History**. See p196.

**The New Territories**
Climb in and out of the coaches and operate the signals at the **Hong Kong Railway Museum**. See p197.

**The Outlying Islands**
Spend the day on **Lantau** island and visit the world's tallest seated outdoor Buddha. See p198.

Arts & Entertainment

Hands-on entertainment at the **Hong Kong Science Museum**. *See p196.*

a great kids' area where they can lie on the floor with their new purchase. There are plenty of food options here, from **Dan Ryan's** (*see p1*, 2845 4600), for the hamburger addict, to the Asian food halls in **Seibu** (Level 1 and Lower Ground Floor; *see p162*). For further eating and shopping ideas, pick up a shopping directory at one of the information boards found throughout the complex.

From Pacific Place you can enter the eastern end of **Hong Kong Park** (*see p68*) by taking the lift to the Island Shangri-La hotel (*see p46*) and exiting through the lobby – this route avoids the walk up the steep hill. The park is a Tardis-like layered space for rest and relaxation. The curtain-waterfall fountain at the entrance is a good place to splash feet, arms and faces. A bit further in you'll find **L16** (2522 6333), a Thai restaurant with tables on a shady terrace, which serves an enjoyable South-east Asian buffet lunch.

At the heart of the park is a waterfall and, above it, the huge, excellent **Edward Youde Aviary** (*see p68*) – actually a chunk of re-created forest through which you descend on a wooden walkway, past an impressively exotic collection of brightly coloured birdlife.

An equally arresting spectacle at weekends is the sight of the massed brides, like living dolls in identical, rented, frilly white 'meringue' dresses, being photographed with their grooms near the Garden Road Registry Office.

If you leave the park at the western end, you can follow the signs to the **Peak Tram** (*see p78*), and climb aboard for a breathtaking climb up the Peak.

## Causeway Bay

Trams have been an essential part of Hong Kong life since 1904 and they haven't changed much over the years. The distinctive double-decker vehicles rattle along the north side of Hong Kong Island from Kennedy Town through Central to Causeway Bay, and they're great for kids – you enter at the back, clamber up to the top and enjoy a bird's-eye view of life on the street. Tickets are just HK$1 for kids under 12 and HK$2 for adults, and you can get off anywhere you want, have a look around and then jump on the next tram.

If you get on in Kennedy Town, your first stop should be an exploration of **Sheung Wan** (*see p69*), where you can wander along Herbal Medicine Street (Ko Sing) and Bird's Nest Street (Wing Lok). Watch as a cocktail of strange ingredients is weighed and wrapped, walk on to **Western Market**, then hop back on the tram. (The ultimate destination is marked on the front of the tram, so if you want to go to Causeway Bay don't get on one marked Happy Valley but take either North Point or Shau Kei Wan). Hop off by **Sogo**, the Japanese department store (*see p163*), for the ace toy and model sections, then cross the road to the Hennessy Centre and into the fascinating toy shop called **Wise Kids** (2506 3328). If you have any energy left continue on through Jardine's Bazaar street market to **Times Square** (*see p165*), another complex of shops of all types, and, for older kids, the well-lit and non-seedy video arcade, Times Zone.

In Times Square, hop on the MTR and go to Shau Kei Wan on the Island line, take exit B2 and walk uphill for about five minutes (or take a cab) to the **Hong Kong Museum of Coastal Defence** (*see p77*). This restored fortress was originally built as a defence against pirates, which were a plague in Hong Kong from the 16th century onwards. It has the narrowest entrance into the harbour; indeed, this is where the Japanese crossed in to Hong

Kong Island in World War II. Kids will love exploring the ramparts and batteries overlooking the eastern harbour, as well as the indoor displays of weapons and uniforms.

For a less militaristic outing in the same area, take the children to **Law Uk Folk Museum**, (*see p194*), a few minutes' walk from the MTR stop at Chai Wan. This 200-year-old Hakka family home has been converted into a folk museum. The rooms are laid out and furnished as they would have been at the time – a huge steamer and wok stand in the kitchen, a waxwork model of a Hakka lady sifting the rice sits in the living room, which is decorated with traditional furniture. The house is dwarfed by the neighbouring 30-storey blocks and is a charming place, surrounded by a well-planted little park tended by Hakka women.

# Ocean Park

Stretched over a peninsula to the south-east of Aberdeen, **Ocean Park** is Hong Kong's answer to Disneyland – until, that is, the real thing opens on Lantau in 2005. There's plenty to see and do, so families can probably fill most of a day at this enjoyable theme park.

The park is divided into seven sections. If you enter through the main entrance you'll find yourself in the Lowland Gardens, which is home to the stars of Ocean Park – the giant pandas An An and Jia Jia. Other attractions include the Goldfish Pagoda, the Butterfly House, the Dinosaur Discovery Trail, the Meteor Attack simulator ride and Discovery of the Ancient World – a walk through extensive re-created 'ruins of an ancient civilization', complete with life-size replicas of gorillas and other jungle dwellers.

Adjacent to the Lowland Gardens is Kids World, packed with gentle child-centric rides, as well as Dolphin University, where you can learn more about everyone's favourite marine mammal, and about the dolphins that have been born at the park.

The Lowland is linked to the Headland by a sedate cable-car ride across a hillside that drops steeply to the shore a hundred or so feet below. The eerily quiet ride is an experience in itself, offering a terrific view over the South China Sea and across Deep Water Bay. Even though they include two rollercoasters, the Headland Rides are pretty low on thrills by modern standards.

Nearby are the more impressive draws of Marine Land. At the Ocean Theatre there

are several shows a day featuring performing dolphins and sea lions – very entertaining if you don't have any moral objections. A recent addition is Pacific Pier, where visitors can watch dolphins and sea lions swimming underwater, and feed them too. The sea theme continues in the rather disappointing Shark Aquarium and the excellent Atoll Reef, a huge, well-stocked and well-explained water tank that re-creates the habitat of a coral lagoon and has underwater viewing points on four levels. The 4,000 fish here represent 400 different species and include an 80-year-old, two-metre (six-foot) long giant grouper.

Further around the headland is Adventure Land, where you'll find Ocean Park's best rides. The Mine Train rollercoaster is genuinely thrilling, while the Space Wheel and Raging River water ride offer slightly less stomach-churning pleasures. For visitors made of stronger stuff, the Abyss Turbo Drop provides a freefall plunge of 60 metres (197 feet). From here, what's said to be Asia's second-largest outdoor escalator (225 metres/738 feet) takes you down to the aviaries of Bird Paradise.

### Ocean Park
*Aberdeen (2552 0291/www.oceanpark. com.hk). Bus 6, 70, 75, 90, 97, 260/ Admiralty MTR then Ocean Park Citybus/ Central Star Ferry Pier then Ocean Park Citybus.* **Open** 10am-6pm daily. **Admission** HK$180; $90 concessions; free under-3s. **Credit** AmEx, DC, MC, V. **Map** p307.

**Arts & Entertainment**

They wear their distinctive hats with the black gauze frill that sways (to keep the flies off) as they sweep the paths.

No visit to Hong Kong is complete without a trip on the water and most kids love a day out on the authentic red-sailed Chinese junk, Duk Ling. The Tourism Board runs free hour-long trips every afternoon. Or take a morning cruise around the harbour and watch the firing of the **Noon Day Gun** (*see p73*). Perhaps the most exciting trip on the water, though, is the dolphin watch; Hong Kong boasts a colony of pink dolphins that live just off the island of Lantau. To arrange a dolphin-watching tour, contact **Dolphinwatch** (*see p40* **Dolphin friendly**), which runs half-day excursions with pick-ups in both Central and Kowloon. This trip is both fun and eco-friendly: Dolphinwatch follows a strict code of conduct to protect the creatures.

Finally, those with cash to splash can take a tour of Hong Kong by helicopter. There are lots of packages on offer – both **Heliservices Ltd** (2802 0200, www.heliservices.com.hk) and **Helitours** (2108 9899, www.helihongkong.com) offer a huge variety.

### Law Uk Folk Museum

*14 Kut Shing Street, Chai Wan, HK Island (2896 7006/www.lcsd.gov.hk/CE/Museum/History/lawuk/ english). Chai Wan MTR (exit B2) then 5min walk.* **Open** 10am-1pm, 2-6pm Mon-Wed, Fri, Sat; 1-6pm Sun. **Admission** free.

## The Peak

Don't rush your trip to the Peak. You can easily base a whole day around this area, with its abundant activities for children. It's all self-consciously touristy, of course, but that's not necessarily a bad thing. Inside the Peak Tower (www.the peak.com.hk/tower), **Ripley's Believe it or Not! Odditorium** (*see p79*) sits next door to the waxwork 'celebrities' at **Madame Tussaud's** (*see p79*). If the kids have an appetite for adventure, take them on the **Peak Explorer Motion Simulator**, a multimedia ride (Level 6; *see p79*). When you're exhausted, you can fall into **Marché** (Levels 6 and 7, 2849 2000) – a restaurant on several floors set out like a market so you can collect the type of food you fancy. It has child-friendly animal chairs, bold murals and a play area with a stunning view of the harbour.

Across the road is the **Peak Galleria** (*see p79*), where kids can stock up on the nastier end of the souvenir spectrum: Mao caps, pigtailed Chinese hats and so on. Amid the shopping frenzy, don't overlook the amazing views over both sides of the island from the rooftop terraces of the Galleria as well as Peak Tower. The Galleria has several eating spots kids are sure to like: **Shooters 52** (2838 5252) on the ground floor

Legions of cuddly toys await at **Teddy Bear Kingdom**. *See p196.*

Arts & Entertainment

dishes up user-friendly American food and has a play area for kids; **Grappa's** (2849 4222) serves delicious pizzas.

The circular path that swings westwards around Victoria Peak along Harlech and Lugard Roads (*see also p78* **Peak of fitness**) is a friendly hike for short legs and offers outstanding views of the city and harbour. There's a nature trail to follow here, and toilets, snacks and drinks are available near the playground halfway round, at the junction of Harlech and Hatton Roads.

You can also climb to the top of the Peak (don't be misled into thinking that the Peak tram terminus is at the Peak itself), a rewarding climb through a series of ascending parks and sculpted trails. If uphill does not appeal, try walking down to Central via Old Peak Road: turn left out of Peak Tower and take the narrow path that zigzags downhill through thick jungle and past some fine old colonial houses; a lovely walk in spring. The path eventually gives way to what must be one of the world's steepest residential streets – this route is not for those with dodgy knees.

## South & east coasts

If your kids have ever been to Disneyland or Alton Towers, it's possible they'll find **Ocean Park** (*see p193*) a bit of a let-down. However, it is in a beautiful location, and it's clean and leafy within. The two giant pandas by the entrance, living in a replica of their native habitat in western China, are worth a look in themselves.

Further south-east, the fishing village of **Stanley** (*see p83*) has been transformed completely in the past couple of years and is now an excellent place to spend a whole day with children. Take a number 6 bus from Central if you want a stomach-churning rollercoaster of a ride over the top of the island – or for a calmer air-conditioned ride, catch the 260. Stanley's narrow market streets are lined with stalls selling factory seconds and Chinese trinkets. Along the waterfront area there are new playgrounds, and a large canopied open space for picnicking. **Murray House** (*see p83*), an old colonial building transplanted brick by brick from Central, has historical displays, and you can take a well-earned break in one of its restaurants, which include a branch of the **Chilli N Spice** chain (*see p134*).

While you're here you can introduce the kids to a Chinese temple – just down from Murray House is the **Tin Hau Temple** (*see p80* **Making waves**), dedicated to the goddess of the sea. It was built in 1767 to protect the

Larking about on the **Peak**. *See p194*.

Stanley fishing community. Inside, the huge yellow incense coils and sculptures of strange deities are fascinating.

Also here is **Stanley Main Beach** (*see p84*), so don't forget to pack the swimming cossies. For the bus ride back, pick up a packet of 'sour plums' from a vendor. These dark red, prune-like dried fruits are the local equivalent of fruit gums, and most children love them.

## Kowloon

The Star Ferry ride between Central and Tsim Sha Tsui costs mere pennies, making it one of the best value attractions in Hong Kong. The Tsim Sha Tsui Ferry Pier abuts the lengthy waterfront promenade in front of the Hong Kong Cultural Centre, which itself offers stunning views across the harbour towards Hong Kong Island. Here, you will find the domed **Hong Kong Space Museum** (*see p86*), with its films on geographical themes (rainforests, glaciers, Everest) and differing levels of adrenaline rush. If you have

Mick Jagger? Jon Bon Jovi? It's anyone's guess at **Madame Tussaud's**. *See p194.*

particularly young ones with you, pop into the adjacent **Teddy Bear Kingdom** (*see below*), a fluffy indoor amusement park dedicated to cuddly bears of all shapes and sizes.

Keep going along the waterfront and you'll eventually reach the **Hong Kong Science Museum** (*see p89*), where kids can spend hours pushing buttons and learning about everything from household appliances to computers. It's very well-designed, hands-on, child-orientated stuff.

To give everyone a real feeling of Hong Kong's history, visit the **Hong Kong Museum of History** (*see p89*). Don't be put off by the appallingly unattractive modern building; inside, a thematic exhibition, 'The Hong Kong Story', traces life from some 400 million years ago to Hong Kong's return to Chinese sovereignty in 1997. It is not the early galleries that will capture the kids' imagination, but rather the street scenes and tableaux from the 19th and 20th centuries, all of which are beautifully presented.

Riding north on the MTR from Tsim Sha Tsui will bring you to the heart of Kowloon. You can exit at Prince Edward to explore the **Flower Market** in Fa Yuen Street, at the end of which is the astonishing **Bird Market** (*see p170* **Market places**). There's lots to fascinate little people here, with a huge variety of South China's most colourful birds on display. Exquisite bamboo cages with blue and white

water pots adorn the stalls, and all manner of bird food is on sale, including live grasshoppers by the thousand, in their own tiny cages. Along the edge of the market sit groups of men reading newspapers or chatting, while on nearby tree branches hang their bird cages. The chirping of the tiny songbirds within is thought to improve by being in contact with fellow birds. When it's time to go home, a cotton cloth is placed over the cage and off man and bird go.

The nearby **Goldfish Market** (*see p92*) is also worth a visit – goldfish of every shape and size – and there's also a Ladies' Market (*see p92*), with acres of stalls filled with girls' stuff.

If more retail therapy is needed, head back to the MTR and catch the train to Kowloon Tong and dive in to **Festival Walk** (*see p165*), Hong Kong's newest mall. It's more than just shops here – an ice rink and cinema are also on the site. When everyone gets hungry there are options from McDonalds to upmarket Japanese, all perfectly child friendly.

From Festival Walk, you can descend into Kowloon Tong KCR station and take the train north into the New Territories.

### Teddy Bear Kingdom

*P1-2, The Amazon, 12 Salisbury Road, next to New World Centre, Tsim Sha Tsui MTR (exit E)/Tsim Sha Tsui Star Ferry Pier.* **Open** 10am-10pm daily. **Admission** varies. **Credit** AmEx, DC, MC, V. **Map** p313 C6.

But there's no mistaking David Beckham...

## The New Territories

Get off the KCR train at Sha Tin for the excellent **Hong Kong Heritage Museum** and the **Ten Thousand Buddhas Monastery** (for both, *see p99*), both of which should appeal to children. The museum is a well-designed space, with an interesting section on Chinese opera. Of all the Buddhist temples in Hong Kong, the Ten Thousand Buddhas is the most likely to seize a child's imagination, if only because it is outlandish. (Beware: it's a long climb, up some 500 steps). As the name implies, there are 10,000 statues of Buddha on this landscaped hilltop. One of its temples contains the embalmed and gilded body of the monastery's founder.

Train enthusiasts can take the KCR to Tai Wo, and then a short taxi ride to the **Hong Kong Railway Museum** (*see p100*), housed in the former quaint Tai Po Market Station. This is a small, hands-on place where kids can clamber in and out of railway carriages and push buttons to make engines run. From here there is a great view up the Tolo channel, which, in the Song Dynasty, was the fishing ground for the Chinese Emperor's most prized pearls. You can also take a taxi to **Kadoorie Farm** (*see p104*), which nestles on the side of Kwun Yum Shan ('Goddess of Mercy Mountain'). This is a beautifully landscaped terraced farm involved in the conservation of Hong Kong's diverse wildlife. It boasts stunning walks, flowers and lots of animals. It's not to be missed, but make sure to call for an appointment.

If the weather is cool enough, and the kids are energetic enough, there are any number of short hikes to be found all over the New Territories. **Sai Kung** (*see p108*) has wonderful beaches and a remote feel. Or go to the Lion Rock Country Park (best approached from Tai Wai KCR station). To climb to **Amah Rock** (*see p98*) is tough but pays off with great views, and from there it is relatively easy to keep climbing up to the Lion Rock itself. For any of these slightly out-of-the-way destinations it is wise to get your hotel to write the names in Chinese characters.

## The Outlying Islands

Walking in wild countryside is one of the great attractions of the SAR's numerous islands. One of the easiest to reach is **Lamma** (*see p110*), a 40-minute ferry ride from Central's Outlying Islands Ferry Pier. Start early, breakfast in Yung Sue Wan in one of the cafés in the narrow street, and then set off on the gentle hike (allow a couple of hours) that takes you past two beaches and over the hill to Sok Kwu Wan. Just outside the village are the Kamikaze Caves (said to have been used to hide small Japanese boats during World War II; *see p111*) and in Sok Kwu Wan you can eat again (great seafood; *see p146*) before catching a boat back to Central.

Arts & Entertainment

For an excursion lasting a whole day take a ferry to **Silvermine Bay** (also called Mui Wo; *see p114*) on **Lantau**, Hong Kong's largest island. If the weather's nice you can catch a bus or taxi to either Pui O or Cheung Sha beach, have a swim, chase some hermit crabs, and clamber over the rocks. Or just go straight to the **Po Lin Monastery** (*see p115*), home to a giant Buddha statue, which sits atop a hill surveying a stunning mountainscape. There is good vegetarian food at the monastery.

Not to be missed is **Tai O** (*see p116*), the little fishing village on the western end of the island. The village straddles two islands, which are connected by a flat-bottomed boat pulled across by a rope. Most of the village houses are on stilts; outside them strange fish hang to dry, half wrapped in pink paper. A bus will take you back to Silvermine Bay and the ferry.

## Festivals & events

Hong Kong offers a variety of annual events that should interest children (*see p186-p190*). Many are based on the lunar calendar, so you'll need to check actual dates with the Hong Kong Tourism Board. **Chinese New Year** (late January/early February; *see p190*) is, at heart, a home-based family celebration, but visitors can always enjoy the big fireworks display (on the second day of the holiday) over Victoria Harbour. Avoid watching it from the packed Tsim Sha Tsui waterfront if you have young kids in tow. Later in the year, the **Mid Autumn Festival** (late September/early October; *see p188*) is celebrated in the streets and parks with lanterns, candles and cake. Go out after dark and you'll see families strolling with younger children thrilled to be up so late to greet the new moon with their lanterns – a touch of real beauty. Victoria Park (*see p74*) is a good place to see the lights and buy battery-operated cartoon lanterns of your own. You might see older kids playing hideously dangerous games with streams of molten wax, which is prone to vaporize and ignite, causing the kind of injuries normally associated with Bonfire Night in the UK. Steer well clear. The **Dragon Boat (Tuen Ng) Festival** (June; *see p188*) is a great spectacle. The shambolic races at Stanley feature a lot of expat participation and a great deal of alcohol consumption, but it's reasonably clean fun. More serious international competition can be seen at the Shing Mun River in Sha Tin.

The **Cheung Chau Bun Festival** (April/May/June; *see p187*) brings alive this little island off the coast of Lantau. Kids love the rush of music, lion dances and especially the children's parade, featuring Cheung Chau's kids riding on floats and stilt-walking over the crowds.

**Stanley Main Beach**. *See p195.*

## Resources

For general queries about any aspect of visiting Hong Kong with children, get in touch with the **Community Advice Bureau** (2815 5444, www.cab.org.hk).

### Child-minding

The majority of four- and five- star hotels offer a babysitting service. Private services are not common in Hong Kong, but **Rent-A-Mum** (2523 4868) specialises in finding well-referenced nannies, babysitters and short-term childcare.

Arts & Entertainment

# Film

Daredevil stunts, sweeping vistas, gritty streetlife… the city looks good on screen.

Although Hong Kong's first film studio opened in 1913, and the first locally produced full-length talkie was shot in 1934, it wasn't until the 1950s and '60s that the city's movie production really came into its own. For two decades its two largest studios, Shaw and Cathay, engaged in intense movie-making rivalry, each churning out over 100 films a year, covering a diverse range of genres, including martial arts, Chinese opera, melodrama and comedy. In 1957, after the death of Cathay's head, Lo Ke Wan, Shaw became the undisputed leader of the Chinese film industry and built an empire of cinemas across Southeast Asia. Charismatic mogul Run Run Shaw – one of the original Shaw founders – ruled with an iron fist, reputedly pushing actors and crew to their physical and creative limits. With no guild to negotiate between studios and performers, some actors and stuntmen turned to the triads for 'representation', creating ties between organised crime and showbiz, which, according to some industry insiders, still exist.

In the 1970s, Shaw's assistant, Raymond Chow, left to form Golden Harvest Films. Its roster of talent included Bruce Lee and Jackie Chan, and, based largely on their work, Hong Kong action flicks began to find a worldwide audience. The local cinema scene reached new heights in the 1980s when Tsui Hark, a prolific director widely respected among fans of period martial arts films, split from Golden Harvest to form the Film Workshop, a production company that went on to hire people such as director John Woo and actor Chow Yun-fat. During the late 1980s and early '90s, Hong Kong films consistently topped the local box office. But the success came to an abrupt end later that decade, as Hollywood blockbusters stole a large share of the audience and local films were increasingly pirated.

Indeed, over the last ten years the number of films made in Hong Kong has dwindled and box office figures for local films have fallen significantly. However, tougher piracy laws and a number of government-backed measures – such as a HK$100 million development fund, and FILMART (a film and TV trade fair set up by the Hong Kong Trade Development Council, www.hkfilmart.com) – have given the industry some hope. Another boost has come from Hollywood studios hot for remakes and distribution rights for local films, among them

*Infernal Affairs* (purchased by Brad Pitt and Warner Brothers), and Stephen Chow's *Shaolin Soccer* (bought by Miramax). Other remake targets include the Pang Brothers' *The Eye* (snapped up by Tom Cruise) and Peter Chan's *Going Home*. Although this injects much-needed cash into the HK film industry, some film fans are dismayed by Hollywood's heavy-handed dubbing and reworking of original local movies (check out the online petition at www.lovehkfilm.com).

Recent years have also seen increased co-operation between international production companies, filmmakers and artists, not only within Asia, but also between Asia and the West. In 2003, Hong Kong, Taiwan and Warner Brothers collaborated on the studio's first Chinese-language film, *Turn Left, Turn Right*, a romance starring Japanese/Taiwanese heartthrob Takeshi Kaneshiro. Other co-productions include *Hero* (HK, China, Taiwan), *Crouching Tiger, Hidden Dragon* (HK, China,

Kubrick Book Café at the
**Broadway Cinematheque**.
*See p202.*

Taiwan, USA) and *Three* (HK, Korea, Thailand). As Hong Kong director Johnnie To said in an interview with the *South China Morning Post*, 'Linking with international movie studios is the way forward for the Hong Kong film industry.'

## ALL THE RIGHT MOVES

The defining characteristic of mainstream Hong Kong cinema is not subtlety, but irrepressible energy, non-stop action, slapstick humour and an almost fetishistic obsession with comic-book violence. Genres are mixed and blended, and current trends and issues tackled in an irreverent way. In a typical season most cinemas will show a selection of cop and gangster movies, a smattering of love stories, a Jackie Chan blockbuster, a comedy or two and the inevitable prequels and sequels... all vehicles for big local names such as Andy Lau, Stephen Chow or various other handsome heartthrobs and starlets, some of whom have made their mark on the international circuit. (*see p201* **HK's acting exports**).

## LOCAL ART-HOUSE

Over the years Hong Kong has produced a number of widely respected art-house directors. Addressing themes such as cultural identity, HK traditions, ties to the mainland, and homosexuality, many of these films have been well received both abroad and locally.

Hong Kong's best-known and most well-established auteur, Wong Kar-wai, is an influential director who has spawned many imitators and established a loyal fan base. Wong's directorial debut was in 1988 with *As Tears Go By*, followed three years later by *Days of Being Wild*. Long-term collaborations with Australian cinematographer Christopher Doyle and designer/editor William Chang have created a distinct visual style, culminating in 2000 with *In the Mood for Love*.

Fruit Chan Kuo, a relative newcomer to the spotlight, had his independent breakthrough in 1997 with *Made in Hong Kong* – famously shot in just two months using non-professional actors. The film won international acclaim both for Chan and its lead, Sam Lee Chan-sam (*Beast Cops, Gen-Y Cops*), and is a critical and compassionate look at the film industry's glamorisation of recruitment to triad life and the breakdown of traditional moral codes.

Ann Hui, one of Asia's top female directors, came to prominence in 1979 with *The Secret*. Her work tackles issues such as identity, local traditions and the impact of history and urban development, and encompasses a range of genres from martial arts (*Romance of Book and Sword, Parts I and II*) to ghost stories (*Visible Secret*, a commercial genre-bending horror film).

Another festival favourite, Stanley Kwan, became an international name in 1987 with the release of *Rouge*, a supernatural romance starring Leslie Cheung and Anita Mui. In 1996 he came out as one of the few openly gay local directors with his film *Yin and Yang, Gender in Chinese Cinema*. Two of his other movies, *Centre Stage* (1992) and *Hold You Tight* (1998), were both prizewinners abroad.

A number of local organisations give support to fledgling directors. The Hong Kong Arts Development Council (HKADC) has a fund for grants, while the Hong Kong Arts Centre offers courses and editing facilities, and hosts the IFVA (Independent Film & Video Awards) Short Film & Video Festival; *see also p205*. Ying E Chi (www.yec.com) is an organisation that promotes and helps distribute local indie films.

## CINEMA-GOING

Hong Kong is home to more than 60 cinemas, from modern multiplexes to dusty one-house cinemas screening anything from the latest Hollywood blockbusters to Middle Eastern art-house. While most venues have excellent facilities, you will occasionally find yourself in an aggressively air-conditioned old hall, where the cleaner insists on starting work ten minutes before the credits start rolling. Even in the best of places mobile phones and pagers are likely to go off and conversations continue regardless.

Daily listings can be found in all local Chinese and English-language newspapers (the *SCMP* provides reviews on Thursdays), as well as *HK* and *BC* magazines – free 'what's on' guides that can be picked up around town (for both, *see p287*). Alternatively, go online to www.cinema.com.hk or www.cityline.com.

Ticket prices vary from HK$50 to $75 according to which cinema you pick and the time you go (add a HK$5-$9.50 booking fee for online/phone bookings made with credit cards). Tuesdays and matinées are generally cheaper – around HK$45 or less – and bookings can be made up to five days in advance. All films are rated according to the following categories: (I) suitable for all ages; (IIA) not suitable for children; (IIB) not suitable for young adults and children; and (III) over-18s only.

Most films are shown in their original version, with English or Chinese subtitles. Children's films, animated films and, less commonly, Mandarin films, are often dubbed, but there are usually two versions shown around town at the same time.

## RESOURCES

For useful websites and suggested reading material about Hong Kong cinema, *see p295*.

Arts & Entertainment

# HK's acting exports

## Jackie Chan

Chan began his career as a stunt man with Golden Harvest studios. His big break came in 1980, when he was given top billing in *The Young Master*, which broke box office records in Hong Kong and Japan. With over 100 films under his belt, including smashes *Rush Hour* (1998) and *Rush Hour 2* (2001), Chan is one of the most bankable stars on the planet.

## Leslie Cheung

This big local star (*pictured*), who sadly took his own life in 2003, played Tony Leung Chiu-wai's petulant boyfriend in *Happy Together* (1997), starred in Chen Kaige's *Farewell My Concubine* (1993), John Woo's *A Better Tomorrow* (1986), Stanley Kwan's *Rouge* (1987), Wong Kar-wai's *Days of Being Wild* (1990) and *Ashes of Time* (1994).

## Maggie Cheung

Cheung mesmerised the world's cinema-goers in 2000 with her role in Wong Kar-wai's *In the Mood for Love*, and appeared again more recently in Zhang Yimou's *Hero* (2002). She also starred in *The Soong Sisters* (1997) alongside Michelle Yeoh in *Chinese Box* (1997) with Jeremy Irons, and in the unusual French film *Irma Vep* (1996), specially written for her by director (and her ex-husband) Olivier Assayas.

## Bruce Lee

The ultimate Hong Kong icon. He had it all: looks, charm and a seductive on-screen presence. Though he was actually born in San Francisco, Lee started his acting career as a young boy in Hong Kong. Films such as *The Way of The Dragon* (1972) and *Enter The Dragon* (1973) made him a household name around the globe. When he died in July 1973 aged just 33, film fans around the world mourned his passing.

## Tony Leung Chiu-wai

This handsome local idol, extremely popular throughout Asia, played opposite Maggie Cheung in both *Hero* and *In the Mood for Love*. Leung, who played lead roles in a number of Wong Kar-wai's earlier films such as *Happy Together* (1997) and *Chungking Express* (1994), also starred in Tran Anh Hung's *Cyclo* (1995) and *Hard-Boiled* (1991).

## Tony Leung Kar-fei

Hong Kong-born heartthrob Tony Leung Kar-fei, who also starred in *Ashes of Time* (1994), caught the eye of a wider audience in 1991 as the paramour in Annaud's *The Lover*.

## John Lone

Another local to reach international screens in the '80s, Lone took the lead role in *The Iceman* (1984), then continued his success with a number of films including Bertolucci's *The Last Emperor* (1987) and Cronenberg's *M. Butterfly* (1993). He also played alongside Jackie Chan in *Once Upon a Time in Shanghai* (1999) and *Rush Hour 2* (2001).

## Michelle Yeoh

Yeoh is famed as being the only female artist whom Jackie Chan allows to perform her own stunts. Born in Malaysia but an honorary Hong Kong star, she gained international recognition for her performances in *Crouching Tiger, Hidden Dragon* (2000) and *Tomorrow Never Dies* (1997), as well as the rather ill-fated *The Touch* (2002).

## Chow Yun-fat

Born on Lamma island, and surely Hong Kong's most debonair export, Yun-fat first became known for his roles as the urbane gunman in a string of works such as *The Killer* (1989) and *Hard-Boiled* (1991). At the end of the '90s he widened his fan base by taking leading roles in *Replacement Killers* (1998), *Anna and the King* and *The Corruptor* (both 1999), and by playing the gentlemanly warrior in Ang Lee's *Crouching Tiger, Hidden Dragon* (2000).

Arts & Entertainment

# Location, location, location

Hong Kong's modern cityscape is spectacularly filmic. William Gibson cited the Kowloon Walled City (*see p94*) as the inspiration for the locations in his sci-fi novels, and there are times when a late-night taxi ride along a flyover threading its way between outrageous skyscrapers and crumbling tenements will take your mind straight to *Blade Runner*. Hollywood, of course, has not overlooked the city's unusual appearance.

One of the first Hollywood films to be made in the territory was *Soldier of Fortune* (1955), starring Clark Gable and Susan Hayward. The opening shot shows Gable at the Barker Road Peak Tram station – the last stop before the Peak terminus, and one of the few locations from that era that remains unchanged. If you take the number 15 bus from the Peak and sit upstairs on the left, halfway down you will see the Chinese mansion used as Gable's residence in the film.

The same year, another big budget film, *Love is a Many-Splendored Thing*, was shot here. Adapted from Han Suyin's autobiographical novel of interracial romance

**Arts & Entertainment**

## Major commercial cinemas

### AMC Festival Walk

*Level UG, 88 Tat Chee Avenue, Kowloon Tong, Kowloon (2265 8545). Kowloon Tong MTR/KCR (exit C1, C2).* **Credit** MC, V.
Deep within one of Hong Kong's newest and largest shopping centres, the AMC complex has 11 screens showing international and local films. It's easy to find from the MTR/KCR, and the seats are comfy.

### Broadway Cinematheque

*Prosperous Garden, 3 Public Square Street, Yau Ma Tei, Kowloon (2388 3188/www.cinema.com.hk). Yau Ma Tei MTR (exit C)/buses along Nathan Road.* **Credit** MC, V. **Map** p312 B3.
Although the screens here are not the largest in town, the Cinematheque offers some of the most diverse listings around, including a great selection of Asian and art-house films, plus regular festivals

and retrospectives. There's also a poster shop on site. Next door, the Kubrick Book Café has a film library, and sells snacks and a respectable selection of film literature and international magazines.

### Cine-Art House

*Sun Hung Kai Centre, 30 Harbour Road, Wan Chai, HK Island (2827 4820/www.cityline.com). Wan Chai MTR (exit A1)/18, 88, 104 bus/buses along Gloucester Road.* **No credit cards. Map** p310 B3.
Another cinema offering an alternative selection, with new films from mainland China often getting their first runs here. It's nothing flash – the seats are a bit shoddy and the air-con can be arctic – but it's cheap and close to the bars of Wan Chai and Causeway Bay if you fancy making a night of it.

### JP Cinema

*JP Plaza, 22-6 Paterson Street, Causeway Bay, HK Island (2881 5005). Causeway Bay MTR (exit E)/ 2A, 8, 103, 170 bus.* **Credit** MC, V. **Map** p311 E2.

and starring Jennifer Jones and William Holden, the film showed a picturesque view of colonial Hong Kong: the bustle of Queen's Road, Kennedy Town and Aberdeen, sleepy Kai Tak airport and glistening Deep Water Bay.

In 1960, William Holden returned to star in *The World of Suzie Wong* with local actress Nancy Kwan. From the opening scene aboard the Star Ferry to the vanished neoclassical architecture of Central, from Wan Chai market to the boat yards at Aberdeen, it's a highly evocative movie. The exterior shots of the Nam Kok Hotel were filmed on Hollywood Road, at its junction with Ladder Street – Man Mo Temple is often visible – and the views from the hotel roof were shot from a location on the Peak. The actual Aberdeen floating restaurant shown in the film has long since disappeared, but the latest incarnation still offers a similar location and experience.

Hong Kong's reputation as glamour capital of Asia has made it a natural setting for the James Bond series. In 1967 Sean Connery showed up to make *You Only Live Twice*, while in 1974 Roger Moore, whose trademark safari suits were made at Sam's Tailor on Nathan Road, arrived to film parts of *The Man With The Golden Gun*, which featured the Hankow Road topless bar Bottoms Up and the Peninsula Hotel.

During the 1990s Hong Kong was the setting for an intriguing mix of films. One of the funniest scenes from that decade is in Clara Law's *Autumn Moon* (1992), when a Japanese tourist asks a local girl to take him to a traditional Hong Kong restaurant and is duly led to McDonalds. Two films by famed director Wong Kar-wai, *Chungking Express* (1994) and *Fallen Angels* (1995), are both interesting for their wild kaleidoscopic views of the Mid-Levels Escalator, Chungking Mansions, late-night bars and cha canting (tea shops). The city was the inspiration for the futuristic metropolis in Mamoru Oshii's animation *Ghost in the Shell* (1995), while the following year Peter Greenaway shot sections of *The Pillow Book* (*pictured left*) in Hong Kong – look out for Nathan Road at night, the Swindon bookshop on Lock Road in Tsim Sha Tsui and the traditional hillside graveyard among the housing blocks near Tsing Yi. The pounding of pile-drivers accompanies Jeremy Irons and Gong Li during their ill-fated affair in pre-Handover Hong Kong in Wayne Wang's *Chinese Box* (1997). Although the film paints a depressing picture of the city and its future, it captures some interesting urban images, especially around the wet markets and the escalator in Central. Ride the escalator up to Lyndhurst Terrace to see the beautiful balconied building on the left where Irons' character was holed up. More recently, Jackie Chan's *Rush Hour 2* (2001) featured stunts involving the trams in Wan Chai, and in 2002 Angelina Jolie's *Tomb Raider 2* featured a spectacular leap from the top of the IFC2 tower.

Tucked in among the shopping malls of Causeway Bay, JP has two large screens and mainly shows the latest Hollywood releases. The cinema's steep incline allows uninterrupted viewing – something Hong Kong's older venues can't boast.

## Ocean Theatre
*3 Canton Road, Tsim Sha Tsui, Kowloon (2377 2100). Tsim Sha Tsui MTR (exit C1, E)/ buses to Tsim Sha Tsui Star Ferry Pier/Tsim Sha Tsui Star Ferry Pier.* **No credit cards.** **Map** p313 B6.
Ocean Theatre's greatest attraction is its enormous screen. For action-packed local chop-socky productions and mega-action hits, this is the place to come.

## Palace IFC
*Podium L1, IFC Mall, 8 Finance Street, Central (2388 6268/www.cinema.com.hk). Hong Kong MTR (exit B1)/Central Star Ferry Pier & buses through Central.* **Credit** MC, V. **Map** p309 D2.

This cinema is easy to locate in the malls beneath this towering building in downtown Central. Despite the small size of its theatres the Palace has well-proportioned screens and comfy seats, and shows a mix of blockbusters and arthouse films. It also boasts a small bookshop and café.

## Silvercord
*Silvercord Centre, 30 Canton Road, Tsim Sha Tsui, Kowloon (2736 6218). Tsim Sha Tsui MTR (exit A1)/buses to Tsim Sha Tsui Star Ferry Pier/Tsim Sha Tsui Star Ferry Pier.* **Credit** MC, V. **Map** p313 B6.
This cosy theatre on the corner of Canton Road and Haiphong Road shows a selection of local and international faves, plus the occasional art-house gem.

## UA Queensway
*Pacific Place, 88 Queensway, Admiralty, HK Island (2869 0322/www.cityline.com). Admiralty MTR (exit C1)/buses through Admiralty.* **Credit** AmEx, DC, MC, V. **Map** p309 F5.

Arts & Entertainment

The Queensway multiplex has the most modern and comfortable seats in town, but be warned – it's also one of the priciest places around.

## Windsor

*Windsor House, 311 Gloucester Road, Causeway Bay, HK Island (2388 0002/www.cinema.com.hk). Causeway Bay MTR (exit E)/2A, 8, 23 bus/ buses along Gloucester Road.* **Credit** MC, V. **Map** p311 D2.

The Windsor cinema plays host to a number of premières and the latest, biggest local and international features. The two-seater benches at the back are part of its appeal.

## Resources & other cinemas

### Agnès b Cinema

*Hong Kong Arts Centre, 2 Harbour Road, Wan Chai, HK Island (2582 0200). Wan Chai MTR (exit A1)/18, 88 bus/buses along Gloucester Road.* **Credit** V. **Map** p310 B3.

Previously known as the Lim Por Yen Film Theatre, this cinema was once the regular venue for art-house festivals, though the number of screenings has declined. However, it still showcases two 'World Film Classics' monthly and holds a regular Hong Kong Film Forum, where local filmmakers talk about their work (mostly in Cantonese). The Arts Centre also hosts the IFVA Short Film & Video Festival in February/March, and regularly screens video and short film productions by young directors. For details check the Arts Centre newsletter, *Artslink*, or the HKAC website, www.hkac.org.hk.

### Hong Kong Film Archive

*50 Lei King Road, Sai Wan Ho, HK Island (2739 2139/www.filmarchive.gov.hk). Sai Wan Ho MTR (exit A)/2A, 8, 77, 110, 606 bus.* **Open** *Foyer* 10am-8pm daily. *Resource centre* 10am-7pm Mon-Wed, Fri; 10am-5pm Sat; 1-5pm Sun. **Credit** MC, V.

The HKFA is home to an exhibition hall, film and information archives and a comfy cinema. Stored in its vaults are over 4,300 films and 85,000 pieces of

## Don't miss HK films

### A Better Tomorrow
(John Woo, 1986)
A stock gangster tale taken to a new level, thanks to Woo's verve and a brilliant performance from Chow Yun-fat. 'The *Citizen Kane* of Hong Kong cinema', according to one film critic.

### A Chinese Ghost Story
(Ching Siu-tung, 1987)
A fantastic tale featuring an ancient tree demon with a life-sapping tongue. Combines tradition with Hong Kong energy.

### Chungking Express
(Wong Kar-wai, 1994)
This beautiful, open-hearted romantic comedy paints an unforgettable picture of Hong Kong in the 1990s. An art-house gem.

### Going Home
(Peter Chan, 2002)
The last short in the pan-Asian collection Three, this stylish and controlled ghost story features stunning cinematography by Christopher Doyle.

### Infernal Affairs
(Andy Lau, Alan Mak, 2002)
The second-highest grossing local film after *Shaolin Soccer*. Stars Tony Leung and Andy Lau in a tale of an undercover cop and a triad spook.

### In the Mood for Love
(Wong Kar-wai, 2000)
A sensuously shot story of unrequited love; full of tension and unspoken passion.

### Made in Hong Kong
(Fruit Chan Kuo, 1997)
An unglamourised examination of triad recruitment, public housing estates and a potential hitman.

### My Life as McDull
(Toe Yuen, 2001)
This charming animation features the comic pig McDull and his offbeat observations of life in the city.

### Peking Opera Blues
(Tsui Hark, 1986)
The female actors shine in this rip-roaring romantic action-comedy. Great stunts too.

### Rouge
(Stanley Kwan, 1987)
Conjuring up Hong Kong past, this clever, warm, funny melodrama has much to say about the city's changing culture.

### Shaolin Soccer
(Stephen Chow, 2001)
The highest-grossing local film ever, this deadpan mix of kung fu and soccer, with Stephen Chow looking uncannily like Bruce Lee.

Pre-show refreshment at the **Windsor**. See p204.

film heritage dating back to 1898. Materials cannot be taken away, but individual booths and a group viewing room are available for a nominal charge. It frequently screens retrospectives of Hong Kong classics, and has held major retrospectives of international filmmakers such as Renoir.

## Festivals & events

The most exciting annual cinematic event is the **Hong Kong International Film Festival** (*see also p187*) in April, which features a wide range of new and old international and local films. In February/March there's the IFVA's **Short Film & Video Festival** (www.ifva.com), featuring work by up-and-coming local talent. French cinema is showcased during May as part of **Le French May** arts festival (*see also p187*) and in June the **FILMART** international film and TV trade fair is held at the Hong Kong Cultural & Exhibition Centre.

To check what's on, look for brochures or flyers in the lobbies of major venues or log on to www.cinema.com.hk, www.cityline.com.hk or the websites of the Arts Centre and Film Archive (for both, *see p204*).

# Galleries

The local art scene may be small, but that doesn't mean it's non-existent.

As international interest in Chinese art continues to grow, Hong Kong's role in the market is shrinking. The trickle of avant-garde mainland works that first found their way to the West via the city's galleries in the mid 1980s has developed into a flash flood of talent that is now surging straight from the source, cutting out the middleman. Dealers are flocking to the emerging art centres of Beijing and Shanghai, leaving Hong Kong bobbing in the wake. But it's not all bad news. The positive result of the city's declining role as an 'open port to the world' is that local artists are getting the chance to express themselves more prominently. Despite what locals might say, Hong Kong does have a visual art scene – you just have to know where to look.

If you're in search of classical Chinese styles you won't find much, unless you head for the touristy shops of Tsim Sha Tsui or Stanley, or limit your viewing to the **Hong Kong Museum of Art** (*see p207*). This government-run space is the continuing focus of criticism from the arts community, who claim it lacks vision. While it's true that the museum's officially appointed view of art is stuck in the gulf between tradition and modernity, and that it only has one space devoted to contemporary art, it nonetheless boasts a good range of calligraphy and an impressive ceramics and antiquities collection, plus a wealth of ink and brush *shui mo* paintings.

But the city also has a healthy representation of works in less traditional styles. This scene started to emerge in the 1960s, when Lui Shou-kwan's fusions of Chinese ink painting with Abstract Expressionism inspired the New Ink Painting Movement, which in turn led others such as Wucious Wong to combine Eastern and Western influences, reflecting the city's schizoid nature as both Chinese and British.

In the 1980s and '90s, this approach was abandoned by a new generation of younger artists. Instead of attempting to compete with the rest of the world, they focused attention to themselves, shedding the ink and brush elements and adopting more Western media to explore the ambiguous identities of Hong Kongers. Not surprisingly, this emphasis on self-identity became pronounced in the lead-up to the 1997 Handover. Fears about the future of the territory and freedom of expression gave way to new art forms, while photography became especially popular with people wanting to record the unique period of history.

A year after the Handover, a new era began with the development of the Oil Street Artist Village in North Point, HK Island, which sprang up after the high rents and commercial focus of established galleries led some local artists to take over abandoned government land to display their work. Unfortunately, it wasn't long before they were booted out. Developers are now aiming to recapture the buzz of Oil Street with a similar venture at the **Ma Tau Kok Cattle Depot** (*see p207*), though its location – in the middle of nowhere by the standards of most Hong Kongers – is proving a stumbling block.

Understandably, spaces in the heart of the city attract more of an audience. In an historic building overlooking the nightlife mecca of Lan Kwai Fong, the **Fringe Club** (*see p222*), with its tiny theatres and galleries, and annual CityJan festival in January (*see p190*), has played a vital role in nurturing the arts scene since 1984. The **Hong Kong Arts Centre** in Wan Chai is another hub. Its main exhibition space, the **Pao Galleries** (*see p209*), is overshadowed by the Goethe Institut's excellent **Goethe Gallery** (*see p207*), which rents a floor in the same building.

Most of the city's commercial galleries are scattered around the restaurants and low-rise architecture of the SoHo district. Enjoy them with a walking tour: the area is a quaint one to explore by foot. Should you be around in the first week of March, try to catch the Art Walk (*see p186*), a charity gallery crawl organised by *HK Magazine*.

Most of these commercial galleries are dominated by Asian art of the decorative kind, although there are exceptions, such as the must-see **Hanart TZ Gallery** (*see p209*), which was responsible for introducing mainland, avant-garde art to the West in the 1980s.

## USEFUL INFORMATION

The **Asia Art Archive** (2/F, 8 Wah Koon Building, 181-91 Hollywood Road, Sheung Wan, 2815 1112, www.aaa.org.hk, closed Sunday) is an invaluable source of information, with exhibition catalogues, artists' monographs, art books and audio and video recordings from Hong Kong, Macau, Taiwan and the mainland.

### Fringe Club

*2 Lower Albert Road, Central, HK Island (2521 7251/www.hkfringe.com.hk). Central MTR (exit D1)/23A bus.* **Open** from noon Mon-Sat. **Admission** free. **Map** p309 D4.

The Fringe has several spaces devoted to art. The Economist Gallery, in the foyer, is a key platform for local artists. Paintings, photography and mixed media works also line the walls of the bar on the ground floor. To the left of the main entrance, up two flights of stairs, is the newest addition: the Volkswagen Fotogalerie. Given the city's obsession with photography, it's a great concept, though infrequent shows have so far left the space underdeveloped, and most people just use it as an access to the pleasant roof garden outside.

### Goethe Gallery

*14/F, Hong Kong Arts Centre, 2 Harbour Road, Wan Chai, HK Island (2802 0088). Wan Chai MTR (exit C)/18, 88 bus/buses along Gloucester Road & Harbour Road.* **Open** 10am-8pm Mon-Fri; 2-6pm Sat. **Admission** free. **Map** p310 B3.

The Goethe Institut's Goethe Gallery is one of the best exhibition venues in Hong Kong. For most of the year, the 'white cube' space is taken up by shows promoting German arts and culture, although there is an increasing amount of high-quality local work.

### Hong Kong Heritage Museum

*1 Man Lam Road, Sha Tin (2180 8188/www. heritagemuseum.gov.hk). Sha Tin or Tai Wai KCR then 15min walk/A41, E42, 72A, 80M, 86, 89, N271, 282 bus.* **Open** 10am-6pm Mon, Wed-Sat; 10am-7pm Sun. **Admission** HK$10; HK$5 concessions. Free to all Wed. **No credit cards. Map** p307.

This out-of-the-city museum of art, history and culture offers more of a grass-roots experience than the Museum of Art. The Chao Shao-an Gallery is devoted to a local ink brush painting master, while other galleries host visiting art shows. *See also p99.*

### Hong Kong Museum of Art

*10 Salisbury Road, Tsim Sha Tsui, Kowloon (2721 0116/www.lcsd.gov.hk/hkma). Tsim Sha Tsui MTR (exit E)/buses to Tsim Sha Tsui Star Ferry Pier & along Salisbury Road/Tsim Sha Tsui Star Ferry Pier.* **Open** 10am-6pm Mon-Wed, Fri-Sun. **Admission** HK$10; HK$5 concessions. Free to all Wed. **No credit cards. Map** p313 C6.

Much maligned for its severe exterior, the Hong Kong Museum of Art isn't much better on the inside. Limited collections, shabby decor and a general lack of explanation often frustrate overseas visitors. Most of the art doesn't seem particularly representative of Hong Kong, especially given the increasing amount of mainland art flooding into the galleries. In its defence, the museum does well with its strong ceramics collection, diverse amount of calligraphy and ink brush paintings, and the recent addition of a jade and gold antiquities collection. *See also p86.*

### Ma Tau Kok Cattle Depot

*63 Ma Tau Kok Road, To Kwa Wan, Kowloon (no phone). Bus 101, 111/Kowloon City ferry from North Point.*

A former cattle depot isn't the sort of place you'd normally associate with high-quality art, but it's here that you'll find some of Hong Kong's more creative individuals quietly at work. Following the closure in 1999 of the famous Oil Street Artist Village in North Point, the government renovated this new site and offered it for cheap rent to the homeless art groups. Unfortunately, the obscurity of the new location has proved a nightmare for luring the public; though it's billed as a 'village', at times it feels more like a ghost town (so check that there are exhibitions on before you set off).

In the central and largest barn is the Artist Commune (2104 3322), an exhibition space dedicated to mainland visual, performance and installation art. Videotage (2573 1869, www.videotage.org.hk) is a new media art collective, whose sleek headquarters are in the barn to the left. Next door is

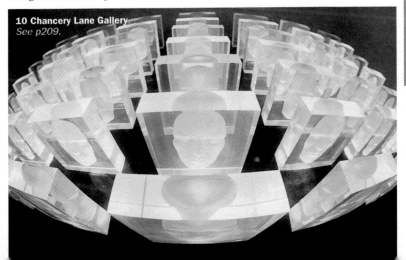

**10 Chancery Lane Gallery.**
*See p209.*

**Arts & Entertainment**

# Sticky fingers

You'll be hard-pressed to spot a painter poised on a street corner with paintbrush and palette in Hong Kong. Anyone seen to be doing anything marginally creative out in the open is likely to be stared at like a lunatic. But hidden in pockets around the city are creative hideaways where people can paint in peace, and even learn Chinese painting traditions along the way. Here are some of our favourites (phone or check the websites for the latest schedules).

The **Meli-Melo Living Arts Café** (G/F, 123 Wellington Street, Central, HK Island, 2541 8816, www.artjamming.com; *pictured*) throws 'Art Jams' every Saturday night from 9pm, which are proving successful with well-paid professionals. Here they get to don an apron, choose from a buffet of acrylic paints and attack a canvas. The all-night get-togethers attract a cross-section of urban dwellers, although the steep admission prices (HK$500 for non-members) might keep genuine starving artists away. The latter may prefer the occasional midweek jams (7-11pm), where complimentary food and wine are served. Family sessions are also offered on Saturday afternoons. Visitors wishing to become members should bring a passport for ID.

At the **YWCA** (3/F, 1 MacDonnell Road, Central, HK Island, 3476 1340, www.esmdywca.org.hk) you'll find an extensive range of classes, including calligraphy and Chinese watercolour painting. Course fees are between HK$250 and HK$1,500; you have to pay a membership fee as well.

**Ng's Art School** (9/F, Oriental Crystal Commercial Building, 46 Lyndhurst Terrace, Central, HK Island, 2815 4344, www.ngsartschool.com.hk) is a friendly centre that offers classes in both Chinese and Western art disciplines. Lessons take place from Wednesday to Sunday and cost around HK$1,300-HK$1,450 for a course of eight.

Hong Kong photographer and artist Norm Yip sometimes holds life-drawing sessions at his home/studio/art gallery **Studio 8** (8B Kamcourt Building, 60-62 Bonham Strand East, Sheung Wan, HK Island, 2540 6267, www.studio8hk.net). A single class is HK$160; eight classes cost HK$1,000. The events are popular with the gay crowd and, while they were not running as this guide went to press, Yip had plans to reintroduce them later in 2004.

Arts & Entertainment

1aspace (2529 0087, www.oneaspace.org.hk), a leading contemporary art organisation hosting well-conceived, curated exhibitions. Also on the site are the On & On Theatre Workshop (*see p233*), an art college and a dozen private studios.

## Pao Galleries

*4-5/F, Hong Kong Arts Centre, 2 Harbour Road, Wan Chai, HK Island (2582 0200/www.hkac.org.hk). Wan Chai MTR (exit C)/18, 88 bus/buses along Gloucester Road & Harbour Road.* **Open** usually 10am-8pm daily; phone to check. **Admission** free. **Map** p310 B3.
The Hong Kong Arts Centre has its own regular programme of exhibitions, but most of the time its highly popular spaces are rented out to private exhibitors. Sadly, because the programming of exhibitions, films, plays and dance productions tends to be fast and furious, many of the curated exhibitions feel rushed and undeveloped.

## Para/Site Art Space

*2 Po Yan Street, Sheung Wan, HK Island (2517 4620/www.para-site.org.hk). Sheung Wan MTR (exit A2)/10, 26, 37A bus.* **Open** noon-7pm Wed-Sun. **Admission** free. **Map** p308 A2.
Located on a side street across from the Hollywood Road Park, this independent art space has been suffering from a lack of funds in recent years, with the result that shows have been declining in quality. The team of mature and well-known local artists who are behind the space persevere nonetheless with the emphasis on installation art.

## University Museum & Art Gallery

*University of Hong Kong, 94 Bonham Road, Pok Fu Lam, HK Island (2241 5500/www.hku.hk/hkumag). Bus 3B, 23, 40, 40M, 103.* **Open** 9.30am-6pm Mon-Sat; 1.30-5.30pm Sun. **Admission** free.
The new wing attached to the old Fung Ping Shan Museum throws occasional visual art exhibitions. *See also p72.*

# Commercial galleries

## Chouinard Gallery Hong Kong

*G/F, 1 Prince's Terrace, Mid-Levels, HK Island (2858 5072). Mid-Levels Escalator/buses along Caine Road.* **Open** 10.30am-7.30pm Tue-Sat; 2-7pm Sun. **Admission** free. **Map** p308 B4.
Patrick Chouinard deals in expressive abstract works from Asia, with a focus on huge Indonesian paintings. Now you'll find two other galleries alongside his corner space: Australian art at the 5 o.p.t Studio/Gallery (2536 9818, www.5opt.com.hk), and the Korkos Gallery (2987 1187, www.korkosgallery.com), which deals with non-traditional artworks such as jewellery, ceramics and installations from international and local artists.

## Galerie Martini

*1/F, 99F Wellington Street, Central, HK Island (2526 9566/www.galeriemartini.com). Central MTR (exit D1, D2, G)/buses along Queen's Road Central.* **Open** 11am-7pm Tue-Sat. **Admission** free. **Map** p308 C3.

Hidden up a steep staircase in a colonial-style building wedged between office blocks, Galerie Martini delights with its monthly exhibitions of quirky international artists.

## Grotto Fine Art

*2/F, 31C-D Wyndham Street, Central, HK Island (2121 2270/www.grottofineart.com). Central MTR (exit D1, D2, G)/23A, 26, 40M bus.* **Open** 11am-7pm Mon-Sat. **Admission** free. **Map** p308 C4.
This relatively new gallery deals exclusively in contemporary Hong Kong paintings, ceramics and sculpture. For those interested in buying, prices are pretty affordable.

## Hanart TZ Gallery

*2/F, Henley Building, 5 Queen's Road, Central, HK Island (2526 9019). Central MTR (exit H, K)/buses along Queen's Road Central.* **Open** 10am-6.30pm Mon-Fri; 10am-6pm Sat. **Admission** free. **Map** p309 D4.
Despite its incongruous location – in an office block in the financial heart of Central – this is one of the city's most important art galleries. It was responsible for introducing Chinese avant-garde art to the West during the '80s and '90s, and the owners continue to show experimental art from Hong Kong, Taiwan and the mainland.

## John Batten Gallery

*G/F, 64 Peel Street, Central, HK Island (2854 1018/www.johnbattengallery.com). Mid-Levels Escalator/buses along Caine Road.* **Open** 1-7pm Tue-Sat; 2-5pm Sun. **Admission** free. **Map** p308 B4.
John Batten writes for various art journals and is a firm supporter of local arts. He shuns mere decorative art, instead devoting his small, street-front space to subtle lyrical abstraction, modernist photography and Asian contemporary art.

## Schoeni Art Gallery

*G/F, 21-31 Old Bailey Street, Central, HK Island (2869 8802/www.schoeni.com.hk). Mid-Levels Escalator/buses along Hollywood Road & Caine Road.* **Open** 10.30am-6.30pm Mon-Sat. **Admission** free. **Map** p308 C4.
This enormous main gallery (and its smaller branch down the hill) exhibits a steady stream of oils of a humorous nature from Asia, Europe and China.
**Other locations:** G/F, 27 Hollywood Road, Central, HK Island (2542 3143).

## 10 Chancery Lane Gallery

*G/F, 10 Chancery Lane (off Old Bailey Street), Central, HK Island (2810 0065/www.10chancerylane gallery.com). Central MTR (exit D1/D2)/23A, 40M bus/buses along Caine Road.* **Open** 11am-7pm Mon-Fri; 11.30am-6pm Sat. **Admission** free. **Map** p308 C4.
This stylish gallery is hidden behind the back wall of the Central Police Station. Owner Katie de Tilly deals with a stellar bunch of international artists, who work in everything from photography to painting and sculpture. She also occasionally lets local artists erect installations in the high-ceilinged space.

# Gay & Lesbian

The city finally has a scene to be proud of – better late than never.

In the last year or so, Hong Kong's gay and lesbian communities have taken on a much more public profile: a HKTB award was given to a two-day itinerary aimed at gay travellers; Hong Kong's first (bilingual) gay issues and lifestyle magazine *Dim Sum* was launched; the Rainbow Action group called for same-sex marriage laws by protesting at the city's Catholic cathedral, and mainstream papers reported plans for the city's first major gay festival (tentatively set for November 2004). After pink businesses and university groups came out in support of the latter, the government, which only decriminalised homosexuality in 1991, said it would also offer its approval if organisers could demonstrate backing from commercial and tourist groups.

While these developments signal a more proactive effort to take gay issues into the public arena, there's still a long way to go before homosexual communities are widely accepted in Hong Kong. Although a network of bars, karaoke lounges, saunas and social groups has long catered to local gays and lesbians, the city's *tongzhi* (literally, 'comrades') have, in the past, generally kept to themselves and been reluctant to lobby for legislation that acknowledges and protects gay rights. Homosexuality remains a taboo in traditional Chinese society: sons and daughters are expected to marry and bear heirs, gay people are rarely 'out' in the workplace, and the confrontational nature of gay rights movements in the West is distinctly at odds with the Chinese value of social harmony.

The gay scene focuses on a half-dozen bars and clubs in and around Central and Tsim Sha Tsui, with more limited chance to meet in the karaoke lounges. Saturday night is the best time to hit the town, with punters following a well-worn party trail along Hollywood Road to three or four venues. Hong Kong's lesbian scene is not very visible and the few karaoke bars and cafés catering to women are all in Wan Chai.

## Clubs & bars

Unless otherwise stated, the places listed below generally cater to men.

### Club 97

*9 Lan Kwai Fong, Central, HK Island (2810 9333). Central MTR (exit D1, D2)/12M, 13, 23A, 40M bus.* **Open** 6pm-4am Fri. **Happy hour** 6-10pm. **Admission** free. **Credit** AmEx, MC, V. **Map** p308 C4.

This once-premier mixed nightspot is still the hang-out for many local stars and celebrities, but its recent makeover into a lounge bar has resulted in a more low-key venue. Every Friday evening, the suited gay brigade turns up for pre-dinner happy hour drinks. After 10pm, it reverts to a mixed venue (for further details, including full opening times, *see p216*).

### Curve

*2 Arbuthnot Road, Central (next to Centrium Tower), HK Island (2523 0998/www.curve.com.hk). Central MTR (exit D1, D2)/Mid-levels Escalator/ 13, 26, 40M bus.* **Open** 8pm-3am Mon-Thur, Sun; 8pm-5am Fri, Sat. **Happy hour** 8-10pm daily. **Admission** free Mon-Thur, Sun; HK$60 Fri, Sat. **Credit** AmEx, DC, MC, V. **Map** p308 C4.

Curve features a comfortable main lounge bar and a second downstairs bar and dance area. The main bar's camp interior of black leather sofas and padded walls is fun and faux chic and, despite the sophisticated additions of designer lighting and dramatic flower decorations, you get the feeling Austin Powers might suddenly make an appearance.

### New Wally Matt Lounge

*5A Humphreys Avenue, Tsim Sha Tsui, Kowloon (2721 2568). Tsim Sha Tsui MTR (exit A2)/ buses along Nathan Road.* **Open** 5pm-4am daily. **Admission** free. **Credit** MC, V. **Map** p313 C5.

Decked out like an old-style pub, with shields, battleaxes and some 1980s beefcake posters, this place attracts a clientele of middle-aged, burly *gweilo* guys and friendly younger locals. The ambience is pretty laid-back, if not subdued. For the other Wally Matt, *see p211*.

### Propaganda

*Lower G/F, 1 Hollywood Road, Central, HK Island (2868 1316). Central MTR (exit D1, D2)/Mid-Levels Escalator/12M, 13, 23A, 26, 40M bus.* **Open** 9pm-4am Tue-Thur; 9pm-5am Fri; 9pm-6am Sat. **Admission** free Tue-Thur; HK$80 Fri; HK$100-$160 Sat. **Credit** AmEx, DC, MC, V. **Map** p308 C3.

This is the only gay disco in town and it welcomes men and women. Given the hefty entry fees, the surliness of door staff and the often-monotonous music served up by the resident DJs, the local crowd has a love-hate relationship with Propaganda, but first-time visitors should be delighted by the fervour and pace on a Saturday night.

### Rainbow Bar

*14/F, Pearl Oriental Tower, 225 Nathan Road (entrance on Bowring Road), Jordan, Kowloon (2735 6882/http://go.to/rainbowhk). Jordan MTR (exit C1)/buses along Nathan Road.* **Open** 5pm-3am

**Club 97**.
*See p210.*

Mon-Thur, Sun; 5pm-5am Fri, Sat. **Admission** free.
**Credit** (over HK$200) DC, MC, V. **Map** p313 B5.
Billed as Hong Kong's only 'official chubbies bar',
Rainbow is a friendly karaoke bar that attracts both
chubbies and their admirers. Late Saturday
evenings can get quite wild as the disco and karaoke
singers compete with each other. Try to grab a table
in the corner for great views over Nathan Road and
across to Hong Kong Island. Rainbow also runs a
sauna in Yau Ma Tei; see the website for details.

### Rice
*33 Jervois Street (corner of Mercer Street),
Sheung Wan, HK Island (2851 4800). Sheung Wan
MTR (exit A2)/buses along Queen's Road Central.*
**Open** 7pm-1am Mon-Thur; 7pm-2am Fri; 8pm-3am
Sat; 5pm-1am Sun. **Happy hour** 7-9pm daily.
**Admission** free. **Credit** MC, V. **Map** p308 B2.
Out of the way in Sheung Wan, this intimate bar
features an interesting rice-themed retro interior and
a dazzling fish tank strategically placed at the
entrance to the loos. A good spot for a quiet drink.

### Tony's Bar
*G/F, 7-9 Bristol Avenue, Tsim Sha Tsui,
Kowloon (2723 2726/www.tonys-bar.com).
Tsim Sha Tsui MTR (exit D2)/buses along
Nathan Road.* **Open** 6pm-5am daily. **Happy hour**
6-10pm daily. **Admission** free. **Credit** MC, V.
**Map** p313 C6.
A new addition to the Tsim Sha Tsui scene, Tony's
is an unpretentious kind of place that attracts a local
crowd but also welcomes visitors. The bar's somewhat cold decor of black vinyl booths and cement
surfaces is softened by the camp addition of sequins
and beads draped over brightly lit lampshades.

### Wally Matt Bar & Lounge
*3 Granville Circuit, Tsim Sha Tsui, Kowloon
(2367 6874). Tsim Sha Tsui MTR (exit B2)/buses
along Chatham Road South.* **Open** 7pm-4am daily.
**Admission** free. **Credit** MC, V. **Map** p313 C5.
More a karaoke bar than a pub, the 'other' Wally
Matt bar (for the new Wally Matt, *see p210*) attracts
a young, local crowd. The bar's entrance is at the
end of an interesting little alley called Granville
Circuit, at the Chatham Road end of Granville Road.

### Works
*1/F, 30-32 Wyndham Street, Central, HK Island
(2868 6102). Central MTR (exit D1, D2)/13, 26,
40M bus.* **Open** 9pm-3am Mon, Sun; 7pm-1.30am
Tue-Thur; 7pm-2am Fri, Sat. **Admission** free Mon-
Thur, Sun; HK$60 Fri, Sat. **Credit** AmEx, DC, MC, V.
**Map** p308 C4.
This bar/club occupies the old Propaganda location
right on the five-way junction near Lan Kwai Fong
and the Fringe Club. The black interior barely
masks the ageing labyrinthine premises, which
attract a mix of ages and nationalities. Busiest on
Friday and Saturday nights at around 11pm.

## Karaoke lounges & cafés

For the adventurous and those seeking an
grass-roots experience, Hong Kong's karaoke
bars make for an interesting night out. There's
little to choose between them in terms of style
and ambience: there's usually a small centre
stage with a microphone for crooners, long
tables with groups playing dice games, and
the occasional beer hostess promoting cheap
drinks. *See also p152* **Look out Elvis...**

### Oasis
*14/F, Evernew House, 485 Lockhart Road,
Causeway Bay, HK Island (2575 8878). Causeway
Bay MTR (exit C)/buses & trams along Hennessy
Road.* **Open** 9pm-3am Mon-Thur, Sun; 9pm-5am Fri,
Sat. **Admission** HK$88 Mon-Thur, Sun; HK$138 Fri,
Sat. **No credit cards**. **Map** p311 D3.
A women-only karaoke 'members club', Oasis
charges an 'all you can drink' cover until 1am.
Karaoke, table dancing and dice games are free.

### Virus
*6/F, Allways Centre, 468 Jaffe Road, Causeway Bay,
HK Island (2904 7207). Causeway Bay MTR (exit
C)/buses & trams along Hennessy Road.* **Open** 9pm-
4am Thur; 9pm-5am Fri, Sat. **Admission** free Mon-
Fri; minimum spend HK$140 Sat. **No credit cards**.
**Map** p311 D3.
This karaoke bar caters mainly for lesbians, but their
gay male friends are also welcome. The noticeboard
outside has information on local groups and events.

**Arts & Entertainment**

Propaganda. *See p210.*

## Why Not Impossible

*12/F, Kyoto Plaza, 491-9 Lockhart Road, Causeway Bay, HK Island (2572 7808). Causeway Bay MTR (exit C)/buses & trams along Hennessy Road.* **Open** 9pm-4am daily. **Admission** free. **Credit** (over HK$200) AmEx, MC, V. **Map** p311 D3.

This sometimes raucous lounge has had its ups and downs. After midnight on Saturday, sentimental karaoke gives way to the fast-track Canto-pop. Opening times can be elastic, so call first.

## Sport & leisure facilities

### Saunas & gyms

For a place the size of Hong Kong, there are an impressive number of gay saunas. This is not surprising given that many local gay men live at home with their families – saunas provide a discreet venue for meeting up and relaxing, and end up functioning as de-facto living rooms.

Finding many of these saunas can be an adventure in itself and will take you on a fascinating trail of high-rise office towers, residential buildings and dubious-looking but harmless stairwells in old buildings.

For more venues, refer to *Dim Sum* magazine or the gay websites listed on page 214. The owners of the Rainbow Bar (*see p210*) also run a sauna.

### CE (Central Escalator)

*2/F, Cheung Hing Commercial Building, 37-43 Cochrane Street (entrance on Gage Street), Central, HK Island (2581 9951). Central MTR (exit D1/D2)/Mid-Levels Escalator/buses along Queen's Road Central.* **Open** 2-11pm daily. **Admission** HK$98. **Credit** AmEx, MC, V. **Map** p308 C3.

This tiny but popular sauna attracts a mix of local and overseas patrons. The entry fee includes a session in a massage chair and tanning bed. The entrance is next to the Dublin Jack pub.

## Chaps Fitness Centre

*G/F, 15 Ming Yuen Western Street, North Point, HK Island (2570 9339). North Point MTR (exit B1).* **Open** 3.30pm-midnight Mon-Thur; 2.30pm-1am Fri; 2.30pm-4am Sat; 2.30pm-midnight Sun. **Admission** HK$138. **No credit cards**.

Chaps is worth a visit thanks to its friendly staff and creative theme nights held throughout the week. Catering to the thirty- and fortysomething crowd and spread over two floors, it's camp and comfy, with a cosy Victorian-style reading room, a mirrored playroom and a Jacuzzi.

### Galaxy

*5/F, Harilela Mansion, 81 Nathan Road, Tsim Sha Tsui, Kowloon (2366 0629). Tsim Sha Tsui MTR (exit A1)/buses along Nathan Road.* **Open** 1pm-midnight daily. **Admission** $56. **No credit cards**. **Map** p313 B5.

Described by a resident wag as resembling a 'mainland hospital ward', Galaxy certainly doesn't win any points for decor. It is, however, a spacious, well-equipped sauna with a private room, three karaoke rooms and the largest dry sauna in the whole of Hong Kong.

### Game Boy

*2/F, Fook Yee Building, 324 Lockhart Road, Wan Chai, HK Island (2574 3215). Buses & trams along Hennessy Road.* **Open** 3pm-midnight daily. **Admission** HK$98. **No credit cards**. **Map** p310 C3.

A favourite spot for both locals and visitors, this place has a large video room with sofas and a cruisy but sociable central shower area.

### Prince House

*Postal address: Shop B, G/F, 9 Old Bailey Street, Central, HK Island (2810 0144/http://quickly. to/prince).* **Open** 4-11pm Mon-Thur, Sun; 4pm-3am Fri; 4pm-late Sat. **Admission** HK$65. **No credit cards**.

A tiny Japanese-style 'cruising den' devoted to rippling muscles and bulges, Prince attracts Central's weekend party crowd who are on their

way to or from the clubs along nearby Hollywood Road. To get here, disregard the postal address and instead go to Staunton Street via the Central Escalator, then turn left down the little alley just near the Eurotreat grocery store.

### QQ Fitness

*3/F King Dao Building, 14 Burrows Street, Wan Chai, HK Island (2834 0554/www.geocities.com/qqsauna). Wan Chai MTR (exit A3)/trams along Johnston Road.* **Open** noon-midnight Mon-Fri; 1pm-11am Sat; 1pm-1am Sun. **Admission** HK$48 before 3pm; HK$98 after 3pm. **No credit cards.** **Map** p310 C3/4.

Set over two levels and recently renovated, this homely place in Wan Chai is a hoot thanks to its karaoke machine, casual sitting room and endearingly cheeky owner. Saturday overnight sessions usually end with a big group cook-up, but it's also a prime lunchtime venue.

### Rome Club

*2/F, Chiap Lee Commercial Building, 27 Ashley Road, Tsim Sha Tsui, Kowloon (2376 0602). Tsim Sha Tsui MTR (exit A1)/buses along Nathan Road.* **Open** 3pm-midnight daily. **Admission** HK$98 HK$118. **No credit cards.** **Map** p313 B6.

Laid out over two floors, Rome Club is one of Hong Kong's longest established saunas, attracting a mix of locals and visitors in the 20-40 age group.

### Seasons Gym

*3/F, Asia Pacific Finance Tower, 3 Garden Road, Central, HK Island (2521 4541). Buses along Garden Road.* **Open** 6.30am-10.30pm Mon-Fri; 6.30am-9pm Sat; 10am-8pm Sun. **Admission** HK$200 before 5pm; HK$250 after 5pm. **Credit** AmEx, DC, MC, V. **Map** p309 E5.

Formerly going under the name of Tom Turk's, this centrally located gym attracts a sizeable gay clientele. It has recently been given a facelift and

# Splashing out

The territory has some excellent gay beaches. The official one is **Middle Bay Beach** (*see p83*) on South Bay Road. To get here, catch the 6, 6A, 6X or 260 bus, or a minibus at Tang Lung Street, Causeway Bay, to Repulse Bay Beach, then walk a short distance along South Bay Road to a long flight of narrow steps down to the beach.

**South Bay** (*see p83*), the next beach along from Middle Bay (and a ten-minute walk along South Bay Road) is mixed but very gay-friendly. It's a nicer beach than Middle Bay, with more shelter and better swimming.

On Lantau there's **Cheung Sha** beach (*see p115*), a lovely, relatively secluded sandy beach on the southern coast of the island. The gay section is located between the netted

areas of Upper and Lower Cheung Sha. To get there, take a bus from the Mui Wo Ferry Pier, get off at the Upper Cheung Sha beach bus stop and then walk back along the beach a couple of hundred metres toward Mui Wo.

Several of Hong Kong's pools attract a gay crowd too. These include **Kowloon Park Public Pool** (Tsim Sha Tsui MTR, exit A1; *see p240*); **Victoria Park Public Pool** (Tin Hau MTR, exit A2; *see p240*) and **Morrison Hill Public Pool** (Oi Kwan Road, Wan Chai, Bus 5, 5A, 10, or buses along Hennessy Road). Pools are generally open 6.30am-noon, 1-5pm and 6-10pm every day, but it's best to phone to check. Most are also closed some months for maintenance. Admission is normally around HK$20.

its indoor pool, large steam room and varied floor classes (yoga, Pilates, step and so on) are all newly sparkly and updated.

### We Club
*6/F, Richmond Plaza, 496 Jaffe Road, Causeway Bay, HK Island (2833 6677). Causeway Bay MTR (exit C)/buses & trams along Hennessy Road.* **Open** 3pm-1am Mon-Fri; 2pm-3am Sat; noon-midnight Sun. **Admission** HK$100 Mon-Fri; HK$120 Sat, Sun. **No credit cards. Map** p311 D3.
In new, larger premises that include a solarium (HK$80 a session) and pleasant sitting area, We Club has a modern, clean, well-run sauna. Tuesday, Wednesday and Thursday are nude nights.

## Massage

Chinese body massage is offered in many of Kowloon's older bathhouses. The following places cater to a 'gentlemen only' clientele.

### Shanghai Onsen
*3/F, Zhongdha Building, 38 Haiphong Road, Tsim Sha Tsui, Kowloon (2375 3861). Tsim Sha Tsui MTR (exit A1)/buses along Nathan Road.* **Open** noon-2am daily (last massages at midnight). **Credit** MC, V. **Map** p313 B5/6.
This friendly, clean and welcoming 'massage only' establishment offers excellent Shanghai-style massages by trained male masseurs from HK$260 for 45 minutes (including steam/sauna, soft drinks and snacks). Manicures, pedicures, back scrubs and foot massages are also available.

### Yuk Tak Bath House
*G/F, 123 Prince Edward Road, Mong Kok, Kowloon (2393 9505). Prince Edward MTR (exit C2).* **Open** noon-midnight daily. **Credit** MC, V. **Map** p312 B1.
Somewhat less salubrious than the Onsen, the Yuk Tak nonetheless offers good massages (from HK$223 for 45 minutes) in a friendly atmosphere. However, the downstairs bathhouse features 1950s decor and most staff speak minimal English.

## Festivals & events

In addition to the monthly Decadance Tea Dance, Hong Kong hosts a gay and lesbian film festival every autumn at the Hong Kong Arts Centre in Wan Chai. The programme covers local and international features, short films and documentaries. Screening times and further information are usually placed in the Arts Centre foyer (*see p226*) and in bars such as Works (*see p211*).

### Decadance Tea Dance
*Queen's Club, Theatre Lane, Central, HK Island (9679 1144/www.hxproduction.com). Central MTR (exit D2)/buses & trams through Central.* **Admission** HK$100 in advance; HK$150 on the door. **Date** 4-10pm 1st Sun of mth. **No credit cards. Map** p309 D3.

Hong Kong's first regular tea dance caters to the muscle crowd, who like to jam the dance floor in one sweaty, pulsating pack. The climax of the evening is a live show with buffed boys and a local diva. The website has details of ticket venues.

## Media

### Films

Several prominent Hong Kong filmmakers have told the stories of gay characters. Titles to look out for include Stanley Kwan's *Hold You Tight* (set and filmed during the uncertainty of 1997) and *Lan Yu* (2001; about a relationship between a Beijing businessman and a poor, first-time hustler). The ironically titled art house hit *Happy Together* won Wong Kai War the Best Director prize at Cannes in 1997 and tells the melancholic and wrenching story of two Chinese lovers in Argentina. Unashamedly melodramatic, *Bishonen* (1998), by writer-director Yonfan, is a stylish gay film, inspired by a real-life scandal in which photos of members of the Hong Kong police force were found in the home of a city patrician. By the same director, *Peony Pavilion* (2001) is a sumptuous period piece about a complex relationship between two women. *Banana Queers*, made in 2002, is a collection of award-winning shorts about Asian gays living in Western cultures. *Women's Private Parts* (2001), directed by Wong Chun-Chun, is a candid take on female sexuality and includes interviews with local lesbians.

### Magazines & websites

The new *Dim Sum* magazine is a bi-monthly, bilingual gay guide with features on visual arts, fashion, music and film, plus a good splash of gossip. The glossy pocket-sized mag includes a handy map siting venues, and can be picked up at most of the bars and saunas listed above.

An offshoot of the magazine is **DS Gallery**, Hong Kong's first gay gallery (3/F, Winning House, 26 Hollywood Road, Central, HK Island, www.dimsum-hk.com, closed Sun). The multimedia space is lit with pink neons and aims to mix art and design playfully with merchandise such as CDs.

Hong Kong's gay community frequently logs on to several excellent sites, in particular **http://sqzm14.ust.hk/hkgay**, a goldmine of information, and **www.gayhk.com**, with a guide to gay bars and saunas. International gay sites **Gaydar** (www.gaydar.co.uk) and **Gay.com** (www.gay.com) also have local chat rooms and personals sections. For **AIDS Concern**, *see p285*. For more general websites, some of which feature dedicated gay and lesbian sections, *see p295*.

# Nightlife

Dance on a table, sip Moët through a straw and dodge the gangsters on Hong Kong's crazy club scene.

## Clubs

As in many cities, the days of dance music mania and the mega-rave have declined in Hong Kong. During the past couple of years, most mass parties have been curtailed by a mixture of tough government licensing policies, high-profile drug busts, overcharging, changing fashions and feuding triad gangs. But all is not lost. Far from it. Top international DJs still regularly stop off here, and the trend for smaller clubs and DJ bars has created a more sophisticated and less trend-driven and drug-fuelled scene. Hong Kong does, however, remain a place where you can party till you drop: some clubs keep the music blasting full-throttle till 10am.

The city's club scene has been through turbulent times. Before 1997 it was dominated by a hard-core group of Westerners. Then dance music exploded among local Chinese, along with consumption of ecstasy (which translates into Chinese as 'head-shaking pill') and, more bizarrely, ketamine (a horse tranquillizer that reduces humans to piles of mush around the dancefloor). Raves with up to 8,000 mad-for-it clubbers took place almost every week, with actors, singers and billionaires' heirs among the throng, happily trashing their designer clothes and waving glo-sticks.

Soon, though, the triads wanted a piece of the lucrative action and vicious gang fights erupted near, and even inside, clubs. This, together with increasing drug use among young people, led to a government crackdown. Licences became harder to obtain and venues fewer. After a few famous singers and socialites were caught in possession of ecstasy the scene lost some of its lustre. Violence, bad drugs and police raids meant a dark mood pervaded and the fun was lost. One entrepreneur lost his shirt after opening the city's first superclub, in Chai Wan. Called Pink, it boasted a fantastic sound system, ultra-cool design and was a mini complex, but closed after just a handful of parties due to a lack of patrons. Promoters also suffered in the dance downturn, as fewer and fewer punters were prepared to cough up the required HK$500 or more to hear names at bigger venues.

In the meantime, some of the more canny promoters have switched to smaller, less-pricey parties (HK$200-$350 is now the norm), while still drawing top spin doctors, such as Sasha and Paul Oakenfold. A crop of talented local DJs has also emerged (*see p217* **Spin city**) and instead of trance the nightlife scene offers more variety: hip hop nights have proved successful and house has undergone a renaissance, especially with the sexy deep grooves suited to the city's swanky smaller clubs.

For the discerning clubber, these small clubs are by far the best bet. Places such as **Drop** (*see p218*), **C Club** (*see p216*) or **Nu** (*see p218*) in Central aren't cheap for drinks but they are well designed, have good sound systems and often bring in international DJs to complement the residents. There's a good mix of locals, expats and overseas Chinese. By far the best nights to go are Thursdays, Fridays and Saturdays.

Niche nights are held in small bars and clubs around town, with everything from drum'n'bass and indie music to dress-up parties and back-

The drink of choice at **Dragon-i**. *See p218.*

Arts & Entertainment

to-school discos. These are usually inexpensive and fun. Big parties are occasionally still held at HITEC (a warehouse-style exhibition centre in Kowloon Bay) if someone like Fatboy Slim comes to town, but these days most parties take place in existing clubs such as **Club ING** in Wan Chai (*see below*) or in spacious bars and restaurants converted for the evening.

## WHERE TO GO

These days it's **Central** that is the party hot spot. **Tsim Sha Tsui** and **Causeway Bay** have some huge clubs, but they are rarely frequented by Westerners and, while most folk are friendly, be sure to mind your manners; you don't want to upset any possible gang members. An argument with one person can lead to 30 waiting at the door for you when you leave. It's the same rule at any club, but don't worry, if you're not looking for trouble Hong Kong's bars and clubs are safer than those in most cities.

**Wan Chai** has many clubs, including Strawberries (*see p220*), La Bamba and Boracays, which open past dawn every day of the week. But consider yourself warned: many bars in the area have their own house bands playing Bontempi organs over records and are so high on the cringe factor that they go way beyond humorous. If you want a real club experience, you'd do best to avoid them.

And if you come to Hong Kong looking for Suzie Wong – the Wan Chai prostitute immortalised in Richard Mason's novel of the same name, you won't find her here. She and thousands like her are long gone. The district she once inhabited has changed dramatically in the past 40 years, and while pockets of sleaze still linger in the area, these girlie bars struggle to make a living (except when US navy war ships make port calls in Victoria Harbour).

The flesh pots are hard to miss. Walk along Lockhart Road near the Luard Road junction and you'll see young 'dancers' and their *mamasans* (Chinese women who act as pimps) standing under flashing neon, cajoling men inside. By all means go in and take a look – but beware: while the bars are no more risqué than those in any Asian city, naïve foreigners often start off buying a poledancer a drink, only to be confronted four hours later with a bill for HK$1,000. These aren't exactly places where you can haggle, remember.

## USEFUL INFORMATION

Details of events can be found in flyers around bars and clubs, in free local entertainment guides *HK Magazine* and *BC*, the *South China Morning Post's* listings section or the paid-for clubber's bible, *Absolute* magazine. The online guide hkclubbing.com is another invaluable resource, featuring details on international and local parties. Indeed, local DJ nights by crews such as the zany Robot team or breakbeat collective Erratica are often much more friendly and fun than bigger parties.

## C Club

*Basement, California Tower, 30-32 D'Aguilar Street, Central, HK Island (2526 1139). Central MTR (exit D1, G)/12M, 13, 23A, 40M bus.* **Open** 6pm-2am Mon-Thur; 6pm-4.30am Fri; 9pm-4.30am Sat. **Admission** free. **Credit** AmEx, DC, MC, V. **Map** p308 C4.
Undoubtedly the best club in the heaving Lan Kwai Fong entertainment district, C Club is sexy in both decor and sounds. The red velvet sofas and drapes are sumptuous to sink into and the dancefloor allows plenty of elbow room. The crowd is dominated by after work suits in the week and can be a bit posey, but the music is good and things tend to loosen up with a more fun crowd after 11pm. Drink prices aren't cheap, but if you want a livelier night than those on offer in the surrounding bars, it's worth paying the extra.

## Club ING

*4/F, Renaissance Harbour View Hotel, 1 Harbour Road, Wan Chai, HK Island (2836 3690). Wan Chai MTR (exit A1, C)/buses along Gloucester Road.* **Open** 9.30pm-5am Mon-Sat. **Admission** *Mon, Tue* free; *Wed* HK$100 (incl 1 drink); *Thur* HK$160 (free for women); *Fri, Sat* HK$100 (incl 1 drink). **Credit** AmEx, MC, V. **Map** p310 B2.
Ladies' night on Thursdays is one of the best times to see the beautiful set who throng here. The dancefloor is well trodden by Prada shoes, but while designer-clad and sophisticated, the crowd is fun-loving and full of twentysomethings. Musically, it runs the gamut from pop to house, via parties with visiting DJs and hip hop nights. The club has a strict anti-drugs policy, which has gone so far as to offer HK$1,000 rewards to customers who snitch on anyone suspected of using the toilet cubicles for anything other than their intended purpose.

## Club 97

*9 Lan Kwai Fong, Central, HK Island (2810 9333). Central MTR (exit D1, D2)/12M, 13, 23A, 40M bus.* **Open** 6pm-3am Mon-Thur; 6pm-4am Fri, Sat. **Admission** free. **Credit** AmEx, DC, MC, V. **Map** p308 C4.
Club 97 was the first club of its type in Central and after 20 years recently underwent a dramatic transformation. The front wall was knocked down and the dancefloor replaced with an 'island bar' surrounded by saddle-shaped stools and illuminated with candles. Leather and velvet sofas, and a surrealist banner artwork complete the transformation from club to lounge, although there is still room to dance to the jazzy house or Latin grooves from the resident DJ. The clientele is not as exclusive as in the '90s – when its door staff were famously tough – but Club 97 still attracts a chic crowd. For the gay happy 'hour' (6-10pm) on Friday nights, *see p210*.

# Spin city

Hong Kong has no shortage of homegrown and adopted DJ talent. Not only have many of the top mixmasters on the local scene played alongside big-name visitors, but some have even guested at top clubs in Europe, America and around Asia. Most famous of all the spin doctors is the pioneering **Joel Lai**, a former Club 97 (*see p216*) resident who now runs and occasionally spins his funky house at Drop (*see p218*) in Central and has a mix CD in the shops.

Young French-born DJ **Eric Byron** also has a CD out and plays uplifting sets in venues around town, among them Drop. Other DJs worth checking out include **DJ Tommy**, **DJ Galaxy**, **Ewan**, **Yeodie**, **Ladystar**, **Chris Sorenson**, **David Lam** and **Roy Malig**, as well as breakbeat champions **bodhi**, **akw** and **Dan Disuye**. Also try to catch **Steve Bruce** and **Simon Pang**, who can often be found playing alternative sounds – from mod to lounge – around the city.

In terms of age, the granddaddy of them all is **DJ Kulu** (*pictured*). In his early sixties and with a wispish white beard, he looks more like the stereotypical wise old Chinese man than top DJ, but he's undoubtedly the oldest swinger in town, playing acid jazz and funky sets right through till dawn at several clubs.

One of the best venues in town to spot talented turntablists scratching their stuff is Queen's (*see p218*) in Central, where they mix with local rappers such as **MC Yan**, of hip hop outfit LMF, and **Calvin Chiu**, who is not yet 20 but has but already performed with rap queen Missy Elliott in Singapore, after winning Hong Kong's 2003 MC Battle.

But without doubt the greatest inspiration to all Hong Kong DJs is **Lee Burridge**. Now ranked in the top 30 of *Mixmag*'s top 100 DJs, Burridge emerged from the fledgling club scene in Hong Kong in the early 1990s. He fine-tuned his sets during 12-hour marathon spinning sessions at Wan Chai's hedonistic and seemingly never-ending club nights, which ran until noon on Sundays at the Big Apple (now Boracays) and Neptunes (now closed). Those days are long gone, but not before Burridge played support to Sasha and Craig Richards at a rave. The pair were wowed by Burridge's mixing and ability to work the crowd, so they encouraged him to up decks back to his native Britain, where they jointly set up the Tyrant club night and brand.

Burridge went from strength to strength, but he attributes much of his success to those heady nights in Hong Kong. His 'local boy made good' story reveals the city to be anything but a clubbing backwater, so dive into the local clubs and listen for yourself.

And if these DJs inspire you and you'd like to learn the tricks of the trade, why not brush up on your mixing skills at the city's DJ training centre, in Kwai Chung. Boasting state-of-the-art facilities and sound-proofed studios, the centre runs short courses for HK$250 an hour, and 16-hour courses for HK$3,000, which includes six hours of lectures. For more information call 2763 1801 or go to www.hongkongdjschool.com.

Arts & Entertainment

## Dragon-i

*1/F, The Centrium, 60 Wyndham Street, Central,
HK Island (3110 1222). Central MTR (exit D1, D2)/
12M, 13, 23A, 40M bus.* **Open** noon-2pm, 6pm-2am
Mon-Thur; 6pm-4am Fri, Sat. **Admission** free.
**Credit** AmEx, DC, MC, V. **Map** p308 C4.

This celebrity hangout, a restaurant-cum-bar-cum-
nightclub, counts film stars Jackie Chan and Zhang
Ziyi among its customers, as well as the city's
wealthiest hipsters. Add to the roster various visitors from overseas, from David Beckham to Macy
Gray, who all drop in to use its private rooms, and
you get the picture. It's the kind of place where you
sip champagne through a straw before dancing in
your Manolos. The brainchild of bleached-blond
party impresario Gilbert Yeung, Dragon-i was
designed by chic international designer India
Mahdavi, and features giant birdcages on the
terrace in keeping with its Chinese theme. Food is
Japanese and old-school Chinese. Expensive but
worth it if celeb-spotting is your favourite pastime.

## Drop

*B/F, On Lok Mansion, 39-43 Hollywood Road,
Central, HK Island (2543 8856/www.drophk.com).
Central MTR (exit D1, D2)/Mid-Levels Escalator/
12M, 13, 23A, 26, 40M bus.* **Open** 7pm-late Mon-
Fri; 9pm-6am Sat. **Admission** free unless there's an
event (Fri, Sat mostly members only). **Credit** AmEx,
MC, V. **Map** p308 B/C3.

This tucked-away club has established a loyal
clientele in the past three years, and for good reason
– it's cool, funky and fun. The watermelon martinis
are fab and, together with the uplifting music policy and swish decor, have kept the club cognoscenti
purring with delight. The atmosphere is friendly and
there's a good crowd most nights of the week, plus
regular visits by DJs from London and New York,
who lay down laid-back and sexy grooves.

## Fly

*1/F, 23-7 Lyndhurst Terrace, Central, HK Island
(2851 9298). Central MTR (exit D1, D2, G)/Mid-
Levels Escalator/12M, 13, 23A, 26, 40M bus.* **Open**
6pm-late Mon-Thur; 6pm-5am Fri, Sat. **Admission**
free. **Credit** AmEx, MC, V. **Map** p308 C3.

The entrance to this chic spot for overseas-raised
Chinese and wealthy locals is easy to miss, a small
door in the middle of a row of shops. Inside, it looks
like four flats converted into a club, which is what
it basically is. It's always crowded, if a little pretentious, and drink prices aren't cheap, but it's a good
place to network and mingle with the cool crowd
grooving to hip hop and R&B.

## Green Spot

*1/F, 1 Wong Nai Chung Road, Happy Valley, HK
Island (no phone). Tram to Happy Valley/5A, 117
bus.* **Open** 6.30pm-3am Mon-Thur, Sun; 6.30pm-4am
Fri, Sat. **Admission** free. **Credit** AmEx, DC, MC, V.
**Map** p311 D4.

Happy Valley's most happening nightspot is a magnet for models, jockeys, minor celebs and hangers-
on. If you want to fit in you'll have to slip your
designer togs on and glam up, as Green Spot is
all about how you look and what you wear. The
high-rollers slide in after meetings at the nearby
racetrack but usually book a private room to ensure
they're not mingling with the riff raff. Pricey, but an
interesting glimpse of the showbiz scene.

## Home

*2/F, 23 Hollywood Road, Central, HK Island (2545
0023). Central MTR (exit D1, D2, G)/Mid-Levels
Escalator/12M, 13, 23A, 26, 40M bus.* **Open** 10pm-
3am Tue-Thur; 10pm-8am Fri, Sat. **Admission** free.
**Credit** AmEx, MC, V. **Map** p308 C3.

Just as everywhere else in Central is closing its doors,
this place is filling up. Running until at least 8am on
weekends, Home is the place for those with no home
to go to – or who simply wish to keep the night going.
It's popular with gay clubbers, so the vibe is energetic
– even more so considering most of the people here
have been partying all night. The music is soulful
(there's no trance), while the large chill-out area at the
back features a giant bed for clubbers to sprawl over.

## Nu

*G/F, 1-5 Elgin Street, Central, HK Island (2549
8386). Central MTR (exit D1, D2, G)/Mid-Levels
Escalator/23A, 26, 40M bus.* **Open** 5pm-late daily.
**Admission** varies. **Credit** AmEx, DC, MC, V.
**Map** p308 B3/4.

This is a split-level club, with a relaxing lounge vibe
upstairs and a thumping club below. Nu replaced the
good, but ailing Liquid, which ran for two years on
the same premises. With the changeover, the decor
has been revamped, with green walls, loungey sofas
and chrome and glass interiors, but the Star Trek-
style soundproof double-door entrance still beams
clubbers in. The crowd of discerning clubbers aged
20-35 is a mix of expats and locals, attracted by the
club's large roster of good local DJs and international guests. Weekends are the best time to come, but it's
good for a quiet drink and dance any weeknight too.

## Pebbles

*G/F, 75 Wyndham Street, Central, HK Island (2522
2628). Central MTR (exit D1, D2, G)/Mid-Levels
Escalator/12M, 23A, 26, 40M bus.* **Open** 5pm-late
Mon-Sat. **Admission** free. **Credit** AmEx, DC, MC,
V. **Map** p308 C4.

Glass-fronted and with chrome fittings and high
stools, Pebbles is typical of Hong Kong's recent rash
of DJ bars. Guest local DJs spin different sounds
through the week, although the decibel levels in this
small space make talking difficult. It attracts a
mixed young crowd either to just drink or dance
(when there's enough room). All in all, a good place
to spend an hour rather than a whole evening.

## Queen's

*1/F, Queen's Theatre, Theatre Lane, Central, HK
Island (2522 7773). Central MTR (exit D2)/buses
along Queen's Road Central.* **Open** 5pm-3am Mon-
Thur, Sun; 5pm-5am Fri, Sat. **Admission** HK$100
(incl 1 drink); women free. **Credit** DC, MC, V.
**Map** p309 D3.

Ladies' night (and a few imposters) at **Club ING**. *See p216*.

This cavernous club occupies the former Queen's Theatre in Central and fully exploits its high ceilings and elevated stage, from which DJs spin hard and fast dance music. The music can be a little too heavy on the progressive and trance for some tastes, and some of the punters look decidedly dodgy, but it's a good venue and the largest club in Central. Well worth a peek for those who prefer something a little more raw than the slick clubs that abound in the area.

### Strawberries

*48 Hennessy Road, Wan Chai, HK Island (2866 1031). Wan Chai MTR (exit B1)/buses along Hennessy Road.* **Open** varies. **Admission** free. **No credit cards. Map** p310 B3.

This is the last club to close its doors each morning in Wan Chai – usually around 9am. Cheesy music (think the tackiest disco mix of already-tacky songs), drunken suits, after-hours hostesses and not-to-be-stared-at punters make this a club of last resort, and yet, strangely, it can be fun – provided you've had a skinful, that is. They even serve breakfast, if you can handle it. Note that you might get charged an entry fee if they don't like the look of you.

### Yumla

*Lower Basement, Harilela House, 79 Wyndham Street, Central, HK Island (2174 2382). Central MTR (exit D1, G)/12M, 13, 23A, 26, 40M bus.* **Open** 6pm-5am Mon-Sat. **Admission** free. **Credit** AmEx, MC, V. **Map** p308 C4.

This great club (which means 'drinking' in Chinese) is tucked away on the right a few steps down cobbled Pottinger Street from Wyndham Street. It's small but offers great music and a friendly vibe. Local DJs play here most nights of the week, with regular breakbeat parties. Expect a good mixed crowd of local and expat clubbers aged 20 to 35.

## Live music

Despite pitching itself as 'the events capital of Asia', Hong Kong has long been a non-event in terms of international music action. It was so far off the map that the annual visit of Air Supply was one of the highlights. Thankfully, things have changed for the better in recent times. From edgy acts like the Chemical Brothers and Primal Scream to superbands like the Rolling Stones, and relative newcomer Norah Jones, the city is now proving a popular stop-off en route to Australia, Japan or, increasingly, China.

The downside is that available venues are not really up to scratch, with poor acoustics, insufficient facilities and inexperienced security staff. Ticket prices are also high, often reaching $1,000 for a seat close to the stage. But having the option is better than no choice at all.

Sadly, following a litany of cock-ups, the city also has a laughable reputation among music promoters and rock stars. Concerts are banned at the 40,000-seater Hong Kong Stadium

because noise levels would be too high for nearby residents – at one gig, audience members were given gloves to soften the sound of their clapping. But October 2003 was a watershed month. A four-week festival backed by $100 million of the government's money brought such acts such as Westlife, Santana, José Carreras, the Rolling Stones, Prince and Neil Young to a temporary stage at the Harbourfront Tamar Site in Admiralty. The event was marred by controversy over alleged inept organisation, overpricing and ticket fiascos, plus a host of other problems, which means it might not happen again, but local promoters hope that the tide has turned and that rock concerts may get support in the future. Also in October, a two-day Rockit festival similar to Japan's successful Fuji Rock Festival attracted 8,000 people to Victoria Park to hear more than 20 local and international acts. Organisers are aiming to make it an annual event.

Months can go by, however, without a decent concert – unless you want to sample some sugary Canto-pop, but a local indie scene does exist – just about. Guitarist singer Paul Wong, formerly of pop rock band Beyond, leads the pack. Others to watch out for are the Pancakes, an innovative female solo act that has landed a record deal in, for some reason, Spain, and electronic duo Slow Tech Riddim.

There are also plenty of student bands and quite a few expat rockers who play local music bars like the **Wanch** (*see p224*) and **Carnegie's** (*see p221*). Several young bands are emerging with enough talent to support international acts. Look out for Uncle Joe, King Ly Chee and From Whence He Came.

Besides Canto-pop, locals tend to be heavily into J-Pop from Japan, K-Pop from Korea and Mando-pop from mainland China. The international charts are packed with Western boy and girl band pap – which is also played in heavy rotation on Asia's two satellite music channels, MTV and Channel [V].

Jazz buffs have had a disastrous couple of years. Several of the city's full-time jazz clubs have closed down, while international acts are fewer, although some big names such as Herbie Hancock have played City Hall as part of the government-sponsored Jazz Up series that runs throughout the year. There is also a plethora of local talent here worth seeing: watch out for gigs by singer and guitarist Eugene Pao, local chanteuse Elaine Liu, trumpeter Mark Henderson – who plays music in the style of the classic 1950s and '60s Blue Note sound – along with guitarists Guy Le Claire and William Tang, and pianist Allen Youngblood. Folk fans can look forward to an annual festival late in the year.

Hotel bands may not sound like much of an option, but some who drop into town are very talented and provide an entertaining night out. Check out **Talk of the Town** (or ToTT's) at the Excelsior and **Cyrano** at the Island Shangri-La (for both, *see p224*). Visiting bands from Cuba and South America or the Caribbean have been known to have even the most supine onlookers up and dancing. Good bands can also be found at the **Music Room – Live** and the **Edge** in Central (for both, *see p222*). More down-at-heel, but offering straight-up fun, are the cover bands who ply some of the packed music bars around town, such as **Insomnia** and **Dusk Till Dawn** (for both, *see p222*), which keep rocking till after 5pm. They're not the classiest places, but if it's good old-fashioned fun and a boogie you want, you'll find it here.

## Major venues

For the following venues, tickets are available through either **URBTIX** (2734 9009, www.urbtix.gov.hk) or **HK Ticketing** (3128 8288, www.hkticketing.com).

### Hong Kong Coliseum

*9 Cheong Wan Road, Hung Hom, Kowloon (2355 7234). Kowloon KCR/101, 104, 110 bus.* **Box office** bookings through URBTIX. **Admission** ticket prices vary. **Credit** AmEx, MC, V. **Map** p313 D4/5.
The glory days of the Coliseum are now over. This 12,500-seat venue is a bit dilapidated, which is a shame as it's still a good place to see major acts – unless you're stuck up in the clouds. Canto-pop stars still perform long runs here, but international acts are laid on mostly at the more accessible Convention & Exhibition Centre (*see p226*). Still, Deep Purple and Santana have played the Coliseum. A further bonus is that you can even get out of your seat and dance if you want, which is not the case everywhere in HK.

### Hong Kong Convention & Exhibition Centre

*1 Harbour Road, Wan Chai, HK Island (2582 8888). Wan Chai MTR (exit A1)/buses along Gloucester Road/Wan Chai Star Ferry Pier.* **Box office** bookings through HK Ticketing. **Admission** ticket prices vary. **Credit** V. **Map** p310 B2.
The largest hall of the HKCEC is now the most popular venue for laying on big acts, and has hosted everyone from Oasis to Ibrahim Ferrer. Unfortunately, that doesn't mean it's a good place for a rock concert. It has been plagued by problems, most notably poor acoustics and crowd chaos. People don't know whether to sit or stand – and security often has little control. Instead of fixed seating, there are portable plastic chairs and as these are mostly laid out on the same level it is difficult to see the stage in the premium seats a few rows back. The owners say they are sorting out the problems, so time will tell whether this can evolve into a good

venue. Ticket prices for concerts here lean toward the high side. All in all, its main advantage is that it is easy to get to.

### Ko Shan Theatre

*Ko Shan Park, 77 Ko Shan Road. Hung Hom, Kowloon (2740 9222/2330 5661). Bus 111, 101, 107, 116.* **Box office** ticket prices vary. **Credit** AmEx, MC, V. **Map** p312 E3.
This 1,000-seat theatre has proved popular with indie bands who can't fill a bigger venue. Since air-con was installed in 1996, concerts have become bearable and improvements to stage, sound and lighting mean good shows can be put on here. Like the Coliseum, though, it is not the easiest place to get to.

### Queen Elizabeth Stadium

*18 Oi Kwan Road, Wan Chai, HK Island (2591 1346). Bus 5A, 10/buses along Hennessy Road.* **Box office** bookings through URBTIX. **Admission** ticket prices vary. **Credit** AmEx, MC, V. **Map** p310 C4.
British popsters Suede like this venue so much they played it three times, but such acts are few and far between. With 3,500 seats, it's good for bands who have sizeable, rather than huge, followings. There's no moshpit and over-zealous security staff often shine torches in the face of anyone who dares to stand up and dance.

## Other rock venues

### Carnegie's

*53-5 Lockhart Road, Wan Chai, HK Island (2866 6289). Wan Chai MTR (exit C)/buses along Hennessy Road.* **Open** 11am-very late daily. **Credit** AmEx, DC, MC, V. **Map** p310 B3.
Nine years is a long time in the HK nightlife scene and yet Carnegie's shows no sign of slowing down. A small stage and cramped space doesn't stop this place rocking most nights. If there's no band, a DJ cranks things up and revellers take to dancing on the bar. Sadly, the second-floor loft – a good vantage point from which to watch the madness – had to be removed in 2003 by order of killjoy officials.

### Chasers

*2 Carlton Building, Knutsford Terrace, Tsim Sha Tsui, Kowloon (2367 9487). Tsim Sha Tsui MTR (exit B2)/buses along Nathan Road or Chatham Road South.* **Open** 3pm-5am Mon-Fri; noon-5am Sat, Sun. **Admission** free. **Credit** AmEx, DC, MC, V. **Map** p313 C5.
This old-fashioned get-down-and-boogie joint hosts cover bands – mostly from the Philippines – playing old and new hits by mainstream acts. Some are surprisingly good, but all become better as the night grows old and more ale is sunk. Bands rotate between Chasers, Dusk Till Dawn and Insomnia, ensuring that all the venues have live sounds every night. The musical style depends on what band you get, but it's all covers. On the downside, all three venues are rowdy and have reputations for being meat markets.

Arts & Entertainment

## Dusk Till Dawn

*76 Jaffe Road, Wan Chai, HK Island (2528 4689).
Wan Chai MTR (exit A1, C)/buses along Gloucester
Road or Hennessy Road.* **Open** noon-around 6am
daily. **Admission** free. **Credit** AmEx, MC, V.
**Map** p310 B3.
*See p221* **Chasers**.

## The Edge

*G/F, The Centrium, 60 Wyndham Street, Central,
HK Island (2523 6690). Central MTR (exit D1, D2)/
23A, 26, 40M bus.* **Open** 6pm-around 4am daily.
**Admission** free. **Credit** DC, MC, V. **Map** p308 C4.
New and noted by the fun-loving crowd, this is a
more upmarket live music venue. Its interior glows
with red lighting and furnishings, while the dancefloor moves to the beat of the talented house band,
which plays both covers and original material. DJs
fill in the breaks between sets and special parties are
occasionally laid on. Ever since Prince played an
after party here, the Edge has moved towards the
centre of the live scene.

## Fringe Club

*2 Lower Albert Road, Central, HK Island (2521
7485). Central MTR (exit D1)/23A bus.* **Open** noon-
midnight Mon-Thur; noon-2am Fri, Sat. **Admission**
usually free. **Credit** AmEx, MC, V. **Map** p308 C4.
Fringe's Nokia Gallery is a reliable space that has
long served aspiring homegrown musical talent.
The venue helped launch the career of successful

local chanteuse Susie Wilkins, and hosts everything
from rock bands to the Saturday Night Jazz
Orchestra, a local collective of Japanese businessmen playing swing. The beer is cheap, and the venue
provides a real pub gig atmosphere that is otherwise
hard to find in Hong Kong. There is normally live
music on Friday and Saturday nights, but it's wise
to phone ahead to check what's on. *See also p66,
p125 and p226.*

## Insomnia

*38-44 D'Aguilar Street, Central, HK Island (2525
0957). Central MTR (exit D1, D2, G)/12M, 13, 23A,
40M bus.* **Open** 8am-6am daily. **Admission** free.
**Credit** AmEx, DC, MC, V. **Map** p308 C4.
*See p221* **Chasers**.

## Music Room – Live

*2/F, California Entertainment Building, 34-6
D'Aguilar Street, Central, HK Island (2845 8477).
Central MTR (exit D1, D2)/23A, 40M bus.* **Open**
6pm-2am Mon-Sat. **Admission** free. **Credit** AmEx,
DC, MC, V. **Map** p308 C4.
Occupying the former Jazz and Blues Club, the
Music Room has a more eclectic offering, from rock
and pop to Cuban to Congo. Besides a house band,
international guests also regularly drop in. The
crescent-shaped lounge surrounding the dancefloor
means you can enjoy the music whether sitting or
shaking, while the Velvet Lounge offers a more
relaxed ambience.

Live life on the **Edge**.

# Canto-pop

For the past quarter of a century, music lovers in Hong Kong have chosen to create their own superstars, rather than adopting those of the West. The genre spawned is called Canto-pop (though some label it Canto-pap). Michael Jackson, while popular, could never match the popularity of idols such as Jackie Cheung and Leon Lai here. Nor could Barry Manilow. Though judging by the clean-cut Canto-pop stars churning out soppy love songs, he would have been embraced if he had been born Chinese.

Until recently, while the names of the idols changed over the years, the content always remained pretty much the same. Then, rival idols like Aaron Kwok and Nicholas Tse began to introduce outrageous costumes and wild behaviour on stage in a belated attempt to stand out from the Canto-crowd. It certainly didn't harm sales: their records continued to shift by the shedload.

Canto-pop came about by serendipity. In the early 1960s Hong Kong was dominated by sentimental Mandarin love songs from mainland China and western pop tunes. Then, as TV sets started popping up in every home, the theme songs to Cantonese dramas unexpectedly became hits, the most famous of which was the theme to *Mad Tides* sung by Roman Tam. As a result, popular local bands like Wynners made the switch from performing English songs to Canto-pop.

Still, it took until 1976 for the genre to become entrenched. Sam Hui's theme song to the film *The Private Eyes* was the catalyst. Suddenly, Canto-pop became the voice of Hong Kong. Featuring the extensive use of slang, Hui's songs were popular because they related to people's feelings and concerns, from love life woes to the concern over rising oil prices.

In the early 1980s patriotic songs to the motherland appeared, and in the early 1990s, when Hong Kong was concerned about the upcoming Handover in 1997, Law Tai-yau made *Queen's Road East*, a humorous, melodic song hinting at the changes to come. But such political posturing is rare.

In the mid 1980s, with growing affluence in Hong Kong, style and personality won out over lyrical content. Although Hui continued to sing about topical issues, such as the local craze for doll-like Japanese girls, other stars played safe and sang Cantonese versions of Western and Japanese classics and hits. Megastars of this genre in the 1980s included Alan Tam, Leslie Cheung (also a highly regarded actor) and Anita Mui, followed in the 1990s by Jackie Cheung, Andy Lau, Leon Lai and Aaron Kwok.

Not only did Canto-pop lack imagination, it also became highly commercialised, as in the West. Instead of bothering with the music, stars began to focus their attentions on their face, hair and clothes. Along with songs about love, unrequited affection and heartbreak, it was all part of a policy to target the youth market. Commercially, it worked.

At the start of the 1990s, Jackie Cheung, Andy Lau, Leon Lai and Aaron Kwok were declared Canto-pop's 'Four Heavenly Kings' by the media. All were squeaky clean, lacked charisma and, by the standards of some Western pop idols, were decidedly boring. Nonetheless, the four 'Kings' were the focus of screaming, obsessive teenage fans, most of whom were girls. Though still well known, the four have more recently been overtaken in popularity by newer names such as Beijing-born singing queen Faye Wong (known for her wild, rebellious look, with tattered clothes and spiky hair), Nicholas Tse (said to be Wong's on-off boyfriend), Joey Yung and Edison Chan Kwun-hei.

As with Western pop stars, local celebrities have started to find themselves at the centre of the odd scandal or two. In 2000, Wynners frontman Alan Tam was accused of having a mistress and love child, while in October 2002 Nicholas Tse was convicted of allowing his chauffeur to claim he was behind the wheel when Tse's Ferrari was involved in an accident. Tse was sentenced to 240 hours of community service, which many people believed too lenient.

But the past few years have been especially sad for canto-pop, with the death of several highly worshipped stars: in October 2002 Roman Tam died of cancer at the age of 52; in April 2003 46-year-old Leslie Cheung committed suicide by jumping from the 24th floor of an upmarket hotel in Central, and in December 2003 Anita Mui died of cancer, aged 40. Newer faces will no doubt continue to crop up, but fans say the golden era has passed, and that the genre will never be the same again.

**Arts & Entertainment**

## Pit Stop

*Harbour Plaza Hotel, 20 Tak Fung Street, Hung Hom, Kowloon (2621 3188/2996 8455). Kowloon KCR/101, 104, 110 bus.* **Open** noon-1am Mon-Thur, Sun; noon-2am Fri, Sat. **Admission** free. **Credit** AmEx, DC, MC, V.

A better-than-average hotel live music joint, the Pit Stop offers a good selection of bands who are capable of performing their own songs as well as the usual covers. Car-racing buffs will dig the decor, which is themed around the world of motorsports.

## Venue

*G/F, 15-19 Luard Road, Wan Chai, HK Island (3105 8990). Wan Chai MTR (exit A1, C)/buses along Gloucester Road or Hennessy Road.* **Open** 5pm-3am Mon-Thur; 5pm-5am Fri, Sat. **Admission** free. **Credit** AmEx, DC, MC, V. **Map** p310 B3.

A flash-looking bar with a small stage, Venue purports to offer an upmarket spot to hear cover bands and sip cocktails or beers. For all the bright lights and chrome fittings, in reality the place has much in common with Wan Chai's more down-at-heel live music joints, but the atmosphere is a little more sophisticated – you won't find people dancing on the bar here.

## The Wanch

*54 Jaffe Road, Wan Chai, HK Island (2861 1621). Wan Chai MTR (exit A1, C)/buses along Gloucester Road or Hennessy Road.* **Open** 11am-2am daily. **Admission** free. **Credit** DC, MC, V. **Map** p310 B3.

Hong Kong's very own Tardis. The Wanch doesn't look much bigger than a phone kiosk, but it manages to squeeze in a band and plenty of punters most nights. Perhaps the city's most famous pub gig venue, it has hosted the debuts of many indie and folk bands who went on to become local fixtures. And it's still going strong.

## Jazz & blues bars

See also p222 **Fringe Club**.

## Blue Door

*5/F, 37 Cochrane Street, Central, HK Island (2858 6555/www.yellowdoorkitchen.com.hk). Central MTR (exit D2).* **Open** 10.30pm-2am Sat. **Admission** varies. **No credit cards**. **Map** p308 C3.

A real jazz and blues den tucked away inside a commercial building, the Blue Door plays host to local and, occasionally, visiting musicians. It provides aficionados with the only weekend hangout to offer a wide range of jazz. All the best local musicians perform here, perhaps because it's small and smoky.

## Ned Kelly's Last Stand

*11A Ashley Road, Tsim Sha Tsui, Kowloon (2376 0562). Tsim Sha Tsui MTR (exit A1, C1)/Tsim Sha Tsui Star Ferry Pier.* **Open** 11.30am-2am daily. **Admission** free. **Credit** MC, V. **Map** p313 B6.

Kelly's Gang brings the sound of Dixieland to Hong Kong every night. The decor is showing signs of age, but it's a friendly pub. And, despite its name, it pulls in expats and younger Chinese as well as Aussies.

## Hotel lounge bars

## Captain's Bar

*Mandarin Oriental Hotel, 5 Connaught Road, Central, HK Island (2522 0111). Central MTR (exit F, H)/buses to Central Star Ferry Pier/Central Star Ferry Pier.* **Open** noon-midnight daily. **Admission** free. **Credit** AmEx, DC, MC, V. **Map** p309 E3.

A great place to relax before or after dinner. Its comfortable yet opulent interior gives way to some down-at-the-heel hip shaking when the resident band runs through jazz standards, or ups the tempo with pop and R&B.

## Cyrano

*56/F, Island Shangri-La Hotel, Pacific Place, 88 Queensway, Admiralty, HK Island (2877 3838). Admiralty MTR (exit C1)/buses along Queensway.* **Open** 5pm-1am daily. **Admission** free. **Credit** AmEx, DC, MC, V. **Map** p309 F5.

The magnificent view alone is worth an evening at Cyrano over wine or cocktails, but throw in the always-excellent band playing jazz and Latin and it has all the ingredients for a great night on – or rather above – the town.

## Eyes

*1/F, Miramar Hotel, 118-130 Nathan Road, Tsim Sha Tsui, Kowloon (2315 5888). Tsim Sha Tsui MTR (exit B)/buses along Nathan Road.* **Open** 5pm-2am daily. **Admission** free. **Credit** AmEx, DC, MC, V. **Map** p313 C5.

Eyes is great if you want to take a peek at the Chinese letting their hair down. Here, expats mingle with locals and visiting business folk from Taiwan and the mainland in a lively setting. There's always entertainment, but if you're here when cabaret act Danny Diaz is in town you're in for a treat of musical impersonations and interpretations, plus plenty of Bob Hope-style comic banter.

## Lobby Lounge

*Kowloon Shangri-La Hotel, 64 Mody Road, Tsim Sha Tsui, Kowloon (2721 2111). Tsim Sha Tsui MTR (exit C1)/203, 973 bus/buses along Chatham Road South & Salisbury Road.* **Open** 9am-midnight daily. **Admission** free. **Credit** AmEx, DC, MC, V. **Map** p313 C6.

Another sumptuous setting, with a decent resident singer to provide background entertainment while you drink or eat.

## ToTT's Asian Grill & Bar

*Excelsior Hotel, 281 Gloucester Road, Causeway Bay (2837 6780/www.mandarin-oriental.com/excelsior). Causeway Bay MTR (exit D1)/buses along Gloucester Road.* **Open** 5-11.30pm Mon-Thur; 5pm-1.30am Fri, Sat. **Admission** free. **Credit** AmEx, DC, MC, V. **Map** p311 E2.

This restaurant-bar-nightclub offers great views, fusion food and fancy cocktails, plus music from a house band or DJ, who manage to get the dance-floor heaving most nights. It's popular with a mix of local and expat residents.

# Performing Arts

Under-appreciated it may be, but Hong Kong's culturally diverse arts scene offers plenty of surprises.

Hong Kong is not a place that one immediately associates with the performing arts. Since colonial days, Western sophisticates have lampooned the cultural crassness of the city's bankers and the philistine pursuits of its Mammon-worshipping property tycoons. Even closer to home, Beijing's intelligentsia has long derided the Hong Kong arts scene and still frequently pokes fun at the territory's popular cultural diet of horse-racing and endless Canto-pop.

At first glance, these stereotypes seem to have some credence. Hong Kong is better known for exporting action film stars than writers, dancers or orchestras; and while lion dance troupes and Cantonese operas are admired for their colour and zest, many visitors would cite the territory's shopping or dining, rather than its performing arts, as its chief tourist attraction.

Hong Kong's performance spaces also fail to suggest a dynamic cultural landscape. Increasingly dated and self-conscious, these venues are no more than functional at best, and far from captivating. Banks, rather than concert halls or theatres, are the city's architectural showpieces, and there is no arts centre or civic building with the cultural promise of, say, the Sydney Opera House or New York's Lincoln Centre.

However, like most things in Hong Kong, appearances can be deceptive. Perhaps overwhelmed by the consumer madness and garish physical density of the city, short-term foreign visitors sometimes fail to grasp the rich and complex cultural ambiguities that lie at the heart of the city. As in Venice or Istanbul – other places where East meets West – Hong Kong has always been an exciting junction of cultures. Resident composers, writers, musicians and dancers have long drawn inspiration from this hybridity and are creating an increasing range of original and unique local compositions. In addition, a number of popular, dedicated and well-funded local performing arts companies – including the **Hong Kong Philharmonic Orchestra**, the **Hong Kong Chinese Orchestra** and the **Hong Kong Ballet** – testify to the city's eclectic cultural tastes.

## TICKETS AND INFORMATION

Tickets for most performances around town can be obtained from **URBTIX**, a ticket agency run by the Hong Kong Government Leisure & Cultural Services Department. For general information on performances and reservations call them on 2734 9009 (10am-8pm daily), or log on to www.urbtix.gov.hk. You can buy tickets over the counter at an URBTIX outlet, or make advanced telephone bookings by providing an ID or passport number (no credit card required). URBTIX has outlets at the Hong Kong Cultural Centre, Hong Kong City Hall (for both, *see p226*), the Hong Kong Academy for Performing Arts (*see below*) and at the New Territories venues listed on page 228.

A local company, **HK Ticketing** (3128 8288, www.hkticketing.com), recently took over the operations of the Ticketek agency and runs several ticket outlets around Hong Kong, including booths in the Hong Kong Arts Centre, branches of the Tom Lee Music Company, and the Fringe Club (*see p226*). The latter is also a good place for information about the city's fringe theatre, folk music, cabaret and poetry performance scenes.

The weekly *HK Magazine* and monthly *BC Magazine* (for both, *see p287*) also provide listings of performances and lectures. The Performing Arts page of the Hong Kong Government Leisure & Cultural Services Department website (www.lcsd.gov.hk) is another useful source of information. The bilingual classical radio station Radio 4 (FM stereo 97.6-98.9) previews arts events during its Thursday evening Artbeat programme (7-8pm).

## Major venues

### Hong Kong Academy for Performing Arts (HKAPA)

*1 Gloucester Road, Wan Chai, HK Island (2584 8500/www.hkapa.edu). Wan Chai MTR (exit A1, C)/buses along Gloucester Road.* **Open** *Box office* noon-6pm Mon-Sat. **Credit** AmEx, DC, MC, V. **Map** p310 A3.

Unique within Asia, this academy brings together schools of dance, drama, music, television and film under one roof. Many HKAPA students have gone on to achieve major success at exclusive international competitions, and worked as soloists and choreographers. The building houses Hong Kong's second major arts venue, incorporating the terrific Lyric Theatre, the intimate Drama Theatre, a studio theatre, a small concert hall and a recital hall. These impressive venues stage both HKAPA student productions and professional performances by local and visiting companies. Frequent free lunchtime concerts on Mondays and free 'Happy Hour' evening performances complete the varied programme (check the website for further details).

### Hong Kong Arts Centre
*2 Harbour Road, Wan Chai, HK Island (2582 0200). Wan Chai MTR (exit A1)/buses along Gloucester Road/Wan Chai Star Ferry Pier.* **Open** *Box office* 10am-6pm daily. **Credit** MC, V. **Map** p310 B3.
Located across the road from the Hong Kong Academy for Performing Arts, the Hong Kong Arts Centre stages mainly avant-garde theatre and community productions in English and Cantonese in its Shouson Theatre and McAuley Studio.

### Hong Kong City Hall
*5 Edinburgh Place, Central, HK Island (2921 2840). Central MTR (exit J3)/buses to Central Star Ferry Pier & along Connaught Road Central/Central Star Ferry Pier.* **Open** *Box office* 10am-9.30pm daily. **Credit** AmEx, DC, MC, V. **Map** p309 E3.
Right next to the Central Star Ferry Terminal, and recently given a much-needed facelift, the City Hall hosts regular concerts and recitals by local and international artists in its concert hall. Its theatre is used for drama and film screenings.

### Hong Kong Convention & Exhibition Centre
*1 Harbour Road, Wan Chai, HK Island (2582 8888/www.hkcec.com.hk). Wan Chai MTR (exit A1)/buses along Gloucester Road/Wan Chai Star Ferry Pier.* **Credit** V. **Map** p310 B2.
The main stage at this venue was the site of the ceremony marking the 1997 Handover. Nowadays, the centre tends to be used for less culturally charged events such as pop and rock concerts. For full programme and ticket details, check with HK Ticketing (*see p225*).

### Hong Kong Cultural Centre
*10 Salisbury Road, Tsim Sha Tsui, Kowloon (2734 2009). Tsim Sha Tsui MTR (exit E)/buses to Tsim Sha Tsui Star Ferry Pier & along Salisbury Road/Tsim Sha Tsui Star Ferry Pier.* **Open** *Box office* 10am-9.30pm daily. **Credit** AmEx, DC, MC, V. **Map** p313 B6.
This buttressed, windowless slab of cement and tiles has been compared to everything, from a crushed carton of cigarettes to a giant urinal. Despite its appearance, this is the territory's premier arts venue and home to both the Hong Kong Philharmonic Orchestra and the Hong Kong Chinese Orchestra, and most of the city's Western opera and ballet is performed in its 2,100-seat Grand Theatre. The com-

plex also includes a smaller concert hall, a studio theatre and an arts library. Free performances often take place in the foyer and forecourt on Thursday evenings and Saturday afternoons.

## Other venues

### Fringe Club
*2 Lower Albert Road, Central, HK Island (2521 7251/www.hkfringeclub.com). Central MTR (exit D1, G)/23A bus.* **Open** *Box office* noon-midnight Mon-Sat. **Credit** MC, V. **Map** p308 C4.
The Fringe Club is the place to see alternative performances in Hong Kong. Housed in a colonial-era former dairy, it's run by a non-profit organisation that supports aspiring artists. The site includes two intimate theatres, a ground-floor bar (which is also a live music venue) and a couple of exhibition galleries. The rooftop bar is one of the best-kept secrets in Hong Kong and occasionally hosts music performances and outdoor film screenings. The Fringe is also the principal venue for the annual CityJan festival, which features live music, and art and photography exhibitions (*see p190*). *See also p222.*

### Kwai Tsing Theatre
*12 Hing Ning Road, Kwai Chung, New Territories (2408 0128). Kwai Fong MTR (exit C)/30, A31, E32, 42, 47X, 91, 93 bus.* **Open** *Box office* 10am-6pm 9.30pm daily. **Credit** AmEx, DC, MC, V.
This newly built theatre in the heart of a New Territories housing estate is one of the best venues in Hong Kong. In the last couple of years it has hosted outstanding performances by local and international talent, including such famous names as Philip Glass, the Royal Shakespeare Company, Marcia Haydee and Cubanismo.

### Ma Tau Kok Cattle Depot
*63 Ma Tau Kok Road, To Kwa Wan, Kowloon. Bus 101, 111/Kowloon City ferry from North Point.*
Formerly a livestock depot, this intriguing 90-year-old complex has been turned into an artists' village (*see p226*) housing workshops, offices for design, multimedia and theatre companies, and two spaces for community theatre performances and multimedia art exhibitions. One of the companies based here is On & On, an educational theatre workshop (*see p233*). For opening times, phone the individual companies.

### St John's Cathedral
*4-8 Garden Road, Central, HK Island (2523 4157). Central MTR (exit K)/buses along Garden Road.* **Open** 7am-6pm daily. **Admission** free. **Map** p309 E4.
This Anglican cathedral frequently stages free lunchtime and evening concerts by a variety of local and visiting vocal ensembles; Christmas and Easter programmes are particularly good. The cathedral also sponsors moderately priced professional choral concerts during festive holidays.

The **Hong Kong Dance Company**. *See p231.*

A corner of old England in the heart of Central: **St John's Cathedral**...

## Venues in the New Territories

To arouse wider public interest in the arts and to cater to the demographic heart of the SAR, Hong Kong's Leisure & Cultural Services Department (*see p225*) organises a rich selection of musical and dramatic performances at venues around the New Territories. In addition to the **Kwai Tsing Theatre** (*see p226*), these include **Tsuen Wan Town Hall** (72 Tai Ho Road, Tsuen Wan, 2493 7463); **Tuen Mun Town Hall** (3 Tuen Hi Road, Tuen Mun, 2450 1105); **Sha Tin Town Hall** (1 Yuen Wo Road, Sha Tin, 2694 2542) and **Yuen Long Theatre** (9 Yuen Long Tai Yuk Road, Yuen Long, 2476 1029).

## Western classical music & opera

The Western classical music scene in Hong Kong is proudly anachronistic and rich, with complex cultural contradictions. In a city driven by free-wheeling capitalism, the main musical bodies enjoy generous government funding and are administrated by civil servants and society patrons. Hong Kong is known for its collective impatience, yet performances by local orchestras are broadcast in their entirety on RTHK Radio 4 without the interruptions of commercials. Although concerts are often marred by late audience arrivals and the occasional ringing mobile phone, classical music audiences are well educated and appreciative, and many of the SAR's music lovers are amateur musicians or choristers. Classical music programmes reflect Hong Kong's eclectic tastes and sentiments: in the same week and same venue, it's possible to enjoy a sensitive performance of an Elgar concerto and a contemporary ode to Chinese nationalism.

## Orchestras

### Hong Kong Philharmonic Orchestra (HKPO)

The Hong Kong Phil is the territory's first and only full-time, professional Western classical music ensemble. The 93-piece orchestra comprises musicians from a range of Asian and Western countries. In the 2004/2005 season, Edo de Waart becomes the HKPO's new artistic conductor. Maestro de Waart intends to woo new audiences by departing from the tried and true and has promised that this city of almost seven million people will have several sold-out orchestral concerts a week. During its season (September-June), the HKPO performs a wide repertoire and is frequently joined by world-class soloists. The company is committed to performing works by emerging local composers such as Law Wing-fai and Daniel Law Ping-leung, and in the last decade has toured North America, Asia and Europe. The orchestra's website (www.hkpo.com) gives information on the season's concert programmes.

venue for frequent free choral concerts. *See p226.*

## Hong Kong Sinfonietta

The medium-sized Hong Kong Sinfonietta (2836 3336, www.hksinfonietta.org) was formed by local musicians in 1990. Many in the ensemble were trained at the Hong Kong Academy for Performing Arts, and the Sinfonietta has become a bridge of sorts between the HKAPA and the HKPO. As such, it is evolving into Hong Kong's second professional (Western music) orchestra and, like the HKPO, regularly performs works by local composers.

## Composers

A growing stable of classical composers, who combine Western forms with Chinese themes, is receiving international recognition. Current names worth noting include orchestral composer Victor Chan Wai-kwong; film and theatre composer Law Wing-fai; Macanese Doming Lam, a celebrated composer of liturgical music; Scottish-born composer, academic and conductor David Gwilt; and Clarence Mak Wai-chu, whose work includes chamber music, electronic music, and music for local contemporary Chinese theatre productions.

## Choirs

### Cecilian Singers

This group, which is named after the patron saint of music, was set up 40 years ago and performs a repertoire that includes a cappella and major choral works. The choir gives four concerts a year in

venues around Hong Kong and performs every Monday evening in St John's Cathedral (*see p66*). For details on concerts and auditions, contact the director/chairman Bethan Greaves on 2575 3931 or go to www.katterwall.com

### Hong Kong Bach Choir

Established three decades ago for a single performance of a Bach cantata, the Hong Kong Bach Choir now performs a wide repertoire, ranging from Palestrina to Elgar. The choir numbers more than 80 singers and welcomes new members (see www.bachchoir.org.hk for details).

### Hong Kong Oratorio Society

This is the oldest, largest and most active choir in Hong Kong. Since it was founded in 1956, the Society has performed more than 80 oratorios and places strong programming emphasis on works from the baroque and classical canons. On average, the choir gives five performances a year. For more information, go to www.oratorio.org.hk

### Hong Kong Welsh Male Voice Choir

Formed in 1978, the choir was the brainchild of a young Welsh engineer who gathered together a small but enthusiastic group of singing fellow countrymen. Since then, the group has grown to 60 members and expanded its geographical base to include singers from around the world. Still, about half the current members are from Wales or have Welsh connections, and the choir's repertoire of songs includes Welsh hymns and folk songs. For membership and programme details, contact the secretary, Mike Wall, at mikewall@so-net.com.hk.

# Chinese performing arts

Hong Kong's distinctive cultural flavour is shaped by many contrasting forces: at the same time it is a high-tech post-modern port, a Manhattan-style cityscape overloaded with corporations, and a place where you can hear a Britten song cycle, see a Pina Bausch dance performance or weep at a Puccini opera. Yet, despite the seemingly pervasive Western cultural influences, much of the city's soul remains forever Chinese, with a performing arts circuit that reflects this traditional bedrock.

Accessing this scene is a rewarding adventure, and with a bit of background knowledge, most operatic, dance and musical performances can be appreciated by non-Chinese-speaking audiences. You can get acquainted with the rituals of traditional Chinese performance at the Folk Culture in Hong Kong exhibit at the **Hong Kong Museum of History** in Tsim Sha Tsui (see p89), which includes a short film of performers in action.

## CANTONESE OPERA (*XIQU*)

The most immediate image of Chinese performance arts is probably the brightly made-up faces and vibrant embroidered silk costumes of Chinese opera. Actors go about their age-old scripts with exaggerated movements, stylised high-pitched vocals and clashing percussion that is compelling to some, an acquired taste for others. Dating back to the 13th century, choreographies are built around the Confucian principles of courage, honesty and piety, with liberal splashes of scandal, doomed romance, sword fighting and acrobatics.

Unlike its Western counterpart, Cantonese opera derives most of its dramatic power from costumes and gestures. Costumes, headdresses and make-up are colour-coded to convey a character's qualities: a black face denotes honesty, a yellow face belongs to a celestial being, and a white nose is a sure sign of villainy. Even an actor's beard (there are 18 varieties) helps to establish dramatic nuance. Most storylines are based on Chinese legends the audience has heard many times over, so it is the quality of stylised gesture, rather than plot development, that engrosses the viewers. Symbolism also helps to propel the storyline – a red cloth draped over an actor's face means that he's just died. If you'd like a bit more information before attending a Chinese opera, visit the Cantonese Opera exhibition in the **Hong Kong Heritage Museum** (see p99).

Local and touring mainland opera troupes give a full calendar of performances in Hong Kong, so check with venues for details

## Western opera

Although there is no full-time resident Western opera company in Hong Kong, it is possible to see four or five opera performances a year. A major event in the **Hong Kong Arts Festival** (see p190) is the production of a grand opera by a visiting company; in past years, the Czech National Opera, Berlin Komische Oper and Los Angeles Opera companies have all appeared.

Innovative and smaller-scale productions of lesser-known operas by composers such as Piazzolla and Janacek have also featured. The **Opera Society of Hong Kong** (www.opera.org.hk) stages an annual full-scale production in the Hong Kong Cultural Centre.

## Classical dance

The dance scene in Hong Kong is surprisingly rich and much of the interest in, and audience for classical and contemporary dance performances come from the region's large number of dance students. In 1979 local dancer Willy Tsao established Hong Kong's first dance company, the **City Contemporary Dance Company**, and after the creation of the **Hong Kong Ballet** and the **Hong Kong Dance Company** the following decade, the local dance scene was complete.

The **Hong Kong Dance Alliance** (2584 8753) is a federation of dance companies, teachers and student groups committed to promoting dance. It publishes the bilingual *Dance Journal HK* and is a good source of information on dance performances.

### City Contemporary Dance Company (CCDC)

Hong Kong's longest established dance company, the CCDC (2326 8597, www.ccdc.com.hk) is dedicated to the development and performance of modern dance. Under its founder/artistic director, Willy Tsao, the CCDC mostly performs a repertoire created by local choreographers and frequently collaborates with artists from other media. The CCDC has a strong education programme and has dance development partnerships with mainland dance schools.

or ask in the HKTB offices. Since many performances take place in theatres in Kowloon or the New Territories, a night at the opera usually includes the cultural experience of discovering parts of Hong Kong less frequented by tourists. The very accessible **Ko Shan Theatre** in Hung Hom, for example, is set in a pleasant park and holds Cantonese opera performances regularly.

Informal opera performances take place before certain festivals in temporary open-air theatres. Productions are not for the faint-hearted: they can last up to five hours, with people casually coming and going and having a chat during intermissions. Chiu Chow communities erect such theatres annually during the **Hungry Ghost Festival** (see p188) – notably in large playgrounds in Kowloon City (opposite the old airport at Kai Tak) and in Hung Hom (off Chatham Road). Enclosures also go up during the festivities surrounding the **Birthday of Tin Hau** (see p187) – one of the largest is in Sok Kwu Wan on Lamma, which regularly attracts some of Hong Kong's biggest operatic stars.

Cantonese opera clubs are a fascinating but dying part of Hong Kong's cultural scene. The half dozen or so that survive cater to older folk in the working-class areas of Kowloon. Not unlike an old-fashioned cabaret, these clubs feature singers who perform a repertoire of favourites without the dramatic assistance of make-up and costumes. Clubs charge a modest entrance of about HK$30 and 'opera' shows (sometimes incongruously accompanied by a go-go dancer or a transvestite) usually take place between 8pm and midnight. Simply go in, take a seat and wait for a waiter to bring you tea and ask for the fee. Many singers have been crooning for a living for years and appreciate a tip.

Opera clubs in the Yau Ma Tei neighbourhood include **Yuet Wan** (120 Temple Street, 2385 2026); **Foon Lok** (47 Temple Street, next to Public Square Street); **Kam Fung Wong** (directly opposite the Foon Lok) and **Koh Sing Club** (on the eighth floor of the same building as Kam Fung Wong). All opera clubs have pictures of female and male singers in gowns on show next to their red doorways. For all four, take the MTR to Yau Ma Tei (exit C).

There are also some regular outdoor amateur opera performance spots around town. The best known is the area near **Public Square Street** on the right side of Nathan Road as you're walking south from exit C of Yau Ma Tei MTR station. ▶

## Hong Kong Ballet

The territory's only ballet company, the Hong Kong Ballet (2573 7398, www.hkballet.com) performs regularly throughout the year at venues including the Hong Kong Cultural Centre's Grand Theatre. Its repertoire includes classics such as *The Nutcracker* and *Lady of the Camellias*, as well as original works created by local choreographers. Like the Philharmonic Orchestra, the ballet maintains close ties with the Hong Kong Academy for Performing Arts. Many of the company's principal dancers are HKAPA graduates and they often choreograph and prepare productions at their alma mater. Stephen Jefferies is the ballet's current artistic director.

## Hong Kong Dance Company (HKDC)

Devoted to promoting Chinese dance, the HKDC has a growing repertoire, including traditional and folk dances, as well as original dance dramas based on Chinese and Hong Kong themes. The latter include works by prominent choreographers, including the enormously popular *Jade Love*. It regularly gives free performances and provides an audience-building programme with visits to

schools and community centres. For information on upcoming performances call 3103 1888 or log on to www.hkdance.com.

## English-language theatre

More than a few of Hong Kong's English-speaking expatriates have complained – without a hint of irony – that the local theatre circuit is limited, impoverished, and just doesn't compare with what's happening in London or New York. They're absolutely right. However, it's amazing that such a comparison is made, given that 90 per cent of the city speaks Cantonese as its first language. While it's never going to compete with the West End or Broadway, and it tends to cater to a well-heeled, middle-aged, expat audience, a reasonably interesting English-language theatre scene does exist here. Most local productions of English-language theatre are performed by community companies such as the **American Community Theatre** (www.act-hk.com), the **Hong Kong Players**, and the **Hong Kong Singers**. There are also

# Chinese performing arts
▶ (continued)

Other venues for both Cantonese opera and Chinese music performances include: **Ko Shan Theatre** (77 Ko Shan Road, Hung Hom, 2740 9222); **Sai Wan Ho Civic Centre** (111 Shau Kei Wan Road, Sai Wan Ho, 2569 7330); **Sheung Wan Civic Centre** (5/F Sheung Wan Complex, 345 Queen's Road Central, Sheung Wan, 2853 2678) and **Tai Po Civic Centre** (1 On Pong Road, Tai Po, 2665 4477).

## HONG KONG CHINESE ORCHESTRA (HKCO)

One of the largest Chinese orchestras in the world, the 58-piece HKCO consists of four sections of traditional and modern Chinese instruments: bowed strings, plucked strings, wind and percussion. The orchestra is designed to promote traditional and contemporary Chinese music, and to experiment with techniques and styles. Its repertoire includes traditional folk music and contemporary full-scale works. Besides regular public concerts in Hong Kong and abroad, the orchestra also offers free student concerts and outreach activities. For more information, check out www.hkco.org/index_eng.htm.

## DANCE

Dance troupes from all over China regularly visit Hong Kong, offering fascinating ancient ritualistic performances – some animalistic, others extremely graceful. The long flowing gown of the Yunnanese female dancer is in marked contrast to the brief jungle-warrior attire of her male counterpart. And, with its deep Muslim traditions, the dancers of Xinjiang province move to an Arabic musical accompaniment and look every bit the desert nomad. Provincial folk orchestras rarely play in events that do not include dance segments.

The best time to see a lion dance, accompanied by costumed drummers, is during the **Chinese New Year** festivities (*see p190*). If you're in Hong Kong during the **Mid Autumn Festival** (*see p188*), you may be lucky enough to see the dance of the Tai Hang fire dragon, a 70-metre-long (230-foot) 'dragon' made of straw and giant incense sticks.

## OTHER PERFORMANCES

Puppet shows, China's earliest type of children's entertainment, are an unusual find these days and come in the form of touring shows. Check the Leisure & Cultural Services Department's website (*see p225*) for programme details. Also worth looking out for is the three-week **Hong Kong Chinese Arts Festival** (*see p188*), which features artists and performing ensembles from around Asia. Ethnic dance and music events are also occasionally held on weekends in the amphitheatre of **Hong Kong Park** (*see p68*) and in **Kowloon Park** (*see p86*).

---

performances by visiting companies, including the Young Vic, Melbourne's Playbox Theatre and Canadian Robert LePage's company. Musicals are also popular and excellent imported productions of *Chicago*, *Miss Saigon* and *Singin' in the Rain* have had successful runs here. One theatrical experience unique to Hong Kong is the performance of monologues by bilingual actors who alternate from English to Cantonese over different performances.

## Hong Kong Players

This is the city's foremost English-language community theatre group. The semi-professional Players are successors to the Garrison Players (a company that was established in colonial days) and the Hong Kong Stage Club. The group mounts three or four productions a year, performing a repertoire that has included works by Shakespeare, Noël Coward and Samuel Beckett. It also stages an annual Christmas pantomime at the Hong Kong Arts Centre's Shouson Theatre. For information on productions and auditions, visit www.hongkongplayers.com.

## Hong Kong Repertory Theatre

This government-supported rep group has put on nearly 200 productions since it was established almost three decades ago. Its works cover a wide variety of Chinese and Western contemporary and classical pieces. Most productions are staged in Cantonese (often with English surtitles), with some in English and Mandarin. For programme enquiries, go to www.hkrep.com.

## Hong Kong Singers

This semi-professional musical performance group has been singing and dancing for Hong Kong audiences since 1931. It originally presented classical concerts and performed Haydn's *Creation* for the troops at Stanley Fort just before the territory

fell to the Japanese in 1941. Nowadays it presents works of less historical gravitas, staging popular musicals such as *Fiddler on the Roof*, *South Pacific* and *La Cage aux Folles*. The group performs at the Hong Kong Academy for Performing Arts, Hong Kong City Hall and the Fringe Club. See www.hksingers.com for programme details.

### On & On Theatre Workshop

Operating out of the Ma Tau Kok Cattle Depot arts village at To Kwa Wan (*see p207 and p226*), On & On aims to be Hong Kong's first company-run theatre. Its mission is to take theatre to the streets and it collaborates on education programmes with youth organisations in Kowloon. Contact the group on 2503 1630 or by email at onandon@netvigator.com.

### Zuni Icosahedron

This independent cultural collective is committed to original productions of alternative theatre, multimedia performance, sound experimentation and installation arts. Performances focus on exploring a range of themes across cultures, media and art forms. The collective has formed artistic partnerships with non-profit making arts groups from Beijing, Tokyo, Taipei, New York, London and Berlin. For information on upcoming performances, phone 2893 8704 or check www.zuni.org.hk.

## Festivals & events

In November 2002 Hong Kong presented the inaugural **New Vision Arts Festival**. It is intended that this superb dance, music and drama festival, which focuses on performers from across the Asia Pacific region, will become a biennial addition to the Hong Kong arts calendar. For the complete range of permanent arts festivals in Hong Kong, *see p186-p190*.

# Sport & Fitness

When you're done flexing your credit cards, it's time to flex your muscles.

Although many Hong Kongers' ideas of after-work sport is multiple reps of beer-glass lifting, interspersed with high-intensity chatting up of the opposite sex, the SAR offers a diverse number of activities for true sports enthusiasts. Few first-time visitors to the territory realise that 70 per cent of Hong Kong is green, which means that along with the usual urban activities such as basketball, badminton and going to the gym, there are also immensely popular adventure sports like trail running, hiking and mountain biking. For a bit of culture with your exercise, try out a martial art, or just take the time to watch the smooth flowing movements of the locals practising t'ai chi in the parks.

If you're in need of some inspiration, get in touch with the **South China Athletic Association** (SCAA, 2577 6932, www.scaa.org.hk/main_new_eng.htm) or the **YMCA of Hong Kong** (*see p235*), both of which offer information on a wider range of sports than we list below, and at very reasonable prices.

For all games halls run by the Leisure and Cultural Services Department, go online to www.lcsd.gov.hk/en/home.php, where you will also find general information on beaches, pools, parks, zoos and gardens, and activities such as water sports and golf. It also has a customer helpline, 2414 5555.

Alternatively, get hold of a copy of *HK Magazine* or *BC Magazine* (for both, *see p287*), which list the week's sports events, or try the tailor-made packages offered by Q Times (2807 1481, www.qtimes.com) or Paul Etherington (2486 2112, www.kayak-and-hike.com). The latter organises trips into Hong Kong's countryside incorporating such activities as mountain-biking, kayaking, speed-boating or heli-hiking.

## Participation sports/fitness

### Archery

#### Hong Kong Archery Club
*1204 Koon Fook Centre, 9 Knutsford Terrace, Tsim Sha Tsui, Kowloon (2739 8969/www.hk-archerycentre.com). Tsim Sha Tsui MTR (exit B2).* **Open** 3.30-7.30pm Mon-Fri. **Credit** MC, V. **Map** p313 C5.

Contact the Hong Kong Archery Club to help kick-start your arrow action. Courses for beginners cost HK$250 per hour; group packages work out a bit cheaper (call for details).

### Athletics

Jogging tracks and athletic clubs abound in Hong Kong, and marathons take place throughout the year. For details of how to get involved, plus a complete calendar of events, club listings and track venues, contact the **Hong Kong Amateur Athletics Association** (2504 8215, www.hkaaa.com). Triathlons are also becoming increasingly popular. The **Hong Kong International Tri** takes place towards the end of the year with sprint and Olympic distance races and is a great place to do your first tri. For more information, check out www.triathlon.com.hk.

### Badminton

Prices at all of the following are HK$59 per hour.

#### Harbour Road Indoor Games Hall
*27 Harbour Road, Wan Chai, HK Island (2827 9684). Wan Chai MTR (exit A1)/18, 25A, 104, 720, 961 bus.* **Open** 7am-11pm daily. **No credit cards. Map** p310 C3.

#### Hong Kong Park Government Indoor Games Hall
*29 Cotton Tree Drive, Central, HK Island (2521 5072). Buses along Cotton Tree Drive.* **Open** 7am-11pm daily. **No credit cards. Map** p309 E5.

#### Sheung Wan Sports Centre
*12/F, Sheung Wan Complex, 345 Queen's Road, Central, HK Island (2853 2574). Sheung Wan MTR (exit A2).* **Open** 7am-11pm daily. **No credit cards. Map** p308 B2.

### Basketball

Concrete courts are dotted around town and you can often find locals having a casual game. It's more comfortable to play inside, though, unless you want to sweat like crazy. The **Harbour Road Indoor Games Hall** and **Hong Kong Park Government Indoor Games Hall** (for both, *see above*) have indoor courts, for HK$236 per hour.

# Bowling

## Kai Tak Bowling Club
*Kai Tak Old Airport, Kowloon (2382 8189/ www.kaitakbowling.com). Wong Tai Sin MTR then short taxi ride.* **Open** 10am-2am daily. **Admission** *Mon-Fri* HK$16 before 2pm; HK$23 2-6pm; HK$29 after 6pm. *Sat, Sun* HK$34 all day. **Credit** MC, V. **Map** p307.

## Olympian City Super Fun Bowl
*Shop 148, Olympian City 2, Kowloon (2273 4773). Olympic MTR (exit D).* **Open** 10am-1am Mon-Fri, Sun; 10am-2am Sat. **Admission** *Mon-Fri* HK$35 before 6pm; HK$42 after 6pm. *Sat, Sun* HK$46 all day. **Credit** (over HK$200) MC, V.

# Climbing

One of the best days out in Hong Kong is to take the old ferry/fishing boat to **Tung Lung** island, walk over the hill to the Technical Wall and enjoy a day's climbing while the waves crash around you. The sport is becoming increasingly popular and there are many other superb climbs across the territory: **Shek O** (granite; good for beginners and bouldering), **Lion Rock** (granite) and **Kowloon Peak** (volcanic rock).

## King's Park YMCA
*Centenary Centre, 22 Gascoigne Road, Yau Ma Tei, Kowloon (2782 6682/www.ymcahk.org.hk). Jordan MTR (exit B2)/buses along Nathan Road.* **Open** 8.30am-10pm daily. **Admission** HK$70 before 5.30pm; HK$90 after 5.30pm. **No credit cards**. **Map** p313 C4.
With 18m (59ft) of wall, this is the best venue in the city for wall climbing, but you need to take an assessment before you climb.

## YMCA of Hong Kong
*2/F, Salisbury YMCA, 41 Salisbury Road, Tsim Sha Tsui, Kowloon (YMCA 2268 7000/climbing wall 2268 7099/www.ymcahk.org.hk). Tsim Sha Tsui MTR (exit E)/buses to Tsim Sha Tsui Star Ferry Pier & along Salisbury Road/Tsim Sha Tsui Star Ferry Pier.* **Open** noon-10pm Mon-Fri; 10am-10pm Sat, Sun. **Admission** HK$80. **No credit cards**. **Map** p313 B6.
You'll have to do a half-day assessment (HK$50, Fridays 6.45-8.30pm only) to get a permit to climb at this 7m (23ft) wall, but after that it's an open house.

# Dance

Salsa lovers can also learn the moves at Club ING on Wednesdays (*see p216*).

## Franky Wong
*The Fringe, 2 Lower Albert Road, Central, HK Island (2521 7251/9410 8652/salsaman@netvigator.com). Central MTR (exit D1, D2).* **Credit** AmEx, MC, V. **Map** p308 C4.

Kai Tak Bowling Club.

*Hong Kong Cultural Centre, 10 Salisbury Road, Tsim Sha Tsui, Kowloon (2734 2009). Tsim Sha Tsui MTR (exit E)/1, 1A, 6, 7, 8, 110 bus.* **No credit cards**. **Map** 313 B6.
Franky teaches salsa at the Fringe on Thursdays (improvers 7-8pm; show moves 8-9pm; beginners 9-10pm) and at the Cultural Centre on Tuesdays (7-10pm). Eight lessons cost HK$800.

## Herman Lam
*1/F, Kai Kwong House, 13 Wyndham Street, Central, HK Island (2320 3605/www.hlamdance.com). Central MTR (exit D1, D2).* **Map** p308 C4.
Get a package and try out all of Herman's classes (ballroom, jazz, rock'n'roll, salsa, tango, rumba…). It costs $HK120 for a drop-in fee, or HK$1,000 for ten lessons. Check the website for times.

## The Point
*15/F, West Wing, Sincere Insurance Building, 4-6 Hennessy Road, Wan Chai, HK Island (2866 9432/ www.thepointhk.com). Admiralty MTR (exit C1).* **Open** 3-8pm Mon-Fri; noon-6pm Sat; 9am-1pm Sun. **Admission** HK$105-$150. **No credit cards**. **Map** p310 B3.
Courses in ballet, hip hop and tap are held at this super-friendly studio.

Want to learn hip hop? Get to the **The Point**. *See p235.*

# Golf

If you have a spare million, then go ahead and join one of the private country clubs for the best golf in Hong Kong. However, if you're only here for a holiday you can play at the following public courses; unlike the private clubs they cost less than the price of a house on the Peak. Note that handicap requirements in Hong Kong are around 36.4 for men and 40.4 for women, though this varies from course to course. China is less strict, and most clubs organise various day or weekend packages there.

### Discovery Bay Golf Course

*Discovery Bay Golf Club Valley Road, Discovery Bay, Lantau (2987 7273/http://hkprogolf.com/discovery_bay.htm). Ferry from Central to Discovery Bay.* **Tee times** *18 holes* 7.30am-1.42pm daily; *9 holes* from 4pm daily. **Admission** HK$1,400. **Credit** AmEx, MC, V. **Map** p306.
Non-members can play on Mondays, Tuesdays and Fridays only.

### Jockey Club Kau Sai Chau

*Kau Sai Chau, Sai Kung, New Territories (2791 3390/3344/www.kscgolf.com). Buses to Sai Kung.* **Tee times** *9 holes* 7.30am-3/4pm daily; *18 holes* 7.30am-1/2pm daily. **Admission** HK$400 Mon-Fri; HK$540 Sat, Sun. **Credit** MC, V. **Map** p307.
This is the only golf course in the area that's open to the public at the weekend. Last tee times vary, so phone to check first.

### Royal Hong Kong Golf Club

*Fanling Lot No.1, New Territories (2670 1211/ http://hkprogolf.com/fanling.htm). Sheung Shui KCR.* **Open** 7am-6pm daily. **Admission** HK$1,200-$1,400. **Credit** AmEx, MC, V. **Map** p307.
Non-members can play on weekdays only (not public holidays).

### Tuen Mun Golf Centre

*Tuen Mun Recreation & Sports Centre, Lung Mun Road, New Territories (2466 2600). Bus 962.* **Open** 8am-10pm daily. **Admission** *Per bay* HK$12 per hr. **No credit cards. Map** p306.

# Gyms & fitness centres

Most hotels have well-equipped gyms that are free for residents, and some also have personal trainers. For spas, *see p180* **Super spas**.

### California Fitness

*1 Wellington Street, Central, HK Island (2522 5229/ www.calfitnesscenters.com). Central MTR (exit D1, D2, G)/12M, 13, 23A, 40M, 43 bus.* **Open** 6am-midnight Mon-Sat; 8am-10pm Sun. **Admission** *Day pass* HK$150. **Credit** AmEx, DC, MC, V. **Map** p308 C4.
Other branches of this high-volume, American-style gym can be found in Causeway Bay, Wan Chai, Tsim Sha Tsui and Mong Kok.

### Fitness First

*G/F, Cosco Tower, Grand Millennium Plaza, 181-3 Queen's Road, Central, HK Island (3106 3000/ www.fitnessfirst.com.hk). Sheung Wan MTR (exit A2).* **Open** 6.30am-11pm Mon-Fri; 7am-10pm Sat; 8am-10pm Sun. **Admission** *Day pass* HK$200. **Credit** AmEx, DC, MC, V. **Map** p308 B2.
This is the biggest Fitness First branch, with all the usual gym facilities on three floors, and steam and saunas in the changing rooms. Other locations include North Point, Quarry Bay and Tsim Sha Tsui.

### Pure Fitness

*1-3F, Kinwick Centre, 32 Hollywood Road, Central, HK Island (2970 3366). Central MTR (exit D1, D2, G)/Mid-Levels Escalator/12M, 13, 23A, 26, 40M, 43 bus.* **Open** 6am-midnight Mon-Sat; 8am-10pm Sun. **Admission** *Day pass* HK$200. **Credit** AmEx, MC, V. **Map** p308 C3.

This new gym comes from the same people behind Pure Yoga (*see p241*) and combines the usual state-of-the-art equipment and classes (sauna, steam and solarium) with Pure Spa, which offers treatments such as facials and massage, as well as the services of a physio and nutritionalist. There's also a juice bar.

## Hiking

There are a myriad of hiking trails throughout Hong Kong Island and Kowloon, as well as on the outlying islands. Some may be along well-trod paths, but you'll still go through lovely countryside on virtually all of them. Try the **Dragon's Back** over to Shek O (*see p82* **Across the Dragon's Back**), or **Violet Hill** followed by the **Twins** (aka the Thousand Steps) if you're feeling super energetic – those will take you over to Stanley. You can end a walk on Lantau at Cheung Sha Beach and kick back at the Stoep restaurant (*see p146*). Local book stores (*see p160*) carry a number of helpful books that explain how to get wherever you want to go.

Extreme hikers might want to join a team for the annual **Trailwalker** event (*see p188*), which takes place each November. It's a gruelling 100-kilometre (62-mile) course, but worth it as all money raised goes to Oxfam. Also contact Paul Etherington (*see p234*), who takes groups through the countryside's tiny villages on a traditional hike, and also arranges helicopter rides to Sai Kung Country Park so you can start your day's hiking in style.

## Horse riding

If you've been to the races at **Happy Valley** (*see p242*) or **Sha Tin** (*see p99*) and are dying for a go yourself, you're in luck. Most horses at schools here are retired race horses – so it's a sure bet you'll have a good ride. The gorgeous scenery is an added bonus.

Most clubs cater to both experienced riders and beginners, but may insist that you prove you know what you're doing before letting you go on a hack on the trails. Some offer reduced rates for children.

### Lo Wu Saddle Club

*Ho Sheung Heung, Sheung Shui, New Territories (2673 0066). Sheung Shui KCR then minibus 51K.* **Open** 8am-noon, 2-6pm Tue-Sun. **Admission** *Mon-Fri* HK$310 per session; *Sat, Sun* HK$350 per group. **Credit** AmEx, MC, V. **Map** p307.

### Pok Fu Lam Public Riding School

*75 Pok Fu Lam Reservoir Road, Pok Fu Lam, HK Island (2550 1359). Buses along Pok Fu Lam Reservoir Road.* **Open** 8am-noon, 2-6pm Tue-Sun. **Admission** HK$360 per hr. **Credit** MC, V.

### Tuen Mun Public Riding School

*Lung Mun Road, Tuen Mun, New Territories (2461 3338/www.lcsd.gov.hk). Buses along Pok Fu Lam Reservoir Road.* **Open** 8am-7pm Tue-Fri; 8am-6pm Sat, Sun. **Admission** from HK$360 per hr. **Credit** MC, V. **Map** p306.

## Ice skating

### The Glacier

*Festival Walk, 80 Tat Chee Avenue, Kowloon Tong, Kowloon (2844 3588/www.glacier.com.hk). Kowloon Tong MTR/KCR (exit C)/buses to Festival Walk.* **Open** 10.30am-10pm Mon-Thur; 10.30am-3pm, 3.30-5.30pm, 6-10pm Fri, Sat; 1-3pm, 3.30-5.30pm Sun. **Admission** HK$50 Mon-Fri; HK$60 Sat, Sun. **No credit cards**.

## Kickboxing

### Fightin' Fit

*2/F, World Trust Tower, 50 Stanley Street, Central, HK Island (2526 6648/www.fightinfit.com.hk). Central MTR (exit D1, D2, G)/buses along Queen's Road Central.* **Open** 8am-9.30pm Mon-Sat. **Admission** HK$200 per session. **Credit** MC, V. **Map** p308 C3.

Both Fightin' Fit branches run martial arts classes, including *muay thai* and karate.
**Other locations**: G/F, 37 Main Street, Yung Shue Wan, Lamma (2982 1861).

## Martial arts

When in China do as the Chinese do – and have a go at a martial art, which here is culture, history and exercise all rolled into one. According to many Hong Kongers it's the best way to start the day, and even just watching the smooth movers on the promenade in Tsim Sha Tsui or in parks all over the city will have you feeling calm and refreshed.

You can try t'ai chi for free on the waterfront promenade in Tsim Sha Tsui (8-9am Monday, Wednesday, Thursday, Friday; call the HKTB on 2508 1234 for details). Otherwise, for karate, tae kwon do, judo, kung fu, t'ai chi or wing chun try the **YMCA of Hong Kong** (*see p235*), **Fightin' Fit** (*see above*) or the **South China Athletic Association** (*see p234*).

## Mountain biking

Mountain biking offers a fantastic high-adrenaline speed experience and many of the biking trails lead through lovely countryside. Lamma island has some quite technical routes. For more details on where to bike, check out the **Hong Kong Mountain Bike Association** (www.hkmba.org) for routes, maps and information, or call Paul Etherington (*see p234*).

Arts & Entertainment

### Flying Ball Bicycle Company

*201 Tung Choi Street, Mong Kok, Kowloon (2381 3661/www.flyingball.com). Prince Edward MTR (exit B2)/buses along Nathan Road & Prince Edward Road.* **Open** 10am-8pm Mon-Sat; 10.30am-8pm Sun. **Credit** AmEx, DC, MC, V. **Map** p312 B1.

### The Bicycle World

*Shop 2, G/F, Connaught Commercial Building, 185 Wan Chai Road, Wan Chai, HK Island (2892 2299). Wan Chai MTR (exit A2).* **Open** noon-8pm daily. **Credit** MC, V. **Map** p310 C3.

### Friendly Bicycle Shop

*Mui Wo Centre, Shop 12, Mui Wo, Lantau (2984 2279). Mui Wo Ferry Pier/Tung Chau MTR then bus/taxi.* **Open** 10am-8pm daily. **Credit** phone for details. **Map** p306.

## Paragliding

Paragliders benefit from Hong Kong's gusty winds, which make it a playground for experienced flyers, who launch off from the Dragon's Back trail near Shek O or from Sunset Peak on Lantau at the weekends. But those same winds make it a difficult place for beginners. To check up on the latest information or for general advice, email the **Hong Kong Paragliding Association**'s chairman, Steve Yancey glblbest@netvigator.com, or log on to www.glink.net.hk/~hkpa for more details.

## Pilates

### Iso Fit

*8/F, California Tower, 30-32 D'Aguilar Street, Central, HK Island (2869 8630/www.isofit.com.hk). Central MTR (exit D1, D2).* **Open** 8am-8pm Mon-Fri, 9am-6pm Sat. **Admission** from HK$450 per class; phone for details of packages. **Credit** AmEx, MC, V. **Map** p308 C4

All newcomers to Iso Fit are given an hour's one-on-one consultation and then can choose between individual or group classes.

## Rollerblading & skateboarding

**Happy Valley Racecourse** (*see p242*) has a track round the outside where you can blade; alternatively, join the joggers on Bowen Road.

### King's Park YMCA

*Centenary Centre, 22 Gascoigne Road, Yau Ma Tei, Kowloon (2782 6682/www.ymcahk.org.hk). Jordan MTR (exit B2)/buses along Nathan Road.* **Open** 8.30am-10pm daily. **Admission** HK$15. **No credit cards. Map** p313 C4.

There's a skate park here with tubes and obstacles (just turn up, bring your own skates). King's Park is also the home of inline hockey (Monday to Thursday, for various levels of ability).

## Running & jogging

The gentle three-kilometre (one-mile) loop on Lugard Road round the Peak (*see p78* **Peak of fitness**) is great for a pre-Sunday brunch run. Otherwise, try Bowen Road, which stretches for four kilometres (one and a half miles) from near Robinson Road to Magazine Gap Road. The views are well worth the effort. Or pretend you're a thoroughbred and gallop round the jogging track at **Happy Valley** (*see p242*). All are traffic-free.

For organised runs, contact Maggie Raynolds at the **Wan Chai Hash** (2559 5955/2537 8389, www.wanchaih3.com) or go to the **Wanch** bar

# Thrill seekers

The newest sport to hit Asia, adventure racing has taken Hong Kong by storm since it began with the first race – the Samsung Action Asia Challenge (for details, see www.actionasia.com) – in 1998, and now has a huge number of local followers. These multi-sport events usually include a combination of trail running, kayaking, scrambling, mountain biking, climbing and abseiling. Hong Kong's wild islands and coastlines are ideally suited to testing competitors without taking them too far from civilisation. As Michael Maddess of Action Asia enthuses, 'Hong Kong is still one of the best-kept secrets in Asia. The parks here offer everything the weekend warrior would want.'

The annual Action Asia Challenge is Hong Kong's best-known home-grown event. It may only be a one-day race but it more than sorts the boys from the men (and raises money for the Action Asia Foundation and underprivileged children too). 'If you can complete an event like this you feel you can take on the world when you cross that finish line,' explains Maddess. Other companies such as Outward Bound and Raleigh International hold similar events, and race organisers like Keith Noyes at Seyon Asia (www.seyonasia.com) are working to make the SAR better known within Asia for its challenging countryside, rather than just its designer shopping malls.

Ready for action at **Big Wave Bay**. *See p240.*

(*see p224*), where the board tells you about the hash's next run. They run most Sundays, starting at 4pm, for about an hour (HK$30 for women; HK$50 for men). Alternatively, try the **Little Sai Wan Hash House Harriers**, who run Wednesdays at 6.45pm (HK$10 for the run; HK$10 for a beer or HK$5 for a soft drink at the end). Runs usually last an hour. If you're interested, contact Stuart Smith (2150 8418, http://home.netvigator.com/~ruggero), or check out www.hkrunners.com.

## Sailing, paddling & kayaking

If you're around at the end of June, you might want to participate in the annual **Dragon Boat Festival** (*see p188*). Spurred on by drums and your fellow paddlers, you'll be taking part in a quintessentially Chinese sport at the same time as straining your back to breaking point. The **Hong Kong Island Paddle Club** (www.hkipc.com/mail.htm) meets regularly to practice dragon boating and outrigger canoeing. **Paul Etherington** takes groups out fun kayaking around the outlying islands around Sai Kung (*see p234*).

There are few more pleasant ways of escaping the hectic bustle of the city than on board a yacht. If you don't have your own craft, check out the boards outside the yacht clubs listed below, as owners often advertise for crew. Experienced crew is preferred but beginners can sometimes get lucky. Both clubs below also run courses; phone for further information.

### Royal Hong Kong Yacht Club

*Kellett Island, Causeway Bay, HK Island (2832 2817/www.rhkyc.org.hk). Causeway Bay MTR (exit C)/buses along Gloucester Road.* **Open** *Phone enquiries* 8am-10pm daily. **Credit** AmEx, MC, V. **Map** p311 D2.

Also based at the RHKYC is Yachting Ventures, which runs a variety of courses (for details, call 9333 8084 or log on to www.yachtingventures.com).

### St Stephen's Beach Water Sports Centre

*Wong Ma Kok Path, Stanley, HK Island (2813 5804/www.lcsd.gov.hk). Buses to Stanley.* **Open** 8.30am-5pm Mon, Wed-Sun. **Credit** phone for details. **Map** p83.

## Scuba diving

Hong Kong might not boast the clearest waters in the world, but it's better than you might imagine. The **Sai Kung** and **Clearwater Bay** peninsulas, **Shek O** and **Po Toi** islands are just some of the many good dive sites, harbouring some 50 types of coral and 400 varieties of sea life. The diving season falls roughly between March and October, when shore, wreck and night dives and various courses are all on offer. Contact the following clubs for details of dives and courses.

### Mandarin Divers

*G/F, Unit 2, Aberdeen Marina Tower, 8 Shum Wan Road, Aberdeen, HK Island (2554 7110). Buses to Aberdeen.* **Open** 9.30am-7pm Mon-Sat. **Credit** AmEx, MC, V. **Map** p307.

### Marine Divers

*3E Block 18, Dynasty View, 11 Ma Wo Road, Tai Po, New Territories (2656 9399/www.marine divers.com). Buses to Tai Po.* **Open** phone for details. **No credit cards. Map** p307.

## Squash

The **Harbour Road Indoor Games Hall** and **Hong Kong Park Government Indoor Games Hall** (for both, *see p234*) both have squash courts costing HK$27 for half an hour.

At **Happy Valley Racecourse**, the race may be over in a flash...

### Victoria Park

*Hing Fat Street, Causeway Bay, HK Island
(2570 6186). Tin Hau MTR (exit A2)/10, 15B,
18, 102, 106, 110, 116 bus.* **Open** 7am-11pm daily.
**Admission** phone for details. **No credit cards.**
**Map** p311 E/F2.

## Surfing

The minute the typhoon signal is hoisted, Hong
Kong's little gang of surfers surge on to the **Big
Wave Bay Beach** (*see p84*) near Shek O and
get ready for the waves. Sadly, when there are
no storm warnings, waves are usually no more
than a foot high. The **Big Wave Bay Kiosk**
(2809 4933) is right on the beach and along with
renting boards also sells food and drinks (board
hire costs approximately HK$100 per day).
Waves at **Long Wan Beach** at Sai Kung
in the New Territories (*see p108*) are usually
bigger and better shaped, but it's quite a trek to
get there. To learn, call Nelson Chan (6036 0360),
whose company, **Surf 360**, holds courses
throughout the year at Big Wave Bay in Shek O.
For surfing gear, head to the **Island Wake
Surf Shop** (20 Pak Sha Road, Causeway Bay,
HK Island, 2895 0022), which also runs courses.

## Swimming

Beaches in Hong Kong are generally clean and
have shops with lilos, snacks and drinks. It's
the water itself that leaves little to be desired,
although some days – and some beaches –
are better than others. **Tai Long Wan** out
in Sai Kung (*see p108*) is an effort to get to –
a sampan from Sai Kung or a fairly demanding
walk through the country park is involved –
but it boasts the clearest water in Hong Kong.

If you camp there you might be lucky enough
to swim in phosphorescence if you venture out
at night, but be careful of sharks. Otherwise,
**Repulse Bay** and **Deep Water Bay** (for
both, *see p82*) are the nearest beaches to
Central. **Big Wave Bay** (*see p84*) near Shek
O is good too. **Stanley** (*see p83*) is better for
water sports than swimming.

If sand in your cossie isn't your thing, try a
day at a swanky hotel pool, which usually costs
around HK$250 for non-residents, or go local
and dive into an outside public pool.

For more pools, check www.lcsd.gov.hk/
LEISURE/LM/beach1/en/pool_address.html.

### Kennedy Town Swimming Pool

*12N Smithfield Road, Kennedy Town, HK
Island (2817 7973). Bus 5B, 10, 101, 104, 904.*
**Open** *Apr-Nov* 6.30am-noon, 1-5pm, 6-10pm daily.
Closed Dec-Mar. **Admission** HK$19; HK$9
concessions. **No credit cards. Map** p307.

### Kowloon Park

*Austin Road, Tsim Sha Tsui, Kowloon (2724 3577).
Jordan MTR (exit C)/buses along Austin Road.*
**Open** *June-Mar* 6.30am-noon, 1-5pm, 6-10pm daily.
Closed Apr, May. **Admission** phone for details.
**No credit cards. Map** p313 B5.

### Victoria Park

*Hing Fat Street, Causeway Bay, HK Island (2570
8347). Tin Hau MTR (exit A2)/10, 15B, 18, 102,
106, 110, 116 bus.* **Open** *Apr-Oct* 6.30am-noon,
1-5pm, 6-10pm daily. Closed Nov-Mar. **Admission**
phone for details. **No credit cards. Map** p311 F2.

## Table tennis

The **Harbour Road Indoor Games Hall**
(*see p234*) hires out table tennis courts at a cost
of HK$21 an hour.

but picking a winner takes longer. *See p242.*

## Tennis

Tennis courts are everywhere in Hong Kong, and they're relatively cheap. Below are some of the best.

### Causeway Bay Sports Ground
*Causeway Road, Causeway Bay, HK Island (2890 5127). Tin Hau MTR (exit B)/buses along Causeway Road.* **Open** *7am-11pm daily.* **Admission** *Before 6pm* HK$42 per hr. *After 6pm* HK$57 per hr. **No credit cards.** **Map** p311 F3.
Six floodlit courts.

### Hong Kong Tennis Centre
*Wong Nai Chung Gap Road, Happy Valley, HK Island (2574 9122). Bus 6, 41A, 61, 63, 66, 76.* **Open** *7am-10pm daily.* **Admission** *Before 6pm* HK$42 per hr. *After 6pm* HK$57 per hr. **No credit cards.** **Map** p311 D4.
17 floodlit courts.

### King's Park Sports Ground
*15 King's Park Rise, Yau Ma Tei, Kowloon (2388 8154). Bus 2C, 103.* **Open** *7am-10.30pm daily.* **Admission** HK$40-HK$70 per hr. **No credit cards.** **Map** p312 C3.
Six floodlit courts.

### Victoria Park
*Hing Fat Street, Causeway Bay, HK Island (2570 6186). Tin Hau MTR (exit A2)/buses along Hing Fat Street.* **Open** *7am-11pm daily.* **Admission** *Before 6pm* HK$42 per hr. *After 6pm* HK$57 per hr. **No credit cards.** **Map** p311 E/F2.
Fourteen floodlit courts.

## Volleyball

The **Harbour Road Indoor Games Hall** (*see p234*) hires out courts at an hourly rate of HK$236.

## Wakeboarding, waterskiing, windsurfing & kitesurfing

Not surprisingly, given the climate, water sports are very popular in Hong Kong. Phone the following for details of tuition and equipment hire.

### Cheung Chau Windsurfing Centre
*Hai Pak Road, Tung Wan Beach, Cheung Chau (2981 2772). Cheung Chau Ferry Pier.* **Open** 11am-6pm daily. **No credit cards.** **Map** p306.

### Wave Star – The Windsurfing Spirit
*Stanley Main Beach (2813 7561/www.hiwindlover. com). Buses to Stanley.* **Open** Mon-Fri (phone for hours); 9.30am-7pm Sat, Sun. **No credit cards.** **Map** p83.
This beach shop has been open for nearly 30 years. Its main instructor is Olympic competitor Barry Ho.

## Yoga

Yoga is extremely popular in Hong Kong, and seems to be the locals' first choice when it comes to stress busting. In addition to the following, **Fitness First** and **California Fitness** (for both, *see p236*) also run classes in yoga. For more listings, see www.yogahongkong.com.

### Pure Yoga
*16/F, The Centrium, 60 Wyndham Street, Central, HK Island (2971 0055/www.pure-yoga.com). Central MTR (exit D1, D2)/23A, 26, 40M bus.* **Open** 7am-9pm Mon-Fri; 10am-6pm Sat, Sun. **Admission** HK$200 per class. **Credit** AmEx, MC, V. **Map** p308 C4.
Pure Yoga, an offshoot of Pure Fitness (*see p236*), runs classes in Hatha, pregnancy and power yoga. **Other locations**: 25/F Soundwill Plaza, 38 Russell Street, Causeway Bay, HK Island (2970 2299).

### Planet Yoga

*20/F, Silver Fortune Plaza, 1 Wellington Street,*
*Central, HK Island (2525 8288). Central MTR (exit*
*D2).* **Open** 7am-11pm Mon-Fri; 7am-10pm Sat, Sun.
**Admission** phone for details. **Credit** AmEx, MC, V.
**Map** p308 C4.

Most of the instructors at this dedicated studio
above California Fitness (*see p236*) are from India.

## Spectator sports

### Athletics

For the **Standard Chartered Hong Kong
Marathon** in February, *see p190*.

### Dragon boat racing

For some Asian-style action, come to Hong
Kong at the end of June and take in – or take
part in– the frenzied **Dragon Boat Festival**
(*see p188*).

### Football

Although its own team may not be among
the world's major players, soccer is extremely
popular in Hong Kong, and international
teams fly into town in January to compete
in the annual **Carlsberg Cup** (*see p190*). For
tournament and competition details, check out
www.footballhk.com.

### Golf

In Hong Kong itself there is only one major
annual event, the **Hong Kong Open**, which
is played at Fan Ling or Clearwater Bay in
November. Slightly further afield there is
also the **Macau Open** in December and there
are various events throughout the year in
Shenzhen, the golfing mecca of southern China.

### Horse racing

Hong Kong loves to gamble, but gambling is
illegal. The only way to have a flutter without
attracting the attention of the police is to bet
with the Jockey Club at one of the horse racing
meetings at the **Happy Valley** or **Sha Tin**
racecourses. It's a high-adrenalin, high-tech
experience with race-goers from every walk
of life – from the blue-collar worker cheering
in the stands to the *tai tais* peering out over
glasses of champagne from the Jockey Club.
Billons go through the books at each meeting,
and a percentage of the profit goes to the
Jockey Club's chosen charities. Among the
major meetings are the **Hong Kong Derby** in
March, the **Queen Elizabeth II Cup** in April

and the **Hong Kong International Races**
in December, all held at Sha Tin (*see p99*).
For details, go to www.hkjockeyclub.com.

### Happy Valley Racecourse

*2 Sports Road, Happy Valley, HK Island (2895 1523/*
*www.happyvalleyracecourse.com). Trams to Happy*
*Valley.* **Open** varies. Closed July, Aug. **Admission**
HK$10. **No credit cards. Map** p311 D 4/5.

Racing in Hong Kong is followed as fanatically as a
religion, and Happy Valley is the altar at which
everyone prays. The high-intensity floodlights,
expectant atmosphere, booming loudspeakers, bil-
lions of dollars, streaming crowds and streaking
horses make for one of the most exciting evenings
out the city has to offer. The minimum bet is only
HK$10, so there's no excuse not to join in. For a
bird's-eye view climb up to the top of the stands – if
your horse doesn't come in, tear your betting slip
and throw it over the edge where it joins thousands
of others in Happy Valley's version of snow. For
close-up, hoof-thundering action stand on the rails,
beer in hand, and cheer your horse round. The season lasts from September to June and meetings are
usually every Wednesday from 7.30pm (check first).

For a whole day's racing, the modern racecourse
at Sha Tin in the New Territories (*see p99*) holds
events on Saturdays and Sundays.

For both venues, log on to www.shatinrace
track.com/calendar.html.

### Rugby

Known throughout the world as one of the
biggest rugby parties of the year, the annual
**Hong Kong Rugby Sevens** (*see also p187*)
brings bedlam to the city at the end of March.
Rugby teams warm up in front of the stands,
run out for the short clash with their opponents
and then, the serious stuff over, run round the
stadium, playing to the hysterical crowds, some
of whom seem to be here to actually watch the
sporting action.

In the days before the big weekend, look out
for the **E-Kong Women's Rugby Sevens
& Asia Championship** and the **Hong Kong
Tens** (www.hongkongtens.com), which focuses
on the best teams from New Zealand, Australia
and the UK.

### Tennis

Three annual tournaments pull in current
champions and crowd favourites from the
past: the **Salem Open** and **Watson's Water
Challenge**, both in Victoria Park, and the
**Cathay Pacific Championships** at the
Hong Kong Convention & Exhibition Centre.
For all local tournaments, check the website
of the **Hong Kong Tennis Association**,
at www.tennishk.org.

# Trips Out
# of Town

# Macau

Gambling may be Macau's mainstay, but the European architecture, fantastic dining and restful hotels are further reasons to visit.

The mainland Chinese peninsula of Macau has one *raison d'être* – gambling. From the gaming tables and one-armed bandits in the casinos to horse and greyhound racing, it's a flutter that most people are here for. But there is much more to Macau than this. Many Hong Kong residents, especially expats, use it as a peaceful and comparatively inexpensive getaway – it's just 70 kilometres (45 miles) from the territory and easily accessible by ferry (or, for those who can afford it, helicopter). The city is home to excellent restaurants, colonial buildings, decent shopping, and plenty of sights and leisure facilities.

Macau is an example of East-meets-West integration refined over more than four centuries, since Portuguese explorers hived it off as a colonial trading outpost. Buddhist temples nestle cheek by jowl with baroque Catholic churches, old coffee shops lie next to traditional Chinese teahouses, and the neon lights of the casinos flash a mere die's throw from classical 19th-century European buildings. Although Macau returned to Chinese sovereignty in 1999, a heavy Portuguese influence remains, which can be seen everywhere from the fusion Macanese food to the city's scooter-filled streets and its 'live-and-let-live' attitude.

Macau's main similarity to Hong Kong is that it is an autonomous Special Administrative Region (SAR) of China. Beijing has its hand on the tiller, but local government is the skipper. Both cities are also free ports (meaning no taxes are imposed on goods imported from other countries) and each is a full member of the World Trade Organisation in its own right.

The similarities largely end there. Macau is tiny, its 25 square kilometres (ten square miles) represent just two per cent of Hong Kong's total land area. It is densely populated, but its 440,000 inhabitants make up just six per cent of Hong Kong's overall population. And while Macau's GDP is high in Asian terms, its currency is pegged to the Hong Kong dollar and it has no stock market.

## EARLY HISTORY

The name Macau is a corruption of 'A-Ma-Gau', meaning 'Bay of A Ma'. Legend has it that A Ma – the Goddess of Seafarers (known in Hong Kong as Tin Hau) – was a maiden who calmed a storm that threatened to engulf a boat. When the boat reached land, its passengers built a temple to her in the inner harbour, which still attracts worshippers today.

Macau was both the first area east of Malaysia to be settled by Europeans and the last to be released from colonialisation. The first recorded Portuguese navigator to visit China was Jorge Alvares, who made it as far as nearby Lintin, an island in the Pearl River estuary, in 1513. Even though he spent ten months on the island, he didn't establish a long-term base there, and it was nearly 40 years later, in 1557, that the Portuguese were given permission by the local magistrate at Heung Shan (in modern Zhuhai) to settle permanently on the Macau peninsula – reportedly in return for assistance in driving away pirates.

Macau, therefore, became the Portuguese headquarters for trade in this part of Asia. As the Chinese had banned Japanese traders from entering their ports (which had been ravaged by Japanese pirates for centuries), the Portuguese became crucial intermediaries in the trading of copper and silver and raw silks. By the early 1600s it was a thriving city, home not only to traders but also Portuguese missionaries determined to convert the Asian communities to Catholicism.

However, Macau's golden era did not last long. In 1637, Japan entered a self-inflicted period of exclusion and trade, and with it the role of the Portuguese declined. By this time the Dutch were also threatening Portugal's domination of world trade. Macau's prosperity suffered and the city became a backwater.

The Portuguese remained, however, and since there were few European women around, the Portuguese men tended to marry Asians, resulting in the distinctive look of the Macanese people. In addition, a local patois developed, which combined Portuguese, Malay, Japanese and Cantonese elements. Sadly, the dialect is dying out – not many people under 70 speak it today. Other elements of the Macanese culture, such as dress, were also derived from Malacca and elsewhere, and until the early 20th century many elderly Macanese women still wore *sarong kebaya* (traditional Malay dress) and lived relatively secluded lives.

Tranquil **St Michael Cemetery**, burial place for Macau's Catholics. *See p247.*

In 1887, although they had already been in Macau for over 300 years, the Portuguese finally formalised their presence in the city by securing a concession of sovereignty from the Chinese. By then Macau was being used as a base by many Europeans and Americans trading with Canton (as Guangzhou was then known). But it was not until the mid 20th century that Macau found true prosperity again, through licensed gambling, which now accounts for 40 per cent of the government's revenue and forms the backbone of the economy. It also made businessman Stanley Ho a billionaire, as he was the sole gambling licensee until 2001, when his monopoly was revoked. That will change in 2005, when two gambling moguls from Las Vegas open their own casino and entertainment complexes (*see p255* **Cash Macau**).

At times, however, Portugal's rule of Macau has been reluctant. Following the Portuguese revolution of 1974, and in a fit of post-colonial guilt, the Portuguese tried to withdraw from Macau, yet, despite years of anti-colonial rhetoric, the Chinese asked them to stay. Portugal agreed to remain in name, but withdrew its troops and declared Macau a Chinese sovereign territory under Portuguese administration. The Sino-Portuguese Joint Declaration – signed in 1987 – finally provided for Macau's return to Chinese control in 1999.

After the signing of the declaration, Macau experienced a few years of unsustained property boom and massive land reclamation schemes were undertaken, completely changing the peninsula's appearance. Bridges were built connecting the mainland peninsula to the islands of Taipa and Colôane, and an international airport was constructed.

Outbreaks of gang in-fighting in the late 1990s earned Macau the nickname the 'Wild East', as Chinese triads flexed their muscles and staked claims to various pieces of business linked to gambling. But the trouble has since calmed considerably and the transition of sovereignty went quite smoothly. Compared to Hong Kong and southern China, Macau was relatively unscathed by the SARS pandemic in 2003. The city authorities won praise for their handling of the isolated cases that did occur.

Now firmly established as a gambling and tourism destination, Macau has spent tens of millions of pounds on new attractions, such as the Macau Tower – the tenth tallest free-standing building in the world – and on restoring old buildings for use as entertainment venues or museums. There is talk of building a bridge to link Macau with Hong Kong and Zhuhai, and in 2005 Macau will host the East Asian games. Its position as the playground of the Pearl River Delta suggests that the financial gamble the government has taken on building for its future is likely to be a winner.

## Sightseeing

Macau has plenty to see, from historic colonial architecture and baroque churches to ancient Chinese temples and ruined forts. The city is split into three areas: the section joined to mainland China, and the islands of **Taipa** and **Colôane**. The heart of the city, with most of the sights and the action, is to be found in the mainland section, while the two islands – particularly the more distant Colôane – offer more peaceful respite.

Trips Out of Town

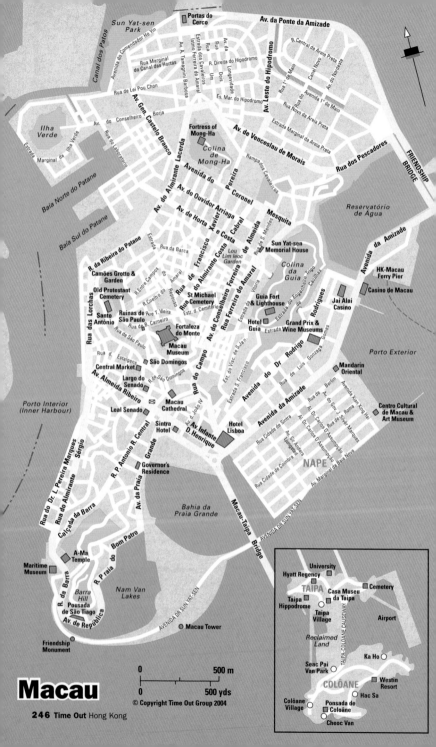

Sun Yat-sen Park
Portas do Cerco
Av. da Ponte da Amizade

R. Central da Areia Preta
Canal Novo
Av. do Nordeste

Canal dos Patos
Av. de Comendador Ho Yin
Rua Marginal do Canal das Hortas
Estrada dos Cavaleiros
Istmo Ferreira do Amaral
Rua A. Tamagnini Barbosa
Rua Dois
Rua da Longevidade
Av. da Direita do Hipodromo
Es. Mar. do Hipodromo
Av. Leste do Hipodromo
Rua 1ª de Maio
Avenida 1ª de Maio
Rua Novo da Areia Preta
Estrada Marginal da Areia Preta

Rua de Lei Pou Chon
Av. Gen. Castelo Branco
Av. do Conselheiro Borja
Av. do abocatoria
Rua da Ilha Verde
Ilha Verde
Estrada Marginal da Ilha Verde

Fortaleza of Mong-Ha
Colina de Mong-Ha
Av. de Venceslau de Morais
Rampados Cavaleiros
Rua dos Pescadores

FRIENDSHIP BRIDGE

Baía Norte do Patane
Baía Sul do Patane

Av. do Almirante Lacerda
Avenida do Coronel Mesquita
Pereira
Rampa dos Cavaleiros
Reservatório de Água

Av. do Ouvidor Arriaga
Av. de Horta e Costa
Rua Francisco Xavier
Cabral
Rua de Almeida
Rua de S. Mendes
Sun Yat-sen Memorial House

Avenida da Amizade
HK-Macau Ferry Pier
Casino de Macau

R. da Ribeira do Patane
Rua da Barca
Estrada
Lou Lim Ieoc Garden

Colina da Guia

R. de Entre Campos
R. Coelho do Amaral
R. Cinco de Reposua
Rua de Almirante Costa
St Michael Cemetery
Rua do Conselheiro Ferreira do Amaral
Guia Fort & Lighthouse
Estrada do Engenheiro Tinga
Cacilhas
Rodrigues
Jai Alai Casino

Camões Grotto & Garden
Old Protestant Cemetery
Santo António
Ruinas de São Paulo
Rua de B. Carneiro
Rue T. Meira
Rua de São Paulo
Fortaleza do Monte
Rua de S. Francisco
Hotel Guia
Grand Prix & Wine Museums

Porto Exterior

Rua das Lorchas

Macau Museum
São Domingos
Central Market
R. de Estalagens
R. de São Domingos
Largo do Senado
Leal Senado
Macau Cathedral
Rua de João IV
Av. Almeida Ribeiro
Rua do Campo
Estrada S. Francisco
Av. do Dr. Rodrigo
Rua de L. Gonzaga Gomes
Mandarin Oriental

Avenida da Amizade
Avenida do Dr. Rodrigo
Rua de... Berlim
Avenida Xian King Hai
Av. do Gov. J. Albuquerque
Rua de Roma
Centro Cultural de Macau & Art Museum

Porto Interior (Inner Harbour)

Sintra Hotel
Av. Infante D. Henrique
Hotel Lisboa
Rua Cidade de Sintra
Al. Dr. Carlos D'Assumpção
Av. Sir Anders Ljungstedt
Al. Dr. Carlos D'Assumpção
NAPE
Rua Cidade de Coimbra
Av. Marginal da Baía Nova

Rua do Dr. L. Pereira Marques Sérgio
R. P. Antonio R. Central
Rua da Praia
Grande
Governor's Residence
Bahia da Praia Grande

Rua do Almirante
Calçada da Barra
Bom Patro
A-Ma Temple
R. P. praia
Maritime Museum
R. da Barra
Barra Hill
Pousada de São Tiago
Av. de Republica
Friendship Monument

Nam Van Lakes

Macau-Taipa Bridge
AVENIDA DR SUN YAT-SEN

AVENIDA DR SUN YAT-SEN
Macau Tower

## Macau

0        500 m
0        500 yds

© Copyright Time Out Group 2004

University
Hyatt Regency
Cemetery
TAIPA
Taipa Hippodrome
Casa Museu da Taipa
Taipa Village
Airport
Reclaimed Land
TAIPA-COLOANE CAUSEWAY
Ka Ho
Seac Pai Van Park
Westin Resort
COLÔANE
Coloane Village
Ponsada de Coloane
Hac Sa
Cheoc Van

## Central Macau

Central Macau's famous waterfront avenue, the **Avenida da Praia Grande**, is an excellent place to start a tour of the city. The grand street once extended in a graceful banyan-lined crescent from the ramparts of São Francisco Battery & Gardens, along the coast to the fortress of Bom Parto, around the cliffs towards the fortress of Barra, eventually reaching the **Porto Interior** (Inner Harbour). Lined with magnificent buildings, the Praia Grande used to be one of Macau's renowned beauty spots. Sadly, extensive reclamation has diminished the beauty of the Praia Grande in recent years, though the southern end of Avenida de República, beyond the Governor's Residence, still gives a tangible echo of what it originally looked like.

Walking down Avenida da Praia Grande, one of the first significant sights is the **Jorge Alvares Monument**, which honours the Portuguese explorer. Here he is remembered by a stone statue that depicts him as a stocky bearded figure in a medieval tunic and long cape, holding a sheathed sword, with the *padrão* (marker stone) he erected at Lintin standing behind him. *See also p7.*

Turn left off Avenida da Praia Grande on to Avenida Almeida Ribeiro and you will reach the buildings of the **Leal Senado** (Loyal Senate; *see p248*). Built in classic Portuguese Manueline style in 1784, it stands on the site of a much older, open-sided Chinese pavilion dating from the very first Portuguese settlement in Macau. It was here that the Red Guards gathered to express their anger during the riots of December 1966. Today the building houses the Municipal Council.

Opposite the Leal is the **Largo do Senado** (Senate Square), the symbolic heart of Macau. Many cultural events take place here, and it's worth visiting in the evening when it is often illuminated for a festival. The square is surrounded by a number of lovely colonial structures, including the **General Post Office** and the charitable foundation **Santa Casa da Misericordia**. Well-preserved Portuguese architecture abounds here – the **Edificio Ritz**, which now houses a branch of the tourist office, is a good example.

A short walk through the square to Rua de São Domingos, on its northern side, will bring you to the church of **São Domingos** (*see p249*), also known as Santa Rosa. Next to it is the **São Domingos Market**, or Central Market, which is one of the busiest, and the most splendidly restored in Macau.

Just east of here, Rua de São Paulo leads to the Jesuit Collegiate Church of Madre de Deus, more commonly known as the **Ruinas**

de São Paulo (or Ruins of St Paul; *see p249*). For many, this is quite simply *the* symbol of Macau – the elaborate stone façade has featured on postcards since the 19th century. The original church was built by Japanese Christians who had fled from persecution in their homeland. Unfortunately, only the stone façade remains, the rest of the building having been destroyed by fire in 1835.

Perched on a hill directly above the Ruinas de São Paulo, the **Fortaleza do Monte** (*see p248*) provides the strongest connection between modern Macau and its colonial roots. Also built by the Jesuits from 1616 onwards, this was the first home of the Portuguese settlers. Dug into the hillside near the fortress is the **Macau Museum** (*see p249*), which tells the history of the peninsula.

From the Ruinas de São Paulo, it's a short walk to the church of **Santo António** (*see p249*). A place of worship has stood here since the mid 1500s, which makes the modern structure on the site today the oldest church in Macau. Churches here seem to be ill fated, having burned down on several occasions. Next to Santo António stand the tranquil **Camões Grotto & Garden** (*see p248*), where locals come to relax. On the eastern edge of the garden is the defunct **Old Protestant Cemetery** (*see p249*), which was established in 1821 to provide for the non-Roman Catholic foreign community. The cemetery was badly needed as tenets of Catholicism forbade the burial of non-believers in consecrated soil, which effectively meant there was no place to bury Protestants in Macau until it was created.

About 15 minutes' walk from the Old Protestant Cemetery, on Estrada do Cemitério, is the lovely **St Michael Cemetery**. This large Catholic cemetery is filled with statues of angels and features some beautiful, elaborate tombs. From the cemetery, walk north along Avenida do Conselheiro Ferreira de Almeida, lined with historic buildings, to the peaceful **Lou Lim Ieoc Garden** (*see p249*), with its ornate mansion and shady gardens. Early in the morning you'll see people here practising t'ai chi or strolling with their birds in cages. Just around the corner from the garden is the **Sun Yat-sen Memorial House** (*see p249*), which is only marginally connected to the rebel and founder of the Chinese Republic. Sun never actually lived in this house, but he did practise medicine in Macau before becoming a revolutionary. From here it's a short walk along Avenida Sidónio Pais to the **Flora Garden**, the largest of Macau's gardens, and one of the most beautiful. Its grounds contain a miniature zoo, lovely landscaped

**Trips Out of Town**

**Ruinas de Saõ Paulo**. *See p249*.

gardens and a pond. This is also the place
to catch the cable car (open 7.30am-6.30pm
daily) up to Guia Hill, at the top of which
you'll find the **Guia Fort & Lighthouse**
(*see below*), which have stood watch over Macau
since 1638. Wander down Guia Hill and along
Estrada de Cacilhas in the direction of the
harbour if you wish to visit the **Grand Prix
& Wine Museums** (*see below*), both housed
in the Macau Forum.

Further south, in among the waterfront
development, stands the **Centro Cultural
de Macau** (797 7215, www.ccm.gov.mo; *see
also p254*), which houses the **Art Museum**
(*see below*) and which hosts an interesting
programme of music, opera, dance, theatre and
film, as well as the annual Macau Arts Festival
(*see p254*).

### Art Museum

*Centro Cultural de Macau, Avenida Xian Xing Hai
(no phone).* **Open** 10am-5pm Tue-Sun. **Admission**
MOP$5; MOP$3 concessions. Free to all Sun.
**No credit cards. Map** p246.
This permanent collection is a showcase for art
works that are related to Macau in some way and
includes such diverse styles as French abstraction
and traditional Chinese art works.

### Camões Grotto & Garden

*Praca Luis de Camões (no phone).* **Open** 6am-
11.30pm daily. **Admission** free. **Map** p246.
The grotto and its gardens are dedicated to 16th-
century Portuguese poet Luis Vaz de Camões,
who is beloved in Macau, despite the fact that there
is no hard evidence that he actually lived here.
(Nonetheless, Macau residents firmly believe that he
did, and that he penned one of his most famous
works, 'The Lusiads', here.)

### Fortaleza do Monte

*Praceta do Museu de Macau (no phone).* **Open**
10am-6pm daily. **Admission** free. **Map** p246.
The fort – reached by walking east from the Ruins
of St Paul – was built in the early 17th century
around the early settlement here, so its walls became
those of the city. It wasn't long before the settlers
found out how strong the walls of the fort were. In
1622, the Dutch attacked Macau, but were ultimately defeated by artillery fired from the fortress, as the
settlers huddled inside. After the military was
withdrawn in 1966, the grounds were opened to the
public. On a clear day the view from Monte takes
in much of Macau and as far north as Zhuhai.

### Grand Prix & Wine Museums

*Rua de Luis Gonzaga Gomes (798 4108).*
**Open** 10am-6pm daily. **Admission** *Grand
Prix Museum* MOP$10. *Wine Museum* MOP$15.
*Joint admission* MOP$20. **No credit cards.**
**Map** p246.
The Grand Prix Museum is home to lots of interesting exhibits from the local Formula 3 Grand Prix
(*see also p258* **Making tracks**), including several
cars. There are simulators that test your driving
skills and TV monitors that let you see what it's like
to drive around the Macau race circuit. The Wine
Museum, displaying (predominantly Portuguese)
wines and wine-making tools, is not as impressive,
though tastings are sometimes possible.

### Guia Fort & Lighthouse

*Estrada de Cacilhas (no phone).* **Open** 9am-5pm
daily. **Admission** free. **Map** p246.
The fort was built in 1637 on the highest point of
the peninsula, overlooking the border with China.
In the mid 19th century, it started a third life as a
lighthouse – making it the oldest on the China coast.
If you want to enter the lighthouse, you need to
get permission from the Marine Department, which
has offices on site.

### Leal Senado

*Largo do Senado (no phone).* **Open** 9am-5.30pm
daily. *Gallery* 9am-5.30pm Tue-Sun. **Admission** free.
**Map** p246.
Chinese and Portuguese officials used to meet here
to discuss trade and other issues relating to the
Portuguese presence in Macau. The name came
about as a result of the Macau Senate refusing to
accept the so-called dual kingdom of Spain and
Portugal. From 1580 until the countries were separated again in 1640 it was the Portuguese flag – not

the Spanish one – that flew in Macau. As a result, in 1654 the city was rewarded with the title Cidade de Nome de Deus, Não Há Outra Mais Leal (City of the Name of God, There is None More Loyal).

It's worth popping in to admire the fine colonial architecture and the gallery, which hosts regularly changing shows of local interest. Today the building is used by the Provisional Municipal Authority but there are public rooms with interesting displays and a lovely courtyard to explore.

### Lou Lim Ieoc Garden

*Estrada de Adolfo Loureiro (580 255).* **Open** 6am-9pm daily. **Admission** MOP$1. Free on Fri. **No credit cards. Map** p246.
This garden, and the ornate house that stands in it (which is now a school), used to belong to a wealthy Chinese family. There are huge shady trees reminiscent of European gardens, but also twisting pathways and ornamental mountains as seen in traditional Chinese landscape paintings, as well as lotus ponds and bamboo groves.

### Macau Museum

*Praceta do Museu do Macau (357 911).* **Open** 10am-6pm Tue-Sun. **Admission** MOP$15. **No credit cards. Map** p246.
Getting to the Macau Museum is actually more rather fun than looking around it, as it is reached by way of an outdoor escalator near the Ruinas de São Paulo. Its extensive, educational exhibits begin with the early colonial years and continue through to modern times, and feature multimedia displays and videos.

### Old Protestant Cemetery

*Camões Garden, Praca Luis de Camões (no phone).* **Open** 6am-11.30pm daily. **Admission** free. **Map** p246.
Many American and European Protestants lived in Macau in the early part of the 19th century, prior to the establishment of Hong Kong as a British colony. Among them was George Chinnery, the well-known China Coast painter, who is buried here; as is Dr Robert Morrison, the first Protestant missionary to China. The cemetery fell into disrepair after its closure to burials in the 1860s, when the new Protestant Cemetery at Mong Ha was established. However, it was gradually restored between the 1950s and '70s by the Vice-Chancellor of Hong Kong University, Sir Lindsay Ride, and his wife Lady Helena May.

### Ruinas de São Paulo

*Rua de São Paulo (358 444).* **Open** 9am-6pm daily. **Admission** free. **Map** p246.
The first Western theological college established in the Far East, São Paulo trained missionary priests before they headed off to work in mainland China and Japan. Constructed between 1602 and 1638 of wood with a stone façade, most of the stone carving was completed by Japanese Christians fleeing persecution in their homeland in the 1630s. All but the façade burned down in 1835.

### Santo António

*Rua de Santo António (573 732).* **Open** 8.30am-5pm daily. **Admission** free. **Map** p246.
This is far from the original structure; numerous fires over the years have necessitated repeated reconstruction. Much of what is here today was built after the 1930s.

### São Domingos

*Largo do Domingos (no phone).* **Open** 10am-6pm daily. **Admission** free. **Map** p246.
This enormous place of worship was built in 1587 by the Spanish Dominicans, which accounts for its distinctively Spanish look. Not long after the church was completed, though, Portuguese friars took over from the previous Spanish incumbents. Upstairs is a small museum of ecclesiastical items, some centuries old and made in Macau.

### Sun Yat-sen Memorial House

*Avenida Sidónio Pais (574 064).* **Open** 10am-5pm Mon, Wed-Sun. **Admission** free. **Map** p246.
This monument to Sun Yat-sen was once home to his first wife. The house contains a collection of flags, photos and other relics.

## Southern Macau

This area is being revitalised and the construction of the **Macau Tower** (*see p250*) on reclaimed land almost links it to Central Macau. As yet, though, the paths and roads are not good enough to make it a simple walk from Avenida da Praia Grande. Instead, it is accessible along the coastal path from the cultural centre. Alternatively, take a taxi and begin your walk of southern Macau here. The tower is a must-see attraction, despite its ugly concrete monolithic appearance, as the views can be spectacular on a clear day.

There are a few attractions to the west of the tower worth visiting. If from the tower you walk past the **Friendship Monument** and keep going around the coast you'll come across the Pousada de São Tiago hotel, which is built into the hillside in the ruins of a 17th-century fort. Further around, on the westernmost tip of Macau, there is the **Maritime Museum** and, opposite, the **A-Ma Temple** (for both, *see p250*). A motorised junk moored next to the museum takes tourists on rides around the harbour on weekends and Mondays.

If you turn back you can head up to Barra Hill and towards Avenida da Praia Grande. Walking towards Central Macau you will pass a stunning colonial building on your left, which used to be the famous Bela Vista Hotel, but is now home to the Portuguese consul in Macau. Continuing along this road, you will also pass **Santa Sancha**, the Governor's Residence.

Trips Out of Town

### A-Ma Temple

*Rua de São Tiago da Barra (no phone).* **Open**
9am-5pm daily. **Admission** free. **Map** p246.
This temple is dedicated to A-Ma, who came to be
known by the Portuguese as A-Ma-Gau, and thus
gave her name to the colony. Although the temple
has several Ming shrines, they are probably 'recent'
additions as the present building is thought to date
from the 17th century.

### Macau Tower

*Largo da Torre de Macau (933 339/www.macau
tower.com.mo).* **Open** 10am-9pm daily. **Admission**
MOP$70; MOP$35 concessions. **No credit cards.**
**Map** p246.
As high as the Eiffel Tower but more than a century
newer, Macau Tower is the city's latest tourist attraction. The concrete column isn't much to look at, but
once you've taken the glass elevator to the 223m-high
(731ft) observation deck, there are spectacular views
over the Chinese border as far as 55km (34 miles)
away (although pollution often reduces the range
dramatically). The viewing platform has glass floor
panels, so it's not for those who suffer from vertigo,
although the revolving 360° Café and the 180°
Lounge both offer more relaxed ways of taking in the
view. Unfortunately there's no guide explaining what
you can see, but the view is impressive nonetheless.

For thrill seekers, adventure holiday specialist AJ
Hackett (9888 858) offers a range of activities depending on your nerve, including a climb up the 90m (27ft)
metal mast on the very top of the observation deck.
For those who prefer to keep their feet closer to the
ground, the tower grounds feature a carousel, an
amusement arcade, a motion simulator and several
bars and restaurants overlooking the waterfront. The
complex also has shops and a cinema.

### Maritime Museum

*Largo do Pagoda da Barra (595 481).* **Open**
10am-5.30pm Mon, Wed-Sun. **Admission** MOP$5.
**No credit cards.** **Map** p246.
The museum is home to a number of ships, including a flower boat, a tugboat, a Chinese fishing
vessel and a dragon boat (still used for racing). It
also has artefacts relating to Macau's seafaring past.

## Taipa

The highlight of this island is the traditional
village of Taipa on the southern tip. The north's
hotel and casino developments are making it
a bit of a bedroom community for mainland
Macau, while it is also home to the horse-racing
track and the airport. You can reach Taipa from
mainland Macau by one of two bridges, the
original (unimaginatively named) Macau-Taipa
Bridge, and the newer Friendship Bridge.

In Taipa Village there is the picturesque
**Casa Museu da Taipa** (*see below*), with its
small collection of period furnishings. The
area around it is great for a walk and often has

musicians or dancing at weekends. Although
it's surrounded by high-rise housing blocks,
life is calm and traditional amid the two-storey
colonial buildings that line the village's narrow
lanes and alleys. A charming market is held in
the square every Sunday.

### Casa Museu da Taipa

*Avenida da Praia (825 314).* **Open** 10am-6pm
Tue-Sun. **Admission** free. **Map** p246.
One of five colonial buildings on the street, this
museum combines European and Oriental design.
The rooms are filled with furniture, paintings, art and
personal artefacts that reflect Macau's dual heritage.

## Coloane

Further away from Macau than Taipa, Coloane
offers the perfect antidote to the hustle and
bustle of central Macau. Connected to Taipa via
a causeway, the less-developed island offers few
sights but more in the way of natural beauty,
with some reasonable beaches and verdant
scenery. The best beaches are **Cheoc Van** and
**Hac Sa** (meaning 'black sand') on the southern
side of the island. Both have lifeguards on duty
(in summer), surfboards for hire and public
swimming pools that stay open late. Hac
Sa is also home to the renowned restaurant
**Fernando's** (*see p252*), while Cheoc Van beach
has a giant swimming pool and a restaurant/bar.
If you want to take a walk on the green side,
then head for **Seac Pai Van Park** (*see below*)
on the western side of the island, where there are
hiking trails, an aviary and botanical gardens.

The village of Coloane, which has been
subjected to less development than that of
Taipa, is centred around a small, tiled square,
at the end of which is the **Chapel of St
Francis Xavier** (*see below*).

### Chapel of St Francis Xavier

*Rua do Meio (no phone).* **Map** p246.
Dedicated to Asia's most famous missionary, the
chapel contains some of his bones. It was built in
1928 in classic Portuguese style, and is decorated
with Chinese artworks.

### Seac Pai Van Park

*Estrada de Seac Pai Van (870 277).* **Open** 9am-
5.45pm Tue-Sun. **Admission** free. **Map** p246.
This large expanse of greenery has a walk-through
aviary, hillside trails, Chinese-style pavilions, a
small botanical garden, a children's playground and
a picnic area.

## Where to eat

Macau is a foodie's paradise. It was serving
fusion food decades before the East-meets-
West cuisine became a global fad. Indigenous
Chinese and traditional Portuguese influences

**Macau Tower**. See p250.

Trips Out of Town

were melded here to create the unique Macanese style, which also incorporates African, South American and South-east Asian spices, with delicious results. The real value of Macau can be found in its many restaurants; big servings of hearty food at prices far cheaper than in Hong Kong. In terms of drink, there's plentiful Portuguese wine at reasonable prices, and excellent coffee in the many cafés here.

The variety of food available here increases every year, and you can now get everything from French and Italian to Indian, Japanese, Mexican and Vietnamese. Macau has good coffee shops for a leisurely drink or quick snacks, while Macanese egg tarts are a delectable local speciality that should not

be missed. In Taipa Village there are dozens of shops selling home-made nougat and cake.

In addition to the following places, the restaurant at the **Pousada de São Tiago** (*see p256*) is also highly recommended.

## A Lorcha

*289 Rua do Almirante Sérgio (313 193).*
**Open** 12.30-3pm, 6.30-11.30pm Mon, Wed-Sun.
**Main courses** MOP$40-$80. **Credit** AmEx, MC, V.
**Map** p246.

Wooden beams and arches provide a European setting for one of the best dining experiences in town. A Lorcha offers great value for money, with giant helpings of traditional Portuguese and Macanese food. It's busy most nights – locals love the place – so it's advisable to make a reservation.

## Café Virginia

*173 Alameda Dr Carlos D'Assumpcão, Rua Gang Fai (715 383)*. **Main courses** MOP$35-$70. **No credit cards**. **Map** p246.
The comfy booths inside this sleek wood-and-glass café are miles away from the rustic charm of most Macau restaurants. Nonetheless, the chef specialises in old-fashioned Portuguese dishes, such as baked *bacalhau* (salted cod) with mashed potato and cream. It also offers a no-MSG guarantee.

## La Comédie Chez Vous

*1/F, 'G' Edf, Avenida Xian Xing Hai (752 021)*. **Open** noon-2.30pm, 7-10.30pm Mon-Thur, Sun; noon-2.30pm, 7pm-1am Fri, Sat. **Main courses** MOP$80-$150. **Credit** AmEx, MC, V. **Map** p246.
La Comédie is in the shadow of the Cultural Centre and sits above its sister café, which serves crêpes, omelettes, sandwiches, coffee and a huge range of teas. Upstairs, the refined Parisian ambiance continues with elegant red and pink decor and a menu offering such classics as foie gras and duck breast. The set menus (from MOP$120) are great value.

## Estrela do Mar

*Travessa do Paiva, 11 Rua do Cunha (322 074)*. **Open** 11.30am-11.30pm daily. **Main courses** MOP$30-$50. **Credit** MC, V. **Map** p246.
A lively and inexpensive restaurant a short walk from Avenida da Praia Grande, this place serves typical Portuguese food, including soups, salads, African chicken, Macau sole, curries and steak. It's nothing flash, but the locals come here in droves, which is always a good sign. Snacks are also available, along with good coffee.

## Fernando's

*Hac Sa Beach, Colôane (882 531)*. **Open** noon-9.30pm daily. **Main courses** MOP$70-$200. **No credit cards**. **Map** p246.
This popular stop-off for day-trippers is so successful you may have to wait for a table. It's a low-key sort of place, and the red brick barn-style back room near the beach is always packed with large groups. The curried crab, prawns, clams and African chicken are all irresistible – especially when washed down with sangria. Transport to Fernando's can be a problem due to its remoteness, but there is a minibus to the Hotel Lisboa, which works out far cheaper than the MOP$100 taxi ride.

## Flamingo

*Hyatt Regency Hotel, 2 Estrada Almirante Marques, Esparteiro, Taipa (831 234/www.macau.regency. hyatt.com)*. **Main courses** MOP$60-$150. **Credit** AmEx, DC, MC, V. **Map** p246.
Showcasing top-quality Macanese cooking, the Hyatt Regency's flagship restaurant is well worth a trip even if you're not staying at the hotel. Sit outside on the veranda next to the ornamental pond or inside in the colonial-style restaurant, and tuck into the likes of African chicken, curry crab and tamarind duck.

**Casa Museu da Taipa.** *See p250.*

## Long Kei

*7B Largo do Senado (573 970)*. **Open** 11.30am-3pm, 6-11.30pm daily. **Main courses** MOP$25-$40. **Credit** AmEx, DC, MC, V. **Map** p246.
Macau has plenty of Macanese and Portuguese restaurants, but Chinese food, unsurprisingly, gets a look-in too. Long Kei has a huge menu (with upwards of 350 dishes), including all the favourites such as dim sum, along with specialities like double-boiled chicken.

## O Barril

*14A/B Travessa de São Domingos (370 533)*. **Open** 8am-10pm Mon-Fri; 9am-10pm Sat, Sun. **Main courses** MOP$45-$66. **Credit** MC, V. **Map** p246.
Starbucks may have taken Hong Kong by storm, but it has only managed one outlet in Macau. Why? Because the Portuguese influence means there are many wonderful coffee and cake shops tucked away up the side streets. This is perhaps the best, and certainly the easiest to find – it's a short stroll up the alley next to McDonald's in the main square. Great coffee, excellent snacks and tempting desserts including rum babas, Macanese egg tarts and crème caramel, are all up for grabs.

## O Manel

*90 Rua Fernão Mendes Pinto, Taipa Village, Taipa (827 571)*. **Open** noon-3.30pm, 6.30-10.30pm daily. **Main courses** $40-$80. **Credit** AmEx, MC, V. **Map** p246.

Taipa Village has more than a dozen good eateries but this is one of the best. Typical hearty Portuguese fare is served up in no-nonsense style by chef/owner Manel. The fish dishes are must-tries, in particular the imported Norwegian cod (*bacalhau*). Go for the baked apple if you have room for dessert.

### Restaurante Litoral
*261A Rua do Almirante Sérgio (967 878).*
**Open** noon-3pm, 6-10.30pm daily. **Main courses** MOP$70-$100. **Credit** AmEx, MC, V. **Map** p246.
Macanese food at its best. The Litoral has a classic restaurant setting, friendly service and magnificent food. Owner Manuela Ferreira brought her home recipes and set up this restaurant to the delight of all who had tasted her cooking. Try the charcoal-black stewed duck with herbs or the African chicken.

### Robuchon a Galera
*3/F, Hotel Lisboa, 2-4 Avenida de Lisboa (577 666).*
**Open** noon-2.30pm, 6.30-10.30pm daily. **Main courses** from MOP$300. **Credit** AmEx, DC, MC, V. **Map** p246.
Run by French super-chef Joël Robuchon, this is Macau's best and most expensive restaurant, boasting a menu and wine list to rival anything in Asia, all for lower prices than in Hong Kong (though it's still not cheap). The gaudy Lisboa Hotel makes a strange home for this restaurant, but nonetheless it's done with taste.

## Nightlife

Macau's nightlife is a mixed bag. While thriving restaurants, casinos, strip clubs and 'massage' parlours are two-a-penny, finding a good bar or club is a bit more difficult. They have always tended to be scattered around Macau, making it difficult to move between them and even if you know the name of place they can be difficult to find. Things eased a few years ago when the waterfront area, known as the Nape reclamation, sprang up between the Mandarin Oriental hotel and the Hotel Lisboa. About 20 bars can now be found on or close to Avenida Dr Sun Yat-sen. To find it by taxi, just say 'Lan Kwai Fong' to the driver (the name is taken from Hong Kong's best-known entertainment district).

There are bars here to suit most tastes, but the area hasn't taken off as much as some had hoped. Many drinking dens are empty even on weekend nights – apart from the odd mainland Chinese tour group dropping in – and considering the low-level of the bands and karaoke entertainment on offer, this is not surprising. Nonetheless, there are a few decent hangouts – you just need to check out a few places first to see which vibe suits you best. The downside is that drinks here are closer to Hong Kong prices (MOP$30-$40 for standard drinks).

The area around the Macau Tower has outdoor restaurants and cafés where you can enjoy a beer, while most coffee shops serve a good range of spirits at half the price of the waterfront bar area. Many of the larger hotels also boast above-average bars and clubs.

In general in Macau, the lingering Portuguese influence means the bars and clubs don't usually begin filling up until the evening is already quite old. People are friendly and you can mingle easily if you want to, but there have been problems in the past for anyone who fails to heed a few simple rules. Macau is a gambling town and gang wars have long been fought here – it is often dubbed the 'Wild East'. Triads tend to leave tourists alone, but it's unwise to get into a needless argument with anyone, especially in the clubs after midnight.

### Embassy Bar
*G/F, Mandarin Oriental, 956-1110 Avenida da Amizade (567 888).* **Open** 5pm-1am Mon-Thur; 5pm-3.30am Fri, Sat; 5pm-2.30am Sun. **Credit** AmEx, DC, MC, V. **Map** p246.
As the name suggests, the Embassy Bar is the classiest watering hole in Macau. Whether it's pre-dinner drinks or an after-midnight boogie you're after, the mood of the bar complements the time of the night. A live band alternates with a DJ spinning tunes, and the sizeable dancefloor is usually heaving. There's also a spacious lounge area replete with low-slung couches. The drinks list is excellent.

### Focus Lounge & Karaoke
*First International Commercial Center, Avenida do Dr Rodrigo Rodrigues (702 172/173).* **Open** 9pm-6am daily. **Credit** AmEx, MC, V. **Map** p246.
Macau's one and only gay venue, this comfy bar near the ferry terminal has a cosy mezzanine seating area and a karaoke machine.

### Signal Café
*Avenida Dr Sun Yat-sen (751 052).* **Open** 8.30am-3.30am daily. **No credit cards. Map** p246.
The largest space in the waterfont area, Signal provides excellent views of the harbour from its first-floor vantage point. But whereas this place was once a DJ bar with a cool clientele, the hipsters have moved on and it's now a more ordinary bar dominated by pool tables. It's still popular with young locals, though, and is a good warm-up place for a night on the town, with comfortable couches and a wide range of cocktails. Prices are about average for the area.

## Shopping

Shopaholics will find plenty to keep them occupied here. With prices significantly cheaper than Hong Kong, Macau's biggest draw is its antiques, furniture and curio shops.

Bargains can be found, but as with anywhere, you have to be careful that what you're buying is authentic and worth the money. Is that Ming Dynasty vase real? To the inexpert eye it's hard to tell, so be cautious of sellers' claims.

Some traders distinguish between antiques and reproductions. Factories over the border in Zhuhai churn out replica tables, chairs, wardrobes and ottomans, while others strip down and restore furniture thrown out as worthless on the mainland for a hefty mark-up to tourists. Yet many of these restored items are beautiful additions to any home, in particular the dark woods, florid engraving and colourful tiled mosaics.

Haggle successfully and you may well end up with a bargain. You can sometimes cut the cost in half or more if you're buying several items from the same shop. Don't worry about carrying them home – most shops can arrange delivery anywhere in the world. As a final word of warning: if you come from a cold climate, make sure the wood has been treated properly to withstand the temperature differences.

Many of these shops are found on the **Rua de São Paulo**, the popular tourist walkway leading to the ruined church. Try **Wa Fat Trade Company** at No.11 for Ming Dynasty-style furniture; **Mobilias e Antiquidades Lu Va** at No.23 for beautiful but expensive antiquities; **Iok Nagi** at No.31 for classical Chinese furniture, and **Mobilias Soi Cheong Hong** at No.38 for leather and wooden boxes. In between are heaps more shops selling furniture and curios such as bamboo birdcages, carved walking sticks and jewellery boxes.

Another popular buy in Macau is knitwear, since manufacturing woollen and cotton garments is a major local industry. Many recognisable labels (usually overruns, discontinued lines and seconds) can be picked up for a snip. Rummage around the clothing shops and stalls in **Largo do Senado** and the market on **Rua de São Domingos** and you may well find something to suit you.

Other items to look out for in Macau include competitively priced electrical goods and gold jewellery (which you'll find in many of the shops lining **Avenida Almeida Ribeiro**), and – for their novelty value – Chinese herbs and medicine.

For more modern and established shops, head for **New Yaohan** shopping centre next to the ferry terminal, which has all the usual department-store offerings, or **Central Plaza** and the **Landmark**, which both brim with trendy shops such as Esprit and Episode.

Foodies will find **Taipa Village** a fascinating stop-off. The nougat and biscuit shops lining the main street sell different flavours of nutty sweets, including an excellent peanut brittle. The Sunday market here offers a much bigger selection of foods to try.

## Arts & entertainment

Macau may be small but it punches above its weight in many areas, the arts included. Along with its many museums, there is also a thriving cultural scene. Occupying pride of place in the waterfront redevelopment is the **Centro Cultural de Macau** (*see p248*), which hosts plays, classical music and arts exhibitions, both home-produced and by visiting performers, artists and musicians. Many internationally renowned artists who visit Hong Kong will stop off in Macau for at least one night, so it's always worth checking to see what's on.

### Festivals & events

Any time of year is good for a visit to Macau, but there are some festivals and special events that could make your trip more memorable if you time it right. Here are a few of the best ones.

**New Year's Eve** is celebrated in Macau with an impressive fireworks display over Nam Van Lakes at midnight, while thousands of people throng the illuminated main square, Largo do Senado.

**Chinese New Year** takes place on the first day of the first moon of the Chinese New Year. Besides the traditional lion and dragon dances, Macau has an edge over Hong Kong in that firecrackers and fireworks are legal for anyone to set off.

In March/April the **Macau Arts Festival** features outstanding dance, painting, theatre, Chinese opera and art. What the shows may sometimes lack in production quality they make up for in colour. For more information, log on to either www.icm.gov.mo or www.iacm.gov.mo.

Macau also has a **jazz festival** every May, with concerts in the Cultural Centre; for information call 596014.

The **International Fireworks Display Contest** in September/October is billed as the largest fireworks competition in the world, with pyrotechnic experts from different countries trying to outblast each other over Nam Van Lakes. Also in October is the **International Music Festival**, which brings in orchestras, choirs and musicians from around the world. Shows are staged around town, in baroque churches and gardens,

# Cash Macau

The vast majority of people who come to Macau come here to gamble. Of course, where most punters lose, Macau gains – casino tax payments account for five billion patacas, or 57 per cent of the government's annual budget revenue. It's no surprise then that Chief Executive Edmund Ho has pronounced gambling the key to the enclave's future economic development, and that the city has licensed an unprecedented expansion of the industry by allowing Las Vegas tycoons Steve Wynn and Sheldon Adelson to build casinos here. Macau will, within a few years, be China's very own Sin City.

Until a couple of years ago Macau was the personal playground of business mogul Dr Stanley Ho, whose Sociedade de Tourismo e Diversões de Macau (STDM) operated all the local casinos under a government franchise. But the 'God of Gamblers' now has to prepare for some stiff competition, although it's a challenge he's happy to take on as more and more gamblers will be attracted to the city: estimates suggest the current ten million (mainly Chinese) visitors a year will double within a decade. For Ho it will mean a smaller slice of a bigger pie.

Wynn Resorts and Adelson's Galaxy Casino have promised to transform the rough and often seedy gambling centre into a world-class gaming and entertainment destination. The change has already begun, with smaller casinos being set up by the American invaders to make a quick entrance into the trade while their grander visions are turned into bricks-and-mortar reality. Ho has fired an early response, opening the Pharaoh's Palace casino, complete with faux Egyptian symbols, on reclaimed land in the Nape area. It's not pretty but it adds to the kitsch casino architecture and is a sign of things to come.

## GAMBLING

Every hour, more than three million patacas are placed in bets at the city's gaming tables. There are now more than a dozen casinos in Macau, ranging from the glitzy to the downright dodgy. There's no entry fee, but foreigners have to be over 18 (locals over 21). There's also no real dress code, but don't wear sandals or carry food, and prepare to have your bag searched.

Apart from the usual casino fare of baccarat, blackjack and roulette, you can try your luck at the Chinese games of *fantan*

(played with a silver cup and porcelain buttons) and *dai siu* (a three-dice game). No photos can be taken inside any of the casinos, and the bets are usually set at a minimum of MOP$50. If you do get lucky, you're not obliged to tip the croupiers, but be warned: they normally skim ten per cent of your winnings as a matter of course. And for those expecting casinos filled with Vegas-like smiles and free drinks, think again: Macau's casinos give you action, but they also give you smoky rooms and a lot of pushing and shoving.

If you plan on visiting just one casino, it has to be the **Hotel Lisboa** (2-4 Avenida de Lisboa, (577 666/377 666). Looking like a Gaudí-inspired spinning top, Stanley Ho's landmark 24-hour entertainment centre constitutes the busiest, smokiest and most anarchic casino in town. As well as casino betting, wagers can be placed on sports such as English Premiership football. The two-floor complex is huge, with over 1,000 guest rooms, plus 18 restaurants, a nightclub and coffee shops. Free shuttle buses run from the Macau Ferry Pier.

## HORSE RACING

Betting on the nags comes second to casinos in Macau and the enclave's racing has long been seen as a poor relation of its Hong Kong equivalent. But the **Macau Jockey Club** at the Taipa Hippodrome (821 188, www.macauhorse.com) has improved its facilities in recent years and upgraded the standard of its horses and riders. Free shuttle buses run to the racecourse from the Hotel Lisboa on race days (several times a week; call the club for details). Entrance costs MOP$20.

## GREYHOUND RACING

Macau's greyhound racing club is one of the largest and best in the world, occupying the former Macau national football stadium (Macau (Yat Yuen) Canidrome, Avenida General Castelo Branco, 221 199). Facilities are first class, with grandstands, private boxes, a VIP lounge and coffee shop. With 14 races on each card, the odds are you'll pick at least one winner during a meeting. Races are held from 8pm on Tuesdays, Thursdays, Saturdays and Sundays. Admission is MOP$10, but an extra MOP$3 will get you into the members' stand.

as well as the Cultural Centre's auditoria, the largest of which hosts a Chinese opera that traditionally closes the festival.

The city's most famous event without doubt is the **Formula 3 Grand Prix** weekend, held in November (*see p258* **Making tracks**).

## Where to stay

Whether you want a cheap bed for the night or to indulge in luxurious surroundings, Macau has a hotel to match your budget. The maxim that you get what you pay for holds true, but many of the lower-end hotels are comfortable, clean and have all the necessary facilities.

Many hotels, including those listed below, can be booked through travel agencies at the ferry terminal either in Hong Kong or Macau. It's rarely difficult to get a room – except around the time of the Formula 3 Grand Prix in November – but booking in advance is always a good idea and often gets you a better price.

Many hotels run free shuttle buses to and from the ferry terminal, airport and major casinos.

### Grandview

*142 Estrada Governador Albano de Oliveira, Taipa (837 788).* **Rates** MOP$980 single/double; MOP$2,180-$6,280 suite. **Credit** AmEx,DC, MC, V. **Map** p246.
This is a good bet if you want a modern hotel with decent facilities for a budget price. Rooms are compact but comfortable and some have a view of the racecourse. There's 24-hour room service, an internet bar and both Western and Chinese restaurants (although eating out is a much better option).

### Hyatt Regency

*2 Estrada Almirante Marques, Esparteiro, Taipa (831 234/http://macau.regency.hyatt.com).* **Rates** MOP$1,800 single/double; MOP$2,300-$16,000 suite. **Credit** AmEx, DC, MC, V. **Map** p246.
The Hyatt's rooms may lack the glamour of those at its sister hotel in Hong Kong, but its facilities go a long way to make amends. As well as tennis and squash courts there's a fitness centre and aerobics studio, but if you've come to chill out there's a large outdoor pool in the lush gardens, plus separate male and female spas offering treatments.

### Mandarin Oriental Resort & Spa

*956-1110 Avenida da Amizade (567 888/ www.mandarinoriental.com).* **Rates** MOP$1,500-$1,900 single/double. **Credit** AmEx, DC, MC, V. **Map** p246.
Probably the best deal in town for those who want to be pampered, the Mandarin Oriental is a destination in its own right. Cheaper than its Hong Kong counterpart, it nonetheless offers impeccable service, luxurious Portuguese-style surroundings and a giant pool. The restaurants and bars here are all good, especially the Embassy Bar (*see p253*), Mezzaluna restaurant and NAAM Thai restaurant.

### Metropole

*Avenida da Praia Grande (493 501).* **Rates** MOP$530-$700 single/double. **Credit** AmEx, MC, V. **Map** p246.
A well-located hotel in the heart of Macau, the Metropole offers affordable rooms with basic but decent facilities, including laundry, a passable restaurant and shuttle bus services. The hotel's main draw, though, is its proximity to many of the city's attractions.

### Pousada de Colôane

*Praia de Cheoc Van, Colôane (882 144).* **Rates** MOP$420 single/double. **Credit** AmEx, DC, MC, V. **Map** p246.
If you want to stay out of town without paying a fortune, then this quiet 22-room hotel near the beach in Colôane could be just the place. It's peaceful, remote and has a (small) pool. Despite a recent refurbishment, the rooms remain a little shabby and it's cold in winter, but staff are very welcoming and the sea-view terrace makes up for any shortcomings.

### Pousada de Mong-Ha

*Colina de Mong-Ha (515 222).* **Rates** MOP$400-$600 single/double; MOP$900 suite. **Credit** AmEx, DC, MC, V. **Map** p246.
A great find for the budget-conscious traveller, this hotel is run by students from the adjacent Institute for Tourism Studies. Service is excellent, but the real charm of this hotel is its beautiful rooms, with carved wooden furniture, large beds and tasteful Portuguese decorations. Each has a balcony and a big private bathroom with decent showers. With its quiet courtyards and close proximity to the 19th-century Mong-Ha fort and gardens, this is an ideal place for a romantic getaway – provided you don't mind going without a pool or a gym. The restaurant also offers a great Sunday lunch buffet for MOP$110.

### Pousada de São Tiago

*Avenida da República, Fortaleza de São Tiago de Barra (378 111/2739 1216/www.saotiago.com.mo).* **Rates** MOP$1,620-$1,960 single/double. **Credit** AmEx, DC, MC, V. **Map** p246.
Built within the ruins of a 17th-century fort, this hotel will seduce even the most world-weary traveller with its beauty and charm. It's the closest you'll get to a boutique hotel around here. Rooms are small but beautifully decorated – in addition to imported Portuguese furniture and tiles, some incorporate the curved walls of the hillside into their design. The pool is tiny, but the excellent terrace restaurant offers good food and a laid-back ambiance.

### Hotel Sintra

*Avenida de Dom João IV (710 111/www.hotel sintra.com).* **Rates** MOP$860-1,260 single/double. **Credit** AmEx, DC, MC, V. **Map** p246.
The Sintra is located in the heart of Macau, a short walk from many of the top tourist sights and casinos. It's moderately priced and although it was built in 1975 it looks almost new, thanks to a mid

**Taipa Village**.
*See p250.*

# Making tracks

Part of the Formula 3 world championship, the **Grand Prix** is the biggest annual event in Macau. During the race, which first ran in 1954, the city's streets are turned into a racetrack, and thousands of people flock from Hong Kong and the mainland to get close to the action and whiff the exhaust fumes as cars whizz past. The event takes place on the third weekend in November and it's hard to get accommodation if you haven't booked in advance (also note that hotel rates tend to go up around this time).

Tickets range from MOP$200-$400 for a single day to MOP$350-$700 for the whole weekend. Tickets are available in person from the Macau Government Tourist Office (9 Largo do Leal Senado), the Tourist Information Counter at Shun Tak Centre, 200 Connaught Road, Central, Hong Kong, and from the Kong Seng Ticketing Network in Macau and Hong

Kong (www.kongseng.com.mo). For general information about the race, call 555 555 within Macau or 7171 7171 in Hong Kong; or log on to www.macau.grandprix.gov.mo.

If you fancy having a go at some motor racing action yourself, head to the karting track at the **Macau Motorsports Club** on Colôane (Estrada Seac Pai Van Kartodromeo de Colôane, 882 126). No experience is necessary – just turn up and pay (MOP$100 for ten minutes, $180 for 20 minutes). After watching a short instruction video, staff will kit you out in helmet and gloves, then you clamber in behind the wheel. Once the engine starts you go around the track. The speed of each kart varies – if it's way too slow take it back to the pit lane and swap – but some reach up to 60 kilometres (37 miles) per hour. The easiest way to get to and from the track is by taxi.

1990s renovation. Rooms are large and some have partial harbour views, but the real reason for staying here is to be in the middle of all the fun.

### Westin Resort

*1918 Estrada de Hac Sa, Colôane (871 111/ www.westin.com).* **Rates** MOP$2,100-$2,450 single/double. **Credit** AmEx, DC, MC, V. **Map** p246. If you want to wallow in the lap of luxury, this resort has it all. Among the facilities are an indoor and two outdoor swimming pools, tennis courts, a health club and an 18-hole golf course. Every room has a big (although not very private) balcony, and many of them overlook Hac Sa beach. It's far from the centre of town, but the emphasis is on relaxation and once you're here, you'll never want to leave.

## Resources

### Hospital

*São Januario Hospital, Estrada do Visconde de São Januario (313 731).* **Map** p246.

### Internet

*Cyber Cafe Varandah, 1/F, Landmark, Avda Amizade (786 987).* **Open** 10am-10pm daily. **Map** p246.

### Police station

*Avenida de Rodrigo Rodrigues (573 333).* **Map** p246.

### Post office

*CTT de Maau, 789 Avenida de Praia Grande, Largo do Senado (356 062).* **Map** p246.

## Tourist information

*Macau Government Tourist Office, PO Box 3006, 9 Largo do Senado (315 566/513 355/ www.macautourism.gov.mo).* **Map** p246.
The MGTO also has information counters at the following locations: Guia Fort & Lighthouse (569 808; 9am-5.30pm daily), Ferry Terminal (726 416; 9am-10pm daily), International Airport (861 436; 9am-10pm daily) and Ruinas de São Paulo (358 444; 9am-6pm daily). Alternatively, you can always try calling the Tourist Assistance Helpline (340 390; 9am-6pm daily).

If you want information before you leave Hong Kong, visit the MGTO at Chek Lap Kok Airport (2769 7970/2382 7110) or at 336 Shun Tak Centre, 200 Connaught Road, Central, Hong Kong Island (2857 2287/2559 0147).

## Other useful information

### Language

The official languages are Mandarin, Cantonese and Portuguese, but English is widely understood (and spoken in hotels and tourist attractions, but not taxis).

### Money

Macau's official currency is the pataca (usually symbolised by MOP$), which is divided into 100 avos. It is indexed to the Hong Kong dollar, with a conversion rate of MOP$1.03 to HK$1, but translates as dollar for dollar in everyday use in shops and bars etc. If you pay in Hong Kong dollars you will often receive your change in patacas.

Foreign currency and travellers' cheques can easily be changed in hotels, banks and at authorised money-changers, which are located throughout Macau. Alternatively, you can withdraw money from one of the city's many ATMs. Credit cards are accepted in many hotels, shops and restaurants.

### Telephones

Local calls are free from private phones, but cost MOP$1 from public phones. You can buy phone cards to the value of MOP$50, $100, $150. Credit card phones are found in busier areas.

To call abroad from Macau, dial 00 + country code + local number (omitting the 0 of the area code if there is one). When calling Hong Kong, dial 01+ the eight-digit number. International calls from Macau are very expensive.

To call directory enquiries in Macau, dial 181 or, for overseas enquiries, 101. The international code for Macau is 853.

### Visas

All visitors must have a valid passport. Citizens of the US, UK, Canada, Australia, South Africa, New Zealand and most European countries do not require a visa for a stay of 20 days or less. Visas are issued for 20 days on arrival, and cost MOP$100 for an individual (MOP$50 for children under the age of 12); MOP$200 for a family visa that is valid for children under the age of 12 years; and MOP$50 per member of groups of ten or more.

## Getting around

However you arrive in Macau, you will probably either hop on to a hotel shuttle bus, bus or taxi to your final destination. Buses cover virtually every corner of the city, are frequent and fares are low, while all taxis are metered and are also inexpensive.

Alternatively, once you are in the centre of town, most places are within walking distance of one another. And if you do get tired, there are always two-seater pedicabs for hire, which cost around MOP$25 for a short trip, or MOP$100 for an hour if you want one to give you a guided tour of the sights – just make sure you negotiate the fare before you get on board.

Once you get out on to the islands of Taipa and Colôane, you might want to consider hiring bicycles, which cost about MOP$40 an hour, from near the Municipal Council Building in Taipa.

## Getting there

### By air

Most of the flights into Macau's airport on Taipa island are from China, Taiwan, Singapore and Korea. On arrival, there are free shuttle buses from the airport to all the leading hotels, as well as buses travelling downtown to the ferry terminal and the border crossing. In addition, there are plenty of taxis.

There are at least 20 helicopter flights per day from Hong Kong, which land at Macau's international airport; the flight time is 16 minutes. The cost of a one-way flight is MOP$1,205 on weekdays, MOP$1,309 on weekends/holidays; ask about one-way rates. For more information, visit www.helihongkong.com.

### By sea

A number of ferries operate more than 100 sailings daily between Hong Kong and Macau, with jetfoils operating round-the-clock services. The jetfoil also provides the quickest seaborne method of making the 60-km (38-mile) journey, taking just 55 minutes. There are two ferry terminals in Hong Kong serving Macau: the China Ferry Terminal in Tsim Sha Tsui and the larger Macau Ferry Terminal on the waterfront west of Central on Hong Kong Island.

New World First Ferry Limited (2131 8181) operates catamarans from the China Ferry Terminal to Macau; fares start at HK$130 (before 6pm) and $161 (after 6pm). Weekends and holidays tend to be busy, so book in advance through a travel agent or www.turbocat.com. On arrival in Macau, there are free shuttle buses from the ferry terminal to all the leading hotels, otherwise check with the Tourist Information desk in the terminal for public transport facilities to your destination. If in doubt, take a taxi.

# Guangzhou

Gritty, far from pretty, but a real Chinese city.

Pity poor Guangzhou – it has such a lowly reputation as a tourist destination, but, as those visitors who make the effort to come here discover, a great deal of that is undeserved. While it's true that people expecting a city of culture geared to the needs of foreign tourists are likely to be disappointed, Guangzhou nonetheless has much to offer. Conventional tourist sights may not be of the standard of those found in other major cities around the world, but take the time to venture away from the main drag and you'll be rewarded. In particular, now that a second subway line has opened, many of the city's markets, such as Huadiwan, are far more accessible than before, and you can easily while away hours browsing, people-watching and absorbing life in a truly Chinese city.

## EARLY HISTORY

Guangzhou (formerly Canton) was a thriving trading port as far back as the second century AD, when Indian and Roman merchants regularly visited. Officially it was part of the Celestial Empire, but because few of the inhabitants were Han Chinese (northerners who traditionally retained power over all other ethnic minorities), it was difficult for Beijing to retain control, and rebellions were commonplace. Guangdong province was largely Chinese in name only and revolts by minority groups continued until the 12th century.

In an attempt to counter the rebellious nature of the region, large numbers of Han Chinese were relocated to the fertile Pearl River delta, along with strong military support from the imperial armies, who had orders to eliminate the indigenous Yi and Miao minorities. Eventually, so many Han migrated south to Guangdong, lack of space meant that many were forced to move again, inland this time to provinces such as Guangxi, Guizhou and Sichuan. These days, the original minorities have all but disappeared, and the only reminder of them is the Cantonese language.

In the 1500s the Portuguese arrived but were not allowed to settle in the city (they went downriver to Macau). It wasn't until the mid 17th century that the British came along, in an attempt to open up the city to trade; they succeeded, but by 1839 opium trade was becoming a problem between the two powers, sparking off the First Opium War in the late

1830s. (During the Second Opium War the city was governed by Anglo-French forces). Guangzhou was also a centrepoint for political developments: Sun Yat-sen, later leader of the nationalist party, was born nearby, and the city was briefly capital under his auspices.

But why the bad press today? It's easy to forget that tourism in China, both domestic and international, is a recent phenomenon. Indeed, it was only 50 years ago that the country was in the throes of a cultural revolution that left 50 million Chinese dead. Until recently, recreational travel was strictly controlled. Government-approved sightseeing was designed to show off the might of China rather than to make a profit or to indulge in the concept of customer satisfaction. For many years Guangzhou's highlights included such communist relics as the Peasant Movement Institute, the Memorial to the Revolutionary Martyrs and the Huangpu Military Academy – suitably patriotic, but not exactly major crowd-pullers.

But things have changed. Ever since China began opening its doors to the rest of the world, Guangzhou has been trying to become a powerhouse of trade and commerce. These days it is growing in importance, and though it hasn't yet arrived, it's definitely on the way. Half demolished and half built, the city has one foot in the past and one in the future. Glistening glass office towers back onto truck stops that double as markets on waste grounds that only yesterday were shanty towns.

Economically, recent years have been tough on the city. After the 1997 Handover of Hong Kong the former colony's economy plummeted, and Guangzhou, only 120 or so kilometres (75 miles) upriver, has faithfully ridden its coat-tails into the slide. Only a few years ago Guangzhou was the number one choice for multinationals wanting to get a foothold in the huge Chinese economy. The expat community, especially those from Hong Kong, were very active in the area, so much so that a number of infamous 'second wife villages' sprang up to cater to the 'needs' of businessmen who spent a lot of time in the city. The glory days of these areas are now long gone. The City of Five Rams is no longer the first choice of entry into the middle kingdom, and this can easily be seen in the recent exodus of Hong Kongers, Taiwanese

and other expats, many of whom have relocated
to Shanghai. Even around notorious Taojin Lu
('Gold-digging Road'), where there were once
five major discos and nightclubs, only one
remains, and even this is a shadow of its
former raucous self.

Nonetheless, for a tourist wishing to
experience the 'real' China, Guangzhou has an
undeniable appeal, provided they bear certain
things in mind. The road system is chaotic.
The city is dirty. The pollution can be all but
incapacitating – on bad days, carbon monoxide
hangs off the flyovers like an untucked bed
sheet. The noise of construction sites, car
horns, squealing brakes on cranky buses,
haggling street vendors, people shouting into
mobile phones, goes on and on… and, like
this list, never stops.

But Guangzhou has something intangible
that Hong Kong has lost. For a start, the locals
have none of the (post-) colonial chippiness of
Hong Kongers. If they do have a chip about
something, it's that they have had to struggle
through a socialist-planned economy while
their Hong Kong cousins have been free to take
the capitalist road. Which is why they're now
doing everything they can to catch up.

## Sightseeing

The two natural landmarks of Guangzhou
are the **Zhu Jiang** (Pearl River), which cuts
through the city from west to east, and **Bai
Yun Shan** (White Cloud Mountain; *see p268*),
which dominates the city from the north.
Its major streets are Huan Shi Lu, Zhong
Shan Lu and Dongfeng Lu, all of which run
east–west. The area south of the river,
**Henan**, offers little for tourists.

The city's traditional heart is in the western
**Xiguan** and **Liwan** districts. These provide
a glimpse of old Guangzhou, with hundreds
of narrow streets and twisting alleys, though
many of these are in the process of being
demolished under the pretence of development.

The districts continue to be a magnet for
Western tourists, who are drawn in particular
to the notorious and atmospheric **Qing Ping
Market**, just north of Liu'Ersan Lu, between
Datong Lu and Zhuji Lu. This is China's most
infamous live animal market, and although it
has been greatly sanitised in recent years,
with many of the characteristic outdoor stalls
moved into modern multi-storey housings, there
is still plenty to gawp at. Many masochistic
tourists come to gawp at the tragic-looking
dogs and cats in cramped cages. Much easier
on the eye are the spice and dried medicine
stalls. Vendors sell scorpions by the bowl
and snakes are everywhere. Souvenirs here

Beautiful architecture on
**Shamian Island**. *See p264.*

Trips Out of Town

# Guangzhou

Hong Kong

**262**

Legend:
- Subway station
- Subway line

## Grid labels
A, B, C (top)
1, 2, 3, 4, 5 (left side)

## Map labels

Wangjia Horologie Market

Guangzhou Provincial Bus Station

XILU

RENMIN BEILU

ZHAN QIANLU

Trade Fair Hall

LIUHUA

HUAN SHI

XIWAN LU

LIUHUA LU

DONGFENG

Nan Hai Yu Chung Restaur

Liu Hua Park

Dong Bei R Restaurant

NAN'AN GONGLU

Yes Disco

XILU

Guang Xiao Si (Bright Filial Piety Temple)

Chenjia Si (Chen Clan Temple)

Chen Jia Ci

LIWAN

ZHONG SHAN QILU

BEILU

RENMIN ZHONGLU

Xi Men Ke

PEARL RIVER BRIDGE

ZHONG SHAN BALU

ZHONG S

LU

LONGJIN ZHONGLU

XILU

HUAGUI

LU

GUANGFU

HUIFU XILU

Liwan Lake

Banxi Restaurant

Liwanhu Gongyuan

PENGYUAN LU

LONGJIN DONGLU

LONGJIN

DUOBAO

Changshou Lu

Dai He Lu Antiques Market

CHANGSHOU XILU

CHANGSHOU DONGLU

Glasses Market

SHISHI

DADE LU

HUANGSHA

LU

BAOHUA LU

Hualin Si (Hualin Temple)

Jade Market

Liwan Plaza

SHANG XIA JIU

RENMIN NANLU

ENNING LU

LIWAN

DISHIPU

DATONG LU

ZHUJI LU

SHISANHANG LU

ZHUANG YUAN FONG

Zhu Jiang (Pearl River)

DADAO

Qing Ping Market

LIU'ERSAN LU

SHIWEITANG

Shiweitang Station

US Consulate

SHAMIAN BEIJIE

Shamian Island

Guanzhou Youth Hostel

White Swan Hotel

RENMIN BRIDGE

Monument to the Martyrs in the Sheji Massacre

NANHUA XILU

Haichu Park

SHANCUN LU

PEARL RIVER TUNNEL

FANCUN DADAO

FANGCUN

BAI ER TAN BAR ST

Fangcun

TONGFU

HONGDE LU

XILU

To Huadiwan Market

are comparatively overpriced, and stall owners tend to be a bit grabby and overbearing (you may want to give an especially wide berth to the pushy antiques dealers).

Just across a number of small footbridges is **Shamian Island**, the former British concession area, which is home to the old British and American consulates (they have both since relocated). Only last century, the movements of foreign merchants were restricted to the small island; the bridges were closed at 10pm and traders lived under the threat of execution if they even began to study the Chinese language. This is also where the buildings of the great colonial trading houses such as Jardine Matheson and Butterfield & Swire are located. To the east is the old French concession. Historic sites worth a look in this area are the old French Consulate, Shamian Park (formerly the French Consul's Garden), Our Lady of Lourdes Catholic Church and the former French missionary residence.

Back across the river, going north, head up Datong Lu, then eastwards along Dishipu and Shang Xia Jiu. Look for a large English sign on Changshou Xilu, just to the east of Liwan Plaza, to find the famed **Jade Market**. Real bargain hunting is best left to the experts, but small bracelets and assorted knick-knacks can be picked up for a few Renminbi. Inside, keep an eye out for the almost-hidden **Hualin Temple** (Hualin Si; *see p268*).

Just north of here, look for **Dai He Lu**. It's often touted as an antiques market, but genuine antiques hunters might be a little disappointed that most of the so-called 'antiques' are mass produced in local factories. Everything from strings of old coins to huge pieces of Qing Dynasty furniture is on offer, though hardly any of it is genuine. Even so, there are still plenty of souvenir shopping opportunities, with ceramic bracelets and amber trinkets cheaper than anywhere else in China. Perhaps the most difficult part is finding a way in through all the demolition and condemned houses. Walk a little up the main road, Wen Chang Lu, and find a way in through Hai Chong Bian Jie.

The area around **Shang Xia Jiu**, just east of Liwan, is another part of the city that has been massively renovated, although it's still uncertain which dynasty spawned the tendency to paint things in pastel shades. This is the old centre of town and is popular with tourists as it is within easy walking distance of Shamian Island (*see above*). Again, wholesale markets dot the surrounding area, including an aquarium market and the haberdashers' street (Guang Fu Zhong Lu). The largely

pedestrianised **Shang Jiu Lu** is a great place to hang out and people-watch. The glasses market close by at 260 Renmin Nan Lu is a wholesale market for spectacles. If you happen to have your prescription with you, this is the place to choose a new pair of frames and lenses for a fraction of the price back home.

Just south of here is a little alley known as **Zhuang Yuan Fong**. At one time this was home to many shops specialising in props and costumes for traditional Chinese Opera. These days, sadly, virtually all of them are gone, and the area has been transformed into the town's most fashionable shopping street for teenagers.

East of Shamian Island, off Yanjiang Xilu (running alongside the Pearl River), **Haizhu Square** is where many visitors begin to understand what a truly enormous range of products are made in the Pearl River Delta. If it has a 'made in China' label on it, then it probably came from this region. Proof of this can be found near the square at the **Haizhu Wholesale Market**. Only last century it was a fruit and vegetable market outside the city limits, but is now where many factories that produce household goods and souvenirs have their wholesale outlets. There are hundreds of small stalls stocking everything from novelty lighters to suits of armour, with plenty of items made using traditional silk, and beautiful 'paper cuts' (rice paper painted with brightly coloured inks, a craft that dates back nearly two centuries). The market is northwest of Haizhu Bridge, to the south of Yide Zhonglu, and west of Qiaogang Lu. The giant statue of the PLA soldier nearby was erected in October 1959 in commemoration of the tenth anniversary of the Guangzhou Liberation (when the communists under Mao successfully drove Chiang Kai-Shek out of the city and founded the People's Republic).

A few blocks east of Haizhu Square, **Beijing Lu** is the Oxford Street of Guangzhou. It was recently pedestrianised, and is a great place to see what 21st-century China is all about. Here capitalism reigns supreme in a country that still refers to itself as communist. As always in China, bargain hunters should avoid the department stores, of which the two largest are Xin Da Xin and Guang Bai, and aim for the smaller outlets. Admittedly, some of the bigger names do have bargains (the second and third floors of **Giordano** are a good place to start), but it's in the one-man shows where the real surprises – and bargains – lie. **Tai Bai** is a good choice for belts, bags and boots as well as just about anything else fashioned out of fake leather. There is an excellent selection of clothes, jewellery, cosmetics and accessories to be found here as well, at very reasonable prices.

Qing Ping Market. *See p261.*

Haizhu Wholesale Market
(and below). *See p264.*

Hai Yin Fabric Market. *See p266.*

For more Western-style shopping, try the **Friendship Department Store** (369 Huan Shi Donglu, 8333 6628). At one time these flagship department stores were the only places that sold imported goods. These days, so many items are made locally for export that Friendship outlets have become dinosaurs from a different age. They not only have the highest prices in town, but also seemingly the most staff, only a few of whom have any real concept of customer service, and just wander around aimlessly. If you really want to buy designer label items, save your money for Hong Kong.

Shoppers in the know generally prefer **China Plaza** (get out at Lie Xi Ling Yuan subway station), the very latest of Guangzhou's mega malls and certainly the trendiest at the moment. Wander the eight floors to get a feel for modern Chinese commerce, and head to the basement for a mass of fashion boutiques, nail salons and fast food. For those wanting to see what China is going to look like in the next century, this is definitely the place to look.

South-east of here, near **Hai Yin Bridge**, the fanciful **Hai Yin Fabric Market** is a treasure trove of fantastic fabrics and a vivid respite from the drab browns and greys found in most of the city. Whether you are looking for a custom-made *qipao* (traditional Chinese dress) or simply a new pair of curtains, this place has everything on its four levels. For the highest-quality Hangzhou and Shanghai silk, begin on the ground floor at A71, where even the most exquisite dragon and phoenix designs start at

just RMB70 a metre. For more choice, head up to B22 and B107, but be prepared for more of a hard sell as these two stalls are more used to dealing with foreign customers. Try B82 for tailoring, and take a look at the multicoloured yarns in B97. The fourth floor is mainly gents' suits tailors, though if you're after a man's suit, Lowu Commercial City in Shenzhen (*see p163*) is probably a better bet as staff there are much more familiar with the needs of foreigners.

South of the river in Fangcun District is **Huadiwan Market** (Huadiwan subway station). From the subway entrance this looks like just another furniture market, but venture further inside and some pleasant surprises await. Huadiwan consists of literally acres of plants, tropical fish and other assorted pets. Songbirds of every colour and description fill the bird market, and repro antique stores fill the spaces in between. Best of all is the bonsai section (the miniature trees are termed *penjing* in China, where they were first developed) and the mysterious but fascinating 'viewing stones' (rocks with naturally occurring strange shapes such as dragons).

For concerts and culture, head east to **Er Sha Dao** (Er Sha Island), a grassy island in the Pearl River that is home to the **Xing Hai Concert Hall**, where international classical stars often appear, and to posh French restaurant La Seine; *see p270*), and the **Guangdong Museum of Art** (*see p267*), which is well below the standard of the **Guangzhou Art Museum** (*see p267*) in Luhu Park.

Tour groups still visit a selection of the city's temples, even though the examples remaining after the chaos of the Cultural Revolution are rather squalid compared to other Asian cities. If you are interested, however, the most famous include the **Temple of the Five Immortals** (Wu Xian Guan; *see p268*), the **Temple of the Six Banyans** (Liu Rong Si; *see p268*), the snappily named **Bright Filial Piety Temple** (Guang Xiao Si; *see below*) and the **Chen Clan Temple** (Chenjia Si; *see below*).

Be warned, though: something depressing you may well encounter are handicapped and disfigured beggars who surround almost every temple. Some of them are delivered to the temples every day by local entrepreneurs for whom they act as professional beggars, taking advantage of sympathetic tourists.

If you're craving some greenery, head for **Yue Xiu Park** (*see p269*) to the north, beside Jiefang Beilu. The park is home to well-known sights as the **Sculpture of the Five Rams**, and the dull **Guangzhou Municipal Museum**. A far more engaging place is the **Tomb of the Nanyue King** (*see p268*), across Jiefang Beilu from the park. This is the burial place of Zhao Mo, the second ruler of the Nanyue Kingdom.

### Bright Filial Piety Temple (Guang Xiao Si)

*109 Guangxiao Lu (8108 1961).* **Open** 8am-5pm daily. **Admission** RMB4. **No credit cards.** **Map** p262 C3.

Founded in 397 BC, Guang Xiao Si is reputed to have been the first Buddhist temple in China; it's certainly the most unkempt temple in the country. Locals come here for good luck rather than to receive any kind of spiritual blessing. Discarded incense is every-where, and the resident monks seem to spend most of their time trying to sell associated paraphernalia. The most interesting thing on the site is the row of small stone lions outside the main temple, all decapitated by Red Guards during the Cultural Revolution.

### Chen Clan Temple (Chenjia Si)

*34 Yin Long Li, off Zhong Shan Qilu (8181 9653).* **Open** 9.30am-5pm. **Admission** RMB10. **No credit cards.** **Map** p262 B3.

Built in the late Qing Dynasty (1894) by the hugely powerful Chen family, this temple is also known as the Chen Classical Learning Academy because it served as both an altar for ancestor-worship and a school to prepare students for the national civil service examination. Decorations include frescoes, carved stone pillars, brick mosaics and clay sculptures on the ridges of the roofs.

### Guangdong Museum of Art

*38 Yan Yu Lu, Er Sha Island (8735 1468).* **Open** 9am-5pm Tue-Sun. **Admission** RMB15. **No credit cards.** **Map** off p263 F4.

This museum opened in 1997 and specialises in contemporary Chinese art (most of it abstract), and also has an interesting schedule of visiting national and overseas exhibitions.

### Guangzhou Art Museum

*13 Luhu Lu (8350 7904).* **Open** 9am-5pm daily. **Admission** RMB30. **No credit cards.** **Map** p263 E1.

Opened in September 2000, this museum combines modern architecture with traditional Chinese design elements. There are nine galleries, various temporary exhibition halls, and a traditional Guangdong garden, connected to the interior spaces by an inner courtyard. The number of fish in the garden pools is astounding and the feeding frenzy that ensues as they all push at once for tossed breadcrumbs is

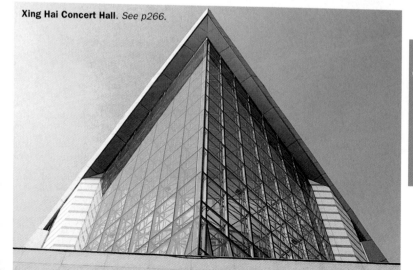

**Xing Hai Concert Hall.** *See p266.*

**Trips Out of Town**

astonishing. There are dedicated galleries for each of four famed artists from the Cantonese school of painting called Ling-Nan that emerged in the late 1800s. Expect exquisite scrolls with pastoral scenes, plum blossoms and bold calligraphy. One gallery is filled with rare Tibetan *tangkas* (tapestries), which were donated by a Hong Kong art collector.

### Hualin Temple (Hualin Si)

*Hualin Xin Jie, off Changshou Xilu (no phone).* **Open** 8am-5pm daily. **Admission** free. **Map** p262 B4.
Founded in AD 526, this temple was rebuilt after the chaos of the Cultural Revolution, and reopened in 1988. It's modest from the exterior, but inside is an impressive collection of life-sized golden buddhas.

### Temple of the Five Immortals (Wu Xian Guan)

*Huifu Xilu (8333 6853).* **Open** 9am-noon, 1.30-5pm daily. **Admission** RMB5. **No credit cards.** **Map** p263 D3.
This temple was originally built in 1377 during the Ming Dynasty in honour of the five immortals believed to be responsible for the quality of harvests. The temple has recently had a complete and rather unfortunate facelift – the central statue now looks suspiciously like moulded cement, although one of the many confusing description plaques dates it to 1113, during the Northern Song Dynasty. At the rear stands a 17m (55ft) bronze bell tower dating from

**Temple of the Six Banyans (Liu Rong Si).**

1374. Perhaps the most interesting feature is a 1907 map of Canton, stored away in a back room. This large reproduction gives an interesting perspective on the city, showing the mint, the imperial archery grounds and the fact that most of this sprawling city was at that time paddy-fields.

### Temple of the Six Banyans (Liu Rong Si)

*87 Liu Rong Lu, off Jiefang Beilu (8339 2843).* **Open** 8am-5pm daily. **Admission** *Grounds* RMB1. *Tower* RMB10. **No credit cards.** **Map** p263 D3.
The main structure in this mediocre Buddhist temple is an octagonal tower that reaches up nine storeys. The staircase is steep and narrow, with a low ceiling that all but guarantees most people will thump their skull at least once. The top storey is closed, but there is no sign explaining this until you've climbed all the way up. Far more interesting are the numerous religious shops surrounding the temple. Beware, though, of con men dressed as monks who offer cheap jade bracelets along with Buddha's blessing and then ask for money.

### Tomb of the Nanyue King

*Jiefang Beilu (no phone).* **Open** 9am-5pm daily. **Admission** RMB15. **No credit cards.** **Map** p263 D2.
For years Guangzhou suffered from a lack of ruins and historical artifacts. Chinese from the northern provinces scoffed at those in the south, referring to them as the 'southern barbarians'. But in 1983, while excavating a low hillside site for a downtown hotel, workers unearthed an ancient imperial tomb, built 2,200 years ago (the Western Han Dynasty) for the second King of the Nanyue Kingdom. The red sandstone tomb itself, along with five chambers, is intact. More than 1,000 articles, including three gold seals, which confirm the identity of King Zhaomo, have been found and are now on display. These include ceremonial jars, copper inlaid doors, jade cups and pendants, the gold seal of the emperor and the remains of the emperor's jade burial suit.

### White Cloud Mountain (Bai Yun Shan)

*15km (9 miles) north of city (3722 6736).* **Open** 9-11.45am, 1.30-4.45pm daily. **Admission** RMB5. *Cable car* RMB25. **No credit cards.** **Map** off p263 D1.
Despite the name, this is hardly a mountain, at only 384 metres (1,259 feet). Pagodas, monasteries and tea houses are dotted about the base, and when the weather is clear, and the pollution not too bad, views from the top are gorgeous. However, it can be hard to get away from other tourists. Some cramped cable cars ascend to the peak – known as the 'Ridge that Scrapes the Stars' (*Moxing Ling*) – but be aware that it is a good three-hour trek down to the base. Recently, bungee jumping, grass skiing and tobogganing facilities have been added to the park, but it is locally famous as somewhere for couples to escape from prying relatives and get intimate in their cars. To get to the park it's best to take a taxi.

Enjoying the spaciousness of **Yue Xiu Park**.

## Yue Xiu Park

*Jiefang Beilu (no phone)*. **Open** 9am-5pm daily.
**Admission** *Park* RMB5. *Attractions* prices vary.
**No credit cards. Map** p263 D1/2.

This was China's largest urban park when it opened
more than 50 years ago. Most domestic tourists
are herded to the Sculpture of the Five Rams, the
symbol of Guangzhou. Otherwise, there is a dull
museum in the park's Zhen Hai Tower (with much
emphasis put on how it was occupied by the British
and French imperialists during the Opium Wars),
and the disappointing Guangzhou Municipal
Museum, which covers the period from the Nanyue
kingdom during the first southern Chinese dynasty
to the days of the foreign concessions on Shamian
Island; along with a football stadium and some plastic pedal boats on the park's three man-made lakes.

## Where to eat & drink

### Restaurants

As the common saying goes, the Cantonese will
eat anything with wings that isn't a plane and
anything with legs that isn't a table. While this
might be a (slight) exaggeration, Guangzhou
locals' love for food is clear. In a recent survey
on dining, people here spent on average nearly
1.6 times more money on eating out than
did residents in second-ranked Shanghai or
third-ranked Beijing. Sadly, though, many
Westerners turn their noses up at some of
the more adventurous dishes here, such
as chicken's feet and endless offal dishes.
Be experimental when it comes to ordering
food and you won't go far wrong.

## Banxi

*151 Longjin Xilu (8181 5718)*. **Open** 6.30am-
11.30pm daily. **Main courses** from RMB100.
*Dim sum* from RMB5. **Credit** AmEx, DC, MC, V.
**Map** p262 B3.

The old (1949) Banxi Restaurant recently had a
facelift and now comes complete with chandeliers
and frosted-glass screens in many of its private
rooms. The staff's English is almost non-existent but
that's hardly a factor when all you need to do is point
at whatever you fancy from the dozens of dim sum
trolleys. There are plenty of curious-looking dishes
to choose from, at prices that that will please even
the most budget-conscious traveller.

## Chuan Guo Yan Yi

*2-3/F, Hua Xin Building, 2 Shui Yin Lu (3760
1325)*. **Open** 10.30am-10.30pm daily. **Main
courses** RMB30-100. **Credit** AmEx, DC, MC, V.
**Map** off p263 F2.

Chuan Guo Yan Yi offers three floors of ultra-spicy
Sichuan selections, the third being dedicated to
authentic hotpots that can only be bettered by getting on a plane and flying directly to Chengdu, the
capital of Sichuan province.

## Dong Bei Ren

*65-7 He Qun Yi Ma Lu (8760 0688)*. **Open**
10.30am-10.30pm daily. **Main courses** RMB30-
100. **No credit cards. Map** p262 C2.

This colourful chain provides an excellent introduction to Manchurian cuisine. However, try choosing from the trolleys before you succumb to the
waitresses' efforts to recommend the most expensive dishes on the menu.

**Other locations**: 36 Garden Building, Tian
He Nan Er Lu (8750 1711); 2/F, 1 Tao Jin Beilu
(8357 6277).

**Trips Out of Town**

No wonder **Dong Bei Ren** pulls in the punters. *See p269.*

### Dong Jiang

*9 Guangzhou Da Dao Nan (8429 7557).* **Open** 11am-2pm, 6.30pm-3am daily. **Main courses** RMB78-300. **Credit** AmEx, DC, MC, V. **Map** p263 D4.

This Cantonese seafood chain has locations all over the city, but the branch just around the corner from the Landmark Hotel is a good place to start. Let a *qipao*-clad hostess seat you at a table and pour you a cup of sweet flower tea, then head back down to the entrance to choose your dishes from the aquariums (don't bother with a menu, just point to what you like the look of). More adventurous diners might like to try fresh water cockroaches (*nong shi*), although the range of shellfish is excellent too – from razor shells and sea urchins to horseshoe crabs. **Other locations**: throughout the city.

### My Home Hunan

*2/F, 77 Ti Yue Xilu (8559 2101).* **Open** 11am-10.30pm daily. **Main courses** RMB30-100. **No credit cards**. **Map** p263 F1.

More fiery dishes, this time of the Hunanese variety, in a space that was recently renovated to reflect the high quality of the food served. If you prefer something more casual, try the small associated noodle shop next door, where a huge bowl of noodles with mushrooms and green vegetables is only RMB8. **Other locations**: 19 Tao Jin Beilu (8358 0544); 181-7 Tian He Donglu (3881 0808).

### Nan Hai Yu Chung

*Ti Yu Donglu, below Tian He Sports Centre (8666 8668).* **Open** 11am-3pm, 5.30-11pm daily. **Main courses** RMB30-200. **Credit** DC, MC, V. **Map** p262 C2.

The two branches of Nan Hai Yu Chung serve some of the best Cantonese seafood cuisine in the province, with some of the highest prices to go with it. Expect plenty of top-end specialities on the menu, including abalone and lobster. **Other locations**: 903 Renmin Beilu, inside Liu Hua Park (3879 6888).

### 1920

*183 Yanjiang Xilu (8333 6156).* **Open** 11am-2pm daily. **Main courses** RMB30-100. **No credit cards**. **Map** p263 D4.

This small restaurant has excellent set lunches with a distinct German flavour – just the thing after a morning exploring Shamian Island and before a hard afternoon of haggling in Haizhu Market.

### Peace

*Parkview Hotel, 2/F, 960 Jiefang Beilu (8667 1731/1732).* **Open** 6.30am-11pm daily. **Main courses** RMB40-80. **Credit** AmEx, DC, MC. **Map** p263 D2.

An appetising and easy-to-follow picture menu makes this friendly place a great introduction to Shanghai-style cooking. This, along with the antique furniture and nattily attired staff, create an excellent dining experience.

### La Seine

*Xing Hai Concert Hall, 33 Qing Bolu, Er Sha Island (8735 2222, ext 888).* **Open** 11am-2pm, 6pm-1am daily. **Main courses** RMB60-200. **Credit** AmEx, DC, MC, V. **Map** off p263 F4.

La Seine is one of the few restaurants in the city with reliable Western fare. The menu also offers interesting fusions of Chinese and European foods, excellent by local standards, but not by international ones. The prices are indicative of the upmarket surroundings.

## Bars & nightlife

It is estimated that around 10,000 punters regularly fill downtown Guangzhou's 500 bars, so if you're heading out for the night, loneliness is unlikely to be a problem. Nor will availability of booze – beer prices are usually quoted by the dozen, 12 bottles usually costing RMB160-360. If you want to buy fewer, expect the price per bottle to be quite a bit higher. Also be aware that few places liven up before 10pm.

Guangzhou nightlife has suffered greatly in the last few years as the municipal authorities continuously change their minds as to where the centre of the things should be, but lately the government is attempting to set up an area similar to Hong Kong's Lan Kwai Fong. It opened a mile-long row of new bars and coffee shops along the south bank of the river on Chang Ti Lu. Unfortunately, the location is way off the beaten track and the promenade of glowing neon has few customers. If they're still open when you arrive, try **D&D One** for its river views, or **Atlantic** for its modern design.

### Babyface

*83 Chang Di Da Ma Lu (8335 5771)*. **Open** 8pm-2am daily. **No credit cards**. **Map** p263 D4.

This is possibly the trendiest spot in town, and is always packed to bursting with fashion snobs and jet-set wannabes. Sadly, the music has gone downhill, with a handful of lazy DJs letting mix CDs do all the work, and you'll have to be prepared for lots of crushed feet, banging elbows and lecherous looks.

### The Wave

*6 He Ping Lu, Hua Qiao Xin Cun (8349 4568)*. **Open** 7.30pm-2am daily. **No credit cards**. **Map** p263 F2.

Currently the favoured *gweilo* hangout, this bar is the last in a row of large converted houses behind the Holiday Inn. Attracting a mix of customers including plenty of expats, the Wave is a great place to find local information. Western DJs churn out a selection of popular hits and dance tunes.

### Windflower

*387 Huan Shi Donglu (8358 2446)*. **Open** 6pm-2am daily. **No credit cards**. **Map** p263 F2.

Recently reopened, this stylish bar in the heart of town used to be the in place for Guangzhou's young and beautiful people, but not any more. Still, the snazzy decor, excellent service and occasional Western DJs make it a good choice for short-term visitors. It's just a shame there aren't many customers to keep you company any more.

### Yes

*2/F, Liu Hua Square, 132 Dong Feng Xilu (8136 6154)*. **Open** 8pm-2am daily. **No credit cards**. **Map** p262 C2.

This is the definitive Chinese disco. Ascend the entrance escalators to be greeted by hostesses in formal gowns. Inside, the deafening throb of imported house and techno hypnotises a sea of locals on the sunken dancefloor. Svelte beauties gyrate on raised podiums, while punters play *sik jong* (liar dice) at their tables. Truly weird.

## Where to stay

Whether you book through a Hong Kong travel agent, a website or directly with the hotel, you're bound to get a discount on published rates.

### Garden Hotel

*368 Huan Shi Donglu (8333 8989/fax 8335 0706/ www.gardenhotel-guangzhou.com)*. **Rates** RMB1,160-1,330 single/double; RMB3,740 suite. **Credit** AmEx, DC, MC, V. **Map** p263 F2.

# Time after time

Ever wonder where the Indians on Kowloon's Nathan Road who conspiratorially suggest 'copy watch, sir?' get all their supplies? Hiding behind Guangzhou's provincial bus station is the **Wangjiao Horological Market**, a wholesale market that deals solely in fake watches and their components. In the main market there are about 300 dealers, each with their own glass-topped counter displaying picture-perfect copies of between 300 and 500 of the world's most sought-after timepieces. You can choose from practically every designer under the sun, from Audemars Piguet to Zeiss, with nearly every name in between. Rolexes come in every colour, style and face design imaginable, as do Bulgaris, Tag Heuers and Cartiers. Competent hagglers should be able to get prices down to about RMB50 a piece; handily, just outside there are plenty of little hole-in-the-wall dealers who can supply a matching designer case complete with velvet lining.

Don't be afraid to explore this area to uncover many other surprises. Catering mainly to small-time dealers from other provinces, many different kinds of specialist wholesale markets are located around the old train station. The station itself can be an eye-opener for tourists who are not yet used to big Chinese cities. Everybody knows that China is the most populous nation in the world, but watching the seething mass of people heading to different destinations can be a little unnerving. Keep your eyes peeled for the shops that sell playing cards, chips and other casino paraphernalia. Even though gambling is strictly forbidden, many entrepreneurs from the rural areas head down here on shopping sprees to kit out their underground gambling dens. Check out all the different sets of marked cards, available along with specially tinted glasses, that unscrupulous dealers use to cheat their hometown buddies out of their life savings.

**Trips Out of Town**

The Garden Hotel is the top business traveller's choice in town, due to its central location, excellent executive floor and the largest convention hall in Asia. Even so, it is starting to need a facelift.

### Grand Palace Hotel

*148 Linhe Zhong (3884 0968/fax 3884 0960/ www.grandpalace-hotel.com).* **Rates** RMB580-800 double; RMB1,080 suite. **Credit** AmEx, DC, MC, V.
Located right by the new railway station, this hotel is a well-kept secret among the more budget-conscious of Hong Kong's business community. That's not surprising given its decent eating and drinking facilities, with both Chinese and Western restaurants, a comfortable bar and a coffee shop.

### Guangzhou City Youth Hostel

*179 Huan Shi Xilu (8666 6889/fax 8667 9787).* **Rates** RMB100 single; RMB150 double. **No credit cards. Map** p263 D1.
This hostel is set on two floors of a new hotel (Guangdong Tourist Hotel) near the old station. There are 80 beds in air-conditioned rooms with en suite facilities, room service, 24-hour access and facilities including a washing machine. Overall it feels more like a hotel than a hostel.

### Guangzhou Youth Hostel

*Shamian Island (8188 4298/fax 8188 4979).* **Rates** RMB50-210 single/double. **No credit cards. Map** p262 B5.
This is one of the best places in town to meet up with backpackers, if that's your thing. Unfortunately, along with being the cheapest place in town, it also has a sometimes surly staff and a steady lack of vacancies. Despite the name, it is not recognised by the World Youth Hostel Federation.

### Landmark Hotel

*8 Qiaogang Lu (8188 6968/gzhuaxia@public. guangzhou.gd.cn).* **Rates** RMB650-1,200 single/ double; RMB1,500-2,000 suite. **Credit** MC, V. **Map** p263 D4.
The hotel was under renovation at the time of going to press, which will surely help improve the rundown interior, but, in the meantime, at least the rooms are clean and it is well situated for tourists. The staff are helpful, but their English is often weak, while the condition of the sub-contracted pool and gym are far from stellar.

### Shamian Hotel

*Shamian Island (8121 2288/fax 8121 8628/ www.gdshamianhotel.com).* **Rates** RMB238 double; RMB288-360 suite. **Credit** AmEx, DC, MC, V. **Map** p262 B5.
This is a reasonable choice if you'd rather not mix with shoestring travellers, although not all rooms have private baths.

### White Swan Hotel

*Shamian Island (8188 6968/fax 8186 1188/ www.white-swan-hotel.com).* **Rates** RMB700-900 double; RMB2,290-2,576 suite. **Credit** AmEx, DC, MC, V. **Map** p262 B5.

Dubbed the 'White Stork Hotel' because of its popularity with American couples coming to adopt Chinese orphans, this place is right next to the US embassy on Shamian Island. All 843 rooms have white marble bathrooms and gold-trimmed fixtures.

## Resources

### Hospital

*Can-Am International Medical Center, 5/F, Garden Tower, Garden Hotel (8386 6988).*

### Internet

Net bars are usually small smoky dens full of loud teenagers. Big hotels are the best choice if you want to check your email as their computers are more likely to have English-language versions of Windows. For local flavour try the second-floor net café on Taojin Lu, opposite Dong Bei Ren Restaurant. There are no English speakers on the staff, but plenty of expats hang out here, and they might be able to help out.

### Police

*Taojin Lu, between Häagen-Dazs & KFC (8359 7560).*

### Post offices

Smaller post offices don't have English-speaking staff, but many of the bigger hotels have their own postal services. These include the White Swan Hotel (*see above*), the Garden Hotel (*see p271*) and the Landmark Hotel (*see above*).

### Tourist information

The days of the national tourist agency CITS (China International Travel Service) are numbered. Once the only bureau for foreign travellers, it stopped being efficient long ago. You're much better off dropping in to the nearest decent hotel where an in-house agency will be able to meet all your needs in English and with a smile. Commissions are negligible and ticket prices competitive. The international hotels all run English-language tours of Guangzhou, if getting on a bus with the blue rinses is your idea of a good time. If you require air or train tickets, then head to a local hotel for assistance.

A locally run agency used to dealing with the needs of foreigners is Xpat Travel Planners (Flat E, 20/F, Regent House, 50 Taojin Lu, 8358 6961, xpats@public.guangzhou.gd.cn).

## Other useful information

### Addresses

Throughout this chapter, and on the map on pages 262-3, we have used the full names of major roads, including prefixes that indicate their location ('bei' means north, 'nan' means south, 'xi' is west and 'dong' is east.) For example, the Renmin Beilu is the northern part of Renmin Street.

### Language

Cantonese is the lingua franca of the city. Most natives also speak Mandarin, while English is spoken at all major hotels and Western bars. Watch out for

Taking a night-time stroll by the river.

young locals wanting to practise their English. Some can be helpful and will happily act as a tour guide just for the chance to speak with you, others are a nuisance and a few are just touts in disguise.

## Media

There are various forms of local English-language media. The official *Guangzhou Morning Post* (no relation to the *South China Morning Post*) offers anodyne business news and the odd tidbit of cultural information. *That's Guangzhou* (www.thatsguangzhou.com) and *City Talk* are both free monthly city mags available at some international bars and hotels.

## Money

The basic unit of Chinese currency goes by two names: the **Yuan** and the **Renminbi** (RMB is used for both; the symbol for Yen – ¥ – is sometimes used to denote Yuan), which is the international name and the one we have used throughout this chapter. (Locals also use the term Kwai, and, just to confuse matters, often translate Yuan/Renminbi/ Kwai as 'dollar', which should not be taken to mean US dollar). One Hong Kong dollar is roughly equivalent to one Renminbi. Although some places in Guangzhou accept Hong Kong dollars, you'll certainly need to change some cash into Renminbi. Tourist hotels, branches of the Bank of China and major entry points all have such facilities; rates vary little. There are a few ATMs around Guangzhou that accept international cards, but don't rely on them. You shouldn't have any problems changing Renminbi back to HK dollars in Hong Kong.

## Telephones

To dial abroad from Guangzhou, dial 00 (not 001 as in Hong Kong), followed by the country code and local number (omitting the 0 of the area code if there is one). It is easiest to find phones that accept IDD calls in the big international hotels, but you'll pay heavily for the privilege. Calls from Guangzhou

to Hong Kong are considered international, but are cheap. The international code for China is 86, while the area code for Guangzhou is 20.

## Visas & consulates

Don't be tempted by so-called 'budget travel agencies' in and around Tsim Sha Tsui in Hong Kong offering visas for China at hugely inflated prices. Legitimate agencies can do it quickly (sometimes on the spot or overnight) for a fairly reasonable price. The cost varies according to how quickly you want the visa, and for how many trips/months, but you should be prepared to pay upwards of HK$200.

Try the alarmingly named but reputable Grand Profit International Travel Agency (705AA, 7/F, New East Ocean Centre, 9 Science Museum Road, Tsim Sha Tsui, Kowloon, 2723 3288) or one of the branches of China Travel Service (*see p276*).

Guangzhou is home to a US, UK and Australian consulate, among others. Overseas consulates in China usually have a well-deserved reputation for being officious, overly bureaucratic and dismissive. This is perhaps not surprising considering the number of bogus applications they receive.
**Australia** *Guangdong International Hotel (8335 0909/5911).*
**United Kingdom** *Guangdong International Hotel (8335 1354/8333 6520).*
**US** *Nan Jie, Shamian (8188 8911/8121 8418).*

## Getting around

### By bike

Bicycles can be rented at various hotels around Guangzhou. But given the traffic and pollution, this is an option best reserved for experienced cyclists. And be warned: although China has only two per cent of the world's automobiles, it accounts for nearly 20 per cent of the world's traffic accidents.

**Sculpture of the Five Rams.** *See p267.*

## By bus

Buses are best avoided, partly because most only have Chinese characters saying where they are heading, but more importantly because locals usually jam themselves in like sardines. Emergency exits do not exist here, and neither does queuing or any other form of communal politeness. Many of the buses themselves should have been retired years ago and few seem to have any dashboard dials that still work. Pickpockets are rife, especially around Chinese New Year, and most other locals will actively avoid sitting next to foreigners at all costs.

## By subway

Now that the second subway line has opened up, getting around the city is much easier. The new yellow line goes from north to south, while the red line goes largely from east to west. Facilities are much like Hong Kong's MTR. Recorded announcements and signs are in English (or a version thereof) and Chinese. You get change from an attendant and go to a machine to get a ticket (RMB2-5).

## By taxi

Air-conditioned taxis with uniformed drivers and clean vehicles cost RMB2.60 per kilometre (RMB2.20 per kilometre if they're not air-conditioned), with a minimum of RMB7. If you don't speak Cantonese, you need to have your destination written for you in Chinese script to show the driver, unless they're taking you from a major hotel, in which case the doorman will tell the driver where to take you. It's best to avoid the smaller and often quite rickety Xia Li cabs and instead flag down a sturdier Santana.

## By train

Guangzhou has two train stations, which can be confusing for first-time visitors. The newer station, in the east of the city (Tian He district), serves mainly Hong Kong and is known locally as *Dong Zhan*. It is new and modern (for China, that is).

The old station is a chaotic, nerve-wracking place on the west side of the city (*Lao Zhan*). The old station serves the hinterland and travellers going to Yangshuo and Kunming.

# Getting there

## By air

Flights from Hong Kong land in Guangzhou almost as soon as they've taken off. It's a 20-minute hop, hardly worth the effort of getting out to the airport – which takes twice as long as the flight itself – and through customs.

The new Guangzhou International Airport, 17km (10 miles) north of the current Baiyun International Airport, is due to open in 2004. Baiyun handles about 30 million passengers a year, while the new project will ultimately cater to nearly three times as many. As this guide went to press, the new high-speed subway link to the airport from the city was about to be unveiled, giving travellers a cheaper way of getting into town.

Do not get a taxi voucher from hotel representatives at the airport; instead, change your money first and get a taxi to your hotel. It can be up to four times cheaper. All the taxis have running meters and it is cheap to go just about anywhere.

## By bus

Bus is second-choice to train when making the journey between Guangzhou and Hong Kong, mainly because the time spent at the border makes the trip a hassle. Going by bus is cheaper, however, with a return journey costing HK$80. Around 20 buses make the journey each way every day, from various hotels around town, including the White Swan Hotel (*see p272*) and the Garden Hotel (*see p271*). Buses leaving the Garden Hotel on the way to Hong Kong stop at either Hung Hom, Chek Lap Kok or Prince Edward MTR.

For those on a budget, upmarket coaches leave for Shenzhen from Guangzhou's Guang Hua Lu bus station every few minutes, costing RMB60. At the terminus, simply cross the border on foot and jump on a KCR (Kowloon–Canton Railway) train headed to Hung Hom or the metro interchange at Mong Kok for another HK$32. Obviously this works equally well in reverse.

If you are really stuck, in a mad rush or have some friends to share the cost with, there are always Guangzhou taxis in Shenzhen looking for a fare back to the city. You can get them down to around RMB400 one way.

## By train

As demand grows, so does the frequency of express trains from Hong Kong to Guangzhou, roughly once an hour. Prices range from HK$190 to HK$260 for first class. The 8.25am commuter train is the newest and cleanest. It is operated by the Hong Kong company KCR (www.kcrc.com) rather than by China Railways, and only takes two hours.

On the return journey check luggage on the second floor and then check in on the fourth floor with your passport and ticket. All formalities including customs are taken care of here.

# Directory

# Directory

## Getting Around

### By air

The largest covered space in the world, **Hong Kong International Airport** (2508 1234, www.hkairport.com) is situated on the levelled island of Chek Lap Kok, just north of Lantau. Designed by British architect Sir Norman Foster, it was completed in 1998 and replaced the old airport at Kai Tak on Kowloon.

Transport to Kowloon, Hong Kong Island, the New Territories and Lantau, as well as to Macau and China, is available from the four-level Ground Transportation Centre.

The **Airport Express** train service operated by the Mass Transit Railway (2881 8888, press 3 for English) is the quickest link, but is also pretty expensive. You can be in Kowloon in under 20 minutes, while the journey to Central (to a dedicated station, which is connected by a subway to Central MTR) takes 23 minutes. Trains run every ten minutes from 5.50am to 12.48am daily.

A one-way adult fare to Kowloon is HK$90 (HK$160 return); to Central it's HK$100 (HK$180). Return tickets are valid for one month. Payment by major credit cards is accepted. Octopus cards (*see p278*) can also be used.

The Airport Express from Kowloon and Central stations offers a free shuttle-bus service for passengers to major hotels every 30 minutes from 6.10am to 11pm, as well as Hung Hom KCR Station and the China Ferry Terminal.

Alternatively, a more leisurely journey is offered by **Citybus** express service (www.citybus.com.hk) to different parts of Hong Kong (A11, A12 to Hong Kong Island, HK$40-$45 single), Kowloon (A21, A22, HK$33-$39 single) and the New Territories (A31, A35, A41, A41P, A43, HK$17-$28 single). Services operate from 6am to midnight and continue with night buses. The N11 goes to Hong Kong Island, the N21 to Kowloon and the N31 to the New Territories. You can buy tickets in the Meeters and Greeters Hall of the Arrivals Hall or you can pay on board with the exact fare. Buses take approximately 35 minutes to reach Kowloon and, given the cross-harbour tunnel and the stops the buses have to make, up to 95 minutes to Hong Kong Island.

**Taxis** are the most expensive way to travel to and from the airport (not least because of the various road tolls, both ways, which are included in the fare). Taxis are located on the left-hand ramp as you leave the arrivals hall. Expect to pay anything between HK$300 and HK$400, depending on your destination and traffic conditions. Red taxis serve Hong Kong Island and Kowloon, green taxis the New Territories, and blue ones Lantau.

New World First Ferry (2131 8181) has a fast **ferry** service from Tung Chung to Tuen Mun in the New Territories. It leaves every 20 to 40 minutes, takes nine minutes and runs from 6am to 11pm daily, costing HK$15 one way. Two buses, the S56 and the S64P, run from

Tung Chung MTR station and Tung Chung New Development Ferry Pier to the passenger terminal at the airport.

**Car parks** (2286 0163/ 2949 1083) have pick-up and drop-off zones and offer complimentary 30-minute parking for departing/arriving passengers in car parks 1 and 4. Parking spaces in lots 1, 2, 3, and 4 are closest to the terminal and have ramps and wheelchair access for the disabled (the cost is HK$16 per hour in the open car park and HK$20 in the covered one). Car park 5 has a fly-and-park facility (HK$200 for a minimum of three days, then HK$70 per day).

Located in the Meeters and Greeters Hall are service counters for hotel reservations and pick-ups, private limo services, the Macau Government Tourist Office, China Travel Service (*see below*) and ferry and train reservations.

If you intend to travel directly on to Macau or mainland China, you can buy coach tickets at the Meeters and Greeters Hall between 7am and 8.30pm (sometimes later) from a variety of companies, including the following:

**China Travel Service** (2261 2472, www.chinatravel one.com) is also the only company at the airport that is authorised to give out visas for travel in China on the spot. For non-urgent visas there's **Global Express** (2375 0099); **Golden Trip Express** (2261 2623); **Eternal East** (2261 0176) and **Gogobus** (2261 0886).

Before boarding the Airport Express or the express bus for the airport, you can check in your luggage (up to 90 minutes prior to take-off) at the check-in halls in Kowloon and Central, though due to security restrictions this is now not allowed for flights by United States airlines or airlines with US destinations; it's worth double checking even with other airlines as the situation is liable to change.

### AIRPORT FACILITIES
A free porter service is available in the baggage reclaim hall. There is also a left-luggage counter (2261 0110, open 6am-1am daily) located in the Meeters and Greeters Hall.

Banks with ATMs and foreign exchange outlets can be found in both the arrivals and departures areas.

HKTB Information Services can be found in the buffer halls and transfer area T2.

Public payphones, card vending machines, courtesy phones and 24-hour help phones are located throughout the terminal.

In-terminal electric vehicles are available in the East Hall, and an automated people-mover in the basement of the passenger terminal travels between the East and West Halls every three minutes between 6am and midnight.

Befitting a modern airport, Hong Kong's is wired for the 21st century. Multimedia lounges provide 24-hour free broadband access to email and the net, and visitors with PCs and LAN cards can also access the internet from almost anywhere in the terminal, with charges being based on time online. In addition, the **CyberMall Cyber Break Café** (2928 6421), with 16 iMac terminals, provides unlimited free internet access. Powerphone connections are available at the Ground Transportation Centre and passenger terminal.

In the Level 7 check-in hall you can find a wireless high-speed internet service at **PCCW** (2888 0088, www.pccw.com), plus items such as mobile phones and phone cards. Also on this level is a branch of **Fortress**, the one-stop electronics shop (2186 6627; *see also p168*).

Facilities for the physically, visually and hearing impaired are provided in the form of toilets, telephone access, escalators, elevators, car parks, drinking fountains, tactile guide paths and wheelchairs and a people-mover (*see above*).

Other facilities at the airport include a police station in the check-in hall (2183 1334, open 24 hours daily), a medical centre (2261 2626, open 7am-midnight) and a lost & found room (2182 2018, open 8am-11pm) on Level 6. Nursing rooms with changing and feeding facilities and children's play areas are on the central concourse, and there are prayer rooms (2182 2024) in the check-in hall. In addition, there are 12 highly comfortable air-conditioned smoking lounges; all are open 24 hours and located in the arrival and departure halls.

## By rail

Trains from mainland China arrive at Hung Hom station in eastern Kowloon. Taxis are available outside the station, otherwise directions to bus services are well marked, and the Hung Hom ferry is a ten-minute walk away.

If you wish to travel by train to China (for which you'll need a visa; *see p276 and p283*), tickets can be purchased at Hung Hom Station or in advance from either of the China Travel Services branches listed below.

## China Travel Services
*1/F, Alpha House, 27 Nathan Road, Tsim Sha Tsui, Kowloon (2315 7188). Tsim Sha Tsui MTR (exit C1, E)/buses along Nathan Road/Tsim Sha Tsui Star Ferry Pier.* **Open** 9am-7pm Mon-Fri; 1-6pm Sat; 9am-12.30pm, 2-5pm Sun. **Map** p313 C2.
*G/F, CTS House, 78-83 Connaught Road, Central, HK Island (2853 3888). Sheung Wan MTR (exit E4)/buses along Connaught Road Central.* **Open** 9am-5pm Mon-Sat. **Map** p308 C2.

## By sea

Ferry services to and from Macau (*see also p259*) dock either at the Hong Kong–Macau Ferry Terminal in the Shun Tak Centre, Sheung Wan, Hong Kong Island (map p308 B1) or the China Ferry Terminal, China HK City, Canton Road, Tsim Sha Tsui, Kowloon (map p313 B6). The latter is also the arrival point for ferries from China.

At the Hong Kong–Macau Ferry Terminal, taxis are available at exit level, while buses are at street level. Sheung Wan MTR station is connected to the terminal; follow the signs and you will find it a short walk away.

At the China Ferry Terminal, taxis and buses are available at street level, while both the Star Ferry and MTR are 15 minutes away on foot.

Tickets for the ferries can be purchased at the terminals. Fares vary according to the type of vessel and class. If you wish to travel on a weekend or public holiday, it's advisable to book in advance – and consider buying a return fare.

## By road

The only way to arrive in Hong Kong by road is from mainland China by a coach service to and from Guangzhou (*see p274*), while Citybus routes link the Shenzhen economic zone (*see p163* **Shopping in Shenzhen**) and Hong Kong.

**Directory**

# Public transport

Public transport in Hong Kong is reliable, affordable, clean and safe. Because of the compact nature of Hong Kong, you can reach most parts within an hour using public transport. That is, as long as you don't get caught in rush-hour traffic (8-10am and 5-7pm) or delayed by an accident or roadworks.

There are three bus companies operating routes all over the territory; the green and yellow minibuses are privately owned. The railways, both underground (MTR) and above (KCR and Light Rail), are connected to housing estates and main shopping and business areas.

All buses, minibuses, taxis and long-haul ferries are air-conditioned.

**Transport Complaints hotline** 2889 9999/www.info.gov.hk/td.
**Transport Department Enquiry hotline** 2804 2600/fax 2248 0433.

## Fares & tickets

Visitors who are planning to use public transport fairly frequently over a week or more can buy an **Octopus card** (a stored-value smart card). Available from MTR stations, it can be used on all public transport systems except for taxis, some minibuses and a few ferries. You pay a deposit of HK$50 for the card, which is refunded upon its return, and then add as much value to the card as you think you will need – you can add more at the machines located in MTR stations or at 7-Eleven stores all over Hong Kong.

Place the Octopus card on the machine displayed in the buses, trams, ferries and minibuses to log in the fare. If you reach your destination before the end of the bus route, place the card on the machine again when alighting to retrieve the rest of the fare.

Some routes take a flat fare with no refunds. Octopus fares work out cheaper than the normal fares by a few dollars and can also be used in convenience stores, parking meters and various fast-food outlets.

For the convenience of visitors, a three-day **Hong Kong Transport Pass** is available, costing HK$220. It can be used for one Airport Express single journey between the airport and most destinations in Central, Causeway Bay and Kowloon, and three days of unlimited rides on the MTR. For an extra HK$20, it can be used on other transport modes. There is also a one-day MTR pass for HK$50, giving unlimited rides. These passes are available at Airport Express and MTR stations.

On many types of tickets, discounts are available for children, students and the elderly – ask when booking.

## Buses

Buses run regularly and frequently, particularly during rush hour. Bus stops display the bus numbers and routes they serve, as well as the fares. If you don't have an Octopus card, make sure you have the exact fare ready, which can vary between HK$2 and HK$15 depending on your destination and the type of bus on which you travel.

For more information call:
**Citybus** 2873 0818/www.citybus.com.hk.
**Kowloon Motor Bus** 2745 4466/www.kmb.com.hk.
**New World First Bus** 2136 8888/www.nwfb.com.hk.
**New Lantau Bus Company** 2984 9848.

## Minibuses

Yellow minibuses with red stripes do not always ply fixed routes, and passengers can get on or off anywhere (except in

restricted zones). Fares can be much higher than on buses, as they are dictated by the whim of the driver, and range from HK$2 to HK$20. Yellow minibuses with green stripes are called maxicabs and travel to residential areas with fixed fares. They, too, can be flagged down anywhere and called to a halt near your destination. A quick shout (of 'lee doe') should be enough to alert the driver that you wish to get off.

## Ferries

Ferries sail between Hong Kong Island and Kowloon, and to the outlying islands, Macau and mainland China. The New World First Ferry Service, better known as **Star Ferry**, provides services to Central, Wan Chai and North Point on Hong Kong Island, as well as to Tsim Sha Tsui and Hung Hom on Kowloon and Discovery Bay on Lantau. A five-minute walk from Central Star Ferry Pier will get you to the Outlying Islands Ferry Piers, where you'll find fast and standard services to Lamma, Cheung Chau, Peng Chau and Lantau. Fares for fast ferries are higher, but the journey time often almost half.

In addition, there are inter-island ferries for island hopping that have fixed fares, as well as a number of small ferries plying their trade between Aberdeen (on the south side of Hong Kong Island) and the outlying islands. Be sure to bargain the fare down.

For more information call the following:
**New World First Ferry** 2131 8181/www.nwff.com.hk.
**Star Ferry** 2367 7065.
**HK Kowloon Ferry** 2815 6063/www.hkkf.com.hk.
**Discovery Bay Transport** 2987 6128.
**HK & Macau Hydrofoil & Turbocat Services** 2859 3333.
**Chun Kee Ferry** (Aberdeen to Shau Kei Wan) 2375 7883.

## MTR (underground)

The **Mass Transit Railway** or **MTR** (2881 8888, www.mtr.com.hk) is clean, fast and efficient. It runs along the north coast of Hong Kong Island, and travels beneath the harbour to Kowloon, the New Territories and Lantau. Trains run from 6am to 1am daily, and generally the maximum fare is HK$13 for an adult single journey (except to Tung Chung in Lantau, which is HK$23, or HK$20 with an Octopus card). The network is made up of five interconnected lines: the **blue** line runs along the harbour on Hong Kong Island from Sheung Wan in the west to Chai Wan in the east; the **red** line runs from Central, Hong Kong Island, under the harbour to Tsuen Wan in the New Territories; the **green** line starts at Yau Ma Tei, Kowloon, looping around to the east to Tiu Keng Leng with an interchange to Tseung Kwan O and North Point on the **purple** line, which starts at North Point and crosses the harbour to terminate at Po Lam in the New Territories. The **yellow** line runs from Central to Tung Chung on Lantau Island.

All MTR stations have been refurbished in recent years, with new coaches, safety doors, and shops selling food, clothes and electronics, plus banks and other services such as dry-cleaning. There are also charts showing fares to destinations, types of travelcard available and the network of train lines.

Throughout this guide, we have given the nearest exit for each destination, but there's a guide map on the wall in each station if you need to check.

## Rail services

Aside from the Airport Express, Hong Kong has several rail systems that fall under the control of the **Kowloon–Canton Railway** or **KCR** (2929 3399, www.kcrc.com). The confusingly named **East Rail** runs from Hung Hom in Kowloon northwards to the boundary with mainland China at Lo Wu, stopping on the way at various towns in the New Territories. These trains run every three to ten minutes starting at 5.30am from Hung Hom until 12.07am, and the maximum (up to Lo Wu) single fare is HK$33 (HK$31 if you use an Octopus card), or double for first class.

The **Light Rail** or **LR** connects the New Territories towns of Tuen Mun and Yuen Long. It runs from 5.30am to 12.30am daily, with single fares between HK$4 and HK$5.80 (less with an Octopus card).

The new **West Rail** links Nam Cheong to Tuen Muen in less than 30 minutes. Trains runs from 5.45am to 12.45am every three minutes during rush hour and every five to 12 minutes during non-peak hours. Fares start at around HK$4, or less if you're using an Octopus card.

Further developments to Hong Kong's rail system are ongoing, with several new lines opening over the next several years. A new East Tsim Sha Tsui station (which is slated to finish at the end of 2004) will connect Hung Hom KCR with Tsim Sha Tsui MTR via an underground passage.

## Trams

Double-decker trams run by **Hong Kong Tramways** (2548 7102, www.hktramways.com) travel along the north side of Hong Kong Island from Kennedy Town to Chai Wan, with a flat fare of HK$2. You enter the tram at the rear and exit at the front, paying the fare before alighting. Tram stops are in the middle of the main road, splitting the two-way traffic.

The **Peak Tram** (2522 0922, www.thepeak.com.hk; *see also p29 and p78*), which is over 100 years old, travels to the Peak from Garden Road, Central. On a clear day it affords a panoramic view of Hong Kong, and makes for a thrilling ride up a very steep slope. Adult fares are HK$20 one way, HK$30 return. Octopus cards can be used for fares on all trams and trains.

All trams run from 7am until midnight daily.

## Taxis

Taxis are plentiful in major areas and fares are reasonable. You will find red taxis on Hong Kong Island and Kowloon, green in the New Territories and blue on Lantau. All of them will go to the airport. Taxis can only stop at hotels or on the road if there are no single or double yellow lines. Although many taxi drivers do speak some English, it is advisable to have your destination written down in Chinese to avoid confusion. Remember to put on your seat belt – the law requires it.

Fares vary according to the colour of the taxi: the basic flag fall on red cabs is HK$15 (and HK$1.40 for every additional 200 metres); for green it is HK$12.50 and for blue HK$12 (both adding HK$1.20 for every additional 200 metres). There are extra charges for telephone hiring, tunnel tolls, the driver's return toll, and luggage placed in the boot (HK$5 for red taxis and HK$4 for blue and green ones – carry your bags with you if you want to avoid this). Tipping HK$5-$10 is optional but appreciated. Avoid trying to pay with larger bills of HK$500 or $1,000 as sometimes drivers don't have change.

If you want to book a taxi call 2861 1008 or 2529 8822.

**Directory**

## Cycling

Don't even think about cycling in the car- and bus-dominated canyons of Central or Tsim Sha Tsui. In contrast, cycling on the islands and in the New Territories can be immensely enjoyable. For information on cycling, contact the **Hong Kong Cycling Association** (2573 3861) or the **Hong Kong Tourism Board** (*see p291*). For cycling permits and rules, go to www.cycling.org.hk.

### Bicycle hire

Bikes can be hired in Tai Wai near Sha Tin in the New Territories and on Cheung Chau island. Rates are roughly HK$30-$50, depending on the type of bike you choose, and a deposit of about HK$100 is often required. *See also p237.*

## Driving

Due to the relatively cheap, efficient and extensive public transport system and hefty parking charges, driving is an option that many visitors pass over. If you do, however, choose to drive, the following information will be of use:

● vehicles drive on the left-hand side.
● traffic signs and street names are in both Chinese and English.
● stopping on a double or single yellow line is illegal except in side lanes, bays or at designated areas and times.
● use of seat belts in cars and taxis is mandatory.
● unless otherwise indicated, the speed limit is 80kmph (50mph).
● drinking and driving is not tolerated, and heavy penalties are in place for those caught over the legal limit of 50 milligrams of alcohol per 100ml of blood.
● mobile phones may not be used while driving.

● an international driving licence is not required by most visitors as they can drive up to 12 months on their home country's valid and current licence (if recognised by Hong Kong Transport Authority), but drivers must carry their passport with the visa stamped in it while driving.

### Transport Department

*3/F, United Centre, 95 Queensway, Admiralty, HK Island (Transport Department Enquiry Hotline 1823/ www.info.gov.hk/td).*

## Breakdown services

### HK Automobile Association

*2304 4911/insurance 2739 5273.*

## Fuel stations

### Mobil Oil

*1 Lockhart Road, Wan Chai, HK Island (2865 3563).* **Open** 24hrs. **Credit** AmEx, DC, MC, V. **Map** p310 A3.

## Insurance

Third-party insurance is compulsory by law.

## Parking

Parking is available on some streets with meters for short-term parking at HK$2 for 15 minutes (or 30 minutes in less busy areas). Cards for parking meters can be bought at 7-Eleven stores and post offices, though Octopus card-operated meters are gradually replacing the traditional meters. Meters operate from 8am to midnight.

Parking is expensive in malls and office buildings, but some restaurants and hotels offer complimentary valet parking. There are several public car parks in the city, including, on Hong Kong Island, at the Star Ferry Pier, International Finance Centre, Pacific Place and in the basement of department stores such as Sogo and Mitsukoshi;

and in Tsim Sha Tsui at Ocean Terminal and Middle Road (behind the Sheraton Hotel). Charges are HK$20-$30 per hour, with a minimum charge of two hours.

## Vehicle hire

Try the *Yellow Pages* (*see p291*) for further ideas.

### Avis

*Head office: G/F, Bright Star Mansions, 85-93 Leighton Road, Causeway Bay, HK Island (International rentals 2890 6988/ www.avis.com.hk).* **Credit** AmEx, MC, V. **Map** p311 E3.

### Toplink

*Head office: Flat F, 20/F, 23 Greig Crescent, Quarry Bay, HK Island (2880 0616/fax 2880 0269).* **No credit cards**.

## Walking

In spite of jostling crowds and fumes from vehicle emissions, irregular sidewalks and steep steps, walking is the way to go in Hong Kong, so a good pair of lungs and stout footwear are recommended. In contrast, walking in the New Territories and on the outlying islands is often a joy and a popular recreational activity with both visitors and residents.

Suggested itineraries covered in this book include, on Hong Kong Island, walks around the Peak (*see p78* **Peak of fitness**) and the **Dragon's Back** (*see p82*).

Bookstore chains like **Dymocks** and **Bookazine**, and the **Government Publications Centre** (for all, *see p160*) sell a range of maps of local and hiking and walking books. The *Hong Kong Guidebook* and *Hong Kong Directory* are both highly recommended. In addition, the HKTB offices (*see p291*) at 99 Queen's Road Central and the Star Ferry terminal in Kowloon sell good maps as well as offering free, detailed street maps.

# Resources A-Z

## Addresses

Addresses in Hong Kong are written: name, apartment floor/house number, name of building, road/street and area. There is no post/zip code. Taxi drivers know most addresses, but you'd be wise to get hotels to write them in Chinese, just in case.

You'll find the relevant floor of the building an intrinsic part of most Hong Kong addresses. G/F (ground floor) is the floor at street level; 1/F (first floor) is the next one up, etc. Variations you might see include G-29, which will be room 29 on the ground floor, and 702, being flat number 2 on the seventh floor.

## Age

The minimum legal age for drinking, driving, sex and smoking is 18.

## Attitude & etiquette

Hong Kong is a cosmopolitan city, but Chinese etiquette prevails. Respect for local

customs and beliefs – such as the importance of family – is evident. Surnames are written first. Elders and men are introduced first. If you want to give a gift, chocolates and money are suitable, but not clocks or watches as they are considered bad luck (the word 'clock' sounds like 'death' in Chinese).

Hong Kong Chinese are used to having foreigners around and are non-intrusive. They are sometimes perceived as being abrupt and rude, but it is only a manner, nothing personal. As in China, keeping face is of paramount concern – to such a degree that it can sometimes seem quite traumatic for a Hong Kong person to admit common errors to a foreigner. If you cause someone to lose face, you too will be perceived negatively. Losing your temper in front of others is seen as loss of face for both you and them. For more on local culture and customs, *see p31-38*.

## Business

Business cards are usually written in English on one side, and Chinese on the other.

Many hotels can print them within 24 hours. They should be presented to a Chinese person with both hands, and received similarly; you should take care to read them. Business meetings and entertainment engagements require suits. Wait for the host to initiate drinking any beverage on offer. Note that no business is conducted during Chinese New Year (*see p190*).

## Business centres & office hire

There are many business centres offering space and communication facilities – the fancier and larger the offices the higher the costs. Terms and conditions differ, so it is worthwhile to phone around two or three to check the rates and services available.

### Harbour International Business Centre

*Room 2802, Tower 1, Admiralty Centre, 18 Harcourt Road, Admiralty, Central, HK Island (2529 0356/www.hibc.hk). Admiralty MTR (exit A1)/buses along Harcourt Road.* **Map** p309 F4.
Contact for secretarial help and office rentals.

### Plaza Business Centre

*35/F, Central Plaza, 18 Harbour Road, Wan Chai, HK Island (2593 1111/www.plaza-asia.com). Wan Chai MTR (exit A1)/buses along Gloucester Road & Harbour Road.* **Map** p310 B3.
Provides 35 fully serviced executive office suites and a full range of secretarial services.

## Conventions & conferences

International conventions, conferences and exhibitions are held throughout the year at the Hong Kong Convention & Exhibition Centre. Bookings are accepted years in advance.

---

# Travel advice

For up-to-date information on travel to a specific country – including the latest news on safety and security, health issues, local laws and customs – contact your home country government's department of foreign affairs. Most have websites packed with useful advice for would-be travellers.

**Australia**
www.dfat.gov.au/travel

**Canada**
www.voyage.gc.ca

**New Zealand**
www.mft.govt.nz/travel

**Republic of Ireland**
www.irlgov.ie/iveagh

**UK**
www.fco.gov.uk/travel

**USA**
www.state.gov/travel

**Directory**

For event bookings and lists of forthcoming events and other information, check its website.

## Hong Kong Convention & Exhibition Centre

*1 Expo Drive, Wan Chai, HK Island (general 2582 8888/information 2582 1818/sales 2582 7919/ www.hkcec.com.hk). Wan Chai MTR (exit A1)/25A, 25C, 961 bus.* **Map** *p310 B2.*

## Couriers & shippers

### DHL

*Head office:11/F, Trade Square, 681 Cheung Sha Wan Road, Kowloon (2765 8111/www.dhl.com.hk).* Drop-off booths are located in the following MTR stations: Causeway Bay (exit F); Admiralty (exit E); Central (exit F); Tsim Sha Tsui (exit D1/D2).

### Federal Express

*Shop 43, 1/F, Shopping Arcade, Admiralty Centre, Queensway, HK Island (2730 3333). Admiralty MTR (exit C1)/buses through Central.* **Map** *p309 F4. Room 606, Harbour City, 5 Canton Road (near Star Ferry) & G/F, Houston Center, Mody Road, Tsim Sha Tsui. Tsim Sha Tsui MTR/ 5, 5C, 6, 7, 8 bus.* **Map** *p313 B5.*

## Translators & interpreters

### Language Line

*Flat 1B, 163, Hennessy Road, Wan Chai, HK Island (2511 2677/ www.languageventure.com). Wan Chai MTR (exit A2, A4)/buses along Hennessy Road.* **Map** *p310 B3.* Can provide European/Asian translation, copywriting, editing and proofreading services.

### Polyglot

*Flat 14B, Times Centre, 53 Hollywood Road, Central, HK Island (2851 7232). Central MTR (exit D1, D2)/Mid-Levels Escalator/ 12M, 13, 23A, 26, 40M, 43 bus.* **Map** *p308 B3.* Offers a wide range of translation and typing services as well as equipment rentals.

## Useful organisations

Chambers of commerce have useful information (including directories) related to doing business in Hong Kong, China and other Asian cities. They also run events such as seminars and workshops. They are also up to date on government business policies and laws. Fees are charged for some services.

### American Chamber of Commerce

*Room 1904, Bank of America Tower, 12 Harcourt Road, Central, HK Island (2526 0165/ www.amcham.org.hk).* **Map** *p309 F4.*

### Australian Chamber of Commerce

*4/F, Lucky Building, 39 Wellington Street, Central, HK Island (2522 5054/www.austcham.com.hk).* **Map** *p308 C3.*

### British Chamber of Commerce

*Room 1201, Emperor Group Centre, 288 Hennessy Road, Wan Chai, HK Island (2824 2211/www. britcham.com).* **Map** *p310 C3.*

### Canadian Chamber of Commerce

*Suite 1003, 1301 Kinwick Centre, 32 Hollywood Road, Central, HK Island (2110 8700/www.cancham.org).* **Map** *p308 C3.*

### Chinese General Chamber of Commerce

*4/F, 24-5 Connaught Road, Central, HK Island (2525 6385/ www.cgcc.org.hk).* **Map** *p309 D3.*

### HK General Chamber of Commerce

*22/F, United Centre, 95 Queensway, Admiralty, HK Island (2529 9229/ www.chamber.org.hk).* **Map** *p309 F5.*

### HK Stock Exchange

*1122 Exchange Square, Tower 1, Central (2522 1122/fax 2295 3106/ www.hkex.com.hk).* **Map** *p309 D3.*

### HK Trade Development Council

*G/F, New Convention Centre, 1 Exposition Drive, Wan Chai, HK Mailing address: 36/F, Office Tower, Convention Plaza, 1 Harbour Road, Wan Chai, HK Island (2584 4333/ www.tdc.org).* **Map** *p310 B2.*

### Japanese Chamber of Commerce

*38/F, West Wing, Hennessy Centre, 500 Hennessy Road, Causeway Bay, HK Island (2577 6129/www.hkjcci. com.hk).* **Map** *p311 D3.*

### US Foreign Commercial Service

*21/F, St John's Building, 33 Garden Road, Central, HK Island (2521 1467). Buses along Garden Road.* **Map** *p309 E5.*

## Consumer

The **Consumer Council** in Hong Kong is an independent organisation that protects consumers' rights and interests, tests products in the market to establish the claims made by manufacturers and retailers, and publishes the journal *Choice*, which details the results of its findings. Visitors and residents can call its hotline below for help with any shopping problems; two other useful organisations are listed here too.

## Central & Western Consumer Advice Centre

*G/F, Harbour Building, 38 Pier Road, Central, HK Island (hotline 2929 2222/2856 3113). Sheung Wan MTR (exit E4)/buses along Connaught Road Central.* **Open** 9am-5pm Mon-Fri. **Map** *p308 C2.*

## Consumer Council

*22/F, K Wah Centre, 191 Java Road, North Point, HK Island (2929 2222, then press 2 for English).* **Phone enquiries** 9am-5pm Mon-Fri; 9am-noon Sat.

## Tsim Sha Tsui Consumer Advice Centre

*G/F, 3 Ashley Road, Tsim Sha Tsui, Kowloon (2926 1088). Tsim Sha Tsui MTR.* **Open** 9am-5pm Mon-Fri; 9am-noon Sat. **Map** *p313 B6.*

## Customs

At the time of going to press, visitors were allowed to bring the following items into Hong Kong duty free:

● 200 cigarettes or 50 cigars or 250 grams of tobacco.
● one litre bottle of wine or spirits.

A doctor's prescription will be required if large amounts of medication for personal use is brought into the country.

The following may not be brought into Hong Kong:
● animals, plants or soil.
● firearms/weapons (which must be declared and handed into custody until departure).
● narcotics.

The following must be declared and duty paid:

● commercial merchandise for trade or import.
● alcohol, cigarettes, tobacco or cigars in excess of duty-free allowances.
● cars.

For more information, go to www.info.gov.hk.

## Disabled

The Hong Kong Government is aware of the need to improve accessibility for people with mobility and sensory disabilities, and measures are being taken to provide facilities in public places and on transport systems. Space being precious, every inch is utilised, so shops, offices, restaurants, theatres and malls are located on every level of a building accessible by elevator, escalator or stairs. Facilities such as braille on tickets and card-processing machines, and LED displays of upcoming stations, are installed in public transport. Priority seats with reachable bells are installed on trams and buses. Taxis can pick up and set down disabled people at restricted roadsides (but they need to get in touch with the Hong Kong Council of Social Services on 2864 2929 for a special certificate). Staff on public transport are trained to assist people with disabilities when requested, and, generally, bus and taxi drivers are helpful.

The **Hong Kong Society for Rehabilitation** provides a transport network, the Rehabus, with a scheduled route service, feeder bus service and dial-a-ride service. (call 2817 8154 or fax 2855 7106). You can also contact the **Transport Department** (2804 2600).

If you feel you are being denied access anywhere, complain to the **Equal Opportunities Commission** (Room 2002, 20/F, Office Tower Convention Plaza, 1 Harbour Road, Wan Chai, HK Island, 2511 8211).

## Drugs

Drugs such as heroin and ecstasy (and also, strangely, the horse tranquillizer ketamine) are a big problem among young people in Hong Kong, as teenagers are vulnerable to triad pushers. As a result, the police patrol areas where there are big parties and conduct random drugs testing. Expats caught with drugs could face imprisonment.

### Anti-Drug Abuse Line
*2366 8822, then press 2 for English.* **Phone enquiries** times vary.

### Narcotics Bureau Hotline
*2860 2888.* **Phone enquiries** 24hrs daily.

## Electricity

The voltage in Hong Kong is 220 volts 50 cycles. Most hotels provide adaptors, or you can buy one from an electrical shop for around HK$20.

## Embassies & consulates

### Australian Consulate
*21-24/F, Harbour Centre, 25 Harbour Road, Wan Chai, HK Island (2827 8881/fax 2585 4457/Immigration 2585 4139/ www.australia.org.hk). Wan Chai MTR (exit A1)/buses along Gloucester Road.* **Open** 8.45am-5pm Mon-Fri. *Immigration* 9.30am-1.30pm Mon-Fri. **Map** p310 B3.

### British Consulate & Trade Commission
*1 Supreme Court Road, Central, HK Island (2901 3000/fax 2901 3066/www.britishconsulate.org.hk). Admiralty MTR (exit C1)/buses along Queensway.* **Open** 8.45am-noon, 2-4.30pm Mon-Fri. **Map** p309 F5.

### Canadian Consulate
*Visa Section GPO 1142 HK, 11-14F, One Exchange Square, 8 Connaught Place, Central, HK Island (2847 7555/fax 2847 7493/ www.hongkong.gc.ca). Central MTR (exit A)/buses along Connaught Road Central.* **Open** 8.30am-5pm Mon-Fri. *Immigration* 8-11.30am Tue, Thur, Fri. **Map** p309 D3.

### Irish Consulate
*6/F, Chung Nam Building, 1 Lockhart Road, Wan Chai, HK Island (2527 4897/fax 2520 1833). Wan Chai MTR (exit C)/buses along Hennessy Road.* **Open** 10am-noon, 2-4.30pm Mon-Fri. **Map** p310 A3.

### New Zealand Consulate
*Room 6501, Central Plaza, 18 Harbour Road, Wan Chai, HK Island (2525 5044/fax 2845 2915/nzcghk@ netvigator.com). Wan Chai MTR (exit A1)/buses along Gloucester Road/Wan Chai Star Ferry Pier.* **Open** 8am-1pm, 2-5pm Mon-Fri. *Immigration* 9am-1pm, 1.30-3pm Mon-Fri. **Map** p310 B3.

### US Consulate General
*26 Garden Road, Central, HK Island (2523 9011/2841 2219/2323/ fax 2147 5790/www.usconsulate. org.hk). Admiralty (exit C1) or Central (exit K) MTR then 10min walk/buses along Garden Road.* **Open** 8.30am-12.30pm, 1.30-5.30pm Mon-Fri. **Map** p309 E5.

## Visas for China

### Visa Office of the People's Republic of China
*Office of the Commissioner of the Ministry of Foreign Affairs, 6-7/F, Lower Block, China Resources Building, 26 Harbour Road, Wan Chai, HK Island (3413 2300/ 3413 2424/fax 3413 2312).* **Open** 9am-noon, 2-5pm Mon-Fri. **Map** p310 C3.
You can apply in person for a visa for mainland China at this office. It normally takes up to three working days but staff can issue one-day visas for a higher fee. Visas cost upwards of HK$400, but it can be cheaper (and quicker) to get one from a travel agent in Hong Kong.

The **HYFCO** travel agency has branches all over Hong Kong, including Room 1909, Lane Crawford House, 70 Queen's Road, Central, HK Island (2526 5305), and Shop B2, Basement, Star House Plaza, 3 Salisbury Road, Tsim Sha Tsui, Kowloon (2730 8608).

**Japan Travel Agency** (Room 507, East Ocean Centre, 98, Granville Road, Tsim Sha Tsui East) can get you a six-month/multi-entry visa for China for HK$400 in one day (2368 9151/fax 2724 4551, open 9am-6pm Mon-Fri).

It's also possible to obtain a visa before you travel. For details, go to www.chinese-embassy.org.uk (UK citizens) or http://www.china-embassy.org (US citizens).

## Emergencies

*See also below* **Accident & emergency**.

### Ambulance/police/fire
*999.*

### Complaints against the police
*2574 4220.*

### Lost credit cards
**American Express** *2811 6122.*
**Diners Club** *2860 1888.*
**HSBC** *2748 4848.*
**MasterCard** *8009 66677.*
**Visa International** Visa card holders should contact the issuing bank in Hong Kong.

### Lost passports
Contact your consulate (*see p283*) after notifying the police on 2860 2000.

### 24-hour crime hotline
*2527 7177, then press 3 for English.*

## Gay & lesbian

For gay-related websites and other media, *see p214*.

### Freemen
*PO Box 2443, Hong Kong (9106 4983/hongkongfreemen@ hotmail.com).*
This gay male social group offers counselling and social activities.

### Horizons
*2815 9268/www.horizons.org.hk.* **Phone enquiries** 7.30-10.30pm Tue, Thur.
Provides counselling and organises social activities such as hiking trips, concerts and movie nights.

### Rainbow Centre
*7/F, 627 Shanghai Street, Mong Kok, Kowloon (2573 1069/ http://rainbowofhk.org). Mong Kok MTR (exit C2).* **Open** 2-7pm Sun.
This is a free, social drop-in centre with books, videos, music and gay information. Rainbow also organises special events such as drag festivals and sleep-over parties.

## Health

Ensure that you have adequate personal medical insurance prior to travelling to Hong Kong. Vaccinations against typhoid, flu, Hepatitis A and B are precautionary. Routine polio, tetanus, mumps, measles

and diphtheria updates are recommended. Check with your doctor about immunisation prior to travelling. For further information, go to the website www.healthinasia.com.

In 2003, from March to May, Hong Kong suffered 1,755 (including 386 health workers and medical students) cases of Severe Acute Respiratory Syndrome (SARS), with a disturbingly high death rate amongst the elderly and health care workers. In June 2003 the disease was finally contained and Hong Kong was declared safe by the WHO, though sporadic cases have since been reported. For more information check out www.info.gov.hk/info/sars/eindex.htm.

## Accident & emergency

The **Hospital Authority One-Stop Enquiry Service** has two 24-hour hotlines (2882 4866 and 2300 6555) giving information on accident and emergency services, hospital fees, help with complaints, hospital phone numbers, locations and transport information.

A full range of A&E services are provided 24 hours a day at the places listed below. If an ambulance is required, dial 999 (*see also above* **Emergencies**).

### Caritas Medical Centre
*111 Wing Hong Street, Sham Shui Po, Kowloon (3408 7911). Cheung Sha Wan MTR (exit A3) then 45M minibus.*

### Matilda Hospital
*41 Mount Kellett Road, The Peak, HK Island (2849 0123). Minibus 1 from Queen's Pier or hospital shuttle every 20mins from City Hall.*

### Prince of Wales Hospital
*30-32 Ngan Shing Street, Sha Tin, New Territories (2632 2211). Bus A41, 73A, 80K, 85A.*

### Queen Mary Hospital
*102 Pok Fu Lam Road, Pok Fu Lam, HK Island (2855 3838). Minibus 54, 55 from Worldwide House, Central/bus 7, 71, 91, 94 from Star Ferry Pier.*

## Complementary medicine

### Integrated Medicine Institute HK Limited
*7/F, Baskerville House, 13 Duddell Street, Central, HK Island (2523 7121). Central MTR (exit D1, D2, G)/buses along Queen's Road Central.* **Open** 9am-6.30pm Mon-Fri; 9am-1pm Sat. **Map** p308 C3.

### Natural Health Association of Hong Kong
*GPO 8268, Hong Kong (www.naturalhealth.org.hk).*

### Optimum Health Centre Alexander Yuan
*2/F, Prosperous Commercial Building, Jardine's Bazaar, Causeway Bay, HK Island (2577 3798/www.natural healing.com.hk). Causeway Bay MTR (exit F)/buses along Hennessy Road.* **Open** 9am-7pm Mon-Fri; 9am-4pm Sat. **Map** p311 D3.

## Contraception & abortion

For advice, call the **Family Planning Association** (2711 9656 in Kowloon; 2574 9523 in Wan Chai).

## Dentists

Foreign qualified and English-speaking doctors and dentists are the norm in Hong Kong. They offer excellent services in private practice and are situated in main commercial and business areas, but tend to be expensive, so make sure you have insurance coverage. A typical consultation costs HK$350-$500. The following two clinics are recommended:

### Dr Eric Carter
*Room 1103, Century Square, 1-13 D'Aguilar Street, Central, HK Island (2525 4285). Central MTR (exit D1, G)/buses 12M, 13, 23A, 40M, 43.* **Open** 8am-4.30pm Mon-Fri; 8am-12.30pm Sat. **Map** p308 C4.

### Dr James Woo & Associates
*Room 1631A, Star House, 3 Salisbury Road, Tsim Sha Tsui, Kowloon (2735 6008). Tsim Sha*

*Tsui MTR (exit E)/buses to Tsim Sha Tsui Star Ferry Pier & along Salisbury Road/Tsim Sha Tsui Star Ferry Pier.* **Open** 9.30am-1am, 2-6pm Mon-Fri. **Map** p313 B6.

*9/F, Lane Crawford House, 70 Queen's Road, Central, HK Island (2869 6986). Central MTR (exit D2)/buses along Queen's Road Central.* **Open** 9.30am-1pm, 2-6pm Mon-Fri. **Map** p309 D3.

## Doctors

The following clinics are both recommended:

### Dr Nicholson & Associates

*Room 402B, New World Tower 1, 18 Queen's Road, Central, HK Island (2525 1251). Central MTR (exit D1, D2, G)/buses along Queen's Road Central.* **Open** 9am-1pm; 2-6pm Mon-Fri; 9am-1pm Sat. **Map** p309 D4.

### Raffles Medical Group

*Room 902, Bank of America Tower, 12 Harcourt Road, Central, HK Island (2525 1730). Central MTR (exit J3)/buses to Central Star Ferry Pier/Central Star Ferry Pier.* **Open** 9am-6pm Mon-Fri; 9am-1pm Sat. **Map** p309 F4.

There are also travel clinics at the Adventist Hospital (*see below*) and Matilda Hospital (*see p284*).

## Hospitals

For hospitals with 24-hour accident and emergency wards, *see p284*. Decent medical care is widely available in Hong Kong thanks to a large number of foreign-qualified local and expatriate practitioners. The private hospitals listed below have English-speaking staff and all operate outpatient departments at the following (approximate) times: 8.30am-4pm Monday-Friday and 8.30am-12.30pm Saturday.

For emergency numbers, *see p284*.

### Adventist Hospital

*40 Stubbs Road, Mid-Levels, HK Island (2835 0566/2574 6211/www.hkah.org.hk). Bus 6, 15, 15B, 61, 66, 76.* **Map** p308 C3.

### Baptist Hospital

*222 Waterloo Road, Kowloon (2337 4141). Kowloon Tong MTR (exit A2)/KCR/buses along Waterloo Road & Cornwall Street.*

### Canossa Hospital

*1 Old Peak Road, Mid-Levels, HK Island (2522 2181). Bus 3B, 12, 12M, 23, 23A, 40/hospital shuttlebus every 20mins from Shanghai Commercial Bank, 12 Queen's Road, Central.* **Map** p308 C5.

## Opticians

*See p182.*

## Pharmacies

Over-the-counter medicines for colds, headaches, fevers and minor ailments are available in pharmacies, such as the Mannings and Watson's chains (*see p183*), in malls and most shopping areas. Most open 9am-6pm daily.

Doctors' clinics are licensed to sell prescription drugs, but if you do go to a pharmacy, be aware that only prescriptions from Hong Kong-based doctors will be accepted. Shops with dispensaries display a red-cross sign.

The Adventist (*see above*) and Queen Mary (*see p284*) hospitals have pharmacies that are open 24 hours a day; those in other hospitals are usually open between 10am and 6pm daily. Hospital pharmacies accept prescriptions from the doctors registered in their hospitals only.

## STDs, HIV & AIDS

### AIDS Concern

*2898 4411/www.aidsconcern.org.hk.* **Phone enquiries** 9am-6pm Mon-Fri. A community-based organisation providing AIDS support, advocacy and prevention programmes.

### AIDS Counselling Service

*2780 2211, then press 2 for English.* **Phone enquiries** 24hrs daily.

### HIV Education Centre

*2501 0653.* **Phone enquiries** varies.

### St John's Cathedral HIV Education Centre

*4-8 Garden Road, Central, HK Island (2523 0531/2501 0653/education centre & counselling 2525 7207/*

*www.csu.med.cuhk.edu.hk/hkaids/sjhiv). Central MTR (exit J2)/buses along Garden Road.* **Phone enquiries** 9am-5pm Mon-Fri. **Map** p309 E5.

St John's run an HIV education centre and free counselling service.

## Women's health

There are well-woman clinics located within the Adventist (*see above*) and Matilda hospitals (*see p284*).

## Helplines

The following helplines are all manned by English-speaking operators:

### Alcoholics Anonymous

*2522 5665.* **Phone enquiries** 6-7pm daily.

### Community Advice Bureau

*2815 5444.* **Phone enquiries** 10am-4pm daily.

### Kely Support Group

*2521 6890/9032 9096.* **Phone enquiries** 9am-6pm daily.

### Rape Crisis/Shelter

*2572 2733, then press 3 for English.* **Phone enquiries** 24hrs daily.

### The Samaritans

*2896 0000.* **Phone enquiries** 24hrs daily.

### SARDA (Society for Aid & Rehabilitation of Drug Abusers)

*2527 7723/English line 2574 3300.* **Phone enquiries** 9am-11pm daily.

### St John's Ambulance

*HK Island: 2576 6555; Kowloon: 2713 5555; New Territories: 2639 2555.* **Phone enquiries** 24hrs daily.

## ID

Visitors and residents are officially 'advised' to carry their passport or other photo ID with them at all times while in Hong Kong. The police do random street checks and if you are found without any identification you are liable for a fine. Some bars and clubs ask for ID if they suspect

**Directory**

you are under age for entry – these tend to be managed or owned by foreigners.

## Insurance

Make sure you have adequate travel and health insurance prior to arrival in Hong Kong, as the territory has no reciprocal arrangements with other countries.

## Internet

In recent years the number of cybercafés in Hong Kong has increased considerably (though there aren't as many as might be expected in a city that has embraced technology – in the form of mobile telephony – so wholeheartedly), and terminals can also be found in cafés and even hairdressers. The HKTB (see p291) offers free internet access at the airport and at its various centres. Many hotels provide broadband internet access in their business centres and in the guest rooms (also sometimes for a fee).

### Pacific Coffee Company

*Shop 1022, Level 1, Southern Retail Podium, International Finance Centre, Harbour View Street, (2868 5100). Central MTR (exit A)/buses through Central.* **Open** *7am-10pm daily.* **Map** *p309 D3.*

This coffee shop chain offers access in all of its branches, free of charge and for an unlimited period of time (as long as there are no queues). **Other locations:** throughout the city.

## Language

English and Cantonese are the official languages (see p294), but away from business and main shopping areas, English is neither spoken nor understood and communicating in restaurants and shops can be a challenge. If you expect to go beyond the main shopping and business areas, ask your hotel concierge to write out the name and destination in Chinese, as well as return directions.

Cantonese, Mandarin and English-language institutes are mushrooming in Hong Kong, though for some you have to be a full-time student to enroll in their Chinese language courses. *See also p290.*

## Left luggage

There are no left-luggage facilities in any of the public transport terminals – except at the airport in the Arrivals Hall (2261 0110). It's open 6am-1am daily and charges HK$35 per piece for up to three hours, or HK$50 per piece per day.

## Legal help

For help in finding a lawyer and basic information on Hong Kong law, call 2521 3333/2522 8018. For embassies and consulates, see p283.

## Libraries

The Urban Council runs a network of libraries with a wide selection of books, newspapers, magazines, videos, cassettes, records, slides and microfilm. For non-residents, a passport, proof of address and a resident guarantor's identity card is required for a three-month temporary library card.

### Alliance Française

*123 Hennessy Road, Wan Chai, HK Island (2527 7825). Wan Chai MTR (exit B1)/buses along Hennessy Road.* **Open** *9am-9pm Mon-Fri.* **Map** *p310 B3.*

### British Council Library

*1 Supreme Court Road, Central, HK Island (2913 5125/5000). Admiralty MTR (exit C1)/buses along Queensway.* **Open** *noon-8pm Mon-Fri; 10.30am-5.30pm Sat.* **Map** *p309 F5.*

### Central Library

*66 Causeway Road (3150 1234). Causeway Bay MTR (exit F)/8A, 15B, 19, 25, 63, 77, A11 bus.* **Open** *10am-9pm Mon, Tue, Thur-Sat; 1-9pm Wed; 10am-7pm Sun.* **Map** *p311 E3.*

### Goethe Institut Library

*14/F, Hong Kong Arts Centre, 2 Harbour Road, Wan Chai, HK Island (2802 0088). Wan Chai MTR (exit A1/buses along Gloucester Road.* **Open** *5.30-8.30pm Mon-Fri; 2-6pm Sat.* **Map** *p310 B2.*

### Urban Council Library

*2-5/F & 8-11/F, City Hall High Block, Central, HK Island (2921 2681/ www.uhkpl.gov.hk).* **Open** *10am-7pm Mon-Wed; 10am-9pm Thur, Fri; 10am-5pm Sat, Sun.* **Map** *p309 E3.*

## Lost property

Call **2860 2000** if you lose anything in the city and you'll be told which police station to contact.

The following are all lost property numbers:

### Airport

*Level 6 (2812 2018). See p277.*

### Buses

**Citybus** *2873 0807.*
**Kowloon Motor Bus (KMB)** *2750 8547/3473 1904.*
**New World First Bus** *2136 8888.*

### Ferries

**Discovery Bay Ferries** *2987 7351.*
**New World First Ferry Service** *2131 8181.*
**Star Ferry** *2366 2576.*

### Taxis

**HK taxis** *187 2920/2574 7311.*
**Kowloon taxis** *187 2920/2760 0411.*

### Trains

**MTR Admiralty Station** *2881 8888.*
**KCR** *2602 7799.*
**LR** *2468 7788.*

### Trams

**HK Tramways** *2548 7102.*
**Peak Tramways** *2522 0922.*
**Public Lightbus** *2804 2600.*

## Media

### Newspapers

Since the Handover, Hong Kong's freedom of speech has been closely monitored – and most agree that it generally hasn't suffered as badly as many people thought it might. However, self-censorship is increasingly and worryingly widespread as the owners of some publications tread carefully to protect their Chinese interests. Of the main English-speaking newspapers, the *South China Morning Post* (www.scmp.com) boasts the biggest circulation and wields the heaviest clout, but its reporting has lost some punch and flavour and appears somewhat subdued. The *HK Standard* has returned, primarily as a business rag, replacing the defunct daily *iMail*.

Of the Chinese language newspapers, three of the most popular are *Apple Daily*, *Oriental Daily News* and *Sing Tao Daily*. These tend to go a step further in their efforts to shock Hong Kongers awake with sensational pictures full of blood and guts spread across the front page on a daily basis. If there is any sex and violence to be had, the Chinese paparazzi are on the scene snapping away before the blood has dried on the pavement.

## Magazines

As you'd expect from the financial hub of Asia, there are piles of locally based magazines reporting on business and finance, including the *Far Eastern Economic Review*, *Time Asia*, *Asiaweek* and the *Asian Wall Street Journal*. Society magazines *HK Tatler* and *B International* are full of pictures of fashionable *tai-tais* attending glossy launches of international haute-couture fashion collections. *Home Journal* takes a peek at the multi-million dollar residences on the Peak, while *Talkies* spreads the latest local and international gossip. There are Chinese versions of *Cosmopolitan*, *Elle*, *Marie Claire* and other British and American publications with Chinese models and articles on beauty and fashion.

There are also hundreds of Chinese publications on technology, cars, fashion, as well as some with 'You've just got to buy me, even though you can't read me' titles like *Cheez!* and *Amoeba*.

*HK Magazine*, published on Fridays, has its finger on the weekly pulse of the Hong Kong world of film, art, clubbing, bars and restaurants, as well as illuminating and confrontational articles on life in the region. *BC Magazine* (www.bcmagazine.net) is a bi-monthly, available on the second and third Thursdays of the month, loaded with information about what's on in the entertainment world and what's happening around town, but without the 'in your face' style of *HK Magazine*. It is the glossier of the two, with a fancy layout and plenty of photos. Both can be picked up for free in bars, restaurants and shops around town. Major international magazines are available, too, albeit at a huge mark-up.

## Radio

**Radio Television Hong Kong (RTHK)**, once government-run, is now publicly funded and editorially independent. It frequently criticises the Chinese government and airs public opinions without restraint on its talkback programmes. **RTHK3** (567AM, 1584AM) is the main provider of English news, finance and current affairs. **RTHK4** (97.6-98.9FM) plays Western and Chinese classical music. **RTHK6** (675AM) broadcasts the BBC World Service. **Metro Plus** (1044AM) is a local station with news and music.

## TV

Two local English-language channels air good documentaries, American

sitcoms, sports, cooking shows, local and international news. **Star TV**, Hong Kong's satellite TV station, and **Cable TV** provide a wider choice of international news coverage and programmes including HBO movies. Hotels rooms often feature a package of cable and/or satellite channels.

## Money

Hong Kong is an expensive place to live due to high rents and the cost of imported merchandise. But some things are cheaper than in other cities in the world, in particular public transport (especially taxis), locally made clothes and other goods, and local food. Visitors from Western countries often find Hong Kong relatively cheap as their currencies have strong purchasing power.

The Hong Kong dollar is pegged to the US dollar at HK$7.80, though this occasionally fluctuates slightly (as this guide went to print it was HK$7.76). Other rates at press time include: AUS$1 = HK$5.81, GBP£1 = HK$13.81, 1 Euro (€) = HK$9.75.

Hong Kong dollar notes come in denominations of 1,000 (orange), 500 (brown), 100 (red), 50 (mauve), 20 (bluish) and 10 (green); new 10 dollar notes are purple. Coins come in denominations of 10 dollars (two-tone, gold circled by silver), 5, 2 and 1 dollar in silver colour, and brass-coloured 50, 20 and 10 cent pieces.

There is no central mint; bank notes are issued by various banks as well as the HK Monetary Authority, and are interchangeable.

Exchange bureaux and banks charge a fee for changing money and cashing travellers' cheques – unless you take the latter to the issuing bank or to American Express (*see p288*).

**Directory**

## ATMs

There are ATMs on virtually every street corner in Hong Kong, as well as at Star Ferry terminals and MTR stations.

## Banks

### Bank of America

*Bank of America Tower, 12 Harcourt Road, Admiralty, Central, HK Island (2847 6111/fax 2597 2919/www. bankofamerica.com.hk). Admiralty (exit B) or Central MTR (exit J3/J2).* **Open** 9.30am-4.30pm Mon-Fri; 9am-noon Sat. **Map** p309 F4.

### Bank of China

*1 Garden Road, Central, HK Island (2826 6888/fax 2810 5963/ www.bochk.com). Admiralty MTR (exit B)/buses along Garden Road.* **Open** 9am-5pm Mon-Fri; 9am-1pm Sat. **Map** p309 E4.

### Citibank

*3 Garden Road, Central, HK Island (2868 8888/www.citibank.com.hk). Admiralty MTR (exit B)/buses along Garden Road.* **Open** 9am-4.30pm Mon-Fri; 9am-12.30pm Sat. **Map** p309 E4.

### HSBC

*1 Queen's Road, Central, HK Island (Customer hotline 2748 3322/2822 1111/2748 9222/fax 2288 2401/ www.hsbc.com.hk). Central MTR (exit K)/buses along Queen's Road, Central.* **Open** 9am-4.30pm Mon-Fri; 9am-12.30pm Sat. **Map** p309 E4.

### Standard Chartered Bank

*4 Des Voeux Road, Central, HK Island (2820 3333/fax 2856 9129/ www.standardchartered.com.hk). Central MTR (exit K)/buses along Queen's Road Central.* **Open** 9.30am-4.30pm Mon-Fri; 9.30am-12.30pm Sat. **Map** p309 E4.

## Bureaux de change

These are plentiful, though banks usually offer better exchange rates.

### American Express

*1/F, Henley Building, 5 Queen's Road, Central, HK Island (2110 2008/www.americanexpress.com). Central MTR (exit K, G)/buses along Queen's Road Central.* **Map** p309 D4. *1/F, China Insurance Building, 48 Cameron Road, Tsim Sha Tsui, Kowloon (2926 1606). Tsim Sha*

*Tsui MTR (exit B).* **Map** p313 C5. **Open** 9am-5pm Mon-Fri; 9am-12.30pm Sat.

### Thomas Cook/Travelex

*8/F, Man Yee Building, 68 Des Voeux Road, Central, HK Island (2545 4399/www.travelex.com.hk). Central MTR (exit C)/buses & trams along Des Voeux Road.* **Map** p309 D3. *Rooms 910-912, 9/F, HK Pacific Centre, 28 Hancock Road, Tsim Sha Tsui, Kowloon (2723 8212). Tsim Sha Tsui MTR (exit A).* **Map** p313 C6. **Open** 9am-5.30pm Mon-Fri; 9am-1pm Sat.

## Credit cards

Credit cards are widely accepted in the city (though hardly at all in rural areas). The majority of large shops, department stores, restaurants, travel agents and hotels take most of the major cards.

For lost credit cards, *see p284* **Emergencies**.

## Natural hazards

Hong Kong's subtropical climate is at its most oppressive during the summer (*see p292*). July to September is typhoon season. During the approach of a typhoon, a system of numbers tracks its progress and defines its severity and the relevant precautions to be taken by schools and workplaces. To indicate the severity of the rain and wind, colour signals are announced. Warnings and weather information are given out on TV and radio channels, or you can call 187 8066.

An **amber** rainstorm warning means that more than 30 millimetres (1.2 inches) of rain an hour is expected; a **red** warning is for 50 millimetres and over (1.9 inches) of rain; while a **black** rain signal warns of rainfall in excess of 70 millimetres (2.8 inches) in an hour. If the latter comes into effect, you can expect roads to become flooded, landslides to take place and public facilities to be closed down.

**Typhoon Signal 1** indicates that a tropical cyclone is within 800 kilometres (500 miles) of the city; **Typhoon Signal 3** means that winds of up to 62 kilometres (39 miles) per hour are expected across Hong Kong; **Typhoon Signal 8** is when the typhoon is close and possibly on the path for a hit with storm-force winds of up to 117 kilometres (73 miles) per hour and gusts of up to 180 kilometres (112 miles) per hour; **Typhoon Signal 10** is as bad as it gets – a 'direct hit' is expected with winds higher than 117 kilometres (73 miles) per hour and destructive gusts as fierce as 220 kilometres (137 miles) per hour. From Signal 8 upwards, you should stay indoors – most of Hong Kong's buildings can withstand such winds, but there's a serious danger of being hit by flying debris or street signs. However, only about 12 maximum severity typhoons have hit the city in the last 50 years.

There are no flies in Hong Kong, but mosquitoes during the summer months can leave you scratching in parks and green areas. As a deterrent, repellents are recommended, but if you do get bitten, try locally made Tiger Balm (available in drugstores) to calm the itching. For suggested vaccinations and health precautions, *see p284*.

Air pollution can be a problem for asthma sufferers, particularly in drier months.

## Opening hours

Generally, office hours are 9am to 6pm Monday to Friday (with lunch usually from 1pm to 2pm) and 9am to 1pm on Saturday. Major banks are open 9am to 4.30pm Monday to Friday and 9am to 12.30pm Saturday. Most government offices are open from 9.30am to 5pm Monday to Friday and 9.30am to noon on Saturday.

Most shops open 10.30am to 6.30pm every day. However, in major shopping areas like Causeway Bay on Hong Kong Island and Nathan Road, Kowloon, shopping goes on until 9pm or later at the weekends. During Chinese New Year (*see p190*) everything shuts down for three days.

## Police

The Hong Kong Police is still largely run and staffed as it was under the British. It is proud of its reputation as one of Asia's best forces. Officers wear grey-green uniform in summer and dark blue in winter. English-speaking policemen wear a red strip under their shoulder badge.

## Police stations

### Hong Kong Island

*Arsenal Street, Wan Chai, HK Island (2860 2000). Wan Chai MTR (exit B1)/buses along Hennessy Road.* **Map** p310 A2.

*10 Hollywood Road, Central, HK Island (2841 6311). Central MTR (exit D1, D2, G)/Mid-Levels Escalator/12M, 13, 23A, 26, 40M, 43 bus.* **Map** p308 C3.

### Kowloon

*190 Argyle Street, Mong Kok, Kowloon (2761 2228). Mong Kok MTR/buses along Nathan Road & Argyle Street.* **Map** p312 B2.

*213 Nathan Road, nr Kowloon Park (2721 0137). Tsim Sha Tsui MTR (exit A1).* **Map** p313 B5.

## Postal services

The Hong Kong postal service (www.hongkongpost.com) is generally reliable and efficient. Airmail letters and postcards to Zone 1 countries (all parts of Asia except Japan) cost HK$2.40 for 20 grams (0.7oz) or less – delivery time is three to five days; to Zone 2 (all other countries) costs HK$3 for 20 grams (0.7oz) or less – delivery time is five to seven days. Local mail costs

HK$1.40 – delivery time is one to two days. International (Speedpost) and local courier services are also available.

For couriers and shippers, *see p282*.

## Post offices

### General Post Office

*2 Connaught Place, Central, HK Island (2921 2222). Central MTR (exit A)/buses along Connaught Road Central/Central Star Ferry Pier.* **Open** 9am-6pm Mon-Sat; 9am-2pm Sun. **Credit** (over HK$300) AmEx, DC, MC, V. **Map** p309 E3.

### Post office

*10 Middle Road, Tsim Sha Tsui, Kowloon (2366 4111). Tsim Sha Tsui MTR (exit E)/buses along Nathan Road/Tsim Sha Tsui Star Ferry Pier.* **Open** 8am-6pm Mon-Sat; 9am-2pm Sun. **Credit** (over HK$300) AmEx, DC, MC, V. **Map** p313 B6.

## Poste restante

The poste restante service operates out of the General Post Office (*see above*) by the Star Ferry Pier in Central. You can collect poste restante mail from 8am until 6pm Monday to Saturday; don't forget to take your passport with you.

## Religion

Buddhism, Taoism and Confucianism have a wide following in Hong Kong and the city is home to many temples. Other religions have facilities and are practised freely.

### Anglican

*St John's Cathedral, 4-8 Garden Road, Central, HK Island (2523 4157). Central MTR (exit K)/buses along Garden Road.* **Services** 7am, 6pm daily. **Map** p309 E4.

### Baptist

*Kowloon English Baptist Church, 300 Junction Road, Kowloon (2337 2555). Kowloon Tong MTR (exit A2)/KCR/Lok Fu MTR/buses along Junction Road.* **Services** 7.30pm Wed; 8.20am, 11am, 6pm Sun.

### Catholic

*St Joseph's, 37 Garden Road, Central, HK Island (2522 3992). Central MTR (exit K)/buses along*

*Garden Road.* **Services** 7.45am, 6pm Mon-Fri; 6pm Sat; from 7am (& every hr thereafter) Sun. **Map** p309 E5.

### Hindu

*Hindu Temple, 1B Wong Nai Chung Road, Happy Valley, HK Island (2572 5284). Bus 5A from Central or Admiralty/tram to Happy Valley.* **Services** 8am Mon-Sat; 7.30pm daily (bhajan); 11am Sun.

### Interdenominational

*Union Church Interdenominational, 22A Kennedy Road, Mid-Levels, HK Island (2522 1515). Admiralty MTR then 12A bus or 28 minibus from in front of Alexandra House.* **Services** 10.30am, 6.30pm Sun. **Map** p308 B3.

### Islamic

*Kowloon Mosque & Islamic Centre, Junction of Nathan Road & Cameron Road, Tsim Sha Tsui, Kowloon (2724 0095). Tsim Sha Tsui MTR (exit A1)/buses along Nathan Road.* **Services** phone for details. **Map** p313 B5.

### Jewish

*Ohel Leah Synagogue, 70 Robinson Road, Mid-Levels, HK Island (2549 0981/2801 5440). Bus 3B, 12M, 13, 23, 23B, 40.* **Services** 6.55am Mon, Thur; 7.05am Tue, Wed, Fri; 8.30am Sun. Rosh Chodesh 6.45am. Shabbath 9am, 6.30pm. **Map** p308 B4.

### Lutheran

*Church of All Nations, 8 South Bay Close, Repulse Bay, HK Island (2812 0375). Bus 6, 66, 6A, 6X, 260.* **Services** 10.15am Sun.

### Methodist

*English Methodist Church, 271 Queen's Road East, Wan Chai, HK Island (2575 7817). Wan Chai MTR (exit A3)/buses along Queen's Road East.* **Services** 7.45am Wed; 8.15am, 11am Sun. **Map** p310 B4.

### Mormon

*Mormon Church, 9-11 Shelter Street (nr Central Library), Causeway Bay, HK Island (2559 3325). Buses along Causeway Road.* **Services** phone for details.
This is a temporary address.

### Sikh

*Sikh Temple, 371 Queen's Road East, Wan Chai, HK Island (2572 4459). Bus 10 from Central or Admiralty.* **Services** 6am, 6.30pm daily. **Map** p310 B4.

## Safety & security

For a city of its size, Hong Kong is remarkably safe – even at night. Violent crime is very rare, and almost entirely confined to triad disputes and domestic incidents. A common petty crime to watch out for is pickpocketing, and even that is not widespread. However, all the normal city precautions apply (particularly in the main tourist areas): don't flash large wads of cash around; don't leave bags where you can't see them (hanging from the back of seats, etc); keep wallets/cash in front pockets, and don't put anything valuable in your backpack.

Although you will come across touts anxious to lure you into their shops in some tourist areas, they are rarely very persistent.

Sexual harassment is rare, and many well-travelled female residents claim that this is the safest city they've ever lived in.

## Smoking & spitting

Smoking is considered anti-social in Hong Kong. Many restaurants, theatres, offices and malls are smoke-free, as is public transport. Hawking and spitting in the street is common in the rest of China, but less so here. Spitting is, in fact, strictly forbidden in public areas and a hefty fine is imposed on defaulters.

## Study

Language colleges in Hong Kong spring up and close frequently. *HK Magazine* (*see p287*) is the most reliable source of information.

Hong Kong has eight universities offering degree programmes in a wide variety of subjects, both academic and vocational. Student unions are visible and active. All of Hong Kong's universities also offer continuing education programmes. Details of

their degree, sub-degree and further education programmes can be found on the websites below.

Smaller institutions run informal courses on everything from jewellery beading to photography. These include the **YMCA of Hong Kong** (2736 0922, www.ymca.org.hk); the **YWCA** (2522 4291, www.esmdywca.org.hk) and the **Island School Evening Institute** (2526 5884, www.island.edu.hk/isei). The latter also runs Chinese-language courses (in Cantonese and Mandarin), as do the **British Council** (www.british council.org.hk), the **Chinese University of Hong Kong** (*see below*) and a number of private language colleges, such as the **HK Institute of Languages** (2877 6160, www.hklanguages.com).

Check the classifieds of *HK Magazine* for full listings.

## Universities

### Chinese University of Hong Kong
*Sha Tin, New Territories (2609 6000/fax 2603 5544/ www.cuhk.edu.hk/en).*

### City University
*83 Tat Chee Avenue, Kowloon Tong, Kowloon (2788 7654/fax 2778 1167/www.cityu.edu.hk).*

### Hong Kong Baptist University
*Kowloon Tong, Kowloon (3411 7400/fax 2338 7644/ www.hkbu.edu.hk).*

### Hong Kong Polytechnic University
*Yuk Choi Road, Hung Hom, Kowloon (2766 5111/fax 2764 3374/www.polyu.edu.hk).*

### Hong Kong University
*Pok Fu Lam Road, Mid-Levels, HK Island (2859 2111/fax 2858 2549/ www.hku.hk).*

### Lingnan University
*Tuen Mun, New Territories (2616 8888/www.ln.edu.hk).*

### Open University of Hong Kong
*30 Good Shepherd Road, Ho Man Tin, Kowloon (2711 2100/fax 2761 3935/www.ouhk.edu.hk).*

### University of Science & Technology
*Clearwater Bay, Kowloon (2358 6000/www.ust.hk).*

## Tax

Hong Kong is a duty-free port; import duty is only payable on alcohol, tobacco and cars (*see p282*). No tax is levied on purchased merchandise or in restaurants, but hotels charge a ten per cent service tax and three per cent government tax (check when you book whether it's included in the rate quoted). There is an airport departure tax for adults of HK$80 (included in the ticket price), and the tax for leaving Hong Kong by boat or ferry (about HK$25) is also included in the ticket price.

## Telephones

### Dialling & codes

The international code for Hong Kong is **852**, so to call the city from abroad, dial the international access code (00 in the UK, New Zealand and Ireland, 011 in the USA and Canada, 0011 in Australia), then 852 and the eight-digit local number. There are no area codes within Hong Kong. For Macau phone codes, *see p259*; for Guangzhou, *see p273*.

To call abroad from Hong Kong, dial the international access code 001, then 44 for the UK, 1 for the USA and Canada, 61 for Australia, 64 for New Zealand and 353 for Ireland, then the local area code (omitting the initial 0 if there is one) and the local number – you'll probably have to precede all this by dialling 9 if you are calling from a hotel. Long-distance IDD calls are the cheapest in Asia, but only if you are calling from a public payphone – many hotels tend to charge an excessive surcharge.

Local calls from public coin boxes cost HK$1 for five minutes (phones accept one-, two-, five- and ten-dollar coins). Local calls from private homes, restaurants, offices and shops are free, but hotels add an extra charge for both local and international calls. If you want to call abroad from a public phone, you'll need to purchase a phone card from one of the HKTB centres (see below), the Star Ferry piers, machines by some phones and from convenience stores like 7-Eleven and Circle K, Mannings and Wellcome (see p177), supermarkets, and PCCW shops (see below). These cards come in denominations of 50, 100, 200 and 300 dollars. Some public phones accept credit cards and Octopus cards (see p278).

## Operator services

**Local directory assistance**
*1081.*
**International inquiries** *10013.*
**Reverse-charge/collect calls**
*from any private or public phone:*
*10010.*

The **Home Direct** system allows direct access to an operator in the country being called, making collect calls cheaper or allowing you to charge the call to your home phone card. The Home Direct access numbers from Hong Kong are:

**Australia** *800 96 0161.*
**Canada** *800 96 1100.*
**UK** *800 96 0044.*
**USA** *800 96 1111 for AT&T;*
*800 96 1121 for MCI; 800 96 1877*
*for Sprint.*

## Telephone directories

Directories are provided in most hotel rooms and by some public phones. There are *Yellow Pages* (which has business listings by category; also available online at www.yp.com.hk) and *White Pages* (with both business and residential numbers listed alphabetically).

## Mobile phones

Hong Kong residents love their mobile phones. In fact, the SAR boasts the world's highest per capita usage of pagers and mobiles. Most dual-band phones work here.

If you want to hire a phone while in Hong Kong, you'll find good rental packages (for a minimum of one week) on offer from **PCCW** shops. On Hong Kong Island these include G/F, 161-3 Des Voeux Road, Central (2543 0603); G/F, 42-4 Yee Woo Street, Causeway Bay (2881 8898); Shop 121-2, New Jade Shopping Centre, 233 Chai Wan Road, Chai Wan (2766 1166); G/F, Hong Chiang Building, 147 Johnston Road, Wan Chai (2892 1997); Shop G4, Max Share Centre, 367-73 King's Road, North Point (2512 8899). In Kowloon they include 168-76 Sai Yeung Choi Street, Mong Kok (2394 8131) and Miramar Hotel, 118-130 Nathan Road, Tsim Sha Tsui (2739 3992).

## Faxes

Most hotels are willing to accept incoming faxes for their guests. Faxes can either be sent from hotels or (generally, more cheaply) from photocopying shops such as **Fit Copy Equipment Co/ Da Fat Stationery** (see p159). The charge is about HK$10 (local) or HK$80 (international) per page.

### Xerox
*New Henry House, 10 Ice House Street, Central (2524 9799). Central MTR (exit H)/buses & trams through Central.* **Open** *9am-6pm Mon-Sat.* **Credit** *(over HK$300) AmEx, DC, MC, V.* **Map** *p309 D4.*

## Time

Hong Kong does not have Daylight Saving Time. Time differences for major cities include:

| | |
|---|---|
| **Chicago** | -13hrs |
| **London** | -7hrs |
| | (-8hrs during DST) |
| **Los Angeles** | -15hrs |
| **New York** | -12hrs |
| **Sydney** | +2hrs |

## Tipping

Tipping isn't a part of Chinese culture, but Westerners have been in Hong Kong so long that it is now widely expected. A standard ten per cent service charge is added to the bill at most restaurants and hotels. Where there is no service charge, tipping is at your discretion, but ten per cent is the usual amount given. Small tips of HK$3-$20 may be given to taxi drivers, bellboys, doormen and washroom attendants.

## Toilets

Toilets in parks, malls, hotels, restaurants, bars, cafés and department stores are usually clean and well maintained. Toilets in some parks/beaches have no toilet paper. In the more Chinese areas, be prepared to squat.

## Tourist information

The official visitors and general city information organisation, the **Hong Kong Tourism Board (HKTB)**, produces excellent maps (including hiking maps), brochures and booklets on eating, shopping and sightseeing, which are available free at its service centres located on both sides of the harbour. A Quality Tourism Services (QTL) decal in the windows of shops and restaurants denotes that the establishment meets HKTB standards and is deemed reliable. The award-winning website www. discoverhongkong.com, is well worth a look prior to arriving in Hong Kong.

HKTB branches are located in: G/F, The Center, 99 Queen's Road, Central, HK Island; and Star Ferry Concourse, Tsim Sha Tsui, Kowloon. Both are

**Directory**

open 8am-6pm daily. Here you can get advice, pick up brochures, maps, events schedules and other information and buy souvenirs.

The HKTB multilingual hotline (2508 1234) is the general line to call for any information on Hong Kong, including directions to a place, or queries about events, addresses or phone numbers.

**I-Cyberlink** is the HKTB's internet access to information about Hong Kong. These information points can be found at the airport on arrival as you leave the terminal and at the HKTB visitors' centres. Most of the information they display is also in the brochures available at these centres and at the airport.

## Visas & immigration

All foreigners entering Hong Kong for employment, business, education or training purposes (as well as their dependants) require a visa. The only exceptions are those born in Hong Kong and those holding a permanent identity card, HKSAR or BNO passport.

For visitors, a visa is valid for a month, though it can be extended, but no employment of any kind is permitted during stays. Visitors are not allowed to change their visitor status to working status after they've arrived in Hong Kong, except in exceptional cases.

Entry permits/visas can be obtained from a Chinese consulate in your country. Visitors must hold a passport that is valid for at least a month after their planned departure from Hong Kong.

In addition, nationals of the UK and British Commonwealth dependent/protected countries do not require a visa for a visit of fewer than three months; neither do American and South African visitors coming

for less than a month, and other nationalities for a stay of less than eight days; but it's best to check to make sure. For frequent visitors, a pass or multiple-entry visa can be obtained.

### HK Immigration Department

*7 Gloucester Road, Wan Chai, HK Island (2824 6111/fax 2877 7711/ www.info.gov.hk). Wan Chai MTR (exit A1)/buses along Gloucester Road.* **Open** 8.45am-4.30pm Mon-Fri; 9-11.30am Sat. **Map** p310 B3.

## Water

Tap water in Hong Kong is considered safe to drink. But residents tend to filter or boil their water before drinking it, not quite trusting the condition of the pipes in their buildings. If in doubt, you can purchase a variety of local and imported bottled water in supermarkets and convenience stores.

Beaches are given a daily pollution rating, as many are below WHO standards, and ocean pollution is a serious problem. Check the reports in local newspapers before setting out to a beach.

## Weights & measures

Hong Kong uses the metric system, although you will sometimes see pounds and ounces in use in supermarkets, as well as a Chinese measurement of weight, the 'catty' (600 grams/21 ounces).

1 kilometre = 0.621 miles
1 metre = 1.093 yards
1 centimetre = 0.3937 inches
1 kilogram = 2.2046 pounds
1 gram = 0.0352 ounces
1 litre = 0.2642 imperial gallon
0 degrees Celsius = 32 degrees Fahrenheit

## What to take

Everything you're likely to need can be bought in Hong Kong, although some items may be more expensive than

they are back home. It's wise to bring all essentials with you – important medication may not be available here, and foreign prescriptions will not be accepted at pharmacies unless endorsed by a local, certified practitioner.

## When to go

Hong Kong has a subtropical climate and there are times of the year when its high humidity can be seriously debilitating, making a visit to the city distinctly uncomfortable. A summary of what to expect during the year follows, but bear in mind that the weather in Hong Kong can be very unpredictable.

**Spring** (March to mid May) is often pleasant, but humidity can be high and some of the heaviest rainfall is recorded during this time. Bring a light jacket or sweater for the evenings, which can be cool.

**Summer** (late May to mid September) is hot and stiflingly humid. Ironically, you'll probably still need to bring an extra layer for when you're indoors, as shops, restaurants, bars and hotels tend to crank up the air-conditioning to icy levels. This is also typhoon season (*see p288* **Natural hazards**) and rainfall is at its highest.

**Autumn** (late September to early December) is usually the best time to visit; temperatures are comfortably warm, and humidity drops to a bearable level. Sunny days and clear skies are relatively common.

**Winter** (mid December to February) can be a good time to come, with temperatures of 13°C to 20°C (55-68°F) and humidity of around 72 per cent. It can get chilly, windy and cloudy, though, so you'll need to bring extra layers.

For daily weather reports and three-day advance forecasts, contact the **HK Observatory** on 2926 8200

# Average climate

| | Temp (°C) | Temp (°F) | Humidity (%) | Rainfall (mm) | Sunshine (hrs) |
|---|---|---|---|---|---|
| **January** | 13-18 | 56-64 | 71 | 23.4 | 152.4 |
| **February** | 13-17 | 55-63 | 78 | 48.0 | 97.7 |
| **March** | 16-19 | 60-67 | 81 | 66.9 | 96.4 |
| **April** | 19-24 | 65-75 | 83 | 161.5 | 108.9 |
| **May** | 23-28 | 74-82 | 83 | 316.7 | 153.8 |
| **June** | 26-29 | 78-85 | 82 | 376.0 | 161.1 |
| **July** | 26-31 | 78-87 | 80 | 323.5 | 231.1 |
| **August** | 26-31 | 78-87 | 81 | 391.4 | 207.0 |
| **September** | 25-29 | 77-85 | 78 | 299.7 | 181.7 |
| **October** | 23-27 | 73-81 | 73 | 144.0 | 195.0 |
| **November** | 18-23 | 65-74 | 69 | 35.1 | 181.0 |
| **December** | 15-20 | 59-68 | 68 | 27.3 | 185.5 |

or **Dial-a-Weather** (187 8066). Also, the website www.underground.org.hk features detailed information about local conditions.

## Public holidays

Many holidays in Hong Kong are Chinese festival days that are subject to the lunar calendar, so the dates tend to change from year to year.

**New Year's Day** (1 January); **Chinese Lunar New Year** (three days in January/February); **Good Friday** and **Easter Monday** (March/April); **Ching Ming Festival** (March/April); **Buddha's Birthday** (April/May); **Labour Day** (1 May); **Tuen Ng Dragon Boat** Festival (June); **HKSAR Establishment Day** (1 July); **Day after Mid Autumn Festival** (September); **China National Day** (1 October) ; **Chung Yeung** (October); **Christmas Day** (25 December); **Boxing Day** (26 December).

## Women

Women in Hong Kong are active and visible, holding high-profile jobs in private and government sectors as well as the legislative council. There are over 50 women's organisations in Hong Kong, ranging from business and professional groups for networking and socialising to charitable ones for community services.

For helplines, *see p285.*

## Organisations & resources

### American Women's Association

*C7, Monticello, 48 Kennedy Road, Mid-Levels, HK Island (2527 2961/ fax 2865 7737/www.awa.org.hk).*

### Association of Business & Professional Women

*GPO Box 1526, Hong Kong (2535 9198/fax 2904 0788/ www.hkabpw.org).*

### The Helena May

*1 Garden Road (2522 6766/ www.helenamay.com). Admiralty MTR/12S, 15C bus.* **Open** 9am-5pm Mon-Fri; 9am-12.30pm Sat. **Map** p309 E4.

### Hong Kong Women in Publishing Society

*GPO Box 7314, Central, HK Island (www.hkwips.org).*

### Women's Corona Society

*GPO Box 8151, Central, HK Island (2549 6966/3197 0130/ sandybay@netvigator.com).*

## Working in Hong Kong

Prior to 1997 British citizens didn't need work visas to get a job in HK, but since the Handover it has become more difficult for all foreigners to work in the SAR. To qualify for a work visa, visitors must prove they have skills that can't be found among HK residents. In addition, the recent economic downturn has led to a record unemployment rate, with the result that jobs are hard to come by, even for locals.

### Work permits

To work in Hong Kong, you have to have a sponsor/ employer apply for a work visa for you. This application is then reviewed by immigration for its validity before a work visa is issued. Be warned that work visas can take up to a year to process.

As of July 2003 dependants can no longer work on their dependant's visa but have to get their own sponsor for working in HK. Permanent residents can sponsor family members provided they meet certain criteria. For more information, log on to www.hk.gov.hk.

**Directory**

# The Language

Cantonese, English and Mandarin are the official languages of Hong Kong.

**Cantonese** is the dialect of the southern Chinese province of Guangdong, from where most Hong Kongers originate and is, therefore, the SAR's lingua franca, being spoken in 89 per cent of households. Three decades ago, it was considered rather low-brow and many Western sinologists predicted that it would fade away after the Handover, as Mandarin came to dominate, but it looks set to stay for good.

Cantonese is very difficult for foreigners to learn because of the seven tones involved, each of which can change the meaning of a word. For example, the word 'gai', when said in different ways, can mean either chicken, street or prostitute. Even for the Chinese, the various tones only avoid confusion up to a certain point: complete understanding is gained from the context.

As it is very difficult to master, many foreigners never bother to learn more than a few essential words of Cantonese, however long they live in Hong Kong. They do get by without it, but with a fair degree of frustration, because – despite the fact that it is an official language – many locals do not speak English.

**Mandarin**, as the Beijing dialect is known in the West, is not widely spoken in Hong Kong. However, a standardised form of it, **Putonghua**, is promoted by the Chinese government as the national language and is, therefore, spoken by 70 per cent of those living on the mainland.

Mandarin was the dialect used by government officials (or mandarins, hence its name) to communicate with each other in days gone by. Putonghua translates as 'the language that can be used everywhere', because it is common to so many of the mainland Chinese. The same – or at least a very similar – language is called Guoyu (national language) in Taiwan and Huayu (Chinese people's language) in Singapore. The differences between these languages are minor, and can be compared with the distinctions between the English language spoken in Britain and that of the US.

What all Chinese dialects have in common is an ingeniously flexible system of non-phonetic writing. In other words, Chinese characters can be read by all Chinese people, whichever dialect they speak.

**Hanyu pinyin**, the official romanisation of Chinese characters, is used in major Chinese cities on street signs (alongside Chinese characters). This is useful for foreigners who cannot read the characters, as it indicates the Chinese pronunciation, but is also confusing because it does not give the tones that must also be used.

Any attempt by foreigners to talk Chinese using pinyin is therefore likely to be unintelligible to the locals. If you are really keen to impress, the only way is to pick up a Chinese dictionary (be it Mandarin or Cantonese), because it also indicates the correct tones of characters.

Having said all that, here are some words and phrases, with approximations on how they should be pronounced: even if your attempt at communication is unintelligible, you will at least be applauded for trying.

## Phrases

| | |
|---|---|
| how are you? | nei ho ma? |
| fine, thank you | gay ho nei yau sum |
| good morning | jo sahn |
| good night | jo tau |
| goodbye | joy gen |
| hello! (on phone) | wai! |
| how much does it cost? | gaydo cheena? |
| too expensive | tei gway |
| I'm sorry (excuse me) | m'ho yi si |
| yes | hai |
| no | mm hai |
| please & thank you (for a service) | m'goy |
| please (invitation) | cheng |
| thank you (for a gift) | doh jeh |
| you're welcome | m'sai m'goy |

## Restaurant & bar phrases

| | |
|---|---|
| beer | beh jau |
| water | soi |
| English tea | lai tcha |
| bill | my dan |
| telephone | deen wah |

## Taxi directions

| | |
|---|---|
| street/road | gai/do |
| turn right | chin yau |
| turn left | chin jo |
| straight on | yat jik hui |
| hurry | fai dee |
| stop | teng |
| wait here | tang hai nee dow |

## Geographical features

| | |
|---|---|
| beach | wan |
| mountain | shan |
| harbour | o |
| headland | tau/kok |
| island | chau |
| village | tsuen |
| rock | shek |

## Numbers

| | |
|---|---|
| one | yat |
| two | yih |
| three | sahm |
| four | sei |
| five | ung |
| six | lok |
| seven | chat |
| eight | baht |
| nine | gau |
| ten | sahp |
| zero | ling |

# Further Reference

See also p204 **Don't miss HK films** and p202 **Location, location, location**.

## Books

### Non-fiction

**Magnus & Kasyan Bartlett**
*Over Hong Kong*
A pictorial record of Hong Kong.

**Austin Coates** *Myself A Mandarin*
A fascinating, often funny, insight into life in Hong Kong in the 1950s, when Coates was a Special Magistrate in Kowloon and the New Territories.

**Maurice Collis**
*Foreign Mud*
An account of the shameful history of the Opium Wars in the 1800s.

**Fredric Dannen & Barry Long**
*Hong Kong Babylon*
Superb insight into the world of Hong Kong movies, with interviews, plot summaries and film ratings.

**Jonathan Dimbleby**
*The Last Governor*
The author, a close friend of Chris Patten, had unrivalled access to the last governor and, as a result, this book provides a compelling narrative of the government side of the final chapter in the city's colonial history.

**Jonathan Fenby**
*Dealing With The Dragon*
A year (1999) in the life of Hong Kong and the author, then editor of the *South China Morning Post*.

**Patricia Lim**
*Discovering Hong Kong's Cultural Heritage*
Half of this book is dedicated to the cultural heritage of Hong Kong; the other half is more like a guide book.

**Jan Morris**
*Epilogue to an Empire: Hong Kong*
An insightful study of Hong Kong.

**James O'Reilly, Larry Habeggar & Sean O'Reilly** (editors)
*Travellers' Tales of Hong Kong*
Fifty tales by travel writers, including Bruce Chatwin and Jan Morris.

**Christopher Patten**
*East and West*
The last governor gives his side of the story of the final years of the colony.

**Russell Spurr**
*Excellency (The Governors of Hong Kong)*
A riveting look at the 28 British governors and two Japanese generals who ruled Hong Kong for 150 years.

**Han Suyin**
*A Many Splendoured Thing*
This book describes Han Suyin's love affair with Ian Morrison, a foreign correspondent for *The Times*.

**Frank Welsh**
*A History of Hong Kong*
A comprehensive history of the city.

## Fiction

**John Le Carré**
*The Honourable Schoolboy*
Exciting Cold War novel set in Hong Kong.

**James Clavell** *Noble House*
Rival *taipans* seek revenge for ancient blood feuds with the CIA, the KGB and China.

**James Clavell** *Taipan*
Set in the 19th century in Hong Kong. Pretty dull, but a popular read.

**Richard Mason**
*The World of Suzie Wong*
This 1950s novel paints an unusually frank picture of the lives of Wan Chai's bar girls.

**Paul Theroux**
*Kowloon Tong*
The worries of expats on the brink of the Handover.

**Nury Vittachi**
*The Feng Shui Detective*
Mystery, comedy and Zen mysticism combine in this book about a travelling feng shui man.

## Macau

**Charles Ralph (CR) Boxer** is an authority on Macanese history and has written a number of books on the subject, most of which – unfortunately – are out of print.

**Luiz Vaz de Camões**
(translated by William C Atkinson)
*The Lusiads*
The story of Vasco da Gama's voyage via southern Africa to India.

**Austin Coates**
*City of Broken Promises*
Historical novel based on the true story of a love affair between a Chinese orphan and the son of the British founder of Lloyd's.

**Austin Coates & Cesar Guillen-Nunez**
*A Macau Narrative*
A concise history of the former Portuguese colony.

**Leila Hadley**
*Give Me the World*
Tells of the author's riotous years of travelling in Asia in the 1950s.

**Jill McGivering**
*Macau Remembers*
Interviews with 30 different people in Macau upon its handover to China.

**Lindsay & May Ride**
(abridged, with additional information by Jason Wordie)
*The Voices of Macau Stones*
This book documents the importance of the stones, statues and memorials dotted all over Macau.

## China

**David Bonavia** *The Chinese*
An excellent introduction to the people of China.

**Jonathan Spence**
*The Search For Modern China*
The definitive work on modern China.

**Tiziano Terzani**
*Behind The Forbidden Door*
A fascinating account by an Italian journalist of life in communist China.

## Film

*See also p204* **Don't miss HK films** *and p202* **Location, location, location**.

## Websites

Note that Chinese characters will appear as question marks if you do not have Chinese fonts on your computer, though most of the following have a link to an English-language version of their site:

**BC Magazine**
*www.bcmagazine.net*
Detailed listings and articles.

**Funhongkong.com**
*www.funhongkong.com*
Listings of activities in the city.

**Health in Asia**
*www.healthinasia.com*
Medical information for Asia.

**Government of the Hong Kong SAR of the People's Republic of China**
*www.info.gov.hk*
Facts and figures on the SAR.

**Hong Kong Tourism Board**
*www.discoverhongkong.com*
Award-winning information site.

**Macau Government Tourist Office**
*www.macautourism.gov.mo*
Macau's tourist board website.

**No.1 Expat Site in Asia**
*www.asiaxpat.com.hk*
Loads of useful information.

**South China Morning Post**
*www.scmp.com*
Online version of Hong Kong's leading English-language newspaper.

**The Standard**
*www.thestandard.com.hk*
Online edition of the English-language tabloid newspaper.

**That's Guangzhou**
*www.thatsguangzhou.com*
A comprehensive guide to Guangzhou.

**Time Out Hong Kong**
*www.timeout.com/hongkong*
An abridged version of this guide.

**Directory**

# Index

**Index**

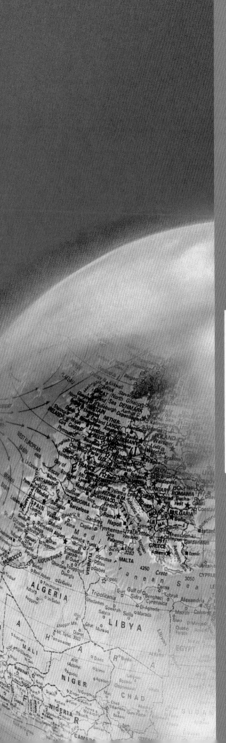

| | |
|---|---|
| Place of interest and/or entertainment | ▨ |
| Railway or bus station | ▪ |
| Park | ▫ |
| Hospital/university | ▨ |
| Post Office | ✉ |
| MTR Station | Ⓜ |
| MTR Station Exit | Ⓔ③ |
| Area | CENTRAL |
| Tram Route | — |
| Elevated Walkway | ▦ |

# Maps

# These books are
# made for walking

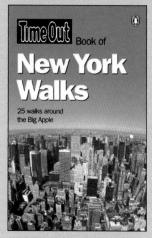

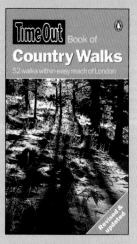

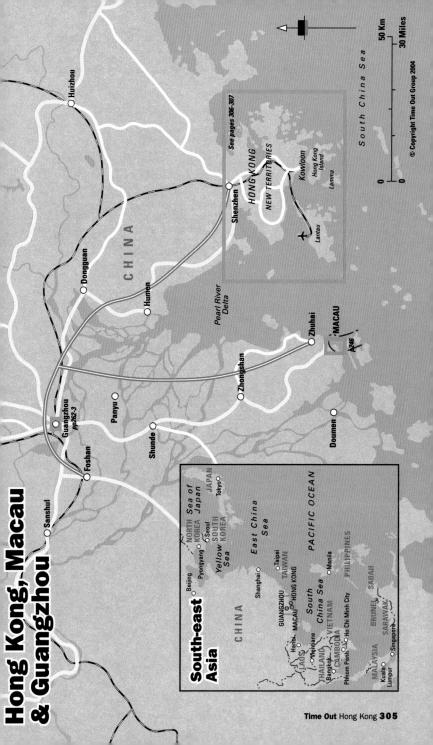

# Hong Kong, Macau & Guangzhou

See pages 306-307

HONG KONG

NEW TERRITORIES

Kowloon

Hong Kong
Island

Lamma

Lantau

South China Sea

© Copyright Time Out Group 2004

50 Km

30 Miles

Huizhou

Dongguan

Humen

Shenzhen

Pearl River
Delta

Zhuhai

MACAU

A246

Zhongshan

Doumen

Shunde

Panyu

Guangzhou
pp262-3

Foshan

Sanshui

CHINA

## South-east Asia

CHINA

Beijing

NORTH
KOREA

Pyongyang

SOUTH
KOREA

Seoul

Sea of
Japan

JAPAN

Tokyo

Yellow
Sea

East China
Sea

PACIFIC OCEAN

Shanghai

Taipei

TAIWAN

GUANGZHOU

MACAU

HONG KONG

South
China Sea

Manila

PHILIPPINES

SABAH

Hanoi

LAOS

Vientiane

VIETNAM

THAILAND

Bangkok

CAMBODIA

Phnom Penh

Ho Chi Minh City

BRUNEI

SARAWAK

MALAYSIA

Kuala
Lumpur

Singapore

# Hong Kong

*Pearl River Delta*

Window of the World

Xintang

Shen Zhen University

Dalingxia

Honey Lake Resort

Shanbu

Shenzhen

Changxingwel

Baishizhou

Chiwei

Xiangnan Beitou

Xineun

Chegongmao

Xiasha

Shatou

Ma Tso Lun

Nanyuan

Houhai

Zucun

Jiushixia

Lok Ma Chau

Kwu Tung

Shenzhen Bay

San Tin

Daniuzai

Shalwantou

Wanxia

Song Ho Park

Shekou

Nam Sha Po

Mai Po

Shek Wu Wai

Lin Tong

Chiwan

The Seaworld

Lau Fau Shan

Fairview Park

Ngau Tam Mei

Mong Tseng Wai

Mai Po Marshes

Kei Kung Leng
572

Lam Tsuen Coun

Sha Kong Tsuen

Wang Chau

Sha Po

Ngau Hom Sha

Ha Tsuen

Yuen Long

Kam Tin

Kat Hing Wai

Ping Shan

Walled Village

Pat Heung

Hung Shui Kiu

Fut Sha Wai

Shui Tsiu San Tsuen

Shek

Ha Pak Nai

Tai Shui Hang

Pak Sha Tsuen

Yuen Kong

Lin Fa Tei

Nim Wan

Kai Lun Wai

Miu Fat Buddhist Monastery

Lam Tei

Ma On Kong

Tai Wo

Ching Chung Koon Temple

Chung Wong Toi

Tai    Lam    Country    Park

N E W T

Pei Tu Temple

Lung Kwu Tan

583

Castle Peak

Tin Fu Tsai

Lung Kwu Chau

Ching Shan Monastery

Tuen Mun

Tai Lam Chung Reservoir

Shek Kok Tsui

So Kwun Wat

Chuk

Yeum M

Siu Lang Shui

Castle Peak Bay

Siu Lam

Tai Lam Chung

Sham Tseng

Airport Core Programme Exhibition Centre

Yue In

Sam T

Uk Mus

Siu Wan

Gordon Hard

Pearl Island

So Kwun Tan

Ting Kau

Tsuen

Pillar Point

Tuen Mun Rd.

Tsing Lung Tau

Ma Wan

Tsing Yi T

Brothers Point

Kap Shui Mun

Tsing Ma Bridge

Shek Wan

Tang Lung

Tsing Yi

Sha Chau

Mo To Chau (The Brothers)

Siu Mo To

Tsing Chau Tsai

Nam Wan

Tai Mo To

Mong Tung Hang

Disney (opens 2005)

Penny's Bay

Hong Kong International Airport

Sam Pak

Chek Lap Kok

Pak Mong

Yi Pak

Discovery Bay

Discovery Bay

Peng Chau

Siu Kau Yi Chau

Kau Yi Chau

Sha Lo Wan

San Tau

Tung Chung Wan

Ma Wan Chung

Ngau Kwu Long

Nim Shue Wan

Tai Shui Hang

Gree Islar

Sham Shek Tsuen

Tung Chung

Tung Chung Fort

Hung Fa Ngan

Trappist Monastery

Tin Hau Temple

Po Lin Monastery & Big Buddha

Lantau North Country Park

Pak Ngan Heung

Mui Wo

Chau Kung To (Sunshine Island)

Tai O

Ngong Ping

Tung Chung Rd.

Lantau

Luk Tei Tong

Silvermine Bay

Hei Ling Chau

Ying Hing Monastery

934

Sunset Peak

869

Lantau Peak

Pui O

Chi Ma Wan

Sai Pok Liu Hoi Hap (West Lamma Channe

Keung Shan

Lantau    South    Country    Park

Cheung Sha

Chung Hau

Lan

Man Cheung Po

Shek Pik Reservoir

Tong Fuk

Chi Ma Wan Peninsula

Tin Hau Temple

Shek Pik

Tong Fuk Miu Wan

Ha Keng

Pak Tai Temple

Power Sta

Tai Long Wan

Shuihau

Cha Kwo Chau

Tung Wan Beach

Cheung Chau

Fan Lau

Kau Ling Chung

Shek Kwu Chau

Cheung Chau

Tin Hau Temple

To Macau

Siu A Chau

Soko Islands

Ha Me

Tai A Chau

0          5 Miles

0          5 Km

© Copyright Time Out Group 2004

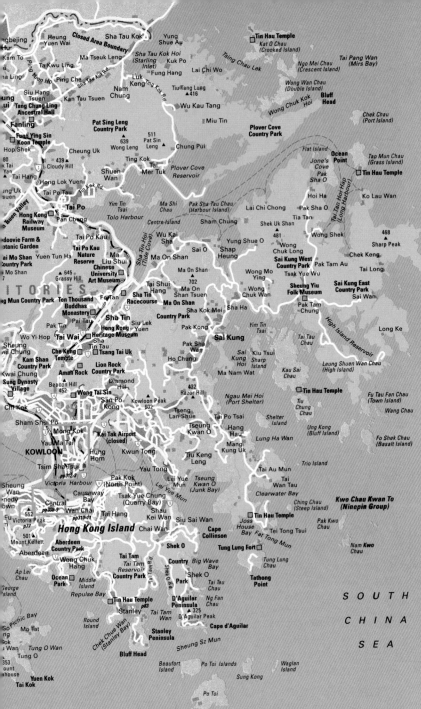

ngbejing  Heung  Closed Area Boundary  Sha Tau Kok
u  Yuen Wai  Yung
Kam To  Ma Tseuk Leng  Shue Au  ☐ Tin Hau Temple
a Ling  Ta Kwu Ling  Ping Che  Sha Tau Kok Hoi  Kuk Po  Kat O Chau  Tai Pang Wan
Wen Hop  Ping Che  (Starling  Fung Hang  Lai Chi Wo  (Crooked Island)  (Mirs Bay)
ui  Siu Hang  Kan Tau Tsuen  Nam  Luk  Tiu Tang Lung  Ngo Mei Chau
Tsuen  Tang Chung Ling  Chung  Keng  ▲416  Wong Wan Chau  (Crescent Island)
☐ Fanling  Ancestral Hall  Wu Kau Tang  (Double Island)  Bluff
Fung Ying Sin  Pat Sing Leng  Miu Tin  Wong Chuk Kok  Head
Koon Temple  Country Park  Plover Cove  Hoi  Chek Chau
Hop Shek  Cheung Uk  639  511  Country Park  (Port Island)
80  439 ▲  Wong Leng  Pat Sin  Chung Pui  Flat Island  Ocean
Tai  ▲ Cloudy Hill  Ting Kok  Leng  Jone's  Point  Tap Mun Chau
Yan  Tai  Plover Cove  Cove  (Grass Island)
Tai Hang  Hong Lok Yuen  Shuen  Mer Tuk  Reservoir  Pak  ☐ Tin Hau Temple
ng Uk  Tai Po Tau  Wan  Sha O
suen  Ma Shi  Pak Sha Tau Chau  Hoi Ha  Ko Lau Wan
☐ Tai Po  Yim Tin Tsai  Chau  (Harbour Island)  Pak Sha O
Hong Kong  Pan Chung  Tolo Harbour  Centre Island  Lai Chi Chong  Tia Tan
Railway  Sham Chung
doovie Farm &  Museum  Tai Po Kau  Wu Kai  Shek Uk Shan  Wong Shek  468
otanic Garden  Tai Po Kau  Sha  Sai O  481  Wong  Sharp Peak
Nature  Liu Shui  Shap  Chuk Long  Chek Keng
i Mo Shan  Yuen Tun Ha  Reserve  Chinese  Heung  Sai Kung West  Tai Long
Mo Shan  University  Ma On Shan  Country Park  Tsak Yue Wu
▲ 645  Art Museum  ▲  Wong Mo  Sai Kung East
I T O R I E S  Grassy Hill  Ten Thousand  702  Ying  Sheung Yiu  Country Park
Buddhas  Ma  Wong  Folk Museum  Sai Wan
n Mun Country Park  Monastery  Sha Tin  On  Chuk Wan  Pak Tam
Pai Tau  Hang  Sha Kok Mei  Chung  High Island Reservoir
Pak Tin  Sha Tin  Country Park  Sha Ha  Long Ke
Wo Yi Hop  Tai Wai  Racecourse  Pak Kong  Yim Tin
Sheung  Hong Kong  Siu Lek  Sai Kung  Tsai
al Chung  Che Kung  Heritage Museum  Yuen  Pak Sha  Tai Tau  Leung Shuen Wan Chau
Kam Shan  Temple  Tin Tau  Wan  Kiu Tsui  Chau  (High Island)
Country Park  Tsang Tai Uk  Ho Chung  Sai  Sharp
Kwai Chung  Amah Rock  Lion Rock  Kung  Island  Kau Sai
Sung Dynasty  Beacon Hill  Country Park  Diamond  Ma Nam Wat  Chau
Village  452  Hill  432  Ngau Mei Hoi  Fu Tau Fan Chau
i Kok  Wong Tai Sin  Razor Hill  (Port Shelter)  Tiu  (Town Island)
San Po  ▲  Chung
Sham Shui Po  Kong  Kowloon Peak  Tseng  Chau  Wang Chau
602  Lan Shue  Tai Po Tsai  Shelter
Mong Kok  Kei Tak Airport  Island  Fo Shek Chau
Yau Ma Tei  (closed)  Kwun Tong  Yau Tong  Tseung  Hang  Ung Kong  (Basalt Island)
KOWLOON  Hung  Tiu Keng  Kwan O  Hau  (Bluff Island)
Hom  Leng  Mang  Lung Ha Wan
Tsim Sha Tsui  Lei Yue  Tseung  Kung Uk  Tai Au Mun  Trio Island
pp312-3  Pak Kok  Mun  Kwan O
Sheung  Victoria Harbour  (North Point)  Lei Yue Mun  (Junk Bay)  Tai  Kwo Chau Kwan To
nedy  Causeway  Tsak Yue Chung  Wan Tau  (Ninepin Group)
wn  Central  Bay  (Quarry Bay)  Shau  Clearwater Bay  Ching Chau
Fu  552  pp308-9  Wan Chai  Kei Wan  (Steep Island)  Pak Kwo
Victoria Peak  pp310-11  Tai Hang  Siu Sai Wan  ☐ Tin Hau Temple  Chau
p77  Chai Wan  Joss  Tei Tong Tsui  Nam Kwo
501 ▲  Hong Kong Island  Cape  House  Fat Tong Mun  Chau
George  Mount Kellett  Collinson  Bay  Tathong
Island  Aberdeen  Tung Lung Fort ☐  Tung  Point
Country Park  Wong Chuk  Shek O  Tung Lung  Lung
Aberdeen  Hang  Tai Tam  Country  Big Wave  Chau
Ap Lei  Tai Tam  Reservoir  Park  Bay
Chau  Ocean  Middle  Country Park  Shek O  Tai Tau
George  Park  Island  Park  Chau
Island  Repulse Bay  ☐ Tin Hau Temple  Ng Fan
So Pichic Bay  D'Aguilar  Chau  S O U T H
g  Mo Tat  Stanley  p83  Peninsula
Round  Tai Tam  ▲ 325  C H I N A
Wan  Tung O Wan  Island  Wan  D'Aguilar Peak  Cape d'Aguilar
ok  Tung O  Chek Chue Wan  S E A
353  (Stanley Bay)  Stanley  Sheung Sz Mun
ount  Yuen Kok  Bluff Head  Peninsula
house  Tai Kok  Beaufort  Po Toi Islands  Waglan
Island  Island
Sung Kong
Po Toi

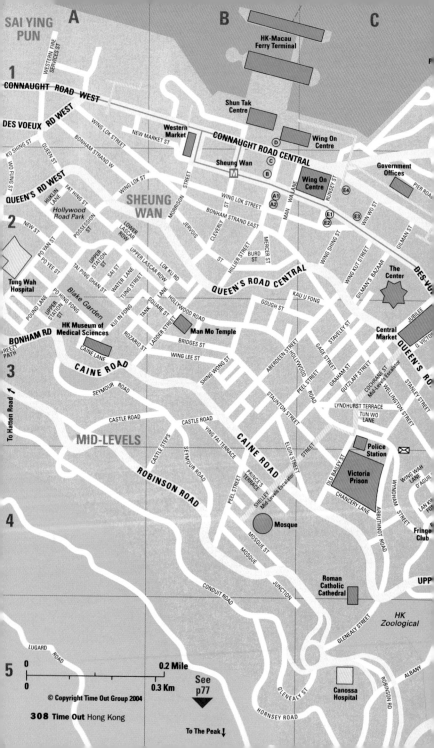

# Central, Sheung Wan & Mid-Levels

Pier 2

Pier 3

Pier
4

To Tuen Mun (New Territories)

To Yung Shue Wan (Lamma)

Pier
5

To Tsuen Wan/Tsing Yi (New Territories)

To Sok Kwu Wan (Lamma)

Pier 6

To Cheung Chau

Pier 7

To Peng Chau

To Mui Wo (Lantau)

MAN

KWONG
MAN

STREET

PO
STREET

Four Seasons
Hotel (opens 2005)

FINANCE STREET

Bus
Terminal

national
ance
ntre

International
Finance Centre 2

MAN CHEUNG ST

Hong Kong
Airport Express
Station

HARBOUR VIEW ST

MAN YIU STREET

Victoria Harbour

To Tsim Sha Tsui Star Ferry Pier

To Discovery Bay (Lantau)

To Tsim Sha Tsui East

CONNAUGHT ROAD CENTRAL

TINGER STREET

CENTRAL

EET W

Exchange
Square

ST E

DOUGLAS ST

General
Post Office

CONNAUGHT
PLACE

Central
Star Ferry
Pier

Queen's
Pier

Edinburgh Place

LUNG WUI ROAD

See
p310

ST

Queen's
Theatre

DOUGLAS LANE

CHIU LUNG ST

(A)

(B)

STREET

THEATRE LANE

(C)

Jardine
House

Swire
House

Bus
Terminal

City Hall

Chinese People's
Liberation Army
Forces Hong Kong
Building

TIM WA AVE

To Wan Chai & Causeway Bay

CENTRAL

(M) Central

(D2)

(D1)

PEDDER

(E)

(G)

(F)

STREET

Mandarin
Oriental
Hotel

CONNAUGHT ROAD CENTRAL

CLUB ST

Central
Building

The
Landmark

HOUSE

CHATER ROAD

(J3)

(J1)

Ritz-
Carlton
Hotel

Bank of
America
Tower

HARCOURT ROAD

ADMIRALTY

CENTRAL

LA ON LAN ST

ZETLAND ST

Prince's
Building

Henley House
(Hanart TZ
Gallery)

Leg. Co.
Building
Statue
Square

(K)

(H)

JACKSON RD

(J2)

Chater
Garden

LAMBETH WALK

Far East
Finance
Centre

DRAKE ST

Admiralty
Centre

(A)

ICE

HSBC
Building

BANK ST

Former
Bank of
China

Cheung
Kong Centre

MURRAY RD

Admiralty

(M)

TAMAR STREET

(B)

DRAKE ST

(D)

ew World
Tower

DUDDELL ST

QUEEN'S
ROAD
CENTRAL

BATTERY PATH

ICE HOUSE STREET

Court of
Final Appeal

Bank of
China Tower

Lippo
Centre

Queensway
Plaza

(C2)

(C1)

KC
spital

LOWER ALBERT ROAD

Li Hall

St John's
Cathedral

GARDEN ROAD

Asia Pacific
Financial Tower

QUEENSWAY

High
Court

Pacific
Place

OAD

Former
Government
House

Lower Peak
Tram Terminal

Flagstaff House
Museum of
Tea Ware

SUPREME COURT RD

Island
Shangri-La
Hotel

JW
Marriott
Hotel

anical
dens

COTTON TREE DRIVE

ST JOSEPH'S PATH

Hong Kong
Visual Arts
Centre

Hong Kong Park

Edward Youde
Aviary

Conrad
Hotel

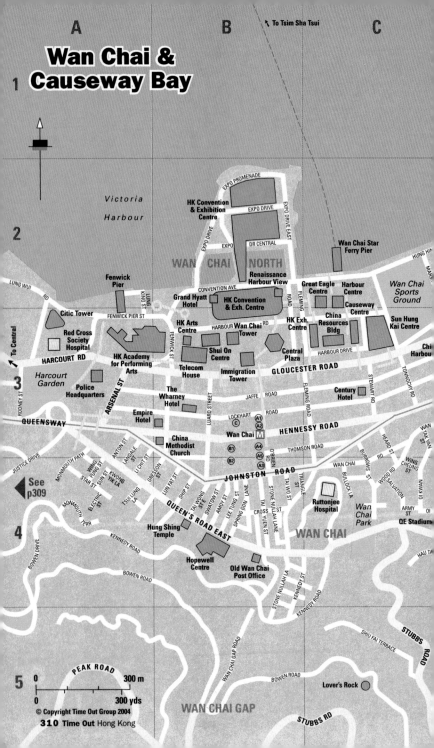

# Wan Chai & Causeway Bay

To Tsim Sha Tsui

**A** **B** **C**

**1**

**2**

Victoria

Harbour

WAN CHAI NORTH

Wan Chai Star Ferry Pier

HK Convention & Exhibition Centre

EXPO PROMENADE

EXPO DRIVE

EXPO DRIVE EAST

DR CENTRAL

EXPO

Fenwick Pier

Renaissance Harbour View

Great Eagle Centre

Harbour Centre

Wan Chai Sports Ground

CONVENTION AVE

Grand Hyatt Hotel

HK Convention & Exh. Centre

Causeway Centre

Citic Tower

LUNG KING ST

FENWICK PIER ST

FLEMING

ROAD

China Resources Bldg

Sun Hung Kai Centre

LUNG WUI RD

Red Cross Society Hospital

HK Arts Centre

HARBOUR RD

Wan Chai Tower

HK Exh. Centre

Chi Harbou

**3**

To Central

HARCOURT RD

HK Academy for Performing Arts

FENWICK ST

Shui On Centre

Central Plaza

HARBOUR DRIVE

Harcourt Garden

Police Headquarters

Telecom House

Immigration Tower

GLOUCESTER ROAD

STEWART RD

FLEMING ROAD

Century Hotel

RODNEY ST

ARSENAL ST

The Wharney Hotel

JAFFE ROAD

ROAD

TONNOCHY RD

QUEENSWAY

Empire Hotel

LUARD STREET

LOCKHART ROAD

HENNESSY ROAD

WAN CHAI

SHARP ST

China Methodist Church

Wan Chai

A1 A2

B1

A4

THOMSON ROAD

HEARD ST

WAN CHAI

BURROWS RD

WING CHEUNG ST

NULLAH RD

JUSTICE DRIVE

MONMOUTH PATH

WING FUNG ST

ANTON ST

LANDALE

LI CHIT ST

LUN FAT ST

SHIP ST

B2

A5

O'BRIEN RD

TAI WO ST

TRIANGLE ST

WAN CHAI

BULLOCK LANE

WO SALVATION

ARMY ST

NAM KONG ST

STAR ST

SUN ST

KWONG YIK LA

GRESSON ST

TAI WONG ST E

SWATOW ST

AMOY ST

LEE TUNG ST

SPRING GDN LANE

STONE NULLAH ST

TAI YUEN ST

JOHNSTON ROAD

Ruttonjee Hospital

Wan Chai Park

QE Stadium

See p309

MONMOUTH TERR

ELECTRIC ST

TSUI LUNG LA

QUEEN'S ROAD EAST

KENNEDY ROAD

Hung Shing Temple

CROSS LANE

KENNEDY ROAD

SAU WA FONG

**4**

BOWEN DRIVE

Hopewell Centre

Old Wan Chai Post Office

SING NULLAH LA

KENNEDY RD

HAU TA

BOWEN ROAD

WAN CHAI GAP ROAD

KENNEDY ROAD

**5**

PEAK ROAD

0    300 m

0    300 yds

BOWEN ROAD

Lover's Rock

SHIU FAI TERRACE

STUBBS ROAD

© Copyright Time Out Group 2004

**310 Time Out** Hong Kong

WAN CHAI GAP

STUBBS RD

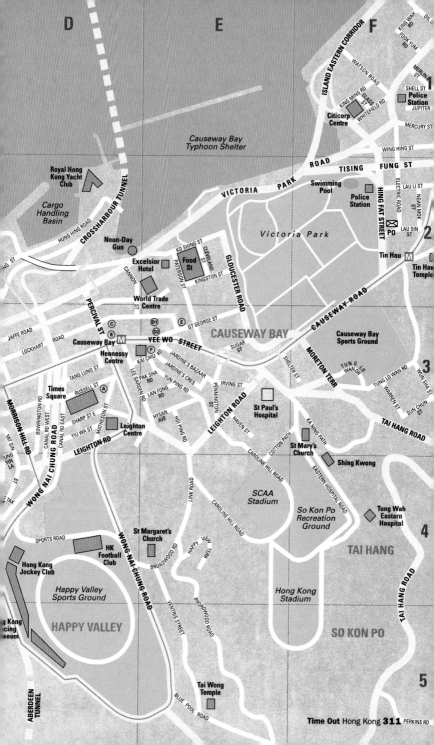

D      E

ISLAND EASTERN CORRIDOR

KING WAH RD

FOOK YUM RD

MERLIN ST

SHELL ST

**Police Station**

JUPITER

WATSON ROAD

KING MING RD

GLASS ST

WHITEFIELD RD

**Citicorp Centre**

MERCURY ST

WING HING ST

ROAD    **TISING**    **FUNG** ST

LAU LI ST

ELECTRIC ROAD

NGAN MOK ST

Royal Hong Kong Yacht Club

CROSSHARBOUR TUNNEL

HUNG HING ROAD

Cargo Handling Basin

ING ST

Causeway Bay Typhoon Shelter

VICTORIA   PARK

Swimming Pool

**Police Station**

HING FAT STREET

LAU SIN ST

PO

Victoria Park

Noon-Day Gun

Excelsior Hotel

Food St

World Trade Centre

CANNON ST

PATERSON ST

KO SHING ST

CLEVELAND ST

KINGSTON ST

GLOUCESTER ROAD

Tin Hau

CAUSEWAY ROAD

Tin Hau Temple

PERCIVAL ST

JAFFE ROAD

LOCKHART

Road

**Causeway Bay** M

C
B

D1

F

E

GT GEORGE ST

**CAUSEWAY BAY**

SUGAR ST

SHELTER ST

MORETON TERR

**Causeway Bay Sports Ground**

TUNG LO WAN DR

TUNG LO WAN RD

WARREN ST

WUN SHA ST

SUN CHUN ST

TAI HANG ROAD

**YEE WO**   **STREET**

Hennessy Centre

KAI CHIU RD

JARDINE'S BAZAAR

JARDINE'S CRES

LEE GARDEN RD

PAK SHA RD

YUN PING RD

LAN FONG RD

IRVING ST

PENNINGTON ST

LEIGHTON ROAD

HAVEN ST

**St Paul's Hospital**

KA NING PATH

COTTON PATH

**St Mary's Church**

EASTERN HOSPITAL ROAD

**Shing Kwong**

MORRISON HILL RD

Times Square

BOWRINGTON RD

CANAL RD WEST

CANAL RD EAST

TANG LUNG ST

RUSSELL ST

A

SHARP ST E

YIU WA ST

MATHESON ST

Leighton Centre

HYSAN AVE

HOI PING RD

**LEIGHTON RD**

WONG NAI CHUNG ROAD

YAT SING

YING WA LA

YAT TAK

CANAL RD

**SCAA Stadium**

CAROLINE HILL ROAD

**So Kon Po Recreation Ground**

**Tung Wah Eastern Hospital**

**TAI HANG**

TAI HANG ROAD

SPORTS ROAD

HK Football Club

St Margaret's Church

BROADWOOD RD

LINK ROAD

HAPPY VIEW TERR

CAROLINE HILL ROAD

**Hong Kong Stadium**

**SO KON PO**

Hong Kong Jockey Club

Happy Valley Sports Ground

**HAPPY VALLEY**

VENTRIS STREET

BROADWOOD ROAD

g Kong cing seum

ABERDEEN TUNNEL

Tai Wong Temple

BLUE POOL ROAD

PERKINS RD

F

1

2

3

4

5

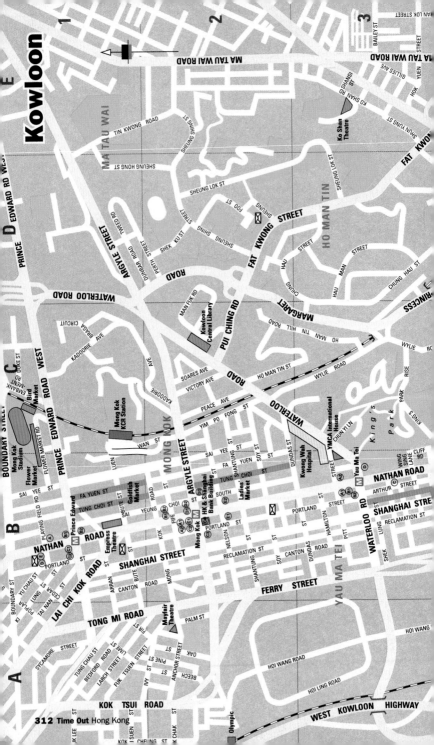

# Kowloon

# Street Index

# Rail
# Transport

**Airport Express**
**KCR Railway**
**West Rail**
**Island Line (MTR)**
**Kwun Tong Line (MTR)**
**Tsuen Wan Line (MTR)**
**Tung Chung Line (MTR)**
**Tseung Kwan O Line**
**Under construction**
**Transfer station**

↑ To Guangzhou

Lok Ma Chau

Lo Wu

Sheung Shui

Fanling

**New Territories**

Tai Wo

Tai Po Market

Wu Kai Sha

To Airport ↗
To Tuen Mun ↗

Tsuen Wan

Tai Wo Hau

University

Kwai Hing

Fo Tan        Racecourse

Kwai Fong

Sha Tin

**Lai King**

Tuen Wan West

Tsuen Wan West

Mei Foo

Tai Wai

Lok Fu        Wong Tai Sin

Lai Chi Kok        Shek Kip Mei

Diamond Hill

Cheung Sha Wan

Choi Hung

Sham Shui Po

**Kowloon Tong**

Kowloon Bay

**Prince Edward**

Ngau Tau Kok

Nam Cheong

Mong Kok

**Mong Kok**

Kwun Tong

Olympic

**Yau Ma Tei**

Lam Tin

**Kowloon**

Jordan

Hung Hom

**Yau Tong**        **Tiu Keng Leng**

Tsim Sha Tsui

East Tsim Sha Tsui

North Point        **Quarry Bay**

To Po Lam ↗

Fortress Hill

Sheung Wan

Tin Hau        Tai Koo        Sai Wan Ho

**Central**

Shau Kei Wan

**Admiralty**        Wan Chai        Causeway Bay        Heng Fa Chuen

Chai Wan

# Hong Kong Island